MW01198984

# IN THE HIGHEST DEGREE TRAGIC

# IN THE HIGHEST DEGREE TRAGIC

*The Sacrifice of the U.S. Asiatic Fleet in the East Indies during World War II*

DONALD M. KEHN JR.

Potomac Books

AN IMPRINT OF THE UNIVERSITY OF NEBRASKA PRESS

This book is dedicated with respect and admiration
to Samuel Milner, historian
*Omnia vincit labor*

# CONTENTS

# ILLUSTRATIONS

# INTRODUCTION

The story of the destruction of the old U.S. Asiatic Fleet in defense of the Dutch East Indies (modern-day Indonesia) in early 1942 is one of multifaceted tragedy. Men and ships were squandered not only for questionable military purposes but, worse, as political gestures to uncertain allies. How and why this small, outdated American force should have been offered up as a sacrifice is the basis for this book.

The need for such a history is obvious enough. Although the campaign took place over seventy years ago, and a number of works have been published that purport to cover it entirely, not one has done a job of exceptional accuracy. The cause for this is twofold. First, few have had adequate access to primary Japanese military records or personal memoirs of the East Indies operations. Second, telling the truth about the backbiting within the joint command known as ABDA has been an undesirable endeavor. Our need for allies in Western Europe during the Cold War saw to that. Both of these inhibiting factors have been addressed and rectified in this work.

American history as written, published, and taught for over seven decades in the United States has also failed to properly comprehend the bravery and dedication to duty shown by its own fighting men in the Java campaign. Most histories of the Pacific War—*even now*—leapfrog from the attacks on Pearl Harbor in December 1941 to the Doolittle Raid of April 1942 or the Battle of the Coral Sea that May, with no mention of the fight for the East Indies or the wasting of the Asiatic Fleet. As an Asiatic Fleet officer who was there observed later, the campaign was a peripheral affair and one in which we did *not* triumph. These factors were thought to explain official and unofficial willingness to overlook combat operations in the East Indies.

Be that as it may, one's patience is taxed by the nonrecognition and ignorance still persisting for those men and the lonely struggle in which they found themselves enmeshed at the beginning of the Pacific War. The narrative history that follows, then, will show the extent to which sailors and officers of the U.S. Asiatic Fleet carried out their challenging, often harrowing, tasks in the opening months of the war. It contains first-person accounts and anecdotes, from the highest command echelons down to the lowest enlisted personnel, never seen in *any* published books or Internet sources. And to make perfectly clear: this work does not detail the air war in the East Indies or Allied small craft or submarine operations. So while it utilizes many previously unused primary records, it is *not* a battle history of the Imperial Japanese Navy, the Royal Netherlands Navy, the Royal Australian Navy, or Britain's Royal Navy. This narrative concentrates on the men and actions of the surface forces of the United States Asiatic Fleet.

It is therefore only fitting here to include a few comments from American participants. Adm. Thomas Hart, final head of the Asiatic Fleet—and in effect its Fabius Maximus—later wrote: "The men of the entire Asiatic command were splendid. They must have realized fairly early on what the outcome of the campaign would be. But, like their officers, they never faltered and kept their fighting edge to the end."[1]

In his own Supplementary Narrative written some years after the war, Hart's successor, Vice Adm. William Glassford Jr., observed:

> It should also be recalled that the Force enjoyed no reinforcement, no replacement of ammunition or torpedoes and no replenishment of stores or supplies of any kind, until after the conclusion of the campaign for the defense of the Malay Barrier. We subsisted as best we could on what could be had locally. As ammunition, torpedoes, and even later, fuel, food supplies, and stores were expended, it became necessary to redistribute what remained on board the surviving ships in order to carry on. There was, however, no dearth of splendid personnel. . . . It should be noted here again, for the record, that this personnel, all of the regular service, acted and reacted in general magnificently throughout.[2]

For final comments, here are remarks by two enlisted destroyermen, from uss *Peary* (DD-226) and uss *Whipple* (DD-217).

*Peary* had arguably the worst misfortune of any of the DesRon 29 destroyers. Badly damaged by bombs in the Cavite Navy Yard two days after Pearl Harbor, she and her crew underwent a miserable ordeal escaping the Philippines. The definition of a hard-luck ship, *Peary* was then sunk only a few weeks later at Darwin when that northern Australian port was devastated by a massive Japanese air raid. *Whipple* in contrast was a remarkably fortunate ship. She and her men escaped the campaign, although severely battered. And while these sailors' remarks may be those of an earlier, less technologically "advanced" generation than ours, they are a generation over which *we* have no moral prerogatives. Quite the contrary.

Billy E. Green, s1/c, operated *Peary's* sonar when not manning one of the destroyer's .50 cal. machine guns. He was lost overboard during the ship's run south when it was attacked and damaged by a trio of confused Australian bombers off Menado, Celebes (Sulawesi today)—one more accidental encounter that the meager Allied forces could scarcely afford. Green would eventually become a POW on Celebes, and there he remained throughout the war.

Many years later he wrote: "I realize most people relate to the cry 'Pearl' but no one seems to ever remember the cry 'Manila' or the forgotten (so-called) Asiatic Fleet of the U.S. Navy. I remember reading the story of David and Goliath in my pre-teens. I think I know how David must have felt when they pushed him out in front of Goliath. I would have settled for a good old fashioned Sling because our worn out old gear was not meant to fight a modern equipped invader."[3]

Joe McDevitt, an electrician's mate, served *after* the Java campaign on the flushdecker *Whipple* but alongside a number of men who had been through that harsh trial. His plain speaking stands out all the more brightly in our self-absorbed, narcissistic era. McDevitt acknowledged that as a youngster without combat experience serving with older Asiatic Fleet veterans, he "looked up to [them]." In an interview he recalled that those men had "put it [the Java campaign] behind them . . . with no negatives," and then carried on with their wartime responsibilities. Yet he also affirmed that the personnel of the Asiatic Fleet "were something unique and different," and that he did not see their like again during his years in the service. Even after seven decades McDevitt remained convinced that "they were heroes; they asked for little. . . . *These* were men."[4]

# ONE

## Prewar

*Hart Assumes Command*

For some thirty months prior to war, the Asiatic Fleet was under the command of Adm. Thomas C. Hart (USNA 1897), an officer with over forty years of service and one of the U.S. Navy's senior admirals. Almost sixty-two, Hart was nearing retirement after several years on the General Board when he was appointed to the Asiatic Fleet's top position (CINCAF, or Commander in Chief, Asiatic Fleet) in early 1939. He had hoped to be offered the command of the entire U.S. fleet. However, President Franklin Roosevelt would not accept Hart—who had previously displeased him—when his name was put forward as the next chief of the *Big Fleet*.[1] It may have been that Roosevelt thought Hart would retire at this setback. If so, he had misjudged his man. Hart's sense of duty and his willingness to face a challenge soon overcame his reluctance. CINCAF was a job Hart never coveted, but he told himself that he was probably "lucky to get what [he was] getting," and a return to sea for two more years appealed to the veteran sailor who did not much care for shore billets. To the Far East and its "not very large command" Hart chose to proceed.[2]

For Thomas Hart was no shrinking violet—with a nickname like "Tough Tommy" he hardly could have been. Hart—described by Samuel Eliot Morison as "small, taut, wiry, and irascible"—was known as a no-nonsense officer and a strict disciplinarian.[3] But he was also fair-minded and knew how to delegate authority. What Hart wanted, and expected, was competence at the very least, from blue-water ship handling to desk-bound administrative matters. Yet when it came to the Asiatic Station, whether concerning base support at Cavite or basic support from Washington, he found little of either that he deemed satisfactory.

All would have agreed that Thomas Hart was his own man—even a "lone wolf"—by any reckoning. And given his seniority he was not much troubled by issues of authority, even if Washington often kept him in the dark regarding strategic thinking in the last years of peace. Thousands of miles from home, and with his new "exalted rank" (as he jestingly called it in his diary), Hart found that, like his small but self-contained fleet, he would often be required to fend for himself.[4]

In matters of national policy he was at times surprised by Washington's decisions—as, for example, when it was announced in the summer of 1939 that the commercial treaty of 1911 with Japan was to be abrogated. However, in his new position he was quickly thrust into such a maelstrom of social activities ("seeing peoples," as he put it) that it muted any second thoughts he may have entertained about such revelations. Meanwhile, international relations in the Far East between the Western powers, China, and the Japanese—always at loading point—would have tested the character of anyone. Many leaders, before and after Hart, would be found wanting.

Now a full four-star admiral, he and Mrs. Hart traveled from the West Coast—leaving July 1, 1939—on board the liner *President Coolidge*. They reached the Far East via Honolulu and Yokohama. In Japan for the first time since 1922, he and his family spent a few days sightseeing before sailing on to Shanghai. There he would assume command of the fleet that was "known as a hard working, hard playing, non-regulation force."[5]

Although the Asiatic Fleet was actually based in Manila, the cooler climate of northern China gave the men and ships a well-earned respite from the torrid Philippine summers. Also the perennially unsettled situation in China had demanded American attention for many years. As such the Asiatic Fleet usually had units moving along the length of the China coastline. Each year submarines and tender went up to Tsingtao, about 350 miles north of Shanghai on the Yellow Sea, with the destroyers generally going on to Chefoo, which was situated on the northern side of the Shantung Peninsula about 100 miles farther on.

However, with the international situation since 1931 deteriorating throughout China and Manchuria—and overt Japanese military operations metastasizing since that time—Shanghai became the focal point of Western diplomatic efforts to counter, or at least stymie, Japan's steadily increasing aggression. While in Shanghai, the Asiatic Fleet was expected to provide the steel backbone to America's occasionally slouching diplomatic posture. Therefore, it was at "dirty, smoky" Shanghai that Hart took command. He broke out his flag aboard the heavy cruiser USS *Augusta* (CA-31) on July 25, 1939. The ceremony on the fleet flagship went off correctly, he noted in his diary, only marred by the light rain falling that day.

When serving aboard ships of the Asiatic Fleet,
'Twas mandatory when at Shanghai not to stick your feet,

Nor swim in the filth of the Yangtze River.
Could cause a sailor to lose his liver![6]

In Shanghai, that polyglot metropolis called "the Mistress of Cathay" by some and "Sodom on the China coast" by others—the largest and wealthiest city in the Orient south of Tokyo—the outgoing commander in chief of the Asiatic Fleet Adm. Harry Yarnell awaited Hart. Yarnell was of the same generation as Hart, and an officer for whom Hart had nothing but respect. Hart also recognized with uncomfortable lucidity the stressful and isolated situation in which Yarnell had performed during his three trying years in the Far East. Yarnell was at times too much the plainspoken sailor for his own good as far as the State Department was concerned, but he was no jingoist.[7]

As for relations with their own allies, Yarnell had on July 20, 1939, written what Kemp Tolley described as a "farewell analysis of the Far Eastern situation," in which the departing admiral remarked of British cooperation: "Her foreign policy in the Far East has been dictated by her imperial and economic interest to a marked degree. She has been willing to support the United States when it was to her advantage to do so, and to support other nations at the expense of the United States, regardless of the ethics of the case, when she felt it the better economic procedure." This trenchant commentary—which was read "with interest" (if little else) by Secretary of State Cordell Hull—says much about the prevailing state of U.S. relationships with other Western powers in the Orient during the prewar years.[8]

As CINCAF since 1936, Yarnell had faced a variety of "incidents" following Japan's expansion of the war in China, notably in the wake of the so-called Marco Polo Bridge Incident near Peking in the summer of 1937. This was a war that the leader of the Nationalists, Chiang Kai-shek, might have avoided, but he at last chose to resist the Japanese in strength. His decision came from a combination of realism and fantasy. First, at Shanghai he enjoyed greatly superior numbers initially, with some 45,000 men deployed against 3,500 Japanese Special Naval Landing Force troops. Second, Chiang clung to the somewhat desperate hope that Japan's aggression would compel the governments of Western investors to intervene. But the Western powers wanted no part of what they knew would become a blood-drenched quagmire. Chiang eventually moved seventy-one divisions totaling half a million troops into the fight, but the Japanese swiftly reinforced their own forces in enormous numbers. A full-scale campaign ensued.

Aerial bombings of Shanghai came in August, with some of the most destructive executed by inept Chinese planes that dropped their own ordnance so haphazardly that they slaughtered thousands of their countrymen, mostly refugees. One salvo of heavy bombs alone killed over seven hundred civilians along Nanking Road, as described by an appalled Western observer, Rhodes Farmer: "Yellow, slowly lifting, high explosive fumes exposed the terrible scene. . . . Heads, arms, legs lay far from mangled trunks. . . . It seemed as if a giant mower had pushed through the crowd of refugees, chewing them to bits. Here was a headless man; there a baby's foot, wearing its little red-silk shoe embroidered with fierce dragons. Bodies were piled in heaps by the capricious force of the explosions. Women, still clutching their precious bundles. One body, that of a young boy, was flattened high against a wall, to which it clung with ghastly adhesion."[9] Ultimately the campaign was a disaster for the Nationalists (KMT), and Chiang lost almost two-thirds of his troops "including 10 percent of the entire trained officer corps."[10]

Although the United States attempted to remain neutral, neutrality kept Americans no more immune than any others. One summer evening (August 20) as she lay anchored off Shanghai, a small antiaircraft (AA) shell landed on the well deck of the Asiatic Fleet flagship, USS *Augusta*. It burst, and a shard hit Freddie John Falgout, S1/c, in the heart, killing him. Almost twenty other sailors were injured as they prepared to set up the evening movie. Later (October 14) Chinese and Japanese air attacks near-missed the flagship, with bomb fragments wounding a signalman on the bridge standing next to Admiral Yarnell. For much of the second half of 1937 and into the beginning of 1938, *Augusta's* logbook read like nothing so much as a war diary. Over the next three months the navy would see dozens of similar encounters and equally unnerving (or maddening) events, and not only in the Shanghai area.[11]

Throughout this period Yarnell sought to reiterate what he believed were the essentials of American policy in China: protection of U.S. citizenry and their interests. During seemingly endless disputes with the Japanese, he minced no words about these issues and tried to impress on them just how serious America was when it came to looking after its own people. As a result, isolationist elements in the States, which were powerful both socially and politically, felt that the commander of the Asiatic Fleet needed to learn to bridle his tongue. Unfortunately for Yarnell, in what would be an oft-repeated strategy, the State Department continued to issue contradictory remarks.

For example the U.S. government scolded Yarnell for speaking his mind on policy, then saw to it that Japanese contracts with Western oil firms for half a million tons (September 23, 1937)—with which to fuel the Imperial war machine—were honored.[12] But the U.S. government had been working hand

4

in glove with the big oil companies behind the scenes for years, struggling to counter the polite criminality of the Japanese, whose aggressive military enterprises frequently hid beneath the flimsiest of legalistic pretenses.[13] Always under pressure, Washington and the oil industry had been maneuvering between the Scylla of Japanese bellicosity and the Charybdis of Chinese banditry for many years prior to World War II.

American public opinion was ambiguous at this time despite the well-publicized *Panay* incident of December 1937. Views shifted somewhat but not as drastically as one might expect. And while anger at Japanese military expansion increased, so too did the belief that the United States had no business becoming embroiled in an Asian war. According to a Gallup poll, 70 percent of Americans still wanted to get the United States—military, businesses, missionaries—out of China entirely. Yet, as we understand today, such poll numbers are often misleading. The pro-China lobby in the U.S. was powerful, with many connections to mass media. Also, Roosevelt had Far Eastern family and ancestry ties that would color his decision making for some years. This would not be the last time that an American administration gave greater credit (both moral and financial) to a foreign country suffering from profoundly flawed internal political issues.

As for his CINCAF predecessor, Hart may have admired Yarnell's willingness to speak his mind, but he also believed that Yarnell's disciplined approach to the Japanese over the years had served him well: "I think the result of Yarnell's firmness and acumen followed through to my incumbency, and since I tried to carry on the same way he had, the Japanese didn't want to stir us up."[14] Yarnell was accorded a "job well-done" in Hart's opinion after the turning-over function on *Augusta*. Coming from Hart, an old-school officer not given to encomium, that was high praise: "He [Yarnell] has been a splendid officer and gentleman all these long, difficult years—going back into the preceding century. The last day of such a career is a very sad occasion."[15]

Hart was a northerner and rock-ribbed Republican with a record of opposing many of Roosevelt's policies, and his conservative views had not escaped the president's attention.[16] Hart likewise felt a marked antipathy for Harold Ickes, FDR's obstinate secretary of the interior (an unapologetic New Dealer) who held fast to the conviction that the U.S. *must* embargo Japan's oil supplies— all the more so when East Coast Americans were then being asked to ration gasoline. Naturally any talk of an oil embargo disconcerted Hart, who, like his boss, chief of naval operations (CNO) Adm. Harold R. "Betty" Stark, believed it would propel Japan into war as "a sure result."[17] Under no illusions regarding his small fleet's feeble strength, Hart regularly criticized administration policies in Washington. But this was done from afar—and generally limited to the pages of his private diary—while maintaining a hard-nosed military posture within his own command.[18]

Of course the U.S. government had its hands full those last two years before the war. It was attempting to manage a policy and public relations sleight-of-hand act that would have tested the skills of any administration or magician: that of appeasing a belligerent enemy while simultaneously supporting an essential ally (Great Britain) and at the same time publically professing U.S. resolve to avoid any foreign wars. And all of this while Roosevelt was deciding whether to run a third-term reelection campaign against violently opposed anti-Roosevelt partisans.

For his part, and despite being often kept in the dark regarding the U.S. government's position, Hart understood the thankless position into which he—like Yarnell before and much like Husband Kimmel later at Pearl Harbor—was being placed. On July 20, 1939, even before reaching his new command, he wrote in his diary that he was "more appalled than ever at the task." Five days later this initial view had not moderated. His job in the Far East was "an unholy mess anyway one look[ed] at it."[19] In fact the situation all along the China coast had been so fraught with problems and "incidents" during Yarnell's tenure that he had not been able to tour the Asiatic Fleet's Philippine installations for two years.

• • •

Over the first year of his command Hart had his hands completely full as he sought to "make do" protecting U.S. interests in the Far East, both economic and military. However, the Asiatic Fleet was little more than the tip of a small, corroded, and weak U.S. spearpoint. Scattered up and down China's immense coastline as well as the length of the Philippines, it had been organized for decades around a few basic (and undersized) components. These were the Yangtze River Patrol—with its subsidiary, the South China Patrol—and its fleet units, which included the flagship (a heavy cruiser from 1931 onward). There were three divisions of old, small World War I–era destroyers plus a squadron leader and tender. These were serviced by the fleet train and augmented by minecraft. The first two organizations consisted primarily of flat-bottomed river gunboats such as *Luzon*, *Oahu*, and *Panay*, and larger seagoing gunboats such as *Tulsa* (PG-22) and *Asheville* (PG-21), with the occasional four-stack destroyer thrown in. After 1938 another expendable unit, the antiquated light cruiser *Marblehead* (CL-12), was assigned to the Asiatic Fleet as well. Then, a year later, the *Lang-*

*ley* (AV-3) moved to the Far East. With the outbreak of hostilities, the Yangtze River Patrol and the South China Patrol both ceased to exist, and their vessels were redistributed. Few would survive the war.

There was also a variable number of submarines, sub tenders, plus associated support vessels and yard craft. Beginning in 1939—when the old *Langley* (converted to a seaplane tender) was sent to the Philippines, along with several lesser tenders (converted flushdeckers *Childs* [AVD-1] and *William B. Preston* [AVD-7]) and the much smaller *Heron* (AVP-2)—a PBY patrol unit began operating out of the Manila Bay area. Based on Sangley Point and Olongapo, the thirty or so PBY Catalinas eventually composed PatWing 10. Last-minute works enlarging various components in Hart's command were under way when hostilities began, but almost all of these activities were undone in the opening days of war.[20] However, for the first year of his tour, Hart saw most of his time consumed by dealing with problems in China.

For some fifteen years prior to World War II, the situation facing the American military in China could be summed up in a line from the annual report of the Navy Department in 1928: "The protection of American citizens has required of the Commanders of our naval forces the greatest amount of tact, patience, and calm judgment."[21] The less flattering truth is that at no time were Western citizens *truly* safe in China. Kidnapping, hostage taking, and murder were all ever-present possibilities. Shanghai, even though largely created and driven by Western influences, was a devil's haven of intrigue and crime in which non-Asians moved outside the European zones ("concessions" or "settlements") at their peril.[22]

When Hart assumed command there were, as usual, more than a few Asiatic Fleet assets at Tsingtao and Chefoo well to the north. An elderly submarine tender—usually USS *Canopus* (AS-9)—with half a dozen ancient submarines (called "pig-boats") and the timeworn light cruiser USS *Marblehead* summered in the former German post at Tsingtao, which was by then under Japanese control. Asiatic veterans liked going up to those cool northern ports, and not only for the agreeable climate. Tsingtao was also one of the few places they could get good quality beef and fresh milk. Popular among the high percentage of midwestern farm boys who had ended up sailors, these were rarities in the Far East.

At the same time many of Hart's aging destroyers were stationed even farther up the coast at Chefoo with their tender, USS *Black Hawk* (AD-9). These Asiatic Fleet ships were an important component of the city's economy, and whenever the destroyers returned to the port—generally in late spring—they were warmly greeted by local merchants and the Chinese working crews who helped with day-to-day routine aboard ship. On a tin can these might include laundrymen, barbers, galley helpers (who provided staples such as chickens and eggs), shoemakers, and tailors.[23] Chefoo also sported the efficient Ah-Fung OK Photo Service, which manufactured heavy, "black dragon" albums. More than a few Asiatic Fleet sailors commemorated their tours in the Far East with collections of photos and ephemera lovingly stored in these distinctive albums with their embossed black leather covers showing paired dragons watching over a sailing junk. Beneath these mythical creatures, unsentimental doggerel celebrated the Asiatic lifestyle:

> Ship me somewhere east of Suez
> Where the best is like the worst
> Where there are no ten commandments
> And a man can raise a thirst . . .
> Around in your ricksha at day break
> Remorseful and bitter with hate
> Back to your ship or your barracks
> Going on duty at eight
> And so the night travel is ended
> And all the nights are the same
> Some more hellish than others
> But none of the nights are tame
> A lure that is soft and luxuriant
> A bidding to the state of the feast
> This is the spell of the Orient.[24]

Some skilled Chinese workers continued in their attachment to specific Asiatic Fleet ships for many years. Almost all had tenacious memories of their Western customers. One destroyerman who had served on USS *Pope* (DD-225) remembered being fitted for a set of dress khakis after the war at Tsingtao, on the hospital ship USS *Repose*. As the Chinese tailor stood on a stool taking his measurements, he suddenly burst out: "Me savvy you! Er-wisha-woo, 2-2-5!" He recalled the sailor as a member of *Pope* from his duty at Tsingtao in the early 1930s. As in any industry, the quality of service varied, but most sailors recalled the excellence and reliability of Chinese tailors and laundrymen in particular. This also extended to the making of custom leather shoes. A Chinese shoemaker from Tsingtao could come aboard and take measurements on his pad one day, thumbing through a dog-eared Florsheim catalog, and deliver a pair of handcrafted leather shoes to the sailor the following day.[25]

And on the coast at Chinwangtao, near the Great Wall—two hundred miles northwest of Chefoo—the sailors took advantage of the U.S. Marine firing ranges to improve their skills with the Browning automatic rifle (BAR), Springfield 1903 rifle, or M1911 .45 cal. pistol. That far north they needed to know their weapons, being so near the Kwantung-leased territory of Japan's proxy state, Manchukuo. From that sinister cauldron bubbled up many of the aggressive policies and actions that the military leaders of Japan fomented and that would ultimately lead to the Pacific War.[26]

By late August 1939, simmering international events were about to boil over in Europe, and these would affect both Hart's responsibilities and the actions of the opportunistic Japanese. During an early visit that summer to Weihai-wei—on the tip of the peninsula, east of Chefoo—Hart learned from the commander of Royal Navy forces in China, Vice Adm. Sir Percy Noble, that due to the emerging threat of war on the Continent, most British warships would withdraw south to Hong Kong. When the European war broke out a week later, Hart sent more of his old tin cans back to Manila and ordered U.S. Marines to Shanghai, where further Japanese provocations were anticipated.[27] Yet, despite such tensions, overt hostilities between the Western powers and the Japanese did *not* break out in the Far East for over two years. As it was, the Asiatic Fleet's old routine continued into 1940.

At Chinwangtao, the nearest port for travel to Peking, standard practice was for U.S. destroyers to send a landing force ashore—this was considered a privilege—arranging for one-half of the men to get leave in Peking, while the others remained at the rifle range to practice. After being transported to Peking by train, the men on liberty stayed at the Legation Guard Barracks. This helps explain the prevalence of tourist photos (and home movies) taken in the Forbidden City by American sailors, marines, and officers.[28] At the same time some of the Asiatic Fleet skippers had friends in other north China ports—small resorts such as Peitaiho Beach, known to sailors as "Potatoville"—and might spend time there, too.

So far as carnal diversions went, in most Chinese ports lonely—or adventurous—Asiatic sailors could take their pick. In any number of bars and houses of prostitution, well removed from stifling, stateside bourgeois hypocrisies, female companionship could be purchased and enjoyed. Such businesses were never reticent about advertising to lonesome sailors far from home. And while all ships made efforts to instruct their crew members in prophylactic measures, venereal infection rates remained high. Alcohol consumption and youthful hormones, in concert with simple ignorance, guaranteed that this age-old naval custom—like brawling and tattoos—would persist to some degree no matter the advice or lectures given.

However, it would be unfair and inaccurate to say that these sailors hadn't enough pride in their professional skills. They took *great* satisfaction in being able to make do with little. They were nothing if not resourceful, self-sufficient, and durable. With so many young men drawn from America's rural communities or hardscrabble inner-city areas during the Great Depression, one would expect that to be the case. Born and raised on remote, isolated plots of ground and tough urban streets, they had few options. And because a culture and economy of cheap, disposable goods did not yet exist, running and repairing machinery and maintaining tools in good working order were often second-nature. This applied to the sailors who were rounders as well as those who remained straitlaced. In fact, these were *the* defining characteristics that many Asiatic Fleet men prided themselves on. It is not claiming too much to state that the men of the old Asiatic Fleet exemplified these traditional nautical values as well as any organization within the U.S. Navy in that period. Raised in the brass-knuckled hardships of the Great Depression under a government that could do little to alleviate their plight, they understood from their earliest years that in this world a man was "on his own." Handouts were to be neither sought nor accepted so long as one remained able-bodied. They kept up their old ships with great care and ingenuity. And when the time came, these same men would fight as courageously as possible with what they had.

By early 1940, spending summer weeks in upper China and winters in Manila had been the customary procedure for the fleet for years, but that routine would be altered. The European war, half a world removed and compounded in the Far East by continued Japanese belligerence, would see to the change. The year 1940 was the last that most Asiatic Fleet units would spend in Shanghai. With the international situation deteriorating almost daily, Hart wanted his ships back to the Philippines, where they would be close to their bases and supplies. He felt that the time had come to train his forces and be concentrated against any possible southward moves by the Japanese. And the south was now Japan's focus.

. . .

After the summer of 1937—but beginning with the annexation and development of Manchuria (as Manchukuo) in 1931–32—the Imperial Japanese war machine expanded its combat operations into China's interior. As for the hated Westerners, *any* pretense for confrontations with the Americans and the British at the treaty ports and settlements along the prodigious Chinese coastline, stretching over two thousand miles from Macau to the Shantung peninsula, would suffice.

Japanese actions were deliberate and preconceived. In adopting the so-called Fundamental Principles of National Policy for 1936, Japanese planners made explicit their aims: throughout East Asia the empire was to "strive to eradicate the aggressive policies of the great powers" (meaning Great Britain and the United States), while at the same time securing the northern areas of China as a buffer zone against any potential Soviet aggression. Similarly, it was vital to promote Japan's "racial and economic development in the South Seas, especially in the outlying South Seas areas."[29]

Although couched in suitably vague language, this important document marked an official attempt to balance the conflicting demands of those Imperial archrivals, the Japanese Imperial Army (Rikugun) and the Imperial Navy (Kaigun). The army was perennially concerned about its expansion into Manchukuo and northern China—with the resultant Soviet reactions and pressure—while the navy increasingly advocated what was known as the Southward Advance. Several middle-echelon Imperial Japanese Navy (IJN) hawks had been instrumental in the creation of the Fundamental Principles of National Policy document. Their influence in particular led to the specific mention of the "South Seas areas."[30] But looming over all was the dire need for those strategic resources that constructed, revamped, and fueled an Imperial war machine hell-bent on dominating the Asian mainland: iron, coal, steel, rubber, and, above all else, oil.

This shift in part occurred because by 1934–35 it was evident that Japan's ambitious plans for developing Manchukuo were faltering. Military goals and those of its commercial business investors were at variance, with the former hoping to establish a strategic resource base with heavy industrialization capabilities—primarily to supply the Imperial Army and Navy—while the latter wanted raw materials shipped to Japan for production, consumption, and export. Having learned little enough from their failures, Japanese schemes for controlling northern China as well as the Southward Advance would replicate the Manchukuo fallacy.[31]

Concurrently, as Sir Robert Craigie, Britain's ambassador in Tokyo recorded, "What history will clearly establish is that it was the settled policy of the Japanese Army to provoke incidents [in China] and to exploit provocations."[32] These "incidents" were invariably glossed over by Japanese diplomats offering the same excuses and false apologies whenever confronted. Behind the friable veneer of polite language, though, lay real menace, and few Western military men or diplomats could not perceive this by 1939–41. Each incident served as a pretext for demands by the Japanese military. These often followed a set pattern: first, apologies; then indemnities; next, punishment for offenders and responsible officers; and finally, withdrawal of local Chinese troops.

Nowhere was this more obvious than at Shanghai. There Western imperialist—but especially British—commercial interests for over a century had coalesced. In China in 1931 some 38 percent of all foreign holdings were British. In Shanghai was concentrated no less than three-quarters of the nearly one billion dollars Great Britain had invested in the country.[33] In combination with its great wealth and distinctive political and governmental structure, Shanghai's huge size—over five million inhabitants—made it "a killing field of brutal economic competition, ideological struggle and murderous political intrigue."[34]

At the end of 1937 new (but no less brutal) proprietors arrived when the Japanese military settled into Shanghai in great numbers following their victory over Chiang's armies. Subduing Shanghai had resulted in some forty thousand Japanese casualties, but it had cost the Chinese many times more than that.[35] From then on, in the wake of the catastrophic economic damage that resulted—foreign trade in Shanghai plummeted 76 percent between July and December 1937—the realists among the Western military all saw the inevitable.

One such clear-eyed individual was Hart's CINCAF precursor, Adm. Harry Yarnell, who told a group of Anglo-Saxon businessmen and local civic leaders in February 1939 that the Japanese were obviously intent on taking over the settlement, and that *when* they came in the United States would not attempt to stop them.[36] He had good reason to say so. In 1938 the Imperial Navy had expanded operations in the north by occupying Tsingtao, Chefoo, and Weihai-wei. These ports had been open to Western fleets, so the presence of IJN forces greatly intensified tensions. The Imperial Navy's Fourth Fleet was responsible for these occupation operations and used Tsingtao as headquarters "and base for the blockade of the North China coast."[37] It was only a matter of time before Japan found a pretext to send its military forces into Shanghai to get rid of the foreigners once and for all.

Therefore, conflict in one form or another could readily be seen by almost everyone, edging across the horizon in Asia as the beams of the "peace-loving" Rising Sun were already casting their long, blood-colored rays over the Far East. Beyond that, when not grappling with yet another "incident" along the Chinese seaboard or on its river systems, Tom Hart had to contemplate the position much farther to the south, in the Philippines and the Netherlands East Indies. And what he perceived there gave him no respite from his misgivings.

Japanese expansionist aims in Southeast Asia, including the Philippines, Malaya, and the East Indies, while not yet fully developed, were also long-standing. When France fell to Hitler's armies in 1940, it took no time for Japan to exploit the situation to its own advantage. By moving into northern Indo-China (present-day Vietnam) late that year on the pretense of cutting off supply lines to China, Japan gave itself a first step to the jumping-off points its military needed to execute its Southward Advance. By mid-1941, emboldened by Hitler's decision to invade Russia, Japan then made an even more rash choice. Led by the same types of extremists who had instigated a variety of "incidents" (*jiken*) throughout the Thirties, it chose to move into southern Indo-China.

Throughout this entire period, the Western powers were often as divided and impotent as they had been in Manchuria a decade earlier. However, FDR was no Herbert Hoover, and the reckless Japanese advance into southern Indo-China triggered precisely what rational Japanese feared it might: an oil embargo by the United States and its allies. Having annually relied on America for 60 to 90 percent of its total available petroleum supplies since the midthirties, Japan's fuel position was markedly vulnerable.[38] With this fateful development in late July 1941, the die was cast for all-out war in the Pacific.

. . .

As for Hart, he took his policy lead from Washington's chief of naval operations, Adm. Harold R. "Betty" Stark, a respected colleague. Stark had helped codify the United States' Europe-first war plans in late 1940 with his "Plan Dog" memorandum—which emphasized the necessity of defeating the Germans first. This plan shifted much of the navy's prewar strategic planning, but with the outbreak of the European war, and with American naval units already involved in screening convoys to England, Stark, like many others, fully expected war with Hitler first.[39]

In the Pacific few if any American naval leaders felt that they were prepared for a shooting war with the Japanese in 1939–41. A strategy of delay was what was *really* being employed behind the smokescreens of diplomacy and stern public pronouncements by both sides. The Japanese used time bought by the deliberately stalled diplomatic talks in Washington to prepare their forces for the Southward Advance, while the Allies—who did scarce justice to that term—struggled to strengthen their defenses.

Most of the major Western powers were still reluctant to openly resist the Japanese, fearing such opposition might lead to an outbreak of hostilities. As Britain's Lt. Gen. Sir H. R. Pownall (later Wavell's chief of staff in ABDA) subsequently observed, the British—preoccupied with North Africa and the Mediterranean—simply *hoped* the war would not happen in the Far East. U.S. planners sought to buy time while American industry geared up for war. For his part, Roosevelt appears to have believed that only by forcing the British and the Dutch into a situation that compelled them to resist the Japanese could those two allies be counted on to fight. The East Indies Dutch wanted no part of any conflict if avoidable. However, they were preparing as best they could— although belatedly—for what Gen. Hein ter Poorten would later describe in a talk with the U.S. military observer and Lend-Lease commissioner Lt. Col. Elliott Thorpe as "the storm that is surely coming."[40]

Australia felt threatened because of its isolated position and sought reassurances from any and all, including the Americans and the Dutch. However, after Pearl Harbor and the crippling of the Royal Navy off Malaya, the Australians had to fall back on a grimly realistic recognition made earlier. This was the Australian chiefs of staff appreciation of February 1941, which envisioned neither Royal Navy nor U.S. Pacific Fleet units coming to their aid in the event of war. It in turn led to the dispatch of small Australian Army units to outlying garrisons at Rabaul on New Britain ("Lark" Force), Ambon in the Moluccas ("Gull" Force), and Koepang and Dilli on Timor ("Sparrow" Force). All were weak, insufficiently armed detachments and would suffer heavy losses in combat and as POWs later.

The United States was endeavoring to increase its military strength in the Philippines, with an emphasis on fighters and long-range bombers. However, that buildup would take time—certainly well into the spring of 1942 after available matériel had been prioritized for Great Britain in the wake of the Dunkirk setback—and this the Japanese understood, too. In the meantime, the United States (like Australia) could transport only small forces to the Far East. These piecemeal units were never sufficient to stop the Japanese advance when it came, but they were enough to provoke a first reaction from their paranoid enemies.

Notwithstanding indecision at the State Department, Hart could scarcely fail to see the threat to his diminutive Asiatic Fleet—tellingly described by *Time* magazine as "grandiloquently named and puppy-sized"—in their exposed position at Manila.[41] Although he continued to receive conflicting (and often delayed) signals from Washington in the year prior to Japan's attack, Hart saw that he would be left largely to his own devices. Moreover, it became clear that substantive reinforcement was not a real priority.[42] Prewar discussions with the British, meanwhile, made it appear that the Royal Navy would be able to furnish heavy ships to firm up the Allied naval spine. This, too, would be obviated by the speed with which Japan moved ahead with *its* plans.

Concurrently, the Dutch had not always been terribly gracious in the use of East Indian waters. Prior to 1941 the U.S. Navy was somewhat reluctant to venture there. American warships were considered provocative to the Japanese—by both the Netherlanders and Washington. The Dutch had already been made uneasy by Japan's assurances in 1940 of support. Though politely veiled in the argot of diplomacy, these were in fact transparent threats. And with persistent efforts at economic penetration in the East Indies during the intervening years, the danger of Japanese aggression was very much alive in Dutch minds.

In 1940 after the fall of Holland in May—but before Japan signed the Tripartite Pact with Nazi Germany and Fascist Italy—Japan's diplomatic statements once more grew angular and sinister. Within days of Holland's capitulation to Hitler, Japan sent a message to the Dutch foreign minister, Nicholas van Kleffens, reassuring him that *Japan* would guarantee the status quo and "security" of the East Indies. The true nature of this generous reassurance was revealed quickly when Japan insisted on greater oil exports from the Dutch. Tasked with carrying out this unseemly business, Ishii Itarō later wrote: "I felt as if I had gone to dun a dying person for a debt."[43] Soon the Japanese would send a delegation to Java to begin economic talks with the Dutch centering on Japan's need for more oil—a *very* great deal more of it, as it turned out. The members of the delegation would find to their consternation that on the subject of oil the Dutch were anything *but* pushovers.[44]

Throughout the spring and summer of 1940, Japan's war machine advanced stealthily across Asia like the opportunistic predator it was. Simultaneously in the Philippines, the American high commissioner, the Honorable Francis "Frank" B. Sayre, and self-assured ex-field marshal Douglas MacArthur seemed mired in their own misconceptions. Sayre and President Manuel Quezon often had an icy relationship, but MacArthur was known to exist in a world all his own. It was a world in which he foresaw a Filipino army (under his command) eventually capable of resisting *any* Japanese invasion. Here MacArthur, as elsewhere in his celebrated career, could not have been more wrong.[45] As Hart noted: "Douglas knows a lot of things which are not so; he is a very able and convincing talker—a combination which spells danger."[46]

In late 1940 Hart finally decided to leave Shanghai for Manila. He put Rear Adm. William A. Glassford Jr., commander of the Yangtze Patrol, in charge on the China Coast. Called "the Duke of Shanghai" for his Anglophile affectations—

which included knee-length white socks worn with service shorts and a pince-nez on a long black ribbon—Glassford would have to manage affairs in China while Hart did what he could to prepare his tiny fleet in Manila.[47] Both men would have their hands very full.

. . .

In Japan during the spring and summer of 1940, the capitulation of Belgium, Holland, and France had the effect of driving undecided and moderate elements within the military and the government (led by the pro-Fascist prime minister Konoe Fumimaro) into the arms of the factions most susceptible to the influence of Nazi Germany. Japanese leaders were being led (or herded) by zealots like Foreign Minister Matsuoka Yōsuke, Gen. Ōshima Hiroshi (Japan's ambassador in Berlin), and Shiratori Toshio, former ambassador to Italy and Scandinavia. These were men of a highly aggressive bent, and they, along with like-minded midlevel army and navy officers, longed to climb aboard the nationalist bandwagon. Many sensible high-ranking officers had been purged over the years from the Imperial Navy, leaving an upper command echelon that consisted of little more than "yes-men." And the mid-echelon hawks were cautious neither in their talk nor in their support of "direct action."[48]

One reckless public statement—which had originated from Shiratori Toshio in 1933—first put the Dutch especially on edge. Shiratori then remarked that "the Japanese Navy would seize the Dutch East Indies oil fields immediately on the outbreak of war, no matter who the enemy might be."[49] Influential within the IJN were a number of hard-line naval bureaucrats who had no doubts regarding this issue. Men of varied rank, such as Vice Adm. Kondō Nobutake, Cdr. Ishikawa Shingo, Capt. Tomioka Sadatoshi, and Cdr. Kami Shigenori, to name but a few, had all admired for years the "efficient" and "direct" manner in which the Nazi military and civilian administrations functioned. Even Rear Adm. Morita Kan'ichi, the top engineer officer in the Combined Fleet, was a dedicated hard-liner. Others, like Rear Adm. Nakahara Yoshimasa—a brother-in-law to Ishikawa Shingo—were less overtly hawkish but willing to move south into the Netherlands East Indies (NEI) should the right situation present itself.[50]

That situation seemed to have arrived in the spring of 1940, with Hitler's swift European successes. Japanese militarists believed Britain was doomed, and that opportunities for seizing possessions from Western imperialists in the Far East would never be better. Understanding the Japanese military's overarching strategic resource requirements, the Netherlands East Indies—where Royal Dutch Shell and Standard Oil had shown that petroleum existed in abundance—was a keystone to proponents of the Southward Advance. Since Japan's war economy demanded oil, rubber, and tin in ever-increasing amounts, Malaya and Singapore would have to be taken preparatory to seizing the East Indies—as would the Philippines, which lay along the flank of Japan's advance. Yet in nothing less than a further stepping stone to catastrophe, several prewar Imperial Navy calculations on oil reserves, production, and potential acquisitions were entrusted at a critical time to one of its most combative middle-echelon officers.[51] More sensible, cautious officials who opposed these fantastic statistics were contemptuously brushed aside.

Still, a few individuals within the IJN exerted some restraining influence. According to official reports, the IJN had concluded that if U.S. petroleum exports were totally banned, Japan's war in China would dry up inside of four months unless Western oil resources were secured along with the ability to transport these successfully back to the homeland. So in May 1940 the Imperial Navy conducted research and table exercises to determine if Western oil installations in Borneo could be occupied by amphibious landings. Though deemed a feasible operation, the navy report ominously stated: "Even then Japan would be able to continue the war for a year at most. Should the war continue beyond one year, our chances of winning will be nil."[52] Navy minister Vice Adm. Yoshida Zengo outlined at that time the real dangers of going to war against the West with a navy that could not hold, protect, and manage the critical strategic resources of the Southern Area.

His reservations availed the Japanese nothing. Vice Admiral Yoshida was then bulldozed aside in September 1940 by IJN hawks eager to conclude the Tripartite Pact with Germany and Italy. The chief leader of this assault on the ministry's senior leadership was one of the Imperial Navy's most baleful characters: Cdr. Ishikawa Shingo. Highly notorious today in Japan, Ishikawa remains little known in the West. Nicknamed Fuki-dan—which we might best understand as "Loose Cannon"—he often lived up to his moniker with catastrophic consequences.[53]

Shrugging off Washington's washy "desire" that he remain near Shanghai, Hart left in late October. He had received no direct orders to stay and was displeased with the State Department's running the show rather than Admiral Stark, the chief of naval operations. Before departing Shanghai he had written in his diary: "I feel that my duty is quite plainly getting south where my Fleet is and helping get it ready for eventualities."[54] Hart knew that he might incur a serious reaction from Washington—perhaps lose his command, given FDR's dislike of him—but he made the choice according to his own sense of responsibility.

As it turned out, Hart *did* hear back from Washington at the last moment, as he prepared to leave. He was pleased that someone "other than the elevator boy" had taken his cable after all.[55] Warily, *Augusta* then steamed south on wartime footing; blacked-out and zigzagging through territorial waters. Alert for any prowling Japanese warships along the way, she encountered none. Hart noted with relief in his diary that the rest of their journey was a smooth one under lovely tropical skies and moonlit nights.

When he arrived off Corregidor on October 21, Hart had still received no word from Washington on larger issues, although his move to Manila had been approved. By then events were "moving pretty fast underneath the paint," he wrote.[56] What little that could be done to get his fleet ready, Hart undertook with a will. Too many of his meager forces had been turned out to pasture, grazing—or lazing, as it were—at Cavite, Olongapo, and Mariveles. In response he made every effort to whip his men and ships into shape right up to December 8. But, as we will see, it was a constant, uneasy struggle.

First, Hart shifted his flag. *Augusta*'s "sweet sister," USS *Houston* (CA-30), came out from the states via Hawaii and Guam. *Houston* (under Capt. Jesse B. Oldendorf) had just completed a refit at Mare Island during which she received her augmented 5-inch battery, degaussing gear, and (at least one) new quadruple 1.1-inch machine cannon mount. Her crew was largely replaced as well. To Hart the alterations to *Houston* were impressive looking at first sight. In action they would prove less so. Any improvements to the gunpower of Asiatic Fleet ships were liable to appear more significant than they really were.

The 1940 flag transition took place in late November, a few days before Thanksgiving. *Augusta* then prepared for her long-anticipated return voyage. When last seen by the other ships of the Asiatic Fleet, the *Augie Maru* was trailing a serpentine homeward-bound pennant, hundreds of feet long, from her mainmast. But her sailors later recalled that as she moved to sea out of Manila Bay the handmade red, white, and blue streamer was quickly torn to shreds by high winds. In that we may feel that there was apt symbolism enough for the Asiatic Fleet.

• • •

Though the ships and men at Cavite—which Hart regarded as little more than "a Penal Colony for officers not wanted at any place nearer home"—were still mired in peacetime bureaucratic formalism, the time was coming when that would be altered forever.[57] Sometimes, as we will see, the learning curve came to an abrupt and violent terminus. And while entire wings of libraries would be required to catalog sailors' tomfoolery—and the men of Hart's fleet were certainly no exception, far from it—a sampling of their prewar escapades may help convey the singular Asiatic flavor.

Under conditions of wartime it would never have been acceptable for a captain like the new skipper aboard the tanker *Trinity* (AO-13) (who had previously served as an executive officer on a destroyer) to bring his heavily laden ship to Manila's Pier One at standard speed carrying 165,000 gallons of flammable avgas. It should not have been acceptable just before the war either. And although the tanker had picked up a Philippine pilot per regulations for taking a ship into port, the captain blithely disregarded the man's suggestions. On the bridge an exchange evocative of Captain Queeg resulted.

"Okay, standard speed ahead," the new skipper ordered. At this the nervous pilot interjected: "No, no, *no*, you're going too fast. . . . Slow down to one-third speed." The confident commanding officer reassured him: "That's alright; *I* can stop it."[58]

In response to this nonsense—for the lumbering *Trinity* was not a frisky 1,200-ton tin can, after all—the harbor pilot exited the bridge, dashed to the side, and leapt back into his boat, yelling, "Not responsible, not responsible!"[59] He had no desire to be near, let alone *on*, the bridge of any ship loaded with that much aviation gasoline heading at standard speed for the docks.

Certain of his ship-handling ability, the self assertive captain said, "*I'll* take it." Only then did he order the engine room to stop the engines and back one-third. The engine room gang told him: "We *have* been going back, captain, since the first bell." At that the skipper apparently heard a little bell himself. He ordered, "Back emergency!" The engine room reply was the same: "We *have* been going back emergency, sir."[60]

The inevitable occurred as *Trinity* "sure took away" no less than 150 feet of pilings and dock space as she smacked into the pier. Luckily a catastrophic event was avoided, for her fuel tanks did not rupture. After this all-too-avoidable fiasco—which would have undoubtedly given Hart more white hairs—the durable, if bruised, old tanker offloaded her fuel allotment in Manila before shambling up to Tsingtao with the balance. It was one of her final prewar visits to that port.[61]

On another occasion, while *Trinity* was in "cold iron" condition at the navy yard—that is, main boilers not in use but with her donkey boiler still going to provide power, lights, and water—a fireman named John Gobidas came up with a new scheme to avoid the misery of his watch. He had found it bad enough in the sweltering boiler room anyway, but that discomfort was compounded by the severe heat of Manila. Having noticed that he "could see the face of boiler from the main deck forward," the diligent fireman "collected a bunch of hand mirrors so he could sit on the main deck and see the pressure gauge and the water level of the boiler." Satisfied with his ruse, Gobidas and the other sailors thought this "cute" until their chief—a no-nonsense old-timer with the euphonious name of H. T. Birchmire—suddenly reappeared on deck. Coming aft and seeing what his artful fireman had done, Birchmire "promptly gave birth to a squealing worm and threw a screaming fit." Resourceful or not, Gobidas was quickly banished to "watching the boiler down on the next deck standing up."[62]

Such rebukes did not make a great impression on the sly—or merely reckless—fireman, however. Less than a week later, with *Trinity* still in the yard, Chief Birchmire went aft to the log room again. He noticed one of his firemen was missing. It wasn't difficult to guess who. Birchmire then astonished a yeoman named Marche Rothlisberger by telling him to climb the funnel and check the cover. (When the main boilers were not in use, stacks were routinely covered.) Although this was a singular request—another sailor remembered that this task was "unheard of for a log room yeoman"—Rothlisberger did as instructed. Sure enough, "there was John Gobidas asleep curled up on top of the cover." He was "hiding and sleeping off a party from the night before." The dumbfounded Rothlisberger—already unnerved by his precarious climb—was so startled by this discovery that he almost toppled from his perch. It was sarcastically surmised that Chief Birchmire gave [Gobidas] "*high* marks that day."[63]

The pressures of his job in handling such individuals must have lain heavily on H. T. Birchmire's shoulders, for the capers of his wayward fireman were by no means unique. There was any number of colorful characters serving on *Trinity* in this period. And the old oiler was merely one ship in a fleet manned by hundreds of such characters.

Chief Birchmire, whose miseries (if not patience) must have seemed to rival those of Job, spent a good deal of his time contending with their foibles. Another episode in prewar Manila involved a veteran carpenter's mate with a name seemingly taken out of a nineteenth-century boy's novel: Orville Chestnut. This character lived up to his colorful name, too. One stifling morning, Chesnutt—known to his shipmates as "the Old Injun"—while suffering from a Ginebra gin hangover, had fallen profoundly asleep filling the ship's forward freshwater tank. Again, it was the engineering chief who had to deal with his wayward underlings.

According to *Trinity*'s Carl Hiller, the freshwater tank overflow vent fed into a cofferdam, which was "a void space which also contained a steam reciprocating pump used to transfer water and also used as a bilge pump for the forward spaces." While the Old Injun snored away his hangover, the ship's bow gradually began to sink. By the time the other men noticed this unnatural trim, the forward tank had fifteen feet of water in it. An exasperated Chief Birchmire then showed up and "taking stock of the situation . . . had the launch take him over to Cavite Navy Yard to either bring back a diver or a hard hat unit for himself."[64]

The long-suffering chief might have saved himself the trouble. In his absence a number of the men, including Hiller, debated whether the submerged steam pump would still operate. It was thought that it might. Then a dare was offered. Hiller, being fearless, a fair swimmer, and also ambitious to move up in rating, "elected to swim down and start the pump." Off went his clothing and into the water he dove, with visions—if successful—of being well on his way to fireman first class. During his first dives Hiller got the suction and discharge valves open, followed by the compartment suction valves and the steam exhaust. "Then came the big test. . . . Start the pump." After a few slow strokes to rid the steam, the engine started very slowly, and "then after the water had cleared the steam cylinders away she went pumping like no tomorrow." Delighted with this successful operation, Hiller wrote: "We pumped the compartment dry and just had finished when here comes old Birchmire." The enterprising young sailor might have seen what would follow: "I never knew a man could turn blue with anger."[65]

It is not hard to imagine the chief's state. Hiller recalled that after being chewed out, Birchmire kept him on his black list for the next three months before they could speak easily again, noting, "For the next year whenever he eyeballed me, he never forgot . . . the fresh water tank incident." Naturally both men avoided any mention at all of pumps.[66]

For other sailors, however, assignment to the Asiatic Fleet came as punishment. An example is the experience of an affable young sailor from the Midwest named Clarence R. Wills. Clarence had joined the navy a couple of years before the war and served on a pair of Pacific Fleet minesweepers. This had not been especially pleasant duty for him since the West Coast waters tossed the little converted four-pipers around like corks and Wills suffered badly from seasickness.

At Pearl Harbor one spring morning he was ordered to paint the crow's nest on his ship, the fast minesweeper USS *Perry* (DMS-17). Unfortunately this simple task did not go well for seaman second class Wills. As he wrestled with his can of gray paint some sixty feet above the deck it abruptly sprang from his grip. When the young Wills looked down in horror at the plummeting can he noticed a figure on the upper platform above the bridge: his commanding officer in whites. The errant paint can landed close enough to splatter the captain's pristine uniform, and Clarence's life would soon change forever.

That same day he was reassigned to mess-cook duty. Later, a veteran chief called for him. Wills, he was asked, how'd you like to transfer to China? The chief's flinty expression told him it was a rhetorical question. Shortly thereafter Clarence boarded the transport *Henderson* heading for the Far East. In June 1941 he ended up on the grizzled oiler *Trinity* at Cavite, along with John Gobidas, Carl Hiller, Old Injun Chesnutt, and Chief Birchmire. However, the more placid Philippine waters agreed with Wills, who mishandled no more paint cans and experienced no further seasickness. Eventually Clarence made yeoman first class.[67]

At the other end of the pecking order, Admiral Hart had known there were serious problems at Cavite when he first visited the facility four months into his command. "I face a sad state of unreadiness, " he noted in November 1939. Nothing seemed to have changed for the better when he got back from Shanghai to what he called the "Filippine Field" in October 1940. Ashore, among Cavite's Sixteenth Naval District bureaucracy, it was more of the same: a heavily formalized mind-set prevailed, ballasted by paper and marked by a clear "lack of brains." This reliance on red tape only produced inefficiency and gridlock. Hart also detected complacency along with what had already been reported as poor morale. These were not qualities for which he had any patience. The grousing at Cavite about Washington's apparent indifference to their remoteness was never going to be acceptable to the old-school admiral. Hart worked to rectify this situation, one that he recognized would be critical to the fleet's proper functioning in Manila. It was never easy, however.[68]

Over the course of his tenure, Hart remonstrated with a succession of rear admirals in command of the Sixteenth Naval District. From the nervous, depressed John Smeallie, who ended his tour by a botched suicide attempt in December 1940, to his old friend from submarines, Harold "Cap" Bemis, who had become a hypochondriac—being invalided out in 1941 due to "colds and indigestion" as the acerb Hart noted—to the hard-drinking Francis Rockwell, Hart found himself saddled with men he regarded as liabilities. Accompanying such headaches were those of mediocre matériel and the struggles of trying to beef up his own forces with whatever slight resources he might wrangle from Washington.[69]

He also had a myriad of issues to deal with that had nothing to do with the efficiency of his own forces. For one thing Hart was nearing retirement age, yet it looked as if the Navy Department might ask him to remain at his post beyond that point. He was not sure if he could manage his responsibilities to the best of his ability, but in general his health—for a man approaching sixty-four years of age—had been excellent.

Apart from that was the matter of war plans. USN plans were one thing, and those that obligated him to act in concert with America's allies—principally Great Britain—were another altogether. There had been talks among the Western powers in 1940 and 1941, but none were very successful and FDR had signed off on nothing, although he had not disapproved any plans either. The first talks with the British (January–March 1941) produced a document known as ABC-1, and it along with RAINBOW 5 (a "Joint Army & Navy Basic War Plan") emerged later that spring as the military's official prewar plans. These plans were approved by the Joint Board, the War Department, and the Navy Department and then sent to Roosevelt for his approval on June 2. Five days later he returned them, neither approving nor disapproving them, saying that Great Britain had not yet approved the ABC-1 report. Roosevelt's military aide, Gen. Edwin Watson, explained that in case of war the papers would go back to the president for his approval. This was a bit of Rooseveltian sleight-of-hand, however, since the British government had in fact approved the ABC-1 report. Lord Halifax informed the undersecretary of state, Sumner Welles, of this in early July. Welles in turn told FDR, but the document remained unsigned.[70]

However, for the isolated Asiatic Fleet forces, cooperation with the Dutch was no less paramount. Therefore, in January 1941 Hart sent his own chief of staff, Capt. William R. Purnell, to Java for a series of conferences with Dutch naval authorities. These talks were in fact merely preliminaries. Purnell was received by Lt. Adm. Conrad Helfrich, Commandant der Zeemacht (CZM, or commander of the navy) on Friday morning, January 10, in Batavia. As Purnell interpreted Helfrich's intentions, they were "exploratory conversations looking toward possible future combined operations."[71]

These talks were tentative, as the qualifiers in Purnell's phrasing indicate, and no definite plans emerged from them. There was an exchange of technical information for the military forces likely to be involved—concerning naval, ground, and air forces of the NEI and the United States, matters such as fuel oil and avgas on hand, Dutch minefields, details of navy yards, seaplane stations, and plans for destruction of petrochemical facilities—but policy matters remained unsettled. Nonetheless, as Hart observed in his diary, both he and Purnell were surprised that the East Indies Dutch had received the American delegation "with open arms!" He wrote, "We rather thought that they would be pretty stand-offish and that P[urnell]'s visit would not be very satisfactory."[72] In terms of military plans they did not amount to much, but they broke the ice and established some semblance of cooperation. One year later the American-

British-Dutch alliance would become formally organized—albeit under traumatic conditions—as ABDA.

During this same period, Hart had another visitor to *Houston*. Capt. John L. McCrea, Roosevelt's naval aide, came out from the states under orders from Stark to personally deliver the WPL-44 ("Rainbow 3") war plans.[73] McCrea remained on the flagship for ten days, waiting for Purnell to return from Batavia. While in the Manila area he also visited High Commissioner Sayre and MacArthur. The former remained hopeful that war could be avoided, whereas the latter believed conflict inevitable.

Later, in April 1941 at Singapore, another round of Far Eastern staff talks took place. These were known as ADB (American-Dutch-British), although representatives of Australia and New Zealand also participated. Hart again sent his chief of staff, Purnell, to attend, but the conference was unsuccessful. American planners and responsible commanders felt that too much emphasis was placed on the defense of Singapore and too little on the Philippines.

At this time Hart noted that he expected his fleet would be left to its own devices when hostilities started, for the Asiatic Station was "a side show—the main tent being over the Atlantic Ocean." But he also wrote: "Now [I] think that as regards our going into this war, it's no longer a matter of *whether* but one of *when*."[74] Yet, within another few months Washington's flip-flopping war plans would undergo another abrupt and radical shift.

• • •

While the planners in Washington and London continued to operate in a maze of mirrors, preparations in the Asiatic Fleet during 1940–41 may be summed up in a single word: inadequate. This to say not that Hart's fleet wasn't put through its paces in the time he commanded but that it was—as in the case of the army under MacArthur—a textbook example of *too little too late*. Regarding the navy's position, the cliché was disturbingly accurate: the Asiatic Fleet was too little—built around only the two old cruisers and thirteen small, weak destroyers of ancient vintage. There was neither a single battleship nor one true aircraft carrier. The auxiliaries, with few exceptions, were also dated and inadequate.

If the Asiatic Fleet possessed any hidden strength, it was thought to lie in its enlarged complement of submarines. By badgering Washington in 1940–41, Hart had managed to acquire several more divisions of modern boats. In the end he had under *Submarines, Asiatic* a total of twenty-nine subs organized in five divisions: half a dozen old "pig-boats" (S-boats) and nearly two dozen more-modern types, including seven P-class and twelve of the big Salmon-class boats. This shift had in fact depleted the Pacific Fleet's force, leaving only some ten boats at Pearl Harbor in late November 1941.

A year prior Hart had been delighted when the large modern boats began arriving in Manila in discreet numbers. The tender USS *Holland* (AS-3) had come out with the last detachment; she had been at Pearl Harbor or on the West Coast for some years prior. She brought Capt. Walter "Red" Doyle, who was to replace Capt. John Wilkes as the commander of the Asiatic Fleet's submarines. USS *Otus* (AS-20), a spanking new merchant vessel that the navy had taken over in late 1940 (as the SS *Fred Morris*), which was being converted to serve as a submarine tender additionally went to the Far East. *Otus* was present in the Manila area at the war's outbreak and received more last-minute conversion work at Cavite.

The hoary *Canopus* (built in 1919) had been the tender for the Asiatic S-boats since late 1924 and was known with affection as "Mama-san" by her crew and veteran submariners alike. *Otus*, on the other hand, was a green newcomer. None of her crew or officers had been on her more than nine months when the war started. Due to the value attributed to the submarine force and its mission— especially in the mind of Hart—none of these auxiliary units were to be dispersed south initially. For the time being CINCAF had decided to hold them in the Manila Bay area to support his submarines.

Yet the submarines of Hart were far from a homogenous organization, and their crews and officers lacked both sufficient tactical and practical experience. One of the many telling lessons in the sub campaign in the Philippines and East Indies would be that of flawed offensive tactics in the service of muddled doctrine left over from the twenties and thirties. Under the command of officers who lacked leadership or aggressive instincts, this was a recipe for failure. And that is precisely what happened. Naturally this situation was much to the displeasure, amounting almost to fury, of Hart, an old submariner himself. As someone who believed very strongly in the ability of his boats to play a significant role in the conflict to come, their poor performance was a sharp blow in a campaign characterized by near misses, almosts, and not quites.

Accounts of prewar exercises for the submarines are ambiguous. Some state that they were almost comically useless, while others claimed that "the submarine commanding officers and second officers had been undergoing extensive torpedo attack training."[75] At times these were little more than ludicrous wastes of time and fuel, as when the boats of Doyle and Wilkes practiced steaming on the surface in formation behind their tender. No less foolish was the prewar dependence on deep submergence attacks—over one hundred feet—and by sound bearings alone. Attacks at periscope depth were discouraged because it was believed boats could not long survive against any targets shielded by aircraft. According to W. J. Holmes, the high brass in the Asiatic Fleet's submarine squadron threatened boat skippers with instant relief from command if they exposed their periscopes during torpedo practice.[76]

Most of the younger officers recognized the uselessness of such exercises. In terms of actual tactical doctrine, many submariners had expected a war against screened enemy combat vessels, not vulnerable merchant ships. The adjustment to unrestricted submarine warfare after Pearl Harbor therefore took some time. American tacticians before the war had unrealistic assumptions in other critical areas as well. They expected far greater casualties to result from enemy antisubmarine warfare (ASW) action—perhaps as high as one in eight when attacking on sound bearings alone—yet at the same time they anticipated high success rates "when the submarine succeeded in making undetected sound contact with the target under good conditions." Then it was believed that as many as one-half of such attacks would succeed. Both assumptions would be found to have been "greatly overestimated."[77]

Accompanying such doctrinal shortcomings were mechanical glitches in the big new subs. The amount of time and energy devoted to rectifying those problems would have constituted a distraction as well. In Hart's view these subs were largely another manifestation of the New Deal navy's reliance on new-fangled gadgetry—an issue he had likewise found on *Houston*—and which irked his nineteenth-century sensibilities.

When war came, the unique circumstances of the Asiatic Fleet—on the front lines with so little offensive capacity faced with the rapid Japanese invasion of the Philippines—meant that Hart's submarine force was considered more *precious* than was realistic. This overprotective attitude had an inhibiting effect on the officers who took them out on their first patrols. Added to all these factors were emerging problems with submarine torpedoes, a defect equivalent to faulty bullets or projectiles that was to feature in one of the Silent Service's greatest scandals as the war went on.[78]

As for the flushdeckers of Destroyer Squadron 29, they were expected to serve as escorts and antisubmarine screens, but few envisioned the aged little ships being employed as frontline offensive weapons, still less that they would be required to fight almost exclusively at night. Hart's destroyermen were well trained, but they were never trained for the type of fighting that they later faced. One skipper even admitted that his destroyer had "never fired a night battle practice with guns or torpedoes," in the two years he commanded the ship prior to war.[79] There were, of course, tactical exercises in the prewar years, but budgetary restrictions and material shortages had always kept these practices brief and perfunctory. The belated emphasis on submarines was another hindrance. Cdr. Henry Eccles later recalled that during the year before the war, "the training of the destroyers in destroyer tactics had been sacrificed in order that we might run as targets for the submarines. We did have a few tactical exercises, but the majority of our operating period was devoted to exercises with submarines."[80]

Hart had seen for himself the poor training conditions prevailing in the Asiatic Fleet shortly after he arrived in mid-1939 and set about addressing those flaws. For some he was seen as a severe taskmaster who pushed the men relentlessly to achieve more efficient performance. Others felt that Hart's regimen was not too harsh, given the lax standards and complacency endemic throughout the Asiatic Station.

*Houston* went regularly on prewar cruises to the southern Philippines; often to Jolo's big Tutu Bay anchorage.[81] The cruiser fired day and night battle exercises—usually targeting small tenders or large, slow vessels of the fleet train—employing her main and secondary batteries. She also made full-power runs, which revealed that, at least for a brief sprint, the old girl could still kick up her heels. On her way out to the Far East in 1940, *Houston* had made over 31 knots, and a year later she was readily capable of exceeding 30 knots.

As for her crew, they never lacked spirit. This often manifested in ways that seemed uniquely Asiatic. After reaching *Houston* in July 1940, Ens. John B. "Lord" Nelson, an officer known for his by-the-book approach, chewed out a young navy bugler for blowing the call to movies when it was time for chow call. The youngster, an Italian from Brooklyn, cracked wise: "Whaddya want for 21 dollars a month . . . Benny Goodman?"[82]

. . .

In late November 1941—the week before the Army-Navy football game—Asiatic Fleet and U.S. Army officers were preparing for their annual party at the Army-Navy Club in Manila. The chairperson that year was Cdr. Thomas Binford (USNA 1920), who at the time commanded the navy's Destroyer Division 58. He had done so since his arrival in the Philippines the previous February.[83] Described as a kind of Colonel Blimp figure, Commander Binford was paunchy and balding but invariably courteous and good-humored. Yet beneath the rotund physique and southern drawl lurked a United States naval officer with high-grade qualities of leadership and initiative. Thomas Binford may have resembled Foghorn Leghorn, but courage and determination he never lacked.

He was well served in late 1941 by *Stewart*'s captain: Lt. Cdr. Harold Page Smith (USNA 1924)—from Mobile, Alabama—among the most highly regarded skippers in the squadron. Deemed "smart, competent, and demanding," Smith was, by all lights, respected and liked by the men on *Stewart*.[84]

The officers and enlisted men of DesRon 29 served at that time under Capt. Herbert V. Wiley (USNA 1915). Good luck had already preserved "High Velocity" Wiley through multiple tragedies. In April 1933 he had been one of only three survivors from the *Akron* disaster, which claimed seventy-three lives when that airship plunged into the frigid Atlantic Ocean off New Jersey after encountering a monstrous weather front. Two years later in February 1935, Wiley was captain of the larger, more sophisticated airship *Macon* when it fell into the Pacific near San Francisco. Miraculously only two lives were lost in the *Macon* crash. Seventy-four members of her seventy-six-man crew were rescued, including Wiley. But the venerable four-pipers of DesRon 29—much like the rigid airship—also represented an outmoded technology that should never have been in frontline service. As a result they, too, would be no strangers to tragedy at sea.

DesRon 29 comprised thirteen elderly World War I–era flushdecked destroyers of the Clemson-class. Many of these tin cans had been on the Asiatic Station since the midtwenties, and not one had been significantly upgraded over its career. In most respects they remained as-built. Interwar budget restrictions and their remote station kept them low-priority vessels. It is still a little stunning to realize just how meagerly equipped they were for offensive operations.

These ships were of the navy's 1916–17 building program "1,200-ton" type. They were each some 314 feet in length by 30 feet in beam, bearing four distinctive high funnels. When new, their powerful engines could push the knifelike hull through the water at an optimal 33–34 knots, although within a very short period in service this fell off to a top speed of 31 knots. By 1940–41 most were extremely hard-pressed to attain 28–30 knots. Throughout their careers, an ideal—that is, most economical—cruising speed was about 15 knots.

Even when new, flushdeckers were plagued by mechanical problems and required constant repairs and upgrades. Boiler brickwork glazed and cracked; their atomizers needed replacing; pumps malfunctioned; turbines lost blades; boiler tubes went bad; fuel tanks leaked. A few ships were built with their 4-inch guns mounted on inversely installed rollers, which meant the guns had to be lifted off and the rollers reinstalled correctly.

Their main battery consisted of four 4-inch/50 cal. guns, which fired a thirty-three-pound projectile to a maximum range of not quite sixteen thousand yards. The destroyers eventually received a modified, if outdated, Vickers or "Baby Ford" (Ford Rangekeeper Mark II) system for director-controlled salvo fire. Difficulties with communications to the gun stations were commonplace and necessitated more alterations. Also, it seems that a few 4-inch/50 cal. guns had an unpleasant tendency to discharge automatically when loaded and then elevated to maximum limit. *That*, of course, also took some getting used to.[85]

There were twelve tubes for Mark 8–Mod. 3 torpedoes (with no reloads); these could be fired electrically by keys on the bridge or at the tubes from the Mark 11–Mod. 4 director. A single, primitive 3-inch/23 cal. weapon—known humorously by the crews as the "peashooter"—was mounted on the fantail. Prior to war these destroyers had three or four .50 cal. machineguns mounted atop their midships and afterdeckhouses, along with a few lighter .30 cal. Lewis guns to augment their woeful AA battery.

Fortunately the entire squadron had received modern sound ("Q") gear in the summer of 1941 for use against subs. They had depth-charge racks, although their wide turning radius did not make them ideal vessels for antisubmarine work. Their original radio systems had been good for anywhere from eight hundred miles (main radio set) down to one hundred miles (auxiliary set); initially they also had a weak radio telephone with a limited range. Many of these communications systems on U.S. four-pipers, however, were replaced in the thirties. And while none of their officers or men were greatly deceived about their combat strength, all understood that they would have to fight these undersized and overage ships *very* well if they were to survive in action.

At war's outbreak Wiley's Twenty-Ninth Squadron was organized as follows:

The Fifty-Seventh Division commanded by Cdr. Edwin M. Crouch in USS *Whipple* (DD-217) (F), with USS *John D. Edwards* (DD-216), USS *Alden* (DD-211), and USS *Edsall* (DD-219).*

The Fifty-Eighth Division under Cdr. Thomas H. Binford in USS *Stewart* (DD-224)* (F), with USS *Barker* (DD-213), USS *Parrott* (DD-218), and USS *Bulmer* (DD-222).

The Fifty-Ninth Division led by Cdr. Paul H. Talbot in USS *John D. Ford* (DD-228) (F), with USS *Pope* (DD-225),* USS *Pillsbury* (DD-227),* and USS *Peary* (DD-226).*

The squadron flagship, USS *Paul Jones* (DD-230), was usually attached to one division (generally DesDiv 59). There was also the squadron tender, USS *Black Hawk* (AD-9), which served as Wiley's administrative HQ.[86]

Binford admired Hart because, although stern, he was a leader who "knew how to delegate authority." Hart made every effort to share as much information as he could with his officers, preferring them well informed rather than kept in the dark. After the war many would credit Hart with perhaps more foresight than he really possessed, feeling their survival had been due to his ability to place them out of harm's way when hostilities started. In fact this was only partially true—for Hart was instructed to get his ships south by Chief of Naval Operations Stark—but it stood out in sharp contrast to the unpreparedness and poor choices made by Douglas MacArthur in the war's opening hours.

In late June 1941 Hart moved his staff off *Houston* and ashore to the modern Marsman building near the Manila waterfront.[87] This change gave his overworked people more breathing room, with better living and working facilities. Furthermore, it reduced stress for the crew of the cruiser, who—like many navy personnel—disliked embarking the extra staff of a flagship. Additional officers present on board *Houston* when it had the flag only meant more misery for the cruiser's weary sailors. They were already being run very hard that year, training more or less constantly for a conflict that most of the men knew was inevitable.[88]

Then, in July 1941, as Japanese aggression intensified with their move south into lower Indo-China, Hart spoke to his officers in Manila. He pulled no punches about the ominous situation in the Pacific: "Gentlemen, I have a feeling this thing is coming." He was not sure how it would start—whether, as he phrased it, "over the water, on the water, or under the water"—but he was certain it would come.[89] It would have been a willful delusion to imagine otherwise. Commander Binford took Hart's comments on the looming conflict seriously, as did fellow officers.

Alternating with other ships on exercises, Binford's *Stewart* had been involved in patrolling the secret minefields around Corregidor at the entrance to Manila Bay after the navy took control of harbor traffic that summer. Along with miscellaneous small craft employed in escorting shipping through the minefields, *Stewart* did this for about six weeks before being relieved around the end of August. At that point other DesRon 29 destroyers took over. This extra duty kept several of Wiley's ships from scheduled overhauls and contributed to their relatively poor condition at war's outbreak.[90]

Such duty was not without its own forms of unwelcome excitement as well, for not only had the ships suffered from lack of yard time, but the men were all undergoing increased pressure for longer periods. The relaxed routine many had known for years in the Far East came to an abrupt end. For the Asiatic Fleet, 1941 was a year of drills, cruises, and training. The "pretty amateurish lot" that constituted his fleet needed discipline with the kid gloves removed, in Hart's opinion.[91] And few in the fleet had any real illusions about the certainty of war. Not many realized, however, the extent to which they had been deceived by their own natural self-confidence and by deep-rooted cultural and racial biases. Soon the enemy would knock more than the proverbial chip off their collective shoulder.

During 1941 precautions at Manila took on a deadly serious cast. Incoming and outbound shipping had begun to be carefully monitored. Unfortunately, in Hart's view the navy—meaning Rear Adm. Francis Rockwell's Sixteenth Naval District command at Cavite—had not done a good job in laying or managing the minefields. But then Hart had routinely been infuriated by what he saw as Cavite's incompetence.[92] He was not alone in this. Ens. Herb Levitt of *Houston* called it "a slothful place."[93]

On July 17 an exasperated Hart had Cavite cease work on laying the minefields—which had begun two days earlier—as the navy yard personnel had made such a mess of the undertaking.[94] This was one more indication of the severe pressures that U.S. forces felt that ominous July. Of course the problems lay not merely with Rockwell and Cavite. Apart from their poor material condition, too many of the ships themselves were indifferently led as far as Hart was concerned. On more than one occasion he expressed this frustration at the dearth of competent skippers in the Asiatic Fleet. "Oh for half a dozen captains or commanders who are real seamen," he wrote, exploding in a diary entry after another ship-handling mishap.[95] And a number of vessels continued to endure personnel shortages. There had still been too few men sent to the Asiatic Station—a time-consuming administrative evolution in the prewar navy's hidebound bureaucracy—and ships continued to be undermanned well into the war's second and third months.

Even Hart's flagship, *Houston*, had suffered from manning problems when her final refit was carried out at Mare Island in 1940. The ship lost a large percentage of her crew at the time—as many as four hundred men were either discharged or reassigned—and only a smaller nucleus of roughly three hundred well-trained men remained. It was then difficult to get a full complement on the ship. Perhaps the reality of impending war in the Far East made men less willing to enlist. The navy put out a call for volunteers, and a draft was sent through the fleet. It brought in only about a hundred sailors, although a number of them were old-timers like Chief Gunners Mate Carl W. "Ace" Miller, an Asiatic Fleet veteran, and Willard Ward and Merrit V. Eddy, both experienced shipfitters. At last a large contingent of raw recruits fresh out of various Naval Training Stations came aboard. Although green they at least filled out the divisions.[96]

With the long-anticipated, and dreaded, oil embargo of late July, Hart's fatalistic mood intensified somewhat. When a convoy came out to Manila in mid-September with AA batteries for the air forces at Clark Field, it was escorted by the powerful new light cruiser USS *Phoenix* (CL-46). Hart coveted these big vessels and even wrote in his diary that he wished he could "retain" one, a sister ship, USS *St. Louis* (CL-49).[97] At that time he did pay a visit to *Phoenix* and spoke with her officers. The ship's chief engineer, Lt. Cdr. J. C. Woelfel, recalled Hart mentioning that he had requested radar equipment from Washington "for the Asiatic Fleet and the P.I. military installations." He had been told that it would be another year before it could arrive. Woelfel remembered the old admiral saying, "It'll be too late then."[98]

In the Philippines moving the old ships to what amounted to a war footing led to more troubling incidents. One such example of near-disaster took place in late 1941 while *Trinity* was returning from Tandjong Oeban near Singapore (where she had topped off her load of fuel oil), as she steamed back into Manila Bay. Reentering the swept channel between the Corregidor and Bataan minefields that evening, with one of the flushdeckers patrolling in the distance, *Trinity* abruptly lost all steering. The situation quickly went from bad to worse, as the heavy, oil-laden tanker began drifting toward the mines. Although these were not contact mines but electrically controlled from shore, they had been activated. In no time frantic signal lights were seen flashing from Corregidor, from Mariveles, and from the now very alert, very alarmed destroyer. The crew of *Trinity* had the presence of mind to drop the ship's anchor, which prevented it from being swept into the minefield. At that point a pair of intrepid machinist mates began a desperate struggle with her antiquated steering gear.

The ship had a unique steering system that was located on the main deck level in the afterdeckhouse. A reciprocating steam engine mounted in the steering assembly turned the rudder and acted as a tiller. This in turn was connected to the bridge steering unit by a telemotor. Machinist Mate Carl Hiller later described what happened to *Trinity*'s "one of a kind" steering system: "The forward end of the unit slid on a quadrant bolt to the deck. Gears from the engine meshed with the quadrant. Loss of steerage was reported to the engine room. . . . They found that the engine was working but the clutch was slipping so the engine was not turning the rudder." An emergency transfer unit was as useless as the bridge wheel. Fortunately, the two adept machinists—one of whom was Cliff Mowrey—managed to readjust the slack clutch, and the steering system resumed proper function again. *Trinity* was then able to up-anchor, back out into the channel, and make her way to her berth, with all her crew breathing much easier.[99]

· · ·

Although Rear Adm. William Glassford Jr. was to become a somewhat unfavorably regarded leader among Asiatic Fleet sailors—who nicknamed him "15-knot Glassford" for what they perceived as his hesitant leadership once hostilities began—the difficult position in which he found himself was scarcely one of his own making.[100] He had not known much in detail about the strategic thinking—or what passed for such—from Washington (*or* in Hart's plans) when he and his small staff reached Manila in early December 1941.

After the blunt November 27 "war warning" from Washington, it was clear conflict was imminent.[101] On instructions from Chief of Naval Operations Stark, Hart began making every possible effort—per the "appropriate defensive deployment" clause in the warning—to get his last ships and people away from China and, where feasible, from the Philippines. At the same time Glassford had to be worked into the larger strategic picture because Hart had decided to put him in charge of a reactivated Task Force Five. TF5 would then function as the striking arm of the Asiatic Fleet. Hart would have preferred to utilize Rear Adm. William Purnell in this role, because he had far more experience and a better knowledge of the fleet's surface forces, but Glassford's seniority became the determining factor.

Upon reaching Manila—following a harrowing sea journey from Shanghai in their flat-bottomed, keelless river gunboats—Glassford and staff were put up at the same hotel where both Hart and MacArthur lived, a few hundred yards from fleet HQ at the Marsman Building. Between December 4, when he arrived, and the start of hostilities, Glassford played catch-up, as he studied revised war plans and discussed the results of conferences with the British and the Dutch. Purnell, Hart's chief of staff, had acted as the navy's primary representative in these talks over the past year, and he informed Glassford of the recent changes to U.S. war plans, most of which came as a surprise: "Perusal of the War Plans disclosed such changes in the traditional strategical conceptions with which we all had been so familiar, that I found myself on most uncertain ground. A then recent modification of the plans revealed that the *British, not ourselves,* would send strong naval reinforcements to the Far East, the inference being clear that we must look elsewhere for support other than to our own Pacific Fleet. Thus for the first time Singapore and British Malaya assumed far reaching importance as a key Far Eastern position for *us* as well as for the British."[102]

And Glassford was not alone in trying to make heads or tails of the latest Washington-London plans. In this period of blurred opacity, no one seemed to have a very clear idea of exactly *what* U.S. commitments were. They were unclear, in fact, from Manila to Oahu to Washington and across the Atlantic to London. In this we see how little concrete had really been achieved among the Western powers between the outbreak of war in September 1939 and December 1941. Indeed, the forlorn Dutch had been requesting *any* form of reassurances from the British and the Americans for military support since early 1940 and had still received nothing very firm.

Glassford, meanwhile, saw that he would probably be thrust into command of TF5 much quicker than anticipated, with little foreknowledge of his actual role: "I had to assume that the Force would operate initially as a unit, independent of any allies. It was evident no plans had been firmed for our joint operation or even cooperation, so far as I was informed. . . . The only thing I really knew was that in due course I was to take command and operate to the Southward, *not* in support of MacArthur."[103]

. . .

On Friday, December 5, Britain's new commander for its Far Eastern naval forces, Adm. Sir Tom Phillips, flew the 1,400 miles from Singapore to Manila for conferences with Hart, Glassford, Purnell, and army leaders. Phillips and staff were sequestered at Cavite, far from the press. There they met in secret with the Americans on the fifth and into the sixth.

MacArthur was present for some of the talks and droned long-windedly about *his* preparations and war plans, plans that would only be fully implemented the following April. Never one to let the truth get in the way of a good quip, he declared, "Admiral Hart and I operate in the closest cooperation. We are the oldest and dearest friends."[104] This was vintage Macspeak, self-aggrandizing and false, but Hart kept a straight face. However, after MacArthur repeated this nonsense to Glassford, Hart made a point to deny its accuracy as the two navy men departed.[105]

The senior admirals, Phillips and Hart, had no lack of mutual respect, yet in that tense atmosphere the meeting at times grew heated. Much of this stemmed from Phillips's insistence that previous U.S.-British talks and RAINBOW 5 allocated U.S. destroyers to the Royal Navy in the event Singapore was attacked. Hart refused at first to accept this and asked Phillips to send three available British destroyers down from Hong Kong. They wrangled back and forth until a kind of agreement was reached. Then fateful news reached Phillips. Air patrols revealed that a large Japanese invasion convoy had been spotted in the Gulf of Siam, presumably heading for Malaya. Phillips immediately began preparations to depart for Singapore. Hart went with him to the dock where he was to be taken to a waiting PBY. One of the last things the American admiral told his British counterpart was that he was ordering one U.S. destroyer division at Balikpapan to head for Singapore, where it would indeed operate with the Royal Navy.

# TWO

## As Is

### *The Asiatic Fleet at War's Outbreak*

With many of his ships already dispersed to the south, the news of a shooting war reached Hart in the predawn hours of December 8. Prodded by Washington, he had tried his best to get most of his fleet out of harm's way when the blow finally fell. Yet a number of American naval vessels still remained in the Manila-Cavite area when the dispatch arrived at 0300 hours of the Japanese surprise attack on Oahu.[1] And even though Asiatic Fleet ships were on a form of alert, some of the men were so stunned to receive the news that their response—like Secretary of the Navy Frank Knox in Washington—was one of sheer disbelief. "They must mean Davao, not Oahu!" one DesRon 29 sailor recalled his communications officer spluttering aloud as he read the message. On *John D. Ford*, Lt. Bill Mack recalled that the message was copied and recopied three times before it could be believed.[2]

At the onset of hostilities Hart's small fleet was scattered across the length of Southeast Asia. The distance from Manila south to Borneo exceeded 1,300 miles. As noted, Hart operated out of his HQ in the Marsman Building in Manila. Capt. Albert H. Rooks's flagship, USS *Houston*, had been sent south on December 1 to Iloilo, a coastal town on the central Philippine island of Panay about two hundred miles from Manila. The cruiser USS *Boise* (CL-47) was off Cebu, scheduled to pick up a convoy there. Her skipper, Capt. S. B. Robinson, had hoped to get his ship away from such an exposed forward position, but Hart had given him direct orders to support the Asiatic Fleet units. *Boise* was not an official Asiatic Fleet vessel, but, like it or not, she would remain attached to Hart's forces for the next six weeks.

Most of the fleet's subs were still in or near Manila Bay, but at least two others were elsewhere: S-36 off Lingayen Gulf and S-39 at Sorsogon Bay. The three submarine tenders—*Canopus*, *Otus*, and *Holland* (AS-3)—were also in the Manila Bay area as were seaplane tenders *Langley* and *Childs*. A majority of the smaller auxiliaries, including minesweepers, inshore patrol vessels (or gunboats), and two valuable oilers, *Pecos* (AO-6) and *Trinity*, along with various salvage and repair vessels remained nearby. Many of the aviation units with their support vessels had already moved south.

Three small units, however, had been ordered *north* toward the Gulf of Siam and Camranh Bay a few days before by FDR, ostensibly to "observe" Japanese movements southward. They were later suspected of being used as lures to provoke the Japanese into firing the war's first shots. One of these, USS *Isabel* (PY-10), was then returning from her (largely unsuccessful) mission as agent provocateur. She had been spotted by a Japanese patrol plane on the morning of December 5 as she approached Indo-China and kept under surveillance. *Isabel* sighted the coastline at 1900 hours that evening but within another ten minutes was recalled to Manila and turned about, her voyage as pointless as it was nerve-wracking. Another ship ordered to take part, the schooner USS *Lanikai*—under an ardent navy lieutenant named Kemp Tolley who had a predilection for covert snooping—was still anchored off Corregidor, unable to reach her patrol station at all. A third small vessel to be used, the schooner *Molly Moore*, was never involved.[3]

Hart wrote in his diary twenty-four hours later: "I immediately told everybody that we were in effect at war 'Govern yourselves accordingly' and then ensued one very long unhappy day." Continuing in his crabbed handwriting, he wrote, "Timing was bad for us: Still evacuating from China. Setting up Glassford in command of Cruisers and Destroyers—with his new outfit scattered over a thousand miles. Reorganizing the Submarines, incident to my last reinforcements. A new—and very slow—District Commandant, etc.... Then of course so many uncompleted preparations—which were started too late."[4]

Within twenty minutes of the notification from Hawaii, Chief of Naval Operations Stark instructed the navy to "EXECUTE WPL [War plan] 46 AGAINST JAPAN." This was soon followed in succession by Hart's orders to execute unrestricted air and submarine warfare against the Japanese. An hour later CINCAF added: "TO SHIPS IN MANILA: DARKEN SHIP X BE PREPARED FOR AIR-RAID AT DAWN." Hart's caution was well placed; within the next twenty-four hours there *would* be air attacks, although they would target the air forces on Luzon of MacArthur's air commander, Maj. Gen. Lewis Brereton, and they would prove devastating. The air raids against Hart's navy yard and small fleet—no less destructive—would occur within two days.

Many of the men's experiences when the war came were routine; others seem remarkably similar. On *Langley* it was the duty of QM1/c Walter Frumerie—a navy veteran since 1934—to take the "war declared" message from the radio shack to "the Old Man" (Capt. Felix Stump) in his quarters. Seventy years later Frumerie could still recall his trepidation as he knocked on the door to Stump's cabin at that hour, and the unnerving timbre of the skipper's voice gruffly asking, "*What* is it?"[5]

Lt. (j.g.) John J. A. "Jack" Michel of *Pope* had grabbed the final boat back to his destroyer after getting his "fill" of San Miguel beer at the Army-Navy Club. He expected, with no pleasure, that his ship would again be conducting mine-field patrols again the following week. Weather conditions on Manila Bay that night were typical according to Michel: "sticky [and] breathless." He eventually fell asleep in his sweltering miniature stateroom, in spite of its dysfunctional ventilator and location next to the forward fire room. In the middle of that momentous night—and no doubt still damp with beery perspiration—he was awakened from his slumbers to be told, "I don't suppose you're particularly interested right now, but Pearl Harbor was bombed and we're at war with Japan." Michel could only mumble, "The bastards," before going right back to sleep.[6]

*Pope*'s sailors, having been on patrol for almost three weeks, were ready that evening to let off a little steam, too. One group—Bill Penninger, Al Disney, Vic Estes, Thomas "Tom Cat" Singleton, Pete Golyer, R. J. "Boogie-Woogie" Smith, and C. W. Sullivan—had rented adjoining suites on the twelfth floor of the Manila Hilton Hotel, stocked them with booze and snacks, set up cots for the extra bodies, and then headed out on the town. That weekend was the annual Filipino Music and Dance Festival and Ball, and the sailors wanted to take advantage of the festivities. The ball's dance was to be held atop the hotel itself.

As it turned out, a big meal in the hotel restaurant, a few cold beverages, and two hours on the streets wore Bill Penninger down early—he had pulled the 0100 to 0500 bridge watch the night before—and he went to bed (avoiding the cots) sometime around midnight. Within another hour or so the others returned. Some were drunk, some disgruntled at the absence of dancing partners, others, as Penninger noted, "just plain unhappy, boozy I guess."[7] The weary Penninger soon drifted off to sleep again, as did his shipmates. It was to be the last good night's sleep they would enjoy for several years.

At 0820 hours on Sunday morning, the men were awakened by a fist hammering on their door. A hotel bellboy cautiously poked his head into the room, telling them they were ordered to return to their ships. Al Disney reached over to the nightstand, grabbed the alarm clock, and hurled it at the door. The bell-hop took off but not before yelling at the sailors: "Navy Department Cavite says so!" The men ignored this, snoozing until the bellboy came back and again told them ("*All* sailors!") to return to their ships. C. W. Sullivan picked up a shoe and bounced that off the door. Once more the messenger fled. But when that same determined bellboy next returned, he brought the Shore Patrol with him, and as Penninger put it, "Those guys *didn't* knock." They burst in shouting at the hung-over sailors: "Up and at 'em!" There was a war on; the Japanese had bombed Pearl Harbor, and the sailors were to get back as soon as possible to their ship. They were to "board any boat [they found] at the landing," where they would be taken out to the destroyer promptly. It was a group of stunned, drowsy, and still-tight sailors who returned that morning to *Pope.* As Bill Penninger later wrote: "My life would never be the same from that day on."[8]

Aboard uss *Trinity* at Sangley Point, Carl Hiller met the onset of the war in a manner equally representative, if slightly more staid. He had received the news following a night on the town with a buddy, his girlfriend, and her sister (the latter being in search of what she called "a clean-cut American").[9] The quartet spent an agreeable evening on the rooftop dance floor of the Great Eastern Hotel dancing and drinking rum and cokes. After midnight Hiller had returned from Manila to the ship by steam launch. When a shipmate, Carl Swanson, came by his bunk and woke him at 0330 hours to tell him the ship was at general quarters and that war had been declared, Hiller told him to go to hell. He then rolled over and went back to sleep. At 0700 he awoke to find that the joke was on him. The United States was indeed at war, and "The Lucky Thirteen"—as *Trinity* was sometimes called by her unsuperstitious crew—would soon find herself in the thick of an active and quite *lucky* career in the Far East.

For Hiller and hundreds of others this turn of events meant an abrupt end to the happy-go-lucky ways they had grown accustomed to during the prewar years: an end to soaking up San Miguel beer or Ginebra gin on the chit system; an end to waking up in a *nipa* shack on weekends next to a tawny-skinned Filipina beauty with the little Tocko lizards scurrying across the hut's ceiling, the sour odor of coconut-oil hair dressing gone bad overnight lingering in hungover nostrils; an end to the sizzling steak dinners served on hot metal platters at the Legaspi Gardens near Pier 7; an end to swimming in the oversized pools in Rizal Stadium; an end to dancing the jitterbug at the cavernous Santa Ana Cabaret and carousing at Cavite's Cascade Bar or the rowdier Riverside Cabaret at Olongapo, followed as often as not by a return in a pony-drawn *caretella* or *calesa* to one's ship, at which point staggering or swaggering aboard might result in anything from fisticuffs to falling head over heels off the gangway; an end to nights in the Intramuros ymca there . . . which, much like those in Shanghai and Hankow, was a home for those sailors and soldiers whose escapades had left them broke; a "so long" to duck-pin bowling at the Dreamland Cabaret in Cañacao, located down the street from the Marine Barracks at the end of the Paseo seawall—owned by Eddie Hart, an ex-pat American married to a Chinese woman and a kind of father confessor figure to many young sailors far from home and family—with the little bowling balls smacking roaches into the gutters as they scuttled from one side of the lane to the other; an end to its zany programs—such as "an All-American Floor Show . . . featuring the most popular entertainers, Miss Helen Webb, who will do the modern hula, and for the first time in Cavite, the celebrated fan dance the way *Sally Rand* does it" and "Carl Hendricks, The Vagabond Singer, In Songs That Never Grow Old"— enlivened by wonderful dance music courtesy of the navy yard orchestra or the band from USS *Augusta* (CA-31); good-bye to the free movies shown each weekend at the navy yard, marine barracks, or naval hospital—or the real thing at the Ideal Theatre in Manila's Plaza, which was air-conditioned and allowed smoking in the balcony; and farewell to the modern air-conditioned restaurant and bar, the Sky Room, atop the new, four-story Jai Alai Club—its graceful and sleek art deco structure designed by an architectural genius from Los Angeles named Welton Becket, who had already been featured in *Life* magazine.[10]

Overnight the well-established Asiatic lifestyle of the U.S. naval forces based there ceased to exist, fading to blurred contours in memory like an aging tattoo. In its place, organization and routine would be replaced by operational confusion, new hardships and stress, a lack of general or specific information, and the simmering anger of having been beaten to the punch by a despised enemy. As at Shanghai, as at Hong Kong, as throughout Malaya and looming like a blood-dark shadow over Singapore, an Asian New Order was poised to overturn and displace decades of white Western dominance.

In precisely what American war planners had foreseen for thirty years, the Asiatic Fleet—old, weak, and susceptible—was left in a dreadfully exposed position, well "out on a limb" with neither time nor matériel on their side, and the Japanese methodically sawing away. Over three decades of work by the U.S. Army and Navy had done nothing effective to alter this fundamental weakness in American strategic plans for the Far East, so for a number of ships and several thousand men, time simply ran out. The vaunted plans of MacArthur to defend the islands— in which he "would meet them at the beaches . . . and fight to destruction," as he liked to boast—were in effect brushed aside in the morning hours of December 8, when his air forces were crippled on the ground by well-timed Japanese air assaults.[11] Attacks on Clark Field by no less than eighty-eight of Japan's Eleventh Air Fleet fighters and bombers, and another one hundred and four enemy planes against Iba Field were devastating.[12] It was, as noted historian William Bartsch aptly termed it, "MacArthur's Pearl Harbor"—although on Luzon the Japanese did a more thorough and decisive job than they had at Oahu.

Hart's precarious scheme for remaining at Manila and operating his enlarged fleet of submarines from that location was likewise dashed in a matter of days. Inside of four weeks the ground forces of MacArthur in the Philippines would be cut off and besieged.[13] Those ships of Hart that escaped found themselves driven south to the Malay Barrier and beyond, back to the arid wastelands of northern Australia, where the desert winds wafted its red, powdery earth to dust the smooth Arafura Sea like a coating of silky blood.

• • •

Thus, in spite of their efforts, Hart and company were still caught flat-footed by the Japanese attacks. Four flushdeckers of DesDiv 59 had remained in the Manila Bay area that first week of December for overhaul and to continue escort duties for shipping. Two of these, *Pillsbury* and *Peary*, were in the navy yard at Cavite under repair following a collision during nighttime exercises in the second half of October. *Ford* and *Pope* operated in the upper bay near Corregidor, around the problematic army and navy minefields that had caused Hart such headaches. These tin cans were also tasked with conducting antisub patrols. The remaining flushdecker in Manila Bay, uss *Bulmer*, had pulled guard-ship duty.

The rest of *Bulmer*'s division (DesDiv 58 plus squadron flagship *Paul Jones*) had already reached the Dutch petrochemical facilities of Tarakan, Borneo. This remote but rich oil field was a tiny island on the northeast coast of Borneo, situated on the Celebes Sea, to the north of Makassar Strait. After leaving Manila on Thursday, November 25, following a warning dispatch from CNO the day before, the destroyers of DesDiv 58—*Stewart*, *Parrott*, and *Barker*, along with *Paul Jones*—had moved south into position with the light cruiser uss *Marblehead* and arrived at Tarakan on November 29.[14] Capt. Arthur G. "Robbie" Robinson of *Marblehead* was senior officer present afloat (sopa) and as such called the shots for all of the U.S. ships there. The 1,300-ton Royal Netherlands Navy minelayer *Prins van Oranje* was also present; she often led Binford's ships through the hazardous minefields around the anchorage.

There is good reason to believe that Hart agreed to send his ships to the various oil ports in Dutch Borneo not merely to protect them from sudden attacks by the Japanese but if necessary to assume control of these facilities. These realpolitik moves were designed to keep the Dutch from turning them over intact to the enemy or without timely, adequate demolitions being carried out. The rapid capitulation of Holland to the German armies in the spring of 1940 had not been forgotten nor had the Nazi takeover of non-German oil installations in Rumania, which were then utilized by the Wehrmacht.[15]

By then Tarakan's drab locale was even less appealing than before the war. Of the principal town, Linkas, *Parrott*'s skipper, Lt. Cdr. Edward N. "Butch" Parker recalled it was "not much of a place."[16] There were few if any bars or clubs for enlisted men to let off steam, although there was a Dutch Naval Officers Club. It was the haunt of a handful of Royal Netherlands Navy (RNN) submarine commanders said to be determined to fight if need be. Described as easy-going, they were also very fond of Bols gin.[17] Luckily *Marblehead* had an executive officer, Cdr. Nick Van Bergen, who spoke fluent Dutch, and he made arrangements with local Dutch officials for his crew to get liberty at Linkas. Radioman Ray Kester recalled of Tarakan, "Not many amenities. Lots of beer and the Dutchmen were good company. Even a 'movie house' that was showing a 'Hop Along Cassidy' western movie. The streets were dirt—mud when it rained—Planked walkways served as sidewalks. This similar to the early western towns in the U.S."[18]

Nonetheless, Tarakan's significance as a valuable (and vulnerable) oil center was well known. U.S. intelligence estimates as of mid-1941 realized that with its refinery complexes situated near the shore and connected by pipelines directly to the oilfields themselves, along with small garrisons weakly defended by minor caliber coastal and AA guns, Tarakan was—like other East Indian oil installations "incapable of resisting even temporarily a swift driving attack in force."[19]

Much of the time the four-pipers continued in a routine that had grown familiar for everyone: patrolling the harbor and holding various drills. On December 1 *Parrott* was sent up to Jolo, three hundred miles northeast, on an unrecorded task and to pick up Asiatic Fleet mail. Three days later at Tarakan Captain Robinson on *Marblehead* clamped down: no more liberties until he received further orders.[20] On *Stewart* a young signalman named Bill Kale wrote in his diary, "Situation at breaking point between Japan and U.S.A."[21] Kale couldn't have been more right. But understanding that hostilities were inevitable did little to reduce tensions. It was felt by all the men, especially the officers. The Asiatic Fleet was thousands of miles from home, far from adequate base facilities, and operating for all intents and purposes on a war footing while being kept in the dark by Washington, and it is a tribute to the self-sufficiency and grit of its men—and the quality of its officers—that they remained as optimistic and sharp as they did during this stressful period of uncertainty.

DesDiv 57—*Whipple, Alden, John D. Edwards,* and *Edsall*—found themselves also dispersed to the south. They, along with the squadron's tender and administrative flagship, *Black Hawk,* had been "loitering" at a Dutch oil port: Balikpapan, 325 miles south of Tarakan. In reality the destroyers were being considered for operations with the British at Singapore, despite Hart's reluctance to lessen his already-miniscule forces.

Hart had continued to hope that it would not yet be necessary to send them north and told Vice Admiral Phillips as much in their meeting at Manila. This was not an altogether honest species of hope, though. Hart's own PBYs flying out of the Manila Bay area had encountered Japanese air patrols for three days running (December 5–7), with the enemy planes "patrolling in the vicinity of the Luzon coastline." The PatWing 10 history further noted: "Each outfit, of course, had their machine guns manned, kept a wary eye on each other and avoided each other like stiff-legged dogs."[22] Hart nonetheless argued with Phillips until the very last moment. He noted that the Royal Navy had extra destroyers at Hong Kong that were not needed there, and as there were only two British capital ships to be screened, a total of six tin cans ought to have been enough.[23]

However, as we have seen, that afternoon Tom Phillips received an air recon report that revealed large Japanese convoys in the Gulf of Siam moving south. At this news he hurriedly departed (via an Asiatic Fleet PBY) for Singapore. Simultaneously Hart relented; his ships at Balikpapan were ordered to sea. DesDiv 57 (under Cdr. Edwin Crouch) and *Black Hawk* (with Captain Wiley on board) were to head for Batavia on the eastern end of Java with ostensible plans that they would there replenish supplies. In fact, this was done to move the four U.S. destroyers closer to Singapore.

The five ships all got under way together from Balikpapan harbor at 2100 hours on the evening of December 7 and formed up in ASW cruising formation around *Black Hawk* for the next four hours. After steaming at 10 knots during this period, the destroyers broke away from the slow-moving tender. Soon afterward *Black Hawk* got new orders from Hart to proceed to Surabaja on the eastern end of Java rather than Batavia.

Between 0106 and 0142 (local zone time) Crouch's division upped its speed from 10, then 15, then 20, and finally 22 knots as additional boilers were lighted off. At 0215 it received word that the war had begun. The division was now told to set course for Singapore, where it would serve with Admiral Phillips's forces. Half an hour later, all boilers now cut in on the main line; the column increased speed to 25 knots and passed Aru Bank Light abeam to starboard some two and half miles off. For the remainder of that morning the ships moved south through the Makassar Strait. At midday the four swung around the point at Selatan, Borneo's southeastern tip, steaming hell-for-leather at 28 knots before heading west into the Java Sea. Then they headed northwest through the Karimata Strait between Sumatra and Borneo, up to the Singapore Naval Base near Seletar on the island's northern shore.

The idea was to include them in the screen for the Royal Navy's heavy ships around which Adm. Sir Tom Phillips's Force Z had been organized: the new and powerful 14-inch-gunned battleship HMS *Prince of Wales*—veteran of the *Bismarck* hunt in May that year—and an older but still-potent battle cruiser armed with 15-inch guns, HMS *Repulse*. These were far and away the most formidable surface units the Allied navies could field in the Far East at that point, which, if nothing else, merely reveals the weakness of those Allied naval forces in December 1941.

The Royal Navy's destroyers of the Local Defence Flotilla then stationed at Hong Kong—*Thracian, Thanet,* and *Scout*—were not only older than the flush-deckers of Hart but even smaller and more feebly armed, if that was possible. *Thanet* and *Scout* departed Hong Kong on the evening of December 8 and made good their escape to the south, but *Thracian* remained behind to deal with minefields and was lost within the week. The brutal truth is that not one of these little ships, either American or British, would have made the least difference to the ultimate fate of Force Z, apart from rescuing more Royal Navy sailors from the warm South China Sea after the two big ships had gone under the waves.

For this was the very fate that Tom Phillips and his small force met on December 10 off Kuantan, Malaya. There they were attacked by Imperial Japanese Navy land-based bombers of Vice Adm. Matsunaga Sadaichi's Twenty-Second Kōkusentai flying out of southern Indo-China. Phillips departed Singapore in *Prince of Wales* knowing that Allied air cover was unlikely, and that he was placing his ships in danger of enemy air attacks. There have been decades of speculation about his actual motives for this rash operation, but most agree that as the ranking naval officer—at a time in which the Commonwealth land and air forces in Malaya were being severely pressed—he felt driven by the need to have the Royal Navy act decisively.[24] In the event Phillips and over eight hundred naval personnel paid with their lives for this temerity. And it was only by the narrowest of margins that Hart's four old destroyers were not caught up in the fiasco as well.

DesDiv 57 arrived at Singapore on the morning of December 10, well after Force Z had departed. Communications were so poor that Crouch's division then proceeded to sea as if to join up with Phillips, but it was soon learned that this was pointless; both heavy ships had been sunk. It took hours to sort the facts out, but the tin cans went on to the location of the sinkings, hoping to help rescue survivors. In Singapore the U.S. naval observer, Capt. John Creighton and his assistant observer, Lt. Cdr. J. S. Mosher, recognized that these destroyers would be in imminent danger of getting "their heads knocked off" the following morning by the same Japanese air forces.[25] After delays and more communications problems, they got a message to Crouch to withdraw before daybreak. DesDiv 57 altered course to the south at speed and returned to the Singapore Naval Base the following afternoon.

Apart from stopping and seizing some Japanese trawlers and sampans on their way back from Kuantan, the most significant action engaged in by these ships was the delivery of a spare ECM (electric code machine) to the U.S. naval observer's office at the naval base, which was done at the suggestion of the British. The device itself had been transported by Lt. J. J. Nix's *Edsall* on orders from Hart and was instrumental in keeping up with heavy radio direction-finder traffic then being gathered by the British at Kranji and the Asiatic Fleet unit at Cavite.[26]

By dispersing his ships to the south, Hart—and Washington—had hoped to avoid having the fleet grouped together and vulnerable if subjected to enemy surprise attacks by air when the fighting started. In the end this seemed a more prescient measure than it perhaps was; the devastation at Pearl Harbor and the airfields of Luzon would ensure that. Yet it also meant that Hart's already-skeletal forces were spread out over hundreds of miles and incapable of a timely assembly. That Hart understood this dispersion *had* to be undertaken tells us that quickly reorganizing his units as a surface striking force was not foremost in his prewar thinking. He would try to employ his ships in the coming campaign in what amounted to a Fabian strategy of delay and attrition. In order to do so, he had, first, to preserve them and, second, to conceal them from the initial onslaught of a skilled and aggressive enemy bent on crippling Allied resistance at the outset.

With the crushing blows suffered at Pearl Harbor, any remotely optimistic thinking settled into the mud like the shattered hulls of Pacific Fleet warships split open by Japanese bombs and torpedoes. Truth as well lay entombed within those oil- and blood-stained waters. Many enlisted men of the Asiatic Fleet, perhaps even a majority, were never to learn of the actual devastation at Oahu for the duration of their service in the East Indies. However, Tom Hart knew. On December 9 Hart wrote the following glum assessment in his diary: "We had to recast our whole situation today: Kimmel's fleet is not going to begin fighting its way westward for quite a time. And MacArthur's air force won't amount to much after the Japs go at them two or three more times, if as successful as yesterday."[27] Although soon accused of defeatism, Hart understood what the Japanese had accomplished within the first forty-eight hours of the Pacific War. More crucially he grasped what his own nation's military had failed to achieve.

• • •

*Houston*, too, received sudden orders to depart Manila in late November, with her final refit unfinished. The last of her quadruple 1.1-inch mounts had only recently been installed, and scores of yard workers and technicians were still laboring from sunup until sundown at Cavite—and often through the night—trying to get her ready for sea. An electrical fire on her searchlight platform may have played a role in the new 36-inch carbon-arc searchlights being left behind on the dock when the cruiser left port. She steamed for Iloilo with only her old searchlights. They had been removed in anticipation of getting the new sets but were taken back on again in her hasty departure. This mix-up did not bode well for her upcoming combat career, but it would have been consistent with Hart's complaints regarding the competence of his yard personnel at Cavite. *Houston* then went south two hundred miles to Iloilo on Panay Island.

Her paint job had been rushed and was likely also incomplete. The previous, bastardized scheme applied earlier that year had quickly faded. It had used a blue-gray paint manufactured locally (known as "Cavite Blue") up to smokestack level; above that a lighter gray was utilized. This was the Asiatic Fleet's variation on the Pacific Fleet's standard Measure 1 scheme and differed only in the dark hue applied. In the Pacific Fleet this was a gray; in the Asiatic fleet, "Cavite Blue" was employed. As of early December, Hart wrote BuShips that this scheme was "now being eliminated and the entire painting scheme involve[d] the application of one color, the present temporary Cavite blue gray color."[28] Although there are relatively few clear images of *Houston* taken after the war began, all show her sporting an abraded and worn paint job of no precisely discernible measure.

At the same time there were concerns about the newfangled AA battery *Houston* had been fitted with during her major overhaul at Mare Island in 1940. As planned since late 1938, her secondary battery was doubled to eight 5-inch guns. A 6,298-gallon fuel oil tank was cleaned out and lined to provide the requisite extra magazine capacity.[29] More significantly, the cruiser received an upgraded fire-control system for those guns. This was a modification of the original Mark 19, in newly enclosed directors mounted above the bridge forward and over the secondary conn position aft. The new Mark 19 incorporated its own range finder—unlike the original system of 1928—and all the guns themselves had cut-out cams installed to prevent shooting into the ship on extreme bearings. This latter feature worried some of the ship's gunnery officers, since they had not yet been in a situation demanding a rigorous test of its efficacy. Additionally, *Houston*'s previous skipper (Capt. Jesse B. Oldendorf) did not like the site of the aft director—above secondary conn, where it was prone to being fouled by exhaust from the cruiser's stacks. He wanted it relocated to the mainmast.[30]

While the prewar navy bureaucracy moved with glacial speed, other retarding factors were at play. One was FDR's use of *Houston* for personal cruises, which meant that cosmetic matters often took precedence over substantive matériel efficiency. The ship—especially when functioning as a flagship or as Roosevelt's "Little White House"—had more energy focused on her crew's deportment, paint jobs, and bright work than on gunnery exercises or antiaircraft drills. It is known that *Houston*'s overhaul and refit time in 1939–40 was compromised by the ship having to wait until the president's travel itinerary could be finalized. In view of FDR's well-known and genuine fondness for the cruiser, there would be a good deal of irony involved in *Houston*'s fate.

Thus, as events transpired, *Houston* went to war with defective 5-inch shells, an unproven AA fire-control system, and no directors at all for her newly installed 1.1-inch "Chicago Pianos." The latter were put on the ship in different yards—one quadruple mount having been emplaced in late 1940 at Mare Island and the others at the Cavite Navy Yard in 1941—but no dedicated directors existed for them. These guns lacked any safety stops, unlike the cut-out cams used on the 5-inch battery, and it fell to one of the cruiser's own officers, Ens. Alva F. Nethken, to fashion a homemade jig that was hoped would keep the 1.1-inch guns from shooting into the ship itself on extreme bearings.

The morale of the men remained high, but their attitudes became a good deal more serious in the course of their extensive training exercises that summer. The ship's assistant engineer officer, Lt. Robert B. Fulton II (USNA 1932), a four-piper veteran himself, remembered the somber mood among new officers arriving on *Houston* in late August 1941. The cruiser was then at Jolo Island in the southern Philippines. On the day before *Houston* changed skippers, a boat brought Fulton and two other young officers—Lt. E. D. Hodge, who would become communications officer, and Ens. Leon Rogers, one of the AA officers—along with Capt. Albert H. Rooks, out to the ship. The ride across the large Tutu Bay anchorage was a time-consuming one, but these officers were silent. Thousands of miles from families in the States and from their bases in

Hawaii and the West Coast, they were struck with the seriousness of their situation. In Bob Fulton's opinion, *all* the men seemed to have been reflecting on the grim business that was obviously near at hand.[31]

Scarcely four months later, as *Houston* sat at anchor in Iloilo's harbor awaiting the fleet's "new boss"—meaning Glassford—Lieutenant Fulton wrote to his parents again in Washington DC. He noted, "Things are just about as tense as anyone wants to make them now." He and everyone else expected something to happen at any moment, but no one had any real idea what, when, or where. Yet even officers were not often privy to good intelligence information. Fulton also expressed (ingenuously, as it turned out) his gratitude for the Royal Navy units sent to Malaya: "Needless to say we are glad to know of the British naval reinforcements in Singapore. We just hope they have a really sizeable force there now."[32] But the British force was not nearly sizable or powerful enough, and the next letter Fulton sent home came nearly two weeks later. By then his world—and that of the entire Far East—had undergone a profound and permanent shift.

. . .

December 8 also altered everything for Bill Glassford. He recalled, "We were taken unawares; the solid ground was blasted right from under us. Never in my experience had I felt so completely at loose ends."[33] Although most of the informed U.S. military leaders in the Far East expected the Japanese to begin hostilities, very few had imagined that Imperial forces were capable of such widespread, well-coordinated, and devastating operations at the outset.

After a swift farewell from Hart, Glassford was put in the admiral's barge around midday along with his staff and baggage. They were then ferried out to his old flagship, the gunboat *Luzon*—anchored off Cavite—for a last-minute visit. *Luzon* was given orders that the Yangtze Patrol had been dissolved and that she and her sisters would join the Inshore Patrol under Cdr. K. M. Hoeffel. From there Glassford went ashore to Cavite and met with Capt. Frank Wagner, commander of PatWing 10, who told him that time was short; a Japanese air attack was expected at any moment. Glassford and staff were next taken by cramped motor launch to a waiting PBY—which he felt was a "sitting duck" moored only a hundred yards offshore. Then, unnerved by the ear-splitting roars of nearby PT-boat engines, which he thought belonged to enemy planes, they boarded the Catalina. The young PatWing 10 pilot, Ens. "Duke" Campbell—described as "a great Viking of a man" by Glassford—after some mechanical misadventures, finally got his heavily laden plane, P-3, into the air. Flying low to avoid enemy raiders, he managed to transport Glassford and company to Iloilo where they joined *Houston*.

Among those units caught in Manila on that momentous weekend were several vessels overhauling at the Cavite Navy Yard. This included two of Hart's modern submarines, uss *Sealion* (ss-195) and uss *Seadragon* (ss-194). Both were in an exposed, defenseless condition.

Other submarines were in the process of being dispersed on their first war patrols, although the majority was still in the immediate Manila area. Lt. Cdr. J. A. Callaghan's *Porpoise* was then at Olongapo having her storage batteries renewed; the aft battery had been replaced but not the forward. It was decided that Callaghan's boat would have to get under way on her first war patrol with the old forward battery unaltered.

The overhauling S-class boats (*Sealion* and *Seadragon*) had been moored alongside each other at Cavite's Machina Wharf. Work had started only fairly recently on this pair. *Sealion* was the more helpless, with her engines dismantled; *Seadragon* was within seventy-two to ninety-six hours of returning to duty. That day she was in the process of being repainted with dozens of drums of paint stacked on her slatted wooden decking.[34]

In addition to these, the bulk of Asiatic Fleet auxiliaries and service vessels, along with Wilkes's other submarines were still present in Manila Bay or Mariveles or Cavite when the war began. All three tenders for Hart's enlarged contingent of boats were present: uss *Otus*, undergoing emergency repairs on a propeller was in the Dewey dry dock at Mariveles across the bay to the west on the tip of the Bataan Peninsula.[35] uss *Holland* was nestled behind the breakwater in Manila Harbor. uss *Canopus* was anchored off the navy yard. That more Asiatic Fleet vessels were not lost over the ensuing days may be seen as an act of divine providence or of stunning incompetence by the enemy. It was *not* due to American sagacity, in any case.

As vulnerable to air attack as *Sealion* and *Seadragon* were, they were no worse off than the two flushdeckers also under repair at Cavite: uss *Pillsbury* and uss *Peary*, both damaged when they had collided in October during nighttime training exercises. Called "P Div" by wags, they, too, were instructed to move south as soon as seaworthy. Hart needed every possible escort for his slow, vulnerable auxiliaries.

Urgency soon turned into emergency when—to nobody's surprise—Japanese bombers attacked Cavite on December 10, wrecking *Sealion* and inflicting moderate damage to *Seadragon*. The helpless destroyers *Pillsbury* and *Peary* received more than their fair share of damage. These bombings destroyed most of the base and the navy yard along with its many parts and stores intended to replenish Hart's fleet, plus the repair and machine shops needed to keep it fighting in the war's initial stage. As many as 185 of the submarine force's Mark 14 and Mod. 1 torpedoes, which had not been moved into bomb-proof casemates, were also destroyed. Another four dozen fish on a lighter next to *Sealion* and *Seadragon* were lost when the lighter sank.

· · ·

Having witnessed the Japanese nighttime attacks of outlying U.S. Army Air Force fields two nights before and the enormous display of exploding bombs and pyrotechnics that resulted, everyone realized that enemy bombers would return soon enough. That first night *Canopus*'s log recorded at 2400 hours: "The crew observed midnight enemy air attack on Nichols Field. Large fires were started instantly, ground defenses replied with heavy but ineffective fire of machine guns and antiaircraft guns but no hits were observed."[36] Her skipper, Cdr. E. L. Sackett, later wrote that the midnight attack "looked for all the world like a good old Fourth of July display. From our anchorage off Cavite, just far enough away to muffle the noise, the showers of red and yellow tracer bullets, the sparklers of antiaircraft bursts followed by the bonfire glare of burning hangars and planes had an unreal quality which made it hard to realize that this was war."[37]

The other four-pipers, *Ford* and *Pope*, meanwhile returned during the night and were waiting off Corregidor at daybreak on the tenth to reenter Manila Bay. Shortly after dawn they came into the bay, which was still teeming with merchant vessels and warships. Very few had remained behind the breakwater, though, since more enemy air attacks were expected. The destroyers then went to the navy yard fuel docks to replenish their oil. As soon as they had finished this task, both moved out into the bay between Manila and Cavite, where they anchored. Each ship's engineering plant was placed on one hour's notice, "with one boiler lighted off for auxiliary purposes."[38]

On the foc's'le of *Pope* an eighteen-year-old sailor from East Texas had been getting some sun following noon chow and was trying to unwind a little after the tense previous days and nights. It was a clear, beautiful day, and Joe Sam Sisk was glad to be topside enjoying the fresh air. Not far from his destroyer he could see one of Captain Wilkes's submarines taking on provisions from a lighter in the bay; its deck was covered with crates of boxed foodstuffs. Suddenly air-raid sirens began screaming across the Manila Bay and Cavite area. "MANY ENEMY PLANES APPROACHING MANILA" was the message copied by fleet radiomen.

December 9 had been a day of several nervous air-raid alarms, all false, but bombers of Vice Adm. Tsukahara Nishizo's Eleventh Air Fleet returned in strength on December 10 for a leisurely and devastating series of attacks. At about 1240 hours the first wave of planes was sighted. As soon as they were recognized as enemy, both *Pope* and *Ford* went to general quarters. The remaining submarines likewise got under way, and several began submerging, seeking shelter on the bottom of the bay. As he went to his battle station, young Joe Sisk on *Pope* would never forget seeing the sub he had been observing lower itself beneath the waves, leaving boxes of supplies bobbing in the glistening blue waters of Manila Bay.[39]

Flying in from Formosa to the northwest, the Imperial Navy land-based bombers came over the area unchallenged but maintained high altitude—estimated at twenty thousand feet—well above AA fire. They then proceeded to single out Cavite and Sangley Point, where they wrought unholy hell on what Admiral Hart called "my poor little Naval Station."[40] Cavite by far received the most severe damage, but the men of PatWing 10 knew that their base at Sangley would not escape the enemy's attention for long. The Japanese had encountered no reason *not* to make a thorough job of it, after all.

Two flights totaling fifty-one medium bombers flew over, in groups of twenty-four and twenty-seven, to make their measured runs undisturbed by flak or effective American interceptors. They concentrated their attention on Cavite and shipping in Manila Bay.[41] One luckless army P-40 attempting to counter the escorting Zeros at low altitude was promptly shot down by U.S. Marine gunners over Bacoor Bay and crash-landed in the waters there. At that moment, 1304 hours, the first string of Japanese bombs landed nearby, almost obliterating the downed pursuit plane and immersing the yard tug *Santa Rita* but otherwise hitting no targets. High overhead, flying in good order and with more precision, another flight of bombers made their run. Their bombs fell at 1313 hours, which proved as unlucky as such numerals might suggest.

· · ·

*Pillsbury* was moored with her port side to the east wall of Cavite's Central Wharf; her sister, *Peary*—with more serious collision damage to her bow—was situated opposite her, with her starboard side moored to the wharf's western wall. Since *Pillsbury* had received less time-consuming injuries, she had priority in repairs because she could then be returned to duty more quickly. Although her condition was far from combat ready, she was closer to seaworthiness than her cohort.

In a precarious and vulnerable "cold iron" state, *Peary* had her engines disassembled and her bow open waiting to be patched. The ship was getting all her services (steam, water, electricity) from the dock. In short the four-stacker was "afloat but incapable of movement."[42] The most fortunate aspect of this nonoperational status was that the bulk of her crew was not aboard her. Many of the men were ashore working in a various repair shops, struggling to help get the ship buttoned back up once again. The destroyer skippers, Lt. Cdr. Harry Keith of *Peary* and Lt. Cdr. Harold "Froggy" Pound of *Pillsbury*, had their own rooms at the Army-Navy Club ashore, although their days were spent with their ships.

On December 10 Pound happened to be in Manila on business at CINCAF headquarters, while Keith was on board his destroyer. *Pillsbury's* executive officer (XO; Lt. R. W. Germany) was senior officer on that tin can. It was just before one o'clock that the inevitable Japanese bombers appeared high overhead and began making leisurely passes over the Cavite Navy Yard. At that height they were undisturbed by AA fire—although some nicked planes fell out of formation, and at least one was believed to have crashed. Maintaining disciplined *V*s they made their drops. Several U.S. ships were able to get under way, including the new sub tender *Otus*, which was moored at the head of Machina Wharf, near the two destroyers. Beginning around 1315 hours, the next forty-five minutes or so saw bombs raining down on the bay, the navy yard, and the helpless ships still there.

Eventually the luck of *Peary* and *Pillsbury* ran out. At about 1350 a string of bombs dropped from high altitude and "fell across the south east end of the yeard [*sic*] making a direct hit on the mast of USS *Peary*, killing or wounding almost everyone on the fire-control platform, bridge, and starboard passageway through and on the galley deckhouse. A severe fire was started on the after starboard side of the well deck and in the starboard passageway."[43] Eight sailors were killed outright, and five officers, including the skipper, Lieutenant Commander Keith, were wounded. The XO, Lt. A. E. Gates, was found unconscious on the bridge and later died. Another fifteen enlisted men on the ship were wounded, while that many more disappeared in Cavite. They were thought to have been killed while ashore helping with the wounded or seeking aid for injuries themselves. The entire navy yard was now wreathed in flames and clouds of smoke. To add to the danger, warheads and air flasks from the nearby torpedo workshop detonated, spraying fragments throughout the area that injured or killed more men.

With no water of her own to fight the flames, *Peary* was aided by a fire hose brought over from *Pillsbury*. Soon *Pillsbury* was able to get under way and moved out into the bay, but *Peary* was incapable of steaming under her own power. At that moment, however, she was saved by an unlikely comrade. The small Asiatic Fleet minesweeper USS *Whippoorwill* (AM-35), commanded by Lt. Cdr. Charles Ferriter (USNA 1924), braved the flames and smoke to render assistance to the severely damaged four-piper. At great peril Ferriter managed to nose his vessel in between burning lighters and barges on one side of the slip so that his men could manhandle a 6-inch hawser from his bow to the stern of the destroyer. In all the chaos several attempts to tow *Peary* out of her berth failed—due to a lack of line at first and then when shrapnel from the explosions nearby severed the next line—but finally, with sailors from *Whippoorwill* leaping onto the dock to help cast away lines from the mooring bollards, *Peary* was taken in tow at about 1445 hours. Slowly and gingerly, past flaming barges and under roiling columns of black smoke, *Whippoorwill* managed to tug *Peary* to a buoy approximately one mile northeast of what remained of the Cavite Navy Yard. With the help of a motor whaleboat from the destroyer, 6-inch Manila lines were secured to the buoy. All told, this "dangerous and mule hauling" work consumed about another hour.[44] At 1545, after the bombings had ended, Ferriter's doughty *Whippoorwill* was moored to the port side of *Peary*. Within a brief period the minesweeper then began sending over water and food to the exhausted and now fully blooded crew of *Peary*. Although they had survived one of the worst possible situations, for the men of USS *Peary* their war would only go from bad to worse.

· · ·

For the remainder of his days, Hart would be haunted and troubled by the memory of ships and men who could not escape. He neither gave his conscience the satisfaction of rationalizing his actions nor had the facts later obscured or falsified to suit his own ego. In his diary after he had reached Java, Hart wrote that for "3,000 people—Navy and Marines," it would be "hell on earth." He felt that he could and should have gotten out about five hundred more but wrote, "I was too Quixotic about it."[45] Hart's honesty notwithstanding, many causes far beyond his control had led to this state of affairs.

Even smaller surface craft, including Motor Torpedo Boat Squadron 3 under Lt. (j.g.) John Bulkeley (USNA 1933) did not escape the bombings' impact. They lost equipment, spares, and most of their drummed 100-octane gasoline. Only nine extra engines were salvaged, and these only because "Bulkeley had had the foresight to store [them] in private garages in Manila." Squadron 3's boats would remain at Manila to very near the bitter end, scrapping with the Japanese as best they could despite matériel shortages and attrition through enemy action.[46]

···

Two hundred miles to the south, anchored off the dingy little town of Iloilo at Panay Island, *Houston* had received news of the war's outbreak in much the same manner as other ships in Hart's fleet. Radioman David Flynn was reading a book as he tried to keep awake during the 0000–0400 shift. At 0315 hours a message came through that he took, automatically and not a little hazily. The priority indicators suddenly caught his attention. "What did that thing say?" he thought to himself as he looked at it again more closely. It was Hart's succinct notification: "JAPAN STARTED HOSTILITIES X GOVERN YOURSELVES ACCORDINGLY."[47] The message was given to Lt. E. D. Hodge, the communications officer, who had it taken to Captain Rooks's quarters. The looming war that all had anticipated was a reality.

*Houston* then had to wait for the arrival of Rear Admiral Glassford (commanding TF5) and his staff, as they were flown in from Manila by PBY. The time went by somewhat uncomfortably for the cruiser's men that day, for they all knew that air or sea attacks were possible at any instant. Rooks meanwhile prepared the ship for getting under way on short notice; he wanted to put as much distance between *Houston* and Iloilo as he could. At about half past six that evening Duke Campbell's lumbering Catalina, P-3, appeared in the distance.

Within three hours more orders were disseminated throughout Hart's dispersed units. Some initial confusion did take place, but these missteps were all minor. At Tarakan *Paul Jones* took down a message reading, "Orders from CINCAF to put war plans in execution. Attack-mission." But such errors were quickly corrected. No one expected the flushdeckers to undertake any offensive operations on December 8, and especially not once the scale and success of the Japanese attacks became apparent.

Notwithstanding the somber reports filtering in, the destroyers of DesDiv 58 and *Marblehead* were promptly set in motion. On *Parrott* Bill Slagle, a young sailor striking for radioman, took the war message to his skipper, "Butch" Parker. Along with *Marblehead*, *Stewart*, and the others, *Parrott* would steam down the Makassar Strait to Balikpapan, Borneo, to await orders. This message was soon clarified to mean they would meet up with other Asiatic Fleet ships coming south out of the Philippines. As might have been expected, the old ships gave trouble at the outset. CDD58 reported to *Marblehead* that *Paul Jones*'s anchor engine was out of commission and would take two hours to be repaired, but in the meantime the anchor could be raised by hand. This was no time to tolerate such delays. At 0530 hours the ships left the Tarakan anchorage, where they were led through the minefields by the Dutch minelayer *Prins van Oranje*. Clearing this area within another hour, the ships stayed together until 0730, when *Barker* and *Paul Jones* split off under new orders: "Directed to rendezvous with *Houston*." *Marblehead*, *Stewart*, and *Parrott* picked up speed as they proceeded to zigzag south on the three-hundred-mile run to Balikpapan.

# THREE

## Manila Abandoned

*South from the Philippines*

After the devastation inflicted on the Luzon airfields and at Cavite and Sangley Point by the bombings of December 8–10, Hart saw his plans for operating out of Manila Bay crumble. The calamity that befell Tom Phillips's Force Z off the coast of Malaya on December 10 only underscored Allied vulnerability to enemy air attacks. Singapore was quickly ruled out. On the tenth, Chief of Naval Operations Stark sent dispatch 101958 to CINCAF with instructions to "retire . . . in the direction of northwest Australia rather than Singapore." From there it was felt Hart could operate his fleet in defense of the NEI (Netherlands East Indies) and Australia "and raid enemy forces and shipping."[1] Therefore, to preserve his auxiliary vessels, Hart ordered those that could to begin moving south to the East Indies and Australia. War plans stated that the Allied powers would make every effort stop the Japanese advance along the so-called Malay Barrier and keep Imperial forces from controlling the Indian Ocean. However, plans were one thing and reality another, and a number of the Asiatic Fleet's auxiliary forces would eventually travel on to Port Darwin in northern Australia.

• • •

Among the handful of American ships narrowly eluding the Japanese stranglehold on Luzon was the venerable tanker USS *Trinity* under Cdr. William Hibbs. On the morning of December 8, 1941, she was moored at Sangley Point's berth number 2 near Cavite, preparing to discharge a large volume of avgas (for the PBYS of PatWing 10) into storage tanks ashore. This poky old vessel, under direction of the Naval Transportation Service and incapable of more than 10 knots, was attached to Hart's command only when west of the 180th meridian. (To the east of this line she came under the Pacific Fleet command.) But slow and ungainly or not, she was valuable. And in striking contrast to the fate soon to overtake many Asiatic Fleet warships, she would lead a charmed life over the next eighty days.[2] That she survived the campaign also meant that her crew was able to provide invaluable reminiscences and details of life and combat in the old Asiatic Fleet before so many of its units were lost in the Java campaign. For these reasons it is worth examining her career a little in the war's first three months.

Like the other ships in Manila, *Trinity* received word of the Japanese attacks well before dawn. Most of her crew had been alerted after receiving the message from Admiral Hart at 0330 hours. By daybreak at least one of her air defense stations was manned—for whatever such efforts were worth. Seaman Frank Barger drew a World War I–era .30 cal. Lewis air-cooled machine gun with loaded pan from the ship's little 8 x 8-foot "armory" and mounted it above the forward 5-inch gun tub, to cover that position in the event of an air attack. There the apprehensive Barger remained all day, sustained only by a couple of sandwiches delivered to his station. He appears to have constituted the tanker's entire AA battery at that time. But not all of *Trinity*'s sailors were as well informed or prepared for the war.

Machinist Mate Wilbur Bingham had somehow failed to get the word and carried on with his usual in-port routine. Up early, he went ashore to find movies for the crew to watch in their nightly shipboard screenings. Returning to the tanker after noon with a load of films, he was met by the officer on duty (OOD), who told him to turn around and take the movies back. Bingham obeyed his instructions, although still without quite grasping the reasoning behind them. When he got back to *Trinity* again, he found that he had missed most of the midday meal, but before he knew it general quarters rang and to his battle station on the bridge he proceeded. There, as he complained to the officer present about general quarters (GQ) being called during lunchtime, he was finally enlightened. The officer exclaimed, "Don't you know that we're at war?" It was only then that the "shocked" young sailor from Iowa learned of the bombings at Pearl Harbor.[3]

Irrespective of any individual's lack of knowledge, most of *Trinity*'s crew had gone to work in earnest that December morning. At 0655 hours her men began pumping out nearly a quarter million gallons of gasoline to the fuel dock. This task was stopped once or twice during the day, but after twelve hours she finished delivering the fuel. Simultaneously, in the course of this chaotic day, some ten or fifteen *Trinity* sailors under treatment at the Cañacao Naval Hospital on Cavite were brought back to the ship by her new medical officer, Lt. Harold S. Miropol.[4] All these men had been hospitalized with severe infections from coral cuts acquired swimming in the waters off Tandjong Oeban—the huge StanVac oil storage facility on Bintan island southeast of Singapore—in late November on the ship's last prewar cruise south.[5] Regretfully, a number of crew members with more serious infections had to be sent *back* to the hospital when *Trinity*'s limited medical facilities "precluded them from receiving adequate treatment." They were left behind when the ship departed.[6] At least three went aboard other Asiatic Fleet ships fleeing in the next few days. Not one of these ships and none of the men survived the war. To elude death on Bataan or Corregidor did not guarantee sidestepping it elsewhere. Other sailors who were *never* accounted for surely suffered the fate of most persons—military or civilian—abandoned in the Philippines: imprisonment or death, with very few making successful escapes.[7]

USS *Langley*, tender for the Asiatic Fleet's air units of VP101 and VP102—which became Patrol Wing 10 (PatWing 10)—had likewise received orders to move south as quickly as she could, but her crew was scattered ashore. In the predawn hours of December 8, one of the unit's shore-based radiomen had turned in after a tiring all-night shift only to find the master-at-arms hammering on his bunk announcing that the Japanese had attacked. The exhausted sailor, a radioman second class, sat up shouting, "Can't you just hold them off until Reveille?"[8] His exasperation and implicit disbelief were reproduced throughout Asiatic Fleet ships that confused night. If dawn brought less illumination to the situation than many hoped, it nonetheless found the fleet busily at work with a will.

*Langley* picked up her men from the Utility Unit, based ashore in a local school building in the General Trias neighborhood of Cavite, and began preparing for the cruise south. As has been noted, though, this operation "was not a headlong flight, but an orderly withdrawal."[9] The men were on edge and knew that events in the Pacific and Asia were moving rapidly and not to their advantage, yet very few had specific information regarding the severity of the Pearl Harbor attacks.

As for the other plane tenders, with the unambiguous "war warning" message from Washington trickling down through the fleet in late November, quite a few of *Langley*'s men were reassigned to *Heron*, *Childs*, and *Preston*. *Heron* and *Preston* then moved to their advance bases in the southern Philippines. *Heron* with four single-engine patrol planes was positioned on the southeastern tip of Palawan Island, and *Preston* with three PBYs had gone to Malalag Bay on the southwestern side of Davao Gulf. *Childs* remained in the Manila Bay area; the morning of the war's commencement would find her at Sangley Point's Coaling Dock.

At 1652 hours, with sunset nearing, tugs assisted *Trinity* in undocking. The tanker then got under way as she prepared to join *Langley* and the Asiatic Fleet's sole fulltime oiler, uss *Pecos* (ao-6). They would be escorted by the remaining DesDiv 59 destroyers, uss *John D. Ford* and uss *Pope* for the journey south to the nei. En route they would link up with other Asiatic Fleet warships, including *Houston*, that would act as their escorts. In the nei they expected to be far out of reach of Japanese air patrols and bombers, but while getting there anything might occur. It was thought that enemy surface units (or airplanes and submarines) might still intercept them.

Even though the Dutch islands possessed some of the richest oil-producing regions in the world at that time, the speed and scope of the Japanese advance quickly made it clear that Hart would need to rely heavily on his own tankers; he also knew that it would be difficult to obtain additional ones from the Pacific Fleet.[10] In a matter of hours the protection and preservation of his aged and humble service vessels became a matter of critical importance. Of eight ships heading south—*Houston, Peary, Pillsbury, Ford, Pope, Pecos, Langley*, and *Trinity*—only *John D. Ford* and *Trinity* were to survive the debacle that would overtake Hart's small fleet in the next eleven weeks.

Departing Manila Bay the three auxiliaries were led past "squat, glowering Corregidor" one last time and on through the lanes in the minefields by *Langley*, which had the senior officer present afloat.[11] Undertaken after sundown, with the vessels maintaining darkened ship conditions, it was a nerve-racking experience for everyone involved. One sailor on *Trinity* recalled that it was the most anxious event in the entire war for him. He was certain the ships would be lost that night and he would end up a pow. But all made it through safely and assumed formation for the lengthy and perilous trip south.

Outside the mined passage they were met by *Ford* and *Pope*, which took up screening positions a mile ahead, *Ford* at 45 degrees off *Langley's* port bow and *Pope* to starboard. For the remainder of that day, they moved sse at 10 knots. They entered the Verde Island Passage by morning; Verde Island light, Pimamalayan light, and Libolon Island were all passed and logged. Then they reached Tablas Strait and continued south. On December 9 at 1445 hours, they sighted uss *Boise* and uss *Houston* with their destroyers, *Paul Jones* and *Barker*, approaching from the south, and turned the convoy over to the cruisers.[12] *Ford* and *Pope* then reversed course and headed back to Manila, as their weary crews—some of whom had been on duty for nearly thirty hours—tried to steal a little rest in catnaps while remaining "on watch, [carrying out] gun maintenance, eating, washing clothes, and always searching the waters for enemy ships."[13] The men off watch soon found that sleep acquired on the top deck, "with the stars as a blanket," was far preferable to that obtained in the stifling quarters below, with blowers running and the red (or blue) lights on all night. Sailors in the wartime navy elsewhere claimed that four hours above deck was considered to be worth eight hours below.[14]

At the speed of the slowest vessel, *Trinity*, the convoy steamed down the length of the Philippines through the Sulu Sea, past the tip of northeastern Borneo, and into the Makassar Strait.[15] It was disheartening to leave the islands in which most of the ships had spent most of their careers—some having been there for two decades—but the men all clung to the truism about running away today to live and fight another day.

As *Langley*, *Trinity*, and *Pecos* (under Lt. Cdr. E. Paul Abernethy) continued south to Balikpapan, *Houston* and *Boise* were told on December 12 to turn back around and meet up with yet another convoy coming south out of Manila Bay—comprising sub tenders *Holland* and *Otus*, patrol yacht *Isabel*, screened by destroyers *Ford* and *Pope*—as it also made its way down to Borneo.[16] At the same time screening forces were sent north from Balikpapan to meet these ships. At midday on the twelfth out came *Marblehead* with destroyers *Stewart* and *Parrott*, steaming northeast up the Makassar Strait. (Glassford was pleased to see the initiative shown by Captain Robinson of *Marblehead* in bringing his ships up to rendezvous without explicit orders.) In these graceless but purposeful movements, the Asiatic Fleet found its way out of the Philippines, heading to what all hoped were more secure ports in the south.

While these ships were repositioned, plans for utilizing Hart's precious few offensive assets were undergoing daily, if not hourly, modifications. Initial thoughts of operating some of his ships out of Singapore with the British quickly changed. They would *all* retire to the East Indies and northern Australia. The command structure had also become absurdly contorted. In general Rear Admiral Glassford (then embarked in *Houston* as ComTasFor5) and Rear Adm. William Purnell (the Asiatic Fleet's nominal, or administrative, commander) would handle most of the command and control functions for the fleet. As later recorded in *Boise*'s war diary: "The mission assigned the ... force was to establish itself along the EASTERN MALAY BARRIER, generally the BALI-DARWIN line, in support of the defense of the NETHERLANDS EAST INDIES and AUSTRALIA, close the EASTERN MALAY BARRIER passages to enemy raiders and raid enemy shipping and forces encountered."[17]

These plans were being recast on the fly as Hart's ships trickled down to the East Indies. At the same time—thousands of miles away in Washington and London—additional schemes were being formulated for the combined Allied command to be known as ABDA. But the urgency of the situation throughout

60

Southeast Asia had not yet fully penetrated the bureaucratic skulls of any of the Allied commands.

Meanwhile, the *Holland-Otus-Isabel* convoy, screened by *Ford* and *Pope* initially and later joined by *Boise* and *Houston*, steamed to Balikpapan, where it arrived on the afternoon of December 14. However, a number of minor mishaps occurred along the way, revealing the inexperience of officers and sailors.

There were, as might be expected, several false sightings of torpedo tracks and submarine wakes. On another occasion *Ford* "accidentally" fired one of her own torpedoes, and although *Pope* maneuvered successfully to avoid it, the convoy's order was disrupted. Then, after reforming, *Otus* lost steering control and fell out of position. On December 11 a rogue wave hit *Ford*, making her roll unexpectedly, which in turn caused a sailor sitting in the 4-inch pointer's seat named Melvin Evans to lose his balance. As Evans reflexively reached out, his hand brushed the firing handle. The gun—number 3, above the galley deckhouse—was loaded and off it went. Another seaman, Richard Taft, who was standing watch with his arm on the gun's barrel was knocked unconscious by the muzzle blast but not seriously injured otherwise. DesDiv 59's commanding officer, Cdr. Paul Talbot, decided his guns should not be kept loaded at all times unless a specific need was recognized.[18]

It was simultaneously noticed, with some alarm, that *Isabel*'s light-colored peacetime paint job made her an inviting target after dark. *Isabel*'s crew went to work overnight with paintbrushes and swabs and by daybreak had repainted her in a highly nonregulation blue-gray camouflage scheme of no specific measure. It was also seen that the men's white uniforms were much too bright in contrast with the destroyers' dark blue decks. Sailors were reduced to coloring some of their older or more soiled clothing in a compound of salt water, boiling coffee, and green dye. The effects were far from prepossessing. Many comments were heard comparing the results to what most men had previously only seen in the used diapers of infants.

The trip south to Balikpapan was its own form of on-the-job training and gave everyone a foretaste of problems to come. Painting the ships under such emergency conditions added its own perils. Early on December 13 *Isabel* suffered a steering breakdown—thanks ironically to a paintbrush that had somehow become wedged in her pilot valve screw—and she fell behind the convoy. By the time this problem was discovered and repaired, *Isabel* lagged some eight miles astern. Due to her small size and limited range, getting to her destination was going to be problematic. As she finally straggled into Balikpapan, after having become separated in bad weather from the rest of the convoy, her fuel tanks were nearly dry and her men reduced to getting thirty minutes of freshwater three times a day.

At the Dutch oil port, *Isabel*'s lowly status meant that she fueled last, and this caused her skipper, Lt. John W. Payne, no little concern since she had made it into the bay only by the barest of margins. Getting his ship replenished turned into an ordeal of its own as there were neither local guides nor enough pilots to bring the ship in. Not until 0200 hours on December 15 was she under way again from the fueling docks at Balikpapan, having threaded her way in and back out on her own. This had been accomplished with her sailors manning a whaleboat ahead of the 245-foot patrol yacht and feeling their way through reefs and shallows ringing the harbor by lead line and boathooks.[19] Thus did the Asiatic Fleet's ships initially meet the preparations of those allies for whom they were expected to do much of the fighting in defense of the Netherlands East Indies. And it was little different for the bigger ships.

"Butch" Parker of *Parrott* and the other destroyers had also reached Balikpapan. Having been compelled to operate during the war's first week in a communications void, they were anxious to finally meet Glassford and get some clear information regarding plans and missions. They had not yet received any details on the attacks at Pearl Harbor or Manila. They reached the Dutch port on "a black night" and transited its minefields in the pouring rain to fuel from *Pecos* and restock stores. Then Parker, Cdr. Paul Talbot (CDD59), Lt. Cdr. H. Page Smith of *Stewart*, and other skippers were called to a meeting on *Houston*. It was the evening of Sunday, December 14, 1941. They felt sure they would then "get the dope" straight from Rear Admiral Glassford.[20]

As Parker later recalled, "We all sat down and waited for the admiral. Glassford came in—a distinguished figure in gray slacks, glasses—pince-nez on a long black ribbon." The first thing that Glassford said took the assembled officers by surprise: "Before we get into the operation, one thing I want to bring out. I was in battleships in World War I. Good practice when you go ashore: always wear at least one article of your uniform." Page Smith also remembered the sartorial advice offered by Glassford: "I suggest when we go ashore in Java we dress as we did in Queenstown, Ireland in WWI. To be distinctive I suggest *gray trousers*." The two destroyermen, Parker and Smith, looked at each other, sharing a single, baffled thought: "Is *this* the dope?" To their astonishment, at that moment it was. "I was struck dumb!" Smith later wrote.[21]

Glassford, who was obviously still rather dazed himself after his abrupt and dramatic voyage from China and equally narrow escape at Manila, "gave [them] no summary of the situation; discussed no plans with [them]."[22] He seems

MANILA ABANDONED

only to have communicated that the ships would leave Balikpapan that night if possible, and that he would issue operational orders upon departure. They returned to their respective ships only to find that there were not enough Dutch pilots to get the ships out through the minefields. It then fell to Parker, who had taken *Parrott* through the minefields several times in the prior two weeks, to lead Talbot's division out.

*Langley* and *Trinity*, screened by *Marblehead* with *Stewart* and *Parrott*, then continued south. After a brief stopover at Surabaja, where radiomen from *Langley* and *Marblehead* helped set up extemporized navy communications, the ships proceeded on to Darwin in northern Australia. Before leaving, radio electrician Charles Snay of *Langley* noted the naïveté of the Dutch civilians, who "all considered themselves saved now that a United States carrier was in port."[23] Signalman Lowell Barty from the same ship remembered that at Surabaja the only immediate difficulty was in monetary exchange, since the Asiatic Fleet paid its sailors in pesos, the Filipino currency. However, he also observed that even early on it was becoming clear to many that the campaign in the East Indies was "a lost cause."[24]

Glassford then took *Houston* down to Surabaja to reorganize his staff and arrange meetings with his Dutch and British counterparts. Events were moving quickly, and all their prewar concepts for defending Southeast Asia were being altered almost daily. Rear Adm. William Purnell and other available staff officers were to be sent from Manila to Java as well. Purnell had been released by Hart to act as chief of staff to Glassford, which in turn freed Capt. Albert Rooks of *Houston* from that additional duty.[25] Unfortunately, the first awkward introductions to the Dutch on Java might well have served as a portent of cooperative issues that would trouble the Allies in the coming campaign.

The Asiatic Fleet flagship arrived off Surabaja's forbidding minefields during the day on December 16, only to be delayed for several hours while the local Dutch squabbled over matters of peacetime protocol for visiting warships. Astonishingly, the "Java authorities" refused to send a channel pilot to bring the ship in through the minefields until, as Glassford noted, "Our identification was complete." Glassford, Rooks, and the men on *Houston* were all discomfited by the "interminable time spent dashing at high speed off the entrance" to avoid becoming a "paddling duck for any lurking enemy submarine."[26] Unknown to them, Cdr. Edwin Crouch's DesDiv 57 (*Whipple, Alden, John D. Edwards*, and *Edsall*) had undergone much the same treatment the previous day when they reached the Surabaja minefields after sprinting down from Singapore following the *Prince of Wales* and *Repulse* catastrophe. The four destroyers wasted over two hours maneuvering at low speed outside the minefields as they, too, waited on Dutch pilots. This delay consumed more precious fuel, just as *Houston*'s high-speed steaming did the following day.

Once in Surabaja, Glassford learned to his disappointment that Purnell's arrival from Manila would be delayed. There was nothing to be done about it, though; he had to press on with his plans. By telephone an early conference was arranged in Batavia with Dutch and British naval commanders: Lt. Adm. Conrad Helfrich and Capt. John Collins, respectively. However, Rear Admiral Purnell reached Surabaja earlier than expected and went aboard *Houston* for a conference with Glassford. At that time Purnell delivered a letter from Hart that "outlin[ed] the general situation in Manila and his plans."[27] A series of hasty trips between Surabaja and Batavia by these U.S. naval commanders ensued.

Purnell went by plane on Thursday, December 18, to Batavia to begin talks with his counterparts. A brief—though by no means particularly clarifying—summary of these discussions was sent to both Glassford and Hart by Nummer, a member of Helfrich's staff. As soon as Purnell returned, it was decided to bring Glassford's small staff ashore at Surabaja; their office was to be established at 15 Reinersz Boulevard, with living quarters for officers at 118 Darmo Boulevard.[28]

On this same day, Lt. Bob Fulton of *Houston*—still healthy and unharmed—wrote his parents again in Washington DC. "The war started with a surprise and shock to most people," he noted, adding, "The losses at Pearl Harbor are unfortunate but should at least serve to blast part of the country into realizing what we are up against." He also wrote (for the last time) that they were hoping for "a short and decisive war . . ." and that afterward "there [would] be somebody who will know how to prevent any repetitions of it." Before long such aspirations would be seen as pointless by most of the more realistic men. And over time Bob Fulton would find that the terrors of war generated yet another, deeper test: that of his religious faith.[29]

On the nineteenth Glassford attended a conference on board the Dutch light cruiser *De Ruyter*, flagship of Rear Adm. Karel Doorman. At this time he was also alerted to the Japanese landings at Miri in Sarawak on British Borneo. One may imagine the atmosphere of chaos and gloom then descending on the Allies in the East Indies. Plans to resist the Japanese seaborne blitzkrieg had to be made on the spot and off the cuff. And it was immediately apparent that Western resources were much too thin to cover the entire length of the Indies from Sumatra to Timor. Although the British wanted desperately to put all possible offensive assets into the west, closer to Singapore, the Americans were not about to allow their small forces to be swallowed up in a futile defense of those colonial possessions, which the British had already squandered decades to *not* secure. Hart's ships would operate to the east of Java in the direction of Australia, while the Dutch and the British attended to those areas westward and up to Malaya.[30]

Between December 20 and 23, Glassford traveled by plane to Batavia, accompanied by a member of his staff, Lt. (j.g.) J. N. McDonald, to confer with Collins and Helfrich, after which he returned to Surabaja. With the entire strategic picture one of such uncertainty, the Americans—according to Glassford—had necessarily once more altered their plans. At this time the navy's thinking was "to retain [its] complete independence of action while wholeheartedly cooperating as practicable with [its] allies."[31] As might be gathered from this contradictory language, such ambiguity would make combined operations with the British and the Dutch anything but smooth over the ensuing two months.

The central and overriding preoccupations of the British were Burma, Malaya, and Singapore. For the Dutch quite naturally it was interdicting Japanese naval forces descending on the East Indies. But unlike the Dutch, the Americans (especially the navy) had painfully experienced what dominant air power could achieve, and they were determined to preserve their remaining forces. Glassford seemed to feel that both the British and the Dutch had already been as stunned and decimated by the Japanese attacks as the Americans. In this (mis)reading he resembled Admiral Hart. Yet even with the loss of Force Z, the British still had a considerable naval presence, and more units were available (from Ceylon and South Africa). The Dutch, on the other hand, had not lost any important surface ships at that point, and this probably contributed to the sharp rhetoric and attitudes of Helfrich and Van Staveren. In time such variables would shift, but in these initial meetings were indications of future discontent among the Allies. And upon such an unsteady foundation of imperfect understanding and conflicting priorities the combined organization of ABDA was to be built.

*Trinity* and others—including USS *Gold Star* of the "Guam Navy" under Lt. Cdr. Joseph Lademan—plodded on from Balikpapan to Makassar, Celebes.[32] Once at Makassar several of the flushdeckers replenished their stores from *Gold Star* and *Holland. Gold Star* was then ordered to Darwin and proceeded without incident to that port—in a train that included *Otus* and *Pecos*, eventually escorted by *Houston* with destroyers *Whipple, Alden,* and *Edsall*—arriving there at midday on December 28, 1941. At Darwin she was taken into the fleet as the base force provision ship. From that time she never moved back up to the East Indies to reenter the combat zone. She was considered too vulnerable and too valuable—although some of this value may be attributed to the stock of Scotch whiskey and beer she allegedly carried. As Glassford later wrote in one of his narratives, due to her precious stores, she soon became known to the fleet at Australia as the *Gold Mine.*

# FOUR

## Birth of a Nasty, Brutish, and Short Life

ABDA *Is Formed*

ABDA was the acronym adopted to designate military forces of the Australians, the British, the Dutch, and the Americans acting together in the defense of Southeast Asia and the Southwest Pacific. It came as the culmination of several weeks of British and American strategic talks in December 1941, when Winston Churchill and his staff visited President Roosevelt and U.S. military planners in Washington DC. At that time the widespread combat operations of the Japanese war machine were well under way, moving south at a pace deeply alarming to the British and the Americans. This joint command between the Allies was to be the first and last wartime coalition among the four primary Allied naval powers in the Far East.

Into that maelstrom of military reversals, illusionary achievements, and real losses was born the unfortunate command known as ABDA.[1] Its lifespan of a mere six weeks may thus be described in the grimmest Hobbesian sense: Nasty, brutish (not "British"), and short. All the same ABDA should be remembered for more than its failures and ultimate defeat. The naval and air forces of the Allied nations all performed with fortitude and courage, fighting against the combined odds of a numerically superior, better organized, and thoroughly prepared enemy. Although the sacrifices of ABDA were swiftly forgotten by higher echelons, the officers and men involved rarely put those experiences out of mind so easily. They, along with family members—and unlike their own countries—refused to allow their lost comrades to be forgotten either.[2]

The Allied ground campaign (especially on Java itself) was another matter and only infrequently redounded to anyone's credit. There the absence of real fighting spirit undercut subsequent arguments by leaders like Lieutenant Admiral Helfrich, who attempted to rationalize his defeat by claiming that another two to three weeks could have made all the difference in turning back the Japanese and saving Java. This was a patent falsehood. Any cursory examination of the NEI campaign will show how disorganized and inept the Allied ground defense was from start to finish, and closer research only amplifies this dreary truth. However, Helfrich's reaction was always to fault someone else and not examine his own failings too closely. If factual veracity had to be discarded in order to maintain this facade and throw the blame elsewhere, then so be it.

Nonetheless, for all of ABDA's failures, its formation did have some positive ramifications, the foremost being the creation of the Joint Chiefs Command. Many years later Gen. George Marshall would reckon the creation of the Joint Chiefs Command one of his three greatest achievements, but at the time— that somber Christmas of 1941—it must have seemed substantially less so. Much of its original impetus was political and came from a desire to show that "the British and American Governments were ready and willing to take bilateral action in the field of military affairs in spite of differences in national policy and notwithstanding the embarrassments they might incur in the fields of domestic and foreign policy."[3] After the war Brig. Gen. Elliott R. Thorpe (former U.S. military observer and Lend-Lease commissioner in Batavia) gave a different perspective when he said that ABDA had been motivated *too much* by the business of politics and media, and that the United States would have been better off, given the doomed position of the East Indies, to have never made *any* assurances to the Dutch.[4]

Superimposed on the difficulties inherent in the defense of several thousand miles of unnumbered islands and waterways by an inadequate number of ships and planes, the situation cried out for a single command, and it fell to the Americans and the British to see that it finally happened. The primary initiative behind this thinking on unified command thus came from Marshall. He believed that a single theater command with one man running it—as suggested by Col. Francis Brink's report—would solve nine-tenths of the Allies' command problems.[5] This may have been a holdover from the hard lessons learned in World War I, when disunity led to repeated Allied calamities. It appears that Marshall felt he was seeing similar quandaries in the opening weeks of the Far Eastern war. Undoubtedly there were influential Allied chiefs, such as Britain's Sir John Dill, who felt much like Marshall in this matter. Other British leaders were reluctant for the overall command to be given to one of their own, believing that they would be unfairly blamed for an unfolding fiasco in Southeast Asia. Churchill, to his credit, would not tolerate this. He felt it was no way for allies to begin their cooperative association in the war, and his view held.

As always, unity came at a high price—the disenfranchisement of the lesser powers—and that cost was controversial. Notable exclusions from these strategic decisions in Washington and London were nations whose territories were threatened by the Japanese invaders: the Dutch in the East Indies; the Indians and the Burmese; the Australians and the New Zealanders. Of these the Dutch and the Australians were the most justifiably annoyed, indeed infuriated, by British and American failure to consult with them regarding strategic planning and the creation of ABDA.[6] They were not only in the line of the Japanese advance, but the NEI was the bull's-eye, clearly a major objective of Japan's war plans. Added to this was unhappiness over the large number of Australians serving in the field for Great Britain—especially in North Africa and the Mediterranean—and Churchill's desire to employ even greater numbers if possible.

There was more to this denial of power sharing than Anglo-American high-handedness though. There was brute necessity. As Adm. Ernest King (COM-INCH) remarked to a group of reporter some months later: "It was obvious that with so many participants in the war, decisions could not be made by a show of hands. Nothing could be accomplished by such means. As the United States and Great Britain were financing the war and doing most of the fighting, they should therefore run the war, make the final decisions, and control the military machine. This is a hard-boiled method bound to cause friction and unhappiness among the smaller nations who thought they should have a voice in the military decisions, but it is the only way to function effectively."[7]

All true enough, although ABDA *never* functioned "effectively." Its brief lifespan was a textbook illustration of strategic and tactical disunity, communications failures, and avoidable personnel losses that left many surviving participants haunted and embittered. It is only natural that in such instances the "fog of war" becomes a convenient extenuating factor. ABDA was in fact a tentative test bed, and it predictably suffered from the flaws of premature, rushed, and imperfect designing. But Marshall and King were correct in one sense. The creation of a unified command structure—precursor to the Joint Chiefs of Staff—was absolutely necessary.

As a consequence of its brief and violent lifespan, few subjects remain as enshrouded in mystery as the ABDA campaign. The Western nations participating in this first attempt at coalition warfare mistrusted one another only marginally less than they did the enemy. Their war plans—to the extent that they had been formulated and codified—were often contradictory. Their various service commands were a mélange of priorities, often under squabbling leaders (even after the celebrated conferences in Washington known as Arcadia), with capabilities ill-matched due to inexperience in joint operations and an almost complete lack of common tactical doctrine.

At the same time, for purposes of Allied propaganda—no other word will do—the Dutch needed to overcome the perception of "little Holland" (i.e., the Netherlands, which had been overrun in a few days by the Germans) and create another public persona, that of "big Holland" (i.e., a nation fully capable of making a significant contribution to the war against Japan). In fact, although this media conundrum continued throughout the war, it was not greatly helped by the campaign in the East Indies.[8]

So swift and confused was the Java campaign that several of the leaders who participated could scarcely recall ABDA in later years. A number of others, including highly placed ones, appear to have had no desire to look back at the ABDA command. Some were clearly reluctant to cooperate with postwar researchers or squelched attempts to gather information.[9] Others simply allowed their memories to fade, as if deliberately wishing to erase this period. For example, Admiral Hart later referred to this "involved subject" after the war as "the Wavell Command" rather than ABDA, which if nothing else suggests precisely who he felt dominated the coalition. Elsewhere he acknowledged how short-lived and forgettable the entire business had been.[10] Even Marshall had clear memories only of his encounters with Churchill and the British chiefs, but actual details of the ABDA command—he never knew Wavell at all, for example—had dimmed. Along with its attendant players, historians and the public have been just as prone to overlook the ABDA campaign in the decades since World War II—that is, those who were sufficiently well informed to even know of its existence.

Nonetheless, after a month of wrangling in Washington and London, ABDA began officially to function on January 15, 1942. Burma (under British leadership) and the Philippines (under MacArthur) were nominally included in the overall structure, but for the U.S. Asiatic Fleet's surface forces the bulk of the campaign would be concentrated along the waters between Sumatra and northern Australia, the so-called Malay Barrier. And they would not be involved in actions much beyond these limits after mid-December, when they withdrew to the NEI.

In overall command of this bricks-without-straw organization was Field Marshall Sir Archibald Wavell (ABDACOM), most recently commanding British forces in India. His chief of staff was Gen. Sir Henry Pownall, and the deputy commander was Lt. Gen. George Brett of the U.S. Army Air Force. The air forces (ABDAIR) were under Air Chief Marshal Sir Richard Peirse, Royal Air Force (RAF), and naval forces (ABDAFLOAT) under Admiral Thomas Hart of the U.S. Asiatic Fleet. Hart's chief of staff was Rear Adm. Arthur Palliser of the Royal Navy. In addition each nation retained its own respective national

A NASTY, BRUTISH, AND SHORT LIFE

commands. Each navy, for example, would operate under its own command except when mixed forces were utilized, at which point Hart would designate a specific commander. This overlapping, shingled command structure—which attempted to placate many and ended up aggravating all—was yet one more obstacle to the smooth functioning of ABDA during its truncated existence.[11]

Many of these plans were being hammered out while Hart was en route from Manila Bay to Surabaja, Java, on the submarine *Shark*. He departed in the early hours of December 26—after MacArthur had declared Manila an open city—and reached the Dutch naval base a week later following a miserable journey. In that interim he was largely without communications and thus unable to rebut the criticisms already being aimed at the navy by MacArthur. So it was without question a weary, dispirited admiral who reached Surabaja in the uncomfortable and overcrowded submarine.[12] If Hart believed he had reached supportive allies, he would soon find the actual situation far from reassuring.

# FIVE

## Overtures in Blood and Oil

*Tarakan and Balikpapan*

In the first ten days of January, as the administrative and operational aspects of the U.S. naval command slowly began to jell—with Hart and Glassford split between Batavia and Surabaja—the Japanese moved ahead according to a carefully plotted timetable. From Davao on Mindanao Island in the southern Philippines, an invasion convoy of sixteen transports screened by the First Escort Unit—built around Rear Adm. Nishimura Shōji's Fourth Destroyer Squadron—moved to the southwest on January 7.[1] They were headed for the long-anticipated seizure of Borneo's critical Dutch oil ports along the Makassar Strait.

First to be captured—and crucially important to Japan's war plans—would be the small island (scarcely eleven by fifteen miles in size) of Tarakan, located about seven hundred miles northeast of Surabaja. The invasion convoy's ships carried the Sakaguchi Heidan (or, Detachment) of the Fifty-Sixth Mixed Infantry Group, along with the Kure Number 2 Special Naval Landing Force (SNLF).[2] Altogether they amounted to over 6,500 men. On Tarakan, the 1,200 Royal Netherlands East Indies Army (Koninklijk Nederlands Indisch Leger, KNIL) defenders under Lt. Col. Simon de Waal would be no match for them in numbers, still less in spirit or combat ability.

On the same day that Wavell reached Java (January 10), the invasion convoy appeared off Tarakan. Two days earlier an Australian newspaperman reporting from Bandoeng spelled the situation out clearly enough: "Perhaps the most menaced point of the whole Dutch Empire in the East Indies is Tarakan, a tiny, palm-fringed island, fabulously wealthy in oil, which lies off the north east coast of Borneo, in a lonely, exposed position."[3] These were all accurate statements; the position was remote, primitive, and vulnerable. It was also incredibly rich, producing up to eighty thousand tons of oil per month from its three fields of over seven hundred wells. Moreover, this product was of legendary purity, requiring little refining at all.

Unfortunately for the Japanese, their convoy had been spotted by a patrol plane of the Dutch Naval Air Force (MLD) by the morning of the tenth. This sighting triggered long-established plans to destroy the installations by sappers and technical staff. To deny their use to the enemy, oil wells, flow lines, storage tanks, and shipping facilities were all put to the torch. Within six hours, by the afternoon of the eleventh, the destruction appeared to have been successful. This work was carried out with the help of Lieutenant Van den Belt, head of a special militarized demolition unit, and De Waal's chief of staff, Capt. G. L. Reinderhoff. They were aided by a reserve captain who was the Bataafsche Petroleum Maatschappij (BPM), or Batavian Oil Company, administrator of Tarakan, Dr. Anton Colijn.[4]

The enemy convoy arrived to find thick black plumes piled up into the sky for miles over the little island. "From the erupting wells smoke and flames rose high."[5] Nonetheless, the Japanese moved in later that day to capture what remained of the oil installations of this important petrochemical complex, coming ashore on the east coast of Tarakan through its dense jungle. This approach was to confuse the Dutch, who anticipated landings on the west side, where the harbor, airfield, and storage tanks were located.

This undertaking went smoothly, although not without its human tragedies. With orders to take the oilfields as rapidly and incurring as little damage as possible, the Japanese commanders and their men had been put under tremendous pressure. All recognized that these were among *the* most critical and central operations for which Japan had plunged headlong into war. Landing on the opposite side of the island from the defenses they were to secure, many Japanese units became lost in the thickets and jungles lining that portion of the island. It hardly mattered; by the next day it was all over.

Allied resistance on the island was generally weak and desultory. By daybreak on the twelfth, the Dutch were offering to surrender. Of De Waal's 1,200 defenders, the invaders captured upwards of 900. Some managed to escape, but by then the maddened Japanese had begun murdering others for refusing to cooperate under interrogation or for suspected culpability when the oil installations were fired. Japanese losses in actual fighting on the ground were miniscule, amounting to but a handful. The bulk of these casualties were eighteen SNLF soldiers killed in a belated bombing attack on the airfield later. Yet a foolish misunderstanding led to a Japanese war crime that cost scores of Dutch lives needlessly.

This tragedy happened when the impetuous Japanese sent a division of minesweepers into an anchorage on the southern tip of the island near Karoengan without first confirming that Dutch coastal batteries had actually surrendered.[6]

Although the Dutch had quickly conceded Tarakan to the invaders, De Waal also warned his captors that not all his units had been so informed. (Telephone communications with the coastal artillery units at Karoengan were known to have been cut.) This move cost the Imperial Navy two vessels.

Leading their division into the bay trailing paravanes—which limited their maneuverability—the 700-ton minesweepers *W-13* and *W-14* were promptly sunk by accurate artillery fire from a battery of four 12 cm (4.7-inch) guns under a transplanted old South African named Van Adrichem. At a range of less than two thousand meters, both ships were quickly disabled by hits in their engine spaces and rudders. *W-14* then suffered multiple "induced explosions" before she drifted onto a mine and blew apart. Dead in the water with many of her officers and crew killed, *W-13* went down under the Dutch shells defiantly firing her own single 12 cm gun and 25 mm battery to the end. Among the losses were 156 IJN sailors and officers on the two ships.[7]

Japanese casualties were heavy enough in these sinkings, but humiliation and rage were greater, and the defenders would pay a gruesome price. Members of Dutch gun crews were rounded up after De Waal persuaded them to lay down their arms.[8] A week later on Sunday, January 18, they were loaded onto a Japanese light cruiser—probably *Naka*—and taken out to sea to a position near the lost minesweepers. Ignoring any thoughts of international law or simple mercy, the infuriated men of Nihon Kaigun demanded vengeance as their prerogative. On the cruiser these helpless Dutch artillerymen were held on deck before being murdered by beheading or bayoneting. The coupled bodies of between eighty-four and ninety men (they had been chained together in pairs, back to back) were thrown into the murky waters off Tarakan. Another one hundred or more are alleged to have been bayoneted on the beaches.[9]

• • •

ABDA had been unable to muster any effective naval surface opposition to the Japanese invasion, and only submarines were available to contest the enemy at sea. Hart at that time was still preoccupied with setting up ABDAFLOAT headquarters. His submarine commander, Capt. John Wilkes, had only recently arrived from Corregidor via one of his remaining boats, as exhausted and dejected as Hart had been when he had reached Surabaja a week earlier. Both men brought enervating cases of the "blues" with them after escaping the dismal situation in Luzon, and both were abruptly thrown into a daunting administrative reorganization on Java. In his diary Hart merely mentioned that the enemy—referred to as "The Rising Tide of Color"—had gone "into Tarakan with a very strong expedition as [the Allies had] for some time been knowing they would."[10]

In ports such as Surabaja the American sailors were not necessarily welcomed with open arms either. A crane operator on *Houston* later remembered friction between U.S. and Dutch personnel in bars, with taunts such as "Aren't you tired of running away?" from Dutch soldiers (who had yet to do any real fighting at all) being typical.[11] It was the beginning of a short, unhappy relationship between the inhabitants of the East Indies, including the Dutch themselves, and Western military forces sent to act as allies.

At that time three American submarines—*Spearfish*, *s-37*, and *s-41*—were vectored by Wilkes from the Philippines and elsewhere to interdict the enemy's Western Invasion Force heading for Tarakan. Not one boat made contact in the foul weather conditions, and the enemy convoy moved into its landing positions unopposed. When indications appeared that the next assault would be at Balikpapan or Ambon, Hart had Wilkes send six subs into the Makassar Strait and three more to the southern end of the Molucca Passage. As we will see, these had only limited success. It was yet one more unsatisfactory performance by the American submarine force, and duly noted by the acerbic, highly critical Helfrich.

From the outset Lt. Adm. C. E. L. Helfrich felt doubly frustrated, first, for being left out of the uppermost command echelons, and, second, for not being in a position to call the shots for *all* the naval forces. In Helfrich's view the initial directives to the U.S. Asiatic Fleet—clearly he meant those devised by Hart—conflicted with Dutch "strategic concepts." Worse, he felt that Hart had arrived from the Philippines in a defeatist frame of mind, or as he put it, "not very hopeful." And, most alarming, the American admiral seemed to already believe that the defense of the East Indies "was a lost cause and retreat to Australia to be expected any moment."[12] From these initial impressions of the Americans, the contentious Helfrich would rarely waver in his subsequent writings.

Meanwhile, in both Washington and Java a handful of Dutch diplomats and high-ranking officials constantly plotted to replace Admiral Hart with Helfrich as commander of the Allied naval forces. Beginning at the start of 1942, Dr. Hubertus van Mook, lieutenant governor of the East Indies, worked for the next month and a half in Washington DC behind the scenes arguing that Helfrich should replace Hart as head of ABDAFLOAT.[13]

As for Helfrich's so-called strategic concepts, they remained vague. One presumes that in using the term he generally meant "concepts" involving the deployment of warships from *other* ABDA nations in East Indian waters under his sole direction, but not necessarily those of his own fleet. That this reading is plausible is borne out by Helfrich's "Secret and Personal" letter to Glassford, dated January 3, 1942. In it the Dutch admiral wrote:

> I wish to discuss with Admiral Hart the action of your submarines from the Philippines. I assume your submarines will be operated from Darwin, but I hope that I may be able to move their base to Soerabaya, Ambon, Balikpapan, and Tarakan. I think we need your cooperation because I am afraid we lost already 4 submarines out a total of 11 (fully manned). Please will you be so kind as to keep this <u>secret</u>. In my opinion we *must* take strong action in the Celebes Sea against the concentration of Japanese forces in Holo [*sic*] which are undoubtedly ready for action against Tarakan, Manado, and so on.[14]

Therefore, the same Helfrich who twitted Hart to his face about the time U.S. vessels spent in port was admitting to Glassford that he had already lost 36 percent of his operational submarines and asking for American help in the very sector that the United States had already decided to patrol. For as the exasperated Hart noted at the time, Helfrich was prone to just such maneuvers. Indeed, in one diary entry (comparing Helfrich to his Royal Navy counterparts), the American admiral called the touchy Dutchman "another cup of tea."[15]

So by all lights, it does appear that Hart had ample cause to feel frustrated by the Netherlander's behavior, which at times bordered (in Hart's opinion) on outright impudence. This also explains the distinct coolness that Hart's superior, Adm. Ernest King, felt toward Helfrich later in the war, along with King's unwillingness to place American warships under foreign command after USN losses in the first months of the Pacific conflict.

Thus it happened that in early January 1942, with the formation of ABDA in its initial, jumbled stages, neither the Dutch nor the Americans had any surface forces available or in position to take action before Tarakan was captured. Their withdrawal of Hart's and Glassford's units from the Philippines left them poorly situated for offensive operations before January 10. Former Asiatic Fleet alternate flagship, *Isabel*, which had only limited combat value, was at Surabaja on January 5, having a boiler patched up. Minesweepers *Lark* (AM-21) and *Whippoorwill* with the destroyers *John D. Ford* and *Pillsbury* were also then at the Dutch port. The latter was still undergoing repairs (when time could be arranged) to her wounds received a month before at Cavite. *Paul Jones* was operating off Surabaja, patrolling with the Dutch destroyer *Van Ghent*. Both of these ships were involved in rescue work after the USAT *Liberty* was torpedoed near Lombok Strait, helping tow the stricken transport on the morning of January 12. The transport eventually went aground off east Bali, where she capsized on January 14, to become a total loss.

*Boise*, accompanied by *Stewart*, *Barker*, and *Parrott*, was engaged in escorting the Dutch liner *Bloemfontein* to Java from Darwin. The latter was carrying 571 men of the Second Battalion, 131st Field Artillery Regiment—a component of the Texas National Guard's Thirty-Sixth Division—which had been brought from the West Coast aboard the transport *Republic* in the *Pensacola* convoy in December. They were then transported from Brisbane to Darwin and from there, more by accident than design, on to Surabaja. As events unfolded, the so-called Lost Battalion would represent the bulk of American ground combat forces sent to Java.[16]

On January 11, after turning *Bloemfontein* over to *John D. Ford* and *Pillsbury* to be escorted into Surabaja's western entrance, *Boise* lay to off the Binnen Light vessel awaiting Glassford and staff. The admiral came to the cruiser in *Isabel*— her boiler repaired—at 1300 hours accompanied by two lieutenants and six enlisted men. That afternoon, escorted by *John D. Ford* and *Pillsbury*, Glassford and *Boise* got under way for Saleh Bay, Sumbawa, about four hundred miles to the east. It was too late to do anything about Tarakan, but information came trickling in that the Japanese were concentrating for more assaults to the north, perhaps at Menado on the uppermost tip of the eastern Celebes or at Balikpapan on the eastern coast of Borneo. Meanwhile, other units of the Asiatic Fleet remained in the northern Australia area, including *Houston* and *Marblehead*. Primarily involved with convoy duties between Port Darwin and Torres Straits, they were too far to the east to offer help in Makassar Strait during early January.

As the dreadful month of December 1941 drew to a close, Robert Fulton of *Houston* wrote another letter to his family in the states. He reassured them that his own health was fine (apart from a mild case of prickly heat), and described his Christmas—such as it was—on the cruiser. He then noted, "The Japs seem to be taking full advantage of their fast start and I am afraid that it will be some time before we can get this over with." As with most of the other men, he lamented the dearth of reliable, timely information, and he worried that false press reports from the enemy might alarm his friends and family back home. At the same time Fulton told them, "Everything that goes on is considered secret, and we have to be ready to do anything on [no] notice at all."[17] Clearly the informational darkness and strain the men were forced to operate under were beginning to take a toll.

As for the disposition of Helfrich's heavy ships, flagship *De Ruyter* was engaged in escorting British convoys to and from Singapore. She was in no position to move north at the time, even had the Dutch so decided. Her elderly sister, *Java*, nicked a prop escorting the merchant ship *Madoera* from Tandjong Priok to Surabaja between January 5 and 7, which put the old cruiser in dockyard hands until January 15.[18]

Strangely—in view of Helfrich's needling of Hart about the time American ships spent in port—the flagship *De Ruyter* would soon find herself, like *Java*, in a Surabaja dock at roughly the same time (January 14–28) getting defects in her steering gear sorted out. Thus the two most powerful RNN units would together miss twenty-two days of operations in January alone. These facts appear to have escaped the attention of Helfrich in his subsequent criticism of U.S. participation. However, they may help explain a legitimate desire by the Dutch admiral to get his hands on U.S. ships at the time, for it seems there were few enough Royal Netherlands Navy warships available. And there was *never* enough air power.

Remnants of MacArthur's battered air forces escaping the Philippines had then reached Java and were doing their best to make their presence felt. Operating out of Singosari field, five miles northwest of Malang in eastern Java, ten B-17s under Col. Eugene Eubank flew missions in the first couple of weeks in January, which tested men and machines. From Malang they staged through the secret Samarinda II field in eastern Borneo and later through the big Kendari II airfield in the southern Celebes, as they struck at Japanese convoys massing in the Davao Gulf area.

None of these lengthy, difficult shuttle missions were particularly effective, and the Japanese timetable was not upset to any appreciable degree. A flight led by Maj. Cecil E. Combs against the convoy heading for Tarakan met severe weather on the eleventh, forcing four of his seven bombers to turn back; the remaining three B-17s were intercepted by Japanese fighters—a pair of which were claimed shot down—but the American planes achieved nothing when visibility proved "too poor . . . for accurate bombing."[19] They dropped their ordnance from twenty-nine thousand feet, and as might be expected, came nowhere close to the enemy.[20]

For better or worse the stage was being set for the American navy's first surface action since the 1898 Spanish-American War. A daring (and to some, foolhardy) mission that would demand "initiative and determination" and much more.[21] In the end, it would fall to a quartet of aged Asiatic Fleet destroyers to carry out this strike. How they arrived at that juncture represents a convoluted tale in itself.

The ease with which Tarakan fell to its invaders did not escape Japanese notice, nor did that with which the precious Dutch oil installations were demolished. The enemy wanted no repetition of the latter at Balikpapan. Therefore, under the twin pressures of time and resources—for the Japanese, even given their strength, were attempting the seizure of the East Indies with limited forces, munitions, and supplies on a drum-tight schedule—the military commanders decided to use their most famous captives from Tarakan as human bargaining chips in the upcoming operation against Balikpapan. These were Dr. Anton Colijn (the son of Holland's well-known and well-regarded former prime minister) and his wife, Aaltje.

Colijn had worked with the Dutch KNIL forces at Tarakan as a reserve captain and helped plan, organize, and implement the destruction of the oil installations. His wife refused to leave what her daughter called "that gloomy place" and stayed behind to work as a Red Cross nurse with about eighteen other female volunteers. Both husband and wife were seized and made prisoners as soon as the island was captured.[22] Neither Colijn nor his wife would be permitted to feel too much satisfaction at their work, however, if the Japanese had their way.

Mr. Naritomi, the local Japanese administrator from Sangkalirang—where the Japanese had a timber and oil concession—had been brought in, and he informed the military officials that the demolition of the oilfields was complete and appeared to be "practically irreparable." The Colijns' captors were enraged at the destruction of the fields that they had sought so earnestly to obtain for the emperor. "Then the fury of the Japanese knew no bound," wrote a Shell Oil historian after the war. "They snapped at Dr. Colijn that they might have sympathized had the Netherlanders destroyed their tools and machinery, as these could have been replaced," but to wreck the wells themselves, thereby befouling the "sacred gift" of oil, was an insufferable insult to Tenno Heika.[23]

Fearing a repeat of this catastrophe at Balikpapan—their next target along the eastern coast of Borneo in the Makassar Strait—the Japanese either decided to utilize or were tricked into employing a traditional method used throughout human history during times of conflict: they would turn Colijn and his wife into hostages. And although she never knew it, the life of Mrs. Colijn would hang in the balance.

To prevent demolition of those invaluable oil installations at Balikpapan, a simple ruse was formulated: Captain Reinderhoff and Anton Colijn would be sent ahead as couriers, with Colijn's wife and the other Red Cross nurses as hostages to ensure that the two men did their utmost. Sources differ as to whether this scheme was concocted by the Japanese or by the Dutchmen. In any event, Colijn and Captain Reinderhoff were to be sent under guard ahead of the Japanese invasion convoy with an ultimatum for the Dutch authorities at Balikpapan. It said very simply—in Japanese and in Dutch—that if the facilities were destroyed not only those responsible at Balikpapan but the captives in Tarakan would be executed. After delivering the document Colijn and Reinderhoff were then to return to Tarakan with the response. What would follow reads like a chapter from one of Robert Louis Stevenson's adventure novels.[24]

On January 16 Reinderhoff and Colijn, accompanied by two Japanese naval lieutenants and two sailors, set out from Tarakan on a small inland craft, the *Parsifal*, for Balikpapan, some six hundred kilometers to the south. With them they brought a written announcement (*Mededeling*) setting forth the enemy demands.[25] On the nineteenth, the *Parsifal* appears to have separated sufficiently from the main body of the convoy—which had been warned by Colijn and Reinderhoff to remain at a distance in order not to alarm the Dutch and initiate demolition plans at Balikpapan—and was spotted by a patrolling plane. This was x-21, a Dornier Do-24 flying boat of the Royal Netherlands Marine Air Force. It would appear the plane received some type of signals from the men at that time. On that day the sea was too rough for a landing, though, and the patrol plane flew off. It would return the next day, on January 20.

However, from this point forward the story begins to assume multiple identities, morphing into different versions of what followed with several variants through the years. It seems that Colijn and Reinderhoff either overpowered or deceived their captors next—some accounts claim the Japanese were drunk—and managed to get them (locked) inside the cabin of the *Parsifal*. They then signaled the plane circling overhead, and with calmer seas it was able to land nearby. Either by leaping into the ocean and swimming or by using a small dinghy, the intrepid Reinderhoff and Colijn escaped to the Dutch airplane, where they were plucked from the water. They were taken forthwith to Balikpapan, where they reported to the KNIL commander, Lieutenant Colonel Van den Hoogenband, who instantly set in motion the demolition plans for the port's oil installations. These two courageous men were not allowed to return to Tarakan but were flown directly to Batavia via one of the MLD Do-24 flying boats, which also carried back a number of demolition experts.[26]

To the Japanese invaders—nervous but resolute—it had all been going well enough up to that point. Vice Adm. Takahashi Ibō, head of Third Fleet and the responsible naval commander overall in the invasion operations (Ranin Butai), wanted the timetable accelerated. He and his staff hoped to move the next invasion convoy on to Balikpapan ahead of schedule. The misadventure with Colijn and Reinderhoff may have made this problematic. This delay was officially ascribed later by the Imperial Army to "lack of air support which was still needed in the Navy's Celebes Island invasion."[27] Whatever the actual cause (and it must be said that such an explanation rings of Japan's endemic interservice rivalries), the convoy did not begin to proceed south until the afternoon of January 21. Again, the "First Escort Unit" under Rear Admiral Nishimura of DesRon 4 in light cruiser *Naka* with three divisions of destroyers would provide support.

As for Colijn's wife, her life was spared and she survived the war unaware of her role as a hostage or the "diabolical" scheme of her Imperial captors. Tragically, the military forces—and civilians—at Balikpapan would not be so fortunate. The shores of the oil port would be stained by the blood of many helpless noncombatants and POWs in the coming days as the Japanese made good their threats.

. . .

Proceeding south, Nishimura's convoy continued to be favored by inclement weather conditions. With close screen for the sixteen merchant vessels provided by nine patrol boats, minesweepers, and subchasers, they had reached a position northeast of Cape Mangkalihat at noon on the twenty-second. Eight hours later they rounded the cape, swinging to the southwest, past Sangkalirang. Having learned little from the Colijn-Reinderhoff affair, another advance operation with two native "secret agents" embarking on a small steamer had been deployed by the Japanese ahead of the convoy some days earlier. They were escorted by the destroyer *Samidare*.[28] These men were to serve as river and road guides for the Surprise Attack Unit, which was to act independently of the main force.[29] The unit was to be sent north into the Bay of Balikpapan, move inland up the river—with critical junctures illuminated by the secret agents along the route—and capture the primary reservoir before turning south to the village of Banoeabaroe behind the defender's positions, thereby cutting off any escape routes.

Despite the meticulous planning of the Japanese, however, and much to their anger, by the time their invasion convoy arrived off Balikpapan most of the oil installations had already been fired. The destruction—planned well in advance and organized by a demolition unit of 120 men with military training—had actually started on January 18 in the Louise oilfields deep in the Mahakam delta north of Balikpapan. At first they dismantled well tubing, cut off to a depth of

150 feet, which were then "dropped down the holes together with pump plungers and accessory rods. To complete the work, the material which lay ready (such as bolts, nuts, and heavy drilling bits) was thrown after them, and finally, a tin containing four pieces of TNT, in order to destroy the casing strings."[30]

As it soon became clear to the Dutch that a full-scale expedition was bearing down on them, more extensive demolitions were carried out, although concentrated on the least productive wells initially. At Balikpapan proper, stills and steam boilers were first wrecked; these were allowed to boil dry to destruction, which was a frightening procedure no one had tried previously. Not knowing how long this might take, the Dutch engineers and sappers there likewise got an early start on the eighteenth. The entire process consumed a day and a half; about thirty hours of "heavy stoking" were required to collapse the shells of the stills, after which the destruction of the boilers themselves took another five to eight hours.[31] Over the following week, however, the destruction of the installations increased throughout the region and at the port itself.

The Dutch at the Louise oilfield then had to destroy "all wells which produced over five tons of oil a day." These were demolished as the others had been. Within a few days "all motors, pumps, dynamos and turbines were blown up." In the distance to the south they could see a sky glowing red "from the burning refineries and supply-dumps" at Balikpapan. There the "frightful destruction" had begun in deadly earnest on the twentieth with the rescue and arrival of Reinderhoff and Colijn.[32]

First, the wharves were set afire, encircled by channels of burning oil ignited by drums of gasoline; factories were then blown up; the paraffin-wax factory, the packed lubricating-oil drum store, the saltwater pumping station were all ruthlessly and efficiently dynamited. The newly constructed tin plant in the Pandansari factory was fired: "The terrific heat caused the gasoline drums lying near to explode. Some of them shot up like fiery projectiles, and howling flames raged at least a hundred and fifty feet into the air."[33] This was followed by the obliteration of laboratories, tank farms, and the power station, with one thunderous explosion following another, shattering windows throughout the town.

• • •

As we have seen, during this period—when Tarakan fell but before the "orgy of destruction" began at Balikpapan—American surface units were scattered hither and yon.[34] Most were well to the southeast along the Lesser Sundas, largely out of position. Only the submarines of Wilkes were on the scene, and they all had problems locating, maintaining contact with, and attacking the

OVERTURES IN BLOOD AND OIL

enemy. For the Japanese, who had enjoyed a fair amount of good luck thus far, intermittent bad weather continued to screen their movements from air patrols above and submarines below.

*Pike* and *Permit* were vectored up to the northernmost coast of Celebes to locate a collection of transports to attack, but they found nothing. *Permit* received a dispatch from CSAF (Commander Submarines Asiatic Fleet) in the late hours of the eleventh instructing her to move down to Kema. She went at her best speed of about 15 knots, cruising on the surface much of the trip, and arrived at daybreak on January 13. The weather did not cooperate; her patrol report read: "Considerable rain made observations difficult during the afternoon." All she saw though her periscope after submerging was a pair of Japanese destroyers on patrol in the distance. The next night—on January 14—she sent another dispatch to CSAF: "No activity here except for DD patrols." The following day, more of the same; there was no convoy, "no enemy vessels."[35]

Frustrated by *Permit*'s messages, CSAF asked her on the sixteenth where she was *exactly*. How far offshore had she stationed herself? *Permit* reported that she was *precisely* 2.3 miles from the coast of Kema, noting that "no vessels of any description were sighted in this area." Less than five thousand yards seems to have been close enough for Wilkes and Purnell to get the picture at last. Yet, with communication gremlins as active as ever, it would still take another full day for the news to be transmitted to Glassford's striking group as it finally headed north.

After splitting off from the *Bloemfontein* convoy, *Marblehead* and destroyers had been loitering to the south at Timor awaiting any news on Japanese moves. At Koepang's lovely bay, the weather was unusually pleasant for the men on *Marblehead* and the tin cans. The cruiser sailors even hoped to steal a few hours of liberty ashore climbing Timor's scenic hills or among the town's picturesque white walls. However, by the morning of January 11, *Marblehead* had learned that a strike was in the offing. She then set off to the north, up through the Alor Strait, between Pantar and Lomblem, before moving east to Sumbawa. A junior officer aboard *Marblehead* wrote of that transit in his diary: "Just before and during sunset we passed through Alor Strait.... It was the most beautiful scene I have ever witnessed. Here was a winding cut heading roughly to the north east. On our left was the island of Lomblem, while on our right was [*sic*] Rusa and Pandai. At some spots it was less than five miles across. The sun set behind Lomblem, making a fine lace of the trees which lined its mountains. A lot of small islands floated around like lily pads. The sea itself was calm as glass and reflected the red-tinted clouds and hills."[36] He would not have many more days for such prose exercises. Personal diaries would quickly become a thing of the past, and soon enough the exigencies of war would catch up with the ship called "Old Knucklehead."

On *John D. Ford* Gunner's Mate Dan Mullin worked hurriedly to augment the destroyer's puny antiaircraft armament. He had located an extra .50 cal. machine gun on the ship and managed to fit it in a .30 cal. Lewis gun mount. He also rigged twin Lewis guns side by side into another mount. The increased firepower of *Ford*'s AA outfit was probably *not* going to save the ship from a determined aerial assault, but it made the feisty Mullin and his shipmates feel less vulnerable. For those with very little in the way of armament, any material improvement, no matter how scant, meant a significant boost in morale.[37]

When last seen *Boise* with her destroyers were continuing west to Surabaja, escorting *Bloemfontein*. There they arrived on the eleventh, and the liner was brought into the port. Once this duty was completed, the cruiser had embarked the commander of Task Force Five, Rear Admiral Glassford and staff, and then proceeded east to rendezvous with the *Marblehead* group. By this time "scuttlebutt" had alerted everyone that offensive operations were imminent.

On the morning of January 13 the ships converged on Saleh Bay, an enormous body of water that splits Sumbawa Island virtually in half. That afternoon Glassford held a conference with his commanding officers where they discussed more than the proper apparel to wear when ashore. They went over their "plans and established necessary security measures." As indicated by primary source documents, the officers shared a pronounced concern with submarines. The following day one of the destroyers' sound equipment picked up a contact, which caused all ships to get under way and stand out of the anchorage. This false alarm turned out to be nothing more than several large schools of fish, numbers of which were killed by the two depth charges dropped by *Pillsbury*.

The following day more info arrived from CINCAF suggesting the possibility of an operation to the north. Elements of a Japanese convoy, said to be twenty transports screened by two cruisers and roughly ten destroyers, had been sighted moving south from Davao. It was believed to be heading for Kema on the northeastern tentacle of Celebes. Glassford called for another meeting with his captains and staff on *Boise*. Swiftly a plan was formed to send in *Marblehead* and four destroyers—*Ford, Pope, Parrott,* and *Bulmer*—as a striking force (known as Task Group 5.2) with *Boise* held to the rear to provide cover on their return with her fifteen 6-inch guns. A cordon of submarines would be deployed across their path as well to ambush any pursuing surface forces. The *Houston* group, including *Alden* and *Edsall*, had left Darwin on the afternoon of Saturday, January 12, was now time steaming west. It was thought that *Houston* might help screen the retirement of *Marblehead*'s group with her powerful 8-inch main battery, but this never became necessary.

That *Marblehead* had been selected for the striking force was a choice that surprised a few of her men as well as some aboard *Boise*. Her skipper, Captain Robinson, reasoned that the "porcupine" armament of the older cruiser may have been a factor in her being utilized rather than the larger, newer, and far more powerful ship. He stated, "We can . . . and I mean to, throw steel from every quarter. That, I consider, reason enough for our entrustment with this job." It was their operational plan that the light cruiser, with her superior fathometer and charts, should lead the force into the tricky anchorage and engage the enemy. The destroyers, after releasing their torpedoes at the enemy's covering forces, would provide illumination for *Marblehead*'s gunfire "quite late and close aboard." The captain believed, or hoped, that the confusion caused by such surprise tactics would allow the American ships to neutralize the Japanese screen, and leave "the troopships . . . at the American's mercy, which, this night, would be in total abeyance." By the same token the Japanese were not expected to react passively, allowing their defenseless transports to be "butchered like tethered pigs."[38] Although Robinson anticipated the enemy would counterattack, he still liked the American chances.

Speaking candidly, he informed his officers, "It is, as a child could see, an extremely dangerous mission. But if we fall upon the enemy by complete surprise, we should be able to create considerable damage, and, perhaps, get away, at least from surface ships." Yet, none of the officers hearing Robinson's remarks failed to recognize that *Marblehead* was also the most expendable cruiser available.[39]

During the afternoon of the fifteenth, Glassford received a dispatch from CINCAF telling him to proceed. "Three destroyers were fueled immediately from *Boise*," and at daylight the following morning all left the huge bay. After some shuffling and additional fueling, TG 5.2 finally "slid out to sea." Described in the inflated language of wartime journalese as "the utterly dedicated and supremely dangerous enemies of Goliath," the four aged destroyers and their big sister, *Marblehead*, headed north across the Flores Sea.[40] On *Pope*, her first lieutenant, Lt. (j.g.) John Michel, realized the obvious in less hyperbolic terms: "Not a man on the ship had been in battle before. There were many thoughtful countenances about the ship, and more than a couple of Bibles were dug up from the bottoms of sea bags."[41]

*Boise* with *Paul Jones* and *Pillsbury* set course in the direction of the Alor Islands, north of Timor. But later that night they copied several critical CIN-

CAF dispatches, which altered everything. After a day of steaming north, as her keyed-up men adjusted themselves psychologically and professionally to their mission, *Marblehead* received an intelligence update in the evening of Saturday, January 17: the game had flown, mission aborted. The disappointing dope had come from the reconnaissance efforts of *Pike* and *Permit*. "On 17 January they reported that the harbor at Kema held no large concentration of shipping, and the attack of the surface striking force was called off."[42]

The voice of Captain Robinson intoned over the ship's squawk box: "Due to the uncertainty of their position we are turning back. I'm sorry. Better luck next time."[43] It was a sharp letdown for the crew and officers of *Marblehead* after their exertions, but perhaps just as well, for her men had scarcely reflected on this turnabout in fortune when the old cruiser began to show her age.

At 1600 hours on the afternoon of the seventeenth, her number 1 low-pressure turbine lost three blades with another six damaged. The ship had to cast loose her propeller shaft to allow it to idle. It was estimated repairs would take three days of around-the-clock work.[44] *Marblehead* and her destroyers began to steam south in the direction of Alor, with her top speed reduced to 28 knots. The other ships, including *Boise*, had retired eastward to obscure Kebola Bay, a remote anchorage off Pantar Strait in the Alor Islands.

With the U.S. ships steaming *away* from projected combat areas, another report soon arrived with more news of Japanese moves to the south. This time, though, it was reportedly "a landing in the vicinity of Kendari Bay," on the southeast coast of Celebes. At that moment Talbot's destroyers were believed somewhat to the northeast of Kendari, and their officers and crews felt no small unease at the thought of enemy forces behind them. *Marblehead* was then "directed to retire on *Boise* pending confirmation."[45] Fortunately the Japanese were not yet prepared to take Kendari, and the Americans would not have to fight their way out.

Coming from the east, *Houston* with *Edsall* and *Alden*—spotted by island lookouts—arrived at Kebola Bay midmorning on January 17. *Boise* (with Glassford embarked) and *Trinity* were anchored in the deep water off the island, where mountains "like inverted paper cups" came immediately out of the sea "to volcanic tips at peaks," their flanks covered in beautiful tropical vegetation. As one of his sailors recalled, Capt. Rooks handled *Houston* "wonderfully, like a destroyer," bringing her six-hundred-foot length through the bay's narrow entrance and easing right up alongside *Trinity*.[46]

From their shacks lining the beachless shore came boats filled with natives selling fruit—bananas, papayas, oranges, and pineapples—which the sailors readily purchased.[47] At the same time *Houston* took on fuel from *Trinity*. In that brief interim there was just enough time for some interaction between the crews. Bill Stewart, s1/c—a sailor from turret number 2 on *Houston*—went to the oiler and had lunch with his brother, Wilber, while the cruiser's thirsty bunkers drank up 232,000 gallons of fuel oil in two hours.[48] CINCAF then decided to send *Houston* and two DDs to pick up a convoy at Torres Strait. Accompanied by *John D. Edwards* and *Whipple*, the heavy cruiser got under way in short order, steaming back to the east. They were heading for a rendezvous with the ss *President Polk*, carrying men and matériel to be brought into the Indies.[49]

Soon thereafter *Edsall*, *Alden*, and *Trinity* set course once more for Darwin. The two flushdeckers were providing ASW screen for the trundling old tanker, which had been drained by her replenishment activities. Along the way they would meet with more excitement than they bargained for.

At 1400 on January 17, *Boise* with *Paul Jones* and *Pillsbury* left Kebola Bay for a rendezvous at sea with *Marblehead*. The definitive communication from CINCAF canceling the Kema strike came that evening and was copied to TG 5.2. Otherwise, it was an uneventful cruise for Glassford's group. Yet the launching of *Marblehead*'s soc floatplane to locate Glassford reveals the primitive state of affairs under which Asiatic Fleet units were then operating. Worried about radio transmissions—or incapable of good ones—and lacking long-range search radar, they had to resort to the shaky expedient of using a floatplane. Yet to launch one of the socs from a ship such as *Marblehead* was not the simple matter it might seem.

An AOM3/c serving with one of these old cruisers recalled the launching and recovery evolutions some years later: "[The] Curtiss soc-3 was a biplane with fabric-covered folding wings with a speed capability of a little over 130 knots slightly downhill. The catapults were compressed air units mounted amidships approximately 16 feet above the water line. Because of the short distance to the waterline, the catapult crew, who were torpedomen, not airdales [*sic*], who tried to shoot us off on an up-roll to keep from shooting us into the water, which they did on a couple of occasions."[50]

Clearly, launching while under way was a perilous business. "During a windless condition, it was necessary for the ship to make turns for close to 30 knots crosswinds, so the aircraft would be headed into same. Once we [the two-man crew, pilot and observer, in the soc] signaled the shooter, the pilot with his left hand on the throttle full forward and his right on the stick partially back, we departed the catapult at about 60 miles per hour. All the poor guy in the back seat could do was to wave his arms like a hummingbird trying to help us get airborne."[51]

Recovering a plane from the water after its mission was another matter altogether. If lucky, the pilot taxied his SOC up onto a sled towed by the ship after the vessel had made a "fast turning circle to create a smooth slick" for the plane to land on. Then, engaging the tow hook to the bottom of the sled and removing the hoist sling from a compartment in the upper wing, "the back seat idiot," who stood astride the pilot, "engaged the boom hook without losing any fingers. He hoped!" Following these tricky actions, positioning the aircraft on the sled was considered "a piece of cake."[52]

Having put her plane into the air with no recorded problems, *Marblehead* made contact later that morning with Glassford's ships. The plane's crew informed Glassford that *Marblehead* and company were about thirty-eight miles to the northeast. The two groups rejoined before midday. At that time it was decided to take the ships down to the more secure anchorage at Koepang Bay again, in view of the seriousness of *Marblehead*'s turbine problems. This consumed many more hours steaming to the south, which brought at least three potential problems: more time required moving the ships back up to the combat theater; *far* more fuel consumed in the process; and the need to transit the Lesser Sundas yet again, which involved negotiating hazardous straits between the numerous islands forming the Malay Archipelago.

It is fairly evident from Glassford's diary entries that he—and probably a number of other officers—were all increasingly apprehensive about the enemy's proximity.[53] Although the Japanese had not yet assaulted either Kendari or Makassar, they would be approaching both within the week. The Dutch and the Americans foresaw these moves with some anxiety. The large field at Kendari II would place enemy bombers within roughly three hundred miles of Flores, easily within bombing range, and one suspects an extra two hundred miles—the distance to Koepang—would have felt reassuring to COMTASFOR5. Admiral Hart later criticized this retrograde movement to Koepang as being "too far in the rear," but under the circumstances and with the information then available, it is hard to fault Glassford or Purnell too greatly.[54]

Late on January 18 *Boise*, *Marblehead*, and the destroyers reached Koepang, where repairs to the damaged turbine of *Marblehead* began immediately. These were of course limited to what the ship's force could handle. Meanwhile, the destroyers maintained antisub patrols. *Boise* launched a pair of planes for the same purpose, and, again, there were numerous false alarms. Meanwhile, over the next thirty-six hours Allied reconnaissance and intelligence—certainly aided by the exploits of Colijn and Reinderhoff—realized that the Japanese would soon be moving another convoy down the Makassar Strait, probably toward Balikpapan.

Messages the next day, however, may have failed to alert Hart and Purnell about the engineering casualty suffered by *Marblehead*'s turbine. Nonetheless, on the morning of January 20, CINCAF informed Glassford to order *Boise* and the four tin cans—after fueling the destroyers as necessary from *Marblehead*—to "START NORTHWEST TOWARD MAKASSAR AT 25 KTS."[55] Over the next few hours this misunderstanding was ironed out. Glassford then directed *Marblehead*, accompanied by *Bulmer*, to follow the striking group at 17 knots.[56] They would proceed along the same route from Koepang Bay to the Postillon Islands—today the Sabalana group, about 120 miles north of Sumbawa—thereafter to await instructions. This would take them via Sape Strait between Sumbawa and Komodo islands. The false starts of prior days were exacting too much fuel and imposing unnecessary strain on ships and men.

In this fuddled situation plans soon changed again. *Marblehead* and *Bulmer* were instructed to head for Surabaja after clearing Sape Strait, rather than move north. Fate would then toss an untimely monkey wrench of its own into this jumbled scenario. Paradoxically, it may be said to have both cost *and* saved American lives in the end.

On the morning of January 21, as *Boise* was passing through Sape Strait, her hull met an "uncharted pinnacle in what should have been 26 fathoms [156 feet] of water." The nearest "charted obstruction" was said to have been 1.2 miles distant. Nevertheless, the lurking coral reef got the better of the encounter. *Boise*'s bottom was torn from the keel plating—in places the keel bulged up for over a foot and a half—for a length of almost 116 feet.[57] In that misadventure the only other available cruiser was taken out of the picture. ABDA's striking force had lost two of its most powerful surface assets at a critical juncture to unlucky accidents.

Bevies of messages flew between the ships and Java's HQ on January 21 and 22. First, it was decided on the scene to divert the remaining ships to Waworada Bay, on the south side of Sumbawa, just west of Sape Strait. Per instructions from Hart and Purnell, *Marblehead*—thought capable of 28 knots under three functional turbines with her damaged unit disconnected—would there receive Glassford and his Task Force Five staff. *Marblehead* was to fuel to capacity from *Boise*. The Reluctant Dragon would then examine her injuries more closely—or, as Purnell requested: "DESIRE FURTHER INFORMATION ON EXTENT OF DAMAGE"—after which she was to proceed to Tjilatjap accompanied by *Pillsbury*, both remaining well south of the Barrier.[58]

Losing *Boise* at this time to a navigational mishap, regardless of responsibility, did not sit well with Hart or Purnell. It was, in truth, a bad patch for the ships of the Asiatic Fleet and would do nothing to elevate their reputation in the eyes of their allies. *Marblehead* was still limited to the use of three turbines, while *Boise* was "out of business" indefinitely. To top it all off, the submarine *s-36* had gone aground in the Makassar Strait and would become a total loss. In his diary on January 21, an incensed Hart would write: "Is not all that a grand series of events for one day?"

Untimely "events" notwithstanding, the remaining naval units under Hart, Purnell, and Glassford had to be positioned for a counterstrike. With the striking force now reduced to the four destroyers of Cdr. Paul Talbot (CDD59), it fell to the hobbled *Marblehead* and her escort, *Bulmer*, to move on to the Surabaja area as previously planned, to cover "as practicable" the retirement of the flush-deckers on their return.

It had come to that: Commander Talbot and his quartet of vintage four-pipers were now on their own as the forward offensive arm of ABDA's surface forces. *Marblehead*'s unofficial historian put it in brave, if inexperienced, words: "The destroyers would start the fight all right, but the old *Marblehead* would finish it in case the destroyers had anything but the most terrific luck."[59]

During the morning of January 23, as they circled the Postillons while waiting for orders, Talbot's ships finally received the go-ahead message. At about ten o'clock the destroyers were instructed by CINCAF to continue north and be in a position off Cape Mandar (north of Makassar and southeast of Balikpapan) at 2000 hours that evening, "PREPARED TO DELIVER NIGHT ATTACK PRIMARY WEAPONS TORPEDOES."[60] A half hour later they formed column, altered course to 015° T., and set a formation speed of 22 knots. Strong enemy air patrols were expected, although the miserable weather gave the battered tin cans much-needed cover during their approach to the jumping-off point. *Marblehead* and *Bulmer* were to remain to the southwest for the rendezvous area northeast of Surabaja near the Brothers Islands after the action.

What would be far more of an issue was the machinery of the elderly destroyers. All were in real need of upkeep, with *Pope* in especially precarious condition. To get to the enemy at the optimal time for a night torpedo attack, the four destroyers of DesDiv 59, including Lt. Cdr. Welford "Willie" Blinn's ship, would need to "average 25 knots, which," according to Blinn, "was a great strain on our overage ships and especially the *Pope* for we were longest out of drydock." That *Pope* was able to maintain station with the others was a tribute to the determination and skill of her black gang. Blinn and his XO, Lt. Richard N. Antrim, both recalled these sailors as "the least spectacular group of men"

OVERTURES IN BLOOD AND OIL

saddled with the most difficult responsibilities, but their pride was amply justified by following events.[61]

Lt. Cdr. Edward N. "Butch" Parker of *Parrott* likewise later wrote: "[My] Engineer Officer reported he never had so many men working on the engines, and that they were in perfect shape."[62] This may or may not have been an overstatement, but as the hours passed boilers and engines all held together—with few glitches—under conditions of pronounced adversity.

. . .

The four ships set off obediently at 1027 hours, swinging around the Postillons. Over the next five and a half hours they battled "heavy northerly swells" maintaining 22 knots. The lightly constructed bridges on all the Clemson-class ships were susceptible to damage when driven through a head sea. Cdr. Holloway Frost had written in his 1930 textbook, *On a Destroyer's Bridge*: "Reduce speed, if necessary, to five knots. Damage to the forward bulkhead of the chart house and the bridge may confidently be expected if this is not done in time. At the first sign of rough weather pull up the metal shutters to protect the non-shatterable glass windows. For, whatever their guarantee, a fine white-capped sea will shatter them into hundreds of pieces."[63] On *Pope*, as the ship slammed into the swells at 22, then 25 knots, this cautionary advice went unheeded. The results were two bridge windows splintered and metal spray shields buckled.[64]

Through the midday mist they were able to get a few navigational fixes, which proved valuable as they steamed north. Sightings of Banawaja and Sabalana Islands (also in the Postillons) helped plot their noontime position. An even better fix was obtained an hour and a half later as they passed inside the De Bril Bank, directly southwest of Makassar. This served the navigators of *Parrott* well in their dead-reckoning calculations for the remainder of the approach to Balikpapan.[65]

For the doughty tin-can sailors it was an uncomfortable approach, "under dark clouds across a rough, rolling sea," yet all were conscious that the heavy weather concealed them from the enemy even though it made them miserable. Gale-force winds and dense rain drove the topside force to seek shelter wherever possible. On *Ford*, "leading her division into a sea that broke monstrously across the bows as [they] rounded Cape Laiking," the gun crew for the number 1 4-inch gun on the foc's'le had to take cover in the well deck.[66] Dan Mullin would remember that "the ships pounded through the waves, water flushed over the decks, and spray carried by the wind reached as high as the gun director platform. Sudden wild lurches caused all hands to grab for support."[67]

None of the men much cared for their odds; even the officers admitted as much themselves: "Personally I felt that our chances of getting back from the attack were pretty slim," wrote *Pope's* skipper, Lt. Cdr. Welford Blinn. Believing—or hoping—if sunk that "it might be possible to swim ashore," he recalled, "I carried in my pocket a number of fishing hooks, a fishing line and a pocket magnifying glass, with which to make a fire in the tropical sun."[68] Lt. William P. Mack, gunnery officer for *John D. Ford*, did likewise. "[He] filled a little box with fishhooks, twine, razor blades, quinine pills, and Dutch money and sewed it inside his life jacket." Mack then attempted to get some badly needed sleep by cramming himself into a corner of two bulkheads, secure against the ship's lively rolling and pitching.[69]

Other men—with time—wrote letters home, but a number had more immediate concerns. These were torpedo men who lovingly cared for their "fish" in anticipation of the battle to come and the engineering force who worked to keep the ships' timeworn machinery running efficiently hour after hour in the dreadful weather. Below decks the machinist mates and their strikers topped off the air at high pressure—nearly 3,000 psi—in the heavy torpedo flasks.[70] There, enduring the nauseating stench of oil in the compressors' crankcases, the three-man teams worked to make certain the correct pressure was raised. Topside, the torpedo men "handled the upper deck connections, going from one to another of their 12 'fish.'" This was critical in assuring that the cranky Mark 8 torpedoes achieved maximum range in their runs.[71]

On *Parrott* Bill Slagle, the young radioman striker who had given "Butch" Parker the message from Hart on December 8, now found that he had no assigned battle station during action. He decided to do what radiomen were trained to do anyway and make a copy of everything he heard that night over the ship-to-ship phones, marking the time after each statement. Although hurriedly scribbled and all but illegible to others, Slagle's notes were to prove immensely useful afterward.[72]

During the afternoon, as the destroyers rammed through the thick weather—having increased speed to 25 knots at 1608 hours—the ships' radiomen were also monitoring PatWing 10 reports. When an unidentified patrol plane was glimpsed in the distance just before sunset through a break in the gray clouds, the men felt some apprehension that the enemy might locate them. Commander Talbot on *Ford* ordered a course alteration, to 035° T., hoping this might suggest that the four ships were enemy destroyers bound for Mandar Bay, north of Makassar. Their greatest concern was that they would be "observed on the afternoon prior to the attack and . . . intercepted before [they] could make an attack on the loaded convoy, which was [their] assigned mission." Soon after they had altered their course, they "received a radio report, in code, indicating the sighting of four enemy cruisers heading north in the exact location in which we had been."[73] They then realized the plane had been friendly and that it had seen the four flushdeckers fighting their way north through the Makassar Straits. True to form, the Asiatic sailors could always find something bright shining through the gloom, taking solace in this misidentification. As one man recalled, "That made us feel good, that we could be mistaken for cruisers even by one of our own planes."[74]

The patrol plane was in fact a PatWing 10 PBY piloted by Dick Roberts and Ed Bergstrom, flying out of Surabaja. The pilots had been instructed to fly north to Balikpapan and report on anything they saw but were given no information concerning enemy activity there or fighters or about friendly forces in the area. After flying up the east coast of Borneo hiding in the clouds as best they could and making a number of reports on the Japanese convoy as it moved south, they turned back across the Makassar Straits and flew down the along the west side of the Celebes. It was on their return leg, after having dipped below the cloud cover that they spotted Talbot's four ships coming toward them in the distance. The time was 1750 hours, and the PBY spent the next half hour observing and reporting on the four-funneled vessels, which they mistook for enemy cruisers. Finally, low on fuel and with the sun sinking, they turned away to Surabaja. It was, as events would show, a fortuitous case of mistaken identity for once.[75]

Through the inclement weather the four old destroyers pushed on, increasing speed just before dark to 27 knots as they entered the Makassar Strait. At 2000 hours *Ford*, *Pope*, *Parrott*, and *Paul Jones* (by column in that order) were running about six miles off the Celebes coastline as they passed Cape Madjene. By then the sea conditions were noticeably moderating, the skies only partially overcast with acceptable visibility again on the surface.

With the rain letting up, Lt. (j.g.) Jack Michel on *Pope* was able to take his turn as OOD during the First Dog watch—1600 to 1800 hours—and remain dry. Few were able to relax, though. Lt. Cdr. Welford Blinn, skipper of *Pope*, wrote in his Action Report: "Considerable anxiety was felt at this time as to the ability of *Pope* to maintain a speed of 27 knots (full power for our time out of dock) because much of our machinery was overdue for overhaul and numerous leaks had developed."[76]

Those men whose stations allowed it tried to steal a little rest before going to general quarters, which was to be set for eleven that night. With the ships' uncomfortable movements this was easier said than done. Jack Michel on *Pope* actually lay down for a couple of hours on the transom in the blacked-out wardroom after his watch, but he could not sleep. Tossing and turning as the waves rolled past, he thought of "every possible calamity that could befall the ship, how [he] would react under fire, and what [their] chances would be of survival."[77]

The navigator on Talbot's flagship, *Ford*, Lt. Norman E. Smith—also her executive officer—would not enjoy the luxury of sleep either. Described as slim, dark, and taciturn, Smith had the intricate job of directing "the way for the *Ford* and the other destroyers toward the pinpoint north of Balikpapan where the Jap convoy would be, just avoiding the Dutch minefields—the whole thing to be done under those black clouds without a chance for a sun sight and with unknown currents shaking [*Ford*]." It would prove an exacting responsibility handled with patience and skill by the meticulous Smith, who "kept a set of jeweler's tools in his cabin and was in the habit of repairing the ship's precision instruments when he had nothing better to do."[78] As it turned out, navigational fixes were obtained by other ships as well, including *Parrott*, which later revealed that their dead-reckoning estimates were more accurate anyway, and the ships pressed on in the darkness, with sea conditions smoothing out as they moved up the strait.

As for Hart's submarines, *Porpoise* and *Pickerel* had detected the enemy convoy broken up into small "detached" groups and heading south on the twenty-second, but they could make no attacks before losing contact. They did inform *Sturgeon*, and that boat found herself in a more advantageous position to intercept the Japanese ships. She was apparently responsible for firing several torpedoes at a large enemy DD in the middle of the night, all of which missed. The big destroyer was in fact *Umikaze* of DesDiv 24, which reported three torpedoes passing beneath her bottom at 0005 hours on January 23.[79]

Although meaningless to Talbot's ships—which were to be sent in regardless so long as the convoy continued to Balikpapan—some news from the boats trickled back in sporadic, often garbled messages to Asiatic Fleet headquarters on Java, where they were relayed by COMSUBAF—again often in poor transmissions—to the ships at sea. Air attacks had more success, though, and that information was definitely sent to Talbot. During the afternoon of January 23, CINCAF messaged the destroyers: "DUTCH AIR MADE SUCCESSFUL ATTACK THIS AFTERNOON STOP," also noting that there were "about 25 ships reported at 0-53S, 117-55E at 1655 (Java time) on course 240."[80]

On that messy day the brave Dutchmen in their old crates had done their jobs well indeed. As later written up in the *Sydney Morning Herald*, a Dutch flier stated: "On January 23 we spotted, through a hole in the clouds, 23 ships—two rows of transports surrounded by cruisers and destroyer—We immediately attacked with four patrols of bombers and two flights of fighters." Nine Dutch B-10 (Martin Model 166) bombers flying out of Samarinda II attacked twice in the afternoon and evening and hit two transports, the *Tatsugami Maru* and *Nana Maru.* "The Japanese put up a heavy barrage. . . . Explosions were followed by a black 'cauliflower' of smoke. The ships began to disperse with the destroyers circling around them like mosquitoes."[81] The *Nana Maru* was set ablaze and had to be abandoned. In obedience to its strict timetable the convoy moved on and left the burning transport behind; one Japanese skipper noted that "she was afire for many hours, and disappeared beyond the horizon."[82] As events unfolded, her flames remained visible from a great distance, and her lengthy incineration aided the American destroyers as they approached later that very night. *Tatsugami Maru* was able to proceed on to Balikpapan with the convoy in spite of her injuries. Once there, her crew's primary attention—like that of most of the Japanese—would be directed to threats from the skies above and the sea below. Too few of the lookouts would think to thoroughly scrutinize the water's surface in the middle of that black night. None seem to have believed the Allied forces had the will or the offensive wherewithal to make a surprise attack. Such overconfidence and naïveté were the most effective protection the Americans could have hoped for.

As the ships of the Japanese convoy began taking their assigned positions within the anchorage—and with some of the destroyers still retrieving their paravanes after sweeping mines—they were surprised by another attacker. This was the Dutch submarine *K-XVIII* (Lieutenant Commander Groeneveld), which, although already spotted by the Nishimura's flagship, *Naka*, had managed to infiltrate the anchorage. At 0200 hours the light cruiser's lookouts saw the intruder about three kilometers away and at first mistook her for a PT boat. They promptly up-anchored and ordered the number 12 subchaser, which was nearby, to investigate the contact. Groeneveld's *K-XVIII* was operating on the surface due to poor visibility that night. Minutes later a torpedo track was sighted approaching *Naka* from her port bow, but she managed to elude it. Nishimura then ordered the number 12 subchaser to attack the enemy, while the cruiser moved off to the east herself. Undeterred, the audacious Groeneveld still had plenty of other targets to choose from.

Within no more than five minutes, by 0215 hours, having just disembarked the first wave of her landing party from the *Sakaguchi Heidan*, the army transport *Tsuruga Maru* (6,988 tons) was struck on her port side by a torpedo from the Dutch submarine. The transport's captain, Kato Shizuo, recalled being stunned by "a deafening roar. . . . The engine room was completely filled with water immediately."[83] At least one crewmember and some thirty-odd army personnel from the assault force were killed. The torpedo had exploded in the number 4 hold, and the ship took on an alarming list to port at once; she then stabilized somewhat but soon began settling by the stern. Kato sent the remaining army landing-party members and all superfluous crew to the *Liverpool Maru*, which was anchored close by.

After reporting the attack, the damages incurred, and that he was abandoning the sinking transport, Kato was the recipient of a wonderfully disconcerting message from the Escort Screen commander (Rear Admiral Nishimura of DesRon 4) that said: "Your report doubtful. Re-check thoroughly." In answer to this absurdity, as his ship settled deeper into the waters beneath him, Kato sent his first officer, Ishiguro Kimiji, back down into the flooded hold. A brave individual—and a fine officer who would later die in combat as a skipper himself—Ishiguro dove into the pitch-black water not once but several times and confirmed what was perfectly obvious: there was an immense opening in the hull and the ship would sink. Kato drily recalled that he wanted to tell Nishimura and his staff, "if they had any doubt, why not check the damage themselves."[84]

Kato saw the remaining personnel off the foundering transport and went up back up to the bridge alone, pondering his fate. After a period of arguing with his officers over whether he should perish with the ship, the sensible Kato allowed himself to live. He and about ten others got into one of the ship's launches, which was moored to a ladder amidships, and moved off to a safe distance where they gloomily watched *Tsuruga Maru* "going down to the bottom of the sea."[85] This, however, was not the end of the adventures of Kato and his surviving crew, or for any others present on the dark waters off Balikpapan that night. The real excitement had not even started.[86]

. . .

At 2215 hours *Parrott*'s navigators obtained a final bearing on Cape William, some thirty miles to starboard. This was "the last navigational aid that was observed prior to the engagement." In the next hour Talbot's formation passed close by the north end of the Little Paternoster Islands in midstrait. Between 2315 and 2330 hours, general quarters was sounded on the various four-pipers, and the men went to their action stations. Most were feeling the apprehensions of soldiers going into their first combat engagement. Soon a glow thirty miles to the north was detected by *Parrott* and several bearings taken and plotted. However, *Parrott* did not seem to know that an air report had already been received (at least by the *John D. Ford* and *Pope*), which suggested this might be a damaged transport. Over the next two hours, as they raced on, this glimmer was eventually recognized as "an irregular burning flame" in the distance. *Paul Jones's* action report later described it as "the bright glow of what was evidently a burning ship." It was in fact the abandoned and burning *Nana Maru*, her flickering immolation helping guide the quartet through the black night.

Another series of lights or fires were visible just after two o'clock. What was thought to be a searchlight was also seen to briefly glimmer on and off, but visibility remained poor due to the haze and smoke drifting to sea from the burning oil installations ashore. Some of these had surely resulted from the attacks on *Tsuruga Maru*. By half past two in the morning, Talbot's ships were beginning to make out the dark shapes of enemy ships in the distended anchorage off Balikpapan, almost ten kilometers long. In column *Ford, Pope, Parrot*, and *Paul Jones* sped at 28 knots into the now-calm waters off Balikpapan. Although unseen at that time, the transports were spread out to their left and slightly abaft. At 0235 *Ford's* lookouts saw what appeared to be a column of several Japanese destroyers passing from starboard to port roughly three thousand yards away. Expecting to be sighted, they were astounded when their ships were permitted to steam on with nothing more than a challenge from a blue signal light on the last enemy destroyer. Talbot's ships did not respond, and the Japanese made no effort to stop them. On into the anchorage the flushdeckers steamed undetected. The Americans had slipped past several cordons of smaller IJN escorts just when the big destroyers of DesDiv 2 and DesDiv 9 were patrolling well to the east of the anchorage.[87]

The destroyermen couldn't miss the acrid stink of burning oil refineries drifting over the water when through the light haze. Talbot altered course to 320° and then 312° T. Suddenly Japanese ships appeared all around them. A few minutes later orders were given (by TBS) to begin firing torpedoes. On the bridge of the lead ship, *Ford*, the skipper, Lieutenant Commander Cooper, then yelled out, "Action port! Torpedo action port!"[88] *Ford* fired two salvos to port, with her chief torpedo man, Gordon Canady, smacking the firing pins himself with a maul.

At about that time an enemy ship—or ships—believed to be destroyer class, passed close by to starboard. *Parrott* unleashed five torpedoes (three from one bank of tubes and two from the other, and set to run at four and eight feet) in two salvos set on broadside (straight) fire at point-blank range. At the rear of the column, *Paul Jones* fired one torpedo herself "at what appeared to be a small cruiser." The enemy ship—evidently this was *W-15*, one of the 700-ton minesweepers from the Eleventh Division—could not have been more than a thousand yards away. To everyone's infuriation these torpedoes swam wide, missing their target, which was moving quickly, and obliviously, away. *Parrott*'s skipper, Lt. Cdr. J. N. Hughes, later attributed this failure to "the rate of change of bearing [being] so great at that close range and [due to the ship's] high speed."[89]

It mattered little, for "numerous shapes were showing up on both sides," and *Parrott* had her pick of targets. She chose one from among "three large ships" about four thousand yards off her port bow, and at 0300 hours fired three torpedoes. The column then altered track slightly to starboard before beginning a large reverse movement to course 185° T. *Ford* and *Pope* had also fired more torpedoes at some of the same black-hulled targets, with a wildly excited Commander Talbot yelling out, "Get that yellow bastard!" as he realized the surprise his ships had achieved. Quickly more and more ships emerged from the darkness.[90] Nonetheless, *Ford* withheld some torpedoes in case heavier enemy screening units were encountered. Before the turn was completed—and within two minutes of firing her torpedoes—a "dull detonation" off *Parrott*'s port quarter was heard, "followed almost instantly by a column of billowing flame that rapidly rose to some three or four hundred feet in height. After some thirty seconds of brilliant, billowing flame the fire began to subside, leaving a tremendous column of smoke above it."[91]

This unfortunate first victim was the 3,519-ton transport *Sumanoura Maru*. Her holds had been filled with mines and depth charges, and she went up in a towering explosion seen throughout the anchorage. Aboard *Pope* Lt. (j.g.) Jack Michel saw the "great mushroom of flame" spewing hundreds of feet into the sky that announced to the Japanese in no uncertain terms the presence of unwelcome intruders.[92] Kato Shizuo and his men in their open boat saw the "fire geysers shooting up," and then what he called "the most dreadful scene": the "explosion of a ship fully loaded with ammunition; the length of the ship as the base, and the height of the masts as the altitude of a rectangular [shape] was filled with fire, and incendiary arrows like fireworks accumulated. When they all subsided into darkness, the ship was nowhere to be seen."[93]

Recognition and signal lights flickered on among the anchored transports and from startled escorts. Suddenly multiple searchlight beams crisscrossed in the night as if the ships were under air attack again. Meanwhile, adding to the confusion, subchasers from Nishimura's escort screen were engaged at that time against Groeneveld's boat.[94] The scene was ideally set for Talbot's quartet of four-pipers.

Although the gigantic blast of *Sumanoura Maru* at first misled Michel—he believed that the Dutch had picked an inopportune time to detonate another oil well—he soon made out the silhouette of a ship beneath the climbing flames and smoke. At that moment he knew it was an American torpedo and that time would soon reveal the flushdeckers' identity.[95] Each ship quickly fired more torpedoes at the dark shapes that lay at anchor around them or at the indecisive Japanese escorts. *Pope*'s chief torpedo man, Harold Netter, hammered the firing pins as if they were never going to be used again.[96] Meanwhile, on all four destroyers, waiting for the torpedoes to strike, dozens of gunners tempered their eagerness to begin firing with the self-restraint that had been inculcated through doctrine and drills. As it turned out, *Paul Jones*'s gunners would never fire a single shot from their 4-inch batteries that night, and would only use up five of her twelve torpedoes.

When *Sumanoura Maru* exploded, the minesweeper *W-16* was near enough to see at least one of the American ships speed past in the darkness, but she could take no action. Upon reaching the area in which the transport had been torpedoed, she found nothing left of the ship above the water. Indeed, there were only nine survivors after the apocalyptic blast. At the same time, *Kumagawa Maru*, an auxiliary supply ship anchored next to *Sumanoura Maru*, got her anchor up when she received the warning of enemy units. She steered toward the shallows along the coast and then altered back to the southwest. This movement took her at first away from the U.S. destroyers briefly but then directly in the path of *Ford*, which had become separated from the other three ships in the division's turn south.

*Ford* had crossed ahead of a minesweeper (probably *W-16*)—which looked to the Americans like a destroyer—and her men believed they had seen torpedoes fired. At the same time *Ford* was moving closer up to the coastline, nearing the ten-fathom line, and there was also fear of wandering into a Dutch minefield. She executed a sharp turn that left the column scrambled, and her three sisters turned inside and more directly south. On *Ford*'s bridge Cooper and CDD 59 Talbot seemed momentarily confused over the disposition of the ships, with Talbot then giving the column to *Parrott* as the others pulled away. Thereafter, and for a period of some hours, *Ford* would be steaming alone, cut off from *Parrott*, *Pope*, and *Paul Jones*. Soon thereafter she came across the solitary *Kumagawa Maru* slowly trundling up from the anchorage.

The Japanese saw *Ford* approaching from their starboard quarter at high speed. In a trice the American tin can opened fire with her 4-inch main battery and machine guns. The assault hit *Kumagawa Maru* about ten times and riddled her stern area with .50 cal. rounds, killing six men. In the blink of an eye the destroyer then sped off to the southwest—having closed to within a few hundred meters during this brief firefight—but not before the Japanese returned the favor. With a display of sharp reflexes and even sharper gunnery, they landed a quintessential Parthian shot, literally kicking the American flush-decker in the rear as it sped away. *Kumagawa Maru*'s gunners walked three salvos right up along *Ford*'s port quarter in a "quick creeping barrage with 50 meter steps" before the fourth hit her fair and square below the afterdeckhouse and the 4-inch gun atop it.[97]

This salvo ignited hand grenades, spare torpedo detonators, a bucket of lubricating grease, and a can of reserve gasoline for the auxiliary radio generator, all of which were whipped into a roaring fire by the ship's speed. High above in the destroyer's crow's nest, Lieutenant Harmon had been blinded for a few moments by *Ford*'s gun flashes, with his little cubicle on the mast jerked back and forth by concussion and the ship's violent maneuvering. As his vision slowly returned to normal, he noticed a bright light aft and looking back saw the "flaming comet tail" of *Ford*'s afterdeckhouse ablaze in the night. Luckily a quick-acting electrician's mate, Vaughn Faber, saved the day by doing the wrong thing. He grabbed a fully charged fire hose, and contrary to all his training—which repeatedly taught the men *never* to spray a gasoline fire with water—turned the hose on the flames. Luckily the powerful stream of water simply flushed the fiery bolus overboard. The concentrated gasoline and oil fire continued to burn in the ship's gleaming wake as it continued on at high speed. This flaming glob attracted the enemy gunners' attention and a handful of shells plunked down around it in the black water while the destroyer made its getaway.

The one Japanese shell hit on *Ford* was not entirely inconsequential. It wounded four men, one of them badly enough to later require hospitalization. This casualty was John T. Darby, RM3/c, who had been sitting in the open hatchway between the auxiliary radio room and the torpedo repair shop. Although the projectile burst within feet of Darby, the open hatch saved his life when he was blown some twenty feet through it and landed against the number 4 (portside) torpedo mount. Darby suffered multiple shrapnel wounds to his back, from his buttocks up to his neck—luckily none spinal—which would put him in the hospital at Surabaja.[98]

*Parrott*'s torpedo attacks consumed less than twenty-five minutes. Around 0308 she had fired a single fish to starboard at "a vague outline at a range of about 2,000 yards." *Pope* and *Paul Jones* also expended torpedoes against the same large target—at 0306 and 0310 respectively. On meeting the hull of the previously damaged *Tatsugami Maru*, one or more detonated. The 7,000-ton ammo carrier blew up with "wreckage hurled over a wide area" and sank within thirty minutes. *Parrott* and *Pope* each fired more torpedoes—three and four respectively—at what was thought to be at least one destroyer off the port beam at 0319 hours. This was in fact a pair of patrol boats, P-37 and P-38, both steaming south of the anchorage at low speed. P-38 recognized the attackers in time to evade the torpedoes fired at her but appears to have masked the Americans from the view of her consort, P-37. The second patrol vessel then mistook one of the four-pipers at first for *Naka* and approached making recognition signals. For this error she paid heavily: one torpedo hit her in the stern and knocked out her power, disabling her guns and searchlights. A helpless target, she was quickly hit twice again by torpedoes in the bow and stern as the U.S. ships wheeled around her. And this time the damage to P-37 was much more severe. She later sank, having suffered some three dozen men killed.[99]

Soon thereafter TBS crackled to life again on the other U.S. destroyers. They reported to Talbot that they had expended all their fish and asked for permission to open fire with their guns. In the wheelhouse of *Ford*, the exhausted Talbot gave his okay.[100] For *Parrott* this order was executed at 0330 hours, when she opened fire to port. She used her 3-inch on the fantail to unload three rounds of star shells to augment the three 4-inch illuminating rounds expended along with three rounds of 4-inch common. Due to her speed, the poor visibility, and the need for concealment, her gunnery was brief; within a minute she checked fire.

*Pope* for her part had commenced with her main battery around 0325, when she fired on a pair of "destroyers" and then against one transport, followed by another DD. With her guns directed by Lt. Bill Wilson from his station above the bridge and spotted by Lt. (j.g.) Jack Michel in the crow's nest, the men on *Pope* believed they hit the transport at least three times before "the combination of high speed and short range made it impossible for the guns to bear on the target."[101] Her gunnery action ended within twenty minutes at the most; in all the old destroyer had fired nineteen rounds of 4-inch common, plus one 4-inch and two 3-inch illuminating rounds, along with all her torpedoes.

Isolated from the others, *Ford*'s gunners, led by Lt. William Mack Jr., Dan Mullin, and others, had been firing throughout their pass to the north as they swung past *Kumagawa Maru*, even as the enemy tagged them in the rear. Above the flaming deckhouse, *Ford*'s 4-inch gun kept firing despite the hit, as did the .50 cal. machine-gun crews on the galley deckhouse. Jack Burshem, a quartermaster manning the big wheel at Aft Steering Station on the forward end of the afterdeckhouse had been knocked flat on his derriere by the enemy shell. Dazed, he did not think he was hurt badly but then felt liquid on his pant leg and realized that he, too, had been hit by fragments. He was able to get back on his feet, however, clinging to the binnacle for support, to continue with his duties.[102]

As *Ford* wound her way alone through the anchored convoy, her aggressive gunners with their machine-gun battery augmented by Dan Mullin's work continued to shoot up virtually everything in their path. This included the transport *Asahisan Maru*, which received a savage machine-gunning along her stern that left upward of fifty men dead.[103]

By that time, well to the southwest, *Paul Jones* had fired the last of the five torpedoes she would expend in the melee. At least one of her three final torpedoes—and probably more—appear to have struck home. At 0322 she had fired two at a transport off her port quarter; one struck the bow of the 5,175-ton Imperial Army transport *Kuretake Maru*, and this ship eventually sank with her stern rising high in the air, taking with her 2 crewmen and over 270 army troops.[104] Acting as lookout high above the water in the crow's nest, Boatswain Mate Warner Guy would not soon forget the experience of *Paul Jones's* part in the battle, with his "ship doing 27 knots in a harbor full of [Japanese] ships."[105] The last fish expended by *Jones* was at one of the two jinxed patrol boats, P-37 and P-38, which challenged the four-pipers as they wove in and out of the convoy. P-37 may have been hit by as many as three torpedoes, so one could well have been from *Jones*. The next day *Paul Jones's* action report would note: "No other suitable opportunities for torpedo fire were presented to this ship."[106] Her part in what soon became known as the Battle of Makassar Strait had ended, but the foxes were not quite free and clear of the henhouse just yet.

As they began "heading for the barn" (as Lieutenant Commander Cooper on *Ford* put it), a final confused enemy patrol boat, P-36, spotted two of the flush-deckers.[107] The crew of the Japanese patrol boat not only mistook the Americans for *Naka* but also briefly mistook its consorts P-37 and P-38 in the distance beyond for enemy ships. Before the befuddled P-36 could get a confirmation as to their identity, a cluster of star shells burst above her. Then, as quickly as they had arrived, the four-funneled vessels steamed past at high speed, their pale gray hulls disappearing into the blackness. Ten minutes later and almost a dozen kilometers to the east, the First Screen Force commander, Rear Adm. Nishimura Shōji in *Naka*, received P-36's puzzling message: "Sighted four enemy cruisers south of the convoy." Having heard nothing for over three quarters of an hour, Nishimura was now baffled. Within eight minutes he asked: "Were the 2nd Destroyer Division ships mistaken for the cruisers?" Four minutes passed, and then P-36 replied—for once correctly: "It was a mistake; the cruisers mentioned were four-stack destroyers." In the interim Nishimura sent a dispatch

OVERTURES IN BLOOD AND OIL

telling the army commander, General Sakaguchi in the transport *Teiryu Maru*, to have the convoy move off a safe distance to the east and await further orders for a dawn rendezvous. At that juncture confusion had assumed dominance over the Japanese forces off Balikpapan. Although by then the four destroyers of Talbot were well to the south-southwest, Rear Admiral Nishimura led *Naka* north to attack the enemy, and as he did so he ordered the Ninth Destroyer Division to follow him. For reasons never explained the destroyers did not comply with this order, and *Naka* headed back alone to unravel the "horrible sight" in the anchorage, as daylight soon disclosed.[108]

In the final period of action *Pope* and *Parrott* become separated, and it took another ten minutes or so for the ships to form column again. *Paul Jones* rejoined them a few minutes later, with "Butch" Parker's *Parrott* leading the other two. For a short period there was some anxiety regarding the fate of *Ford*, but voice contact through TBS was soon made, and retirement courses were given and acknowledged. It would still be several hours before Talbot and Cooper in *Ford* caught up with the other three.

As dawn began to illuminate the horizon, the three flushdeckers under Parker came barreling out of the strait at 28 knots. The Americans, astonished by their luck but with no wish to push it further, hoped to put as much distance as possible between themselves and the enemy ships and planes they expected would pursue them at daybreak. They also wanted to link up with *Marblehead* quickly, since even her primitive AA battery would have offered more protection from air attacks than they could muster themselves. Most of the destroyermen anticipated that Japanese naval units would attempt to intercept them, and *Marblehead*'s torpedoes and 6-inch main battery in addition to a couple of extra flushdeckers would help even out those odds. One of the destroyer skippers would later joke that the men were all so focused on watching astern for enemy pursuers that "had a mountain loomed up in front, they would have hit it!"[109]

With the tin cans running at 28 knots, *Pope* then experienced an engineering casualty. Blinn's ship was forced to reduce speed temporarily to repair a feed-pump steam line. This limited the destroyers to roughly 20 knots for half an hour while *Pope*'s engineering force worked doggedly to fix the problem. Her black gang "almost suffocated in a stifling, heated, steam-filled atmosphere," as they labored to keep the engines functional, suffering several cases of heat prostration in the process.[110] At 0545 hours "Willie" Blinn's ship could resume high-speed steaming, and all three four-pipers increased to 25 knots.

By that time *Ford* was spotted in the distance, emerging from the darkness five miles off *Pope*'s port quarter. Moving at a good clip, she overtook her three division mates an hour later and reassumed her position at the head of the column. By blinker light CDD59 Talbot began assembling inventory numbers from his division on fuel, water, ordnance, and more importantly, enemy ships sunk or damaged. At the same time tired sailors and officers topside turned fatigued eyes to the south in search of their rendezvous mates. Where was *Marblehead*?

It produced some unease at first when an unidentified patrol plane was seen about five miles distant. The men tried to signal it but got no satisfactory response. This was a cause for concern, but twenty-five minutes later another scout plane—of U.S. cruiser type—appeared seven miles away, and correctly identified itself. This floatplane signaled that *Marblehead* was forty miles to the south. With this news Talbot's weary destroyermen breathed a collective sigh of relief, and the flushdeckers reduced speed to 23 knots. On board *Parrott* Butch Parker's wound-up men then relaxed enough to play a popular Dinah Shore recording ("Yes, My Darling Daughter") over the public address system for reveille.

At just after 0800 the light cruiser's mast tops poked over the horizon ten miles away. Soon her escort, *Bulmer*, was seen as well. When they moved ahead to take their stations, much of the tension on the four-pipers evaporated and the spirit of the Asiatic Fleet sailors manifested itself in a series of good-natured wisecracks with *Marblehead*'s signalmen. "Well-done!" came a message from the cruiser, adding: "Wish we could have been at the party." The quartermaster on *Parrott*'s afterdeckhouse didn't miss a beat, replying: "First party I was ever at with no lights except fireworks. It was so dark I couldn't find the girls!"[111]

Over that day and the following night, a more normal routine was resumed on the flushdeckers; most of the men were able to clean up, change clothes, and eat a decent meal. On *Ford* cooks worked through the morning to make hot steak-and-egg sandwiches for the crew; these were delivered in wire baskets to those still standing watches up on the deckhouses or down in the sweltering engine spaces. Cauldrons of strong coffee stood brewing, ready to be delivered in pots to the men of each mess. By then the ships had reduced speed to an economical 15, then 14 knots, due to both fuel considerations and the problematic turbines of *Marblehead*, which were still giving trouble. The destroyermen did not care for this reduction in speed and worried that it might enable Japanese ships of greater power to catch up with them, but no enemy attacks materialized. Requests for "maximum air coverage" were sent out to Java, but as usual none were forthcoming.[112]

Throughout the day more messages were transmitted to Surabaja and Batavia as the destroyers laid out their accomplishments as clearly as they could to

Glassford (COMTASFOR5), Purnell (CINCAF ADMIN), and Hart. They thought they had surely sunk five or six enemy ships, perhaps more. In this early estimate they would later be proved largely correct. Even BBC radio broadcast the results: "From the Eastern Front! Good news, good news!" And, for once, mass media told the truth: "Four American destroyers infiltrated into the middle of a Japanese invasion force at 0300 hours this morning.... A total of six ships are known to have been sunk, and many more damaged."[113]

A petty officer on *Parrott* named Aloysius Mondschein recalled malicious local gossip: "There had been a story around that we weren't at Makassar." Mondschein, who was in charge of the main electrical switchboard on the old four-piper, had seen plenty of the night fight with his own eyes: "Saw Jap ships all around. I saw about six myself. Our first shot hit an oil tanker. It went up in flames. Then a transport was hit; I saw it go down." As the four destroyers came back into the swept channels through the Surabaja minefields, Mondschein knew something else that would tell the tale: their empty torpedo tubes.[114]

. . .

At 0810 hours on Sunday, January 25, Talbot's four destroyers reentered the minefields off Surabaja; by 1130 they had tied up to the dock. Lt. (j.g.) J. S. Slaughter on *John D. Ford* wrote many years later: "Our success reached Surabaja prior to our return. This was first apparent when we passed a Dutch destroyer and they saluted us with enthusiasm. By contrast when we had entered a month earlier their salute seemed more like a 'birdie.'... Then our boss, Admiral Hart was waiting for us on the dock. This was the first time we had ever seen him."[115]

The brow on *Ford* had just been set up forward of the galley deckhouse when the official party of American and Dutch officers, including Admiral Hart and staff, came aboard. Hart could not have been prouder. Before the ships even reached port, he had already begun writing up several "congratulatory despatches to the young fellows who ha[d] contacted the enemy so very effectively."[116] As Hart came aboard, telling the dead-tired men to carry on, Dan Mullin could not restrain himself, blurting out, "We got a couple for you, Admiral." Hart smiled and with a wave replied, "More than a couple from what I hear."[117] He was then taken below by Lieutenant Mack to visit Commander Talbot, still in his bunk suffering from the effects of his near heart attack.

Talbot was being tended by Harry Zlotolow, CPhM, for what was clearly a cardiac episode during the return. As he was leaving the bridge, his complexion had become ashen and his breathing labored. While attempting to descend the ladder, Talbot suddenly collapsed. The men helped get him into his bunk, after which he appeared to fall into a profoundly exhausted sleep. After visiting *Ford* on January 25, Hart noted in his diary: "Talbot who commanded carried the show off all right but returned an utter wreck and is probably finished; 46–47 is too many years for that sort of thing."[118]

Both the more seriously wounded radioman, John T. Darby, and Commander Talbot were then put in the U.S. naval wing of the Central Burger Ziekenhuis (hospital) at Surabaja. Darby would recover sufficiently from his wounds to be evacuated. Talbot was flown soon thereafter to Australia, where he would then be sent back to the States for additional treatment and recovery before resuming his career.

When CINCAF visited *Parrott*, Aloysius Mondschein noted, "When Hart saw that all our torpedoes were gone, he had no doubts in the matter."[119] On the same four-piper young Bill Slagle's handwritten notes that he had taken during the engagement while stationed in the radio room—he had no assigned battle station—suddenly came to the attention of the destroyer's communication officer and her skipper. After returning to Surabaja, Butch Parker and his subordinate "dashed into the radio shack." Slagle recalled, "[They] looked me in the eye and asked me if I had been copying anything of the last night's action." Before the unnerved radioman striker could finish his stammering reply, Parker cut him off: "Slagle, if you have anything, give it to me!" Slagle reached into a bottom drawer where he had stashed his "little souvenir" from the previous night's battle, fished out his scratchpad, and handed it to the captain. Parker glanced at it for a moment, then barked: "I can't read this damned mess. Bring it to the wardroom." The men went into *Parrott*'s small, stuffy wardroom, where Slagle read his notes out to the two officers. As he was doing so, Parker broke in and inquired whether the notes were helping flesh out the picture. His communication officer replied, "Captain, this is *just* what we need. He has it *all*." They thanked Slagle as they finished, but when Bill reached for his pad, Parker placed his hand over it, and that was the last Slagle ever saw of his own handwritten notes to the Battle of Balikpapan. Several days later "Butch" Parker thanked Slagle again, however, telling him that the notes had been instrumental in completing the report for Admiral Hart.[120]

Although Hart was delighted with the results, he had to admit—along with the "honest" destroyer officers, "that they did not do nearly enough damage." This severe appraisal sprang from the view that the flushdeckers had encountered a perfect opportunity and had they "done everything just right, [they could have] sunk everything that the Japs had there."[121] In this appraisal we may discern the effects of adrenaline as clearly as sober analysis. It was unlikely, under even the most perfect circumstances, for the destroyers steaming at high speed in pitch darkness, firing old World War I–era torpedoes, and armed with undersized main battery guns, to have destroyed *all* fifteen of the enemy transports.

Nonetheless, their results were quite respectable: they had sunk or incapacitated *Sumanoura Maru, Kuretake Maru, Tatsugami Maru,* and *P-37*—the bomb-damaged *Nana Maru* burned herself out before going under the waves—and they had ravaged both *Asahisan Maru* and *Kumagawa Maru,* while the intrepid Groeneveld's *K-XVIII* sank *Tsuruga Maru* on her own. It was believed that their torpedo attacks should have been more effective, but given the age and performance characteristics of the Mark 8–Mod. 3 torpedo, this seems unrealistic, too.[122] In any case, the Japanese were not about to let the forces of ABDA rest on their laurels for any length of time. Balikpapan was taken in spite of these reverses, and the enemy's timetable suffered no appreciable setback.

In the Western press, though—starved for positive news in the weeks after the disasters at Pearl Harbor, Luzon, and Malaya—needlessly fulsome accolades came soon enough. Within a fortnight *Life* magazine ran a full-page article titled "The Sea Battle off Makassar Strait" and wrote that it had been "a modern kind of sea engagement that may rank in results with Jutland and Lepanto. . . . The Japs assembled in the Celebes Sea a great armada of perhaps 100 ships. They carried probably 100,000 soldiers." This colorful padding was followed by more of the same, although leavened with a teaspoon of truth: "On January 23 the huge fleet poked into the north end of Makassar Strait. It was hit at once by American-made bombers flown by Dutchmen." Following a description of the raid, more inflated claims were made: "By January 28, at the most conservative count, they had sunk 13 ships and damaged 18 more, drowning thousands of Japs." Continuing to engage in wishful thinking, the article next surmised that Allied forces "may have hit the [enemy] aircraft carrier, so that the Japs had almost no air protection."[123] This exaggerated reporting was rampant throughout the early months of the war in the Pacific, and while not confined merely to the Western press, it was especially unfortunate in the East Indies, where civilians were led to believe that a far more energetic and successful campaign was being conducted than was the case.

After returning Talbot's destroyers remained moored together at Surabaja's Holland Pier for the better part of the next four days. Hart and staff, along with various Dutch naval officers, including Rear Admiral Doorman, visited them all. Although the destroyermen were able to rest, eat around the clock, and prepare for liberty, they had more pressing immediate duties. Ships were promptly fueled; they had come back into port with nearly empty tanks. *Ford* received

108,000 gallons, 95 percent of her total capacity. They resupplied, cleaned their guns, and restocked magazines. Always conscious of the ships' advanced years, engineers took apart pumps and compressors and cleaned valves, hoping to avoid more engineering casualties. On *Pope* the crew hung stagings over her side for a quick paint job. The men knew better than to waste this valuable time; they might be called back into action at any moment.

Liberty was granted to one-quarter of the crew at a time; this began the following afternoon (January 26), and the sailors, as always, made the most of their free time in bars and clubs in town, where the Dutch had suddenly grown less distant and cool. It seemed to dawn on the locals and Dutch military personnel that the Americans were not reluctant to fight after all. Almost overnight RNN sailors and officers appear to have altered their opinions. They made certain now that the Americans knew where their clubs were and that they were received with more cordiality than previously.

On *John D. Ford* a neat hole three inches in diameter was found in one of the stowed life rafts, where *Kumagawa Maru*'s gunners had put a shell into the afterdeckhouse. Elsewhere on the damaged flushdecker the affected areas had been scrubbed, patched, and repainted within hours and now looked almost as good as new.

Jack Michel from *Pope* went over for a visit and noted that the compartment showed little more visible damage than scorched paint. He there encountered Jack Burshem, a former crewmember of *Pope*, who had been struck in his rear end by fragments while stationed atop the afterdeckhouse. When asked about his wounds, Burshem hemmed and hawed before stating that he was having trouble sitting down. Michel soon discovered that *Pope*'s crew had already been over to *Ford* and given Burshem the business about getting his "fat duff" in the way of those Japanese shells.[124] Burshem, nonetheless, seems to have had the last laugh since he spent several nights ashore "in the sympathetic arms of a generous native girl" who tended to his wounds . . . and more besides.[125]

# SIX

## First Sortie of the Striking Force

*Flores Sea*

January ended with time clearly running out at Singapore, and Hart's attention—when not distracted by the machinations of Helfrich, Van Stachouwer, Van Mook, and others—turned east to the Japanese advance on the Moluccas and Celebes. Tarakan, Balikpapan, Menado, and Kendari had all fallen; Ambon was soon to be taken.[1] Hart and others had anticipated these moves, but none were countered, either by ABDA submarines—which were in general "a day late and a dollar short"—or by offensive ABDAIR forces.

Not surprisingly, by this time Allied attitudes were darkening. As a sub commander noted, "We realized that this war was too big for submarines and the pitiful Asiatic Fleet to win alone."[2] He was right; in the short term, the men of ABDA were well on the way to being written off. Stated reassurances from the high brass in the second week of February ("You can be certain you are not forgotten men") must have been received with dismay by the isolated Americans caught up in what was clearly a losing business in the East Indies.[3]

As matters stood, all that Hart and Helfrich could bring to bear against the enemy was a combined force made up of American and Dutch warships. And as in other branches of ABDA's slapdash coalition, this would prove another case of getting insufficient assets to the combat zone too late to deter the enemy. There were multiple causes for this failure. Most of the ships, even the more modern units, were getting run down by the amount of convoy duty they had been compelled to undertake. This was especially true of Hart's aging destroyers and cruisers. And by the end of January it was becoming clear that the main Dutch ports with adequate repair facilities—Surabaja and Batavia's Tandjong Priok—would soon come within range of Japanese land-based bombers and fighters. This situation necessitated the utilization of many obscure bays and harbors spread along the Malay Barrier and beyond, from Sumatra to northern Australia, with all the navigational problems these locations brought. Evading enemy air patrols meant running vessels through any number of dangerous straits between the Indian Ocean and the Java, Bali, Flores, Celebes, and Timor Seas. This brought its own set of difficulties, as the campaign's numerous accidents and groundings show.

Like it or not, the Allies had to undertake more offensive operations. According to Hart, forming a cruiser-destroyer striking force was an American idea, which appears to have had a simple enough explanation: British and Dutch warships were preoccupied during January with escorting convoys; mostly in support of the defense of Malaya. After the British withdrew onto Singapore Island, more ships became available for use in the striking force, although there, too, Helfrich behaved in what Hart believed was a disingenuous manner. "Helfrich was still found disposed not to be entirely frank as regards the state and readiness of his forces," wrote Hart of this period later in his narrative.[4] Meanwhile, Wavell—or "the Chief" as his men called him—was preoccupied with Singapore and made two rather dangerous trips there himself in the second half of January alone.

While in Surabaja on January 25, visiting his men in the aftermath of the Balikpapan destroyer strike, Hart became aware that enemy forces were still positioned in the Makassar Strait area and might be vulnerable to more attacks by ABDA units.[5] The next day he went to Batavia for a conference with Helfrich (CZM) and Collins (commodore commanding China Force, CCCF). Hart realized that he could not put together an adequate force made up solely of American ships in time, and that the Dutch had five cruisers and destroyers concentrated in the Karimata Strait (to the west between Borneo and the Bangka-Belitung islands), so he asked Helfrich about the possibility of using those vessels for a sortie against Makassar Strait. This suggestion was rejected by Helfrich, who stated that these Dutch ships were *not* a striking force and that their orders had been changed. He gave no further explanation or disclosed any of his intentions for the employment of those ships. This incident, in a nutshell, may be said to have represented the cooperative principle of ABDA as described by many who were there: "Let the other guy do it." It also provides an ironic counterpoint to Helfrich's subsequent criticisms regarding Hart's unwillingness to keep American ships at sea.

Nonetheless, Hart should still have had enough ships for the job in late January. Convoys into Singapore were coming to an end; British and Dutch vessels were being freed up for offensive operations. He seems to have taken Helfrich at his word about the Dutch ships, but in another few days the situation changed again. Suddenly Rear Admiral Doorman's ships *were* available, after all.[6] This

FIRST SORTIE OF THE STRIKING FORCE

was doubly galling because in the interim Capt. "Robbie" Robinson in *Marblehead* and four flushdeckers—*Stewart, Barker, Bulmer,* and *Edwards*—had attempted another northern foray only to call it off prematurely due to high night visibility under a full moon and having been shadowed during the day by Japanese air patrols.

The destroyermen at first felt tremendously let down when the operation against Balikpapan was canceled late in the afternoon of January 31, but within hours, after returning to Surabaja, they understood that the odds were not necessarily in their favor. U.S. moods whirled like a weathervane in a thunderstorm. Bill Kale on *Stewart* began by complaining in his diary: "Well, we've lost so much damned face." But a few hours later he had changed his tune: "We are pretty well satisfied that had we attacked last night, we would have come out of it pretty badly. . . . Captain Robinson [of USS *Marblehead*] officer in tactical command of this group, is a pretty smart cookie."[7]

Privately Hart's mood fluctuated, too. At first he was concerned that Robinson's ships might be "going into a hornet's nest to attack" and then, in the wake of the ships turning back, Hart worried that "Robbie" had not been "sufficiently venturesome." He also found the "wording" of Robinson's dispatch announcing the mission's cancellation problematic and was apprehensive that it might make a poor impression in Java.[8] His long experience and grasp of the professional, political, and diplomatic ramifications of each operation—and more critically, every written dispatch—told him that when handled in too perfunctory a manner, such communications could carry inordinate weight during times of crisis.

. . .

At just this time Hart was being distracted both internally and externally, by political intrigues within ABDA along with ongoing problems with Washington DC and the Navy Department. Naturally this made focusing on the job at hand more problematic. The political intrigues were emanating from Dutch sources in Java (Helfrich, Van Stachouwer) and Washington (Van Mook). Their constant complaints to the administration and the navy were beginning to tell.

Admirals Stark and King had given Hart a considerable amount of leeway in running the campaign at sea in the East Indies. But for the prickly Dutch—as they watched their outposts falling one by one, with their thinly distributed resources being whittled down—this meant little enough. In their eyes Hart had never been aggressive enough. With the war going badly for ABDA in every dimension—air, sea, and land—Hart had no effective countermeasures against either military or political criticisms. Even his attempts to garner support from Wavell, with whom he was on good terms (or so he thought) came to nothing. Hart later admitted that he misjudged Wavell's willingness to act at all. In fact, he did not expect "the Chief" to take *any* action. But in assuming Wavell would behave in a complacent manner, he turned out to be dead wrong.

Wavell, although disinclined to " open up his mind" to Hart, had sent a dispatch to London it seems after all. Somehow this message, or a permutation of it, was thrust in the face of American leaders there by none other than Churchill. This communication amounted to a "lack of confidence" vote by the Dutch (which was not disputed by the British) regarding Hart's ability to handle his assignment effectively. Wavell declined to show the dispatch to Hart, so an additional degree of uncertainty went along with his uneasiness about being cast in "a bad light."[9]

During an awkward face-to-face meeting with Wavell at Lembang, the British general hemmed and hawed, once more muttering something vague about Hart's age. Hart was personally disappointed that Wavell had bent beneath the political pressures of the day, but he seems to have understood it. Hart had never been an officer who quailed at the burdens of responsibility, including the consequences of his own "too blunt" personality.

Undoubtedly both men realized that the Dutch were dead-set on getting Helfrich into the top position of ABDAFLOAT, regardless of just how this took place. The Netherlanders seemed then quite prepared to sacrifice Hart's reputation just as casually as they would later exonerate Helfrich and Doorman from any responsibilities for the much heavier losses and reversals that took place on their watch. Although he had good reason to distrust Helfrich, it is not clear that Hart wanted to recognize the desperation and delusions affecting the Dutch on Java when he accepted command of ABDAFLOAT and, as he put it, "climbed up in this damned saddle."[10]

And to be fair to the Dutch, we must understand that Hart had already told Wavell more than once that he had never wanted to act as ABDA's naval commander in the first place. In other words the fact that he *would* be replaced surprised him far less than the *means* by which the shift was accomplished. Having had a command that he never solicited thrust on him, Hart seems naive to have expected this would guarantee he would not be taken out "in a manner which reflected adversely on [him]."[11]

At the same time (on Tuesday, January 27) he had been ordered by Washington to reorganize what remained of the old Asiatic Fleet, with Rear Adm. William Glassford Jr. given command of the new organization. It would be known as the U.S. Naval Forces in the Southwest Pacific, and "Tubby" Glassford was to be raised to the temporary rank of vice admiral. So it required no clairvoyance to see that the stage was being set for Hart's replacement. He mused in his diary the next day that he might soon be "dropping out of the picture."[12]

His pride understandably wounded, Hart admitted to some sleepless hours thinking about it all during this crisis, but such unease seems to have passed quickly enough. His conscience was clear, and he could not see any "considerable mistakes" he had made. The same enemy tactics—driven primarily by air superiority—that had forced the American navy and air force out of the Philippines were now routing the British in Malaya. He had no reason to expect that the defense of the East Indies would be any different. As the Japanese war machine ground its way south, allied opposition on land seemed to weaken. There was less resistance on Malaya and at Singapore than on Bataan and Corregidor; there would be far less still in the East Indies.

Beneath Hart's glib comments and generally unruffled facade one perceives a sense of relief as well. He knew that the top job at ABDAFLOAT was at best a thankless task and at worst a career-murdering one. His primary concern in that sense was to emerge with his professional reputation intact. Most of his apprehensions regarding his "allies" turned out to be correct; he expected to be blamed. And it does appear he understood that both Stark and King backed him—even if FDR did not. But with the situation heavily skewed by political considerations, even the hands of the navy's top brass were being yanked around by forces beyond their control.

It was never a matter of winning a war with the Japanese in the East Indies. Those delusions—willfully entertained by others on Java for reasons that would later look ugly and indefensible—Hart had the sense to ignore. By the end of January he was writing in his diary that it was time to "face and accept facts." An eagerness to distort the truth in order to manipulate propaganda or exculpate failures was not second nature to Hart; he was no Douglas MacArthur. All the same Hart was not one to openly criticize his own government, still less the U.S. Navy. His duty and responsibility lay elsewhere, and the consequences of this hard truth he accepted.

. . .

While distracted by these political imbroglios, Hart had to get on with the business of fighting a war. And even though he had delegated most of the operational duties to Purnell and Glassford, in this last instance he again felt compelled to lead personally. In a conference of his commanders in Surabaja on

Monday, February 2, Hart thought that he detected some reluctance on the part of Glassford to make another thrust into the Makassar Strait area to attack Japanese convoys there.[13] This perception may not have been fair to Glassford, but Hart remained perturbed by "Robbie" Robinson's failure to press home his mission in *Marblehead*. He wanted no one to accuse the U.S. Navy of pusillanimous behavior, least of all the Dutch and Helfrich. Helfrich had needled him on more than one occasion, and it rankled. That this first foray by the Combined Striking Force (csf) had a political component to its timing—given Dutch complaints about leadership—is also indisputable.[14]

With no British participation, along with Bill Glassford's seeming lack of enthusiasm—and with the Dutch willing to put in nearly half as many ships as the Americans—Hart saw that command of the Combined Striking Force went to a Dutchman: Rear Adm. Karel "Tank" Doorman. Hart stated that the decision was based on the willingness of the Dutch to finally throw that many ships into the fight and Doorman's familiarity with the waters in which the force would operate. And in early February he knew of no good reasons why Doorman should *not* command the striking force.

The plans were for another night attack against Japanese shipping near Balikpapan, which was now up to twenty transports, three cruisers, and ten destroyers, according to air reconnaissance on February 1. It was hoped a Balikpapan-style raid might hinder the enemy's next move, which was thought to be against Makassar or possibly Bandjermasin.

Rear Admiral Doorman and his chief of staff, Cdr. J. A. de Gelder, produced a four-page "Operation Order No. 1" late on February 3, which detailed the deployment of forces, steaming formations, urgent signal codes and radio frequencies, and offensive tactics to be employed along with retirement procedures. On that day the ships were anchored to the east of Surabaja in Bunder Roads off Gili Radja Island, south of Madura. The csf as then assembled was without question powerful enough to inflict significant damage to the Japanese in Makassar Strait. It would be led by Doorman in his flagship, *De Ruyter*, along with light cruiser *Tromp* and three rnn destroyers designated DesDiv 1: *Van Ghent* (F), *Banckert*, and *Piet Hein*. The Asiatic Fleet ships participating were cruisers *Houston* and *Marblehead* and flushdeckers of Cdr. Thomas Binford's scratch DesDiv 58: *Stewart* (F), *Barker*, *Bulmer*, and *John D. Edwards*. An American pby flew Rear Adm. William Purnell, acting head of Hart's Asiatic Fleet units, out to the anchorage that afternoon to confer with the various commanders.

After topping off several warships, *Pecos* was to remain in the Madura Straits area. A Dutch tanker, tan 8 (formerly *Petronella*), was to arrive in Surabaja on

February 5 and steam one hundred nautical miles south of the Barrier below Alas Strait in the Indian Ocean. That tanker was to then move up to Pandjang Island in the northern end of the strait off the northwest coast of Sumbawa, where she would be "available for fuel" after the mission. *Pillsbury*—still without half of her torpedo battery, lost in the December 10 bombing at Cavite—would remain with *Pecos* as her screen. *Paul Jones* stayed behind to escort the Dutch steamer ss *Tidore* east along the Lesser Sundas, where the two vessels would find their own adventure.[15]

Even before the CSF could sortie, however, dozens of Japanese bombers flew over, heading west. Although they were targeting Surabaja's naval base and its port facilities as well as ABDA airfields on the eastern end of Java at Malang that day, the Japanese pilots had also sighted the mass of warships through the broken clouds south of Madura. This inadvertent sighting was to have deadly consequences for the CSF.

The lack of Allied air power throughout the theater, and the pressure exerted at all points on ABDA's defenders by the aggressive forward deployment of Japan's air forces, rendered all Allied surface units vulnerable . Seizure of most of the important airfields in Borneo (near Kuching, at Samarinda II, and the Balikpapan area) and Celebes (in Menado and Kendari II) before the end of January and the first week in February had thrust the Imperial Navy's Eleventh Air Fleet (Kōku Kantai) to within striking range of Java itself. Despite repeated attempts to reinforce the planes of ABDAIR on Java, the Allies' losses were far more critical at this stage of the war than those of their enemy. In sheer numbers ABDAIR and ABDAFLOAT were overmatched; in qualitative terms the Japanese machines were not only superior but also being flown by better pilots.

The Allies also suffered from an absurdly primitive air warning system on Java that provided little or no adequate response time. The viable model of British radar-based systems, which was well recognized by Hart and others to have worked in the Battle of Britain, would not be utilized in either the Philippines or the East Indies on any meaningful scale.[16] This is not to say they were never *any* radar units in the East Indies, but the system was not prioritized by U.S. planners before December 1941. And after December 8 the United States did not enjoy the luxury of additional time to see it implemented on a scale that might have made a difference.

On February 4, 1942, the Combined Striking Force was moving out to sea with no more protection overhead than a vague reliance on cloud cover and flimsy hopes that enemy air patrols would be inefficient. Such wishful dreams were futile. Heavy losses by the Dutch and American fliers the previous day in the air and on the ground had left ABDA's Java air forces shaken and disorganized. They would be able to give no support to Doorman's force.[17] On the other hand, Japanese air recon patrols had been functioning with effectiveness since the outbreak of the war.

Lack of air support was sorry enough, but within the Asiatic Fleet a different species of negligence was unfolding. It involved matériel flaws that impaired the ability of America's young men to do the job they had otherwise been well trained to do. On this single issue a good deal more of the campaign's outcome would hinge. It would have significant ramifications—*all* of them bad. This problem concerned *Houston*'s secondary battery of eight 5-inch/25 cal. guns, and the antiaircraft shells they had been allotted prior to the war.

In order to better understand this "scandal"—and its far-reaching consequences—we must reverse time some six months to examine its background.

· · ·

In a short, perfunctory ceremony on the morning of Saturday, August 30, 1941, as the cruiser *Houston* lay at anchor off Jolo Island in the southern Philippines, Capt. Jesse B. Oldendorf turned command over to Capt. Albert H. Rooks. Within fifteen minutes, at 0833 hours, Oldendorf left *Houston* and boarded the light cruiser *Marblehead*, where he would begin his journey back to the states and his next assignment. For the next hour Captain Rooks held inspection of his new command. At 0940 hours the crew secured from inspection. One hour later *Marblehead* stood out.

At this time none of *Houston*'s officers could have failed to see the seriousness of their situation. As for the crew, many of whom were inexperienced youngsters, they knew that they had lost a skipper they liked and respected, so it was only natural that they should have wondered what kind of man Albert H. Rooks was and how well he would fill Oldendorf's shoes. Although the recognition would take some months, in the end almost all would find Rooks as fine a skipper as any they ever encountered.

When Oldendorf turned command of *Houston* over to Albert Rooks, the two officers had little time together to discuss the knotty situation in which they found themselves. However, we do know that they took this opportunity to exchange information and views on the ship's armament and personnel. Oldendorf, a popular skipper of the "hail-fellow-well-met" type, and known familiarly as "Oley"—he was remembered by one of his sailors as "a big, good-natured Swede"—pointed out to the serious, scholarly Rooks that should he ever "get in a scrap" the ship's survival would most likely be determined by her

5-inch battery. Oley said it was therefore imperative that those guns be kept in tip-top shape and their crews thoroughly trained.[18] This was sound, practical advice. It meant, among other things, that he believed the ship's primary duty would be escorting convoys and thus her greatest danger would probably come from the air. It also implied that Oldendorf had absorbed to some extent the hard Royal Navy experiences suffered off Greece and Crete.

*Houston*'s air defense officer since June 1940 was Lt. Cdr. W. Jackson Galbraith (USNA 1929). He had previously served—from July 1939—on USS *Indianapolis* (CA-35), where he acted as one of her AA battery officers. Galbraith joined *Houston* in Hawaii when she was a unit of the so-called Hawaiian Detachment (of the Pacific Fleet cruiser Scouting Force) and stayed with her at Mare Island in 1940 to keep an eye on the AA battery upgrades the ship received there, including the quad 1.1-inch machine cannon. Tellingly, he considered these "already obsolete" at the time.[19] All the same, it would fall largely to Galbraith to get the ship's AA systems and men functioning and properly trained. In the months preceding the war, his complement of men on the 5-inch battery nearly quadrupled. These grew from the original eighty-man complement—made up of forty navy men and forty marines—to about three hundred in all, which gave each gun almost four complete crews.

From the time the ship left Mare Island to return to the Philippines in October 1940, her secondary and light batteries were drilled on a fairly regular basis. *Houston*'s USMC detachment (in the ship's Seventh Division) manned two of the 5-inch guns aft, one of the four 1.1-inch mounts, and half of the .50 cal. battery—the machine guns on the foremast. Navy personnel took care of the rest. As one may guess, it was neither hard to get the Marines to maintain their guns nor to make them fire them in exercises. In fact G/Sgt. Walter Standish, who ran the .50 cal. machine guns on their foremast platform, and Pfc. Jim Slocum often had to be reminded not to overdo it in drills. When war came, they would prove equally enthusiastic.[20]

The problem with 5-inch/25 cal. shells had first come to light in the late summer of 1941: a report from one of the West Coast fleet schools for gunnery revealed the discovery that a large batch of those projectiles had defective fuses. Test-firings indicated a failure rate (i.e., nonexploding shells) of up to 75 percent.[21] When the report reached Galbraith, he sent his senior gunner, James Hogan, chief gunner's mate (CGM), below to the 5-inch magazines to double-check the cruiser's allotment. Hogan soon found that *all* the ship's secondary ammo was from the faulty batch. *Houston*'s gunnery officer, Cdr. Arthur Maher, was then informed. These men, duly alerted but keeping this disturbing knowledge to themselves, went directly to Captain Rooks. Rooks promptly wrote a letter reporting this matter, which was in turn shown to Hart—who endorsed it—and sent it on to the Navy Department. At that point bureaucratic complacency and denial appear to have taken over. Requests to test-fire some of the ammo were turned down; the navy's cautious stance on firing live ammunition in addition to conservative Depression-era fiscal policies seem to have dictated that this was not permissible. Prior to war, ships were not allowed to fire live combat ammunition in gunnery exercises but were forced to use cheaper practice rounds. Unluckily, *Houston* had both navy regulations and the shortness of time stacked against her. In February 1942 her mission would change and with it the crucial importance of her AA battery's ability to defend the ship and her charges. The all-too-predictable results were to prove catastrophic.

• • •

At 0130 hours on February 4, 1942, Rear Adm. Karel Doorman's four cruisers got under way from Madura Strait; they were preceded by the destroyers of Commander Binford (*Stewart, John D. Edwards, Barker,* and *Bulmer*), which had already left, clearing the anchorage about a quarter of an hour earlier. Binford's ship had been delayed by the transfer of a Dutch naval officer for liaison duties: Lt. 3rd Class Jacobus Leborus, RNN, came aboard less than fifteen minutes before *Stewart* departed. The same business took place on Robinson's *Marblehead,* as they waited until 0046 for the arrival of their RNN liaison officer. It then took almost two hours to get through the extensive Dutch minefields east of Surabaja.

The RNN personnel were taken out to the anchorage in a Dutch motorboat, at which point they were simply asked if they had any preferences about the American ship they boarded. Sub-Lt. "Ted" Luxemburg, who spoke four languages, agreed to go to *Marblehead.* There, over the next few days, when not on duty, he would share a cabin with one of her junior officers. Luxemburg had been recalled from Japan (where he had been studying since 1938) in the spring of 1940, when the Germans invaded Holland. He was sent to Padang, Sumatra, where he lived in Dutch barracks (built "around 1895" as he recalled), before being transferred to Surabaja. There he underwent training in the navy's officer training school and ended up as a signals officer for liaison purposes. Luxemburg was one of many such liaison personnel, but his adventures and ultimate survival would prove almost unique.[22]

At night the ships were steaming at a cautious and fuel-conserving 13 knots. General quarters was sounded on *Marblehead* at 0450. By dawn a cruising formation had been assumed, with the flushdeckers ahead of the main body, acting as an advance antisubmarine screen. A trio of Dutch destroyers—commanded by Lieutenant Commander Krips in *Van Ghent*, along with *Piet Hein* and *Banckert*—operated as the rear screen. Later the ships began zigzagging at a fleet speed of 15 knots.

The day was warm with moderate seas and skies mostly clear; overhead were scattered cumulus clouds, and on the water floated a slight surface haze. To the south the blue-gray peaks of Bali and Lombok, about sixty miles away, could be spotted occasionally, while to the north the green heights of Kangean Island, some thirty-five miles distant, soon became visible as well.

The mood aboard the U.S. warships was captured by a chief yeoman serving on *Marblehead* who wrote, "From January 7th [the date he joined the ship] until February 4th we had not seen any real action and all of us were very desirous of getting a punch at the Japs. . . . We were now sure that we were going to make a pretty heavy attack and the entire crew was very much elated and hoped we would be able to deal them a very heavy blow."[23] At that stage many of the Asiatic Fleet rank and file still held the belief that it would be a very short war against the despised Japanese. On *Houston* Eugene T. Wilkinson, a second-class seaman from Colorado, stated: "We thought the war would be over in six weeks. We really did."[24] A few more hours into the morning of February 4 would bring such American naïveté to a violent and terrible end once and for all.

Doorman's operational orders had arranged for cruising formations, rudimentary signals, and how the ships were to react to various potential attacks from air or by submarine.[25] *De Ruyter, Houston,* and *Marblehead* were to keep planes aloft to provide more or less continual air patrols overhead from dawn until nightfall.

At 0935 hours the ships received a message by signal hoist from Doorman that Japanese planes could be expected; the information was at least an hour old at that time. *Houston's* fliers went to their SOCs immediately, and preparations began to get her planes airborne. In less than fifteen minutes—and with two of *Houston's* SOCs still warming up on her catapults—the first enemy aircraft were visible in the distance. *Marblehead* got Doorman's message just as *Houston* signaled, "Strange aircraft sighted bearing 023 true."[26]

At first nothing more than metallic specks, this was soon seen to be several groups of twin-engine bombers flying in shallow nine-plane Vs. They all approached from the north at approximately ten thousand feet. These were medium attack bombers of the First, Takao, and Kanoya Kōkusentai flying out of newly seized Kendari II airfield in the southeastern Celebes. A total of sixty Japanese planes had taken off that morning—twenty-four Type 96 Nakajima (NELL) and thirty-six Type 97 Mod.1 Mitsubishi (BETTY) bombers—armed with a mixture of 250 kg (551 lb.) and 60 kg (132 lb.) bombs.

The Japanese naval air branch had not ignored the sighting of the previous day but had in fact thrown almost all available bombers at the ABDA force. They had to have sufficient range to make such an attack, as the CSF was well over five hundred miles from Kendari, but this does not appear to have caused any difficulties. The medium bombers employed—G3M NELL and G4M BETTY types—had far more range than necessary. They had taken off at daybreak and experienced no great difficulties locating the ABDA warships. Once they had spotted the Allied ships, the Japanese fliers took aim at *Houston*, the largest vessel in the group. Following Doorman's operations plan, his formation then split apart, with cruisers turning to port and starboard. It was felt that by attempting individual maneuvers each ship might better avoid the attacks.

*Houston* was able to catapult one of her SOCs, flown by her senior aviator, Lt. Tommy Payne, because it was already on the starboard catapult. But it would be the only one of her planes to get off the ship that day. And since the Mark 19 director could not begin tracking the Japanese bombers until they approached to within fifteen thousand yards, director crews and gunners had little time to prepare themselves. As soon as the leading flight of enemy aircraft came into range, *Houston*'s 5-inch secondary guns promptly opened fire. The first group of shells fired was from half the battery, and of the four projectiles expended, only one exploded. Thereafter this percentage—roughly one shell in four detonating—held throughout the engagement. That their shooting was quite accurate only made the bad performance of their shells that much more disappointing. Although this defect in her 5-inch ammo would leave *Houston*'s crew "very much downcast," the men continued to fire steadily at their attackers.[27]

The cruiser's gunnery had one other unfortunate effect, and not on the enemy. Although the SOC flown by Payne had been successfully launched from the disengaged—starboard—side of the ship, the plane of Lt. Jack Lamade on the port catapult was having engine trouble. This brief delay proved ruinous. When the portside 5-inch guns opened fire, their muzzle blast first tore the fabric off the tail section of Lamade's SOC on the catapult; subsequent salvos ripped even more surfaces from the Seagull.

Below, on the quarterdeck, Lt. (j.g.) Walter Winslow's SOC was being hauled into position to be lifted by crane onto the cat for launching. His observer, Elmo Bush, AOM3/c, was already in the rear cockpit attending his customized twin .30 cal. machine-gun mount.[28] Winslow and Bush would come no closer to getting into the air that morning. The startled Lamade and his observer in their plane on the port catapult could do nothing but sit and witness what next occurred with great rapidity. At that time, and far quicker than the *Houston*'s gunners had expected, the enemy's first string of bombs fell screaming along-side the ship. An order ("per doctrine") for all but gun and fire-control crews to seek cover had been given, but many men were still taken by surprise.

For the men of *Houston* this initial exposure to heavy air attacks was terri-fying. The nine 551-pound bombs landed close enough to deliver thundering body blows to the cruiser's twelve thousand tons. They sprang hull plates and popped rivets inside compartments, while tons of seawater knocked men off their feet topside in mountainous cataracts thrown over the ship from fore-mast to flight deck. From the engine rooms—where gauge lines and pneumer-cators were broken—to the men passing ammo on the 5-inch batteries who were swept off their feet with shells still in their arms, the ship was given what amounted to a massive haymaker.[29] Inside the main battery gunhouses and down into their handling rooms and magazines, men could only remain at their sta-tions and grit their teeth as the bombs fell. In the blink of an eye over a thou-sand young, largely inexperienced sailors and officers on *Houston* learned the hard lesson that enduring an aerial bombardment was a nerve-racking experi-ence over which one had little control.[30]

Jack Lamade and his observer leaped out of their now-useless SOC on the port catapult. Swiftly they helped strip the plane before it was catapulted over the side as a fire hazard. According to Walter Winslow the little biplane still managed a pretty takeoff even when unmanned. It almost looked as if it might make a stable landing on the sea, but at the last second a pontoon dug into the waves and the Seagull cartwheeled into the water, where it sank rapidly. Top-side, the portside AA gun-crews had not been told that the plane was being jet-tisoned, and they were stunned, believing that the SOC had failed on launch and killed both crew members.[31]

At the same time Lieutenant Payne's solitary Seagull climbed away, intent on avoiding any errant "friendly fire." For the remainder of the attacks Payne stayed at between one and two thousand feet, dipping in and out of the clouds as he observed what was a most sobering introduction to the realities of ships operating at sea against enemy bombers without adequate air cover. Below he had seen his ship inundated by walls of explosions and towering splashes that appeared to lift the cruiser's hull from the sea. With the detachment of a pro-fessional, though, Payne could not help but admire the accuracy of the Japa-nese bombs, noting: "No error was greater than ten mils."[32]

Meanwhile, a more ominous setback came to light as a result of these near misses: the tremendous jolts had dislodged the forward Mark 19 AA director on its mount, jamming it in train. When the first string of bombs had fallen—

striking "in a straight line" according to Lt. (j.g.) Leon "Buck" Rogers—the stolid junior division officer tried to reassure his men and "beef up morale." In a voice as rich as the Kentucky bourbon whiskey for which his hometown of Louisville had long been renowned, Rogers drawled, "They didn't even come close!" This was immediately met with an excited reply by one of his phone talkers, a young seaman first class named George Stoddard, who exclaimed, "Oh yeah? They looked awful close to me!"[33]

It soon became evident that Lee Rogers and his men could do nothing to free the director by themselves. It was as if fate had conspired to produce the one scenario that the cruiser's gunners had long recognized as a potential Achilles heel for *Houston*. No one had ever cared for the position of sky aft (the Mark 19 director just abaft the second funnel), and as early as March 1940 Captain Oldendorf had noted this as a problem. At the time the navy had done nothing to remedy the matter, and that director would remain there. But most of the other Northampton-class cruisers had their after directors sited atop the mainmast when they were refitted, which afforded much better vision and freedom from the effects of funnel smoke. Being compelled to rely solely on the after Mark 19, as awkwardly placed as it was on *Houston*, was something her air defense personnel would have hoped to avoid. Of course this unwieldy situation was exactly what happened. Following that first stick of bombs to fall near her in the entire war, *Houston*'s forward director was rendered useless; all the 5-inch guns were then placed under control of the aft director.

There was then an interval of some minutes between attacks. The men on the cruiser had time to undertake what damage-control measures they could. Broken phone leads were repaired and seawater cleared from decks; telescopes and instruments that had been doused with seawater in the aft director were wiped clean. Commander Maher had officers sent to each 5-inch gun to double-check fuse settings, making certain the shells were being correctly seated for fuse pot loading and "to prevent improper fuse cutting and consequent duds."[34] It was futile but better than doing nothing, and it gave the men a sense of trying to deal with the problem. Elsewhere men picked up chunks of steel from the decks believed to be from their own antiaircraft guns. Olen Minton, s1/c, a rammer man on the number 2 5-inch mount, found such metal shards. At least one other gun-crew member had been momentarily stunned when struck on his helmet by a fragment.

The aft director's position was above secondary conn between the aft funnel and the mainmast, and above the boat-deck battery of 5-inch guns. In secondary conn was a small group of men, probably not more than four in all, and commanded by Lt. J. C. Patty Jr., the secondary control officer. It, too, was a problematic location, with poor visibility for its single spotting scope, which was easily obscured by smoke. Immediately overhead was Lieutenant Commander Galbraith's air defense position—what would have been designated sky control in most large ships—although he and his assisting officer, Capt. Frederick Ramsey, USMC, were both out in the open, watching the skies from a pair of metal seats bolted to the deck. Inside the director of sky aft itself, Lt. Russell Ross (known by his men as "The Old Lieutenant") and crew struggled to keep enemy planes within sight. Nearby was the gun telephone talker, Raymond Sparks, s1/c, and he had heard Galbraith's loud expletives as that initial burst of 5-inch shells had failed to detonate properly. From Captain Ramsey—a man as self-composed as Gunny Standish was excitable—Sparks and others would hear no such outbursts.

As these events unfolded aboard *Houston*, the *Marblehead* was being subjected to much the same tactics from the enemy bombers and would suffer a very similar fate that morning. Like the other ships, *Marblehead* was steaming in column almost due east (87° T.) at 15 knots, zigzagging in accordance with the Dutch plan, with *De Ruyter* and *Houston* ahead and *Tromp* aft, when strange aircraft were sighted at 0949. They were far off to the northeast and approaching at high altitude. *Marblehead* immediately went to air-defense stations, set watertight condition ZED, and lighted off her remaining six boilers for full power. Her men began pumping 4,200 gallons of highly flammable avgas over the side. Within minutes the first flight of enemy planes was seen splitting up into groups of nine aircraft each. Two minutes went by while the cruiser's men prepared themselves and their ship, then "full speed" of 20 knots was ordered. *Marblehead*'s boilers and turbines did their job; she had power to make 27 knots by that time. At 0958 *Houston* opened fire—she was soon beneath the bombs herself—and *Marblehead* began firing inside another two minutes. "Flank speed" was then called for, and the ship swung left, maneuvering independently as her gunners began firing.

The light cruiser was nearly a decade older than her larger cousin, and both her main battery and her antiaircraft batteries were correspondingly weaker and more primitive. Her chief AA weapons at that time consisted of a battery of seven old 3-inch/50 cal. guns, hand operated and with no really adequate or efficient director control. These were all sited in her waist alongside the ship's second and third funnels, three to a side. Another single weapon was located aft on the superstructure above the 6-inch twin turret, where it could cover a wider arc of the sky. Ammunition was brought up by hand from the 3-inch magazines below in trains of men and delivered to the guns through hatches on the main deck. This was a laborious and clumsy process, but *Marblehead* managed to make the best of the system. Her gun crews fired at as good a rate as one could have expected under the circumstances. At the height the Japanese planes were flying, however, the effective range of *Marblehead*'s old 3-inch guns was negated.

Atop her foremast, towering over the bridge, was a large rectangular structure—or "birdbath"—in which four .50 cal. mounts were sited. These machine guns had none of the range needed to make effective antiaircraft weapons against bombers flying at high altitude, but that didn't matter: *Marblehead*'s gunners were spoiling for a fight. As on the other Asiatic Fleet vessels present—from the 12,000-ton bulk of *Houston* down to the flushdeckers displacing one-tenth as much—it would prove very difficult to prevent those antsy young gunners from firing during the battle.

The American destroyers had also scattered, and although far beyond the capabilities of their light AA weapons, several ships opened fire anyway. On *Stewart* a predictable result ensued. As one of her sailors wrote: "We were zigzagging at 25 knots. . . . We small ships were not in danger, the Nippers were after the cruisers. Some dope on here blasted away with a machine gun, and the whole damned machine gun battery fired. Result, they shot down some of our antennae."[35]

When the next wave of attacks unfolded, the antiaircraft batteries did manage to wing at least one Japanese bomber, which staggered out of formation and, smoking, plummeted to the sea. Other planes were thrown about by the AA bursts, but only one plane was verifiably shot down. Commander Maher of *Houston* later wrote: "It went into a large spiral and crashed into the sea."[36] This incident is also mentioned in documents from *Marblehead*, in which the Japanese pilot was thought to have attempted an early variant of later kamikaze tactics, as he seemed to try to fly the doomed bomber into that cruiser. The plane did not strike anything but water, however, and there were no survivors. Nonetheless, for the two cruisers left from Hart's original command—forming the brittle core of his surface forces—eight weeks of good luck would be reversed in mere moments.

· · ·

Although the Japanese bombers were able to operate undisturbed by either ABDA fighters or AA fire, it must be said that they executed their tasks with skill. To hit a speeding warship maneuvering in the open sea from such heights was a relatively rare event in the Pacific War. Despite press claims, American B-17s would not be able to do it four months later against the forces of Vice Admiral Nagumo as his vaunted Kidō Butai approached Midway for their day of reckoning. Aboard the Allied ships that mild, sunny morning off Madura, few sailors realized the severity of the test they were about to face.

In clusters of nine—three trios of bombers flying in flattened Vs in each group—the Japanese passed overhead, testing the antiaircraft fire from their targets and estimating the best angle for attack. *Houston's* AA was accurate even if it was too thin, and only one bomber fell from its formation into the sea below. However, this failed to disrupt or discourage the Japanese. At 1026, as both American cruisers continued to fire energetically at the bombers, another run was made on them. A minute or so later it was evident that the Japanese had made another drop. Over *Marblehead's* loudspeaker system blared the chilling alert: "Bombs coming. Lie flat."

Beneath this particular salvo, steaming at 29 knots and wriggling across the ocean like a snake, the old cruiser attempted to evade the bombs. But within seconds her luck would run out. At about 1027 seven bombs straddled and struck the ship with devastating effect. The near miss of a 250 kg (551 lb.) bomb off her port bow caved in and smashed her thin bottom plates, causing extensive damage as it opened a multitude of rivets and seams to the sea. This torn plating formed a giant intake that funneled tons of seawater into the ship. With the cruiser still steaming at high speed, this damage produced serious flooding throughout her forward sections. The flooding in turn soon affected her stability, which was precarious to begin with due to her overloaded design and upgrades she had received over the years. Eventually all compartments from frame 47 forward to the stem were completely or partially flooded.

Although they may have been smaller weapons—of 60 kg (132 lb.)—the direct hits were far worse. One struck her starboard upper deck between her bridge and forward (number 1) funnel. It first sliced through the side of a motor launch stowed there—leaving one of its metal fins embedded in the boat's wooden hull—then punched through the steel deck, which activated its fuse mechanism, leaving a neat hole ten inches in diameter in the deck. The bomb then exploded with a high-order detonation on the main deck below.

The explosion caused heavy, widespread damage in the ward rooms, officer's country, barber shop, canteen, and tailor's shop. Below decks the downward effects of the blast destroyed the sick bay, while fragments also penetrated the hospital quarters, entering fuel oil tanks beneath these compartments, which in turn led to fires and widespread oil flooding throughout the ship. Upward the force bowed the upper deck almost twelve inches and sprang more rivets and seams, which opened fuel bunkers, leaving that area coated in oil. The uptakes for her funnel were jarred out of kilter by half a foot. Fires started immediately, and damage-control parties went to work to combat these as a first priority.

Even at some distance, this one bomb hit "threw men around like chaff" in the midships repair party under Machinist Mate First Class Dale Johnson.[37] They were stationed in a starboard compartment on the main deck level above the aft engine room. A sailor lying next to Johnson was blown almost fifty feet down a passageway. Another crewman getting a drink of water standing at the scuttlebutt had it blasted from beneath his mouth but was otherwise unharmed.[38]

A second bomb went through her deck "on the fantail, abaft the after twin mount and close to port."[39] It passed through the chief petty officers' quarters and detonated in her hand-steering compartment, killing everyone in it and wreaking extensive damage through numerous aft compartments. The power machinery for the rudder was damaged and jammed at 30 degrees, locking the ship in a tight turning circle. She received more bombing attacks while her rudder was frozen in this position, but mercifully no more hits were registered.

The blast aft had simultaneously peeled back the steel deck alongside her 6-inch gunhouse like so much plastic and thrown it up against the guns themselves. Its weight then brought the damaged section back down in a massive wave of rippled metal, with the ravaged compartments below exposed. The twin aft gunhouse was instantly rendered inoperable. In those brief seconds fifteen young men in the hand-steering compartment and elsewhere were either killed outright or mortally wounded. Several dozen more were injured, and a number of them would require hospitalization.

It was evident to everyone that the old ship had been struck a potentially mortal blow. Within minutes Captain Robinson messaged Doorman that his damage was serious. The ship was already settling forward due to the opened hull plating and had quickly taken on an 8-degree list to starboard that had increased to 11 degrees by 1044. De Meester's *Tromp* dutifully approached more than once to take off survivors if necessary. With the light cruiser locked in tight circles billowing volcanic clouds of black smoke and down by the head from flooding forward, it appeared to many that *Marblehead* might well have to be abandoned.

Yet through it all her AA guns kept up their fire, indeed firing with such rapidity that 3-inch ammo supplies were soon depleted. Additional parties were created from 6-inch battery personnel and other sailors who "formed in the wardroom country and began bringing up ammunition from the forward 3-inch magazine group and running it aft on the port side and up no. 2 hatch to the guns."[40] The men on *Houston* reported that they saw the ship inundated in bomb splashes, completely blocked from view by towers of seawater erupting all around *Marblehead*, but when she emerged all her 3-inch guns "were still throwing them out like a machine gun." It was through the fortitude of such men as those gunners and her damage-repair parties that the enduring reputation of *Marblehead* took root. For the sailors and officers there was "no confusion and excitement. Those that were not wounded helped take care of those that were and the rest went immediately about the task of keeping the ship afloat."[41]

Above, flying in their disciplined formations, the Japanese made a long circle and next singled out the largest undamaged ship present, *Houston*. At a few minutes past 1100 hours, the Japanese planes were seen approaching again from the cruiser's port side. Stationed outside the director of sky aft, Capt. Frederick Ramsey had remained imperturbable in the face of many near misses on the ship. One of his young marine sergeants, Charley Pryor, recalled that Ramsey was "cooler than a bowl of cracked ice." After one particularly jarring near miss, Ramsey quipped: "You know, if they get any closer, I'll have to climb down." He was prescient in this remark, but not for the reason he made it.[42]

The AA gunners of Houston were now relying on their aft director solely, and in this interval a grim species of Murphy's Law came into play. Due to stack gasses and the angle of the planes' flight, the aft Mark 19 director could not obtain an accurate range—one of the worst possible developments at the worst possible time. Altitude and speed could only be roughly estimated, which naturally hindered the effectiveness of her already-compromised AA fire.

When and if the bombs were perceived to be on the verge of landing very close to the ship—and whether operating the guns or not—the men were all given the order to take cover or lie flat, just as on *Marblehead* earlier.[43] High above in the uncontested sky, this V of bombers passed over to make its run. As the planes unloaded their ordnance, the men on *Houston* noticed that one of the bombers lagged slightly behind the formation. Down screamed another salvo of 60 kg and 250 kg bombs. These smacked the sea off the cruiser's starboard side and threw tons of water over the men in the 5-inch battery and 1.1-inch gun tubs. These gun crews noticed that some of the bombs detonated when striking the water, creating gigantic splashes; others exploded well beneath the surface, while a few appeared not to explode at all and left much smaller impacts on the sea.

For a split second it appeared that *Houston* had again eluded her attackers, but a number of sailors topside observed that one last bomb emerged belatedly from the trailing plane. No more than a tiny silver flake when first seen, it announced its proximity with a heart-stopping shriek. This bomb was later thought to have hung up in the plane's bomb bay before dropping or had a bent tail fin. It fell out of the salvo pattern, and although some of the men felt it might miss the ship, it was soon apparent that it would come *much* closer. On his 5-inch gun (number 3), Olen Minton sought cover at the last instant as he heard the bomb whistling down. However, for almost seventy young sailors and officers there was no time left; what remained of their lives would be crowded into a single blazing instant.

In its perverse course the bomb first nicked a port yardarm on the top of the mainmast—where the men in *Houston's* machine-gun nest had a clear view and heard the unforgettable noise of its transit. Earl Joe Snyder and Marvin Bain, both first class, were up there working the .50 cal. guns. Snyder would never forget the shower of sparks that flew out from torn iron and steel as the bomb punched through everything in its path.[44] It then struck the searchlight platform and searchlight control, killing a young seaman named Bruce Adkins as he lay flat seeking cover, before exiting and leaving a 14-inch diameter hole in both Adkins and the deck. Slightly deflected, it next emerged to "cut a hole in the leg of the mast about ten feet long," then blasted down through the roof of radio 2 (the aft radio transmitting room) and on through its deck, with two more holes left in its path.[45] When a slight distance above the upper deck and at a point behind the number 3 turret—which had been trained out to port—it detonated with a thunderous crump. This explosion was soon followed by a large volume of "sickening yellowish smoke" pouring out of the gunhouse.[46]

Yet there were men not a great distance from the hit who were uncertain that the ship had been badly struck at all. Also at 5-inch gun number 3, located on the flight deck's starboard side forward, Robert Martin, a seaman first class, was acting as rammer man in gun captain Jim Kenney's crew. Martin felt the bomb hit but was unaware of its severity until he saw wounded and dying men staggering out of searchlight control. One of the men who emerged from searchlight control was Coxswain Donald "Pappy" Trim, who gave Lieutenant Commander Galbraith—at sky aft—the thumbs-up signal to indicate that he, at least, was all right. Another sailor, Floyd Arnold, s2/c, a member of the portside aft 1.1-inch mount, never even heard the explosion. This fact he later attributed to the 5-inch battery "roaring right over [their] heads." All he had been aware of was "a puff of smoke" aft. Meanwhile, Arnold's mount had fired enough to rupture the water jackets on its 1.1-inch guns that day but had not hit any of their high-altitude attackers.[47]

On 5-inch gun number 7, starboard side aft, manned by the marines, the first loader was Pfc. James "Packrat" McCone. "Packrat" along with other gun-crew members had taken cover when their gun reached its full elevation and bombs were seen falling. Sheltering in a passageway along with his gun captain, Cpl. Kelton B. George, was another marine, Pfc. T. J. McFarland. The bomb's blast fired splinters and fragments through the passageway. Dazed, George and McFarland looked down to find themselves splattered with blood. Which one was wounded? It was Corporal George; both of his arms had been seriously lacerated by flying slivers of lead paint. He was able to tell the others he had been hit before losing consciousness. McCone was uninjured, and George was then taken to an improvised triage set up in the number 1 mess hall.[48]

Pfc. Marvin "Robbie" Robinson, a hot shell man on his 5-inch gun, sought cover under one of the ship's boats nearby. After the bomb exploded, he looked back to see "sulphurous, sickly yellow smoke" billowing out from the gunhouse.[49] Others sheltering around the boats were not as fortunate: Coxswain Robert Kraus and Seaman First Class Ed O'Leary—the latter a notable "problem child" with many disciplinary infractions—were huddled at a motor launch when the ship was hit. Bob Kraus was seriously wounded, but O'Leary had put in his final appearance before the captain's mast; he was killed on the spot.[50]

Those close to the bomb had no doubts about its effect, however. To some it appeared the entire aft end of the ship had been destroyed. Nearby there was a terrific blast and concussion. Turret 3's gunhouse crew and those of the after damage repair party, who were sitting on the main deck just below, took the brunt of the explosion. Most were slaughtered instantly. In the aftermath, chaos and confusion dominated for the first few moments. Men not injured were stunned by the concussion or blinded by dust, smoke, and fire.

The turret had been trained out 20 degrees to port in order to fire her 8-inch guns at approaching, low-level torpedo bombers, should any try to attack her, a measure believed to be an effective deterrent.[51] On the rear side, near the turret officer's booth, sat Lt. George E. Davis Jr., the Third Division and turret officer with his legs dangling over the hatchway. He had positioned himself there— with fatal bad luck—to observe for torpedo-armed planes.

The powerful explosion killed Lieutenant Davis instantly, blowing his body and the hatch door to the turret officer's booth across the back of the gunhouse. It blew off the armored rangefinder "ear," which protruded from the rear of the gunhouse, and riddled the thin (0.75-inch) side plating in about two hundred places with small fragments, most an inch to three inches in size. These white-hot shards of metal were injected into the upper gunhouse, where twenty men of Lieutenant Davis's turret crew were stationed. They had little to do in an air attack yet had to be prepared to fire on a moment's notice.[52] Within the gunhouse's upper chamber were several forty-five-pound silk bags of smokeless propellant in the powder pockets, fully exposed, along with 8-inch projectiles. Hot fragments ignited the powder bags, resulting in a violent conflagration inside the gunhouse that burned to death most of the men and severely injured others.

Due to the high mortality within the gunhouse, accounts of the explosion there will never be understood in precise detail. What we do know is this: the center gun's rammer man was Bill Kohl, GM3/c, and he was positioned near the rear wall of the gunhouse, where he operated the chain drive to ram the loaded projectiles into that gun. Slightly above and in front of him on a small metal seat sat the turret captain, Roger Poirier. Nearby was another friend of Bill Kohl: Eugene "Smitty" Smith, s1/c. These men were injured by the bomb's explosion and intense flames that followed. Poirier was by far the most seriously wounded, with severe burns and a gaping shrapnel wound in his back said to be as big as a man's fist. Smith and Kohl were also both burned, though not as badly.

Most of the turret crew perished outright. Poirier attempted to activate the sprinkler system inside the turret before he escaped the inferno—despite his horrible injuries—but it was too damaged to function properly. These few surviving men tumbled out of the opposite side of the gunhouse, trying to evade the fire and smoke. Poirier quickly collapsed on the deck in agony, begging to be killed.[53]

The bomb's force obliterated the deck, creating a gaping hole in it some twelve by eighteen feet, and sent blast, fragments, and fire into the group of sailors waiting just beneath the gunhouse as they congregated around its barbette. These men of the after damage repair party (Repair III) were under Chief Warrant Officer Joseph Beinert, Chief Shipfitter Joe O'Neal, and Chief Carpenters Mate Maurice "Dutch" Weller. This force was wiped out almost to a man. Only Charles Collings, SF2/c, Merritt V. Eddy, CM2/c, and a machinist mate who "happened to be in a corner where the air compressor was"—survived the explosion.[54] The grim irony here is that the repair party had taken that position beneath what should have been the overhang of the gunhouse, imagining that it offered more protection. Yet with the turret trained out to port, the deck under it was left exposed, and in just that vulnerable area the bomb spent its force.

In different sections of the ship nearby, fragments and blast caused more casualties; some were trivial, others were fatal. The ship's assistant physician, Lt. Clement D. Burroughs, was stationed in a compartment aft with another sailor in anticipation of handling wounded cases, but both had already been thrown about so violently in the bombing attacks prior to the hit that they had left the compartment and were lying flat in a passageway. When the bomb

FIRST SORTIE OF THE STRIKING FORCE

struck, there was a "dense cloud of smoke"; Burroughs was hit in the finger by a small steel sliver but not badly hurt. As he gathered himself, looking through the haze, he began to see murky shapes moving toward him. These ghostly figures then became "men running around with their entrails showing, and men with their skulls caved in."[55]

Some 150 feet forward from the bomb hit, several other crew members were in the port hangar. These were pharmacist's mates whose dressing stations were set up there and men who had taken shelter, including a group from V Division. Among these was Elmo "Joe" Bush, the aviation ordnance mechanic. Sweating out the aerial assault with his shipmates, Bush never heard or felt the bomb explode. Suddenly a man stumbled in, his face bloody from wounds. This was Harold Brown, BM1/c, one of the few men from Third Division who had survived, and he was slipping into shock. He could only gasp, "We have a pretty bad hit back there! Some of you better go see about it."[56] Just then Lt. (j.g.) Walt Winslow appeared, having come aft from his position on the signal bridge, where he had been attempting to film some of the action with his 16 mm camera. Winslow was met in front of the hangar by the ashen-faced Bush, who said, "Mr. Winslow, come quick. . . . We got hit aft and a lot of boys are hurt bad!"[57] Fighting back their fear, these men, along with a group of others that included aviation machinists John W. Ranger and Charles P. Fowler Jr., Chief Aviation Machinist Cumming, and Joseph R. Smith, PhM1/c, all proceeded aft quickly along the upper deck.

A formidable, powerfully built young man, John Ranger had a personal motive: one of his closest shipmates, a childhood friend named Russell Shelton (with whom he had grown up in Gillespie, Illinois) was stationed in the gunhouse. In the hope that Shelton had survived, Ranger sprinted back toward the smoke and flames.[58] For all these men it was to be their initiation into war's ugliest reality, leaving memories seared into their minds for the rest of their lives.

Once aft they came upon what Bush called "a horrible sight": a hole that looked to be "twenty feet across" had been blown in the upper deck. Within it, amid "I-beams curled around like toothpicks" and "lying atop a pile of debris made up of bunks and lockers" were dead men, mutilated body parts, human limbs, all sloshing back and forth in a half foot of water from ruptured mains. Bush looked down into the mass and saw the corpse of a man he knew well: shipfitter Vic "Moose" Winters, eyes still open, staring sightlessly up at the frightened young sailor. Next to the gaping hole, turret 3 was a blazing pyre, with clouds of "yellow, powder cellulose smoke" billowing out.[59] Men in shock, dazed, or badly injured were milling around the turret; some were prostrate on the deck, but nothing was being done to combat the fire. The ship's flag had been blown off by the explosion, and as he went back, Ranger had grabbed an American flag from a motor launch and lashed it to an aft stanchion. *Houston* was wounded, but she was still a U.S. Navy man o' war. Lacking any protective clothing, he ignored the smoke to enter the scorched gunhouse in search of Russell Shelton.

Cdr. Arthur Maher came down from spot 1 on the foremast, for he realized that the fires were a serious threat to the ship should they begin "cooking off" 8-inch shells or reach down into the magazines. As he stood beside the ravaged turret, Maher began issuing orders to uninjured crewmen. Ranger in the meantime managed to play the contents of several carbon dioxide bottles on the flames inside to help smother them. Then he grabbed the nozzle of a heavy red fire hose from Charles Fowler. It was clear from the moment he looked inside turret 3's smoking charnel house that Shelton could not have survived, but Ranger did not stop. He, like Maher, understood that the heat might set off more explosions that could doom the entire ship. Standing astride the hatchway, engulfed in ochre-colored smoke, without gloves or breathing apparatus, the burly aviation machinist ignored several commands to get out as he continued to hose down the interior as best he could, even as gun grease sizzled on the 8-inch projectiles. At the same time Fowler kept Ranger soaked by spraying him with another hose as he fought the fire.[60]

Below deck two often-overlooked survivors of Third Division were no less heroic. Jack D. Smith, s1/c, along with Czelaus Kunks, GM2/c, in a compartment next to the after handling room (D411M) managed to get flash doors shut, while sprinkling the hoists and reporting the fire over their battle phones. Smith later said he estimated some sixty bags of propellant burned in the conflagration. "I do not know where in the powder line the burning was stopped. . . . I know Deits [Edward Dietz, s1/c] was in After Transfer Room and he survived. That is outside the Powder Circle."[61]

Once the flames and smoke had been controlled, repair parties moved in to try to separate the survivors from the dead and to remove bodies, or what remained of them. It was an exceedingly grisly business that none of the living would ever forget. To flay already-raw nerves, fire-hoses then set off an electrical circuit causing the center 8-inch. gun to fire, further terrifying everyone.

Warrant Officer Carpenter Louis E. "Chips" Biechlin, a fourteen-year navy veteran and leader of the forward repair party, went back with his men to help those beneath the turret on the main deck. Biechlin had between thirty and forty men divided into various subgroups within the repair party working under him; there was a firefighting group with hoses and axes, asbestos gloves, and suits; a shoring group with ropes, timbers, and mauls; an electrical group; and finally, first-aid men and stretcher-bearers (who were made up almost entirely of *Houston*'s Chinese mess attendants). They would confront a frightful task when they reached the devastated areas.

The first thing Biechlin saw was a young sailor, "a boy, seaman second class, his face and part of his head was shot off. . . . his brains were still in the brain pan, but there was no face."[62] The scene grew no better as Biechlin and others moved among these men, sifting the wounded from the dead. Not far away, his closest friend, Chief Warrant Officer Joseph "Bos'n" Bienert, had been mortally wounded, his body riddled by fragments with one leg nearly severed. Among the first to reach Bienert was Al Neitsch, MM1/c—a sailor who knew the chief warrant officer (CWO) well—and he put a tourniquet on the chief's leg.[63] But by the time Biechlin reached the area, Bienert had been moved into a forward compartment where Doc Burroughs did what little he could. Joe Bienert—well known and highly regarded throughout the *Houston*—was given a shot of morphine but died within two hours from his severe wounds.

Red Reynolds, S1/c, came down from his 5-inch mount on the starboard side and helped Biechlin remove another sailor from the turret's shell deck. Described by Red as "boiled alive," the wounded man's skin came off and stuck to Reynolds's hands as he moved him. This unfortunate young man, though blinded by fire, was still conscious and mumbled to Reynolds and Biechlin, asking who they were. He wanted to thank them properly "if he came out of it." He did not but also died after receiving an injection of morphine while the triage was being set up in number 1 mess hall.[64]

Ship's baker Theodore "Itch" Schram came aft from the mess hall, where he had been working with the 5-inch ammo handling detail. Standing next to a clothing locker as he passed empty shell casings, Schram was spared serious injury by the thinnest of margins. The bomb hurled fragments through bulkheads and into the locker next to him only to be absorbed by the heavy clothing inside. When he reached the devastated compartment where the after repair party had been stationed, Schram first came across the seated body of a senior chief, Delray Hankinson, CCst (PA). The chief had been hit in the head by a fragment as he stood against a bulkhead. The steel shard came through and struck the back of his skull, killing him instantly and in effect scalping him. He slid down into a sitting position, where he was discovered by Schram. When Lt. Cdr. J. K. Chisholm, the ship's paymaster, came back and asked about Hankinson's whereabouts, the unnerved Schram told him: "He's over there with his head in his face! Go look for yourself."[65] Nearby were two dead shipfitters from the repair party: Francis B. Schultze, his skull perforated by shrapnel, and "Moose" Winters, disemboweled, with his entire back blown off. When Warrant Officer Biechlin tried to lift Winters's body out, he grabbed a handful of intestines. To add another layer of peril to this Grand Guignol, the entire area was swathed in severed electrical wiring, much of it live and extremely dangerous for the repair parties wading into the half-foot of water that had accumulated on the deck from broken mains.

Carpenters Mate Merrit Eddy had one of the closest calls with death in that crew space (D-202-L) where the repair party had assembled, and he left the most telling account: "Collings, myself and Johnson were sitting with our backs against the ventilation blower casing almost under the ladder leading to the main deck. We sat side by side looking aft toward the turret handling room aft of us with Johnson sitting between us." When the bomb exploded Eddy registered a bright flash but heard and felt nothing; he was rendered unconscious instantly. "When I regained my senses, I was all alone," he recalled. "Both Collings and Johnson were gone and there were bodies lying all over the compartment in front of me. There was a large hole slightly aft and above where I was sitting. I could look up directly at the side of No. III gun turret. [Roman] Gorney was lying at my feet with the back of his head missing. I got up in a state of bewilderment and half panic and somehow managed to find my way out of the compartment and onto topside."[66]

Eventually breathers showed up, and both Ranger and Fowler donned them to reenter the darkened, smoldering gunhouse of turret 3. They found no one alive within the upper room; what remains there were of the dead were dismembered or badly charred. Floyd Arnold recalled: "Everyone was burnt to a cinder and we could only find men's shoes, some hands and a few rings . . . and that's about all there was."[67] The bodies of two young sailors in the port and starboard powder flaps were the most problematic; these were tight, claustrophobic spaces to begin with and usually had small men assigned to them. There the sailors had been trapped by the flames. It took a strong back and an even more durable stomach to climb into those "pockets" and dislodge the men's corpses. Skin hung down in brown shreds from muscles of sailors who had been roasted alive. A noisome stench of broiled human flesh and entrails permeated *Houston*'s aft decks and gunhouse. This sickening odor would never be removed satisfactorily before the cruiser was lost.

The remains of the turret officer, Lieutenant Davis, were the hardest to identify. His body had been horrendously mutilated by the bomb's volcanic blast, resembling nothing more than a "dressed hog" according to Elmo Bush.[68] One white canvas shoe riddled by fragment holes with the lieutenant's foot in it was said to have been located. Another clue was found in a shirt collar that had his laundry number, 1402, on it. Three days later somebody discovered Lieutenant Davis's hand still wearing his academy class ring embedded in a bulkhead.

· · ·

This single heavy bomb had done its work. Blast and fragments killed and wounded almost seventy men, and it put turret 3 out of action. The hit seriously damaged three of the four large searchlights aft on the mainmast and wrecked two of the ship's motor launches. It ruined the crew's head—injuring several men in the process—and damaged the aft radio transmitting room; it perforated a cold storage compartment for meat—all of which, apart from tinned five-pound containers of Armor and Wilson ham which the men ate promptly, quickly spoiled—and it destroyed a number of lockers with men's personal belongings and clothing. Yet, structurally, *Houston* was in no danger of being lost. She could still steam at full power; her engines and boilers were all intact, and her steering unaffected. Near misses had sprung a few hull plates, resulting in small but manageable leaks. *Houston's* personnel losses amounted only to about 6 percent of her total complement.

The jammed roller paths on her AA director and the defective 5-inch projectiles were a more serious issue. It is quite probable that her air defense officers and the captain all recognized—with no small degree of unease—that to a large degree the ship's very existence relied on the effectiveness of her AA battery. It would have been clear to everyone that this was now radically compromised, which in turn placed the cruiser and her crew in peril.

The ship's two doctors, Epstein and Burroughs, aided by Raymond "Rainy" Day, PhM2/c, and others worked throughout that afternoon and into the night trying to save lives, but more men died from their wounds. Several others were clearly not going to survive if not hospitalized. As soon as the severity of her wounds, and those of her crew, were understood—and with *Marblehead* clearly fighting for her life—Captain Rooks decided to take the ship out of harm's way. Although Surabaja was nearer and possessed better repair facilities, it was decided to steam south through the Barrier, then several hundred miles west to Tjilatjap to place the ship as far away from enemy air attacks as possible. Fortunately, the mercurial East Indian weather altered, concealing the ship beneath sheets of rain as she made her way back.

Located on the southwestern coast of Java, the diminutive port of Tjilatjap had seen better days, but the arrival of war had forced it into a position of importance—a position for which it was ill-suited. In the words of Dutch naval historians Frans Luidinga and Dr. Nico Guns:

> The harbor was suitable for ships with a draught of 30 feet. It lay at the mouth of the river Donan. There was an inside channel approximately 3 miles long, where the piers were located. . . . Right before the bend in the Donan River, new wooden piers, sheds and a shunting yard had been built. On the new pier stood 18 1.5-ton cranes and 2 10-ton cranes. These brought ashore the cargo that had been loaded from the cargo ships onto lighters. Around the bend were the old piers, sheds and railroad tracks. A bit farther stood the BPM (Bataafse Petroleum Maatschappij) oil installations.[69]

They might have added that its harbor lay within a contorted series of sharp bends as ships entered from Schildpadden Bay, and this twisting, narrow entrance was lined by sand banks and shoals that made groundings an all-too-common occurrence.

Upon returning to Tjilatjap, *Houston*'s carpenter force—led by Biechlin—worked around the clock to build coffins for their dead shipmates, now arrayed on the fantail under canvas tarps. They lacked enough of their own lumber to complete boxes for so many bodies and were forced to obtain more wood—local mahogany—at the Dutch port. This made a difficult and sorrowful job that much more unpleasant, for the mahogany was uncooperative, being both hard and brittle. Biechlin had to improvise "small strips of wood and nails to hold the coffins together." The veteran warrant officer worried about the boxes coming apart during burial services with the remains of his friends inside. As one of the marines remembered, Biechlin insisted on building Joe Bienert's coffin personally.[70] Merritt Eddy, CM2/c, recalled that not only had the local shipyard provided some ready-built coffins in addition to the mahogany, but "yard personnel pitched in and helped [them] build the remaining coffins needed."[71]

At the same time Hart was keeping abreast of these grim developments as best he could at ABDACOM's slipshod HQ in Lembang. The news—mostly bad—spluttered in through the overtaxed communications systems that had been hurriedly rigged between Lembang, Bandoeng, and Surabaja. All that Hart knew from February 4 to 7 was that *both* of his cruisers had been hit hard, and there was even some doubt whether *Marblehead* could make Tjilatjap safely. Simultaneously he learned—somewhat to his displeasure—that Rear Admiral Doorman had also turned all his undamaged warships for home. Hart had clung briefly to the hope that even with *Houston* and *Marblehead* knocked out,

Doorman might go ahead with an attack on Japanese forces at Makassar. As Hart was soon to learn—and as even Helfrich would acknowledge—Karel "Tank" Doorman had been quite disturbed by the bombings, and he continued to suffer from their aftereffects for the remainder of the campaign.

. . .

As if this situation was not gloomy enough, Hart then found support from Washington being cut out from beneath his very feet. Not altogether unexpectedly he learned from Ernie King that the navy had been "forced into a bad position in Washington" and that it would be best if he "requested detachment on account of health." This development had no doubt resulted from the contrivances and intrigues of Helfrich, Van Mook, and Van Stachouwer, finally taking effect after two months of behind-the-scenes machinations. Hart was expected to depart the command around midmonth and was given a few days to tie up loose ends. That he showed almost no surprise indicates that he had foreseen the blow for some time in advance. Glassford would then take over the remaining U.S. naval forces. They would operate under the control of Helfrich, who had finally been allotted the command that he felt *he alone* deserved all along.[72]

Hart was to later call it the most difficult thing he had ever done in his long naval service. For the men of the old Asiatic Fleet, it was more bad news at a critical moment. As a destroyerman wrote, "Tommy Hart gone! Were [we] to be thrown to the wolves?"[73] In this sharp reaction, even among the poorly informed lower ranks, was contained more than a kernel of bitter truth.

. . .

After dumping fuel oil from her forward tanks and pumping and bailing her flooded spaces, *Marblehead* reduced her draft forward enough—from thirty-two to twenty-one feet—to enter Tjilatjap's small, crowded harbor. She, too, brought her share of dead and wounded. One of the men who returned to port that day was her Dutch naval liaison officer, Sub-Lt. Ted Luxemburg. He had survived the enemy air attacks unharmed, but like many others his belongings had not. Luxemburg made it to Tjilatjap with nothing more than the clothes on his back. After replacing his kit as best he could—a cap, pair of shorts, a shirt someone gave him, some skivvies—Ted received verbal orders to report to the American destroyer USS *Whipple*, which was then operating out of the port. By the time he reported to the flushdecker on February 8—along with a RNN quartermaster named Delorms—Luxemburg had managed to acquire some decent clothing. Properly dressed, he presented himself—at attention with a formal salute—to *Whipple*'s skipper, Lt. Cdr. Eugene Karpe. The response of Karpe, whom Ted recalled as "a good chap," was memorable: "Oh, for god-sakes. . . . What's your Christian name?" And at that the formalities were dropped. Luxemburg was then able to relax as he went about his duties. At action stations he was on the bridge, but much of his time was spent roaming "all over the damn ship." The men of *Whipple*, he said, were "very disciplined." Unlike his time spent on *Marblehead*, though, Luxemburg did not sleep in a cabin at night. Instead, like a number of the other men, he preferred to bed down on the upper deck under open sky, for the same reason that numerous men in the Asiatic Fleet slept on deck: in anticipation of the not-improbable event that their ship should be sunk.[74] Many, if not most, expected *just* that.

As for the bomb-battered old cruiser, immediate structural repairs were sorely needed, but her injured personnel were first priority. *Marblehead* was moored ahead of *Houston*, and her wounded men—almost four dozen—were disembarked at the dock on February 6 and put onto Dutch military hospital trains marked with large red crosses. *Houston*'s wounded had already been loaded onto hospital cars overnight. These sailors were then sent via rail to Jogjakarta about two hundred kilometers to the east, where there was a Dutch hospital with staff who could attend to their injuries. There they would come under the care of a U.S. naval reserve medical officer named Corydon Wassell, who took his orders to look after these men in both the most serious and the literal senses.[75]

Other grim duties also had to be dealt with at Tjilatjap: the funerals for the navy's dead. Those of *Houston* were carried off the ship in their coffins early on Friday, February 6, as the crew stood on the quarterdeck. Almost four dozen men in the funeral party each held small crosses in remembrance of their fallen shipmates. Maurice Hurd, RM3/c, held the memorial cross of Louis J. Zimba, GM3/c. Many years later Hurd would write that he could not "help but recall the incidents at Tjilatjap, the funeral procession to the little beautiful graveyard that sloped down to the water. . . . We marched slowly through the dusty streets of that town while natives lined the way. Certainly the most melancholy procession. Reaching the grave site I recall a few Dutch women who sympathetically watched. The boys were lowered away without tears, but with heavy hearts. I particularly noted the position of Theodore Duane Daniels, a very good friend of mine. I intended some day to tell his family. I never did."[76]

To make matters worse it was an oppressive day, sweltering and thick with humidity. The men trooped behind Dutch army trucks loaded with the forty-six coffins. The cruiser's band played Chopin's funeral dirge as the coffins were offloaded, and a full honor guard accompanied the procession. In cadence they marched in twos, in reverse order of rank, through the dilapidated town, past the local natives and on to the small cemetery near the beach. Services were held by Chaplain Rentz and the local Dutch Catholic padre. But the tropical heat and fatigue took a toll. Two sailors in the funeral detail passed out from "parade ground stress." Lt. (j.g.) Harold Hamlin Jr. dressed the men down as "a bunch of schoolgirls" to get them back into what he considered good order.[77] This hard-hearted approach infuriated Jack D. Smith at the time, but military discipline prevailed. Quickly, the bodies were all interred in the military section of the European graveyard, with the coffins of Lieutenant Davis and Chief Warrant Officer Bienert at the top of the rows.

Dealing with *Marblehead*'s structural damage proved a serious engineering challenge. It was recognized after a meeting with Dutch officials and naval architects on the scene that the largest floating dry dock at Tjilatjap had insufficient capacity to take the cruiser. They would have to improvise something, and how this was arranged would be both ingenious and risky. It was thought possible to raise a portion of her bow in the dock but leave much of her hull submerged. At this precarious angle, under such unstable conditions, a danger always existed that the ship could slide backward stern-first into the water again. No one liked the situation very much, but under the circumstances it was a gamble that had to be accepted.

The work on *Marblehead* was necessarily improvised; the men simply hadn't the time to attempt more. "All that could be hoped for was to slam some kind of patch over the hole in her bow and make a getaway before the Japanese came."[78] Engineers and specialists from *Black Hawk* pitched in to help, and local Javanese yard workers performed heroically. Meanwhile the local Dutch priest came on board to perform services for the personnel. A Dutch cargo-passenger ship in Tjilatjap, the *Tjitjalengka*, opened her commissary to the bedraggled sailors. It was said that "by showing some consideration for the steward's financial welfare," the men could obtain a fried chicken, tomato sandwiches, or even a cold quart bottle of the highly regarded Dutch beer.[79]

After a week of round-the-clock work, the mauled cruiser was ready for sea. Getting underway on Friday the thirteenth and aided by two Dutch tugs, she had the kind of ill-luck one associates with that day. *Marblehead* had not yet cleared the Tjilatjap minefields when near-disaster struck. Her after tug had cast off, but the towline to the fore tug then parted, leaving the cruiser adrift in the narrow channel with no steering gear. The remaining tug attempted to run another line to the cruiser but "put herself in a position across the bow."[80]

The result was a sharp collision that bent the cruiser's stem, flooding the forward peak tanks. The old cruiser gingerly negotiated the channel steering by engines and then set course for Ceylon.

With her crew fighting a constant battle against flooding throughout the journey while "ridding the ship of oil soaked wreckage and debris," *Marblehead* staggered on toward India. Repairs to her steering continued. By the time she reached Trincomalee (February 21), the ship was "in a reasonable state of cleanliness above the first platform deck," and her flooding was under control. Also progress had been made on the steering motor.[81] When she finally returned to the States in early May, *Marblehead* would be docked for most of the remainder of 1942, but her survival alone—a lasting testament to the self-sufficiency and toughness of Asiatic Fleet personnel—had truly been a "miracle of miracles."

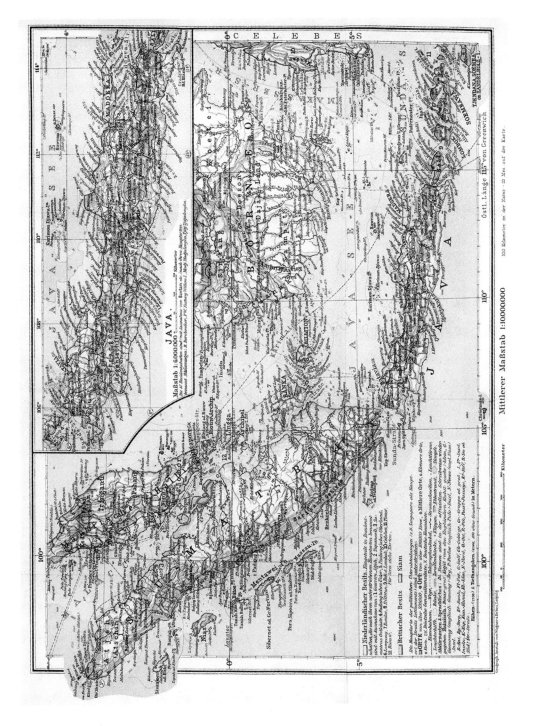

1. This detailed World War I–era map of the East Indies shows almost all the areas in which the Asiatic Fleet operated during the Java campaign other than the waters around Australia. University of Texas–Austin, Perry-Castañeda Library.

2. Adm. Thomas C. Hart, commander in chief of the U.S. Asiatic Fleet. Photo by Josepho, Shanghai. University of Houston, M. D. Anderson Library, Special Collections.

3. A humorous but informative hand-drawn map of the Asiatic Station in the 1930s. Author's collection via the Ben Odum Asiatic Fleet album, Navy Memorial, Washington DC.

4. This large 1939 photo of the officers and crew of *Edsall* was taken at a party in Chefoo. The skipper, Lt. Cdr. Abel C. J. Sabalot, and several of his officers are in the center. Author's collection via the Ben Odum Asiatic Fleet album, Navy Memorial, Washington DC.

5. USS *Parrott* prewar. This flushdecker had an active campaign in the East Indies and featured in several important engagements. U.S. Naval History and Heritage Command, 80-Cf-21525-11.

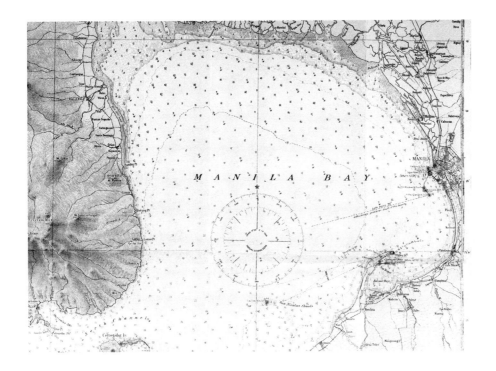

6. (*opposite top*) The calm tranquility of this prewar image of
uss *Pillsbury* in an unknown Philippine anchorage gives no
indication of the gruesome and violent death awaiting her in the
Indian Ocean in early March 1942. Author's collection via the
Ben Odum Asiatic Fleet album, Navy Memorial, Washington DC.

7. (*opposite bottom*) Another ship's party photo taken at the North
China port of Chefoo in the late 1930s. This shows sailors (and
at least one chief) from uss *Pope* enjoying "wine, women, and
song" in the traditional Asiatic Fleet fashion. The smiling sailor
getting his glass filled is Ben Odum, the owner of the photo album
in which this image was found. Author's collection via the Ben
Odum Asiatic Fleet album, Navy Memorial, Washington DC.

8. (*above*) Prewar map showing the Manila Bay area and its
major military points, from Mariveles Harbor (lower left near
Corregidor) to Cavite, Sangley Point (lower right), and Manila
itself. www.fold3.com.

9. Aerial view of prewar Cavite from the northwest looking across the bay toward Bacoor in the distance. Author's collection via Otto Schwarz.

10. USS *Houston* departing for her final refit at Mare Island in 1940. This rare photo—which shows that the cruiser had already received her new AA directors but not her 1.1-inch gun tubs—was taken over the fantail of a Pacific Fleet Brooklyn-class light cruiser. Author's collection.

11. High Commissioner for the Philippines, the Honorable Francis B. Sayre, and Adm. Thomas C. Hart, CINCAF, on board the flagship *Houston* during a prewar meeting. Author's collection via Otto Schwarz / USS *Houston* Survivors Association.

12. A rare, previously unpublished photo of *Houston* at Cavite in 1940–41, with most of her final upgrades showing. Author's collection.

13. (*opposite top*) This slightly blurred photo shows the August 1941 change of command ceremony aboard *Houston* in which Capt. Jesse B. Oldendorf (saluting) turned over command to Capt. Albert H. Rooks. Visible in the first row, left to right, are *Houston* officers Grosskopf, Epstein, Rentz, Maher, and Gingras (dark glasses). Both Chaplain Rentz and Senior Engineer Officer Gingras would perish in the Battle of Sunda Strait. Author's collection via Otto Schwarz.

14. (*opposite bottom*) Five *Houston* "V" Division pilots are shown here next to one of the cruiser's SOC floatplanes. The men on either end (Deane to the left and Keys to the right) were not on the ship when war broke out, but the three between them (Payne, Lamade, and Stivers [left to right]) were. Payne and Stivers spent the war as prisoners of the Japanese. Lamade was left behind at Australia in February and could not rejoin the ship before she was lost. Author's collection via Otto Schwarz.

15. (*above*) One of *Houston*'s SOC floatplanes shown in March 1941 off Cavite with the navy's three enormous radio towers at Sangley Point visible in the background. Author's collection via Otto Schwarz.

16. Old Peking was a major attraction for Asiatic Fleet personnel on leave, as shown in this prewar photo of the entrance to the Altar of the Sun. Author's collection via the Ben Odum Asiatic Fleet album, Navy Memorial, Washington DC.

17. This prewar picture found in a destroyerman's photo album shows how torpedoes were sometimes transferred. Just this method was employed when *Black Hawk* delivered the final allotment of Type 8 torpedoes to DesRon 29 flushdeckers off Christmas Island in late February 1942. Author's collection via the Ben Odum Asiatic Fleet album, Navy Memorial, Washington DC.

18. An unabashed Anglophile, Rear Adm. William Glassford Jr. was the last commander of what had been known for decades as the Asiatic Fleet during the final weeks of the East Indies campaign. Official U.S. Navy photograph, University of Houston, M. D. Anderson Library, Special Collections.

19. Cdr. Thomas Binford, commander of DesDiv 58 in the Java campaign (shown here later in the war as a rear admiral), acted decisively in the final hours at Surabaja to extricate four ships and save seven hundred American officers and enlisted men. He later retired a vice admiral in the 1950s. www.fold3.com.

20. Shown next to a triple torpedo mount on either *Pope* or *Edsall*, destroyermen in the Asiatic Fleet like this youngster were self-sufficient and durable characters. Author's collection via the Ben Odum Asiatic Fleet album, Navy Memorial, Washington DC.

21. Competitive sports were always important to Asiatic Fleet sailors. Filipino Guillermo Sabadisto, MATT1/c, on USS *Pope* (DD-225) won the fleet flyweight boxing title in 1939. Author's collection via the Ben Odum Asiatic Fleet album, Navy Memorial, Washington DC.

22. Marion "Elly" Ellsworth works
a signal lamp later in World War II.
Author's collection via M. Ellsworth.

23. Old, ungainly, and ponderous,
the oiler USS *Trinity* (AO-13) was
nicknamed "Lucky Thirteen" by her
crew, and with good reason. She was
one of the few ships to escape the
East Indies cauldron intact. Her men's
reminiscences form an important
component in this history. U.S. Naval
History and Heritage Command, NH
105649. Donation of Capt. Stephen S.
Roberts, USNR (ret.), 2008.

24. Lt. Nicholas "Ted" Luxemburg, RNN, served as signals liaison officer on *Marblehead* and after her bombing was transferred to the destroyer *Whipple*, where he was a participant in the *Langley-Pecos* fiasco and was one of the lucky few who survived that ill-fated operation. Author's collection via Ted and Nick Luxemburg.

25. Future adversaries meet a decade prior to World War II. The Japanese light cruiser *Naka*—later Desron 4 flagship of Read Adm. Nishimura Shōji in the East Indies campaign—steams past *Houston* off Shanghai in early 1932. Author's collection.

# SEVEN

## Abortive Efforts East and West

*Bangka Strait Sortie and Timor Relief Convoy*

As February moved into its second grim week, another series of reverses would paint the ABDA picture in even more somber tones for Hart and his hard-pressed Asiatic Fleet personnel. Increasingly the men came to understand the situation as one of inevitable tragedy. This was frequently expressed through an old slaughterhouse wisecrack: "Did you hear that gate clang shut behind us?"

On February 8 Hart was flown down to Tjilatjap in a "very uncomfortable" personal plane to visit his damaged cruisers. From the outset he knew that *Marblehead* would have to leave Java but decided that "Houston [would] stay in service, minus one turret, for a time at least." Aboard *Houston*, as on *Marblehead*, although the crews were noticeably more serious after the bombings, Hart realized that "there [was] plenty of determination in them."[1]

Also at Tjilatjap was the Dutch flagship, *De Ruyter*, and Hart spent some time attempting to shore up Rear Adm. Karel Doorman's spirits. He saw that the Dutch admiral was still quite apprehensive about air attack while at sea and contrasted this concern with the American skippers, who worried about their ships being bombed while in port. Doorman, in Hart's view, remained too much the "cloistered, war-college type of officer" who lacked "the dash and drive" for risky offensive operations. However, he saw no reason to withdraw or replace Doorman as the striking force commander. In truth, Hart believed that after so much critical talk from the Dutch regarding the U.S. Navy ("asking why the American Fleet does not win the war"), it was better—"politically speaking"—to let them have one of their own "in the saddle."[2] It's hard to blame him for this attitude. It was a view shared by other high U.S. Navy commanders and government officials as well. The Dutch navy would finally get what it said it had wanted all along in the East Indies: command.

At Tjilatjap Hart examined both ships along with the fleet surgeon, the material officer, and his assistant, Lt. Cdr. Harry Keith (former skipper of *Peary*).

As Hart went through the cruisers' ruined compartments, men were hard at work trying to affect what repairs they could. On *Houston* Gunner Hogan and two of his best men had actually managed to put the forward AA director back into operation. This repair involved removing the mount's brass weather stripping and was considered so effective that the stripping from the aft director was also removed.[3] This was done while Hart and Commander Maher were in Captain Rooks's quarters discussing the ship's status. The news about the director was received by Hart and the senior officers at that time and was probably *the* critical factor in the decision to keep the battered cruiser in action.[4] Without functional AA directors, whatever value *Houston* still retained for convoy duty as an antiaircraft battery would have been negated.

During this period Lieutenant Commander Keith was involved in procuring a large slab of half-inch steel plate to patch *Houston*'s bomb-damaged after-deck next to turret 3. He had found the plate about three or four miles outside Tjilatjap and arranged to have it brought to the docks. But unknown to Keith, it had to be done by sheer muscle power, involving fifty to one hundred local Javanese transporting the heavy steel manually. This operation took many hours, but the plate finally reached the ship later that night.[5]

Elsewhere aboard *Houston*, Lt. (j.g.) Harold S. Hamlin, officer for turret 1, saw that his sailors were "really upset by the realization" that the thin 7/8-inch side plating on the gunhouse offered little protection other than "to keep off spray and fish." The so-called treaty cruisers, also known derisively as "tin-clads," were not called such for nothing. The destructive power of heavy bombs had been brought home to them in the most graphic manner conceivable.[6] Hamlin, along with Lieutenant Commander Galbraith and the junior air defense officer, Lt. (j.g.) Leon Rogers, made sure to keep their men—and many others as well—working hard to keep their minds off such negative reflections. Yet such thoughts were evident for those able to read between the lines. Bob Fulton wrote his parents another letter from Tjilatjap on February 10, and he spoke for many of the officers and enlisted men when he said: "It is too bad the American public doesn't know the real picture out here."[7]

Just before departing for India on February 1, *Boise* had off-loaded 1,200 5-inch projectiles and another 200 3-inch for her fellow cruisers. The shells were left in Tjilatjap at a Dutch magazine. These were gladly acquired by the men of *Houston*, who had learned the mortal dangers of being saddled with inferior ammunition. They took on approximately five hundred rounds of the *Boise* ammo, bringing it in by hand through cargo hatches and stacking it in the mess hall. Either from fatigue or inattention the men also took aboard much of the 3-inch ammunition, which became mixed in with the 5-inch projectiles. When the mistake was recognized, the smaller shells had to be removed and off-loaded again.[8] Nonetheless, the gunners of *Houston* were able to go back into operation with antiaircraft ammunition that worked as designed. This in itself helped preserve the ship in its final weeks.

• • •

While *Houston* and *Marblehead* were licking their wounds at Tjilatjap, another ABDA cruiser-destroyer striking force was to be sent north to contest the Japanese invasion convoys coming down from the Anambas Islands to land on Sumatra. Led by Rear Admiral Doorman in *De Ruyter*, it was a reasonably powerful group, comprising five cruisers—*De Ruyter, Java, Tromp, Exeter*, and *Hobart*—and, originally, ten destroyers; four Dutch and six American. They were to rendezvous at the southeastern Sumatran port of Oosthaven (present-day Bandar Lampung) before proceeding north to contest Japanese landings—and presumably any Imperial Navy covering forces—off the north end of Bangka Island. There the enemy could attempt to move inland up the Moesi delta toward Palembang and its massive oil fields. It was still believed that such convoys might be stopped by determined naval counterattacks. Since the Dutch thought that the southern entrance to Bangka Strait had been mined by the enemy, a lengthy, roundabout route was chosen through Gaspar Strait between Bangka and Billiton islands.

As events played out, and according to written notes made a few days later, a twenty-four-hour delay for which Hart was responsible probably cost the striking force its best opportunity. Hart wrote: "Council was divided on the subject at ABDACOM Headquarters, but the decision was in my hands." He then admitted, "I think I made a mistake in the 24 hour delay" but also noted that the additional day allowed Doorman's group to be reinforced by *Exeter*, *Hobart*, and *Java* and—perhaps more tellingly—gave the destroyers extra time to arm themselves fully. This gave the striking force "considerable gun-power," he noted. However, as warfare has always revealed, offensive weapons rarely achieve decisive results in the hands of a leader lacking determination.[9]

Also, as time and again during the Java campaign, the naval forces of ABDA were too dispersed for timely reaction to enemy moves. And once more a sloppy operational accident would take its toll. Four U.S. destroyers of DesDiv 58—*Stewart, John D. Edwards, Barker*, and *Bulmer*—had been milling around on the southeastern end of Java awaiting other units of the Dutch navy, but these never appeared and the flushdeckers were ordered back to Surabaja. Unknown to them, there *were* Dutch ships farther to the west, lying low along the underbelly of Java. In such hiding places the RNN had tried to keep some of its tankers and oilers concealed from enemy air patrols. In one of these remote bays a number of Dutch and American ships had gathered to fuel and prepare for their next mission.

This time the collision involved Doorman's flagship, *De Ruyter*, in this instance with the Asiatic Fleet four-piper *Whipple* off Prigi Bay (also known as Segoro Wedi, between Sempoe and Patjitan). *De Ruyter* had left Tjilatjap on February 11 to meet with a tanker, the TAN 8 (ex-M/V *Ambo*), at this obscure anchorage. In this action it appears that once more a retrograde movement cost the ABDA Striking Force time and opportunity. *De Ruyter*'s collision with *Whipple* took place in the overnight hours as the force was exiting the bay during a blinding rainstorm. Ted Luxemburg recalled hearing and feeling "a helluva bang," and one more ABDA naval asset had been scratched from combat duty. The four-piper—which had long suffered from bow problems, dating back to a 1936 collision with fellow tin can *Smith Thompson* in the Philippines—was damaged badly enough to be out of action for ten days.[10] With her bow bent back to frame 10, both peak tanks flooded, and partial flooding of her paint and chain lockers, *Whipple* then limped westward at six knots, escorted by *Pillsbury*. In Tjilatjap she entered the 8,000-ton floating dry dock on Friday the thirteenth after *Marblehead* had departed. With *Whipple* under repair, *Pillsbury* would move across Sunda Strait to Oosthaven, there to meet up again with *Parrott* (which left Tjilatjap as soon as *Whipple* reached the dry dock) and the reconstituted DesDiv 58—coming from Surabaja—along with the remaining Allied ships of Doorman's striking force.

Most of the Americans were not exactly sure what their mission was to be; the sailors thought they were probably going to Oosthaven to help assist in evacuations. The port was a railway terminus, and crowded with fleeing civilian refugees as well as military units departing Sumatra. By this time near-panic was setting in. It was becoming more and more evident that the "impregnable fortress" of Singapore would likely fall. The British and the Dutch could talk all they liked of last stands and such, but at no stage was *any* fighting of that type seen by ABDA's ground forces. On the contrary, in the back of everybody's mind loomed the spectacle of miraculous deliverance at Dunkirk just two years earlier.

It is hardly surprising that many sailors could not help but feel embittered and abandoned. Bill Kale aboard the destroyer *Stewart* captured the temper of many when he groused in his personal log: "Someone has to fight this damned war, the new ships and heavy armed ships are back in the States eating gee-dunks [ice cream] and we fellows on these 22 year old four stackers have to do the dirty work. It's just dirty politics in the Navy Department somewhere."[11]

Higher up in the command, ABDAIR's chief, Air Marshal Sir Richard Peirse, sent a lengthy message on February 10 to the Air Ministry in London laying out his precarious situation. He had too few planes overall, and those he did have were being destroyed piecemeal by Japanese air raids. In the previous two days he stated: "15 Hurricanes were destroyed on the ground due to lack of adequate air raid warning system; almost total lack of AA defense and extreme difficulty of dispersal and camouflage since we have been forced to operate from Dutch makeshift aerodromes surrounded by swamps and jungle." American help had not materialized either, he noted. "Today there are only some 17 P-40s in Java operational." Although Peirse appeared preoccupied with defending Singapore and Sumatra, the situation across the East Indies was clearly slipping out of his control. He concluded this downbeat message claiming that "25 percent pilots and 50 percent Hurricanes required per squadron to make good wastage."[12] No such numbers would ever reach Java, although attempts were made and many lives lost in the process.

By this time the enemy had already initiated para-drops to seize the invaluable oil installations near Palembang many miles up the Moesi River in Sumatra.[13] Amphibious landings from coastward would soon follow. Although outnumbered by KNIL defenders, Japanese paratroopers managed to arrive undetected over the area, aided by the mind-boggling obliviousness of Allied fliers and "dense smoke rising high from oil burning in Singapore, which was on the verge of falling, [which] greatly limited visibility all the way to the estuary of the Moesi River."[14] In some instances groups of Royal Australian Air Force (RAAF) Hurricanes flew right past the Japanese paratroop transports—these were license-built copies of Lockheed 14s, which the Allied men naturally took to be Hudson bombers—without recognizing or attacking them. On the ground, equally disturbing chaos and folly ruled.[15]

As before in Borneo and Celebes, infantry resistance by ABDA's forces was weak and sporadic; incidents of panic and friendly fire were not uncommon. Meanwhile, surviving RAF and RAAF fighters and bombers sent to attack the transports off Muntok and the Moesi estuary flew back to the Pangkalan Benteng ("P1") airfield only to find it "utterly deserted" until realizing it was in the process of being overrun by the Japanese.[16]

At length the Royal Dutch Shell and Standard Oil refineries at Pladjoe and Sungei Gerong were seized by fewer than two hundred Japanese paratroopers.

Although a spirited counterattack by KNIL forces retook them briefly, these gains were abandoned within two days. Allied demolition efforts were spotty again, and Japanese specialists were able to preserve most of the installations from serious damage. Both of the invaluable airfields at P1 and P2 were eventually lost as well. At the same time, and despite repeated air attacks, Japanese army advance units moved up the Moesi, Sela, and Tela Rivers in landing craft from the mouth of the Moesi on the afternoon of the fourteenth. These units linked up with their paratroop counterparts by noon the following day. On the morning of February 18, the main body of the Thirty-Eighth Division had begun its advance from Muntok on Bangka Island up the Moesi River. It landed at Palembang ten hours later, its units having encountered little Allied resistance except when Djambi was captured. Surviving British and Australian air force assets were quickly withdrawn to western Java on February 16, and the entire area conceded to the enemy by the eighteenth, giving the Japanese another of the East Indies' most productive and valuable petrochemical complexes. So concluded the critical phase of Operation "L," the seizure of Bangka Island and Palembang. The Japanese later claimed to have acquired no less than a quarter million tons of oil at Palembang. Whatever the exact total, it was a staggering loss to ABDA and the Dutch East Indies.[17]

While the Dutch and their allies were being defeated by ground and air at Bangka and Palembang, Tom Hart—in his final days as ABDAFLOAT—and his successor, Helfrich, made a belated attempt to contest the landings. A naval striking force under Doorman was to proceed to sea on the afternoon of the fourteenth from Oosthaven, swing up through Sunda Strait, and then head north for Gaspar Strait separating Bangka and Billiton islands. It was hoped the force could drive headlong into enemy convoys known to be converging on Muntok in the upper end of the Bangka Strait. Hart believed the men could do some real damage even in daylight. He knew perfectly well that air attacks were probable, but if ever there was a time for "grave risks" it was now. Whether Doorman would be equal to the task remained to be seen.

. . .

By about 1300 hours on February 14, *Stewart* with *Barker*, *Bulmer*, and *John D. Edwards* reached Teluk Boetong Roads off Oosthaven (also called Lampung Bay) and anchored. They were followed into the anchorage by *Pillsbury* and *Parrott*, which arrived together some thirty minutes later. Rumors of a strike north against Japanese surface units rather than convoy escort duty were now circulating, and the mass of Allied ships seemed to give credence to such talk.

Also present were *De Ruyter, Java, Tromp, Kortenaer, Van Ghent, Piet Hein,* and *Banckert.* Another two cruisers—British and Australian—HMS *Exeter* and HMAS *Hobart* had been detached from convoy duties to join the striking force. A pair of British minesweepers showed up, but these vessels were too slow for offensive operations and would be left behind. The six flushdeckers added an imposing five dozen or so torpedoes to the group, which it was believed would be of much value against the enemy.

With the fall of Palembang imminent, *Trinity* had been sent to retrieve a last load of oil. Escorted by *Edsall* she was a few hours out of Tjilatjap when she got news of the paratrooper attacks at Palembang. Understandably alarmed by this news, her commander requested new orders and was instructed to return to the Javanese port. It was her final close shave during the Java campaign. Ordered then to Abadan in the Red Sea area, *Trinity* departed, waddling slowly across the Indian Ocean, her part in the East Indies debacle over. Unmolested, the elderly tanker finally reached her destination. Although they later recalled being closer to Palembang than they in fact were, the crew of "The Lucky 13" would never forget their narrow escape. Nor could they fail to see how fortunate they had been to get away, in contrast to so many of the men and ships left behind.

Back in the combat zone, the two ships with senior commanders, *De Ruyter* and *Hobart,* got under way from the Lampung Bay anchorage just after 1600 hours. *Parrott, Pillsbury, John D. Edwards, Stewart, Barker,* and *Bulmer* soon followed, along with the other Dutch ships. Heavy rains and cloud cover made navigation and station keeping no easier. The striking force moved into its night cruising formation and despite the foul weather steamed on at a brisk 20 knots. At 0310 hours the ships changed course to the northwest, slowing to 15 knots. Within another half hour the flushdeckers also began dumping their gasoline stores in anticipation of the coming engagement.

To get through the treacherous Gaspar Strait at night—long known as a highly dangerous approach—in adverse weather conditions while steaming at a good clip was not merely tempting the gods of misfortune but tweaking their noses. These spiteful deities had watched over the naval forces of ABDA throughout the Java campaign and missed no chance to visit mischief on the coalition's naval units. Another opportunity for such ill luck would follow soon enough through the choice of this ill-advised route. For three dozen miles to southward below the four channels that make up Gaspar Strait, an abundance of rocks, shoals, reefs, and sandbanks stud the Java Sea between Bangka and Billiton islands. Seven decades earlier navigational guides had noted: "In thick or bad weather, it is possible to proceed through Bangka Strait without risk;

but Gaspar Strait can never be approached at such times without incurring considerable danger."[18] The Dutch were willing to assume these risks and on them fell the consequences.

Lt. Cdr. H. Page Smith's *Stewart* (ComDesDiv 58 Binford embarked) was struggling to maintain its position in the bad weather as the ships entered the so-called Stolze Channel (Selat Baur today), which is the easternmost of the channels and generally considered the safest. Her helmsman, Bill Kale, reported that it was "dark as hell, and hard to keep station" as the four-piper moved through the shallow, reef-studded waters behind the Dutch destroyers. Apprehensive, Lieutenant Commander Smith wanted to let more experienced RNN ships lead them through this perilous stretch. Unfortunately at around 0520 hours the inevitable occurred. A Dutch destroyer ahead came to a sudden halt, then sounded a warning with three horn blasts. It was the starboard ship, *Van Ghent*, and her career in the Royal Netherlands Navy had come to a sad conclusion. The 1,600-ton Admiralen-class destroyer had run hard aground on Bamijo Reef in the channel's east side at 17 knots and would never again steam with her sisters. *Stewart* had to back engines two-thirds and swing left to avoid a similar fate. She then moved warily past at five knots, noting that the Dutch ship was by then smoking badly from both funnels. *Van Ghent* was also leaking oil and had experienced a few small explosions. Page Smith's flushdecker lingered for about ten minutes, with the crew "trying to get [their] bearings," but it was soon apparent that *Van Ghent* would have to be left to her fate. In line astern in slightly deeper water, one of the remaining Dutch destroyers, *Banckert*, signaled that she would remain behind to give what assistance she could. However, as *Van Ghent*'s ASDIC officer, Lt. Abraham van der Moer ruefully noted, "We had no choice but to abandon ship."[19] *Stewart* now resumed her northward course.[20] *Parrott* had also seen the Dutch destroyer aground, logging it at 0540 hours. Then *Parrott* swung around and, without pausing, continued on with the others.

This "bad business" in Gaspar Strait was yet one more operational accident that the thin forces of ABDA could scarcely afford. To make matters worse, *Van Ghent* was one of only two Dutch destroyers in Helfrich's fleet equipped with ASDIC—the other being *Witte de With*—so her loss was keenly felt. While *Van Ghent*'s entire crew was transferred to *Banckert*, and sensitive materials destroyed or salvaged throughout the day, *Stewart* and the others carried on to the north. It took an hour for *Stewart* to overtake the formation, which had moved some eight miles ahead of her. At 0700 she resumed her position in the antisubmarine screen. By this time the ships were on a course nearly due north, zigzagging intermittently at 20 knots. The weather remained uncomfortable with rough seas and limited visibility.

To make matters more difficult, *Barker* and *Bulmer* were both suffering from engineering problems. The former had troubles with her oil drain pump from her reduction gear sump tank, while the latter was fighting condenser leaks throughout the sortie. As a result each destroyer had to operate on one engine for extended periods as her engineers worked to repair each casualty. In contrast to the oft-repeated criticisms of Helfrich both during and after the campaign, it should be noted that such engineering setbacks did not keep these American ships from combat operations.

*De Ruyter* had meanwhile catapulted off one of her scout planes at dawn and at 0837 hours reported that it had spotted a force of ten enemy cruisers and destroyers forty-five miles north of Bangka Island moving at high speed to the northwest. Doorman chose to press on, continuing north at between 15 and 20 knots and once again zigzagging according to various RNN plans. The ships sighted by *De Ruyter's* plane were most likely the cruisers and destroyers of Vice Adm. Ozawa Jisaburo as they rounded up the eastern flank of the twin Japanese invasion convoys moving south from their jumping-off points at the Anambas Islands and the Natuna Archipelago. At virtually the same time Ozawa had sent out air patrols from his flagship, the heavy cruiser *Chōkai*, and one of these soon spotted the ABDA force. It reported three cruisers and five destroyers steaming north through Gaspar Strait. Upon receipt of this information Ozawa ordered the main body of the invasion convoy back to the north while he called in air support in the form of bombers from the light carrier *Ryūjō*, which had been attached to his force. Additional bombing attacks by land-based air forces would also be vectored in later. Doorman was about to receive a sharp lesson in the efficient employment of air support during naval operations, something ABDAFLOAT consistently failed to achieve.

It is worth noting that—as Henry Eccles on *John D. Edwards* later wrote— none of the flushdeckers had "access to any reconnaissance reports to give us any information as to the strength or disposition of the enemy forces."[21] He was correct, although some reports that contained surprisingly accurate information arrived later. But by then it no longer mattered; Doorman had never closed to within gun range of the transports or their covering forces.

Instead, much as feared, Japanese bombers appeared. Bill Kale, spotting as he lay flat on the port flag bag at the rear of *Stewart's* bridge, recorded: "1200— Well, just what we expected, only in a different form. Planes, first raid twenty-four planes. They tried for the *Exeter*, but those damned Limeys put up such a burst of AA fire that it scared them away."[22] Notwithstanding his good fortune up to that point, Doorman had seen enough. At 1243 "all ships countermarched to course 185° T." and headed south maintaining their high speed.[23] The ill-conceived, irresolute venture against Japan's Sumatran invasion convoy had ended after less than an hour of action. Ozawa was then able to turn his ships around and head for the Moesi River estuary.

But for Doorman and the striking force, the ordeal was far from over. They were bombed at intervals throughout the day. Several sticks of bombs straddled the four larger cruisers but scored no direct hits. The crew of *Parrott* thought they saw smoke from a fire on the stern of *Java*—the result of "apparently one hit"—but this was not so. The four-pipers continued to take evasive action at high speed when air attacks developed. During that afternoon *Parrott's* AA gunners were busy repelling Japanese planes for over five hours, only firing their last projectiles—six rounds of 3-inch common—at 1712. For *Barker's* Robert Moyers, the battle seemed a blur of popped rivets during the bombing attacks, water shipped down the stacks, and "guns that wouldn't elevate adequately to return fire." Yet for the old four-stacker's tight-knit crew, "none of the things were as important as 'getting their job done.'"[24] The final enemy aircraft—seventeen long-ranged G4M (BETTY) medium attack bombers of the Kanoya Kū from southern Indo-China—bombed *Exeter* at 1730 hours but had no better luck. In fact they were roughly handled by ABDA's gunners and lost two damaged machines later to crashes and landing mishaps.[25] Doorman's striking force then resumed "night cruising formation" to continue its withdrawal.

Although the Allied ships bunched up in the Gaspar Strait bottleneck during their return, their luck held and no further damage was suffered. Eccles on *John D. Edwards* remembered: "We all got through the strait safely, passing the *Van Ghent* which was on fire and blowing up as we went through." The sight of the abandoned Dutch destroyer's wreck pouring black smoke into the sky was symbolic of the entire sortie, but even this did not prevent some of the more naive sailors from briefly imagining that they had done "fairly good."[26] Such comforting delusions were not part of Rear Admiral Doorman's makeup, though, and as he came back to Batavia, he remarked that he expected to be judged harshly for his withdrawal.

As for Adm. Thomas Hart, he had by then been pushed out of his command and was preparing to leave for Ceylon on the damaged light cruiser HMS *Durban*. On the evening of February 14, Hart said farewell to his officers after a dinner given at the Hotel Savoy at Bandoeng. The next morning he was driven down to Batavia and then left alone at the dock "like the newest recruit."[27] Fortunately for Hart, the young skipper of *Bulmer*, Lt. David Alonzo Harris, was also nearby and had the admiral taken out to *Durban* in the destroyer's gig.

On board the British cruiser Hart scrawled that night in his diary:

> Admiral Doorman . . . went out with a mixed force—all three nationalities—of five cruisers and ten destroyers which were a pretty powerful lot. Doorman went up to near the most promising hunting grounds but didn't drive right into there—Of course the Jap air found him and sent in quite a bombing attack. It did no damage, however, and then—mind you—Doorman simply headed for home. Of course I should not criticize for I was not on the spot and the force might not have found any game if they *had* driven in. However:– I had previously guessed that Doorman was not the kind of man for that kind of job. At any rate Helfrich can now blame no one but the Dutch for the mis-carriage [*sic*] if there was one.[28]

For Thomas C. Hart, his brief tenure as commander of ABDA's naval forces had ended. This came after a month of internecine backbiting that did nothing to help the Western cause and probably aided the Japanese with the delays and disharmony generated. In response to the British and the Dutch commanders who criticized him as an "old man [with] . . . no kick in him at all," "Tough Tommy" would have the best revenge: he lived another three decades before dying in his ninety-fourth year.[29]

· · ·

Having buried her dead in the European cemetery and offloaded ten more wounded men to be sent inland to Petronella Hospital, *Houston* left Tjilatjap for northern Australia again.[30] On the evening of February 11, after discussions with Glassford concerning the disposition of U.S. ships, Hart noted in his diary, "We are sending *Houston* back into the war." With the pressing need for convoy escorts, it made some sense to keep the ship in the combat zone a while longer. George Hedrick, QM2/c, recalled, "*Houston* was still classed as 80 percent a fighting ship, good for convoy duty."[31] He was right, and her secondary battery would be most important in that duty. In order to bolster her AA capabilities, she had taken on about five hundred rounds of "good" 5-inch/25 cal. ammo left behind earlier at Tjilatjap by *Boise*.[32] She then made the journey to Darwin without incident, arriving at the harbor on February 14.

At Darwin's primitive harbor, *Houston* was moored alongside a lengthy L-shaped pier, with one of "the tubs they called transports" to be used in the relief convoy on the other side of the pier.[33] These four ships were the USAT

*Meigs* (12,568 tons) along with *Mauna Loa* (5,436 tons), *Portmar* (5,551 tons), and a British vessel, the *Tulagi* (2,281 tons). While men and matériel from the First Battalion, 148th Field Artillery Regiment, were being loaded onto their transport, an army band dockside played all day during the work. *Houston* also took aboard supplies, which included an allotment of USMC uniforms originally destined for the Philippines left behind earlier in the war. This clothing was welcome because many sailors had lost their uniforms and more when the ship was bombed.

As so often the majority of *Houston's* crew was employed in this hurried evolution. And Darwin was still suffering from labor shortages and work stoppages. However, with fewer supplies to load, *Houston's* sailors—including her bandsmen—sweat-soaked and in their crudely dyed T-shirts and dirty dungarees, finished their work first. At the sight of the spick-and-span army musicians on the opposite side of the pier "in full uniform with laced gaiters, standing up straight and playing in formation," *Houston's* band members could not resist. They rushed down to their quarters, grabbed their instruments, and ran back up to the dock. There they stood behind their counterparts, reading the sheet music over the army bandsmen's shoulders to play along with them.[34]

By the middle of the night, the loading on the four transports had been completed. In addition to the American units, an Australian Pioneer Battalion was to be sent to Timor, but only after opposition by senior Royal Australian Army leadership was overcome.[35] As so frequently in ABDA's brief history, the recognition of critical strategic vulnerabilities came too late, and even when it happened, there were inadequate forces to address the deficiencies. On Timor as at Rabaul and Ambon—or for that matter at Palembang, Balikpapan, Kendari, and Makassar—the ABDA coalition was short-sighted *and* short-handed. However, there was a sense that Timor was crucial to the defense not only of Java but to Australia's security as well.

The convoy, with its four transports escorted by *Houston*, four-stacker *Peary*, and two Australian sloops—HMAS *Warrego* (U-73) and HMAS *Swan* (U-74)— departed Darwin just before two in the morning. The route to Koepang was some seven hundred miles by sea and was thought safe since no Japanese attacks had yet occurred south of the Barrier. But this small, slow group would not make one quarter of that distance before being detected and attacked by the vigilant Japanese naval air arm. The pitiful state of ABDA's forces was clearly indicated by the presence of the much-damaged *Peary* in this convoy. Walter Winslow on *Houston* considered that the four Allied warships "were hardly qualified to escort a convoy in peacetime."[36]

If the ability of the Imperial Navy to locate this convoy so quickly seems uncanny and suspicious, perhaps it should, for no sooner had the ships left harbor than at 0330 hours on February 15, the IJN flying boat squadron operating out of Ceram was notified. Five big Kawanishi H6K Type 97 (MAVIS) four-engined flying boats of Tōkō Kū took off. Eight hours later, while flying at four thousand meters over the Timor Sea, the convoy below was spotted. One MAVIS was ordered to keep the Allied ships under observation, and she ended up staying over the convoy for three hours. By radio she reported back to her headquarters, dodging occasional bursts of AA fire from *Houston*, ducking in and out of clouds.

On the cruiser Lieutenant Commander Galbraith remembered, "A big 4 engine Jap flying boat picked us up and remained with us about 2 or 3 hours. Fighters from Darwin were requested." This request would have been the message sent by Rooks at 1145 to the RAAF airfield soon after realizing that the convoy had been detected. The message also gave his location, northwest of Darwin. Roughly three hours later, a single American P-40E appeared. This was 2nd Lt. Robert "Blackie" Buel of the Third Pursuit Squadron (Provisional). He had taken off for the convoy at 1400 hours. Buel had some trouble locating the MAVIS, and *Houston*'s AA gunners fired several single rounds in the flying boat's direction to help guide him. Galbraith later stated: "The big flying boat had made only one approach and had turned away when our guns flashed. This maneuver threw our deflection off. . . . Finally she came in at about 8 to 10,000 feet and as we began to fire, she turned away gradually, until she passed about a mile ahead and continued out of sight."[37]

The Type 97 had dropped her 60 kg bombs and was turning for the long flight back to base. At that moment, low on fuel and with her men preparing to eat their lunch, crew member Takehara Marekuni recalled "a single-engined fighter raced towards [them] from the right front." Although he was the plane's navigator, Takehara also doubled as tail gunner, and he hurried back to the aft section's 20 mm cannon. Buel had slipped around to attack from the rear and was pouring machine-gun rounds into the big flying boat, wounding the radio operator and setting fuel tanks afire. Evidently not suspecting the tail stinger of the MAVIS, he walked his plane straight into a full clip of 20 mm shells fired by Takehara. After expending all fifty rounds, Takehara had shoved another clip into his gun when he looked back and saw white smoke streaming from the U.S. fighter. He and the others then watched the doomed P-40 crash into the sea. At the same time the big Japanese flying boat lost altitude itself and fell toward the water.[38]

Lieutenant Commander Galbraith on *Houston* and others had seen the MAVIS disappear into the distance pursued by Buel's fighter. Within five minutes "a large bright flame was observed on the horizon." There was so much black smoke on the horizon, in fact, that general quarters was called on the cruiser. Quartermaster George Hedrick Jr. remembered: "Preparations were made to engage surface craft which never showed up. Later we came to the conclusion that this smoke must have been made from the flying boat after it hit the drink." Walter Winslow similarly saw "a brilliant flash of fire and considerable black smoke" in the distance. All hoped and prayed that the solitary American had won the exchange.[39] Yet it would be half a century before the truth was finally revealed about this obscure engagement in the skies south of Timor.[40] "Blackie" Buel never returned to Darwin, and the MAVIS never made it back to Ceram. In the early nineties it was found that Buel, alone and unsupported, had indeed attacked and shot down the huge flying boat but at the cost of his own life.

While it is proverbial that there are no atheists in foxholes, it would seem few exist in the engine spaces of warships during combat either. During the voyage back to Darwin, Lt. Bob Fulton penned another letter home to his folks in Washington DC. After the terrors of February 4 and February 15–16, *Houston's* assistant engineer officer openly acknowledged his religious belief to his family—no doubt recognizing just how mortal the circumstances in which his ship and her crew had been placed: "As time goes on I am more and more thankful for a Christian Faith, and for my parents who brought me up in it. It is certainly the only thing one can depend on these days." Fulton had been known to have his black gang kneel on the engine room gratings and join in prayer before engaging the enemy. After the chilling experiences of February that they had undergone, it is perhaps not terribly difficult—even for nonbelievers—to understand this. In the same letter he admitted: "All the news we get here is still bad," then adding, hope against hope, "but I suppose things will change once help from the states begins to arrive."[41]

However, that help would not reach the East Indies. After the campaign, surviving officers who had escaped, such as Cdr. Henry Eccles of *John D. Edwards*, would look back on such assurances with no small degree of bitterness. They were appalled by the official talk from Washington about new ships, new planes, and new troops, none of which arrived in time to make any real difference.

# EIGHT

## Axidents, Surprisals, and Terrifications

*The Battle of Badoeng Strait*

By the second week in February the ABDA command understood that it was just a matter of time before Japanese planners would target islands east of Java. Both Timor and Bali possessed strategically located airfields and were recognized as vulnerable.[1] The Japanese considered Timor more important as an Allied staging point, but Bali was closer and less strongly defended. For its part Allied intelligence suspected such enemy preparations were under way in Makassar as early as February 9. Unfortunately, ABDA's naval units were once again too widely dispersed for an effective counterblow.

The Combined Striking Force under Rear Admiral Doorman in *De Ruyter*, which attempted to intervene in the Japanese landings on Sumatra via the Gaspar Straits, drew most of ABDA's available warships away to the west during the period of February 13–16. In that interim Singapore, beset to the end by denialism and incompetence bordering on idiocy, fell after little real fighting to the Japanese under Gen. Yamashita Tomoyuki. An unprecedented number of Allied troops—upward of 130,000 men—surrendered. None in the command echelons of ABDA doubted that Sumatra and Java would be next.[2]

As noted *Houston* departed Tjilatjap on February 10 bound for Darwin. The cruiser reached the northern Australian port on February 13 under orders to escort another convoy. That was the ABDA effort to reinforce Timor, and it came too late. Concurrently, with no overt surface opposition, Japan's Southern Operations plans proceeded apace.

ABDA air reconnaissance eventually detected an enemy convoy forming at Makassar around mid-February. For reasons of speed and security the Japanese then broke it up into smaller elements. The first advance group comprised two transports, *Sasago Maru* and *Sagami Maru*, escorted by four destroyers of DesDiv 8, *Ōshio*, *Asashio*, *Michishio*, and *Arashio*. Aboard the transports were men of the

Forty-Eighth Infantry Division's Kanemura Detachment, a reinforced battalion-sized force that had been hastily assembled for immediate deployment to Bali.

The flagship of the Eighth Destroyer Division was *Ōshio*, commanded by Cdr. Kikkawa Kiyoshi (Fiftieth *ki*), who would prove one of the IJN's ablest tin-can skippers over the next year. Capt. Abe Toshio (Forty-Sixth *ki*) flew his division commander's flag in Kikkawa's ship. As was the frequent practice in the Imperial Navy, the four ships were of the same type—members of the Asashio class—and thus formed a more homogenous unit tactically and administratively. The Asashios were relatively modern—all completed between 1937 and 1939—and robustly built big destroyers at 2,370 tons full load displacement. Almost 390 feet long and capable of speeds up to 35 knots, they carried as armament a main battery of six 5-inch/12.7 cm guns in three twin gunhouses, and eight 24-inch Type 93 torpedoes in two quadruple mounts, with eight reloads. In early 1942 these fine vessels would have been more than a handful for any Allied destroyers that could have been fielded in the Far East.[3]

They were all able to slip out of Makassar on the evening of February 17 undetected. This was unfortunate because an American submarine, the old pigboat S-37 (SS-142) under Lt. J. C. Dempsey, had been patrolling a mere two miles off the southern entrance to Makassar on the sixteenth. That same evening, Dempsey's boat was ordered to move south and "patrol inside Lombok Strait."[4] She then missed sighting the Japanese convoy until it had passed ahead of her as it moved south. With that her ability to strike it had also passed.

On the morning of February 18 ABDA patrol planes spotted these ships roughly 140 miles southwest of Makassar, southbound in the direction of Timor—as was surmised—or possibly Bali. Initially misidentified as two unspecified vessels accompanied by four cruisers, they were found again at three that afternoon. All six of the ships were sighted less than 100 miles northwest of Bali and moving in its direction at fifteen knots. Lagging behind the prey was S-37, still en route from Makassar to Lombok Strait.

Rear Adm. Kubo Kyuji (Thirty-Eighth *ki*) in the light cruiser *Nagara* served as commander of the First Auxiliary Base Unit (Dai Ichi Konkyochi-tai) and had overall command of this phase of the invasion operations. This responsibility included distant cover for the convoy. For this duty Kubo was allotted three Hatsuhara-class destroyers of DesDiv 21, *Hatsushimo*, *Wakaba*, and *Nenohi*. Kubo's ships remained at some distance, loitering in the Bali Sea behind the transports and four destroyers of DesDiv 8 during their approach. While the ships were crossing, air cover was provided by A6M Reisen (Zero) fight-

SURPRISALS AND TERRIFICATIONS

ers of the Twenty-First Air Flotilla and the Third Air Group's Tainan Kū flying out of airfields recently captured in the Makassar area.

As the convoy's destination soon became apparent, Helfrich and Doorman were reduced to last-minute ad hoc planning. With so little time they scrambled to organize their dispersed forces, then at opposite ends of Java, for a strike. At Tjilatjap was Doorman's more powerful group—*De Ruyter* (F) and the light cruiser *Java*, along with the Dutch destroyers *Piet Hein* and *Kortenaer*, and two American four-pipers, *Pope* and *John D. Ford*. The modern RNN flotilla leader *Tromp* (a 4,000-ton light cruiser) and four U.S. flushdeckers of a revamped DesDiv 58—*Stewart, John D. Edwards, Parrott*, and *Pillsbury*—were ordered to rendezvous at Surabaja. An additional pair of Dutch destroyers, *Witte de With* and *Banckert*, were also at Surabaja, but neither one could be included in the attacks. *Witte de With* needed overhaul and could not be readied before February 22. *Banckert* had been damaged in an air raid on the eighteenth; she then entered a Surabaja dry dock from which she never again emerged functional as an Allied fighting ship.[5]

Doorman called a conference late in the afternoon of February 18 in Tjilatjap to detail the hasty and improvised operational plans with his commanders.[6] He had received general instructions from Helfrich to "make a nighttime raid" on the Japanese forces in the straits, and get clear of the area before daylight and back to Surabaja, or as close as possible, the next day. It was also felt that some air cover might be provided if this tactical sequence was followed, according to Helfrich's postwar *Memoires*.[7]

The Americans in Tjilatjap were represented by Lt. Cdr. Edward N. "Butch" Parker (ComDesDiv 59), embarked in *John D. Ford*, and the two destroyer skippers, Lt. Cdr. J. E. "Jocko" Cooper of *Ford*, and Lt. Cdr. Welford "Willie" Blinn of *Pope*. Parker was a hard-nosed but capable and respected leader who had been given command of DesDiv 59 after Talbot's health failed. Welford Blinn was conscientious and well regarded by his officers and crew. Jacob Elliott Cooper was something else. He was a strict, often abrasive officer with a foghorn voice and no favorite of the men who had to serve under him. However, his bravery and competence were never debated. "Jocko" Cooper would earn one Navy Cross, two Silver Stars plus one gold oak leaf in lieu of a second Navy Cross for his service during the war.

Both U.S. destroyers had undergone cursory maintenance and resupply from their tender *Black Hawk* in Tjilatjap on February 12. At that time both ships also loaded a full complement of Mark 8 torpedoes, twelve each. These heavy torpedo batteries made the ships useful participants for a nighttime, high-speed hit-and-run attack against transports, just as they had done at Balikpa-pan a month earlier. On the other hand, their small size, unreliable machinery, and weak gun armament made them quite vulnerable to any Japanese surface vessels larger than a patrol boat. None of the skippers were especially optimistic about the odds facing them; all were feeling the pressure and strain of prolonged operations in the combat zone. Several still believed that they would never escape the Java cauldron alive. For obvious reasons, though, they kept such misgivings to themselves.

Tactical details of the operation, such as they were, had been left up to Rear Admiral Doorman by Helfrich. In truth the constraints of the situation had as much to do with the structure of his tactical arrangements as his own thinking. Thus, with his forces spread out over many hundreds of miles, two separate groups would attack "with an ample time margin between," as Helfrich later wrote.[8] On paper the operation looked like it *might* have potential; certainly the ABDA forces had numbers in their favor, sending three cruisers and seven destroyers against a Japanese screen of no more than four cruisers or destroyers.

In execution, however, it turned out to be nothing of the sort. Instead of concentrating his ships and attacking with torpedoes *before* gunfire—as would have been more effective—Rear Admiral Doorman had chosen to send in his forces in piecemeal attacks using different sections with dissimilar tactics. His two cruisers, *De Ruyter* and *Java*, would attack in the first wave with shellfire, accompanied to the rear by the destroyers *Kortenaer*, *Piet Hein*, *Ford*, and *Pope*, which would—it was hoped—expend their torpedoes to maximum effect. About two hours later a second striking element coming down from Surabaja and comprising the Dutch light cruiser *Tromp* with flushdeckers *Stewart*, *Parrott*, *Edwards*, and *Pillsbury* would follow up. In that wave, though, the destroyers would lead the way using their torpedoes, with the light cruiser trailing them, employing its battery of six 5.9-inch guns and eight 40 mm cannon.

According to his own account, Helfrich was somehow then persuaded by his staff to include a third wave of eight Dutch motor torpedo boats (MTBs) from Surabaja. These were tacked on as an afterthought it appears; they were not in Doorman's original conception. It is hard to see what was to be gained by such an arrangement, which, while courageous enough, would leave the Japanese forces well alerted by the time the third wave—which in the end amounted to little more than a ripple—arrived. Perhaps the Dutch imagined that only residual surface forces would be left to combat at that point or perhaps cripples to finish off. Last but not least, it seems that his scheme would have had the potential to create more confusion among the attackers than among the defenders. Yet the exigencies of time negated second thoughts, and ABDA's striking units moved ahead to carry out Doorman's brave if maladroit plans.

After a meandering journey from Oosthaven and Ratai Bay on the eastern end of Sumatra, where his ships had been sent following the unsuccessful Gaspar Strait sortie, Commander Binford (ComDesDiv 58) in *Stewart* was called to a quick conference aboard *Tromp* at Surabaja by her commanding officer, Cdr. J. B. de Meester, on the morning of February 19. The Dutch officer then laid out Doorman's operational plan to him in the barest terms: they would "press in right at the enemy transports" in three waves, with the first to hit at ten o'clock, the second—which would be Binford's group—at midnight, and the third at two in the morning.[9] The mission called for the ships to then retire north through Lombok Strait to Surabaja following their attacks. Binford had no time to evaluate, let alone criticize or revise, these plans. But plans were one thing, their execution another. And this group of engagements would feature its share of what a naval veteran from an earlier era referred to as "axidents, surprisals, and terrifications."[10]

· · ·

To the west Doorman's ships began emerging from Tjilatjap's clotted little harbor late on the evening of February 18. The destroyers pulled out some two hours prior to the heavy ships. It was after midnight when the two Dutch cruisers cleared the channel. Outside they were met by *Ford*, *Pope*, and *Piet Hein*. With bad luck dogging all of ABDA's naval missions, another mishap then took place. The unlucky *Kortenaer* grounded herself on one of several sandbars near the entrance to Schilpadden Bay and was written off as part of the attacking forces. A sailor from *Ford* later wrote: "Scratch one big beautiful modern destroyer."[11] It was hardly an auspicious start to the operation, but it was neither the first nor the last time such ill-luck would visit the ships of ABDA. The remaining ships then formed up into their "night cruising disposition" and headed east on the four-hundred-mile run to Bali.[12]

By midnight, however, and unknown to Doorman's force already at sea, the Japanese convoy had arrived off Bali's southern coast in the area of Sanur. Once more the Japanese had been the beneficiaries of poor weather, which made finding and tracking them far more troublesome to the Allied forces. After their uneventful but anxious journey—in which the sailors on the destroyers were "very tense and alert"—the ships reached the anchorage. First Class Petty Officer Watanabe Daiji on *Michishio* later recalled, "We could see Bali Island where the landing operation would be carried out. We started unloading war supplies immediately."[13] His memory was accurate; *Sasago Maru* and *Sagami Maru* began disgorging their troops at 0030 hours on February 19.[14] With a precision and energy typical of Japan's operations in the first phase operations, the little convoy had made good time from Makassar, covering the approximately four hundred miles in just over twenty-four hours. However, amphibious operations as conducted by the Japanese were still primitive affairs, and unloading was largely carried out by hand. The landings would consume some seventeen hours over the course of that day.

As the Japanese had approached Bali, they were made aware of the presence of enemy submarines. All four Japanese destroyers were busily pinging away at contacts real and imagined. And with every justification, as it turns out, for there was in fact a trio of ABDA boats searching for the enemy convoy in the waters around Bali. In addition to Dempsey's S-37, a British sub, HMS *Truant*, commanded by Lt. Cdr. Hugh A. V. Haggard, had been sent into the area, as had the Asiatic Fleet's USS *Seawolf* (SS-197) under Lt. Cdr. Fred Warder. *Truant* had departed Surabaja on February 18—too late to get into position before the ships reached Bali, as it transpired—reaching a point some fifty miles north of Cape Bungkulan at midday on the nineteenth. By noon on the following day she was in the northern end of Lombok Strait, where she had no success finding Kubo or the transports at that time and played no further part in contesting the invasion operations until several days after Bali had fallen.[15]

S-37 made the northern entrance of Lombok Strait and encountered such severe conditions as she began struggling down the turbulent waterway that Lieutenant Dempsey was compelled to temporarily turn back. The boat would remain in the upper entrance, away from the bad currents—said to be as much as 7.5 knots—and attempt to intercept enemy units known to be in the area. At 1531 hours on February 19, S-37 spotted one enemy transport escorted by a single DD moving south but was unable to make an approach. In less than an hour she then heard pinging, and two Japanese destroyers that had appeared began stalking her. At that point the sub took evasive tactics, which shook off her pursuers.

Dempsey then decided to move down through the strait in the direction of Sanur. At just after eight o'clock, as she entered Badoeng Strait, Dempsey's boat went aground off the northeast corner of Lembongan Island between Bali and Nusa Besar (Penida). It took fifteen minutes of backing and shifting ballast for S-37 to grind her way off the reef. Forty minutes later—with the sub trailing a lengthy oil slick from her scrape on the bottom—her men saw two enemy destroyers not two thousand yards away steaming southeast. These vessels were fortunately avoided, with Dempsey duly concerned about his telltale slick. Inside of thirty minutes he resurfaced and received a message from ComSubAF telling him to head north out of Lombok Strait. He disregarded this communication since for some time "firing from the vicinity of Benoa Channel had been seen and heard," and Dempsey felt he might yet ambush an unwary transport or escort. But this was not to be. Lurking in Badoeng Strait the next day—February 20—Dempsey's boat was depth-charged repeatedly while overhead could be heard enemy pom-poms firing and bombs detonating in the water as the Japanese ships were attacked over many hours by American bombers.

*Seawolf* had a similarly miserable experience. That boat had fought its way down Lombok Strait into position south of Tafel Hoek over a fifteen-hour period the previous day. In no respect were the waters around the idyllic island an ideal hunting ground for submarines; Warder described it in his patrol report—in consummate understatement—as "a bad business," noting that tidal information on its "violent" currents was "very meager and not accurate."[16]

That evening *Seawolf*'s men saw fires burning near Benoa on the southernmost shores of Bali. Warder assumed these flames to be Dutch demolitions in reaction to the impending landings. In the middle of the night *Seawolf* received a dispatch from ComSubAF to move in closer to the reported landing areas. This took her back to the north near Nusa Besar and Bali, with "Fearless Freddie" spotting his first destroyer through the black night's heavy rain at 0240 on February 19. It was another three and a half hours before he got a better look at the tin can: an Asashio-class vessel was his guess, and his identification was precise. The ship was circling at low speed, distance estimated to be ten thousand yards.

No sooner had this recognition taken place, though, than Warder's boat twice smacked into the bottom of Badoeng Strait near Serangan Island. First, running in what her instruments read as sixty-three feet of water, she slammed herself onto the beach like a grounded whale; it took several tense minutes to gingerly back out. Twelve minutes later a second mishap overtook the boat when *Seawolf* was raked the length of her starboard side, the jolt knocking many the men off their feet. Although perilous and unnerving to surface among enemy forces in broad daylight, Warder had no choice. He quickly ordered "All Stop" and brought the boat up to find himself "fenced in with coral patches and discolored water" on all bearings. After gathering his wits, and spotting what seemed a channel of egress, he edged the boat forward and by 0654 had "all shoal water cleared."[17] On the horizon, through heavy rains, he could make out the silhouette of a large enemy destroyer or cruiser about six miles distant, heading southwest. In the murky weather, however, it did not spot him and soon moved out of sight.

Another six hours of fumbling around in the violent, eddying whirlpools of the strait elapsed, exhausting men and machinery, with only a few glimpses of solitary destroyers on patrol gained. Then, at 1256, *Seawolf*'s gunnery officer, Ens. "Red" Syverson, caught sight of masts. Warder took over on the periscope and soon found both enemy transports in Sanur Roads—with all four enemy destroyers there, several milling around in a protective patrol—between 1350 and 1417 hours. One destroyer was no more than 1,800 yards away; Warder was able to examine her closely. She lay motionless with AA batteries fully manned and gun crews all eyeballing the broken cloud cover or looking toward the beach. Nearby a transport—which would have been *Sagami Maru*—already showed signs of the one hit and several near misses she had sustained earlier that morning from American bombers. He could see that she was listing to starboard and down by the stern.

Ninety-six minutes later Warder was in position to attack both transports and did so, firing four torpedoes from his forward tubes at *Sagami Maru* and *Sasago Maru*. There were no hits, but the torpedo tracks gave away his location, and the destroyers pounced on *Seawolf* within minutes. They unloaded over forty depth charges on her, jarring the men and the boat quite severely but luckily causing no damage of note beyond a multitude of small leaks.

Petty Officer Watanabe, who as a member of the gunnery department's range-finding team in *Michishio* might have been one of the enemy crewmen Warder had seen looking skyward, later wrote: "After a few hours of work, the sky was getting bright. Just about when we thought that this landing would culminate in success, all of a sudden, B-17s flew over us and bombed the convoy."[18] The destroyermen had participated in operations against Malaya, British Borneo, and Ambon, but this was their first experience of air attack, and they found it every bit as unnerving as their Western counterparts had already. "Repeated bombings by enemy airplanes delayed our landing operation," Watanabe later said. "The landing operation did not go smoothly even though we were eager to complete it quickly."[19] He likewise acknowledged the disturbing presence of enemy submarines as the afternoon wore on, which led to "the situation getting worse and dangerous." All the same the truth is that in spite of these attacks—and the pounding rains that obscured visibility—the troops were eventually put ashore at Sanur in good order against no resistance. There, on the beaches "unloading operations were completed" on the afternoon of February 19 by about 1600 hours.[20]

With great determination the same U.S. planes on that sortie later returned to Malang, where they were refueled and rearmed, and departed once more at 1240 hours for their second mission of the day against the Japanese ships at Denpasar. En route they encountered broken cumulus clouds from ten thousand to thirty-five thousand feet. One bomber had to abort its mission due to a cracked cylinder head; it returned safely to Malang at 1510 hours. The other two Americans made their runs at greater altitude this time; they each dropped eight 300 kg bombs from twenty-five thousand to twenty-seven thousand feet. This persistence paid off in wounds inflicted on both *Sagami Maru* and *Sasago Maru*; the former received damage to her engine rooms that left her with only half of her power plant operational and her speed reduced to seven knots, while the latter took a near miss to port that further hampered her unloading. Later that evening both transports finished their unloading operations; the more seriously damaged *Sagami Maru* departed first, escorted by *Michishio* and *Arashio*.

On Bali matters were even less satisfactory for the Allies. By midmorning the airstrip at Denpasar was seized; its six hundred or so local defenders had fled almost immediately at the first notice of Japanese landings. Instead of destroying the field as planned, engineers misinterpreted orders from the Dutch commander and failed to set off demolition charges in time. For some unaccountable reason they thought that he wanted the operation postponed.[21] This appalling confusion—so typical of the East Indies ground campaign across the entire theater—helped give the Japanese the extra time they needed to capture the valuable field intact. Eastern Java, with its many Allied airdromes, was now laid open to Japanese air attacks barely an hour's flight away. Moreover, the enemy's ability to use Denpasar airfield—for the energetic Japanese had, with their usual alacrity, flown planes into Bali to utilize the field on February 20—would prove instrumental in numerous sightings and attacks carried out over the following fortnight against Allied vessels in the Indian Ocean.

· · ·

With no time to spare Cdr. Thomas Binford's destroyers got under way from Surabaja's Holland Pier at 1430 hours on the nineteenth, following the last of that day's air raids. They left via the dredged eastern channel (Oostervaarwater) and after negotiating the Dutch minefields and various sunken vessels joined *Tromp* at the lightship. Then, in Binford's words, they "steamed fast" ESE across the Strait of Madura. The ships rounded the northeastern tip of Java with its spiny trio of capes—Patjenan, Djangkar, and Sedano—with *Tromp* leading, before proceeding down into the narrow Bali Strait at 2100 hours. Their orders were explicit: they *had* to be off "Point A"—at the bottom of the Badoeng Peninsula at Tafel Hoek—just after midnight in order to be in position to begin their offensive sweep. As for the men aboard the U.S. four-pipers, they were "electrified" to learn that they were indeed heading south for Bali, "to attack enemy transports and escorts." As one officer aboard *Stewart* later recalled, "At last it appeared we might have a good chance of getting in some good licks of our own against the Japanese."[22]

During the same day Doorman's force was moving together along the south coast of Java at a brisk, if occasionally ragged, pace. No plan for zigzagging had been distributed by Doorman, nor was any ever transmitted during the day. It was therefore up to the Americans to attempt to conform as best they could to the Dutch ships' changes in course and speed. These flaws in communications gave the destroyer officers an uneasy feeling about Dutch leadership going into battle. One U.S. lieutenant mused to himself that if they received no messages during the approach, it was very unlikely they would get anything more during action.

At sea during the day, like all the other destroyer officers, Welford Blinn of *Pope* was concerned chiefly about the enemy's escorts. Were they cruisers, destroyers, or what precisely? Then he learned that Dutch air reports "indicated that there were four cruisers with the landing force at Bali and [they] were directed to set [their] torpedoes for cruiser depth (which would also take care of heavily laden transports)." This would be another mistake that may have cost the U.S. destroyers better success. Blinn certainly thought so after the war, writing, "Unfortunately our principal torpedo targets would be destroyers and our deep running torpedoes missed under them, probably."[23]

At 1600 hours as they approached Bali, *Ford* and the other ships altered course to 60° T. and increased speed to 25 knots. Two and a half hours later Rear Admiral Doorman's ships moved into their attack formation, which spread the ships out in a column some four miles long. *De Ruyter* and *Java* led the striking force, with one thousand yards between the two cruisers; they were followed at five thousand yards by *Piet Hein*; behind trailed *Ford* and *Pope* at a distance of two thousand yards, the two flushdeckers five hundred yards apart. It was an exceptionally dark night, and although the seas were not heavy, currents in Badoeng Strait—then as now—would prove swift and treacherous. Within another thirty minutes the U.S. destroyers went to general quarters.

As far as communications in action were concerned, Doorman had already informed the Americans that he would not send messages to them regarding changes in course and speed. Thereupon the U.S. commanders decided to maintain contact with their own ships through TBS. *Ford* used "Jocko" as her codename; *Pope* was "Willie"; and ComDesDiv 59—Lt. Cdr. Edward N. "Butch" Parker, in *Ford*—was simply "Nine." Among the Royal Netherlands

Navy striking groups, communications would also prove imperfect. The *Tromp* group, in the second wave, for example, never received any messages from Doorman's first wave or the U.S. ships and was therefore "in the dark" in more ways than one that night.[24]

The first ABDA force soon sighted Tafel Hoek and altered course to swing around the peninsula off the ships' port beam three miles distant. They next turned back to the east, with *De Ruyter* leading and the others conforming to her movements. She and *Java* were some three miles ahead of the four-pipers. At 2215 the American ships were moving "along southeast coast of Bali Island" on a course of about 020° to 025° T. at 25 knots. Just before darkness fell, *Pope* executed the standard precaution of cutting loose her topside gasoline used to fuel the ship's whaleboat.[25] Writing after the war, Blinn said he remembered jettisoning the drums "just about the time [they] entered the south end of the Strait."[26]

Excitement was building up in at least one group of American crews and officers; for many, after some ten weeks of war, this would be their first surface action against the enemy. In the second wave, Lt. (j.g.) Lodwick "Wick" Alford on *Stewart* had scribbled in his journal, "Funny feeling going into battle."[27] For others who had already been in combat, it was not quite the same. Lt. (j.g.) Jack Michel, in the first wave, remembered, "There was not the same tension we all had felt on the eve of our first action. This time it was just an air of expectation."[28] Another sailor has described the men's attitudes as resembling those of firemen; they were trained professionals engaging in a highly dangerous, often mortal business, but they were not necessarily frightened before action.

On the other side of Bali, in the northern approaches to Badoeng Strait, Rear Admiral Kubo was anxious to get his transports—now split into two groups—away from the landings and back out to sea for Makassar, far from the American bombers and "nest of submarines," which had delayed his mission.[29] The bomb-damaged *Sagami Maru* and her two escorts, *Arashio* and *Michishio*, had already started moving slowly up the strait to the north and were then a dozen or more miles ahead. It would be some time later before *Sasago Maru* could get under way, screened by *Ōshio* and *Asashio*.

An hour or so after weighing anchor and steaming off, the men of *Sasago Maru* either realized that they had forgotten several landing craft at Sanur or were "asked" (by the army transport commander) to go *back* and retrieve the eight landing barges that they had neglected to pick up. To correct this "blunder" they had no choice but to comply with the army's request and turned around at 1900 hours; *Ōshio* and *Asashio* returned with *Sasago Maru*. This reversal, which would cost the Japanese more than time in the end, ate up three precious hours.

They arrived back at the landing area at 2000 hours. Within fifteen minutes the transport had started laboriously reloading the barges on what all remembered as "a very dark night." As another Imperial Navy veteran wrote later, "Recovery of small craft made slow progress in complete darkness and without lights."[30] This was almost completed by 2220. While this was happening, the two destroyers resumed their patrols off the anchorage. No sooner had they begun this task than strange ships emerged from the south some six kilometers distant.

As *John D. Ford* had steamed up to Balikpapan against the invasion convoy the previous month, the flushdecker's executive officer and navigator, Lt. Norman Smith, drily observed to a shipmate that "the average life of a destroyer in action is fifteen minutes."[31] For one of the ABDA striking force's destroyers this night Smith's dour assessment would prove accurate, nearly to the minute.

. . .

Up the strait Doorman's first wave steamed at over 20 knots, with all eyes straining for a first glimpse of the enemy. They should have understood that to see and shoot first was to obtain a critical, potentially life-saving, advantage. What the Dutch ships in the van were about to learn in the most unforgiving way possible was that by opening the battle with star shells and searchlight-directed gunfire they would be giving themselves away. And unless they shot exceptionally well and with killing effect, they might soon be on the receiving end of Japanese gunnery and torpedoes. This was, again, contrary to U.S. doctrine and may well have been a chief factor in losses suffered by the Dutch that night.

Separated in their patrol formation by two or three kilometers, Ōshio led *Asashio*; both were slightly northeast of *Sasago Maru*, which lay closer to the shore. Neither destroyer had yet built up any speed; they were each still steaming slowly when at 2223 hours lookouts on *Asashio* "sighted the silhouettes of ships . . . six kilometers to the south." These were quickly identified as "two Java-class cruisers steaming up to the north at high speed."[32] Within seven minutes, when the range had closed to two thousand meters, and before *Asashio* could get enough power up for a chase, one or both of the Dutch cruisers fired star shells, which landed between the destroyer and the shore. The Japanese then launched a red-orange flare, and as it slowly drifted down over the dark waters, the chaotic naval engagement known as the Battle of Badoeng Strait was joined.

*Asashio* (Lt. Cdr. Yoshii Goro, Fiftieth *ki*) swung due east and at 2231 returned fire with her 5-inch battery, passing ahead of the Dutch cruisers as they swept past. *Java* had opened fire with her main battery from 2,200 yards at the same time that the star shells were employed. A fragment from one 5.9-inch salvo—

fired by *Java* evidently—then struck the searchlight of *Asashio*, but she sustained no other damages.[33] Lieutenant Commander Yoshii in *Asashio* and Commander Kikkawa in *Ōshio* would then give ABDA's forces a lesson in tenacity and execution that had few rivals during the Java campaign.

By crossing in front of the Dutch ships, *Ōshio* and *Asashio* had masked much of the enemy's heavier batteries, thereby negating any advantage they might have had, while being able to fire full six-gun salvos themselves. Although Japanese sources do show that the destroyers fired liberally that night, it seems that *Ōshio* was not yet in a position to open fire. Even so, it is highly probably that the hot welcome they offered *De Ruyter* and *Java* disinclined those two ships to prolong the engagement.[34]

This swift, sharp engagement was over in a matter of five minutes or less; *Java* and *De Ruyter*, having fired no more than a dozen salvos, made no attempt to "engage the enemy more closely" and sped on at 27 knots into the night. The crew of *Asashio* could not determine the effects of her gunnery but reported, "We have engaged two Java class in Lombok Strait."[35] Many have written that *De Ruyter* did little or no firing that night as a consequence of focusing her attention (it is said) to the starboard side of the strait. This seems a feeble rationale, and one difficult to accept. However, regardless of whatever firing she may or may not have done, the results were zero. *Java* for her part appears to have expended only nine 5.9-inch salvos from her main battery and in return was struck once amidships on her port side. The trailing American destroyers thought that *Java* had indeed taken on an enemy vessel at short range to port, as indicated by what they perceived to be 40 mm fire from her Bofors battery seen in the distance. In any case *Java*'s damage from the single 5-inch hit, which struck in the aft quarter along the waterline, was inconsequential, and she suffered no reduction in speed. Both cruisers had altered slightly to the northeast in the exchange of gunfire before heading north at high speed. They rounded Bali's northeastern cape marked by volcanic Mount Seraya, then swung up Lombok Strait for the return journey to Surabaja.

*Ōshio* had been caught out of position as the cruisers blew past, but she was now fully alert. Heading to the southeast and gathering speed a few moments later, she was prepared when more enemy warships abruptly appeared in successive waves out of the black night. At 2235 her crew made out a single destroyer to the south trailing a smokescreen, distant about six thousand meters coming her way.[36] This was the solitary *Piet Hein*, moving almost due north. *Ōshio* next turned south to put herself in position to attack this ship. Slightly ahead of her, perhaps two kilometers distant off her starboard bow and following a roughly parallel course, steamed *Asashio*. The Japanese destroyers had made no attempt to pursue the Dutch cruisers but remained on station, alert to emerging threats. The self-discipline and rigorous prewar training of the Japanese crews would soon pay off.[37]

Through their course alterations, *Asashio* was inside *Ōshio* on their loop back to the southeast, which placed her closer to the intruding destroyer. The two ships had evidently been spotted from *Piet Hein* as well, for she had bent to the northeast under pressure from the enemy ships crossing ahead of her. At 2240 hours she enveloped herself again in smoke just as the gunners on *Asashio* opened fire from the pointblank range of 1,500 meters. *Piet Hein* began firing with her 4.7-inch battery and at the same time fired three torpedoes at the transport, which registered no hits. On the bridge of *Ford*, peering through his binoculars, C. E. ("Kelly") Bowen, CSM, also witnessed the twisting *Piet Hein* firing to port against several enemy ships. He told Lt. Cdr. "Butch" Parker that her targets looked like a transport, a destroyer, and a cruiser.[38]

What *is* certain is that the firing at this point on both sides suddenly became quite intense, with both ships firing from short range, and *Asashio* even able to employ her 25 mm machine cannon. Not surprisingly the larger Japanese destroyer—often mistaken by both sides as a cruiser—with its more alert and better trained crew, got the better of the exchange. *Piet Hein* took several hits that (at least momentarily) disabled her. Her survivors reported that one shell had exploded in the aft boiler room, which required her engineering force to shut down one turbine. At this the destroyer quickly lost speed as she swung back to the south. It is believed—and evidence suggests—that the turbine may indeed have been restarted after a few minutes, with the ship resuming way just before a catastrophic detonation took place.

During this exchange *Ōshio* did no firing, as she was then perhaps a kilometer off the disengaged side of *Asashio* and still slightly to the rear. There was no real need for her to intervene, but she would soon speed up and eventually overtake her section mate. The wounded *Piet Hein*'s desperate maneuvers had placed her in an ideal position for a torpedo attack from *Asashio*, and at 2245 hours Lieutenant Commander Yoshii's big destroyer pounced like a leopard on an injured gazelle. *Asashio* fired a spread of 24-inch torpedoes from very short range ,and at 2246 one of these massive weapons detonated against the thin hull of the crippled Dutch destroyer. *Ford* and *Pope*, who were trailing, noted that after some "radical maneuvering" *Piet Hein* had come to the right, then "erupted in a great ball of fire on her port side."[39] *Ford* had closed to within one thousand yards of the Dutch ship and was forced to make a sharp turn in order

SURPRISALS AND TERRIFICATIONS

to keep her in view and to clear her smoke. *Piet Hein* was by then nearly dead in the water, burning amidships and emitting clouds of black funnel and white chemical smoke. Her fighting career had lasted not more than fifteen minutes.

These events were registered by both the other ABDA and Japanese units many miles distant. Well off to the southwest, Commander Binford approaching in *Stewart* "saw flashes over the horizon [and] a deep glow."[40] Simultaneously, nearly twenty-five kilometers to the north, *Michishio* and *Arashio* had received transmissions that their sisters were in action against enemy ships. On orders from Rear Admiral Kubo, they reversed course at 2400 hours, sending the damaged *Sagami Maru* alone on her way north.[41] It would take some time to get back to the fight, but both destroyers did not hesitate in returning.

Off Sanur *Ford* and *Pope* made more changes in speed and direction in order to avoid the blazing Dutch destroyer. At this time the Americans fired their first torpedo salvos. As she cleared *Piet Hein*'s smoke, *Ford* fired three fish to port at what was believed to be a transport; *Pope* unleashed two of her own in the same direction within the next couple of minutes, range estimated to be four thousand yards. However, *Pope*'s next two were expended "to port at a ship believed to be a light cruiser of Yubari class or a large destroyer."[42] Although each tin can had lookouts topside who claimed they saw hits, there were in fact none.

At about this time *Pope* was forced to stop to "prevent running over *Ford* and *Piet Hein* who had slowed radically."[43] It was clear to all that the Dutch ship was doomed, and would have to be left behind. A number of American officers had noted with rather frigid professional detachment the grim results of *Piet Hein*'s simultaneous employment of gunfire and torpedoes; it was seen as a "tactical error" for which the ship paid a heavy price. (At that point *Pope* had fired no main battery rounds at all.) Not quite so dispassionate were the Asiatic Fleet enlisted men topside. They clearly felt moved by the fate that had befallen their fellow tin-can sailors on the Dutch destroyer now enveloped in fire and smoke. They knew how easily it might have been their lot.

Both *Pope* and *Ford* were then wheeling in an arc to the northwest—still finding any chance of forcing the tight passage to be impossible—and doing their best to keep up a speed of 27 knots. It was soon clear that they could not push through the strait, and they looped back to the southeast, under fire, in the direction of Nusa Besar. For the next quarter of an hour, the pair of American four-pipers would be in for the chaotic ride of their lives, and one far more nerve-racking than they had experienced off Balikpapan. Enormous splashes—often mistaken for 8-inch shells—began to erupt on all sides as the two little ships zigzagged south.

*Asashio* and *Ōshio*, now fully engaged, began chasing them on a roughly parallel course not more than two miles away, slightly off their port quarter. The Japanese were pouring out fire in full six-gun salvos that bracketed both American destroyers. Tracers from enemy secondary batteries flew over *Ford* "like a flock of wild geese," according to her gunnery officer, Lt. William Mack Jr.[44] High up in the crow's nest, seventy plus feet above the water, Jack Michel thought *Pope* had been caught "in a cross fire of heavy batteries."[45] Towering waterspouts from salvo straddles collapsed like avalanches on the ship's open control platform, knocking the men stationed there to their knees. Above the wardroom amidships and atop the afterdeckhouse, 4-inch gun crews fought to stay on their feet as the ships drove down the strait. Tense but disciplined, with officers and chiefs exercising great restraint, the men awaited any possible opportunity to bring their guns into action. Still, the swift and violent destruction of *Piet Hein* had shown that self-control was a necessity if the two destroyers were to escape annihilation in the Badoeng Strait buzz saw.

The crews of the Japanese ships required no less self-discipline and composure at that moment. In Cdr. Kikkawa Kiyoshi, skipper of *Ōshio*, they had one of the Imperial Navy's finest destroyer commanders. Although short of stature, Kikkawa was well known for his fighting spirit and "iron nerves," and he lived up to his reputation that night in the strait's narrow waters. Taken by surprise in complete darkness, Kikkawa had nonetheless ordered his destroyer "to flank speed without hesitation," and heading for the enemy, *Ōshio* "made a wide turn in the dark sea, [and] rained shells . . . upon the enemy one after another."[46]

By 2254 hours both IJN destroyers were gaining on the flushdeckers, which were now about three kilometers away and attempting to conceal themselves in a smokescreen generated by *Ford*. The adverse visibility conditions caused multiple sighting errors. *Pope* had fired one torpedo to port a few minutes earlier at what was reported "a heavy ship near land." Although Blinn wrote afterward that "two men stated they saw an explosion followed by fire on this vessel," he admitted, "results not observed on bridge."[47] This firing went unnoticed by the Japanese, and it certainly hit nothing *but* land, if that. Running at high speeds the Japanese thought their shells were "sure hits" on the enemy, but the low silhouette and lithe maneuverability of the Clemson-class ships once again stood them in good stead. *Pope* and *Ford* ducked in and out of the smoke at 27 knots, dodging salvos, and holding their fire to keep from giving themselves away unnecessarily in the pitch darkness.

Those on board *Ōshio* and *Asashio* could not be certain that only two enemy ships were in the smoke; at times they believed they were facing two *pairs* of four-funneled destroyers. (More than a few postwar histories in Japan show four or five Allied destroyers present at this juncture in the engagement.) After seeing the two Allied DDs emerge from their smokescreen again at 2300, both Ōshio and Asashio resumed heavy firing. Dan Mullin on Ford recalled: "Shells were falling on each side. The enemy was on target and Ford and Pope zigzagged to the southeast, with water splashing both sides, but no shells hitting."[48]

It was at this uncomfortable time that the men on Ford noticed a loud banging near their ship's midsection on the disengaged side. To their consternation they found that "a fragment from one of the near misses [had] cut the after falls on the whaleboat hanging from the davits on the midships, starboard side." The motor whaleboat, its after support severed, was dangling stern-first into the water and slamming against the ship's hull. This alone might have damaged Ford's thin and venerable plating, but it was also directly obstructing the number 1 (starboard forward) torpedo mount. In true Asiatic Fleet fashion, an intrepid trio of sailors led by the veteran Chief Torpedo Man Gordon K. Canady clambered out with nothing more than a hatchet and knives and managed "at great risk to life and limb . . . to cut the belly band and the falls to drop the boat from the speeding, wildly maneuvering ship."[49] The MWB tumbled into the strait and quickly disappeared aft, swallowed up in the darkness as the destroyer sped on. Butch Parker remembered: "As the whaleboat had been buffeted with considerable force for some time, and then dropped into the sea while the Ford was making 30 knots, it seemed most likely that the whaleboat was seriously damaged and had promptly sunk."[50] Few of the men gave the boat much thought after that; there were other things on the water to occupy their attention.

By 2300 hours Commander Kikkawa in Ōshio was showing the "cool judgment and indomitable spirit" for which he was known. His big destroyer had reacted beautifully, and running at what must have been very close to her maximum speed (of 35 knots) she had not only overtaken Asashio—which had cut inside her path earlier to engage Piet Hein—but now pulled ahead of the struggling flushdeckers like a thoroughbred racehorse passing an overaged pair of cow ponies. Aboard Ford a seaman second named John Fish was stationed on the open platform above the bridge, observing through the gun director's optical rangefinder. Suddenly he caught a glimpse of something odd in the darkness and haze. "I see something on the starboard bow. . . . It's big—could be an island or a ship," he told gunnery officer Lt. William Mack. The lieutenant relayed the sighting to the bridge, where the captain's talker, J. W. Gelvin, Y1/c, repeated it aloud for all to hear. Navigator Lt. Norman Smith replied sharply, "No island there, Commander."[51] It does not appear to have occurred to the

American destroyermen that one of the Japanese ships could have outrun *and* outmaneuvered them, but this seems to be exactly what transpired. The enemy destroyers had run rings around the U.S. ships as literally as the flushdeckers had around the Japanese at Balikpapan.

*Ford* then alerted *Pope* to this sighting, asking how many torpedoes Blinn's ship had left. *Pope* replied she still had all six starboard fish. Parker told Blinn to hold onto them in case they ran into anything. Within five minutes they did just that. Abruptly, "out of the black, black night" both flushdeckers were suddenly bathed in what Dan Mullin on *Ford* called "the paralyzing, frightful beam of a powerful searchlight."[52] On the bridge of *Pope* Welford Blinn was no less startled: "*Ford* was illuminated and we were partially illuminated by bright searchlight from a large cruiser at a range of 2,500 yards on our starboard bow." One of the signalmen on *Ford*'s bridge gasped, "It's the *De Ruyter!*" For fifteen agonizing seconds both destroyers turned on their recognition lights as the frightened men crouched instinctively—and absurdly—behind the canvas windbreaks atop *Ford*'s open platform above the bridge. Parker and Blinn resorted to this dangerous action since neither skipper had any way of knowing if the imposing vessel now off their starboard bows was a Dutch cruiser or a Japanese destroyer. The big shape answered their fighting lights by unleashing what seemed to be "a well-concentrated 8-inch salvo."[53]

With only the hand of divine providence—or those of fallible Japanese gunners—to protect the U.S. ships, the first batch of shells landed several hundred yards over *Ford*, blocking her from *Pope*'s view—and alarming some of that ship's company—but the next salvo was closer to *Pope*, splashing her with water. Taking the ships in a screaming left turn and with *Ford* making smoke, the DDs fired eight torpedoes to starboard: three by *Ford*, then five more by *Pope*. (*Pope* would have fired all six but suffered a misfire in one tube.) Chief Torpedo Man Canady on *Ford* had swung his maul on three fish, firing them manually, even before he received the order from Cooper and Parker. Given permission to operate in "local control firing" as far as he was concerned, Canady knew he wanted the torpedoes in the water as soon as that searchlight beam illuminated his ship.[54]

It was also high time for the gunners on each four-piper to open up with their main batteries and machine guns. On *Ford*'s galley deckhouse, Dan Mullin and his men "lit up the night with their blinding flashes" firing five rounds of 4-inch as well as controlled bursts from their .50 cal. machine gun at the murderous spotlight. *Pope* "opened fire on the cruiser [*sic*], firing three salvos (seven rounds) which were believed to be hitting."[55] These were spotted by Jack Michel on *Pope*, who noticed the first group of shells "were hitting a bit aft," and he compensated for this by spotting the next salvo "to the right to bring the forward part of the enemy ship under fire."[56] After three excruciating minutes the big searchlight went out.

The two Japanese destroyers were not hit. Indeed by then they felt that they had "caused considerable damage to the enemy."[57] When *Ford* and *Pope* veered off to escape their salvos, *Ōshio* and *Asashio* assumed (incorrectly) that the four-pipers had headed back north. This would have been the logical thing to do . . . had they been Imperial Japanese Navy vessels or *really* determined to get at the transports. However, witnessing the destruction of *Piet Hein*—a much larger ship than either of the flushdeckers—had convinced Parker, Cooper, and Blinn that their only chance was to run through the strait's southern end and then back to Tjilatjap. With not a little wishful thinking involved (believing they'd sunk the transports and damaged at least one enemy cruiser) and clearly unprepared to face any more Japanese "giants" in the confined waters of Badoeng Strait with just 4-inch guns and .50 cal. machine guns, they chose self-preservation.

As *Ford* steamed out of the strait, with her men still wound up from their narrow escape, Butch Parker understood the close call he had just avoided and also the peril he had (inadvertently) put his ship and men in by turning on recognition lights when illuminated by that huge searchlight. It was not a sensation he cared for, nor one that he or any of his men wanted to repeat.[58]

Both U.S. destroyers had turned away from the enemy after firing torpedoes and were then briefly heading northeast in conformity with prebattle plans to exit north through Lombok Strait. This took them toward Nusa Besar (Penida Island) for about four minutes until Parker decided against it. There were just too many enemy units in that direction. He opted instead to return via the same route and messaged Blinn to that effect: "Get in as close to the land as you can. We will run out the south, repeat, south entrance on course one six zero."[59] Replying "Wilco," *Pope* altered to conform; Blinn's action report verified this, stating that they changed to "course 160° T., retiring from action in company with *Ford*."[60]

For *Ford* and *Pope* their active part in the Battle of Badoeng Strait was finished. Adhering to doctrine—and common sense—they had fired a total of only twelve 4-inch rounds at the enemy, but they had expended almost all their torpedoes. Butch Parker had gotten them out alive, it was true. Both ships' crews believed—or, as in matters of faith, one should say "hoped"—they had inflicted serious damage on the enemy. In truth, though, such damage was virtually nonexistent. Worse, their actions had not impaired Japanese operations to capture Bali in the least.

To the north *De Ruyter* and *Java* continued at a good clip through Lombok Strait and reentered the Bali Sea, then steamed westward back to Surabaja. *Piet Hein*, still afloat (partly, or in parts), wallowing in flames and smoke, drifted with the currents somewhere between Semamwang, below Sanur, and Cape Sari on Nusa Besar. Her surviving crew had been separated by the fires and destruction amidships from the tremendous explosion caused by *Asashio*'s killing torpedo hit. Those men in the aft part of the Dutch destroyer were cut off from their officers and the bridge by these fires; believing the situation to be hopeless, they soon decided to abandon ship. For some thirty-odd sailors of *Piet Hein* this would prove a most "fortuitous" choice in the end.[61]

· · ·

The battle was not over, however, but merely entering its next phase. From Surabaja via Bali Strait the second wave of light cruiser *Tromp* (Capt. J. B. de Meester) with Commander Binford's four destroyers—*Stewart, Parrott, John D. Edwards,* and *Pillsbury*—began their approach according to plan. At midnight *Tromp* dropped back and took up her position three thousand yards astern of the destroyers, where it was felt she could be more effective with her heavier 5.9-inch main battery once the four-pipers had delivered their torpedoes. Fifteen minutes later the American ships went to general quarters. After another half hour they rounded Tafel Hoek, heading due east at 25 knots. At 0110 the ABDA force turned up into the strait, altering course to 20° T. and increasing speed to 27 knots. Visibility meanwhile remained poor in the inky night.

Binford and his men could see gun flashes in the distance and hear the reports of salvos. They had earlier seen—across the low-lying areas of Tafel Hoek—flickering searchlight beams and "flashes over the horizon." Obviously there was some kind of action ahead, presumably "hot combat," as an officer on *Stewart* wrote afterward.[62] At 0102 hours *Stewart*'s XO, Lt. Clare B. Smiley, took the conn. Within ten minutes his destroyer and the others altered course to the northeast.

Binford's ships than began picking up several jumbled TBS conversations. Binford could make out "Butch" Parker's voice, and what he could understand was contrary to their original plans. "Something about returning to the south," he later remembered.[63] This was the plain-language information Parker had sent out hoping to warn Binford and De Meester that his ships were exiting on an opposite course and to avoid any collisions or friendly fire accidents.[64] It also explained why Parker chose to steer as close as possible to the far side of the strait, away from Bali—not only for concealment but to reduce the possibility of such potential errors.

The firing that Binford and his ships heard and saw would, by all indications, have been coming from the two obstreperous Japanese destroyers *Ōshio* and *Asashio*. After circling *Ford* and *Pope* the IJN units had turned back to the north and rejoined in column at 2312. This maneuver would take them back in the direction of *Sasago Maru*, which they may have assumed was the destination of the American ships as well. What resulted was a source of even greater confusion to researchers and historians and has not been correctly understood for over seven decades.

Within three minutes the speeding Japanese destroyers saw what they thought was another pair of enemy ships steaming along in the same direction—to the north, that is—at a distance of about 3,500 meters. To the men of these two enemy DDS *Ōshio* and *Asashio*, what they saw appeared to be moving as if to cross their bows from right to left. At 2316 intense "saturation firing" was opened on the "enemy ships" and continued off and on for another twelve minutes while the two Japanese destroyers executed a lengthy, flattened figure-eight maneuver.[65] One of the enemy ships immediately burst into flames—within a minute—and seemed to sink. Then "a fire also broke out on the [other] DD." *Ōshio* and *Asashio* continued to fire on this second, burning ship as they made their course changes from north to south and back again. The burning ship was thought to have sunk by 2340 hours. But as we now know, no Allied units were then in that stretch of Badoeng Strait.

What *Ōshio* and *Asashio* were so aggressively attacking may have been remaining sections of *Piet Hein*, which had stayed afloat after being split apart by the Type 93's massive one-thousand-pound warhead fired some thirty minutes before. Indeed, this is precisely what Japanese track charts indicate. Such an effect would be consistent with damages suffered by other small(ish) vessels—such as the Dutch tin can *Kortenaer* or the Japanese minesweeper *W-2*—that were hit by these fearsome weapons during the Java campaign.

When the second supposed destroyer (or other half of *Piet Hein*) sank at 2340 hours, *Ōshio* and *Asashio* reversed course once more. Together they proceeded northward and arrived off Sanur at 0010. They took up their protective stations again, moving slowly athwart the center of Badoeng Strait from east to west. They would continue these patrols for the next ninety minutes or so.

This was occurring at approximately the same time that Rear Admiral Kubo had messaged the second section of DesDiv 8—*Michishio* and *Arashio*—to detach itself from *Sagami Maru* and head for Lombok Strait again. Accordingly the two ships had done so by 0015 hours; it would take them exactly two hours to reach the area of battle and undergo their long-awaited baptism of fire. However, aboard one of the Japanese destroyers, its excited crew would find their initiation a more blood-drenched ordeal than ever anticipated.

. . .

Simultaneously, through the black night came Binford's 1,200-tonners, steaming at 27 knots—with *Tromp* bringing up the rear—and, again, every eye alert to the enemy's presence. At approximately 0134 hours the Americans spotted what they suspected were the silhouettes of two ships, visible only as two slightly darker smudges against the background of the Bali coastline. They were distant perhaps five kilometers or less. Only rarely in the Java campaign were Asiatic Fleet vessels lucky enough to spot their adversaries first at night. Perhaps the crew of the Japanese destroyers were distracted or fatigued after their earlier exchanges; probably the low profile of the smaller Clemson-class ships concealed them once more. This Allied advantage was short-lived, though, and not fully exploited.

With this unknown pair of ships well ahead on his port bow, Binford altered course away to 30 degrees—this may have given his torpedo men a better angle—as his gunners examined the suspicious shapes. The portly, sunburned Mississippian—described as resembling "an apple on two toothpicks"—was on the bridge dressed in the standard Asiatic attire of the period: a pair of white shorts, a white short-sleeved shirt, and his white officer's cap.[66] Three feet away from Binford was his navigator and xo, Lt. Clare B Smiley, who stood shoulder-to-shoulder with the helmsman. Lt. Cdr. H. Page Smith, the "calm and cool" skipper of *Stewart*, was positioned just behind the sailor at the wheel, William E. Kale, sm2/c. Later, in the darkness, chaos, and noise of battle, it would be the light tapping of Smith's fingers on Kale's shoulders—right for starboard rudder, left for port—that directed the ship's course.

*Stewart's* men were preparing to fire torpedoes but could not yet discern any targets. In near-total darkness, running at high speed in a narrow waterway, the tension aboard all these warships—American as well as Dutch and Japanese— was almost unbearable. Events were unfolding with sobering rapidity; it was only with extreme difficulty that Binford refrained from having Lieutenant Commander Smith order his men to turn on the searchlight.

Underneath the men on *Stewart's* bridge, in the destroyer's small radio room, the lone sailor on duty, Marion "Elly" Ellsworth, s1/c, felt figuratively and literally "in the dark." Locked in by himself, sealed off from the sights but not the sounds of action, he had already made the disagreeable journey down into the loud, sweltering engine rooms to get water for the acid-lead batteries that powered his radio equipment. Back at his station, only the thin steel bulkhead of the angled bridge structure separated him from foc's'le and its number 1 4-inch gun. (Ellsworth often doubled as number 3 loader on the gun crew of the ship's forward gun.)[67] But on this night the radioman striker had been shut away in the radio shack. There he could see nothing at all of the action yet still feel the rough-riding little ship twisting and turning at high speed as he listened with some apprehension to the confusing noises of combat while working to monitor the radio traffic. He received and transmitted numerous messages regarding course alterations, speed changes, sightings, and groundings, all blurring together in the course of what he would recall as "*Stewart*'s wild ride."[68]

Standing out in the open at his position atop the bridge, Lt. (j.g.) "Wick" Alford, *Stewart*'s gunnery officer, looked through his 7 x 50 binoculars at the silhouettes, thinking to himself, "This is the enemy and it is now or never." He was absolutely right. At that moment Alford was also getting a better look at the two ships than his men on the fire-control director. It wasn't pointing in quite the same direction as his binoculars, he noticed. Over the headphones he asked the trainer on the director, Eugene Stanley, s2/c, if he could see the enemy: "Are you on the target? Do you see the ships?" Stanley replied: "No, I do not." Alford tried to help Stanley bring the director to bear on the target, saying, "Come right, come right!" As he did so, the Americans' brief element of surprise evaporated.[69]

Off their port bow Binford and the others on the "*Stewie Maru*" suddenly saw a flashing light wink in the blackness—undoubtedly a signal light. He asked a signalman on the bridge if he recognized it. The sailor responded that he thought it was sending Japanese code. Binford got on the TBS to inform the others, but as the range closed, the excited bridge signalman blurted out: "Commander, those are Jap ships and more than one!" Binford's decision was made for him, and the orders were given: "Fire one spread when ready!" A moment later, at 0136 hours, six torpedoes jumped into the water from the portside battery of *Stewart*. Six more shot out from mounts number 2 and 4 on *Parrot* at 01361/2, while *Pillsbury* launched three.[70] (The fourth flushdecker, *John D. Edwards*, did not launch torpedoes at this time and would experience problems a few minutes later when she attempted to do so.)

Not more than two minutes had elapsed since the first dark shapes off the Balinese shore were noticed by lookouts on *Stewart*. These lights also solved the difficulty that director trainer Stanley had been having. He instantly yelled out, "On target!" as the signal lights in the distance gave him the aiming point he needed.

On *Stewart* her torpedo officer for the port battery, Lt. Archibald Stone, clicked his stopwatch as the fish slid out of their tubes toward the enemy; it was expected, or hoped, that explosions would result within the allotted time. The destroyer's men topside seemed to hold their collective breath as the seconds ticked off in anticipation of hits. But nothing of the sort resulted; to their dismay all fifteen torpedoes had missed their targets. Although there were many "loud oaths and groans of disappointment," according to Wick Alford, the men had no time for protracted grumbling.[71] Binford realized that he would have to illuminate the enemy ships, which were by then almost abeam of his destroyers.

The stout commodore gamely clambered up to Alford's position by the fire-control director atop *Stewart*'s bridge structure. He wanted to make certain for himself that everyone was prepared for the hell that was about to break loose. Then their positions would be revealed by their own searchlights and gun flashes. Alford quickly reassured him, as he had Lieutenant Commander Smith that his gun captains—Charles Gilchrist, James Lindly, and Pershing Sales—and their associated gun crews were on target and prepared. It was critical that the searchlight's use be followed as swiftly as possible by gunfire. Hitting first and hitting hard in naval combat—especially at night—was often the difference between survival and destruction.

At 0143 hours Binford gave the order, "Commence firing!" With that *Stewart* opened the shutters on her searchlight, and her eager 4-inch gun crews opened fire with a full three-gun salvo. *Parrott*, next in line, followed her example. This operation went according to plan, but seeing what they had captured with their searchlight beam took many of the men aback. There loomed the sinister forms of not one but two large vessels, thought to be cruiser-sized—and infuriated ones at that. Within moments the Japanese ships snapped open their shutters to counter-illuminate these intruders. After registering on each other, as if to make certain of no accidents, the enemy searchlight beam swung out over the black water and lit squarely on the little American ships now barking at them.[72] To the men on the American ships it seemed they were staring *up* at the super-structures of the enemy vessels even at that distance, so large were their adversaries. From 3,200 meters range—with the searchlights of Binford's division providing excellent aiming points—*Ōshio* and *Asashio* opened fire, as they discharged more torpedoes. At such a range the Japanese ships' practiced 5-inch batteries should have been on target, and so they were. The startled American destroyer column broke up almost immediately.

*Pillsbury*, under "Froggy" Pound, veered out of line to the right firing torpedoes and guns as she sought to escape the searchlight beam. This led to a near-collision with *Parrott*. Emergency backing bells went off in *Pillsbury* as she maneuvered wildly trying to get out of the enemy's illumination. At the same time she made smoke and fired another series of rounds from her main battery. Meanwhile *John D. Edwards* attempted to launch a spread of six torpedoes but succeeded in getting only four into the water, for two of the old Mark 8 fish jammed in their tubes.

*Pillsbury* would not rejoin the formation until the end of the action, having suffered a series of mechanical failures, but she was far from being out of the fight. Her revolutions indicator went out with one of her first salvos; it stayed out for the next ninety minutes. This made it impossible to determine her speed accurately. Her engine room lights and gyro repeater light were knocked out by gunfire concussion—they, however, came back on shortly and resumed proper function. But her TBS receiver was also damaged early in the engagement and did not work properly thereafter. All the same her separation would prove a fortunate accident—one of few for the ABDA forces that night—as the fighting continued.

*Stewart* and *Parrott* were both firing their 4-inch/50 cal. batteries for all they were worth as they tried to dodge enemy salvos. At these gunfight ranges—as low as two thousand yards—in which the ships were now engaging, the factor of sheer blind luck came into play. Chasing salvos at that distance was a complete impossibility; the U.S. ships could only rely on their low profiles and nimbleness to elude destruction. For "Elly" Ellsworth in the radio shack on *Stewart*, it was a cacophony of sounds, with the loud noises of "blowers and engines going full blast." He recalled, "[I] did not know if noise was from our guns or from shells and shrapnel bouncing around the ship [and] also the twists and turns of the ship made you wonder what was going on."[73] Yet to have been topside, where men had a better idea of the action, would have been far less safe.

By then the American ships were heading roughly northeast, their column broken, with the two Japanese destroyers swinging in behind them steaming from west to east across the strait. *Tromp* was a couple of kilometers to the rear at this stage but closing fast. One of her officers later said he could see the American destroyers ahead, illuminating the night with their gunfire, but paradoxically claimed the Dutch had received no reports on what was happening.[74] Her gunners were also expecting action to starboard and thus had her 5.9-inch main battery trained in what would prove the wrong direction as the fighting unfolded. The aggressive reaction of the enemy ships pushed the ABDA groups away from Sanur and the transports' anchorage, and in so doing deflected the Allies' offensive thrust within the first fifteen minutes of action. Although more fighting and more damage—along with many more casualties—would follow, the purpose of the ABDA attack that night in Badoeng Strait was decided before *Tromp* ever opened fire. From the outset Binford, Smith, Pound, Eccles, and Hughes realized that only the hand of fate—or Almighty God, in the eyes of some—hung over their ships that night to keep them from destruction.

One of the first 5-inch projectiles fired by *Asashio* or *Ōshio* either hit short in the water or caromed before bursting in the air forward of *Stewart*. This sprayed shell fragments throughout the front of *Stewart*'s upper portside superstructure, "banging all around the bridge," as one sailor wrote soon afterward. A shard entered the pilot house cutting through the shield on the port wing of the bridge. Inside that small enclosure the ship's XO and navigator, Lieutenant Smiley, was helping conn the ship. The fragment ricocheted around the bridge where it sliced through the electrical wiring to the standard compass and bent a stanchion before striking him in the right shin. Bill Kale, the helmsman, heard Smiley exclaim, "One of those sons of bitches got me in the leg!"[75] Standing nearby, Commander Binford noticed that his XO did not fall instantly. Although bleeding seriously, Smiley continued to perform his duties.[76] When Lieutenant Commander Smith realized the severity of Smiley's wound, though, he sent him below, ignoring his objections. Reluctantly, the exec left the bridge, aided by Donald McClune, CPhM, and another sailor.

Before McClune could finish seeing to Smiley's wound, the ship had registered another casualty. Several fragments from the same burst or one immediately thereafter showered the director platform above the bridge, striking the director trainer. Hit in the head and through his pea coat in midchest, young Eugene Stanley was killed outright. Alford reported to the officers that his director trainer was down, and McClune was sent up. After the pharmacists mate examined the fallen seaman, noting a piece of shrapnel embedded in his skull and the large, fatal wound to his lungs and heart, a stretcher team went up to remove the body. Stanley's place was promptly taken by the chief fire-control man, Fred Allison, and the destroyer's gunners continued to get off their salvos.[77]

At roughly 0147 *Stewart* was again straddled, blasted with numerous fragments, and struck squarely by enemy shells. The hits did not register with great violence, but Lieutenant (j.g.) Alford at his post, Commander Binford, Lieutenant Commander Smith, and Bill Kale on the bridge were all certainly aware of them. The most serious was a direct hit three feet above the waterline on the port side aft, which nicked an exhaust steam line that helped power the steering engine. This particular shell appears to have exploded in a low-order detonation; it entered the thin hull just underneath the port propeller guard, making a sizable entrance hole, and a handful of fist-sized fragments exited the opposite side. Damage within the compartment was not excessive, though, and there were no personnel casualties. Another shell struck the port whaleboat in its davits and blew it in half, leaving the deck covered with sawdust and debris; to Alford the dangling boat "looked like a fish that had been bitten in two by a shark."[78] The steering engine room and aft living quarters for the crew were filled with so much steam from the punctured steam line that they could not be entered. As one sailor recalled, the steering engine room was "steaming like a damn boiler."[79] Yet, miraculously, the destroyer's steering engine continued to function despite the loss in steam pressure and the ingress of seawater.

Within a few more minutes as the Japanese ships pulled away aft, and his own guns could no longer bear on them, Alford had his men check fire. *Stewart* had expended half her torpedoes and something less than forty shells in the first short, sharp exchange. A lull then occurred, lasting not more than ten or twelve minutes but sufficient to give the men on *Stewart* a chance to look to their damages. During this break Alford called up to his foretop spotter, Ens. John T. Brinkley, positioned in the crow's nest on the mainmast over seventy feet above the water. Brinkley in spot 1 was safe and sound, having done a good job at his post thus far. But it was not his imagination that led Alford to believe he detected a slight quaver in the young ensign's voice over the phones: even at that height Brinkley's small compartment—not much larger than barrel—had already been struck multiple times by shell fragments. While the Japanese destroyers' direct hit on *Stewart* should have wrecked her steering, it had not; yet a self-inflicted injury on *Parrott* would indeed cause her to lose steering a few minutes later, with what might have been dire consequences.

As the American ships proceeded up the waterway at 28 knots on course 65° T.—although with *Pillsbury* well separated from the others by then—a few cursory damage control measures were taken. Page Smith of *Stewart* sent Lt. Francis Clark aft to determine the nature and extent of her wounds. These were accurately assessed by Clark, and the ship continued to maintain station with *Parrott* and *John D. Edwards*. At 0157 the ships altered course to 75° T., and at 0201 the remnants of *Stewart*'s bisected whaleboat were cut away. This relatively quiet interlude came to an end when they noticed *Tromp* astern running a bright blue recognition light—much too bright as soon became apparent.

The Dutch warship was steaming northwest of Lembongan Island at very nearly maximum speed—as much as 31 knots—when her gleaming blue light alerted *Asashio* and *Ōshio* to her presence. They spotted the cruiser about 3,200 meters off their port bow, moving in the same northeast direction as they were headed. Once more the Japanese hit first, and they hit decisively. At 0211 hours *Asashio* and *Ōshio* opened searchlight-directed gunfire with their 5-inch batteries, followed by a brace of torpedoes. These initial salvos wrecked *Tromp's* bridge area fire-control systems outright. Binford, several thousand yards ahead in *Stewart*, could see *Tromp* "getting clobbered."[80] The captain of *Pillsbury*, which had fallen behind, thought that the Japanese destroyers and Royal Netherlands Navy cruiser were fighting it out "practically astern" of her.[81]

From that point on this well-designed and modern Dutch vessel—said by warship expert H. T. Lenton to be "without doubt the finest example of flotilla cruiser of optimum size to be built"—was in for the fight of her life.[82] Over the next five minutes Japanese shells struck her upperworks eleven times. These hits killed two officers—Lieutenant First Class Van Eck and Sub-Lieutenant Kriesfeld—along with eight ratings and wounded another thirty men. It did not take long for *Tromp* to switch to local control for her 5.9-inch battery and 40 mm Bofors AA weapons, and when she did return the enemy's salvos, her designers were vindicated. For a few blazing moments *Tromp* lived up to her famous name, as "she put up an absolute wall of fire."[83] The cruiser poured out several dozen rounds from her main battery and many hundreds more from her Bofors guns at her two attackers. At the same time her captain managed with several sharp turns to avoid the destroyers' potentially lethal torpedo spread. Unwisely, though, *Tromp* had compounded her predicament by switching on a large searchlight early in the action, thereby giving the enemy gunners another aiming point. This error seems to have cost more lives and further damage before the light was either shot out or switched off.

A gunner on *Tromp* named Johann Teppes later recalled that by firing in local control her men "did the best they could . . . and because of the close, short range took many bites out of the enemy."[84] This was a perfectly fair assessment; *Ōshio* paid for her combativeness at about 0216 hours, when a shell from *Tromp* tore into Captain Abe's flagship. This 5.9-inch projectile struck in the "number two turret powder supply room" located beneath the mainmast, killing seven men, and very nearly destroyed the ship. Commander Kikkawa's intrepid destroyer was able to continue in action, later resuming her post in the strait, but the damage was serious enough. *Ōshio* was probably lucky not to have suffered a catastrophic detonation in her magazines.[85] Within a few minutes the gunnery exchange abruptly ceased; *Asashio* and *Ōshio* swung away to the east. They decided that "the enemy ship was considered to have been seriously damaged," and it was time to return again to *Sasago Maru*.[86]

At that moment the second section of DesDiv 8, *Michishio* and *Arashio*, finally reached the scene. They had steamed down the strait pall-mall, observing "flashes of an artillery duel" in the distance as they approached. The crew of *Michishio* could see flashes off their port bow as *Ōshio* exchanged salvos with *Tromp*, and it was from that quarter that they expected action. Most of her men still felt that they were several minutes away from action, but in fact these two destroyers were about to stumble headlong into the battle. Yet through no fault of their own the crew of one Japanese ship was going to pay a heavy price for arriving at the wrong place at the wrong time.

Unseen, Binford's column—or what remained of it, with *Stewart*, *Parrott*, and *John D. Edwards*—had moved up the strait on the opposite side in the dark shadows of Bali to within five thousand meters of the Japanese pair. *Parrott* then noticed a flashing light forward on the starboard beam. At about 0207, a lookout on the lead destroyer, *Michishio*, sang out, "Starboard, white waves!" They suddenly (though not quickly enough) spotted the flushdeckers some 40 degrees to starboard, all moving at high speed with the narrow stems of the flushdeckers throwing up huge bow waves. Quickly the order came to illuminate. In the searchlight beams the Japanese could see "two U.S. destroyers with four smoke stacks . . . sailing north."[87]

Watanabe Daiji, the young rangefinder operator on *Michishio*, was one of the first men to see these vessels. His immediate reaction was a common one by Japanese sailors and airmen in the East Indies naval campaign; mistaking them for *Marblehead*-type ships because of their four funnels, he thought to himself, "An enemy cruiser!" More accurately, though, Watanabe noticed in this instant of illumination that the American ships' hulls were a very light color, to his eyes a shade closer to white than gray. Without hesitating further he called out, "47, 47!" indicating a range of 4,700 meters. The Japanese destroyer went into a hard right turn at high speed as she prepared to launch torpedoes. This evasive reaction caused *Michishio* to list so much that her main battery could not bear; her lighter weapons could and did open fire. Although noticed by the U.S. ships, her automatic guns were ineffective.

At the same time, though, shells from *Arashio* landed well ahead of and over *Stewart*. Binford's flushdecker altered to 85 degrees and found the enemy ships off to starboard passing them on an opposite course. In a matter of minutes he fired six torpedoes from the starboard tubes. At about the same time, *Parrott* also loosed a half dozen of her torpedoes to starboard. The Japanese clearly saw these firings and altered course to elude them. This predictably threw off their gunnery somewhat; their salvos were landing in the vicinity of *Stewart* but not too close—unlike the opening exchanges earlier with *Asashio* and *Ōshio*, when Lt. Cdr. J. N. Hughes of *Parrott* wrote: "The enemy fire control was amazingly accurate."[88]

In the ensuing minutes the three American ships switched on their searchlights and poured out fire from their main and secondary batteries. With the range now down to 3,500 meters (3,850 yards) numerous 4-inch and 3-inch shells flew through the night at the Japanese duo, along with hundreds of .50 cal. machine-gun rounds until "the sky became scarlet from fires, explosions, and shells."[89] They found the lead target, *Michishio*, most often, and on her they wrought the most severe damage, much of which was captured in graphic detail later by Watanabe Daiji.

First, an early salvo from *Stewart* and company ate into one of the engine rooms of *Michishio*; she suffered three hits there. These killed or severely burned most of the destroyer's engineering force, bringing the ship to a halt. Clouds of smoke and steam billowed upward in the night; on *Stewart*, Lieutenant (j.g.) Alford could see that "the left-hand ship"—which would have been *Michishio*—throwing off "great columns of smoke . . . so [they] knew great damage was done."[90] She soon lost way, and then her electrical power went out. While lacking power, and with her remaining guns being served by hand against her antagonists to starboard, out of the darkness another U.S. ship suddenly materialized, trapping *Michishio* in a killing crossfire.

This was "Froggy" Pound's solitary *Pillsbury*, which had arrived unseen from the opposite quarter. At about 0215 hours, from the point-blank distance of 1,600 meters, *Pillsbury* opened fire and pumped out dozens of 4-inch shells and hundreds of .50 cal. machine-gun rounds at the luckless Japanese ship. The first shell to hit struck *Michishio* on the port bow, but the next three did murderous work. To the Americans it looked like one long series of orange explosions along her upperworks. On *Stewart* Binford peered out to starboard and said he saw "great flames" on the ravaged enemy ship. *Michishio* had been raked from bridge to fantail; entire AA crews were wiped out topside by these hits and associated "induced" explosions. Next she lost steering due to rudder damage. On her bridge a 4-inch shell from *Pillsbury* removed the legs of the chief searchlight operator, Chief Petty Officer Masano Yutaro, before penetrating the bulkhead of the forward radio room, killing more sailors and injuring the ship's skipper, Lt. Cdr. Ogura Masami.

No sooner had Watanabe been sent below from his post to more fully assess damage than he found flames curling around a torpedo in its tube. The terrified young sailor expected the ship to be destroyed at any moment, but when a very courageous, and unnamed, IJN petty officer single-handedly began fighting the fire, Watanabe (who believed he would be killed anyway) "without hesitation" jumped in to help extinguish the blaze. After that "crisis" he made his way back up to the bridge, where he glimpsed the legless body of Chief Petty Officer Masano.[91]

Below, the main deck was strewn with bodies of the dead and injured as the ship settled deeper in the water from her damage. Her ninety-six casualties included thirteen men killed—including her chief engineer—and eighty-three wounded.[92] Communication between the aft and the forward sections of the ship had been lost. Before the night was over, *Michishio* would be flooded almost to main deck level, with water lapping her gunwales from amidships aft to the stern. It was feared the ship's keel might have been severed or damaged to such an extent that the vessel could split in half. Watanabe also saw corpses floating in the sea, though whether these were of the enemy or his own shipmates he could not say with certainty.[93]

As the Japanese destroyer's crew fought to save their ship and themselves, the Americans were undergoing ordeals of their own. None were more dramatic than *Parrott*'s. Lt. Cdr. J. N. Hughes's destroyer had just completed firing five of her six starboard torpedoes at 0219 hours—one tube had a misfire, and her chief torpedo man smacked his maul on the wrong breech in the confusion and darkness—when her rudder jammed. This happened just as an enemy searchlight beam revealed a large rock directly ahead. Hughes called for an emergency back-down, but too late. With the ship's gunners firing wildly to protect themselves, the destroyer slammed into the shoals, briefly grounding herself. The impact was such that men were knocked off their feet as 4-inch projectiles rolled across slippery decks. Chief Walter Padgett, a member of the forward repair party who was doubling as an ammunition handler, lost his balance, with a shell cradled in his arms. Thrown through the starboard lifeline, Padgett went "ass over tea-kettle" into the waters of Badoeng Strait. Cries of "Man overboard!" were disregarded; at that moment the ship had more pressing concerns.[94]

Caught in the enemy spotlight, salvos were landing close enough to douse *Parrott*'s men topside with water. Meanwhile her engineers and electricians worked to shift steering control. Her gunners continued to fire in defense of their now-motionless ship; even the 3-inch "peashooter" on her fantail blasted away, deafening the men working in the steering compartment just below. This changeover to after steering took several agonizing moments, with the scene still "bright as day" in the enemy's searchlights.[95] Then, with a shudder and a lurch, as the ships' screws churned up the shallows astern, the ship backed off from her "soft grounding" and broke free. At the same time, inexplicably, the

Japanese ceased firing. Lieutenant Commander Hughes later stated that he considered this a clear manifestation of the grace of God and nothing less. The skipper ordered his engineers to give him every possible amount of power, and *Parrott*'s engines reacted as they had for many years: like a quarter horse, the old destroyer soon leapt to full speed as she resumed her course up the strait, having by then fallen a fair distance behind *Stewart* and *Edwards*.

Machinist Mate John Chupak on *Parrott* emerged from the "oil stinking, shuddering hollow drum" that was the destroyer's aft steering compartment, where he had helped make the mechanical adjustments necessary to switch to aft steering. He was covered in grime, blood, and vomit, for he had been stunned by the 3-inch gun firing in close proximity to his head as went below—which had the effect of a punch in the face that left him bleeding from his nose and ears—while the nauseating stench of fuel oil in combination with the brain-shaking vibrations of the claustrophobic compartment had made him violently sick to his stomach. Addled and filthy, Chupak climbed out onto the main deck just as the ship lurched from its brief grounding and away from the enemy searchlight. At that moment a Japanese near miss sent a pillar of water arching over the ship that doused Chupak, helping him regain his senses. For a fleeting moment the gritty machinist had a ringside seat at the climax of the action. In the distance to his right, he could see *Pillsbury* "silhouetted in its own gun-flashes" as she fired on *Michishio*—the enemy ship described by the machinist as "on fire from stem to stern . . . and dead in the water"—while aft of these he saw "another fire-fight," which would have been *Tromp* and her two adversaries. Chupak did not know the individual identities of these vessels at that moment, but his eyewitness account jibes perfectly with events. The steadfast machinist mate's memory at arguably the climactic moment of the complex and confused Battle of Badoeng Strait is one of U.S. naval history's more remarkable visual snapshots.[96]

Binford's destroyers soon checked fire and strove to gain more speed. Both groups, Allied and Japanese, were now moving in different directions, bloodied and battered. And at that point the ABDA forces were intent on one thing only: to get clear of the Japanese hornet's nest they had stirred up and back to the relative security of Surabaja. The captain of *Stewart* had asked his acting chief engineer, Chief Machinist Mate Paul Seifert—standing in for engineering officer Lt. Francis Clark, who was topside on a torpedo mount—for all he could get from the old destroyer's engines earlier that night. Seifert and his black gang had seen that the boilers, turbines, and pumps responded heroically. Although Binford went through the formality of asking Wick Alford's and others' opinion about returning to look for more enemy transports, it was evident that he and Lt. Cdr. H. Page Smith knew that without any torpedoes it was high time to retire to Surabaja.

The ships swung to the north at 28 knots, then veered west at 0317 hours, securing from general quarters. Rounding Bali again, they made for Madura and on to Surabaja. "Froggy" Pound and *Pillsbury* rejoined before daybreak, with that tin can's various mechanical failures having made no impact on the efficacy of her gunnery or the crew's fighting spirit. Her luck had been fantastic that night, but more, and greater, darkness was fated for this rugged old four-piper and her crew.

At daybreak—around 0525 hours—a lookout on *Stewart* watching astern saw a dark shape three or four miles off the starboard quarter in the half-light. He reported to the bridge: "Something [is] following us." The exhausted Binford, who had not slept in two days, thought to himself, "Jap? A cruiser to wipe us out?"[97] Thankfully, it turned out to be the battered *Tromp*—still capable of high-speed steaming—moving up on the flushdeckers. And a mile or so behind *Tromp* was another ship. This was Lieutenant Hughes and crew in *Parrott* attempting to rejoin after their steering mishap. All five vessels soon closed up, and the destroyers maneuvered to assume screening positions as the ships steamed west to Java. The men on the four-pipers could clearly see the grievous wounds suffered by the intrepid Dutch cruiser. *Stewart*'s helmsman, Bill Kale noted "three huge holes in her starboard side and shrapnel holes all over [the cruiser]." In the admiring eyes of the U.S. helmsman, *Tromp* remained a "mighty fine fighting ship."[98]

In the early morning sunlight weary sailors on the American ships released from watch or off duty looked to their damage. Above waterline the condition of *Stewart* was a sobering sight. Sailors and officers found her entire upper deck littered with fist-sized fragments from Japanese shells; number 3 stack had at least two fat holes in it. "Elly" Ellsworth came out of the little radio shack he had been cooped up in during the battle and looking aft "observ[ed] the hole and the steam escaping from the stern." One of *Stewart*'s torpedo tubes had a deep gouge several inches long in it; a blower in the starboard passageway had received additional "ventilation" courtesy of Japanese fragment. In the hard-hit aft steering compartment, a wooden hand-steering wheel had been torn "into splinters" by the 5-inch shell that deranged that area. On the morning of the twentieth, though, there was still too much steam and heat in the steering compartment, as well as in the adjoining crew's quarters, to make a closer examination until the ship could dock and her engines and boilers shut down.[99]

Binford was himself speckled with powder marks on every exposed inch of skin and all over his whites, as if he had been standing beneath an oversized pepper shaker. Lt. (j.g.) Wick Alford likewise had reddish spots on his face and hands from powder particles. When a shipmate teased him, saying said he should receive the Purple Heart for these "wounds," the good-natured Alford declined, but he did wonder aloud how he had made it through in one piece. Ensign Brinkley's crow's nest high on the foremast had suffered four shrapnel holes. The shaken spotting officer told his shipmates that he had survived through sheer luck; he just happened to have been squatting down in the steel barrel's confines when the fragments struck it. Had he been standing upright, it might have been a different story.

As for the Japanese ships involved, the badly shot-up *Michishio* was later found by *Arashio*, which began to tow her back to Makassar, with support from Rear Admiral Kubo's light cruiser *Nagara* and her three destroyers. The best speed possible was only eight knots. Proceeding individually in some cases, the Japanese ships eventually reached Makassar between the early morning of February 21 (*Sasago* and *Sagami Maru*) and February 22 (*Nagara*, *Asashio*, damaged *Ōshio*, and *Arashio* towing *Michishio*). It had been a costly operation in terms of injuries to their vessels, but the mission was completed successfully. Japanese air units were flying out of Denpasar airfield soon thereafter to help seal the fate of Java.[100]

In terms of combat effectiveness, the performance of *Asashio* at Badoeng Strait remains one of the most impressive, if lesser-known, achievements in the southwest Pacific during the first year of war. She was fought with superb coolness, precision, and tenacity by her skipper and crew that night. Indeed, it may fairly be said that *Asashio* singlehandedly controlled much of the battle's critical first phase. The ABDA naval forces had nothing to match it, really, yet they wanted so desperately to believe they had been victorious that they acted as if they had routed the enemy.

Anxious to redeem its reputation after the setbacks at Pearl Harbor and the ongoing Philippines catastrophe, the U.S. Navy was liberal in awarding medals for the Badoeng Strait action. Commanders Thomas Binford and Henry E. Eccles, Lieutenant Commanders Edward "Butch" Parker, Jacob "Jocko" Cooper, H. Page Smith, "Froggy" Pound, and Lieutenant John Hughes all received the Navy Cross; "Willie" Blinn of *Pope* got a Gold Star in lieu of a second Navy Cross. Lt. Clare B. Smiley and Machinist Paul Seifert of *Stewart* both received the Silver Star, as did *Parrott*'s gunnery officer, Lt. John V. Wilson.

In the chaos of close-range combat, under fire repeatedly and taking hits as well, the Americans all imagined that they had given as well as they got. Post-action accounts would say they had seen numerous shell hits, torpedo explosions, enemy ships blowing up, and the like. They believed they had sunk one or two transports, engaged and damaged several "Nip" destroyers and cruisers, and wrought havoc on the invasion forces. It was not the first or the last time when such self-deception colored Western (or Japanese) accounts after battle. Naturally, the U.S. officers and sailors wanted to imagine they had broken up the Japanese landings. But in truth—and this was a bitter truth—they had accomplished almost nothing at Badoeng Strait to keep the enemy from seizing Bali and its invaluable airfield at Denpasar.

As the war progressed, American claims would not need to be inflated, whereas those of the Japanese required ever-greater deceptions. In early 1942 the "fog of war" that cloaked the action that night in Badoeng Strait also concealed the reality of multiple failures (tactical and operational) for the inexperienced ABDA naval forces. What the darkness could *never* disguise and should not be forgotten, however, was the courage and determination—the "true grit"—of the Asiatic Fleet's remaining surface forces as they carried out their sacrificial duties. Few American ships were faced with such a daunting, or thankless, mission during the Pacific War—or one rendered so invisible by supervening political factors.

Unfortunately, the gremlins of misfortune were waiting when *Stewart* entered a Dutch floating drydock that afternoon at 1445 hours to begin repairs. Within two hours, after being improperly blocked, she keeled over at a 37-degree angle into the waters of the dock. She was far too damaged to be saved at that late stage of the campaign and had to be abandoned, with her crew split up among other ships. The part of her crew reassigned to *Pecos*, *Edsall*, and *Pillsbury* was doomed to a man. On *Stewart*'s bridge Bill Kale noted Capt. Page Smith's heartbroken expression. After all they had come through, to then lose the old "*Stewie Maru*" through such a needless accident was an agonizing reversal of fortune to her men and commanding officer. In one further irony, subsequent American demolition efforts failed to wreck *Stewart* completely. In 1943 the industrious Japanese salvaged her for use as a patrol boat. At war's end, much altered but still a tough Cramp boat, she was found near Kure (as PB-102), recovered, and returned to service in the U.S. Navy.

# NINE

## Disaster at Darwin

### *The Fate of* Peary

News—and especially bad news—trickled slowly to the lower decks of the Asiatic Fleet in those days, and the sailors on the four-pipers did not learn of the devastating Japanese bombing raid on Darwin until well after the Battle of Badoeng Strait. For many it was not until they went into Surabaja itself several days later that newspapers and the grapevine revealed what had happened on February 19 to the Australian port and town. It was also at that time that the enlisted personnel found out, or at least heard rumors about, the Japanese landings on Timor.[1]

A number of American and Australian vessels were caught flat-footed and defenseless in the Port Darwin anchorage and sunk, including the veteran Asiatic Fleet tin can USS *Peary*. Regarding her story, it may be fairly said that *no* other U.S. destroyer serving in the opening months of the war in the southwest Pacific endured greater hardships on its way to a tragic end than this old-timer.

*Peary* had been badly damaged by the Japanese air raid on Manila on December 10 and was unable to resume normal patrols until almost two weeks later. Her skipper, Lt. Cdr. Harry Keith, had been wounded; eight officers and enlisted men were killed outright on the ship; another fourteen were missing and presumed dead, thought to have been killed ashore at Cavite during the bombing attacks. A replacement for Keith was soon found: Lt. John M. Bermingham, former executive officer of *Stewart*—who had completed his Asiatic Station tour of duty and was waiting for orders to return him to the States. He was a veteran destroyerman and knew his way around the small but handy world of flushdeckers. More importantly his appointment pleased the crew of *Peary* no end, as they had feared receiving an inexperienced "spill-over" officer from Hart's staff.[2]

On December 26, 1941, after several requests to depart, *Peary* and Bermingham (along with *Pillsbury*) finally received orders from Rear Adm. Francis Rockwell to rejoin other Asiatic Fleet units in the East Indies. This should have preserved the ship and her crew from the cruel fate that would soon overtake those left behind in the Luzon area. As events played out, however, the voyage south itself became a nightmare, one resembling an outlandish scenario concocted by a writer of fiction.

Just before departing the destroyer took aboard nine "passengers" for the trip: two ensigns and seven enlisted yeomen and radiomen. All were members of Hart's "Purple Gang" (from the secret radio intelligence unit working in their underground installations at Monkey Point on Corregidor). They brought out several bags of sensitive material, along with a radio receiver and one ECM. These were welcome additions, as *Peary* was still short of much equipment, having lost all her radio receivers in the December 10 bombing attacks.[3] Yet even in this situation more bad irony prevailed; *Peary* would be hounded by communications gremlins throughout her torturous odyssey to the south. Despite having an augmented communications team with the code breakers from Corregidor, she could not receive or transmit messages on any clear or consistent basis.

Lacking proper sonar gear and stripped of one-half of her torpedo battery—as was USS *Pillsbury*—the game old destroyer with her extra passengers started south. Unlike *Pillsbury*, which reached Balikpapan late in the afternoon of December 28 after a prosaic trip with no encounters, *Peary*'s course would be neither straightforward nor uneventful. Steaming at sea only by night and concealing herself along the Philippine shoreline by day with her upperworks now heavily camouflaged in green army paint obtained just before leaving Manila, *Peary* departed at a sprint but finished by inching her way crabwise down through the Celebes and Moluccas.

The story of her trip south is that of 2,100 miles of anxiety, misery, and determination, along with some good and much bad luck. In the course of this close-run escape, she was snooped and bombed by Japanese planes, attacked by "friendly" Australian bombers whose crews mistakenly assumed she was an enemy, then assaulted by fever-bearing mosquitoes, and all of this while generally incapable of exchanging messages with her own forces. On the morning of January 3, 1942, the bedeviled old four-piper reached Darwin harbor at last, where she was greeted and led into the anchorage by her sister, *Pillsbury*. The crew felt overjoyed to have reached safety, even if it was the wilds of the northern Outback. But within another week *Peary*'s horrible luck returned: twenty-eight sailors and officers became ill with a virulent form of malaria or dengue fever, contracted when the ship had anchored off remote Maitara Island, near Ternate in the Halmaheras, to make repairs after her friendly fire incident. Eventually nine men died, victims of one of the ABDA campaign's stupidest

IFF errors.[4] It was, as Dan Mullin later wrote, "a terrible price to pay."[5] Yet even then *Peary* had not experienced the worst that fate had in store.

· · ·

For the balance of the destroyer's brief wartime career, *Peary* operated primarily around Darwin. Throughout the rest of January she helped by escorting ships in and out of the harbor; standing watch while divers made attempts to gain access to the sunken submarine *I-124*; patrolling and transferring Asiatic Fleet sailors and officers to various other ships as they reached Darwin. Some of her communications division went ashore—along with men from *Marblehead* and *Langley*—and aided in the establishment of radio facilities there.

On January 29 she took a "special duty" contingent of U.S Army personnel, sixteen men in all, from Darwin to Timor. There they were to deliver 5,300 gallons of avgas and another 50 gallons of lube oil to RAAF forces in the middle of the night on January 31. As might have been expected given the ship's snakebit campaign thus far, this secret mission did not go too smoothly either. When the motor whaleboat, manned by five sailors under veteran bosun G. W. Inlay—an old coxswain—took men and supplies ashore, it broached in the high surf and could not be brought back to the ship. Bermingham waited for the tides to shift and seas to moderate before picking the men up. *Peary* then high-tailed it back to northern Australia. But there was no *real* safety for *Peary* at Darwin, and she had less than twenty days to live.

In the first two weeks of February, as other units left for Java, *Peary* underwent a limited overhaul by engineers from *Black Hawk*, who replaced her sonar gear. By midmonth she was incorporated into the Timor relief convoy along with *Houston*. After her return from that aborted mission, she found herself back in the crowded anchorage, along with the seaplane tender *Preston* and a variety of transports, support vessels, and Australian ships. She pulled briefly alongside *Houston* in Darwin harbor, and some of the men on the two ships were able to visit before heading back out to sea.

Lt. Bob Fulton, the senior assistant engineering officer aboard *Houston*, took the opportunity to spend a little time with his naval academy classmate, Lt. Matt Koivisto, then serving as executive officer on *Peary*. They were both 1932 graduates of Annapolis. As we have seen, it was Koivisto who skippered *Peary* as acting CO after her captain, Lt. Cdr. H. H. Keith, was seriously wounded during the December 10 air raids on Cavite. He had done an excellent job and was recognized for his "efficient and courageous" handling of the ship in Japanese bombing attacks. Following the assignment of Bermingham as captain, Koivisto became the XO.

Before being sent to the Far East, Bob Fulton had spent three years on flush-deckers in the Atlantic. He knew them, especially their engine rooms, inside and out. Now, sitting in Koivisto's tiny stateroom on *Peary*, the two friends chatted; they had undergone somewhat similar experiences. Both ships had been damaged by bombing attacks, and each had suffered personnel casualties. Both men understood only too fully just how far from relief and safety they were being asked to operate. Still, in the manner of genuine classmates—indeed Koivisto had been described in *The Lucky Bag* as the very best of roomies—they shared what they could. Koivisto took out the last of his Prince Albert smoking tobacco in its distinctive flat red can. Fulton produced his penknife, and after spreading out the remaining tobacco atop the little metal desk in the cabin, the men divided it up into two portions. There simply was not time for much else. Soon enough Fulton had to return to his duties on *Houston*. This prosaic meeting between the two former Annapolis classmates would be the last time they saw each other alive.[6]

The two ships departed at ten that night and steamed west back to Java. But outside Darwin *Peary's* sonar picked up a sound contact, and she began stalking the suspected submarine. After dropping depth charges and in the process burning up more fuel, her captain decided to return to port to replenish her fuel tanks. It was a fateful and fatal decision.

Thursday morning, February 19, was clear and sun-bright with few clouds, the sea smooth, and visibility extreme. It was, therefore, very good weather for an air raid. Local American fighter pilots and navy personnel along with their Australian counterparts at Darwin were all taken unawares initially; the typical reaction of numerous individuals when they looked up to the sky off to the north as they first heard and saw approaching planes was, "No worries, they are Yanks." One USAAF pilot who managed to get airborne in his P-40E still thought the enemy planes were U.S. Army A-24 dive-bombers or even AT-6 Texan trainers until they got within a few hundred yards and the red meatballs on their wings became apparent. Thus the entire raid on Darwin was a textbook case of the advantages of a stealthy and aggressive strike against primitive alert systems, faulty communications, and inadequate defensive firepower.

A sister flushdecker, converted to a small seaplane tender, the USS *William B. Preston*, was anchored not far away from *Peary* with a trio of her PatWing 10 PBY Catalinas floating nearby. Twenty men from *Preston*, including her skipper, Lt. Cdr. Etheridge Grant, had gone ashore earlier that morning. At least one of the Cats was being serviced by her crew. This was, of course, standard procedure, but as *Preston's* official ship's history later stated, "At 0945 . . . the ship's routine was altered by the appearance of 90 Japanese bombers."[7]

A mechanic named Tom Anderson standing on his plane's lower wing looked up from his work and eyeing the approaching planes remarked that it was good to see reinforcements arriving. He then stated that the navy must have finally sent out a carrier, but in the next breath corrected himself: "Those aren't reinforcements. Those are Japs." No sooner had he uttered these words than he and his pals saw three Zeros peel off to begin a strafing attack on the helpless PBYS in the water.[8] So began the disastrous day of February 19 for Allied service personnel then at Darwin, Australia.

At 0957 the small Australian minesweeper HMAS *Gunbar* became one of the first victims of the attackers when she received a brisk machine-gunning from *Kaga* fighters that turned the little ship under Lt. Norman Muzzell, RANR (S), "into a colander." They knocked out her sole AA weapon—an ancient .30 cal. Lewis gun said to be "as old as the hills"—and left bullet holes throughout the vessel, including "a whole line like a cheese" right across the captain's bunk. The crew was reduced to firing back with Lee-Enfield rifles, while Muzzell shot at the planes with his 45 cal. pistol, all of which he later compared to "throwing peanuts at a tiger."[9]

Surprise in the harbor was so complete that *Peary* never even managed to get her anchor up.[10] The immobile ship was an ideal target and suffered the fate of such; struck by five Japanese bombs, she exploded, splitting in half and drifting slowly from her moorings. *Peary* "ablaze from end to end, with numerous explosions" finally sank beneath a massive plume of black smoke from her burst fuel-oil tanks.[11] On her upperworks men fired their machine guns to the last against marauding enemy planes as they swept over the chaotic harbor. Five officers, including skipper Lieutenant Commander Bermingham, and her XO, Lt. Matt Koivisto, along with over eighty members of her crew were killed.

At 1040 hours the "all clear" sounded, but the harbor and town of Darwin were left in shambles. Some fifteen ships had been sunk or damaged, roughly twenty planes destroyed, and three hundred to four hundred persons in all appear to have been killed, although exact casualty figures have never been agreed upon. In the military forces there were many examples of true heroism, while in the civilian population numerous cases of cowardice, looting, and drunkenness. But the chaotic conditions also bred rumors and misinformation, and many decades would pass before a clear picture began to emerge. For the hard-luck *Peary*, however, it was a heartbreaking termination to her long career—and like the fate of other Asiatic Fleet ships, emblematic of that organization's larger tragedy.

# TEN

## Six Days to Oblivion

### *The* Langley *Episode*

In this ill-conceived operation, the elderly, slow, and lightly armed U.S. Asiatic Fleet seaplane tender USS *Langley*, which was of no real combat value—although crewed by many experienced officers and men—was sent by muddled orders from ABDA planners into waters and airspace dominated by the enemy. There she met a predictable fate. U.S. military commanders were equally complicit in facilitating the debacle, but the real impetus came from American and Dutch politicians in Washington and London, along with the Dutch naval command. This was a case of politics and propaganda overriding military strategy, for the choices that were made functioned as political gestures rather than strategic—let alone operational or tactical—schemes. The Curtiss P-40E fighters that *Langley* transported were not going to change Java's fate, and American planners clearly understood this. Even so, they allowed the mission to take place. Not only *Langley*'s fate tells the tale; the disposition of surviving vessels—in particular that of the cruiser *Phoenix*—reveals the true strategic imperatives of the United States and Great Britain at this juncture. Contemporary and subsequent accounts concerning the mission, including many reports in the press and published histories for several decades afterward, fail to take into account these realities.

Although *Langley* suffered only light casualties at the time of her abandonment—thanks to fine ship handling and courageous rescue work from the U.S. destroyers with her—the operation quickly went from bad to worse. Through American efforts to succor their Dutch allies, two more U.S. vessels in addition to *Langley* were needlessly lost, this time with a tragic and heavy human toll.

In 1950 Lt. Adm. Helfrich, whose rash decisions led to the fiasco, conveniently overlooked reality as well as his own culpability when writing his *Memoires*. In chapter 24 ("The Very Last Days") of volume 2, he mentions that the USN survivors of *Langley* picked up by the two destroyers "arrived safe and sound at Tjilatjap" after the sinking.[1] This mindless error showed his regard for the over 650 American lives squandered needlessly in the *Langley* episode alone. After over seventy years, such an incomprehensible error as this deserves to be rectified. The *Langley* mission may therefore quite properly be seen as symptomatic of the ABDA campaign's failures overall and as such deserves to be recognized by posterity for the miscarriage it in every respect was.

• • •

The entire operation was marked by disarray from its shaky start to its grim finish. It was conceived at the highest political levels—coming after a promise made by Roosevelt's factotum, Harry Hopkins, who headed the Munitions Assignments Board, during early February to the Netherlands' minister Hubertus van Mook. Making an end run around military planners, Hopkins assured the Dutch that thirty-five fighters would reach Java that month, to be followed by another sixty-four the following month.[2]

The mission would also involve the British supreme commander (Wavell) and an American lieutenant general (Brett) acting as his deputy; a meddlesome Dutch admiral of the Royal Netherlands Navy (Helfrich) whose attention faltered at the worst possible time; two more American admirals (Glassford and Purnell) who, although in charge of the U.S. ships' movements, often appeared to have known less than any of the others. Ultimately not *one* of these senior officers may be said to have understood the plans and operation from inception to conclusion. They were allies united in bewilderment, if in nothing else.

• • •

In order to place the operation within its historical and operational context, we must look back over a short period in the abbreviated lifespan of ABDA. In late January 1942, General Wavell at ABDACOM realized that Japanese air and naval forces would soon be in positions to directly attack Java or block reinforcements from Sumatra to the west and Timor to the east. This realization also impacted the Allies' ability to reinforce Malaya, which was always the foremost concern of Wavell and his largely British staff. *Their* primary objectives really had little to do with the defense of the East Indies but much to do with getting convoys and supplies to Singapore. Once the fall of Singapore had become inevitable, their concerns gravitated west to Burma and—more critically—to India. By the time the focus of their flickering attention shifted back to the East Indies, the day of the white man in the Orient and the southwest Pacific would be far

SIX DAYS TO OBLIVION

gone into night. A new sun, radiating blood-red shafts, was preparing to rise over much of the Far East.

Japanese pressure was being exerted across the East Indies at multiple points more or less simultaneously—like pythons crushing prey—each movement by the victim only allowing the predator greater area on which to exert its might. By sea, air, and land the forces of Imperial Japan were advancing. They menaced Balikpapan and Bandjarmasin in lower Borneo; they moved down from the Moluccas to the waters above northern Australia along the Timor-Ambon axis; they approached the critical harbors and airfields of Kendari and Makassar, Celebes. Dutch ground resistance (where it existed at all) was generally feeble; these key points were seized at no great expense to the Japanese. Their successes gave them airfields and port bases that would allow preparations for a massive, dual-pronged attack on their primary objective: the island of Java itself.

Simultaneously, the use of Port Darwin in northern Australia by the Allies as a forward staging base was seen to be less and less secure. The ability of Allied—or in this instance, American—planners to assemble and fly operational warplanes (primarily, but not exclusively, P-40E fighters) from Brisbane on the east coast across the vast Australian continent (a distance of at least 2,000 miles) to Darwin, and along the chosen route via Timor's Penfui airdrome, Sumbawa's Waingapoe landing strip, and Denpasar airfield on Bali, thence into Java (another 1,600 miles) was suspect from the very start.

Losses of planes and personnel to noncombat accidents in addition to increased Japanese air activity all along the ferry route compelled Wavell and Brett to search for different means to get matériel to the front. This unpleasant realization was brought to Wavell's attention—and subsequently to Washington and London—by heavy Japanese air attacks in early February, which diminished the small number of Allied planes in the East Indies still capable of resisting Japan's air offensive. As it was, when the enemy made his first substantial air raids against Surabaja and environs on February 3, the United States had scarcely more than a dozen P-40ES on Java to resist them and *no* other reinforcements closer than Darwin.[3]

Hence, throughout the campaign, as Allied fighter and bomber strength melted away under recurrent enemy pressure, Wavell and his subordinates were driven to countenance increasingly reckless schemes for reinforcing the East Indies. For the Americans this situation had resulted first and foremost in ignoring a cardinal precept of AAF doctrine: avoiding the piecemeal distribution of its forces into combat. Eschewing their own doctrine, inexperienced AAF reinforcements were sent to the East Indies in small groups that added very little to ABDAIR's combat effectiveness at any given time. Many were chewed up en route by operational accidents or swiftly destroyed once in the combat zone. A single incident at Denpasar, Bali, is but one of several yet remains a representative example.

There on February 5, after a laborious odyssey from Australia and across the Lesser Sunda Islands, a group of thirteen desperately needed Twentieth Pursuit Squadron (Provisional) P-40ES arriving on Bali was jumped by ten A6M Zeros of Third Kū flying out of Kendari, Celebes.[4] The A6Ms were escorting thirty-one bombers of the Kanoya and Takao Kū sent to bomb the airfield. It was a stroke of misfortune for the Americans—dogged throughout the campaign by example after example of plain bad luck—and one of fortuitous timing by the aggressive Japanese. Caught by surprise as they were being refueled, few of the American fighters had managed to get airborne. In the swift and ruthless enemy attacks, seven U.S. planes were destroyed in the air and on the ground, with three others damaged.

It was a jittery trio of Warhawks that made the short flight west to "safety" on Java two hours away. Of these a duo of riddled mounts landed at Perak Field near Surabaja, and the third plane some sixty miles off-course at the heavy-bomber base at Singosari. Two of these young pilots arrived in a state of obvious psychological trauma, severely distressed by what they had undergone at Denpasar.[5] One flier, 2nd Lt. Dwight Muckley, in reply to airmen at the field who asked how he was after his awkward landing on two flat tires, had blurted out: "I'm all shot to hell!" And so he was. Both wings of his mount were riddled with holes as if a screwdriver had punched through every square inch; the aileron cables were "dangling down, swinging in the breeze." Elevator and rudders had seized up as a result of machine-gun hits. There was a cavity "a foot square" in the fuselage; the prop itself had multiple holes; and not two inches from the pilot's head a rearview mirror had been cleanly excised by an enemy round.[6]

By this time the green AAF pilots had begun to fully comprehend, to their horror, the meat grinder into which they were being fed. Tellingly, even this pitiful small-scale fiasco represented a substantial loss of assets to the depleted air forces on Java. Within another two weeks, following the devastating air raids on Port Darwin, and after enemy amphibious and para forces captured Penfui airdrome at Koepang and then seized Denpasar (both on February 20), this last viable flying route from Australia into the East Indies had been effectively truncated.

These blows on the eastern half of the ABDA region, so inevitable and rapid in the wake of Singapore's fall and the seizure of Palembang to the west, would have strained the resolve of any command, but they made clear the fate of the

East Indies. Yet still more sacrifices—in the name of Allied unity, for political factors were at play as well—would be required. Most would come at sea, and by far the heaviest losses would be suffered by the forces of the United States. Almost *all* of these would take place when American men and ships were put at the disposal of the Dutch. Largely as a result of the confused and calamitous end to the ABDA campaign, no such command arrangements would again be tolerated by the U.S. Navy as the war progressed, a fact whose significance appears to have later eluded the full understanding of British and Dutch naval commanders and political leaders.

. . .

In late January 1942, through rumors and misinformation, both MacArthur and Wavell seemed to believe that an Allied aircraft carrier was either available or preparing to operate in the vicinity of the East Indies. For these two desperate army officers, each beleaguered and constantly beset by requests for more air support—*any* straw, no matter how slender or nebulous, seemed worth clutching.[7] Thus the pressing situation in the Far East led to a succession of poor decisions at the headquarters of ABDA and in Washington.

The misapprehension concerning the presence or availability of an aircraft carrier stemmed from multiple causes. Any number might have formed the basis for such a "rumor." One was Operation OPPONENT. This took place on January 26 and 27, near Christmas Island south of Java, when the British flew off two squadrons of RAF Hurricane fighters from the carrier HMS *Indomitable*. These planes, forty-eight in number—from 232 and 258 Squadrons—were reinforcements in the battle for Singapore and were quickly vectored to that island via Batavia and Palembang. News of their presence on Java should have been a routine matter at ABDA; they were in fact led into the island by RAF Blenheims flying out of Batavia along with a single British PBY Catalina. From Kemajoran airport they moved north to Sumatra in penny packets, there to be squandered against the more numerous and adaptable enemy fighters. It should be noted, however, that the British never allowed *Indomitable* to approach within sight of Java, and screened by three destroyers—HMS *Nizam*, HMS *Nestor*, and HMS *Napier*—the big carrier promptly wheeled about and returned to the safety of Trincomalee, Ceylon, on February 2.

It is also unquestionable that Wavell had asked on January 30 for "a striking force which should include at least one aircraft carrier, [and] should be stationed at Darwin." He may or may not have been thinking of the *Indomitable* operation at the end of January, but he also mentioned a request to the

U.S. chiefs of staff for an American carrier to transport planes and also possibly be utilized in the proposed Darwin striking force.[8] But the U.S. Navy had no serious intention of allowing one of its precious few fleet carriers to operate in proximity to the doomed East Indies.

A few days later, on February 7, 1942, the Admiralty noted in a list of British naval forces allocated to the ANZAC area that HMS *Hermes* was to be sent to Australia with those units. These included—among others—the Australian cruisers HMAS *Australia*, *Canberra*, and *Adelaide*, plus the New Zealand light cruisers HMNZS *Achilles* and *Leander*, along with one U.S. heavy cruiser and two destroyers. Soon enough this plan for *Hermes*, too, was dropped; she would remain in Indian waters. And there she would be sunk a little over two months later by swarms of Vice Adm. Nagumo Chuichi's carrier dive-bombers during the Imperial Navy's momentous "C" Sakusen (Operation C).

A third event might also have given the impression that a carrier was in the East Indies. Thirty-nine crated Hurricanes reached Batavia's Tandjong Priok on February 6 aboard the British aircraft transport HMS *Athene*, arriving from Mauritius. These fighters were then partially assembled and towed to the civil airport at Kemajoran, outside Batavia. From there they were dispersed to various locations, and almost all would be lost or captured by the end of the campaign. A conflation of stories in any form could have readily produced just such an impression on MacArthur's command or that of Wavell.

There is no question that MacArthur and others in the army were still insisting throughout January that the navy could reinforce his besieged command by sea. Many army officers on Corregidor saw the navy as having deserted them in their greatest time of need. To Adm. Ernest King, the paranoid MacArthur (who had a history of belittling Hart—at one time even referring to the Asiatic Fleet's "combat inferiority," in a particularly fatuous prewar letter) complained that Hart was not cooperating in helping resupply the Philippine command with ammunition and supplies for the army.[9] However, Hart, the whipping boy of choice for the minions of MacArthur as well as the Dutch, had expected such reactions.[10] With his usual clear-sightedness Hart knew the risks involved and hoped to manage them more sensibly. His personal diary recorded on January 10, 1942, that since he believed he would never again see *any* planes he sent to MacArthur, a submarine would have to be used—even though he understood this would "have no effect on the final outcome of the campaign but, based wholly on sentiment, [he] must make the try." One of his big, new fleet submarines—badly needed elsewhere—would be the means.[11]

Eventually Marshall and Eisenhower were both drawn into the squabble, as they felt the need to send direct orders to Hart (via Commander in Chief King) to comply. This King did, although with no pleasure; he had as much use for British and Dutch complaints about Hart as he did for those emanating from MacArthur.[12] Nevertheless, such was the grip held by MacArthur on Washington and the press, even after his "four star fiasco" on Luzon, that there were *still* standing orders—following ABDA's dissolution—for the navy in the southwest Pacific to keep one submarine in hand at all times for making the perilous trip to and from Corregidor.

For his part Hart satisfied his own conscience by ensuring that his subs evacuated as many naval personnel and nurses as possible on each trip. Exasperated, Eisenhower in his papers only mentions the possibility of such resupply operations costing (as he rather cynically put it) " merely a submarine."[13] Meanwhile, Dutch admiral C. E. L. Helfrich continued to fume, spreading his toxic grievances.

Helfrich had complained that he felt as if he wasn't "boss in his own house" with Adm. Thomas Hart of the U.S. Navy—a man he saw as elderly and tired—running ABDAFLOAT from Java. Not satisfied with overt grumbling, Helfrich continued his own covert operations against his ABDAFLOAT superior with more behind-the-scenes machinations. Within another few weeks this noxiousness took effect in Washington and London. Hart would be moved out, and Helfrich brought in as ABDAFLOAT's commander. Then, in a matter of days, Helfrich would be able to exhibit his own aggressive operations against the Japanese (of which he was prone to *talk* much), albeit with fighting assets supplied by the very allies he had made such determined efforts to undermine.[14] True to form, after the campaign ran its bitter course Helfrich blamed everyone but himself for the loss of Java.

The shabby communications on Java likewise played a gremlin's role at this time. During the second week in February, Wavell (ABDACOM) exchanged messages with Washington (CCS) in which one transmission was either misinterpreted or contained a garble that led him to believe—however briefly—that he would be furnished an American aircraft carrier for transporting planes to Java. Wavell, like many high-echelon commanders, was prone to believe what he liked to believe for as long as possible. If this fantasy with the imaginary carrier was any indication, he also tended to hear what he wanted to hear. But committing a fleet carrier was something the U.S. Navy would never have seriously considered for a moment, and several more messages had to be transmitted over another week before the misunderstanding was rectified.[15]

Such hard actualities notwithstanding, it appears that Wavell, and undoubtedly the Dutch, had not abandoned the idea of seaborne shipments altogether. Brett's notes of the ABDA commanders' conference on January 31 explicitly referred to Dutch requests for a supply of P-40s.[16] Though nominal allies in ABDA, they were working from entirely different motives. Nevertheless, this idea would prove as stubborn to dislodge as it was impossible to implement.

Therefore, after his initial communications in late January and early February, Wavell decided to notify CCS on February 9 that he wanted to send in crated planes aboard the HMS *Athene* (as had been done previously) and about three dozen assembled, ready-to-fly P-40E fighters via the Asiatic Fleet's seaplane tender USS *Langley*. Neither ship was a true aircraft carrier—although *Langley* had been one, in fact the U.S. Navy's first, years earlier—but they would serve the Dutch and Wavell's purposes as ersatz carriers in a pinch. Obviously ABDACOM was scraping the bottom of an almost-empty naval barrel by then.

This decision, given the vast territory of ABDA and the primitive quality of communications, took time to implement.[17] Wavell gave the job to his chief deputy, Lt. Gen. George Brett. And Brett (an army air force general) along with Maj. Gen. Julian Barnes in Australia—who commanded U.S. forces there—then set the wheels in motion. The result was a five-vessel convoy designated MS.5 that would transport "the headquarters and ground personnel of a bombardment and two pursuit groups and numerous service units in addition to planes."[18] A more jumbled plan with a greater potential for disaster would be difficult to imagine.

And where was ABDAFLOAT leadership throughout this period? As we have seen, an untimely interregnum had occurred with the ouster of Hart and the installation of Helfrich as commander of naval forces.

• • •

*Langley*, then under Cdr. Robert McConnell, had been stationed at Darwin for the previous six weeks as a member of the fleet's Service Force. Apart from her normal duties as a tender for the PBY flying boats and what remained of the fleet's Utility Squadron, she ostensibly served as one point in a radio communications loop or "progressive message system" for Asiatic Fleet vessels. Radio Darwin, which was actually established in the week of January 2–8, 1942, and initially utilizing radiomen from *Marblehead*, was a temporary expedient for receiving and resending messages "until USN Radio Station Surabaya/Kandangen was fully active and provided primary communications with the Asiatic Fleet and Corregidor."[19] In her role within this relay system, *Langley* would send each message *blind*—three times but with no receipts in order to prevent direction finding by the enemy—from there to Java and on to Corregidor and back again.

That the antiquated old ship, a converted collier of pre–Great War vintage, should be performing such duties says something about the communications problems then facing the United States in the southwest Pacific. As further proof, the diary of Hart indicates that even he was receiving messages only intermittently from Washington after he had reached Java safely aboard the submarine *Shark*. These technical headaches, which persisted on Java and throughout the East Indies, were never to be satisfactorily remedied during the campaign. Hart's supplementary narrative prepared after the war noted that "great difficulty at the ABDA GHQ lay in communications, which constitutes the essential tool of command, and it was a particularly adverse condition of the Naval command function."[20]

In addition to servicing a handful of battered PBYs from PatWing 10, *Langley*'s mixed complement of SOC Seagulls, O2SU Kingfishers, and J2F Ducks was operating in utility duties and on antisubmarine patrols off the approaches to Darwin.[21] Her planes, for example, had been involved in the January 20, 1942, stalking and destruction of the Imperial Navy's *I-124*, a large mine-laying submarine then engaged in operations throughout the waters off northern Australia. Several corvettes from the Royal Australian Navy had done most—and in truth the best—of the work, but *Langley*'s planes had helped track the sub and acted in concert with the Asiatic Fleet destroyers, USS *Alden* and USS *Edsall*, which also participated in the sinking of *I-124*.[22]

The town of Darwin was a remote, fly-blown place—hot, dry, and red-dirt encrusted. Most civilians had already been evacuated. An RAAF squadron was stationed there but had little awareness of war's realities even at the end of December. As noted, local Australian longshoremen routinely went on strike, often leaving military personnel to bear the burdens of unloading and loading supplies.

On December 31, 1941, Lieutenant General Brett flew in for a brief visit at the location. He spent the morning of New Year's Day going over the port, docks, and airfield; the plan was for the establishment of an "advance depot" there. Brett noted that although the Australians were "pleasant and cheerful," they were also "not very serious," and as he put it, "don't know the war is on." After this short visit, Brett flew out at 1300 hours on January 1, 1942; later that afternoon he arrived at Brisbane, where he was met by Brig. Gen. Henry B. Claggett "and some RAAF people." He then held a long confab with Barnes and Brereton to talk over their responsibilities, such as these were understood.[23]

*Langley* remained in Darwin fulfilling her role as communications hub and PBY tender as well as employing her utility planes in air patrols over the port and its approaches. After this period of dull routine, lasting about six weeks, *Langley*'s war abruptly shifted into a higher gear. When ABDACOM plans for ferrying fighters finally came through—whether to India or Java was undecided—the tender was ordered to proceed down to Fremantle, leaving the bulk of her own planes behind. She departed on February 11 and went as hurriedly as her elderly GE turbine-electric drive could manage; her best speed then was about 13 knots.

At Fremantle she was to be loaded with P-40E fighters of two squadrons (the Thirteenth and Thirty-Third Pursuit Squadrons Provisional), which were being flown across the continent from Brisbane. *Langley* would then join convoy MS.5, transporting AAF pilots and planes of two other squadrons then en route Melbourne to Fremantle. The P-40E pursuit planes of the Thirteenth and Thirty-Third Squadrons, flying tangentially along the coast, would arrive on February 17. All three components of this complicated plan were scheduled to join up in Fremantle, where the planes and pilots would be taken aboard *Langley* and the tender join up with the other ships in the convoy.[24]

The original MS.5 convoy was made up of four transports accompanied by one warship and had departed Melbourne at 1630 hours on February 12. These vessels were the USAT *Holbrook* (ComConvoy) and SS *Sea Witch*—both American—with two Australian ships, SS *Katoomba* and SS *Duntroon*. The Brooklyn-class cruiser assigned as escort, USS *Phoenix*, was a sister to *Boise*. Aboard *Holbrook*, *Katoomba*, and *Duntroon* were the men of the Thirty-Fifth and Fifty-First Pursuit Groups, while *Sea Witch* carried the bulk of their fighters—twenty-seven—along with almost half a million rounds of .50 cal. ammunition for the planes. There were ten more P-40Es on *Holbrook*.

The other ship selected by Wavell, the British transport *Athene*, would arrive sometime later. She was then picking up more fighters in Australia. *Athene* had departed Batavia on February 10 after unloading thirty-nine RAF Hurricanes, steaming east across the Indian Ocean to Fremantle some six days later, thence to Melbourne to load more planes.[25]

Seeing the implications of Java's probable loss in early February (and especially after the Bali fiasco), Major General Barnes, commanding U.S. forces in Australia, along with Wavell and Brett at ABDACOM, realized that the United States' ability to send more planes to Java along the previous island-hopping route was becoming less tenable by the hour. Both Brett and Wavell had better reasons to look to the flanks of ABDA as points for establishing new flying bases from which to operate against the enemy. Believing Java doomed, the British were naturally preoccupied with concerns about Burma and its proximity to India after the collapse at Singapore. Wavell's prior assignment in India as well as his background as an army commander meant his attention—and indeed that of ABDA's British-dominated GHQ in general—would remain fixed on soil held by the British, and most of that was much closer to India.

Airfields in Burma to the west and near Darwin in the east were then being considered for bomber operations. Men and planes, many of which were originally thought to be going to the Philippines or to Java, would have to be shipped from Australia to India. Others were coming by sea from the states to Africa, where they would be assembled and then flown to the ABDA theater. But the window of opportunity in which bombers could be brought into Java was being lowered swiftly. Indeed, General Marshall sent the suggestion to Wavell on February 11 that the Nineteenth Bombardment Group (H) be transferred from Java away to Burma. Fighter protection was the first priority, and it was believed that these could be supplied in Burma from shipments originally intended for the NEI. In this thinking Brett, too, had agreed, as he had wanted to set up a heavy bomber force in the Akyab-Calcutta region. These flip-flopping priorities would have life-and-death consequences for the MS.5 convoy and *Langley*.[26]

In this interval Adm. Thomas C. Hart was "relieved" as head of ABDAFLOAT late in the second week of February—with the explanation given out that he had "requested" the change (he had not) and that ill health was a contributory factor (it was not)—whereupon Lt. Adm. Helfrich of the Royal Netherlands Navy took command. A few days earlier Bill Glassford—promoted temporarily to the rank of vice admiral—assumed command of the U.S. naval presence, which had been renamed United States Naval Forces in the Southwest Pacific (a designation disliked by Asiatic Fleet veterans.) Hart, who was still at Lembang, noted (doubtless with some mischievous pleasure) that after all the machinations and infighting, Helfrich still had to be personally told by Wavell in a "pretty summary [manner] . . . to take over at once!"[27] It seems that the Dutch admiral, like many of his fellow NEI countrymen, was still not inclined to move quickly or decisively. And oblivious to these changes, the *Langley*'s mission moved ahead, as though along fixed steel rails leading to catastrophe.

As should have been foreseen, within days the patchwork MS.5 plan began to fray and unravel. Between February 14 and February 22 (the latter being the date of the convoy's departure from Fremantle), the Japanese seized invaluable oil installations and airfields in and around Palembang, Sumatra, west of

Java. At the same time, farther north at Singapore, the British garrison, neither "impregnable" nor resolutely defended, surrendered on February 15 in the greatest military failure of Britain's long history, with over 130,000 prisoners taken by the Japanese. At sea an ABDA striking force sent to the vicinity of Bangka Island to counter the Japanese advance on Sumatra was bombed north of the Gaspar Straits and turned back after less than an hour of combat, never coming to grips with the enemy.

Further to the east a relief convoy carrying U.S. and Australian troops from Darwin to Koepang, Timor, likewise suffered heavy air attacks, and although heroically defended by *Houston*, these ships had to return to the Australian port, their mission aborted. Next Darwin itself received a devastating air attack on February 19 that left numerous vessels in the harbor sunk—including that most unlucky of destroyers, USS *Peary*—port facilities ravaged, airfields and planes wrecked, and the town terrorized by the bombings.

In another couple of days the Japanese landed on both Timor and Bali. On the former island, IJN paratroops were again utilized; as at Menado their performance was unimpressive, and they suffered heavy casualties. After being dropped on the north side near the village of Usua, east of the airfield at Penfui near Poeton, they floundered before finally reaching the airfield. Meanwhile larger army forces landed on the southern side of the island and moved inland to complete the pincer movement.

At Bali air units of the Imperial Navy were operating out of Denpasar airfield by February 20. The Japanese navy and air forces by then controlled virtually *all* vantage points to the west, north, and east, and their submarines were operating with impunity to the south of Java in the Indian Ocean from the Bay of Bengal to the western coast of Australia.

Seeing the handwriting on the wall—in its clear, towering letters—and with every possible justification, Brett informed the other ABDA commanders on February 16 that "a U.S. carrier [was] not now available" and made the decision on February 17 to reroute MS.5's destination from Java to India.[28] In this he at first appeared to be supported by his superior at ABDACOM, for Wavell later messaged both the CCS and the British chiefs of staff on February 21, "No more fighters can reach from east and consignment from *Indomitable* cannot arrive in time."[29]

But this missive was quickly rescinded the following day, February 22—the day that MS.5 with *Langley* sailed from Fremantle—when Wavell and Brett held a conference with Governor-General Van Stachouwer and other Dutch chiefs on Java in order to discuss the impending dissolution of Wavell's ABDA head-

206                                     SIX DAYS TO OBLIVION

quarters. Reaction and downward pressure from political leaders in Washington and London came almost immediately. Over the next few days the Dutch (in Java and from their government in exile in London) continued to argue with the British and Americans "that the situation in Java was not irretrievable." In Washington Marshall and the War Department, thinking perhaps more of MacArthur and the besieged men on Corregidor at that point, paid lip service to heroic defensive campaigns by reiterating their determination to "support the NEI defense by every practicable means." General Brett—by then thoroughly flummoxed—was informed to that effect.[30] Next Wavell at ABDACOM intervened and formally overruled Brett, choosing to send *Langley* and *Sea Witch* into Java after all. In this quid pro quo the higher echelons had succumbed to misguided political sentiment at the expense of realistic military goals.

The Dutch, oscillating between the unfounded hopefulness of Van Mook in Washington, the determination of Van Stachouwer and Helfrich, and the gloom of Ter Poorten and many KNIL officers in Java, had persisted in their irrational conviction that the island could be held. How or why this should have been believed is difficult to grasp now. ABDA's naval forces, even with those added units of the United States and Great Britain, were too small, too weak, and too widely dispersed to defend the entire archipelago. The fighting in the skies above Java was increasing losses of Allied warplanes daily, though under any circumstances the naval forces operated almost entirely without even minimal air cover. And notwithstanding the bold talk of Lieutenant Admiral Helfrich, the Dutch had shown absolutely no more tactical skill in their naval operations than the British or the Americans. The misadventures of Doorman's abortive Gaspar Strait strike in midmonth and the ineffective night fight off Bali a week later proved this conclusively.

To imagine that a small number of planes would be adequate to delay the Japanese advance long enough for greater Allied reinforcements to arrive was delusional. In time, had it been required, the Japanese could and would have brought far greater air and naval forces to bear on the island.[31] Dutch commanders of the KNIL on the ground knew full well that their own organizations were of uncertain quality. Clearly few native troops had displayed any real desire to fight the Japanese. As for the indigenous population of the East Indies, it was as a whole unsympathetic if not openly hostile, to its Dutch masters, as events were soon to prove.[32]

At the same time, and as recorded by a number of American officers, *even* within the heart of ABDA at GHQ, rumors were rife that local civilian leaders on Java might be contemplating a "compromise" of some type with the invaders. Nonetheless, official news organizations on the island, controlled by military censors enforcing such *non-sense*, were forced to play along. And given the pervasive spying and infiltration by the Japanese and their collaborators on Java, it is conceivable that these rumors were actually disinformation. In any case this irresolute, bewildering atmosphere did nothing at all to reassure the U.S. commanders or their personnel that further sacrifices were either reasonable or desirable. On the contrary most had only the sickening feeling that they were being left out on a limb and, what was worse, might be thrown away for nothing.

In the first hours of February 21, Headquarters Southwest Pacific Command sent the following message: "1. U.S.S. LANGLEY and S.S. SEAWITCH are to be sailed from FREMANTLE with M.S. 5 escorted by U.S.S. PHOENIX (.) 2. Destination of all ships in M.S. 5 is BOMBAY repeat BOMBAY (.)"[33] As might have been expected, America's allies in ABDA, long disgruntled, were more than a little displeased. Against all evidence and reality, the Dutch on Java believed—or claimed to—that they could hold their homeland. They were wrong, clearly, but the political exigencies of war—and a losing war at that for the Allies—demanded faith in something other than the facts or truth.

After so much wrangling over these assets, no one should have been surprised to learn that when MS.5 departed from Fremantle at noon on February 22, its orders had *again* been altered. It was to set course for neither Java nor Burma but instead for India. However, the amount of contradictory evidence concerning the exact plans for this convoy remains daunting even now. The war diary of *Phoenix* records that during a conference on February 21, the "sailing orders" to take MS.5 to Bombay were cancelled, and it was decided to send *Langley* and *Sea Witch* in "to Java port Tjilitap [*sic*] without escort."[34] It seems clear that this alteration was through pressure by the Dutch in Washington, London, and Java.

Apparently the Dutch had grown even more incensed when they learned that Brett wanted to send *all* the airmen and *all* the fighters in the convoy to India. They protested hotly, and a compromise was reached. These objections may have been prompted by a blithely misinformed remark from "Hap" Arnold, who told the Dutch (including Rear Admiral Renneft, the naval attaché, and Colonel Weijerman, the military attaché), "*Langley* is not taking pursuit planes to Java." Yet, on February 23 Van Mook was still objecting to the Joint Chiefs of Staff in Washington that it was "essential to get in fighters from the *Langley* and the *Indomitable*" to Java.[35]

Believing that reneging on assurances already given to the Dutch would reflect badly in the public eye during a time of crisis, and feeling the deep

SIX DAYS TO OBLIVION

need for positive news at a time of negligible achievements, Washington permitted the fate of *Langley* to be sealed. As Wavell put it in a carefully worded message transmitted to CCS and the British chiefs on February 22: "The withdrawal of ABDA HQ will NOT repeat NOT mean stoppage of warlike supplies to Java." Similarly, the War Department informed Brett on February 25 that "the purpose ... to support the NEI defense by every practicable means ha[d] not repeat not been changed."[36]

Another micro-example of the macro-confusion then reigning over the entire mission—and of the fickle nature of fortune—was the embarkation on *Langley* at Fremantle of six AAF men from the Fifty-First Group. They had no sooner gone aboard than they were recalled, and their places taken by twelve enlisted men from the Thirty-Fifth Pursuit Group. At the suggestion of one of his officers (Capt. Ivan McElroy), Major Sanders had agreed to send five handpicked crew chiefs from the Twenty-Sixth Fighter Squadron "to go on the *Langley* to be sure they treated the P-40s with the care they needed."[37] Captain McElroy would embark with them. McElroy went aboard the tender with his bunk locker, along with the other five enlisted men; some of them complained that the last-second assignment made locating their toolboxes difficult. Just as they settled into their temporary quarters, a messenger arrived telling McElroy to report *back* to Sanders on the *Holbrook*. He gathered up his (by then thoroughly angered) men and their scattered possessions and returned to Sanders to see what the change was about.

It turned out that Major Sanders and McElroy had previously encountered interservice problems. A self-important U.S. Army lieutenant colonel by the name of Baird, assigned as permanent commander of troops aboard *Holbrook*, had already provoked the two AAF officers during the trip by trivial complaints that quickly led to open confrontations. It seems that as soon as Baird had learned of the six chiefs leaving to board *Langley*, he took the opportunity to resume his personal head butting with Sanders. At that point the piqued Sanders recalled the six men, telling McElroy in exasperation, "I can take care of my men, or I can take care of that SOB, but I can't take care of both. I need you here to help me." Another skirmish between the two officers and Baird was the result, and according to McElroy this led to a "Mexican stand-off that lasted all the way to Karachi." Nonetheless, many years after the event McElroy admitted, "In the final analysis, I should thank Lieutenant Colonel Baird for saving my life along with the five crew chiefs."[38]

One other "lucky" soldier was Meredith "Red" Wood, who remembered only the brevity of the men's time aboard *Langley* and their consternation. He explained by saying that he and the other AAF crew chiefs had looked forward to the "good quarters, good chow," and of even greater importance to the men, the expanded freedom on the tender, dangerous mission or not. They had felt that they "more or less . . . would be on [their] own. Anything to get off the crowded troopship." Subsequently, after his disappointment had subsided at not getting his "wish to ride with the Navy," Wood saw things differently. He would later write, "We were grateful and thanked God for the queer quirk of fate that had saved our lives."[39]

A diary kept by Major Sanders in this period revealed his misgivings about the operation; and he acknowledged both the dangers involved and the odds stacked against them, writing that they were undoubtedly "sailing into most dangerous waters."[40] Others were less perceptive or too naive to feel rattled. Another crew chief of the Thirty-Fifth recalled, "Everybody was bucking to go where the action was. Little did we know the fate that was in store for those who went."[41] Still others had their own hairbreadth escapes from catastrophe, such as Pvt. Don Van Cleve, an aircraft mechanic in the Sixteenth Fighter Squadron (part of the Fifty-First Group) who had helped load the P-40E fighters onto *Langley*. Initially embarked on the ship, Van Cleve was returned "at the last moment" to *Duntroon* when Major Sanders "changed his mind about letting [them] go with the P-40s and the *Langley*, which probably saved [their] lives."[42]

Another handful of soldiers in the air groups that were part of the *Langley* detail had been granted liberal shore passes at Fremantle. Two chiefs from the Thirty-Fifth Group who missed the *Langley*'s departure, gung-ho sergeants Jack Ellwood and Iver "Curly" Ellefson, described seeing the convoy depart the harbor without them as a "bitter moment" but later acknowledged that it was "a blessing in disguise."[43]

As conceived by the American planners—before these plans were altered the first time by Brett—*Langley* and *Sea Witch* were to steam west across the Indian Ocean with MS.5, then detach themselves from the convoy on February 25 somewhere near the Cocos Islands, and set course north-northeast for Java.[44] It was hoped that by leaving the convoy at such a westerly point to steam back up to Java, they might avoid detection or confuse any enemy snoopers.

If allowed to proceed according to the plan, the two ships would traverse the final ten hours into Java under cover of darkness—their only means of security from Japanese submarines and airplanes—during the night of the twenty-seventh and arrive in the early morning hours of February 28. Those were the original plans, such as they were, when the ships departed Fremantle. Yet within hours Lieutenant Admiral Helfrich, acting in his new capacity as ABDAFLOAT, did what he had wanted to do since the war first broke out: he reached out to "grasp" another warship, in this case an American ship. Helfrich stepped in without consulting or notifying Vice Admiral Glassford, and interfered with the new timetable by sending direct orders to *Langley* to leave the convoy the night of the twenty-second and begin the dash into Tjilatjap alone, in order to reach the port a day earlier. *Sea Witch*, carrying her large allotment of .50 cal. ammunition for the fighters, would adhere to the original timetable and break away on February 25.

According to Helfrich's own explanation given later in volume 2 of his *Memoires* (1950), this change was prompted purely by his sense of urgency: "I was in a hurry . . . Therefore, I ordered [*Langley*] to leave the convoy earlier and . . . to take the shortest route going to Tjilatjap, to debark the planes as soon as possible." After describing some of the last-second efforts being made at Tjilatjap to unload, assemble, and fly the P-40Es, he remarks: "There were no reports of Japanese forces in the Indian Ocean, south of Java."[45] Although this was patently false, as IJN submarines had operated in the Indian Ocean for some time, attacking and sinking Allied shipping, one may give Helfrich the benefit of the doubt here, especially in view of the poor quality of intelligence and communications on Java and throughout ABDA.[46] But by then the short, unhappy life of ABDA was coming to its messy, inevitable conclusion.

On February 23 the British informed the Dutch that they would dissolve the formal command known as ABDA at midday on February 25. Thereafter Helfrich, as CZM, would retain nominal control over the Allied naval forces, with the British (under CCCF/Collins) and the Americans (under COMSOW-ESPAC/Glassford) cooperating to the best of their abilities. Rear Adm. William Purnell, with members of his staff, was flown by PBY to Broome, Australia on February 25, the same day that Wavell left for India.

Meanwhile, south of the Barrier, the Japanese were deploying submarines. Five boats had entered the Indian Ocean around February 20 via Lombok Strait—*I-53*, *I-54*, *I-58*, *RO-33*, and *RO-34*—and spread out "in the waters ranging from the southern entrance of the Sunda Strait through the waters off Tjilatjap to the southern entrance of the Lombok Strait."[47] Then, a separate division of Japanese submarines designated Group "C"—*I-4*, *I-6*, and *I-7*—departed Staring Bay at Kendari, Celebes, about the same time that convoy MS.5 left Fremantle. By February 25 they were situated along a line some three hundred nautical miles southward from Soemba Island, moving west in search of enemy vessels and acting as a "vanguard" for the heavy surface units under Kondō and Nagumo that followed.[48]

. . .

The MS.5 convoy got under way around midday with orders stating "destination all ships Columbo [*sic*] with ultimate destination Bombay which was subject to change." As *Langley* slowly and "majestically" passed by *Duntroon*, a uniformed Australian Army band on the dock played a "lively 'Beer Barrel Polka'" followed by both national anthems. One of the army's mechanics, Sgt. Charlie Lamb, remembered the scene all too clearly: "Each ship dipped its ensign in salute as the Old Covered Wagon, with its cargo of landed-based fighter planes, glided past." American officers on *Duntroon* saluted as "the most soul-moving rendition of the 'Star Spangled Banner'" was played. A hundred yards away on the flight deck of the *Langley* they could see the four dozen AAF pilots and chiefs arrayed in a single line at attention under a brilliant blue sunny sky.[49]

At 1346 hours on Sunday, February 22, the convoy escort, USS *Phoenix*, proceeded out of Fremantle's harbor. After clearing Rottnest Island, *Phoenix* took station with the convoy, forming cruising disposition number 1. All then set course westward at 270 (T), before altering northward to 312 (T), steaming at a moderate 12.5 knots.

Slightly less than twelve hours later, in obedience to urgent orders from Lieutenant Admiral Helfrich—sent via the Australian Commonwealth Naval Board (ACNB)—*Langley* left convoy MS.5 and began to make her way alone and unescorted north to Java at 13 knots. According to the deck log of *Phoenix*, the tender had detached herself from the convoy at 2305 hours. This was in accordance with the ACNB message received by *Phoenix* at 2124 instructing *Langley* to leave the convoy and proceed to Java "with all dispatch."[50] *Phoenix* communicated these orders to *Langley* at 2155. That these orders went through to *Phoenix* via ACNB may have indicated a desire to keep Helfrich's grasping hands off that cruiser. She was technically a member of Glassford's Southwest Pacific command at that time, but per ABDA agreements, *Phoenix* could have been subject to direct control by ABDAFLOAT (Helfrich) whenever operating in ABDA's area.

As for the ordinary sailors on *Langley*, few realized the real danger until it was too late. They were healthy, optimistic young Americans and had no doubt they would win the war against Japan. Immediate fears for their own lives appear to have been rare enough. Quartermaster Walt Frumerie said in after years: "I didn't know anybody who was afraid of getting killed."[51] Most of the enlisted men, perhaps armored through simple ignorance, had a "positive attitude" like that expressed by Lowell Barty, SM3/c, from West Frankfort, Illinois, who had been on *Langley* since July, 1939. He would state later that, come what may, he was "absolutely" sure he would make it.[52]

As it turned out, until she got within 150 miles or so of the island, *Langley*'s trip was uneventful. The weather was mild and apart from scattered rainsqualls, the Indian Ocean with its fearsome reputation for massive and miserable seas was relatively tranquil. The hoary "Covered Wagon," as she was known by her sailors, was a tough old bird and earlier in her career had weathered severe conditions off Alaska and on her journey from the West Coast to Manila. In 1940 she had steamed through a monstrous Pacific typhoon that brought green water over the flight deck, fifty-five feet above the waterline. She thus made this portion of her last journey in good form. This may have reassured or deceived some of her less experienced men; others of course knew better.

These more knowledgeable men aboard her, such as Cdr. Lawrence Divoll, her executive officer—who had been on the Asiatic Station since the summer of 1939 (and a skipper of a four-piper himself the year before coming to the tender)—realized they were entering a killing zone alone and unaided. Luckily, as in Commander Divoll's case, not all her men were naive or complacent. Several diligent *Langley* sailors worked to complete improvised shields on the four 3-inch/50 cal. guns that had been mounted on the tender's reduced "flight deck" at Cavite before the war. They did so by welding sheet metal and boiler-plate forms around the mounts, filling them with concrete for protection against splinters and strafing.

These AA weapons were all under *Langley*'s gunnery officer, Lt. Walter Bailey (USNA 1931), although the 3-inch guns were directly commanded by Ens. Lanson Ditto. These were her primary "heavy" antiaircraft weapons, but the ship had retained her quartet of ancient 5-inch/51 cal. deck guns, in pairs fore and aft, for surface targets. These old 5-inch "bag guns" were under the command of two young reserve ensigns, J. R. Asdell (forward) and Michel Emmanuel (aft). For aerial targets such low-angle weapons were of no use, yet during the mission they too—if only for reasons of morale—were fully manned.

She also had four .50 cal. machine-gun mounts, along with men wielding the .30 cal. Browning automatic rifle (BAR) placed at various points on the upper decks, but they would be impotent against high-level bombers. All her .50 cal. machine guns were sited atop the open signal bridge structure, with one water-cooled mount in each corner. This location, too, would eventually cause problems. In the center of the signal bridge a crude control station had also been erected, in the form of a sheet steel tub. Inside the tub was poised Lieutenant Bailey, the gunnery officer, and his talkers. Many of the other men manning the four machine guns were largely signalmen who were normally stationed atop the signal bridge anyway. Among these was Lowell Barty. The young signalman would be a significant eyewitness to numerous occurrences over the next three days.

Finally, those 3-inch guns aft on the "flight deck" possessed no real central fire control; an ingenious, although rudimentary, system had been set up in a sandbagged pit in the middle of the deck between these guns. This was Ensign Ditto's action station. His crew included a talker, John Kennedy, y3/c, and two other sailors who operated the improvised fire-control mechanism. (Kennedy, a graduate of Northwestern University and aspiring flier, had been on the ship only since January 10, 1942, but he was also fated to play a memorable role in the events to come.) After receiving data from the operators and Ensign Ditto, Kennedy would relay the info to the 3-inch gun crews via phones.[53] Time would tell how useful this device and the other improvised antiaircraft defenses would prove to be.

On the ship, sailors and airmen did have some interaction. Bill Warnes, a radioman second class with two years on *Langley*—after two years on the flushdecker *Alden*—spoke with a few of the AAF ground crew and at least one pilot about that newfangled contraption called radar. None of the Asiatic Fleet ships had been outfitted with it, although both *Boise* and *Phoenix* did have fire-control radar, which was a closely guarded secret and very rarely mentioned. The AAF technician with whom Bill Warnes talked "was quite familiar" with the system and described how it worked to the fascinated navy radioman. It was also apparent to Warnes that the system the airmen knew was of a different type than that which was being utilized on navy ships.[54]

Although American and Dutch postcampaign accounts of the *Langley* incident are amply detailed, they are replete with "facts" that do not match reality. Neither the *Memoires* of Helfrich nor the various documents written by Glassford—and there were several—agree closely with narratives by U.S. officers involved or with the logbooks of the ships that survived. In some cases the discrepancies are minor—as, for example, when Glassford states that convoy MS.5 and *Langley* departed Fremantle on the evening of February 21, when in fact the ships departed at about midday on the twenty-second. Others are of alarming proportions, for example, when Helfrich inexplicably claims that "almost the entire crew" of *Langley* rescued by *Whipple* and *Edsall* had then "arrived safe and sound at Tjilatjap harbor." As we will see, this was either a fantastic piece of ignorance or a fabulous misreading.[55]

Early on February 26 Glassford notified *Langley*: "FOLLOWING INFOR-

MATION FROM DUTCH AUTHORITIES FOR YOUR INFORMATION ONE
PLANE STARTS DAYLIGHT TWENTY SIX FEB TO MEET YOU X PLANE
WILL CONVOY YOU AND BRING DUTCH DESTROYER WILLEM VAN DER
ZAAN NEAR YOU TO ACT AS ESCORT X ONE PLANE WILL ALSO ESCORT
YOU ON TWENTY SEVENTH."[56]

Another message soon followed about half an hour later when Glassford sent the following orders to *Whipple* and *Edsall* in Tjilatjap: "AT ABOUT 1630 GH/26TH WHIPPLE AND EDSALL DEPART THIS PORT PROCEED TO ARRIVE LAT 9-50 S. LONG 109-25 BY 0600GH THERE RENDEZVOUS WITH LANGLEY ESCORT HER TO THIS PORT X ON COMPLETION THIS TASK PROCEED TO RENDEZVOUS WITH AND ESCORT OUTBOUND CONVOY OF MERCHANT VESSELS IN ACCORDANCE ROUTING FURNISHED X REMAIN WITH THIS CONVOY UNTIL TWENTYEIGHTH THEN RETURN THIS PORT XX."[57]

It appears either that the Dutch and Americans were not coordinating the movements of their escorts or that someone had envisioned *Willem van der Zaan* screening the ship part of the way and the two flushdeckers the remainder.

*Langley* had held up her end of the bargain, but as she closed Java, she was subjected to more inefficiencies on the part of the Dutch—who had assured Glassford that the ship could and would be protected as it approached Tjilatjap—which jarred the plan off its careful timetable to disaster. These snafus began at about 1500 hours (zone -7.5 hours) on February 26, when two Dutch flying boats were spotted overhead; one of these planes signaled to *Langley* that her surface escort was approximately twenty miles to the west. Reading between the lines in Commander McConnell's subsequent report on *Langley's* loss— "the escort, which proved to be the Dutch minelayer *William van der Zaan*"— makes it appear that this rendezvous with the Dutch ship was not necessarily foreseen.[58] *Langley*, zigzagging at thirteen knots was then forced to alter course, losing more valuable time in the process.

When she finally linked up with the Royal Netherlands Navy minelayer *Willem van der Zaan*, it was discovered that the Dutch vessel was suffering from boiler difficulties and could make no more than 10 knots herself. A relatively new vessel (launched at the end of 1938), the 1,400-ton minelayer's power-plant issues would prove all the more ironic in the outcome of this thoroughly snakebit operation. Her anemic pace clearly rendered *Willem van der Zaan* useless as an escort—since time was the cardinal issue, especially regarding *Langley's* rendezvous with the two U.S. destroyers—and Commander McConnell decided to press on to Java alone.

The communications also tell us that Glassford was trying to have the pair of DesDiv 57 four-pipers accomplish two different duties more or less simultaneously. In his anxiety to provide escort for *Langley's* arrival as well as for merchant ships departing Tjilatjap, he set into motion a negative cascade of factors ensuring that nothing would succeed as planned.[59] Splitting and doubling duties for the war-worn old destroyers was in itself a recipe for failure.

Sometime after dark *Langley* received yet another message from the commander of U.S. Naval Forces Southwest Pacific (COMSOWESPAC), reiterating the understanding that *Willem van der Zaan* and two PBYs would provide cover for her final approach into Java after all. Whether these problems with communications were technical glitches (such as the delayed reception problems noted in Admiral Layton's war diary) or simply horrible planning, the end result was the same. Compounding the confusion by obeying this piece of inanity, the old ship reversed course yet again and plodded back to link up with the even slower Dutch vessel. By then night had fallen. According to McConnell's report later, "When the *Van Zaan* [*sic*] was sighted orders were received that the *Langley* was to rendezvous with the USS *Whipple* and USS *Edsall*. Course was again altered to make for the previous rendezvous."[60] It does not take a genius to understand, or a Big Blue computer to analyze, the frustrations and anger that the men and officers aboard *Langley* must have felt as their mission's carefully plotted schedule crumbled around them under the corrosive effects of such stupidity.

Each wasted hour meant miles lost and cover of darkness squandered. Aboard *Langley* the revised timetable now estimated the tender and her escorts would be reaching Tjilatjap at 1700 hours on the twenty-seventh, which meant steaming the final one hundred miles or so in full view of any Japanese planes or ships. *Langley* would now approach Java protected by one ancient tin can (*Whipple*), which had only just emerged a few days earlier from a Tjilatjap dry dock after its collision with the Dutch flagship *De Ruyter*; and another (*Edsall*) suffering from a leaking stern, sagging firewall bricks, and a rattling propeller shaft, leftovers from much hard steaming and an unwise depth-charge attack carried out in shallow waters a month earlier off Darwin. (In fact, *Edsall* had had *no* useful dockyard time during the campaign.) And neither of the two destroyers carried its full allotment of torpedoes. *Whipple* went into the mission with only four torpedoes in her tubes, while *Edsall* retained nine of hers. The PBYs overhead, when they appeared—whether U.S. or Dutch—were of negligible offensive value, although defensively they should have been able to provide sightings and advanced warnings of submarines, airplanes, or enemy surface forces. However, even this task proved impossible.

At the same time, once her troops on the ground at Bali had secured the area, Japanese naval air groups moved with alacrity to the newly seized forward airfield at Denpasar and initiated operations against eastern Java and out over the Indian Ocean almost immediately. Reconnaissance planes, Tainan Kū A6Ms—the fighters had arrived on February 20—followed by Third Kū fighters, and Type 1 Rikko (BETTY) bombers of the Takao Kū would soon seek out worthwhile targets among incoming or fleeing Allied shipping in an enormous six-hundred-mile arc.[61] ABDAIR's counterattacks against Bali were piecemeal and of little consequence; ABDAFLOAT operations at sea had fared no better in the engagement of Badoeng Strait. The Japanese noose was tightening around Java where there would be no effective Allied remedy.

Later, in the middle of the night, *Langley's* crew was called to general quarters when two mysterious white flashes were observed off the port bow; the ship "altered course 90° to the right and emergency full speed rung up." Through a series of dense rainsqualls the tender held this course until the men felt sure any possible contact was lost. Thereafter, "course was again set for the rendezvous and condition two of readiness set." Before sunup the ship went again to general quarters, which was relaxed at dawn "when all was found clear." At that time *Langley's* skipper set condition 1 in all AA and broadside batteries, and condition 2 "in ship control, engineering departments and remainder of ship's organization."[62]

In Dutch headquarters at Bandoeng the situation took on an even more wretched complexion when the *Langley's* plight came to the attention of the head of Java Air Command, Major General Van Oyen. He recognized the danger the ship would be in approaching the island during daylight over such a lengthy period and attempted to contact Helfrich. However, Helfrich could not be located for a response. Perhaps he felt those arrangements had already been made—with the *Willem van der Zaan* and two PBYs—or, what is more likely, he was preoccupied with the confusing and difficult situation then developing north of Surabaja in the Java Sea as the Japanese Eastern Invasion Convoy began its approach to the island. To his credit Van Oyen then communicated with the head of what remained of the ABDA command, the Dutch army's Lieutenant General Ter Poorten, and offered to utilize fighters from Andir airfield near Bandoeng as cover for the tender's approach. Ter Poorten denied the request, and Van Oyen appears to have protested, but to no avail. Ter Poorten's reasoning was that all available fighters were needed for protection over the striking force under Rear Admiral Doorman then searching unsuccessfully for the enemy invasion forces in the Java Sea.[63] In view of the miserable application of Allied air units in the Java Sea engagements later that day and evening, this is all the more ironic. South of Java, as the cool dawn melted into a mild morning, *Langley* would begin the final and most perilous leg of her journey.

Within a very brief period, at about half past six, two four-stack destroyers were sighted approaching from the north. These were *Whipple* (Lt. Cdr. Eugene S. Karpe)—with ComDesDiv 57 Cdr. Edwin C. Crouch aboard—and *Edsall* (Lt. Joshua James Nix), both of which had departed from Tjilatjap at 1640 hours the previous day. Overhead two Dutch PBY Catalinas were also seen. At 0700 hours the flushdeckers had taken station on *Langley's* bows, *Whipple* to port and *Edsall* to starboard. The formation began zigzagging while maintaining speeds of 11–12 knots. A large course deviation was made while *Edsall* checked a submarine contact report; she rejoined the other two ships at 0744 hours, and they resumed course north to Tjilatjap. It had become a fair weather day of good visibility with scattered altocumulus clouds high in the porcelain-blue vault overhead and moderate winds from the east-northeast. These were conditions pleasant enough for a sea cruise but far from ideal for anyone wishing to conceal himself from the eyes of possible predators. It did not take long for those keen eyes to find the three ships.

. . .

Making efficient use of their time that morning—unlike the Allied ships—the Japanese began reconnaissance patrols over the Indian Ocean out of Denpasar airfield. A Third Kū Type 98 (Mitsubishi C5M) single-engine patrol bomber took off early and by half past seven had spotted *Langley* and her two escorts. She stayed in visual touch over the ships for almost thirty minutes and then—after taking her time looking elsewhere—at 0843 hours turned back for home. As she did, the Type 98 transmitted a reasonably accurate contact report to the airfield of a carrier with "many planes" on her deck accompanied by a destroyer and a cruiser.[64] Their course, speed, and distance were all noted by this attentive snooper. It was not the first or last time a four-piper destroyer would be mistaken for a four-funneled *Omaha*-class light cruiser like the Asiatic Fleet's *Marblehead*.

Fifty-two minutes later at 0935 hours sixteen Takao Kū Type 1 (BETTY) bombers took off from Denpasar; their targets were the three Allied ships some 360 nautical miles away. These attackers were led by Lt. Adachi Jirō in the First Chūtai of nine bombers, along with seven more BETTYs of the Fifth Chūtai under Lt. Tanabata Yoshinobu. Each medium bomber carried two 250 kg armor-piercing bombs and two 60 kg antipersonnel bombs. The round-trip flight of some 800 miles or so was well within the operational range of these extremely long-legged planes.

SIX DAYS TO OBLIVION

Fifteen minutes later six A6M Type O fighters accompanied by one Type 98 recon plane, all of Third Kū, under Lt. Yokoyama Tamotsu took off to escort the bombers. Within eight minutes, by 1003 hours, these planes rendezvoused over Blambangan on the eastern tip of Java with another nine A6Ms plus one more Type 98 also from Denpasar, of the Tainan Kū, led by Lt. Maki Yukio. This group of ten planes had originally been vectored out for a sweep against Tjilatjap but was now being sent to help attack the incoming Allied ships. Together they winged across the Indian Ocean on a bearing of 265° T., with their estimated interception time some two hours.[65]

*Langley* by then had spotted her lone stalker as well, and the officers at least knew that the implications were ominous. "About 0900 an unidentified plane was sighted at high altitude," McConnell later recorded. It flew from the east and returned in the same direction. In view of its uncertain identity a message was sent to COMSOUWESPAC (dispatch 270237) requesting fighter escort, "as it was apparent [their] location, course, speed, and point of destination were definitely known to the enemy, and that attack could be expected." At the request of Commander McConnell, executive officer Divoll got on the ship's loudspeaker system and informed the crew that the situation had become quite serious and the ship was likely to "catch hell," so he wanted each man "to concentrate and do his job." He ended by wishing them all good luck.[66] They were soon going to need it. For the aging "*Langlee Maru*" the hour was finally at hand to unreeve her lifeline.

• • •

A little over two and a half hours later, the easternmost ship, *Edsall*—off *Langley*'s starboard bow—first spotted enemy planes approaching from that direction. At about 1140 hours Lt. J. J. Nix's destroyer sent an emergency "aircraft sighted" signal, which was relayed to *Langley*. Nine twin-engine land bombers were seen flying at high altitude, estimated at fifteen thousand feet, in the distance to starboard. They pulled around to approach the formation from astern. The American ships had been zigzagging on a base course directly north but would act independently during the attacks.

On *Langley* Commander McConnell was conning the ship from atop the open signal bridge through voice-tube communications with the OOD on the navigating bridge below. He and the other experienced officers on the thirty-year-old tender understood full well that their only *real* defense lay in maneuver. Their inadequate AA guns and jury-rigged fire-control system would not save them.[67] Nonetheless, McConnell gave the "commence firing" order as soon as the enemy bombers began their approach. This command was relayed to the 3-inch gunners by Chief Yeoman (AA) Gustave Peluso, a talker stationed on the bridge with the skipper, Lieutenant Bailey, quartermaster Walt Frumerie, and about a dozen other men. Apart from his headphone set, Peluso was wearing, like many others, a kapok life vest and a flat World War I–era Kelly helmet. Like many others, too, he was still surprised by the falling enemy bombs. For his part Quartermaster Frumerie maintains that up until that point the men had all expressed a "positive attitude" about their chances and few were openly fatalistic. But such naive optimism was about to be altered forever.[68]

A thousand or more feet beneath Lieutenant Tanabata's formation of seven G4Ms, the black bursts of 3-inch shells from *Langley* were exploding harmlessly; her AA guns lacked the altitude to reach the enemy even if they had possessed the tracking ability. Tanabata's Chūtai had been able to proceed untroubled as if on an exercise. The two Asiatic Fleet destroyers escorting the tender were even less effective as AA platforms; their ancient 3-inch/23 cal. "peashooters" did not possess half the altitude necessary to thwart the bombers. At this time neither *Whipple* nor *Edsall* had opened fire. Also within visual range but equally impotent were the two Dutch flying boats. All they could do was observe the inevitable from what they may have felt was a safe distance.[69]

At 1154 the first stick of bombs fell from Lieutenant Tanabata's Fifth Chūtai. On the deck of *Langley* these could not be observed, but according to McConnell when the enemy planes' "angle of elevation reached about 80° the rudder was put full right."[70] The old ship shimmied and shook as she went into the turn; alongside her port bow seven 250 kg bombs came shrieking down. These all detonated, with two of the closest exploding not more than one hundred feet away. The concussion knocked dozens of men off their feet in the ship. From the steering engine room to the radio shack, sailors, officers, and airmen were tumbled as the old ship was jolted, then vibrated stem to stern like a three-million-pound iron and steel tuning fork.

Although the skipper's report stated later that *Langley*'s injuries were "superficial," in fact the tender had received serious damage. The near misses had sprung plating in the hull adjacent to her engine rooms, and flooding through her bilges—of a slow but persistent nature—threatened to put her electric motors, which were sited near the bottom of the ship, out of commission. Men labored to stop leaks and reroute broken lines, their tasks rendered all the more problematic by the unknown sources of many of the leaks and the inability of bilge pumps to keep up with the flooding. However, within fifteen minutes and through Herculean damage-control efforts—overseen by the damage control officer, First Lt. Cdr. Tom Donovan—they thought the ship just might be able to hold her own. McConnell was not optimistic about their chances, but as soon as the planes moved out of range, he had the ship resume zigzagging.

Within less than ten minutes, the second group of bombers (the First Chūtai, under Lt. Adachi Jirō) began their first run on *Langley*. They started at 1210 hours, but McConnell handled the ship so well, maneuvering "radically on the last stage of the approach," that no bombs were dropped.[71] This gave the Americans a brief respite, and the skipper got on his headphones and sent Commander Divoll, the executive officer, below to the engine rooms to see what was really happening there.

Divoll's battle station was aft steering, near the two stern 5-inch/51 cal. guns on the poop deck of the ship. He descended to the engine room and spoke briefly with engineering officer, Lt. N. B. Frey. The entire area was soaked with water from broken lines and patches, while seawater sloshed in the bilges mere feet below, threatening the engines themselves. But before he could get any information to the bridge, Lieutenant Adachi's next pass over the ship had taken place and the bombs of his Chūtai were already in the air dropping toward *Langley*. McConnell—an experienced aviator himself—ordered hard right rudder when he felt the optimal dropping angle had been reached. He had not been quick or precise enough, however. In the blink of an eye the bad odds in this entire mismanaged and ill-conceived mission finally caught up with "The Old Covered Wagon" and her dogged crew.

Of the cluster of bombs dropped during Lieutenant Adachi's second run, no less than five struck the old tender fair and square while three others were near misses. As McConnell later told reporters: "The *Langley* was literally smothered with bombs."[72] It was a devastating salvo from which a ship as aged and poorly compartmentalized as *Langley* could not hope to survive. The first bomb struck on the starboard side of the main deck just forward of the starboard jib crane. It destroyed a motorboat that had been left behind by *Marblehead* at Darwin, starting fires in four other inboard boats stowed on the deck. It also blew a ten-foot hole in the main deck, destroying steering control from the bridge and slicing phone lines, as it butchered 3-inch gun crews and shattered stacks of ammo boxes. Men were scythed down by fragments on the signal bridge as well. Walt Frumerie remembered seeing a radioman striker who lost one of his eyes to shrapnel; that injured sailor would not be among survivors later.

Lt. Walter Bailey, the gunnery officer stationed inside a metal tub near the captain, was hit squarely by a large chunk of steel. Although he collapsed, Bailey did not immediately lose consciousness.[73] Signalman Lowell Barty was manning one of the machine guns emplaced on the signal bridge, and the .50 cal. weapon was torn from his hands by the blast, knocking it out of its mount. At the same time he saw fragments strike Lieutenant Bailey. One of the few unharmed gunners, Barty was the first person to reach the fallen lieutenant. Bailey was bleeding freely from the hole in his chest, and Barty noted this blood had air bubbles in it, indicating that his lung had been punctured.[74] Soon a pharmacist's mate arrived to tend to the severely wounded officer, and though his injuries were ultimately fatal, Bailey's end would prove a remarkable testimony to the sheer animal durability of the human body.

The next two bombs—the second and third—fell in proximity to each other. The second exploded on the port side of the elevator, where it torched a pair of P-40E fighters on the main deck, another motor whaleboat at davits, plus a motor launch in it skids, and then set on fire two more fighter planes lashed down on the flight deck. The third bomb struck the port side after the corner of the elevator and the port side of the main deck where it, too, set planes afire along with the *Langley* gig. A fierce inferno fed by ruptured crankcase oil next resulted on the port side that claimed an unknown number of lives; many were thought to have been army air force personnel sheltering near their planes.

As the first three bombs tore into the tender, two more near misses were registered next to the port side and another on the starboard side. McConnell later reported, "The side of the ship was pierced below water line by near misses. The ship listed 10 degrees to port. Castings to sea connections on fire, and bilge pumps were broken but repaired. The gyro-compass system was destroyed. The steering from the bridge was disrupted. . . . Engine-room flooding—source of water unknown. The forward part of the ship, port side, riddled by near misses and taking water as well as port side of elevator flats."[75]

Bomb hits number four and five were devastating. The fourth struck some eight feet below the flight deck on the outboard section of the portside stack sponson, "shattering aircraft in vicinity on flight deck with splinters."[76] These P-40Es were severely battered and erupted into flames, their undercarriages crumpled and collapsing, with wounded and mortally injured men strewn all around. Many men in the damage-control party were killed or wounded as well. Bill Warnes remembered coming out of his battle station and seeing many of these injured men, including a disemboweled first class electrician's mate. Warnes was then sent to ascertain the condition of the ship to whatever extent he could, given the smoke, flames, and chaos.

In the meantime a group of six Third Kū A6M (Reisen) fighters flew in low for strafing runs, while three others remained above to fly top cover. These

SIX DAYS TO OBLIVION

half-dozen planes led by Lt. Yokoyama Tamotsu dove down, although not all actually attacked. They spewed 20 mm cannon fire along the length of *Langley*, wrecking more P-40ES, scattering personnel, while wounding and killing other sailors and army men. Luckily, the strafing attacks were not pressed home with much enthusiasm. McConnell's report stated that only one fighter made "a determined attack."[77] Return fire from *Langley*, although improvised, was far from nonexistent, but even these half-hearted strafing runs caused more damage.

Radio electrician Charles Snay had come out of his station in the crypto room—next to the radio shack—to see whether communications could be restored. On his way to the signal bridge, he organized a mass of men who were milling aimlessly outside the radio and crypto rooms into extra stretcher-bearer parties and damage-control teams. Next the energetic Snay helped "Damage Control Unit Number 1" fight one of the fires in a launch when the Reisen under Yokoyama appeared. As he recalled years later: "The party scattered momentarily—and then came back. One of the 'Asiatic' seamen was slow in getting back and I asked him where-in-hell he had been." He didn't blink an eye: "I got under that deck rivet over there before one of you officers could."[78]

At 1242 hours Snay was back in the radio room, where Claud Hinds Jr., RM1/c, had been transmitting messages since the bombers were first spotted overhead. Bill Warnes, RM2/c, and Leland Leonard, CRM, had both reentered the room in the meantime to report on specific damages to the ship. They had been knocked off the air for a couple of minutes by the first salvo and had switched to batteries for a brief time; these would hold up only for another forty minutes. Remarkably, however, throughout most of the engagement—from first sighting to abandonment, a period of roughly an hour and a half—transmissions of the attacks were sent out by *Langley*'s persevering radiomen.

It was clear almost immediately to Commander McConnell, executive officer Divoll, damage-control officer Donovan, engineering officer Frey, and others that the tender had been severely damaged, and only the utmost exertions would save her from foundering. *Langley* was already listing some 10 degrees to port, and neither her fires nor her leaks were under control; her engine room motor pits continued to flood through the bilges and their overworked pumps. Though the fire rooms were less affected by flooding—being situated several feet higher than the engine rooms—when water reached four feet in the port motor pit, the motors had to be shut down to avoid a catastrophic explosion. As soon as that happened, the battered ship lost way. Although she was less than one hundred miles from Tjilatjap, *Langley* had come to the end of her road.

What then followed was, in effect, a series of catastrophes set into motion through well-intentioned motives. In retrospect the *Langley* fiasco resembled a chain-reaction vehicular disaster on a foggy highway, one in which a single wreck of modest damage and few injuries leads to multiple crashes that cost numerous casualties, with most of these deaths among good Samaritans attempting to render aid.

• • •

Also steaming off the Javanese port that Friday—in fact she was escorting the tanker *Pecos* en route from Tjilatjap to Colombo, Ceylon—was Lt. John Nelson Hughes's destroyer, *Parrott*, and at 1330 hours her log recorded: "Commenced receiving over TBS conversations between *Pillsbury*, *Whipple*, and *Edsall* indicating *Langley* had been bombed and was sinking and aid was given her survivors by ships in the vicinity. Informed *Pecos*."[79]

This final notation is crucial. *Pecos* (Lt. Cdr. E. Paul Abernethy), scarcely thirty miles or so distant, had also copied some of *Langley*'s last transmissions as she came under attack as well as those telling of the ship's abandonment and the rescue of her survivors by *Whipple* and *Edsall*. Upon departing Tjilatjap en route to Colombo, Abernethy had set a course of 195° T., but when reports first reached him of the attacks on *Langley*, he altered to 270° T., chugging due west at all of 12 knots in order to put distance between his ship and any Japanese air patrols. *Pecos* was not fully laden with oil, but on instructions from Glassford (via Captain Hudson at Tjilatjap) she had retained diesel—for the submarines—and at least 1,400 gallons of gasoline. Abernethy had ballasted the ship and turned on steam "in the top of all oil tanks and kept on for four (4) hours so as to drive out all vapor."[80]

He had also augmented life-preserving stores by taking on board a large number of bamboo poles, which were secured to the upper decks. Passengers, such as wounded men from other Asiatic Fleet ships, were limited to ambulatory patients only.[81] The precautions taken by Abernethy—who had grown increasingly skeptical of his ship's chances due to delays in Tjilatjap caused by difficulties with Dutch authorities there—would prove fully justified. On the afternoon of February 27, Abernethy knew his ship was too close to the position of *Langley* and that *Pecos*, too, might just as easily be sighted by enemy planes.[82]

At the same time, several hundred miles to the northeast, Rear Adm. Karel Doorman's Combined Striking Force was engaged in its futile search for the Japanese Eastern invasion convoy. According to Dutch air commanders later, all available air forces—including planes that might have offered more protection for *Langley*—had been drawn off to the north into the Java Sea area closer to Surabaja in anticipation of the Japanese invasion and in support of Door-man's CSF. This absence of combat air cover over *Langley* during the critical daylight hours as she steamed into the southern coast of Java would represent the final, ironic failure by the Dutch to protect one of the valuable assets they had badgered the Americans to send to Java.

At 1315 hours Crouch in *Whipple* sent a message to Glassford (COMSOW-ESPAC): "LANGLEY HAS FIRES UNDER CONTROL ANY [*sic*] IS PROCEED-ING NORTHWARDS ABOUT SIX KNOTS X EXPECT ADDITIONAL ATTACKS ANYTIME."[83] This shows that for some time efforts were being made to pre-serve the tender, yet it soon became evident that this was not a realistic goal. Still afloat but burning and with a marked list to port, McConnell's *Langley* was never going to make it to Tjilatjap, and the officers aboard her knew it. The old ship, according to McConnell's own handwritten explanations later, "was heel-ing progressively; rapidly at first to 10° then slowly to 15°–18°. . . . The *Langley*'s list was increasing and it appeared that unless the crew were cleared from the ship that a large loss of life would result should it capsize."[84]

Men struggled in smoke and fire to manhandle five of the ruined P-40ES off the flight deck's port side and into the ocean in a desperate effort to keep the ship stable. At the same time, "counter-flooding was resorted to but the list could not be corrected."[85] McConnell and his officers reasoned that it was time to get the men over the side to *Whipple* and *Edsall* before more enemy air attacks materialized. They thought—correctly, in fact—that the bombers and fighters that attacked them had probably come from Bali. The officers cal-culated that they might have two hours at most before any other planes could arrive again, but they did not rule out the possibility of Japanese carriers in the region either. If that were the case, they might be attacked again at any moment.

At 1300 McConnell told one of his officers to pass the word to prepare to abandon ship. In the confusion and poor communications then rampant, this led to people going overboard prematurely. Both *Edsall* and *Whipple* were keep-ing a close eye on these individuals as they left *Langley*. All seem to have been picked up successfully from the water by boats from *Edsall*. At 1325 *Whipple*'s logbook reported that the men were abandoning *Langley*, but McConnell's actual order was not issued until about five minutes later. At this time Crouch fired off another message to Glassford: "LANGLEY REPORTS MAY HAVE TO ABANDON SHIP 500 MEN X AM STANDING BY X REQUEST ADDI-TIONAL DESTROYERS THIS VICINITY LAT 08-57 S 109-00 E."[86] In the radio shack *Langley*'s communications men were pounding out their final messages. At 1329 Hinds sent: "WE ARE SECURING SOON AS SHIP IS LISTING AD

COMM SHOT T HELL . . . NERK NERK NERK."[87] One minute later the men under Chief Radioman Leland Leonard signed off for the last time. Then, at 1333 hours, CDD57 in *Whipple* sent another message to COMSOWESPAC: "AM RESCUING SURVIVORS X WILL DESTROY LANGLEY."[88]

The augmented and contradictory requirements under which *Whipple* and *Edsall* were operating only further complicated the scenario. Both Purnell and Glassford believed that the destroyers' primary mission was to protect ships departing Java for Australia and India. However, for the men at sea south of Java—Cdr. Edwin Crouch (ComDesDiv 57) and Lt. Cdr. Eugene Karpe in *Whipple*, Lt. J. J. Nix in *Edsall*, Cdr. Robert McConnell of *Langley*—the picture was a cloudier and more threatening one. With so many principal officers operating under the increasingly urgent pressures of time in such a communications and information fog, it was perhaps inevitable that hasty, half-informed decisions would lead to catastrophe. Yet on the afternoon of February 27, few of these men could have foreseen the scale of the disaster that would come over the next forty-eight hours.

Benefiting from the temperate weather and sea conditions, those still on board *Langley* got off the ship with few problems. And while it was neither an exceptionally orderly nor a chaotic, helter-skelter abandonment, it did happen swiftly due to concerns that the listing tender might suddenly capsize. Signalman Lowell Barty just jumped "feet first" off the signal bridge, which was the same height from the water as the flight deck, and swam to *Whipple*.[89] Walt Frumerie went off close to the bow on the port side via a line hanging near the wheelhouse; the rope lacerated his fingers as he slid down into the water wearing his heavy life jacket. In no time he was picked up and taken to one of the destroyers, which happened to be *Edsall*. On the deck of that ship one of J. J. Nix's destroyermen handed Frumerie a Dutch cigarette—which to the exhausted quartermaster tasted "the best ever"—while another gave him an extra pair of cutoff dungarees.[90]

Although almost all the crew were off the ship and picked up by *Edsall* and *Whipple* within thirty minutes, there were a few setbacks. Severely injured men from *Langley*—including Lt. Walter Bailey—had been put in the number 1 motor whaleboat while still in its davits, and as it was lowered along the angled, listing hull's starboard side, a line aft, weakened by shrapnel or shock, came loose and spilled the boat down stern first, emptying its wounded into the sea. Able-bodied sailors immediately went into the water to rescue these men—a number of whom were enfeebled by morphine—and all were thought to have been picked up promptly by boats from *Whipple* and *Edsall*. The four-pipers were slowly motoring through the masses of survivors, scooping them up one by one or in clusters. Rescues proceeded with an increasing sense of urgency, since no one knew when and in what numbers the enemy planes might return.[91] However, wounded men and pharmacist mates were not all that fell into the Indian Ocean during the abandonment of *Langley*.

During this interval one of the more unusual events took place, which would soon garner attention in the press and eventually pass into legend: the preservation of several bags containing tens of thousands of dollars in Australian, Dutch, and Philippine money—navy payroll funds that the *Langley* had been carrying. Most of the money was conveyed successfully to *Whipple*, although waterlogged in some instances, but a number of bags opened and spilled their contents into the sea. Relatively few of these bills were grabbed by sailors in the water, most of whom were understandably preoccupied with saving themselves. The most famous example of rescuing Uncle Sam's funds—and also ship's records—came in the person of John Kennedy, Y3/c, the same young sailor who acted as Ensign Dittos's phone talker on the main deck gunnery-control station during the bombings. As he prepared to get off the ship, Kennedy was handed a large canvas bag filled with some $50,000 and various records by *Langley's* pay clerk, A. J. Randall, and ordered to get them to one of the destroyers.[92] This Kennedy managed to do once he was in the water by locating a chair floating upside down, between the legs of which he wedged the heavy bag and pushed it ahead of him as he swam. As Kennedy later told newspapers when the story gained public notice, "They were grateful about saving Uncle Sam's money, but mostly about the records which would have been troublesome to duplicate."[93]

Other aspects of the abandonment were less amusing. Just as the last men were leaving *Langley*, a lone figure floating in a kapok life jacket was spotted in the water near the port side. He was unconscious, his head lolling back. To everyone's astonishment he was recognized as Lt. Walter Bailey. No one could understand how the gravely wounded officer had come to be there after the MWB had fallen into the sea on the opposite side, but he was soon pulled from the water and transported to *Edsall*. There he was attended by the DesDiv 57 medical officer, Lt. Charles G. Butler, but he never regained consciousness.[94]

Radioman Bill Warnes had come up to the well deck after being released from his duties in the gyro room and was debating how best to get off the ship. As he sat with his feet in the gunwales peering down *Langley's* starboard side into the water below, he felt reluctant—as did many sailors—to leave the ship that been his home since January 1940. At that moment *Langley's* XO, Cdr. Lawrence Divoll, who was helping oversee the abandonment, walked past and noticed

Warnes. The destroyer *Whipple* was scarcely fifty yards away, and in the calm seas most men were making the swim to her without difficulty. When Bill told Divoll that he was having trouble making up his mind, the xo said, "Here, let me help you" and gave Warnes a sharp push. That took care of the radioman's decision-making quandary. Into the sea he went and swam over to *Whipple*; he later told newspapers: "There was nothing to it."[95] The destroyer by this time had several hundred extra men on board, most of whom were told to go below decks and not move about unnecessarily. As events played out, the lucky Warnes would be rescued by *Whipple* not once but twice.

Without question the options then facing McConnell (and his fellow commanders) were almost entirely bad ones. The two destroyers were overloaded, far from port, and would soon be running low on fuel—especially for any high-speed steaming—and they remained virtually defenseless against aerial assault. Time was against them, too, with the looming possibility of new air attacks. It did not escape McConnell's attention that *Whipple* and *Edsall* were both "useless against high-flying aircraft and of but doubtful value against dive bombers or torpedo planes." Survivors later recalled that there were concerns, too, about having so many men—over three hundred—on board *Whipple* with her chronically fragile bow. As McConnell later wrote in explication to Adm. Ernest King (commander in chief, COMINCH), "The decision to abandon the *Langley* at the time was the only practical solution, albeit, the hardest to make. It is felt further that the crew did their utmost, not only in fighting the ship but also in their efforts to repair damage and keep the ship going. They moved intelligently and effectively in overcoming many fierce fires and in effecting repairs with the means available and were defeated only by the failure of the drainage system to combat the ingress of water."[96]

Commander McConnell, accompanied by a handful of his crew, was in the final boat to push off from *Langley*. He had been moved and distracted by persistent cries of "Come on, captain!" from his men still in the water and already on board the destroyers, and he felt that "this solicitude for the commanding officer was interfering with the rescue work and adding to the jeopardy of the two destroyers." He had then accepted the necessity of getting off *Langley* and using the destroyer armament to "accelerate her sinking . . . as it was considered that this would be the most effective method in any event."[97] At 1345 the order of "over the side" was also given, and McConnell went to *Whipple*. After all crew were seen to be clear of *Langley*, he returned to the tender to verify destruction of code books, bridge publications, and the general signal book and saw to it that the all-important ECM was dumped overboard. Satisfied that these essential actions had been completed properly, McConnell went once more to *Whipple*. By 1358 hours all of *Langley's* men were on board *Whipple* and *Edsall*.

Although *Langley* was down by the bow and listing to port, she exhibited no immediate signs of going under. To hasten her sinking—which in turn would allow the two destroyers with their survivors to get away from the scene—*Whipple* fired nine rounds of 4-inch into the ship at 1428 hours. These shells, which seem to have accomplished little, were followed by a single torpedo at 1432, which struck the ship on her starboard side "aft of the starboard jib crane in the magazine area." This hit caused the ship to begin returning to an even keel, but the tough old bird still remained stubbornly afloat. At 1445 *Whipple* expended a second torpedo, which went "into the port side, striking below the stack sponson and setting a fierce fire at the break of the poop deck." This hit apparently caused more damage, as the ship was soon seriously aflame from amidships aft and settling lower into the sea. McConnell, Eugene Karpe, and Edwin Crouch had seen enough at that point. The two torpedoes fired by *Whipple* represented half of her total—"a serious reduction in [her] fighting power"—and the men were eager to put miles between themselves and enemy planes. *Whipple* then turned her bows due west and increased revolutions, which she maintained for the next three hours.[98] During the ensuing minutes Crouch sent another message to Glassford: "ALL SURVIVORS ABOARD WHIPPLE EDSALL HEADING WEST 25 KNOTS TO CLEAR AREA X 25 WOUNDED 6 SERIOUSLY X COMMANDER MCCONNELL RECOMMENDS TAKING PERSONNEL TO FREMANTLE FOR FURTHER USE X ADVISE."[99]

The advice given to the American officers at sea south of Java soon became a tangle of jumbled communications and conflicting priorities. These overlapping orders—and who precisely was giving them—have not been previously recognized. For reasons never adequately explained, both COMSOWESPAC ADMIN at Tjilatjap and COMSOWESPAC at Bandoeng were still busy transmitting messages, but regardless Crouch's request to proceed to Australia with his survivors and wounded was denied.

Less than two hours later *Parrott*, which was then still escorting *Pecos*, received word to instruct the oiler to proceed to the lee of Christmas Island, about 250 miles south of Tjilatjap. There *Pecos* was to anchor and receive the survivors of *Langley* from the two old tin cans. *Whipple* recorded the message as well, and she altered course at 1755 hours to 235° T., steaming at fifteen knots to meet *Pecos* the following morning.[100] However, COMSOWESPAC ADMIN had already sent the same information some twenty minutes earlier to Crouch (ComDes-Div 57) in *Whipple*.[101] It does seem that the appearance of Japanese submarines, surface raiders, and land-based airplanes over the Indian Ocean with the resultant loss of *Langley* may have rattled these officers. A number of smaller U.S. vessels were then at sea just outside Tjilatjap.[102] It must have suddenly become apparent to them that the situation was rapidly deteriorating and serious American and Allied casualties might ensue. At the same time they were hit by more communications gremlins, and these continued to plague their radio transmissions until the very end.

These technical problems appear to have caused COMSOWESPAC ADMIN to send a cranky "urgent" message out later that night with the suggestion, "GIVE DIRECTIVE TO PILLSBURY TULSA ASHEVILLE LARK WHIPPOORWILL X I BELIEVE THEY ARE NOW NEEDLESSLY SEARCHING FOR LANGLEY AND WILL BE EXPOSED TO ATTACK X." At the same time COMSOWESPAC ADMIN believed that the earlier message to Crouch regarding the disposal of *Langley* survivors and wounded had been "UNDELIVERED OR DISREGARDED." If it had not been received and acted on, there was concern that it could "INTERFERE WITH [Crouch's] VITAL MISSION OF PROTECTING TROOP SHIPS."[103] With so much confusion, it took little for yet one more monkey wrench to be thrown into this already-jumbled mix.

In the early afternoon of February 27, just as *Langley* was receiving the coup de grâce from *Whipple*, Lieutenant Admiral Helfrich sent another "most immediate" message to his Allied confederates requesting that the "oiler *Belita* be diverted to Cocos Island forthwith."[104] Whether this request was simply another attempt by the Dutch to maintain their offshore fueling dispositions is unclear. What *is* now understood, however, is that the British and the Americans—perhaps without Helfrich's direct knowledge—were also working to rescue a party of high-ranking Royal Navy and Royal Air Force officers who had been shipwrecked on a tiny island north of Bangka off the coast of Sumatra since mid-February. Rear Admiral Spooner and Air Vice Marshal Pulford were among a group of men who had left Singapore at the last moment in a British motor launch (ML-310) and made their way south, seeking to evade prowling Japanese air and sea patrols that were trying to interdict and destroy such evacuees. "No Dunkirk at Singapore!" the Japanese propaganda machinery boasted, and their naval and air forces made great efforts to enforce this declaration. Duly attacked, ML-310 ended up beached and wrecked near Chebia (also spelled Tjebea), and its occupants were left to fend for themselves on the small, inhospitable, and malarial island.

As the Java Sea and Indian Ocean battles were raging to the south, an American submarine—Red Coe's old pigboat, S-39—was informed of the men's

SIX DAYS TO OBLIVION

presence on this remote island.[105] The submarine was vectored up to determine if they could be found and extracted. If so it was tentatively planned to next transport the party to the Cocos Islands, where they would be put aboard a British oiler there. That ship, of course, was *Belita*. However, the oiler was a solitary and undefended ship, and with this extra value added to her complement, she required more protection. The job of acting as her antisubmarine escort then fell to *Whipple*. Presumably this would also have permitted the hard-pressed destroyer to replenish her fuel oil tanks before proceeding on to her next assignment. Yet many adventures were to come for both Red Coe's S-39 and Eugene Karpe's *Whipple* before either could prepare navigational plans for that rendezvous.

Other Asiatic Fleet vessels had received multiple duties to carry out, too. Later that same evening at 2230 hours, Lt. John Hughes's *Parrott* left *Pecos* to return to Tjilatjap, where she was needed to help escort the merchant ship *Sea Witch* into the port. That merchant ship had been allowed to come into port under the cover of night, and although *Parrott* did not locate her until eight the next morning, this reliance on darkness probably preserved the ship and her cargo of crated P-40E fighters.[106]

At the same time as *Parrott* was taking station off the port bow of *Sea Witch* for the final hours into Tjilatjap along with "Froggy" Pound's *Pillsbury* to starboard—and after cruising through "scattered wreckage . . . apparently from *Langley*"—two of their sister flushdeckers (carrying the men who had just called that very debris their home) were meeting *Pecos* at Christmas Island some 250 miles to the south. In what should have been fairly routine business, the ships were to exchange personnel—with the remaining AAF personnel, pilots, and mechanics all being transferred to *Edsall*—and then go about their individual missions. *Pecos* with her survivors and wounded was to set course for the western coast of Australia, either Exmouth Gulf or Fremantle. *Whipple* would be sent deeper into the Indian Ocean to meet *Belita* at the Cocos Islands. *Edsall* was to return the AAF men to Tjilatjap, where it was thought they could still help assemble and fly the remaining P-40Es that were then being brought in on *Sea Witch*. To Glassford and staff this may have seemed a reasonably practical disposition of these remaining forces.[107] But again it was a scheme that only guaranteed catastrophe.

Unknown to the naval command in Java or the men at sea, Japanese surface forces of considerable power had already steamed through the Malay Barrier and were now searching for targets of opportunity in the Indian Ocean south of the Indies.[108] Elements of one enemy task group—identified as "two cruisers and two large vessels"—were spotted early on February 28 150 miles south of Java.

This sighting report was sent by COMSOWESPAC to *Edsall, Whipple, Parrott, Pillsbury, Pope,* and *Phoenix.* Unquestionably these ships were Vice Adm. Kondō Nobutake's Southern Force group known as Main Body. It was composed of three cruisers from Sentai 4—*Atago* (F), *Takao,* and *Maya*—battleships *Kongō* and *Haruna,* DDs, and oilers. Kondō was in fact the ranking Imperial Navy admiral in the "Southern Area" (Southwest Pacific) and CinC of the Second Fleet, from which the Southern Force was formed. Along with Main Body, Vice Admiral Kondō had been allocated another extremely powerful offensive asset when he and his ships teamed out of Staring Bay, on the southeastern side of Celebes on February 25. This was the heart of Japan's First Air Fleet, with its associated support vessels, under Vice Adm. Nagumo Chuichi and known as Kidō Butai.

This strong carrier force was assigned to sweep the waters below Christmas Island, alert to fleeing Allied ships while at the same time preparing for another massive air raid—this one to be directed against Java's last tenable port, Tjilatjap.[109] Nagumo's Mobile Force was built around the nucleus of the Imperial Navy's carrier forces. The First Air Fleet's heavy carriers *Akagi* (F) and *Kaga* of CarDiv 1; the smaller but no less potent *Sōryū* (F) and *Hiryū* of CarDiv 2; along with a support force of two upgraded fast battleships of Sentai 3, *Hiei* (F) and *Kirishima,* and two modern heavy cruisers from Sentai 8, *Tone* (F) and *Chikuma.* Additionally it contained a screen force, under the DesRon 1 flagship, light cruiser *Abukuma,* with nine large, new destroyers. Six fueling vessels were also sent out on the operation. Against such a crack organization—already involved in the Pearl Harbor attacks and raids on Rabaul, Ambon, and Darwin—the combined Allied navies in the East Indies and Indian Ocean could offer no effective response. The fragmented and war-weary forces of what had once been the old U.S. Asiatic Fleet were by that time little more than moving targets.

On board *Abukuma* an Imperial Navy sailor recorded his impressions in the "flowery language" much favored by Japanese newspapers, magazines, and other propaganda organs. The chosen title for his little booklet—which begins in November 1941 with the Pearl Harbor operation and concludes in April 1942 with the Doolittle Raid—was "The Southern Cross," and its dozen or so pages contain a somewhat bewildering yet fascinating amalgam of poetic declamations juxtaposed with precise military observations.[110] He wrote of the transit into the Indian Ocean: "The fleet, keeping a strict anti-submarine patrol in the sea areas where enemy submarines navigate, advanced between the islands which intersperse the Ombai Straits. . . . These waters, ripple-free as flowing oil, reminded me of the Inland Sea. . . . Words at such a time fail to express what I feel. Wild ducks flying together, clouds floating majestically, a great school of dolphins—the very picture of peace. Could it be that a bloody war was being fought on such a sea? It is not surprising that we felt a sense of wonder."[111]

As the Japanese task force steamed between the Barrier islands, scores of other young sailors, Dutch, British, Australian, and American—then one thousand miles to the west—were having less flowery thoughts about the events they faced and experiencing an utterly different species of "wonder."

• • •

Roughly four hours after informing Glassford of his situation following the abandonment of *Langley*, Crouch sent a follow-up message to COMSOWESPAC. At 1842 hours he transmitted the following: "FURTHER CHECK SHOWS 485 SURVIVORS ABOARD BOTH SHIPS X SIXTEEN MISSING X FIRED TWO TORPEDOES INTO LANGLEY AND CLEARED AREA TO AVOID FURTHER AIR ATTACK X LANGLEY ON FIRE AND HEAVY LIST TO PORT WHEN WE LEFT BUT DID NOT ACTUALLY OBSERVE HER SINK X REQUEST AIR RECONNAISSANCE CHECK AT DAYLIGHT WHETHER SHE ACTUALLY SUNK X TOTAL SIXTEEN TWIN ENGINED BOMBERS AND SIX FIGHTERS ATTACKED WHEN HEADED EAST X TWO TORPEDOES LEFT ON WHIPPLE XX."[112] Crouch and McConnell were here attempting to clarify their decision making for Glassford in case he felt the tender had been abandoned prematurely. As it turned out, this was precisely the conclusion drawn by Glassford later, and it would cause no small degree of embarrassment—and the potential for much worse—to Cdr. Robert McConnell.

At sea, their minds preoccupied with enemy air patrols and the likely presence of submarines, the harried American commanders—Crouch, Karpe, and McConnell—sought to reach a plan for the transfers. The two flushdeckers spotted Christmas Island at daybreak and at 0755 requested the services of a pilot as they approached Flying Fish Cove. At 0840 the British pilot, a Mr. Craig, came aboard *Whipple*. At that point one further hindrance arose when he informed Crouch and Karpe that a Japanese submarine had been spotted off the island the previous afternoon. With the broken-back hulk of the torpedoed merchant ship *Eidsvold* plainly visible—grounded just off the cove—this new information complicated matters.[113] The men were now not only worried about an enemy sub but apprehensive that their radio communications might be compromised. It was decided to transfer the men while the ships were under way, and in order to keep their plans secure, they would send a boat carrying *Langley*'s first lieutenant, Lt. Cdr. Thomas Donovan (USNA 1928), to *Pecos* to tell them in person of the change in the transfer procedure.[114]

The transfers of AAF men from *Whipple* to *Edsall* took just twelve minutes; this was completed by 0920. Donovan then got into Craig's pilot boat for the short ride over to *Pecos*. As the boat carrying Donovan, Craig, and two natives approached *Pecos*, a line trailing aft fouled the propeller and the little craft lost power. It was close enough to the sea ladder on *Pecos*'s port side, however, for Craig to leap onto the ladder, but as he did so he pushed the boat away from the oiler.[115] The short, heavyset Donovan made no attempt to jump. He and the two native boatmen were left powerless and adrift as they worked frantically to clear the propeller. Their boat then drifted around to the stern of *Pecos* and out of sight to the two destroyers. At that moment the entire scenario for transferring the survivors was shattered—and indeed the fate of both *Pecos* and *Edsall* sealed—when a trio of Japanese twin-engine bombers appeared flying high in the sky from the east.

All three ships scattered out of the anchorage area at best speed, for it was apparent that the three medium bombers were preparing for an attack. The planes—G4M BETTYS—were from the same Takao Kū unit flying out of Denpasar that had attacked *Langley* the previous day. At 1039 hours their bombs came shrieking down. However, they all struck along the Flying Fish Cove shoreline close to the piers and docks; not one of the ships was hit or near missed. In the confusion and excitement of this sudden and unexpected bombing attack, though, Lt. Cdr. Tom Donovan was forgotten. As Donovan later wrote: "So the boat with me as a passenger was adrift and abandoned."[116] The first lieutenant from *Langley* had what may be seen as either marvelous fortune or the most terrible luck. Marooned on Christmas Island for a month before it was seized by the Japanese, he became a prisoner of war. Yet facing a long and wretched incarceration, Donovan was still far more fortunate than hundreds of men who had just steamed off over the horizon in *Whipple*, *Edsall*, and *Pecos*. With this "turn of the screw" the fate of many of those young sailors and air force personnel would be sealed, yet what became of them remained a profound mystery for over seven decades.

Heading for a timely rainsquall spotted to the east, the three ships fired back at the high-flying bombers as they sought cover under the clouds, but luckily for them the Japanese pilots had no real interest in their ships as targets.[117] Although they flew over the Americans menacingly, no more attacks were made. Nonetheless, the alarmed gunners on *Whipple* still expended 23 rounds of 3-inch AA ammo, plus 1,050 rounds of .50 cal. and 287 rounds of .30 cal. ammunition at the enemy planes during this short interval, and it may be fairly assumed that gunners on *Edsall* did much the same. All the U.S. naval officers expected additional enemy air attacks now that the Japanese had been alerted to Allied ships at Christmas Island. By the same token, with the sighting of a large auxiliary and two destroyers, it probably appeared to the Japanese that the island's forces may have been in the process of receiving reinforcements. Accordingly, the Japanese were not then finished with operations directed against Christmas Island.[118]

As they emerged from the rainsquall, the three ships were relieved to see that the enemy planes had departed. However, a submarine periscope had been reported off *Whipple*'s starboard quarter during the bombings, and this extra threat—although probably imaginary at that time—was a constant concern for all the men. The belief that they were being stalked by at least one Japanese submarine was not far from anyone's mind throughout the next couple of days and would have tragic consequences in the end.

The senior officer present was Cdr. Edwin Crouch (ComDesDiv 57) in *Whipple*, and he chose to have the three ships head south, deeper into the Indian Ocean, at the best speed possible by *Pecos*—about 12 knots—and transfer the survivors while under way. This maneuver would hopefully put distance between the American ships and the Japanese forces—wherever they were—and make the three vessels less vulnerable to submarine attack. This change in plans went out in Crouch's dispatch to Glassford just after noon: "SHORE STATION BOMBED BY THREE PLANES X PECOS AND DD'S NOT HIT X SURVIVORS NOT TRANSFERRED WE ARE ALL HEADING SOUTH 12 KNOTS TO CLEAR AREA WILL TRANSFER SURVIVORS AFTER DARK IF SEA CONDITIONS PERMIT X EXPECT MORE ATTACKS THIS AFTERNOON X WE ARE BEING SHADOWED BY ONE PLANE XX."[119] Under the circumstances this decision appears reasonable enough, but at least two or three other issues would emerge, all of which had serious consequences.

As Crouch's message implied, weather conditions soon worsened; the Indian Ocean quickly became turbulent, with high seas and 26-knot winds. This made it impossible to transfer the men while under way that afternoon and forced the ships to steam deeper into the Indian Ocean. On *Edsall*, for example, Walt Frumerie knew the dangers of being topside in such weather, and he remained below decks for the most part. On the more crowded *Whipple* the men were told to not move about the ship too freely for fear of stressing the destroyer's newly repaired bow. Karpe was also conscious of the precarious stability of his ship, which, like all four-pipers was prone to excessive rolling in any but calm seas.

Another factor was the number of seriously wounded men on board: three each on *Edsall* and *Whipple* who needed to be hospitalized promptly. Eight hours after his midday message to Glassford, Crouch sent another transmission: "HAVE HEADED SOUTH SINCE NOON TWELVE KNOTS NO FURTHER

ATTACKS X SUBMARINE PERISCOPE SIGHTED NORTHEAST POINT OF ISLAND X IMPOSSIBLE TRANSFER WOUNDED AND OTHERS TONIGHT DUE SEA CONDITIONS X 32 ARMY 12 MECHANICS ON EDSALL OF WHICH 31 AND 10 RESPECTIVELY AVAILABLE FOR DUTY X THREE WOUNDED EACH DESTROYER REQUIRE URGENT HOSPITALIZATION X RECOMMEND DESTROYERS PROCEED AHEAD BEST SPEED TOMORROW TO EXMOUTH GULF DISCHARGE SURVIVORS SEND SIX WOUNDED TO HOSPITAL BY PLANE X."[120]

As this message should make evident, Crouch and his fellow officers had no desire to linger in *any* proximity to the East Indies. One may also read between the lines of this message sent that night and perceive Crouch's hope that *Edsall*'s foolish assignment to return to Tjilatjap might be called off as well. But in Glassford they had a commander who was (like Hart) of the old school in the sense that he placed more value on obedience and the strict adherence to orders than to flexibility in a crisis.[121] It appears he took the U.S. commitment to aid Helfrich and the Dutch quite seriously.

Headquartered in Bandoeng, Glassford—the career officer whose years of service in Asia had involved no small amount of diplomacy as well as operational duties—would have been trying to keep several very different balls in the air at once. This challenge involved accommodating his naval command superior, Lieutenant Admiral Helfrich, as well as his chief of staff, Rear Admiral Palliser of the Royal Navy, acting in a spirit of cooperation while at the same time making efforts to not squander American lives or valuable military assets in what was clearly a losing proposition. Yet it would not be long before both Glassford and Palliser recognized that the operational reversals on February 27–28 in the Indian Ocean to the south and in the Java Sea to the north represented the beginning of a swift downward spiral. Beyond that point it was really a matter of struggling to control the free fall. Any effective opposition to the Japanese was by then out of the question.

Unfortunately for the crew of the destroyer *Edsall*, their lives appear to have been viewed as expendable. But by then Glassford was growing increasingly exasperated at the actions of a number of his commanders at sea and was more than likely looking for potential scalps to take when the dust settled. On the original copy of Crouch's message sent that night (dispatch 281230) regarding his suggestion to take the destroyers at best speed to Exmouth Gulf, Glassford scribbled: "This was not approved. He was ordered continue efforts transfer the survivors to *Pecos* then proceed on his vital mission—escort of troop convoy."[122] What this tells us—and has not been properly recognized previously—is that the urgency of protecting ships leaving Java with Allied evacuees had at least as much to do with Glassford's decision to return *Edsall* to Tjilat-jap as getting the AAF crews into Java. In *that* sense it was not an unreasonable or rash plan. It was, however, implemented far too late and as such allowed just the right number of factors to tumble into place to doom *Edsall* and every soul on board her. In the meantime, the schedule of the tanker *Belita* served to act as a kind of naval deus ex machina, preserving the entire crew of *Whipple* and, ultimately, over two hundred survivors of *Langley* and *Pecos*.

Glassford's commanders south of Christmas Island were told to expedite the transfer of survivors to *Pecos* and continue on their individual assignments. The wounded would have to be placed in the care of *Pecos*'s medical team—aided by *Langley*'s doctors (Cdr. Robert Blackwell, Lt. J. F. Handley, and Lt. [j.g.] C. W. Holly Jr.) and pharmacist's mates if necessary—and the rest of the men would need make do as best they could. For one badly injured Asiatic Fleet officer it was already too late. At 2200 hours on February 28, Lt. Walter Bailey finally succumbed to his wounds on board *Edsall*. The following morning, before dawn, he was buried at sea, the ceremony presided over by Commander Divoll. Shortly thereafter the transfer of *Langley* survivors—including wounded men—from *Whipple* and *Edsall* to *Pecos* took place "while the weather was rather rough but accomplished safely with no ill effects on the patients."[123]

These transfers occurred between approximately 0520 and 0800 hours despite high seas and wind, with one destroyer acting as an antisubmarine patrol for the other during the actual boat trips to *Pecos*.[124] Once the transfers were completed, at about 0830 the three ships split off on their respective missions. *Whipple* altered course to 279° T. and changed speed to 17 knots for her rendezvous at the Cocos Islands with *Belita*. Lt. J. J. Nix's *Edsall* steamed off slowly to the north, carrying the AAF personnel, with the intention of lingering south of Christmas Island during the day before making a high-speed run overnight into Tjilatjap. The oiler *Pecos* set course for Fremantle at 160° T., which would take her some 130 miles from the northwestern shoulder of Australia and beyond the range—it was hoped—of those land-based enemy bombers on Bali.[125]

On the previous day (28 February) Glassford had taken stock of his remaining forces and sent a lengthy message to CZM/Helfrich as well as to CCCF/Collins regarding their disposition. Among much else it also stated: "WHIPPLE EDSALL SOUTH OF CHRISTMAS ISLAND WITH LANGLEY SURVIVORS ON BOARD X WHEN TRANSFERRED WHIPPLE PROCEEDS TO COCOS ISLAND TO PROTECT BELITA EDSALL RETURNS TJILATJAP WITH FIGHTER CREWS X."[126]

That there had been no important alterations to these plans—at least up until 0830 hours on March 1—is verified by the actions of *Pecos*, *Whipple*, and *Edsall* the following morning. One suspects that Glassford was content to allow *Edsall*, the junior destroyer in her division after all—and still retaining nine torpedoes—to undertake this perilous assignment while the division flagship under Cdr. Edwin Crouch—which was known to possess only two torpedoes and had a tender bow as well—was sent off to meet *Belita*. COMSOWESPAC was not simply dividing up his already slender forces but also dicing and mincing them, yet in the end this dispersion may well have preserved *Whipple* and saved several hundred more men from *Langley* and *Pecos*, too. To the profoundly unfortunate *Edsall* fell the lot of sacrificial victim.

By way of contrast with *Edsall's* fate, an examination of the peregrinations of the light cruiser USS *Phoenix*—a relatively new vessel and a far more potent military asset—may be enlightening. In the same communication to CZM of midday on the twenty-eighth, Glassford made a reference to the whereabouts of *Phoenix*, that powerful, modern warship on which Helfrich had seemingly placed such emphasis for weeks. The COMSOWESPAC message told the Dutch admiral: "PHOENIX ABOUT LAT 11 SOUTH LONG 92 X WHEN RELIEVED THIS AFTERNOON BY ENTERPRISE WILL PROCEED TOWARD JAVA X."[127]

Here, too, Glassford was giving an honest accounting that nevertheless hid his real intentions—and for this the men of *Phoenix* ought to have been very grateful to him—since the actual mission assigned to *Phoenix* was indeed to "proceed toward Java" but most certainly not to come into Helfrich's hands. After turning over convoy MS.5 to HMS *Enterprise*, she was to return to a rendezvous point in the Indian Ocean well south of Java and escort Allied ships steaming for Australia. Whether Helfrich actually believed at that stage that *Phoenix* would operate under his control is another issue. While Helfrich's post-campaign memoirs and letters suggest as much, it is unlikely that either Glassford or the Royal Navy commanders (Collins and Palliser) held such a belief.

*Phoenix* duly completed her escort duties with convoy MS.5 and was relieved by HMS *Enterprise* on February 28. She then turned back in the direction of Java. However, she had received changes in her orders three times between Friday, February 27, and Sunday, March 1. Each one altered her course farther away from the island and deeper into the Indian Ocean. First she was to move east along the 10th parallel, then along the 13th, and finally the 15th. At no time was she encouraged to actively seek out engagement with enemy forces, and one gets the very distinct impression that she was deliberately kept away from Java and Helfrich's "grasping" hands. While this was good luck for *Phoenix* because there were two formidable Japanese task groups at sea, it would also represent the worst irony to the men of *Langley*, *Pecos*, *Edsall*, and *Pillsbury*, since the big cruiser was never able to come to their aid. When the few Asiatic Fleet survivors did reach Fremantle at last, their reaction to the sight of *Phoenix* anchored in port, having never fired her guns in anger or aided in the rescue of a single soul, did not go over well.[128]

. . .

As we have seen, *Edsall*, *Whipple*, and *Pecos* had taken different courses when they split up at 0830 hours on the morning of March 1. Both destroyers were probably expecting alterations to their respective assignments, since they clearly understood that COMSOWESPAC HQ on Java was on the verge of shutting down. *Whipple*'s action report says as much explicitly, stating that after four hours of steaming west she simply altered course to the southwest at 1247 hours, then— "on advice of Commander Destroyer Division Fifty-Seven" [Crouch]—changed course to the south at 1324, "due to numerous messages originating from Commander Southwest Pacific relative to retirement from Java and in expectation of change of orders from same sources."[129] What neither she nor the others understood was that they were all murderously close to Vice Admiral Nagumo's Kidō Butai, and that the carriers, battleships, cruisers, and destroyers of that organization were, like all bored predators, hungry to locate worthy targets.

As usual Nagumo had launched patrols from his escorting cruisers that morning at dawn. The long-ranged floatplane from the heavy cruiser *Tone* searched areas toward Christmas Island. It reported seeing a wrecked merchant ship there—this would have been the *Eidsvold*—adding, "Other than that, no enemy [is] sighted." On its return leg, however, three more sightings were made in rapid succession by *Tone*'s sharp-eyed observers. Two small merchant ships were seen to the northwest of Kidō Butai between 80 and 110 miles away, moving slowly to the southwest. Next the floatplane "sighted a third enemy ship" at 0937 hours.[130] This lone vessel was steaming quite deliberately at about 8 knots in the opposite direction, toward Java. There is little doubt that this was Lt. J. J. Nix's destroyer *Edsall* lingering well off Christmas Island. Closer still to the Japanese, *Pecos* was plowing south at her best speed of about 14 knots, but she had yet to be spotted by the task group air patrols. However, on that fateful Black Sunday, the first victim of Nagumo's force would be neither an American vessel nor a warship.

A medium-sized merchant ship was discovered in a position much closer to the Japanese task group, which was then spread out over tens of kilometers across the ocean in a roughly inverted T-shaped formation as it began sweeping south-southeast at 0830 hours that morning. At the head of the IJN force was the 5,500-ton light cruiser, *Abukuma*, flagship of DesRon 1 under Rear Adm. Ōmori Sentarō, the screen force commander. The three-funneled *Abukuma* had a handful of her destroyers spread out abreast and on the flanks. Additionally, each of the four carriers in Kidō Butai nestled in the heart of the formation had its own dedicated guard destroyer. Heavy gun power for Nagumo's group was supplied by the support force: BatDiv 3's second section, the fast battleships *Hiei* and *Kirishima*—under Vice Adm. Mikawa Gun'ichi in *Hiei*, also support force commander—and the two newest heavy cruisers of the Imperial Navy, sisters *Tone* and *Chikuma*, of CruDiv 8, commanded by Rear Adm. Abe Hiroaki in *Tone*. These long, lithe, and powerful cruisers were designed for advanced scouting duties with their augmented complement of floatplanes and as such were positioned out on the flanks. The two battleships of Mikawa—the same admiral who would gain notoriety later as the victor of the Battle of Savo Island in August 1942 off Guadalcanal—were in column toward the rear of the formation.

As the morning unfolded with few (if any) military targets nearby, Vice Admiral Nagumo had planned to refuel his ships, unless they became engaged. The mobile force had been at sea for several days, and fuel would have been running low. Moreover, that far from their forward base—Staring Bay near Kendari, Celebes—Nagumo and his skippers were all quite conscious of their exposed position and vulnerability even though they had little concern about any Allied forces they might contact. It was presumed—and rightly—that the majority of U.S., British, and Dutch warships that had not been destroyed in the battles around Java would try to escape to either Ceylon or Australia. And while the Japanese worried continually about submarines, they still did not know enough about conditions in Tjilatjap to justify an air raid in force, which was what Nagumo had been instructed to do. Nagumo seems to have reasoned that any personnel seized from the fleeing Allied merchant vessel found that morning might provide details on shipping and the general situation at Tjilatjap. He therefore dispatched the heavy cruiser *Chikuma* with two destroyers from DesDiv 18, *Shiranuhi* and *Ariake*, to deal with the merchant ship. On this morning, though, nothing would go smoothly or simply for the Japanese task group either.

• • •

The unlucky merchantman was in fact the Dutch *Modjokerto* (8,082 tons), from the Rotterdamsche-Lloyd line, and her fate would end as darkly as any ship lost that day. Captain Jacobus Verhagen's ship with the distinctive icebreaker bow was one of several dozen merchant vessels ordered out of Tjilatjap on the night of February 27. It is believed that the ship was to be routed to Bombay, but her immediate orders had changed like other merchantmen in the southern Javanese port at that time. Many of these ships were instructed to proceed to sea and take up holding positions some 400 kilometers (about 250 miles) offshore until they received further instructions from the Dutch authorities. For *Modjokerto* her position that day placed her almost directly in the path of Nagumo's hunters.

On the morning of March 1, when southeast of Christmas Island, *Modjokerto* reported that she had been spotted by a Japanese scout plane.[131] This sighting in turn led to the appearance of *Chikuma* with the two destroyers. *Shiranuhi* reported to Rear Admiral Ōmori (screen force commander in *Abukuma*) and Vice Admiral Nagumo that the merchant ship was a "7,000-ton class" vessel and had not behaved correctly when challenged; the destroyers were therefore "going to sink her." Rather than come to a halt meekly and destroy her radio equipment, *Modjokerto*—which had not revealed her nationality when the enemy ships appeared—then transmitted an SOS signal when the enemy ships first fired on her. What is more, she may have even returned fire against these assailants with a single 3-inch gun mounted on her bow. This was at roughly 1000 hours, when her message stated that she was being attacked by surface forces. For this temerity *Modjokerto* was dealt with swiftly and severely. The pair of DesDiv 18 destroyers fired rather ineffectively at first, apparently at long range, but their 5-inch shells—even when they hit the target—were not effective. This continued until 1013, when *Chikuma* came up and began pouring the first of forty-nine 8-inch armor-piercing projectiles into Verhagen's ship. Many of these AP rounds went through her unarmored merchant hull, but they seem to have had the desired effect. At 1015 hours *Modjokerto* sent out another message, off frequency, which was picked up accidentally by her sister merchant vessel *Siantar*, then roughly one hundred miles northwest of *Modjokerto*. This final message was fragmented but included the word *sinking*. Another Dutch merchant vessel fleeing Java also copied that last signal. *Zaandam*, about three hundred miles from the coast, picked up at least two of these messages from *Modjokerto*. The last one told the tale: "I am sinking."[132] The records of *Chikuma* for that day confirm that the merchant ship indeed sank some ten minutes later, at 1025 hours. For the men under Captain Jacobus Verhagen, it would have been better had they plunged into the depths with their ship.

Although *Modjokerto* carried a crew of about forty-two, a dozen men must have been lost in the shelling and sinking. Japanese records state that thirty minutes after her reported sinking, a number of survivors were spotted "aboard a cutter (or cutters) in the vicinity of the ship." At that time *Ariake* was ordered by Nagumo to "capture the crewmembers."[133] She did as directed, but it should be remembered that Kidō Butai was continuing to move south, so that *Ariake* became separated by many miles over the next few hours. Next, with one encounter leading to another, yet another sighting was reported. This one caught Nagumo's attention.

"Appears to be an enemy merchant ship, 207°, 70 NM from *Akagi*, course 180. Speed 14 knots." Whether through a desire to give his eager fliers some practice, or because he felt the enemy vessel worthy of attack, Nagumo then ordered aircraft from *Kaga* and *Sōryū* to "immediately scramble and sink this ship."[134] Some Japanese accounts, however, stated the ship was believed to be a "special service vessel," and it seems probable—given the spirited AA fire coming from it—that air spotters understood the ship was not merely one more fleeing merchantman. It was Cdr. E. Paul Abernethy's oiler *Pecos*, packed to overflowing with the survivors of *Langley*, and like the doomed seaplane tender her final hour had also arrived.

On board *Pecos*, as hundreds of sailors tried to adjust to their new home within the hours after parting company with *Whipple* and *Edsall*, a Japanese patrol plane's droning engine was heard. The silvery aircraft was then seen circling high in the eastern sky. Although *Pecos*'s AA gunners opened fire briefly, no one topside had any doubts that they would soon be under attack yet again.[135]

In the interior of the tanker a chow line had formed as cooks began trying to feed as many of the hungry men as possible. Standing in line was Walt Frumerie, the veteran quartermaster from *Langley*. Also waiting in line—where it snaked topside—Lowell Barty, SM3/c of *Langley*, was hoping to get some food into his stomach, and like others he heard the scout plane approach. As soon as the snooper was recognized to be enemy, GQ sounded again and men ran to their stations. On the bridge of *Pecos* Commander Abernethy, his navigator, Lt. F. B. McCall, and Commander McConnell held a brief confab. Abernethy then altered course to 225° T. and asked for maximum speed, which was about 14.5 knots, hoping to put distance between *Pecos* and the Japanese carrier force that he felt must be nearby. He had no doubt that they would soon be attacked. The surviving officers and crew of *Langley* seconded these opinions. Within another hour and forty-five minutes everyone's suspicions were confirmed.

It is an index to human exhaustion—or perhaps merely in the nature of all predation—that the men on *Pecos*, even with scores of additional pairs of eyes from the *Langley* survivors also on the lookout, were still taken by surprise when the first eighteen enemy dive-bombers arrived over their ship. Few more graphic examples of the need for radar may be found in surface encounters during the war's opening months in the Pacific.

From the carriers *Kaga* and *Sōryū* came two flights of nine planes each; these were Type 99 (VAL) dive-bombers (*kanbaku*), each carrying one 250 kg bomb. Attacking "out of the direction of the sun," they fell on the old oiler in several waves over the next hour and a half, inflicting severe damage but without stopping her and certainly not sinking her—despite their combat reports to the contrary.[136] Of the nine planes from *Kaga*, one direct hit was claimed, along with eight near misses. *Pecos*'s maddened gunners gave a good account of themselves, though, hitting four of the *Kaga* VALs with their AA fire in return. "During the battle one enemy plane was seen to be smoking and I believe several others were hit," stated Commander Abernethy later, and in this claim he was both honest and accurate.[137]

Regardless of such spirited resistance, no amount of AA gunnery from the slow, antiquated oiler was going to preserve it against determined bombings. *Kaga*'s attacks led to flooding in the ship and reduced both her speed and her maneuverability. *Pecos* had taken on an 8-degree list to port after these first hits, but "the list was corrected by pumping water into tank #15 and transferring oil from tank #18 to tank #17 . . . and gasoline was drained from the 1,400 gallons tank at the foremast."[138] Nonetheless, these injuries made the next bombing runs all the more effective; they would inflict serious damage to Abernethy's ship.

The nine *kanbaku* from *Sōryū* arrived about an hour after those of *Kaga*, and their results were far more destructive. Although they seemed to attack at "irregular intervals," these planes delivered their bombs with murderous accuracy. The first hit wiped out men in the fire-control position atop the bridge, shattered the glass bridge windows, and inflicted lacerations on all personnel there. This bomb so badly concussed the assistant fire-control officer, Ens. W. J. Crotty, that he had to be taken forcefully from the bridge and turned over to the ship's medical staff. Dr. R. P. Blackwell of *Langley* later wrote: "[Ensign Crotty's] face was flushed and he complained of headache and he was suffering from concussion due to air pressure from bomb explosions."[139]

Another hit caused even more alarming damage; it knocked out steering control. Abernethy gave orders to the after station to take control, but within half a minute steering was returned to normal. Moments later another *Sōryū kanbaku* glided in from the sky and delivered its bomb with terrible precision. "The explosion sounded as if someone had slammed the Gates of Hell," wrote Abernethy.[140]

*Sōryū*'s planes scored four direct hits in all—causing damage and inflicting scores of casualties—and a bruising near miss on the ship's port quarter that killed many of the gun crews on the after deck and wrecked a boiler in one of the fire rooms. The tanker's maximum speed dropped to about 10.5 knots, and her portside list increased to 15 degrees, but *Pecos* had not been stopped. After more heroic damage-control work managed to get several of her fires under control and reduce the list, the ship's pumps seemed to be coping with the flooding. Abernethy felt *Pecos* might still have an outside chance of surviving, but in any event he was determined to persist, or as he wrote later: "I vowed that the ship would continue to fight and would stay afloat as long as possible so as to prevent the Japanese carriers from engaging other ships."[141]

One *Pecos* crewmember, Bob Foley, CM3/c—in a damage-repair party—was sent between attacks with messages to the bridge, passing through the foc's'le mess hall as he went. There he had seen a buddy, Emory Nelson—a painter—getting a drink of water at the scuttlebutt. It was the last time the two friends would see each other alive. Within moments after Foley had moved on, one of the four bombs from *Sōryū* struck the forward section of the ship, and Emory Nelson was "splattered," as Foley would later graphically express it.[142]

A lull of about one hour came before the third wave of Japanese dive-bombers arrived from *Hiryū*. These bombers would be followed by those of the flagship *Akagi* in the final attacks. In that interim the desperate men of *Pecos*, often aided by *Langley* survivors, went about their firefighting and damage-control work with a will. It was then that Abernethy noticed thick black smoke pouring out of one of the bomb hits forward. He told *Langley*'s executive officer, Cdr. Lawrence Divoll, "There are 400 tons of aircraft bombs covered with dunnage down there—if you don't get that fire out pretty damn soon, we're going up in a hell of a big blast!" Divoll collected a sailor he knew, Robert "Chris" Christensen, S2/c, to help him. Described by Divoll as "a bad actor from *Langley* with two BCDs [bad conduct discharges] under his belt," Christensen grabbed a long fire hose, while another *Pecos* sailor supplied a rescue breathing apparatus. Down the trunk leading to the hold they went. Christenson may have been a disciplinary problem previously on the *Langley*, but he was without question a significant hero that day on *Pecos*. He put on the breather, seized the charged fire hose, and entered the smoking "inferno." As Divoll later wrote, "After it seemed like a very long time the black smoke turned to white, and to steam, and Chris crawled out." He was in a state of near-collapse due to lack of adequate oxygen in his breather, its mask clotted with mucous, but after reviving somewhat, he managed to growl, "Your damn fire is out!" The executive officer had him brought up to the main deck, where the fresh air helped restore him. Men on *Pecos*—among others the oiler's gunnery officer, Lt. Carl Armbrust—recalled afterward that the forward hold had been full of " a lot of ammunition," including torpedoes and torpedo warheads along with 6-inch and 8-inch projectiles.[143]

At the same time Abernethy, recognizing the seriousness of *Pecos*'s condition, also began having his officers take preliminary steps for getting men off the ship. He had little doubt that the attacks would continue and that sooner or later *Pecos* would have to be abandoned. Abernethy would also have been concerned about the breakdowns in discipline among some of his passengers.

During the height of the second-wave attacks—at about 1315 hours, and before the fourth bomb hit—a number of *Langley* survivors aft suddenly became unnerved and began going overboard. Several rafts and two after motor whaleboats were lost in the panic. This false "abandon ship" was quickly countermanded by Abernethy and his officers, but not before upward of a hundred men, many of them *Langley* survivors, went over the side. Of the others who went overboard at this time on rafts and in the other boat, not one would be among survivors rescued later.[144]

All hands not engaged in firefighting, damage control, or manning guns were instructed to begin bringing any items that would float up to the weather deck. Simultaneously the ship's doctors and pharmacist mates started preparing wounded men by taking them to the quarterdeck area.[145] "Some wounded men were placed in the passenger's compartment of the captains' gig," Abernethy would later write in his report, "even though it was known that her engine was inoperative. Other wounded men were lashed to officer's kapok mattresses and a man assigned to watch for each of them and to assist if possible."[146]

During these attacks and in the intervening lulls, Abernethy's executive officer, Lt. Cdr. Lawrence J. McPeake, remained a steadfast and heroic figure, reorganizing gun crews, directing repair parties, and even taking over one of the .50 cal. machine-gun mounts himself after its operator had been wounded. At about the same time Abernethy had directed one of *Langley*'s extra radiomen, Charles Snay, to see if he could help with transmissions since there seemed to be no acknowledgment of messages sent out by *Pecos*. (Unknown to Abernethy at the time, a transmitter, power amplifier tube, and cable had all been knocked out by concussion from bombs.) Charles Snay turned out to be another unsung hero that day, and it is clear that he helped briefly restore radio function to *Pecos*. The *Langley* radio electrician worked for an hour to fix the malfunctioning transmitter, and between 1414 and 1428 hours fragments of the distress calls sent out by *Pecos* reached the *Whipple*, then about seventy-five miles off to the northwest. These messages, which Snay continued to transmit until just before the ship sank, were instrumental in preserving the lives of over two hundred survivors.[147]

As the radioman was sending out his desperate calls for help ("NERK V NIFQ BOMBED SINKING CONDITION LAT 1430 LONG 10630 NPO NPO NPO

NERK NERK V NIFQ") the third wave of Nagumo's dive-bombers, nine more *kanbaku* from *Hiryū*, arrived over the doomed oiler, now head down and moving sluggishly through the choppy seas. The planes attacked in tightly spaced runs, with their bombs falling all around *Pecos*, but only two near misses forward near the starboard bow registered any damage. In return the furious gunners on *Pecos* hit no less than seven out of the nine VALs in these attacks with their AA fire. The three *chūtai* of *Hiryū*, under Lt. Shimoda Ichiro completed their bombings runs at 1450 hours and headed back across the sea to the carriers, now barely forty minutes away.

Waiting patiently in the sky above during these attacks—and observing through spaces in the clouds—was the last flight of enemy dive-bombers. These nine *kanbaku* were from Nagumo's flagship, *Akagi*. Within five minutes of the completion of *Hiryū*'s bombings, they too fell on *Pecos* and delivered the coup de grâce. In attacks led by Lt. Chihaya Takehiko, the first seven bombs missed the ship completely, but the final two delivered mortal blows.

One hit near the starboard side aft near the exposed prop and blew men off the ship, killing most of the aft gun crews as well. The other near miss shattered the hull forward at the port bow inflicting structural damage that led immediately to a pronounced list and unstable forward trim. Regaining altitude a few of Chihaya's planes circled over the mortally wounded oiler until 1525 hours to verify the effectiveness of their attacks. Four other *kanbaku* made their way back the short distance to *Akagi* bearing multiple bullet holes. All nine eventually landed safely again aboard the flagship. At this stage the Japanese planes were only about fifteen minutes from the dying *Pecos*, with Vice Admiral Nagumo's force *much* closer than has been realized previously.

In the wake of these crushing, final hits and near misses, Abernethy knew that his ship was doomed. He gave his communications officer, Lt. J. L. Lacomblé, instructions to open up the emergency and any other radio frequencies for broadcasts requesting help. These were sent in plain language, as *Pecos* had already been under attack for several hours and Abernethy correctly presumed that the Japanese knew his identity and location.

At 1530 hours Abernethy finally gave the "abandon ship" order. The oiler by then was markedly down by the bow, with seawater pouring into her shattered forward sections. If there was any good luck, it was probably the absence of any serious oil fires from *Pecos*'s ruptured tanks. Roughly ten thousand gallons of diesel were still retained aboard the oiler, and those tanks, too, had been opened to the sea. A number of survivors later recalled being sickened when they floated into patches of diesel fuel released into the ocean.

SIX DAYS TO OBLIVION

Most of the men had moved aft to higher positions before leaving the ship. Even with *Pecos* waterlogged and sinking, they seemed to reluctant to depart. Bob Foley had been below decks helping fight multiple fires with one of the repair parties. At one point a couple of men in his repair team went into a $CO_2$ filled compartment to try to repair broken lines and put out a stubborn blaze. A sailor Foley recalled as "Jim Long" (James H. Long, CM2/c) emerged completely addled by lack of oxygen and bounding through the hatchway ripped off his steel helmet and swung it at Foley. However, the powerfully built Foley could handle himself; he decked the disoriented Long, who then came to his senses.

The bomb explosions had already left several tiny brass slivers in Foley's shin and fingers, but it would have taken much more to stop the tough Minnesotan. All the same, when he came up from below and saw the water had reached "chin-deep" level in the portside well deck, Foley decided it was high time to get off.[148] Opposite Foley, on the starboard side, Creal Gibson had seen that "the bow of the ship was submerged almost up to the radio shack . . . down by at least 45 degrees, with the stern high in the air." He said, "I did not have to jump, I was awash [sic] right off the deck." Then, to his terror, Gibson found that he could not push away from the hull, and that he "was being held there by the suction of the sinking ship." Only by a "super effort" was the "desperate" Gibson able to work his way through "all kinds of debris floating around" and thick, obnoxious oil "to be able to swim normally."[149]

One of many other sailors congregating aft and having trouble making up his mind to abandon ship was *Langley*'s signalman, Lowell Barty. He had jumped from the signal deck of *Langley* when she sank, but now the situation was entirely different. There were no accompanying destroyers a few hundred feet away to swim to, no boats to pick up the survivors, and the rolling seas were glazed with heavy oil and diesel fuel. On *Pecos* he had been helping the .50 cal. gunners aft by carrying belts of ammo to their positions. However, as the *Pecos* lurched downward beginning her final plunge, Barty, too, rushed to the stern, tossed away his flat helmet, and leaped off. Nearby were a few balsa rafts with ropes attached floating in the sea, and he managed to swim to one of these. It was late afternoon by then, and dusk was coming on. He grabbed a free line and held on for dear life in the rough seas.[150]

Also among the men who had gone aft to the stern of *Pecos* as she started to plunge was Bill Warnes, RM2/c, from *Langley*. He swung himself over the side and slid down a line to the starboard shaft bearing and from there dropped into the sea.[151] *Pecos* then upended almost vertically, her stern rising up some fifty or sixty feet; for a few moments she stayed poised in that position, with the gruesome sounds of machinery and objects breaking loose within her hull audible to the men all around her. Then as Bill Warnes, Bob Foley, Lowell Barty, Creal Gibson, Commander Abernethy, and many others looked on, she began, without rolling, to sink straight down into the depths of the Indian Ocean.

Not far away drifted a powerless motor whaleboat that had floated free from the portside main deck forward of the bridge. Minutes before the ship went under Gus Peluso had had the presence of mind to grab an ax and cut the lines that attached it to a guy wire. The lucky Peluso then won a coin toss with a shipmate to see which one got to join the whaleboat. He piled into the forty-foot boat with twenty-six other men, many of them seriously wounded, along with the navigator, Lt. F. B. McCall, and the first lieutenant, Lt. J. B. Cresap. Also present were two doctors, Yon (from *Pecos*) and Blackwell (from *Langley*). Once in the sea, however, it was discovered that the boat had no oars, and the sailors had to row furiously with wooden boards found floating in the water to clear the sinking oiler. "We made it by about ten feet and paddled like hell," said Peluso. All the same they were tossed mercilessly by the rough seas—with waves estimated to be ten feet high—and severely hampered by a damaged rudder as well.[152] To add to the danger, two or three Type 99 dive-bombers from *Akagi* made strafing runs on the ship and the men in the water.

Clusters of swimmers congregated around anything they could find that floated—tables, lockers, bamboo poles, doughnut rafts, shoring timbers—and clung to these desperately despite the waves and the sickening fuel spilt into the sea during the attacks. Most of the men became coated in oil, although not all did. Bill Warnes recalled that he did not. But he was spared one misery only to be engulfed by another: he drifted through patches of diesel fuel (for submarines), which *Pecos* had been ordered to retain.

Commander Abernethy had gone overboard from the bridge wearing his life jacket, merely stepping into the sea as the ship began its death plunge. His executive officer, Lt. Cdr. Lawrence McPeake—who had been firing a .50 cal. machine gun himself at the strafing enemy planes—and Lt. Carl Armbrust, gunnery officer from *Pecos*, were nearby and went into the water with Abernethy. McConnell and Divoll left the ship from a spot on the starboard side between the bridge and the poop deck. The two *Langley* officers were edging uncertainly down the listing hull, but Divoll hesitated, worried about being pulled into the revolving starboard propeller. To some of the sailors already in the water, including Walt Frumerie, quartermaster Ordell Dickinson, and Roy "Breezy" McNabb, both officers seemed reluctant to get off the ship. Frumerie, Dickinson, and McNabb had tied their life jackets to a cane fender that floated free.

McNabb then yelled out to McConnell, "C'mon, Mac, they can't kill a good Irishman!" At that McConnell yelled back, "Okay, Breezy!" and told Divoll it was time to go. The two officers went off the side into the water together.[153]

It was 1548 hours when the battered USS *Pecos* sank, leaving a field of debris and several hundred men floating in a sheen of heavy bunker oil and diesel fuel. Creal Gibson had only just cleared the oil around the ship and gained some distance when he looked back and saw the "stern slip down into the sea." He remembered that awful moment in terms most sailors could understand: "One of the most devastating things a sailor can witness is to see his ship that was his home at sea, a beautiful ship to behold by those who served on her, and a work of art by those who created and built her, take the final plunge and disappear into the ocean." Gibson turned out to be luckier than most, for even without his kapok jacket he found his way through the oil and debris to a life ring. It was made for perhaps twelve men but had at least twenty-five or thirty on and clinging to it. For nearly seven hours he, too, held on in the pitching sea. Eventually regaining his courage and self-confidence, he believed that he "would be able to stay afloat long enough to eventually be picked up."[154]

For some of the other men with him, the ordeal would be too much. Gibson recalled, "I do not know how long we were drifting in the water. The conversation between the men was very depressing. Some wanted to leave this group and try to make it to a larger group that was close by; some just wanted to give up, and in fact there were a few that just let go, said good-by and then they were gone."[155] Walt Frumerie remembered that as dusk came on he and the others were "worried." Bob Foley, who was by then also covered in fuel oil, said the melancholy thought that he "would never see [his] parents again," passed through his fatigued mind.[156]

Off to the northwest *Whipple*, cautious but resolute, was steaming back in the direction of *Pecos*'s last broadcast position. Somewhere to the northeast and much nearer (between the oiler's sinking position and her attackers) was Lt. J. J. Nix's *Edsall*, which must also have been heading for *Pecos*. Many miles closer, though, were Japanese ships under Vice Admiral Nagumo, and they, too, knew of *Pecos*'s location and her survivors in the water. Until now it has not been recognized just how close Kidō Butai was to *Pecos*. Thus memories of some American survivors in the water never registered as much sense as they might have had this proximity been correctly understood.

A message went out from Vice Admiral Nagumo in *Akagi* to Rear Adm. Ōmori Sentarō (commander, Screen Force) in *Abukuma* at 1700 hours [1530 hours USN]—just as Abernethy's ship appeared to be sinking—and it instructed him to "dispatch two DDs and capture the survivors of the U.S. tanker *Pecos*. Search for the survivors until sunset. If unable to find them, then return. The enemy's position at 1600 [1430 hours USN ] 205° 20nm from *Akagi*." These orders were then forwarded by Ōmori to the first section of DesDiv 17, destroyers *Tanikaze* and *Urakaze*, along with the added injunction, "after capturing survivors of *Pecos*, sink her."[157]

Off toward the last reported position of the oiler the two big destroyers duly steamed. For a couple of hours they "searched an area covered by heading 150 through 220 degrees, speed 0 to12 knots. However, [they were] unable to sight an enemy ship." As darkness fell, *Tanikaze* radioed that they would discontinue the search at 1830 and turn back to rejoin the task force.[158] Naturally they had no desire to linger at low speeds, burning up fuel and loitering in seas thought to have enemy submarines present. Yet little did they—or the Americans in the water—ever realize just how close they had come to each other.

In the *Pecos* whaleboat Lieutenants Cresap and McCall along with doctors Yon and Blackwell were preoccupied with tending wounded sailors and with jury-rigging something to keep the boat from wallowing helplessly in the high seas. With evening coming on, Lieutenant McCall eventually managed to set up a small sail in the stern and stream a sea anchor. These improvised measures were only marginally effective, but they did keep the boat from rolling excessively and taking on more water.[159]

As we have seen, one of the sailors also in the struggling motor whaleboat was chief Gus Peluso. He had witnessed men fighting back to the last minute on *Pecos* as well as men "who didn't move fast enough." When *Pecos* went down, they were "lost in the suction." Peluso also recalled seeing "one doughnut raft with twelve men hanging on to the sides . . . [the] sea dotted with swimmers." He noted that although it was still light, there was "a moon coming up over the horizon." Soon thereafter, as his boat rode up out of the troughs to a higher position on the waves, Gus Peluso spotted something else. Looking to the west he saw "two destroyers in the red sunset." Given what we now know to be the facts, it is not unlikely that the chief had glimpsed *Tanikaze* and *Urakaze* as they searched for the men from *Pecos*. Peluso remembered that he and the others "couldn't be sure they were destroyers because of the distance—8 to 10 miles away." The chief yeoman, whose eyesight was better than his ship identification skills, also believed he saw "*Marblehead* . . . with its four stacks . . . going away from [them]."[160] Of course this was not *Marbly*. But if Gus Peluso had actually spotted a ship with multiple funnels off to the west, it could have been either Rear Admiral Ōmori's own flagship, *Abukuma*, leading the Japanese task force as it steamed past the point where *Pecos* sank or—and more mysteriously—the only other American warship (and one sporting four funnels) in the immediate area.

At the same time Peluso and many more survivors in the sea began to notice other noises: sounds of gunfire and bombs exploding in the distance, which were soon followed by shock waves they felt through the water. Some of the men thought they might have been from submarine attacks. Peluso believed as much: "People in the water could feel concussion from depth charges." However, these "rumbling noises" were not from depth charges alone. "We could hear noises of battle distinctly . . . the crack of six-inch and eight-inch guns," Peluso later recalled.[161] What those men adrift in the warm, choppy seas heard and felt at that very time was nothing other than the Japanese attacks on Lt. Joshua James Nix's old destroyer, *Edsall*.

· · ·

As *Pecos* was being claimed by the Indian Ocean, the Japanese force simultaneously noticed something else unexpected. At least one enemy ship, perhaps two—and seemingly of light cruiser type—had been spotted behind Kidō Butai. It was thought to be "pursuing" them. First seen at a distance of thirty kilometers (just over sixteen miles) off to the west-northwest, this sudden appearance seems to have perturbed Vice Admiral Nagumo. His ships all went to battle stations again. On *Abukuma* the anonymous author of "The Southern Cross" recalled, "As we took up our posts, full of fighting spirit, the big guns of *Tone* in the rear were already firing and shortly thereafter the *Hiei* also opened fire."[162] In this he was more or less accurate. However, it was *Chikuma* that had first opened fire, followed shortly by *Hiei* and *Kirishima*. Rear Admiral Abe's flagship, *Tone*, which was farthest from the enemy ship, would not find the target and begin firing for another half hour. Without any question, though, these were the sounds heard and rumblings felt by the survivors of *Pecos* floating in the Indian Ocean mere miles away.

This small and elusive four-funneled target, which had not been "following" or "tracking" the Japanese task force at all, was indeed USS *Edsall*, and to that ship—still bearing the AAF crews of *Langley*'s lost P-40Es—fell the role of sacrificial victim in the most tragic sense. We can never know whether Lt. J. J. Nix's destroyer had reached a point where he felt the *Pecos* survivors might have been floating only to be surprised by Nagumo's support force, or if the destroyer by sheer inadvertence had wandered into the rear of the Japanese task force formation. What we *do* know is that she had been spotted by air patrols a few minutes prior—allegedly by an *Akagi* plane over Kidō Butai—and that she came from the direction of *Pecos*'s sinking.[163] On the IJN track chart of this strange engagement—based on the highly detailed records of Sentai 3—*Edsall* appears as if steaming to the northeast, having appeared on the starboard quarter of Nagumo's task force, which was then following a course of 165 degrees to the southeast. This suggests that the four-piper may have been searching for signs of *Pecos* survivors in the water when the Japanese heavy ships began firing on her. And this places her *much* closer to the position of Gus Peluso and the men in the whaleboat from *Pecos* than ever previously realized. In any event the skipper of a Dutch merchantman, the *Siantar*—sunk a few days later off the northwestern coast of Australia—claimed (after he was rescued) that his ship had picked up a transmission from *Edsall* that reported she was under attack, having been "surprised by two Japanese battleships."[164]

What came next was extraordinary but foredoomed. When the first heavy shells of the Japanese began falling around her, *Edsall* had taken off like a jackrabbit. Beginning at 1558 hours, the two Japanese heavy cruisers of Rear Admiral Abe and two battleships of Vice Admiral Mikawa relentlessly dogged the old destroyer—at first mistaken for a light cruiser by *Tone* and *Kirishima*—for an hour and a half, firing over thirteen hundred shells in the long stern chase. They were not able to stop Nix's elusive and plucky tin can, which fought back to the best of her ability, firing her 4-inch battery and launching torpedoes against her pursuers.[165] Eventually though, as darkness approached, and no doubt apprehensive for the safety of not only his warships but his replenishment force as well, Nagumo was compelled to request—"seething with rage" according to one account—more help from his Sea Eagles. From *Kaga*, *Hiryū*, and *Sōryū*, a total of twenty-six unescorted Type 99 *kanbaku* took off in three waves. Although one of *Kaga*'s *chūtai* overshot the wriggling destroyer on its first run, all three waves claimed hits and near misses with their 250 kg bombs soon enough. *Edsall* then rapidly lost power and steering control, curving back toward her assailants before going dead in the water. Aided by the bombings and *Edsall*'s many evasive maneuvers, which had narrowed the range, the cruisers and battleships caught up with her and poured a series of salvos into her immobile hull. The battleships checked main battery fire and continued at medium ranges (from 15,900 down to 12,500 meters) from their 6-inch secondary batteries. As if exhausted by her lengthy final action, *Edsall* at last turned onto her starboard side and sank at 1731 hours. Eight survivors, all enlisted men, were recorded as being picked up by *Chikuma* from a large number of survivors in the water.[166]

According to "The Southern Cross" the engagement, as seen from *Abukuma*, unfolded as follows: "Finally we sighted the two enemy cruisers which were following astern [note that somehow the solitary destroyer *Edsall* has grown into two lurking cruisers].... They [sic] at once made a quick 180° turn and fled into the clouds and mist."[167] Official records of *Chikuma* actually state that the enemy destroyer went into a rainsquall, and the Japanese cruiser soon entered it as well for approximately ten minutes. "The Southern Cross" went on:

> Apparently it was considered too much trouble to finish them [sic] off with artillery fire; so our Sea Eagles rose with one flap of their wings from the decks of the carriers. In a few moments they sent the enemy to the bottom and came triumphantly back. In a short time the *Tone* rescued members of the enemy crew from the same ship [now there is but one enemy ship] and returned to its group.... We, who had not fired a single shot while we watched the artillery fight of the other ships, grieved with vexation beyond description staring at the sky.[168]

The operational records of Sentai 3 as well as *Tone* and *Chikuma* paint a different picture, recording in unexpressive terms the contours of this very unusual and very obscure action: how they were ordered to attack *Edsall* by Nagumo and operated under the tactical control of Mikawa in *Hiei* that afternoon; and how *Tone* "attacked the enemy vessel from its east, and *Chikuma* from its west, [and] at 1900 [1730 USN] they sank the enemy vessel." Also, the records note that despite being well beyond her own gun range—some twenty thousand meters from the battleships—the destroyer still fired her midships and aft guns, while the forward gun remained "in the tie-down position." Finally the concluding remarks make a sheepish admission: "For long range gunfire against an evasive small maneuverable enemy vessel running freely in open waters, the accuracy rate was not so favorable, and more shells were unexpectedly expended than had been assumed."[169]

Adrift in the open whaleboat, Gus Peluso and others were hearing and feeling the attacks on *Edsall*, although with no understanding of which ships were involved. One of Peluso's recorded memories told the tale as graphically as any: "[We] didn't see any airplanes, but did see great plumes of smoke."[170]

For the eight *Edsall* men picked up from the sea that afternoon by *Chikuma*—like those seized from *Modjokerto* earlier that same afternoon—survival would prove to be a strictly contingent matter. On that Black Sunday, the men captured from *Modjokerto* and *Edsall* would eventually share a common fate; indeed they would end up together in the most absolute sense.

In "The Southern Cross" we find a passing reference that sheds light on another mystery—as far back as July 1945, that is—but has never been properly recognized. This is the mention of the fate of *Modjokerto*'s survivors. In the aftermath of *Edsall*'s sinking, the sailor from *Abukuma* wrote, "In the meantime the destroyer *Ariake* came back with 27 crewmen and other persons from the merchant ship which had previously been sunk."[171] (The precise identity of which Japanese destroyer picked up survivors from *Modjokerto* had not been known to Western researchers until 2009.) These explicit details in "The Southern Cross" are verified by the message log of Rear Admiral Ōmori's flagship *Abukuma*, as we will now see.

According to official IJN records, just as *Edsall* had been spotted that afternoon and Mikawa's support force ships had turned to pursue her, Vice Admiral Nagumo in *Akagi* received more news from the merchant ship sinking earlier in the morning. At 1600 hours the destroyer *Ariake* sent the following information to Rear Admiral Ōmori in *Abukuma* and to Nagumo: "1) Captured the skipper, chief engineer and 28 others. 2) Situation as follows: a) Nationality Dutch, ship's name MODJOKERTO, tonnage 8,082, armed with one 3-inch high angle gun and two machine guns. b) Departed Tjilatjap, on her way to Colombo. Transmitted SOS when fired upon. c) Although they are under interrogation as to the situation(s) at Tjilatjap and her mission, etc. they have not yet confessed."[172]

It is not known exactly what type of information Nagumo hoped to gain by this interrogation, but his ships would remain at sea prowling the waters well south of Java for another week before turning back for the Celebes. On March 5 Kidō Butai launched a massive air attack on Tjilatjap, further damaging the town and shore installations and sinking ships in the harbor there, although none were of any appreciable size.

Two days later the "Flying Column" (*betsudo tai*) detached itself from Kidō Butai and paid Christmas Island an early-morning visit. Battleships *Kongō* and *Haruna* with two destroyers of the DesDiv 17 lobbed a few shells at the island for twenty minutes, wrecking a heavy oil tank, a power station, and its remaining communications. Meanwhile about forty *kanbaku* of Rear Adm. Yamaguchi Tamon's Second Carrier Division (*Sōryū* and *Hiryū*) sought out targets south of Sunda Strait. These Type 99 dive-bombers found and destroyed the large Dutch passenger ship *Poelau Bras* (9,278 tons)—which was sunk with heavy loss of life—as well as the smaller Norwegian cargo vessel *Woolgar* (3,050 tons). The wretched *Woolgar* was transporting several thousand tons of coal and explosives and was accordingly blown to smithereens and sank in a matter of minutes. Later in the afternoon floatplanes from the "Flying Column" flew to Java and "reconnoitered Tjilatjap Harbor (from an altitude of 600 meters)," where they observed "five large merchantmen, three medium-size, fifteen small-size merchantmen, two DDs, three flying boats. All of them were sunk, grounded or afire."[173] To the south and east they saw warehouse buildings, the train station, and other facilities burned down or still partially aflame. The last viable port for evacuations from Java had been rendered unusable.

On March 9 the "Flying Column" rendezvoused with Nagumo's Kidō Butai south of Sumba Island, and all proceeded on to Celebes. When they returned to the spacious Staring Bay anchorage on March 11, 1942, the sailors and officers they had captured from both *Modjokerto* and *Edsall* were then turned over to the Special Naval Landing Forces based at Kendari.[174] There the reasonable treatment these prisoners had received at the hands of the Imperial Navy would cease.[175] Of those POWs, *all*—roughly three dozen men—would be butchered on the afternoon of March 24, 1942, by SNLF troops at an inconspicuous *kampong* called Amoito near the big Kendari II airfield. This was merely one in a bloody series of Japanese war crimes in the East Indies campaign and would remain one of that campaign's most obscure atrocities for almost seven decades.

• • •

While the men rescued from *Modjokerto* and *Edsall* may or may not have thought that they had been truly saved, the survivors of *Pecos* had few reasons at that hour to hold out hope. As the sun fell below the horizon, hundreds were still adrift on the choppy seas—the oiler had upward of seven hundred men on board when she sank—most of these soaked and choked by heavy bunker oil. Dozens were losing faith along with their ebbing strength as they clung to whatever they could grasp in the huge oil slick left behind after *Pecos* disappeared.

Wearing his heavy kapok life jacket, Bob Foley was among a group of about twenty men hanging on to wreckage; all were being exhausted by the high wave action. So, too, Lowell Barty, who was "tired out" clutching a balsa life raft's line in the "very rough" seas.[176] Creal Gibson and another small knot of sailors continued to bob up and down in the increasingly high waves—"the swells were fifteen to twenty feet high," he believed—clinging onto their life ring.[177] Undoubtedly a number of men were praying for a miracle of some sort. Their prayers were to be answered, yet deliverance would not come to all the men in the water. A grim quid pro quo in human life would be the result.

At 1757 hours Lt. Cdr. Eugene Karpe's *Whipple* altered course to the southeast, hoping to approximate the last known position of *Pecos*, and pressed on at twenty knots. Throughout the afternoon, her crew had "kept busy making knotted lines and cargo nets for use in the rescue of survivors." Then, at 1916, *Whipple* spotted a "red flare dead ahead about five miles." The Very star had been fired by Ens. Michel Emmanuel of *Langley*, floating in the water with a cluster of men around a raft holding injured survivors. After sundown Emmanuel had been doggedly firing flares at half-hour intervals. One of these had been spotted by *Whipple*'s lookouts. Six minutes later *Whipple* "sighted several lights on both bows," started her sound gear, and went to general quarters, while slowing to five knots. About this time, in the drifting whaleboat with Lieutenant McCall and others, Gus Peluso thought he saw the four-piper, too. He found a copper waterproof flashlight and quickly "sent a message in Morse code . . . and said that *Pecos* had hundreds of survivors to the right of the moon's path."[178] *Whipple* soon replied by signaling "DD" and cautiously closed to pick them up. At 1931 hours the destroyer stopped all engines; by 1935 Peluso, Lieutenant McCall, Doctors Yon and Blackwell, and the other men in the motor whaleboat were alongside. They quickly affirmed that most of the survivors were in an enormous oil slick on the flushdecker's "starboard hand." The timing was, to say the least, fortuitous. Destroyers *Tanikaze* and *Urakaze* had been no more than a few miles distant when they called off their own search for the survivors at 1830 hours to rejoin Nagumo.

Karpe, acting as "good shepherd," edged his ship in carefully, "maneuvering to get among the survivors and pick up as many as possible." On the deck of *Whipple* dozens of sailors and officers were "lining the rails to fish out battered and exhausted people." Heroism takes many forms, and several men did far more than throw lines out to the survivors. These were the sailors who, as Karpe later wrote, "took their life in their hands when they took out lines to people who would otherwise have been unable to reach the ship." He named nine enlisted men from *Whipple* (Kusnic, Speers, Gibbs, Daubert, Oliver, Lewis, Jones, Covell, and Yost) who "were in the water several times carrying lines to people on rafts that were too far out from the ship to be reached by heaving lines."[179]

Soon McConnell, Divoll, and Abernethy were also picked up. As Abernethy recalled, "What a sorry sight we were as we got on board *Whipple*! Everyone rescued was covered in oil from head to foot. All of the spare fresh water and soap on board the *Whipple* was used to remove this smelly mess. It took me half an hour just to get the stains off my teeth."[180] For the next two hours and six minutes, Karpe steered his ship by engines as it moved among the oily seas speckled with clusters of floating men. Those who had survived the sinkings of *Langley* and *Pecos* to be rescued again were often saved through sheerest chance; there was no rhyme or reason to it.

Creal Gibson's group, floating around the life-ring raft, were thrown a line and told to secure it to the ring so that all the men could be picked up together.

Nothing of the sort happened, and a more perfect representation of blind Fortune spinning on her globe could scarcely be imagined.[181] Men struck out desperately in the pitch-black night through the water, clutching at the line and attempting to use it to drag themselves to the ship and on board. Gibson left the raft and swam up to a cargo net dangling over *Whipple*'s hull but was knocked off three times by other men climbing over him. He recalled, "Finally I got a hold and started up the net. Someone grabbed my arm and pulled me up onto the deck." To Gibson's astonishment the *Whipple* sailor who had seized his arm in the darkness was a childhood friend named Wilfred "Bill" LeBeau who had been raised in the same Chicago orphanage as Gibson and joined the navy with him prior to the war. Gibson later stated, "One can never imagine at that moment our reaction and the feelings toward each other."[182]

In Bob Foley's case it was a matter of choosing to leave his group when *Whipple* had closed to within fifty yards and swimming for the ship alone. The others in his group did not swim with him, and they were never rescued. As he approached the ship's side, high waves pitched him up to within four feet of the upper deck. A rope draped over the bow appeared to be within reach, and Foley grabbed it; he was then dragged aboard. As the exhausted sailor reached the narrow foredeck and stood up, the clasps on his waterlogged life jacket suddenly popped off and the heavy kapok vest tumbled over the side where it "sank like a rock."[183]

Walt Frumerie, too, had been among the happy few. He had seen a ship approaching on the edge of the horizon, the silhouette of its four funnels bobbing in and out of view above the swells. Walt did not know its identity, but when *Whipple* came close enough he, too, found his way up a cargo net. Once on deck he experienced what many of the other sailors already knew: "the best feeling ever."[184] Well might Frumerie have felt so, as the rescue operations were about to be unexpectedly, and tragically, cut short.

Among the very last men picked up—and therefore among the luckiest—were Lowell Barty and his friend, Reginald Mills, GM3/c. Although exhausted by the rough waves and sickened by exposure to oil, they still hung on to lines attached to a balsa life raft holding a number of other survivors. An unknown officer had taken charge of this group and had attempted to keep the men together throughout the ordeal. Then, abruptly, as *Whipple* crept gingerly among the survivors picking them up, she began to gain speed again and move away. At 2141 she "picked up propeller beats bearing 130° T.," at which time Karpe went to standard speed and prepared for a depth-charge attack on the suspected submarine. The men in the water were ignored as *Whipple* made several clumsy and unsuccessful attempts to drive off the sub. Only one of the first two depth charges dropped left the rack properly. Then, between 2153 and 2156 hours, the destroyer "commenced rescuing survivors again." In that brief interim Reginald Mills and Lowell Barty saved themselves. "Better swim for it!" someone yelled, and the two sailors made for *Whipple*, which had closed again to within fifty yards or so. Behind them remained the others on the raft with the furious officer shouting, "I'll shoot the first guy." But Mills and Barty ignored his threats and swam for their lives. They managed to reach the side of *Whipple* and had just got up into the cargo netting—although not before other panicky sailors climbed over Barty and knocked him off—where they were dragged up on to the deck. None of the other men in their group were rescued. Seventy years later Lowell Barty would recount his hellish experiences after the sinking of *Pecos* and claim that the survivors' rescue by *Whipple* had unquestionably involved "a lotta luck, man!"[185]

Only a few more sailors had made it to *Whipple* when the destroyer began again maneuvering to drop depth charges. Karpe dropped two more depth charges; of these only one exploded. However, the repeated sound contacts meant time was running out for the remainder of those men still in the water.

One of the most profoundly troubling decisions a captain could conceivably face then fell upon Lt. Cdr. Eugene Karpe. Was he to depart and leave several hundred men behind, saving only those he had picked up already? Or remain in a vulnerable position, slowly rescuing more men while he risked losing *Whipple* and all on board her? A brief consultation with McConnell, Abernethy, and Crouch on the bridge decided the issue. *Whipple* was now by herself— the final survivor out of the four ships involved in the foolhardy mission and its aftermath—weakly armed, with only two torpedoes left, and severely overcrowded. Neither her bow's structural weakness nor her precarious fuel situation could be overlooked. In the view of all four commanders the seeming presence of enemy submarines was the determining factor. "On advice of the Commanding Officers, USS *Langley* and *Pecos* and the Commander Destroyer Division Fifty-Seven the area was cleared and it was deemed inadvisable to proceed with any more rescue work while submarine was in vicinity."[186] The ship's engines came to life, and her sharp hull cut a path through the oil slick with its bobbing, desperate men. On the decks of *Whipple*, as they steamed for clear water, those who had been rescued would now learn from their own consciences the price of their deliverance. In order to preserve the few, a great many would be left behind to die; there was simply no other alternative. Karpe increased speed to 16 knots and turned *Whipple* to the southwest.

SIX DAYS TO OBLIVION

It is just as well that Karpe and the other men never knew that they had been a fraction of that distance from the forces of Vice Admiral Nagumo. They ran southwest for a few miles, then altered to due south and upped speed to 19 knots for about five hours before increasing to 20 knots just before two in the morning. They held that course and speed for the next eighteen hours as the men tried to recover, and officers took a head count of survivors. Profound ironies were not uncommon. Among the 230-odd men rescued was the British civilian harbor pilot from Christmas Island, Mr. Craig, who as Karpe dutifully noted, "could not be returned to his station."[187]

*Whipple* continued on a southern course for two full days, "to put as much distance between *Whipple* and Japanese aircraft carrier." All the men were deeply apprehensive throughout the daylight hours, expecting to be discovered by enemy patrol planes. They were not spotted, however. Karpe then reduced speed to 15 knots late on March 2, and on the following morning at 0734 hours *Whipple* "set course for Fremantle." The ship cut speed to conserve fuel and eventually zigzagging was dispensed with during the final hours of steaming.[188]

In the cramped pilot house of the four-piper, McConnell asked for Walt Frumerie to come up and help Karpe navigate the tricky entrance past Rottnest Island into Fremantle. For most of the campaign many of the ships had been forced to make do with out-of-date British Admiralty and Dutch charts, but *Whipple* had none for entering port there. Quartermaster Frumerie had helped McConnell take *Langley* in and out before and felt confident that he knew the course.

On the evening of March 4, no more than three hours after Binford's division wheezed into port, *Whipple* and her weary, oil-stained passengers at last reached Fremantle safely. The solitary old tin can's fuel tanks were almost empty. When mustered the rolls showed 147 men saved from *Langley* and 84 from *Pecos*, along with the pair of wounded AAF pilots, Lieutenants Dix and Akerman, for a total of 233.[189] Killed and missing amounted to well over 450 officers, sailors, pilots, and ground crew. Unknown to any at that anticlimactic moment in Fremantle was the annihilation of *Edsall* with her entire crew and all air force personnel. That added at least another 185 dead—technically missing in action—to the botched and bungled mission.

The surviving men were taken ashore and transported by buses to a military camp, where they were given a good meal and clean bunks to sleep in. On the following day they were issued clothing items to replace those lost in the calamity. But there was a war on, and most of the survivors had to be returned to duty in short order. A handful stayed in Australia to be assigned to new sea or shore billets. Still others went back to the States, as did a handful of the Asiatic Fleet officers who had emerged from the East Indies crucible safely (if not free from psychological scars). Within a day or two of reaching Fremantle, many were put on the huge American troop transport USS *Mount Vernon* (AP-22)—formerly the luxury liner SS *Washington* (34,000 tons and 20 knots)—to begin the long sea journey back across the Pacific. *Mount Vernon* made stops at Adelaide and at Wellington, New Zealand, before proceeding east again. Several surviving USN commanders, including McConnell, Abernethy, and Binford, wrote up their action reports while traveling on this large and spacious converted liner. The bulk of the big ship's passengers was made up of survivors from *Langley*, *Pecos*, and PatWing 10, with an assorted sprinkling of men from other Asiatic Fleet ships such as *Houston*, *Marblehead*, and *Holland*. From *Langley* and *Pecos*, Dr. Blackwell, Commander Divoll, and Lieutenants Armbrust, Cresap, and McCall returned on *Mount Vernon*, as did the assistant U.S. naval observer from Singapore, Lt. Cdr. J. S. Mosher.

Some of the enlisted men returning on *Mount Vernon* soon found that even they had decent accommodations. Bob Foley went back as a passenger in state-room AB-338, a far cry from the old rust bucket he had taken to the Far East in early 1941. Bill Warnes of *Langley* was able to go ashore in Wellington, where he made the acquaintance of a local woman with whom he stayed in touch for a few years afterward. None of these survivors, however, would easily forget the friends and shipmates they had left behind in the heaving seas of the Indian Ocean that black night south of Java.

For these men the hellish Java campaign was over physically if not psychologically. But the culmination of the tragedy would occur to the north, above the Malay Barrier, in the Java Sea. And for that part of our narrative we must again revisit events beginning in mid-February leading up to the campaign-ending battles that occurred between February 27 and March 1, 1942.

# ELEVEN

## Chaos and Night

*The Battle of the Java Sea*

With the failures of the Gaspar Strait engagement to the west and the Battle of Badoeng Strait to the east, ABDA's flimsy defenses were being torn apart by Japan's simultaneous pincer operations as they descended on Java. Constant pressure by the enemy's air and naval forces was then brought to bear on both flanks and from the north. Within a few more days Japanese submarines would act as a vanguard for a major naval incursion into the Indian Ocean to the south of Java, thereby completing that island's encirclement and sealing its fate. The period between the melee in Badoeng Strait and the start of full-scale operations against Java a week later was one of disordered regrouping for the Allies. As throughout the campaign, poor communications and misuse of what meager intelligence they *had* been able to obtain kept the ABDA forces from affecting any meaningful response to their adversaries.[1]

On the afternoon of February 21—following their involvement in the action off Sanur in Badoeng Strait—*Ford* and *Pope* were steaming west to Tjilatjap, where they would fuel from *Pecos*. After that they had been instructed by Glassford to proceed to Christmas Island, there to rendezvous with the sub tender *Holland* and DesRon 29 tender *Black Hawk* (Capt. Herbert V. Wiley, COMDESRON 29 embarked) in order to replenish their torpedoes. They were additionally ordered to transport fifty RAF personnel who had escaped from Singapore to Java and deliver them to *Black Hawk* for evacuation to Australia. These men had been accommodated temporarily aboard *Pecos* at Tjilatjap; there they were given some items of clothing and allowed to clean themselves up after their rapid evacuation from the doomed "fortress." Twenty-five each then came aboard the destroyers later in the afternoon at Tjilatjap and were served the evening meal with the crew. The ships were under way shortly—by 1630 hours—and the RAF personnel accommodated below in the forward crew compartments. Both destroyers worked up to 20 knots; time was short, and they were needed elsewhere.

Christmas Island is an isolated green speck in the Indian Ocean, with neither enough natural resources or size to be of any real value—except to millions of small red crabs—but the Americans and the Japanese had still kept their eyes on it through submarine and air patrols. In late February it was nonetheless felt to be distant enough from enemy air patrols to offer a relatively secure location for *Ford* and *Pope* to take on more torpedoes. They met up with *Black Hawk* and *Holland* and a pair of screening four-pipers, *Barker* and *Bulmer*, the next morning. The submarine *Stingray* was also present. Within another couple of hours the ships lay to without anchoring off Flying Fish Cove on Christmas Island's northeast corner. To add a surreal touch, many thousands of seabirds swarmed over the ships, flying out from their nests in caves along the sheer walls of the cliffs. Finding a suitable location for transshipping their passengers was another problem; the cove, situated on the lee side of the island—where the only piers had been constructed—was scarcely better than the weather side. Before disembarking the RAF men were at any rate fed a good breakfast on the destroyers of chipped beef on toast ("SOS"), oatmeal, tea, hard rolls, and coffee. They were then put into *Black Hawk*'s fifty-foot motor launches and taken through the moderate sea and wind to the old tender, getting drenched in the process but probably greatly relieved to be finally leaving the wretched East Indies for Australia.[2]

Unknown to the U.S. sailors, the impoverished state of communications between the allies in ABDA could have led to more serious problems. British observers in their small contingent stationed at Christmas Island were evidently not informed of these ship movements. They saw the seven strange ships approaching the island but could not identify them and reported them to their superiors at the ACNB (Australian Commonwealth Naval Board).[3] The naval board then sent a message to HMAS *Perth*, which had just released her convoy to proceed back to Fremantle on its own while she moved northwest towards Java. The Australian cruiser under Capt. Hector "Hec" MacDonald Laws Waller, a veteran skipper of the hard fighting in the Mediterranean, received this news from the watchers at Christmas Island after dark on the twenty-second of February. He chose to wait until dawn the next day before launching a scout plane for reconnaissance but informed his crew that he anticipated meeting an unknown ship early the next morning, and "if he did not receive the correct reply to his challenge he intended to shoot first and ask questions later."[4] *Perth* then had orders to proceed with all dispatch to Batavia's Tandjong Priok, but Waller had no intention of being waylaid on the journey to Java. The fate of *Perth*'s sister, HMAS *Sydney*, was still painfully fresh, not least in the mind of Hec Waller.

For a few hours anyway a brief glimmer of hope that they might be getting away from the combat zone had rippled through some of the American destroyermen as they headed for Christmas Island, but the subsequent orders to restock their torpedoes soon told them otherwise. There was good reason for these orders. It was evident that the ships would be returning to the front-lines; the ABDA surface forces needed every torpedo they could possibly find, and both *Ford* and *Pope*, although weary and long overdue for machinery over-hauls, would find themselves pressed into service yet again. *Barker* and *Bulmer* were more fortunate; their existing condenser woes were aggravated by near misses from Japanese bombs in the Gaspar Strait sortie and allowed both four-pipers to be sent out of the danger zone.[5]

• • •

Lieutenant Admiral Helfrich (ABDAFLOAT) and staff had decided to split the remaining naval units into eastern and western striking forces, based out of Sura-baja and Batavia's Tandjong Priok respectively. This decision was based on intel-ligence obtained through air reconnaissance and submarine reports that showed large concentrations of enemy shipping at Jolo—thought to be "between 80 to 100 ships"—and another massive convoy coming down from Cam Ranh Bay in French Indo-China (Vietnam).[6] Unfortunately the February 16 redistribution of ABDA's submarine forces at the insistence of Helfrich had left the Makassar Strait wide open, with the result that the Japanese East Java convoy was not detected for some time.[7] Nonetheless, Helfrich believed that the heaviest enemy concen-tration would fall on Java's eastern end, and on that basis he wanted his strongest surface force concentrated there at Surabaja. This decision would prove ques-tionable, too, as Surabaja was by then becoming an almost daily target of Japa-nese bombers flying out of captured airfields in the Celebes.

As for the remaining units left over from the western striking force at Batavia—with the exception of HMAS *Hobart*—most were elderly, small, and weak. ABDA's naval commanders, including Helfrich, rightly considered them less suitable for offensive operations at sea. These were all ships of First World War vintage: the light cruisers HMS *Danae* and HMS *Dragon* and two old destroyers, HMS *Scout* and HMS *Tenedos*.[8] Their principal remaining value lay in use as convoy escorts—much like the American flushdeckers—and most certainly not as offensive weapons against more-formidable surface opponents. A contingent of Austra-lian minesweepers also operated out of Batavia and along the upper reaches of Sunda Strait on the Java side near Merak, but these ships were too slow—their top speed being well under 20 knots—for any striking force missions.

It was becoming all too evident that, as in Malaya, defending Java against the "hardy, tough, enduring, almost fanatical" Japanese was a losing proposition.[9] The highest echelons made no bones about it. On February 13, after less than a month on the job as ABDACOM, Wavell sent a message to Churchill that confirmed Hart's belief that the British were primarily focused on the western end of the ABDA theater (meaning from Burma to Sumatra), saying, "If Southern Sumatra is lost prolonged defense of Java becomes unlikely. . . . We must reinforce Sumatra until it is clearly useless to do so. Subsequent reinforcement of Java would probably be unprofitable."[10]

On February 16 Wavell sent more grim news. By the eighteenth, as Roosevelt and Churchill pondered Wavell's advice—and with Churchill devastated by the fall of Singapore—it was still clear that the importance of Burma and Australia far outweighed that of Java. Churchill saw Britain's chief responsibility laying to the west, beginning with Rangoon and on to India and Ceylon. As for the Americans, they would probably be called on to help defend Australia. Most already anticipated that MacArthur would exercise overall command there, once he had been extricated—as was even then planned—from the doomed Philippines.[11] The United States would utilize Australia as its principal springboard for any campaigns northward to retake territory seized by the Japanese. Roosevelt evidently felt at no time that the continent was greatly threatened and informed Australian prime minister Curtin on February 23 that he believed the gravest danger was "against the Burma or left flank, and that [they could] safely hold the Australian or right flank." He assured Curtin that more "American fully equipped reinforcements [were] getting ready to leave for [his] area" and that he was, "working on additional plans to make control of the islands in Anzac area more secure, and further to disrupt Japanese advances."[12]

Clearly the high command in Washington and London had written off the East Indies well before the Japanese invaded; and additional reinforcements—if they went at all—were going to be minor and piecemeal at best, regardless of official proclamations.

. . .

At the same time Japan's East Java convoy at Jolo in the Sulu Archipelago—just three hundred miles northeast of Tarakan—had already begun moving south. After departing early on the nineteenth, it would reach Balikpapan on February 23 for a very short refueling stop before resuming its course down through the Makassar Strait the same day. Its assigned invasion sectors—designated "D" and "E" in Area Number 3—were near Kragan, about ninety miles west of Surabaja.

The Japanese were indeed preparing to envelope Java from both the eastern and the western flanks. The Imperial Army (Rikugun) planned to attack at each end of the island and swiftly destroy the Allies' capacity for resistance. This was in keeping with the overall strategy employed by the Japanese war machine for the entire first stage, in which simultaneous attacks were undertaken in order to crush any possible Western counteroffensive.[13] Considerable resources were assigned to the invasion, regarded as one of the most critical to Japan's first stage operations. And as they were prone to do, the Japanese had also included "feinting maneuvers" in their plans. In their air operations these consisted of pre-invasion air attacks. Imperial Navy air units were to bomb enemy installations at Cheribon, Tegel, Semarang, and Probolinggo along the central northern coast of Java as diversionary actions.

Rikugun forces were led by Lt. Gen. Imamura Hitoshi, commander of the Sixteenth Army. He and his staff were in the specialized landing ship *Shinshu Maru* in the West Java convoy.[14] As with the other first stage operations, Imamura's plans were made up according to a precise and exacting timetable in which speed was of the essence.[15] Shipping bottoms, fuel, and air support were all calculated along narrow margins by the Japanese. If they were to succeed in their audacious first stage operations, striking Hawaii, the Philippines, Malaya, and ultimately the East Indies, they needed minimal losses of shipping and minimal expenditures of both fuel and ammunition. And as it turned out, these simultaneous operations in the East Indies—or what the Japanese termed "parallel operations"—were going to require more resources than were immediately available as of late January, and this worried Japanese planners, in both the navy and the army.

The division of army and navy responsibility had been decided by the central agreement drawn up by the Imperial Headquarters in a joint conference in Tokyo on November 12, 1941.[16] By then, however, most of the necessary military assets for the so-called Southern Operations were already assembled in Indo-China, and detailed operational plans had been in place for some time. Due to the speed with which the campaigns in the Philippines and Malaya had progressed, however, plans for the actual invasion of Java were agreed on by the Imperial Navy and Army between January 24 and 28 in conferences at Manila. The so-called Manila Agreement was then signed on January 30. This original outline relating to the seizure of Java envisioned landings by the main body of the Sixteenth Army at Merak and Bantam Bay—designated Number 1 Area—to take place on "H-Day" as of February 21, 1942. The Number 2 Area, which was at Patrol (or as it commonly appears in Western accounts, Eretan Wetan, located roughly seventy-five miles east of Batavia), was to mark the invasion point for the Shoji Unit, also on February 21. To the east the Forty-Eighth Division's landings would occur near Kragan two days later, on February 23—this was the Number 3 Area. In Saigon, where Lieutenant General Imamura's Western Convoy forces were assembling, the army received photoreconnaissance charts of the landing sites from Japanese naval air force specialists on February 10. Extra copies also went to the seaplane carrier *Kamigawa Maru*, then at Cam Ranh Bay. A variety of factors ultimately pushed back these original invasion dates about one week to the night of February 28–March 1.[17]

Overall naval operations by the Java Invasion Force (or Ranin Butai) were under the command of Vice Adm. Takahashi Ibō (commander in chief of the Third Fleet) sailing in the cruiser *Ashigara* and usually escorted by two destroyers of Destroyer Division 6, *Ikazuchi* and *Akebono*.[18] For the operations against Java his principal subordinates in escorting and protecting the invaluable convoys were five rear admirals with their associated commands: in the Western Convoy, Rear Adm. Hara Kenzaburo of the Fifth Destroyer Squadron (who also commanded the direct escort group, or "Third Screen Force") and Rear Adm. Kurita Takeo of the Seventh Cruiser Division. In the Eastern Convoy, Rear Adm. Takagi Takeo in the Fifth Cruiser Division (Sentai 5) had overall control, with the support of Rear Adm. Nishimura Shōji of the Fourth Destroyer Squadron and Rear Adm. Tanaka Raizo of the Second Destroyer Squadron.

To augment its offensive power, Vice Adm. Ozawa Jisaburo of the Malaya Butai had allotted a squadron of four Mogami-class heavy cruisers and requisite screening destroyers under Rear Admiral Kurita to the West Java forces once air reconnaissance determined the number of Allied surface units still in Batavia. As we will see, petty turf wars and personality clashes among the Japanese naval commanders and their staffs in this stressful period would soon lead to difficulties as the West Java force approached its destination.

The East Java covering force of Rear Adm. Takagi Takeo's Sentai 5 centered around his flagship, the 15,000-ton heavy cruiser *Nachi*, accompanied by her sister, *Haguro*. The Eastern Convoy was protected by two destroyer squadrons: the Second under Rear Adm. Tanaka Raizo in light cruiser *Jintsū* with eight destroyers, and the Fourth, commanded as before by Rear Adm. Nishimura Shōji in *Naka*, leading another half dozen DDs. It was Nishimura's ships (also known as "First Screen Force") that provided direct escort for the East Java convoy. There were also four minesweepers and the usual allotment of auxiliaries, consisting of tankers, seaplane transports, torpedo boats, subchasers, and minelayers. However, Tanaka's Second Squadron would arrive quite late on the scene as it turned out. This delay was because the Japanese had decided to proceed with the capture of Timor—a "key defense base in the perimeter"—in order to secure their eastern flank. This far-flung operation left a number of their already scanty naval units widely dispersed immediately prior to the Java invasion.[19]

• • •

The seizure of Timor (Ku-Go Sakusen) was undertaken in the same period as the landings on Bali.[20] It would be primarily an Imperial Army operation, with two separate forces being landed to seize airfields near Koepang (Kupang) on the western end of the island, which was Dutch territory, and to the northwest at Dili in Portuguese Timor. The Koepang-bound convoy of four marus with the bulk of the army's 228th Infantry Regiment embarked left Ambon in the Moluccas at 0500 hours on February 17, escorted by four destroyers (*Kuroshio*, *Hayashio*, *Tokitsukaze*, and *Amatsukaze*) and two minesweepers (nos. 7 and 8); they were joined at sea by *Kunikawa Maru* coming from Kendari. The smaller Dili convoy carrying the remaining army elements departed from Ambon in the Moluccas during the middle of the night on February 18, screened by destroyers *Ushio* and *Sazanami* and later joined by *Akebono*, steaming also from Kendari with other transports. Positioned south of Lomblem Island, the Eleventh Air Fleet's seaplane carrier *Mizuho* provided air cover.

Also involved in covering the convoys were the heavy cruisers of Sentai 5 under Rear Admiral Takagi, *Nachi* and *Haguro*. They left Staring Bay outside Kendari on the seventeenth, and after a feint toward the Moluccas had moved south through the Banda Sea and down through the Strait of Ombai at dusk on February 19. They then swung southwest along the upper coast of Timor, past Dili, then south again around Koepang before making another sweep farther south below Roti. These movements would have put the two cruisers in some proximity to *Houston*—then heading due west for Tjilatjap—but no contact was made. That was just as well for Capt. Albert Rooks's *Galloping Ghost*, but she would meet the two formidable sisters soon enough—in fact just days later—in the Java Sea.

As usual the Imperial Navy wanted to share in the successes of the East Indies campaign, and therefore a para-drop component was added at Timor as well. In the early morning hours of February 20, some 307 naval paratroopers of the Yokosuka Third SNLF flying out of Kendari were dropped east of Koepang, close to Desaoe, about twenty kilometers from the airfield; the next morning another 323 were also dropped nearby. The vanguard of the first group, consisting of the Fukumi Unit's Nagamine and Takasaki platoons, fought through some surprisingly tough Allied resistance on the outskirts of a village called Babau, where they sustained a number of casualties. Nonetheless, they were able to overcome this opposition in short order. Both air-dropped groups then linked up to seize the Poeton airfield outside Koepang, where they arrived on February 22.[21]

To the north Japanese army units had an easier time of it; they had been landed at Dili and moved inland against light defensive fighting. Major objectives were seized by midday on the twentieth. The chief naval action here came not from ABDA surface forces—there were none—but from some vexing artillery batteries overlooking the harbor area. The Dutch First Field Artillery Battalion had brought in a battery from Malang in East Java armed with Krupp 75 mm guns, and these had fired on the ships offshore. Perhaps recalling the foolishness at Tarakan a month earlier, *Ushio* and *Sazanami* promptly conducted a fifty-three-minute shore bombardment in the first hours of February 20. Both destroyers would then remain in the Dili harbor area until February 24, carrying out antisubmarine patrols, after which they returned to Makassar on February 25.

. . .

Well over one thousand miles to the west, seven American ships—*Barker*, *Bulmer*, *Black Hawk*, *Holland*, *Stingray*, *Pope*, and *John D. Ford*—lay to at 1328 hours on February 22 off Christmas Island's Flying Fish Cove. From *Black Hawk*, beginning at 1422 hours, *Ford* received eight torpedoes and *Pope* eleven. These were delivered by motor launch in sections, warheads not attached, and it was then up to the destroyermen to assemble them properly aboard their own ships. It was a clumsy and stressful process hoisting them aboard. The crews of *Ford* and *Pope* noted that *Black Hawk*'s nervous sailors appeared to be in a great hurry to get the transfers completed so their ship could leave the area as quickly as possible. Lt. (j.g.) Jack Michel on *Pope* remembered, "There was something unseemly about this; like telling a condemned man to hurry with his last breakfast. It was annoying too because the men were working at top speed, and without the advantage of power-driven cranes."[22]

Adding to this air of tension, torpedo men on *Ford* noticed that the delicate weapons—which had been sent to Darwin from Brisbane via army transport—had received some rough treatment at the hands of the "Hawk," which made fitting the warheads to the air flasks more of a challenge than it should normally have been. Several had to be filed repeatedly and then banged into place with sledgehammers. *Pope* experienced more trouble with this matter than *Ford*, so Lieutenant Commander Cooper sent over his top men with their own gear, Gordon Canady, CTM, and James Sigel, TM1/c, to help out. They were able

CHAOS AND NIGHT

to demonstrate the technique for *Pope's* Harold Netter, CTM, who then took over with his own crews. Canady and Sigel returned to *Ford* and carried on there with their work preparing the weapons in their tubes. Topside, men not required for these fittings discreetly moved to the bow and stern of the flush-deckers, feeling that *should* an accidental explosion or enemy submarine attack occur, they might have better chances for survival there.[23]

At 1830 hours that evening the ships had finished up most of this ticklish work and were again under way, destination Sunda Strait and from there into the Java Sea and on eastward to Surabaja. They completed arming their fish as they steamed north.[24] Well off to the southeast, a *Walrus* amphibian was cata-pulted from HMAS *Perth* at 0900 hours on the following morning, the twenty-third, in search of unidentified ships reported near Christmas Island. She found *Holland*, *Black Hawk*, and their escorts, the four-pipers *Barker* and *Bulmer*, and their identities were established.[25] Satisfied that he was not going to encounter any enemy raiders, "Hec" Waller then set course for Sunda Strait. *Perth* would have been some hours behind the American ships, which had transited the straits overnight in darkness.[26]

. . .

The flushdeckers steamed east along the northern coastline of Java the follow-ing day and reached Surabaja early on the morning of Tuesday, February 24. They anchored just before noon, having completed their circuitous peregri-nations around Java in something like ninety-six hours.[27] Behind them *Perth*, making good time, had reached Batavia's Tandjong Priok that same morning.

This route taken by the Asiatic Fleet ships—and the necessity for it—affords a good look at the negative factors that ABDA's naval units were facing daily. They had been sent from Tjilatjap to their hurried deployment into battle at Badoeng Strait; then the long retrograde journey back to Tjilatjap for fuel, fol-lowed by a subsidiary mission within another journey of several hundred extra-neous miles out to Christmas Island in order to replenish torpedoes; finally the lengthy trip to Surabaja via the long way 'round, through Sunda Strait . . . consuming even more fuel in the process and putting additional wear and tear on the old ships' worn machinery and exhausted men.

Within hours of reaching Surabaja's Tandjong Perak harbor, as they neared Holland Pier, the naval installations were attacked yet again by unopposed Jap-anese bombers. *Ford* and *Pope* anchored well out in the harbor, away from dock areas. Their tired crews kept the ships "heaved in to short stay," with just enough chain to hold the anchors but able to get under way quickly in case the enemy bombers targeted the ships in the harbor.[28] That raid appeared to be concentrated mainly on the warehouses and fuel storage area, but at Rotterdam Pier, the freighter *Kota Radja*, with her holds filled with rubber, was hit and caught fire, sending thick billows of choking, inky smoke into the sky. She was towed out into the harbor away from the wharves, and there attempts were made to sink her with gunfire from one of the smaller Dutch auxiliary vessels. Thirty shells had the same effect that Japanese projectiles would later have on Dutch merchant ships intercepted elsewhere around Java: they simply did not do the job.[29] The ship's cargo continued to burn stubbornly, sending up a heavy black column. Most survivors would recall the caustic stench of incinerated rubber, as the pall from this ship settled over the harbor, where it seemed to last for days. The American destroyers were not in immediate danger, but it did no one's nerves any good. When the bombers departed, *Ford* then shifted, tying up next to *Pope*, which had moved over to the dock.

By this date, although bunker oil was still plentiful at Surabaja—in many tens of thousands of tons—the ships were beginning to have trouble obtaining enough fuel. The cause for this difficulty was not only the damage to docks and fueling lines but also a shortage of native workers. Most had refused to remain in the navy yard through daylight hours, having been terrified by the persistent Japanese bombings, and would only work—if they would work at all—during the night. The previous week Bill Kale on USS *Stewart* had written in his diary when his destroyer reached Surabaja: "The air raid alarm is on, so there are no natives on the docks to handle our lines. All those people think we are crazy to come in and tie up during an air raid."[30] Of course, in *Stewart*'s case, they had little choice in the matter; they *had* to have fuel if they were going to continue offensive operations. *Ford* and *Pope* were only marginally more fortunate in that they were not quite so pressed for time when they reached the harbor on the twenty-fourth.

It was also at this time that they learned of the indefinite results and losses suffered in the fight at Badoeng Strait. *Stewart* remained capsized at a 35-degree angle in the floating dry dock, and men from *Ford* and *Pope* were told to help themselves to whatever useful items they could remove from her. By then she had been pretty thoroughly stripped, and neither Lt. Bill Mack's party from *Ford* nor that of Lt. (j.g.) Jack Michel from *Pope* would come away with anything of much use. They went over to the ruined ship the next day, February 25, with no intention of remaining long, as they considered the dry dock a likely target for enemy bombers.

According to the report later submitted by Lt. Francis E. Clark (USNA 1937),

CHAOS AND NIGHT

her former engineering officer, "all storerooms, holds, and compartments had been thoroughly ransacked and all items of any great value, including spare parts, machine tools, radio spares, etc., had been removed."[31] Mack's men found a few tins of smoked oysters and some five-gallon oak kegs of drinking water from one of *Stewart's* life rafts, which they took. Michel and his sailors obtained nothing more substantial than a new Beauty Rest mattress for a fellow officer, but before he could get it off *Stewart* and into *Pope's* motor whaleboat, another air raid by Japanese high-level bombers occurred. Into the Dutch air raid shelters ashore they all piled as the bombers worked over the navy yard and docks for an hour, obliterating much of the seaplane base landing area near Morokrembangan but leaving the ships untouched in the harbor. When the men emerged, *Kota Radja* was still burning furiously, her heavy smoke providing the Japanese with an ideal homing beacon—as if they needed one—while the ancient Dutch coastal battleship *Soerabaja* sat on the bottom of the harbor, her upper works forlornly poking above the oily waters.[32] Not far away the 8,600-ton Dutch hospital ship *Op Ten Noort* was receiving emergency repairs after having been bombed and seriously damaged by the Japanese several days earlier in flagrant disregard of international law. (She would be fated to play a consequential, if tragic, role in later events.) At least one British mobile Bofors 40 mm gun was set up dockside at the Holland Pier—of the Twenty-First Light AA Regiment—but it appears to have done little firing against high-level bombers. As Jack Michel drily observed viewing the destruction and inertia there, "The place was inclined to instill a pessimistic outlook."[33]

By this stage of the campaign, the remaining PBYs of PatWing 10 operating out of Morokrembangan at Surabaja had been reduced to a trio of machines, and of these only two could still fly patrols. A third ship was being fabricated from the cannibalized parts of wrecked planes. Another pair of planes had moved to the south of the port at a remote scatter base. With the enemy controlling the airspace north of Java in all directions and given the tremendous vulnerability of the PBY type, all patrols were now flown after dark. Capt. Frank Wagner (COM-PATWING 10) had moved his HQ to Bandoeng, as it had been clear for a week or more that Surabaja was rapidly becoming untenable as a base, with daily bombing attacks in broad daylight by the Japanese. Within a short period, though, Wagner would again shift his command from the hills of Bandoeng down to Tjilat-jap on the south coast, as had COMSOWESPAC Glassford himself on February 18.[34] Clearly this reduction in the strength of PatWing 10 affected reconnaissance and intelligence at a critical time. In the days to come Allied weakness in the air fully revealed itself. Poor scouting capabilities over the Java Sea were so compounded by inferior communications systems and lack of offensive assets that the enemy's East Java invasion convoys were able to close to within one hundred kilometers of the coast without being seriously challenged.[35]

A handful of Dutch auxiliary oil tankers remained in the Surabaja area, however—among them the *TAN 4* (ex-*Pendopo*) and *TAN 5* (ex-*Aldegonda*)—and *Paul Jones*, *Ford*, and *Pope* were able to fuel from *Pendopo*, although not quite to full capacity. Many ships reported experiencing trouble getting enough oil at Surabaja during the final week of the naval campaign. For the most part this was due to broken fuel lines and problems with valve fittings, all compounded by the shortage of local dock workers.[36] As Cdr. Thomas Binford wrote after the campaign, "All four pipelines in the area were put out of commission and in the end there was only one dock left capable of fueling Allied ships."[37] This deteriorating situation regarding fuel would have further implications later for the U.S. four-stackers. However, as difficult as matters had become by then at Surabaja, by the final week of February they were far worse at Batavia's Tandjong Priok and at Tjilatjap. An inventory of fuel oil stocks compiled that morning by Glassford and sent to Capt. H. V. Wiley (COMDESRON 29) showed only 1,020 tons available at Tandjong Priok. At Tjilatjap there was twice that amount; at Surabaja almost 10,000 tons, with another 10,000 inland at Tjepoe.[38]

...

While Glassford and his commanders were struggling with how best to dispose of the wrecked *Stewart* as she lay in her Surabaja dry dock, the cruiser *Houston* was also forced to make the long, circuitous voyage around Java to reach the same harbor. Steaming west at speed from Darwin, she had reached Tjilatjap—that "veritable witches' cauldron"—on the evening of February 21.[39] Outside the minefields another freakish near-accident took place when a British PBY dropped at least one depth charge in the bay near the cruiser as she came in. Alarmed, Rooks and his officers thought an enemy submarine was under attack and turned the ship out to sea again. Half an hour later, when the all-clear was sounded, they found out that the PBY had been forced to unload her depth charges in preparation for an emergency landing after having been hit by Dutch AA fire. The Royal Navy Catalina landed safely, but it sported a four-foot hole in one of its wings, courtesy of the jumpy local gunners. This delay would cause more problems for *Houston*, as it turned out.[40]

It next took over two hours to locate the Dutch harbor pilot, C. B. Droste, who had gone home to eat dinner by that time. He then pleaded with Rooks not to bring the ship in after dark. Rooks, understanding the urgency of getting away promptly, would not hear of it. In he brought *Houston*, but this determination came with a price. As the cruiser swung her six-hundred-foot length north around the bend of the docks and into the Kali Donan (river), she hit a bank of hard sand and grounded herself. It ate up several more hours for tugs to dislodge the big ship, after which she moored alongside the oil jetty, which was connected by pipeline to the nearby storage tanks.

Any relief at this achievement, though, was short-lived. It was soon found—much to the disgust of *Houston*'s "Oil King," Chief Frank Ellis, and his weary men—that the time lost through the PBY incident and the grounding had conspired against them: by that hour no local personnel were available to help fuel the ship. The cruiser's own engineering force had to fend for itself. The engineers worked through the night to replenish her oil tanks. Like most of the American skippers familiar with Tjilatjap, Captain Rooks was wary of being bottled up in the crowded, narrow harbor, and he had resolved to be out as early as possible the next morning.

The strain of such prolonged operations on *Houston*'s aging machinery put everyone at risk. During this stop at Tjilatjap, Albert Elmo Kennedy, F1/c, was nearly killed when a rotor on a centrifugal pump in one of the engine rooms disintegrated. In action Kennedy's battle station was marginally safer; he was with the after-damage repair party under Ens. Alva F. Nethken, with his friends Robert Kalinowski and J. O. Burge. Events at this time caused Kennedy to speculate, along with his fellow shipmates, that the unwillingness of the navy to commit modern ships then operating in the southwest Pacific to the Java campaign—such as USS *Phoenix*—indicated that *Houston* had already been given up for lost.[41] After the cruiser departed Tjilatjap, there would be good cause for such dark thoughts.

By 0730 Rooks had the ship under way again, heading out to sea on a westerly course that some believed would take them to Christmas Island, too. At dusk, however, the cruiser altered course to due north. Beneath the waterline, in the broiling confines of the number 1 engine room, Jack Leroy Smith, WT2/c, noted the "terrific sudden change of the rate of flow of water into the boilers" as the black gang under his boss, Chief Water Tender (PA) Archie Terry, increased power for the high-speed run through the narrow waterway between Sumatra and Java.[42] There would be no respite; it was back into the battle zone for the war-weary *Galloping Ghost*.

Topside, Lt. Walt Winslow had been curious about the ship's destination that afternoon and finally asked Cdr. John A. Hollowell, the cruiser's navigator, where they were headed. The conscientious older officer put his arm around

Winslow and made an enigmatic reply, as if talking to himself: "Son, we're going to hell. . . . We're going to hell." While the "puzzled" Winslow was understandably filled with "deep concern" by this ominous remark, it is clear that *Houston*'s senior officers—who knew they were going to Surabaja—then felt they and their ship were well and truly expendable.[43] As for many of the enlisted men, such as Albert Elmo Kennedy and Jack L. Smith, they felt that the brass in Washington had "walked out" on them a week before when Admiral Hart was recalled. That their ships had been turned over to Helfrich was nothing but a betrayal as far as they were concerned.[44]

After transiting Sunda Strait without incident, *Houston* steamed east hugging Java's northern coastline, always alert to the possibility of enemy air contact. Fortunately that leg of her journey was uneventful. In the midafternoon hours of February 24 the cruiser reached Surabaja. She passed through the extensive Dutch minefields and entered the grim-looking harbor, fouled by the stench and smoke of burning rubber from *Kota Radja*'s cargo, as yet another Japanese air raid took place. *Houston* docked at the big Rotterdam Pier just as the all-clear alert was sounded.

A number of ships were still in the harbor, even though the port installations had been reduced by Japanese air attacks over the previous three weeks. Various American and British headquarters had been shifted piecemeal to the west, as we have seen, and there is little question that events were now moving with great rapidity. All military commanders expected an invasion by the Japanese within a matter of days. Yet at Surabaja the crew of *Houston* would find more startling contradictions indicative of the muddled priorities of the Allied coalition.

Although heavy and light AA units were set up around the Surabaja port area—Dutch and British—none were really sufficient to deal with the Japanese level bombers flying high overhead. When *Houston* arrived with her battery of eight 5-inch/25 cal. AA guns, she had the range and firepower to affect bombers at altitude. To the astonishment and chagrin of *Houston*'s men, however, the Dutch requested that while in harbor the cruiser restrict her firing arcs "on certain bearings" in order to avoid endangering civilian areas within the city.[45] This seemed to the cruiser's men a howling absurdity. They were well aware of Dutch criticism of American naval participation throughout the campaign, and now, when they could bring assets to the table, they were being told to limit their contribution.

Some crewmen on the U.S. ship recalled having the impression that the local Dutch resented the cruiser being in the harbor, as if *Houston*'s mere presence had *attracted* the Japanese planes. Other men stated that it was not unusual for

Dutch personnel to wave at them as though pleading with the big American ship to go away, hoping that this might dissuade the enemy bombers from further attacks.[46] In confirming this defeatist atmosphere, Walter Winslow wrote, "Apart from the distant wail of sirens, Surabaja and the entire area surrounding the navy yard remained silent. It was like a city of death."[47] Within another day similar observations would be recorded by sailors aboard the Australian light cruiser HMAS *Perth*, as she arrived in Surabaja's Tandjong Perak harbor from Batavia, along with the 8-inch gunned British cruiser HMS *Exeter* and three destroyers, HMS *Electra*, *Encounter*, and *Jupiter*.

These units from the Royal Navy had been ordered from Tandjong Priok at Batavia on the morning of the twenty-fifth by CCCF Collins, but they were delayed by the inability of *Hobart* to complete fueling due to the enemy air attacks that had damaged the oiler *War Sirdar*. In any case Collins's instructions were of a general nature; they told the British ships—which for several hours were assumed to include HMAS *Hobart*—to "steer towards EAST JAVA SEA at 20 knots. Further instructions follow."[48] In the end, they departed without *Hobart*, which was a significant loss to Doorman's Combined Striking Force but which undoubtedly preserved the Australian light cruiser.

The Dutch under Lieutenant Admiral Helfrich had decided to concentrate all warships at Surabaja, there to operate under Rear Admiral Doorman. Helfrich—with the dissolution of ABDA at noon on that day in command of the Allied naval forces, under his old RNN title of CZM (*commandant der zeemacht*)—had at last received the air reports, which revealed what appeared to be enemy invasion convoys moving down Makassar Strait toward eastern Java.[49] The enemy's speed and course estimates were read—or misread—on the twenty-fifth by Helfrich and his command to put the Japanese invasion convoy off Madura Island by the morning of February 26. With this in mind Helfrich chose not to wait for the *Exeter* group coming from Batavia but ordered his available forces to sortie that evening. Accordingly, Doorman under his title of EC (*eskader commandant*, or squadron commander) took *De Ruyter*, *Java*, *Houston*, and seven destroyers—*Witte de With*, *Kortenaer*, *Paul Jones*, *John D. Ford*, *Pope*, *Alden*, and *John D. Edwards*—out from Surabaja at 1800 hours for a high-speed sweep east along the northern coast of Madura Island, where the Dutch expected the Japanese to land. This CSF naturally found nothing, but it did burn up more precious fuel and further exhaust the already-fatigued officers and men.

By 0600 hours the following morning the ships had returned to Surabaja; U.S. destroyer skippers immediately began making efforts to again fuel their ships. It was the same story, the same struggle to obtain enough oil. With fuel lines shattered at the Holland Pier, they had to use Dutch tankers. By 1340 hours *Ford* had taken on over 47,000 gallons from *Pendopo* (TAN 4), which brought her total up to more than 112,000 gallons on board. In midmorning another Japanese air raid had taken place, and *Houston* was near-missed by several bombs but not hit as she continued her energetic AA firing.[50] It was during these raids that the destroyer *Paul Jones* under Lt. Cdr. John J. Hourihan provided accurate and useful sighting info to *Houston's* gunners.

*Jones* had just finished receiving over 50,000 gallons of fuel herself from *Pendopo* and was anchored away from the docks and tankers. She counted twenty-six attacking bombers. One string of bombs landed about three thousand yards away, closer to *Houston*, but luckily nothing approached Hourihan's ship.[51] Afterward Capt. Albert Rooks sent a message to COMSOWESPAC Glassford informing him of the situation on his ship: "CONSIDERABLE SHRAPNEL CAME ON BOARD X 1,571 ROUNDS FIVE-INCH REMAIN ALL BEING OF DEFECTIVE LOT X."[52]

These details tell us that *Houston* had taken aboard a large amount of *Boise's* "good" 5-inch ammo at Tjilatjap earlier that month. *Houston's* AA crews fired 933 5-inch rounds against Japanese air attackers defending the Timor relief convoy in midmonth. It also indicates *Houston's* limited lifespan as a useful escort; Rooks undoubtedly would have known that without his secondary battery, the ship lost most of her value. In this sense the message by Rooks may also be read—between the lines—to indicate that in his judgment it was time to get the cruiser out of the East Indies. But by this stage of what was undeniably a losing campaign, the navy was not about to send another valuable warship (such as *Phoenix*) into the cauldron of the East Indies to be squandered for nothing. The stage had been set, the cast selected, and the script all but completed. It only remained to play out the final scenes in the drama's last act. And a less awful ending was not in keeping with the conventions of great tragedy.[53]

*Exeter* and *Perth* with destroyers meanwhile arrived at Surabaja in midafternoon on Friday, February 26, with the trio of British DDs preceding the two cruisers into the anchorage by thirty minutes. The remaining Royal Navy units to the west at Batavia—*Hobart, Danae, Dragon, Jumna, Yarra,* and several older destroyers—were to be held there as an ad hoc striking force for the time being. It was clear that these ships could offer little real resistance to Japanese covering forces, and undoubtedly the British hoped to be able to get them away from Batavia as quickly as possible to aid their convoys fleeing eastern Sumatra for India.

To the Australians arriving in Surabaja on *Perth*, the allied forces gathered there appeared potent. In addition to *Houston* there were the two gray and green camouflaged Dutch cruisers along with several RNN destroyers and five American four-pipers. The Aussies thought the Dutch warships fine-looking vessels, and several mistook *Houston*, with her great length and big tripod masts, for an American battleship. The battered and rust-flecked four-pipers may have been viewed with some skepticism, but their service in Australian waters and their earlier exploits at Balikpapan and Badoeng Strait told a different story. Along with the well-publicized veteran British cruiser *Exeter* and screen of three relatively modern Royal Navy destroyers, the sailors thought their fleet a reasonably formidable one. However, the best analogy may have been supplied by another veteran who saw the Combined Striking Force as a group of college all-stars who had never scrimmaged, let alone competed together, yet were being sent out to face a crack Notre Dame team.[54] Whatever their individual abilities, the critical absence of practiced teamwork in the CSF would prove a serious defect in combat.

Simultaneously, the British destroyers found the same trouble getting enough fuel that the American ships had encountered. As Lt. Cdr. T. J. Cain, senior survivor of *Electra* later wrote: "Sourabaya, stinking from air raid [meaning the noisome pall from *Kota Radja* no doubt], was no sailors' rest. It took *Electra* three hours to negotiate the minefields."[55] During the late afternoon conferences ashore, commanding officers voiced concern that they might not have enough time to receive sufficient fuel to sortie as planned that evening. Captain Oliver Gordon of *Exeter* later reported that due to damage to oiling berths in Surabaja, the Royal Navy destroyers had "experienced difficulty in obtaining fuel, but all eventually fuelled though some were unable to complete to full stowage."[56]

Gordon and Hec Waller were to be the last commanding officers to arrive at the afternoon conference called by Doorman at Dutch Naval HQ. This was in a new location at the Netherlands Indies Electricity Company's head office, known as the ANIEM, about two or three miles from the harbor.[57] They were driven through heavy Surabaja traffic in what was later described as the most hair-raising and life-threatening automobile ride either officer had ever experienced. Since they were not going to arrive on schedule, though, Doorman had changed the time of the conference from 1500 hours to 1700. Captain Rooks was already present, as were the skippers from *De Ruyter* (Lacomblé), *Java* (Van Straelen), *Witte de With* (Schotel), and *Kortenaer* (Kroese). Cdr. Thomas Binford of DesDiv 58 and Lt. Cdr. Edward "Butch" Parker (as division commander and junior division commander respectively) represented the DesRon 29 destroyers.

While waiting for Gordon and Waller to arrive, several Dutch officers went off to visit their families, probably well aware of the fate that lay in store for many of them. Evidently Butch Parker and Tom Binford both appeared so "forlorn" that Cdr. Antonie Kroese of the destroyer *Kortenaer* offered to take them to his home to meet his family. He drove them in his own car. There they met his beautiful and charming blonde wife and two young daughters, about four and six years of age. The two little girls modeled their tin helmets, which they were wearing to school. In his garden Kroese was constructing a makeshift air-raid shelter for his family because he hadn't enough money to send them away from Java to safety elsewhere. As recorded by Parker, "Cruiser" Kroese was an amiable and informal officer, wearing shorts, and also, of all things, barefooted that afternoon. This all-too-brief social interlude, mellowed by a Scotch and water or two, was much appreciated by the weary U.S. destroyer officers. (Binford had decided to allow his other skippers to remain with their ships in the harbor, in the hope of giving them some much-needed rest and to assist, if necessary, with any problems in acquiring fuel.)[58]

When they returned to the RNN headquarters, Parker spoke informally with another Dutch officer about the prospects of holding Java. The impression he received was not inspiring. An army of only twenty-five thousand reliable men, and with very few airplanes to defend the island, had led *this* Dutchman at least to the unpleasant realization that it might be up to the combined naval forces to fend off the Japanese invaders. Obviously such thoughts on the afternoon of February 26 were hardly encouraging.[59]

Gordon and Waller at length reached the headquarters along with the three British destroyer skippers, and Doorman began the conference. Butch Parker offered the following description of Rear Adm. Karel Doorman: "[He] a large, serious man. . . . His English was sufficiently good and permitted him to conduct our conferences in our language."[60] Doorman's remarks were brief and to the point; although his demeanor did not show it, they were also far from optimistic. The enemy was concentrating his forces for landings at either end of Java; the Japanese had control of airspace, with planes operating from captured fields in Borneo, Celebes, Sumatra, and Bali; it was thought that at least one Japanese Kongō-class battleship was among the Imperial Navy's covering forces in the Makassar Strait and another ship of the same type at Singapore; he informed the commanders of various Dutch minefields near Madura Island and plans for more mines to be laid that day off Toeban, up the coast roughly fifty miles northwest of Surabaja. Parker and Binford already knew that reconnaissance from U.S. patrol planes was going to be no real help; they'd spoken to Captain Wagner of PatWing 10 earlier that afternoon on their way to the conference, and he had told them he was down to a single Catalina. Both American destroyer commanders also suspected that Japanese aircraft carriers were probably loose in the region, based on the tremendous air raid on Darwin the previous week.

Doorman's operational orders for the Combined Striking Force were necessarily quite simple and rudimentary, and the scope of what they entailed shows how seriously outmatched the remaining Allied forces were at that point. He wanted the ships to be under way by 1900 hours and formed up by 2100 to sweep eastward at 25 knots along the northern coast of Madura Island again. (This was just what they had done the previous day and night.) At such speed they should reach the tip of Madura by midnight, at which time he would reverse course and sweep westward to Rembang and continue along the length of Java, with the ships returning not to Surabaja but to Batavia's Tandjong Priok.[61]

At sea they were to operate in a scorpion-like formation with the column led by *De Ruyter*, followed by *Exeter, Houston, Perth,* and *Java*. The three British DDs would spread out ahead like pincers, with both Dutch DDs attached, and Binford's five flushdeckers bringing up the rear to act as the stinger in the tail as it were. It was Doorman's hope that his cruisers and modern destroyers might be able to draw off the Japanese convoy escort during a night battle, thereby allowing the flushdeckers with their heavy torpedo batteries to get at the vulnerable transports. Binford's memory of the tactical plan differed only in that it presumed the other ships would all make attacks first: "In case of contact British and Dutch destroyers to attack at once and retire, then cruisers attack and retire, then U.S. destroyers come in and deliver a torpedo attack."[62]

That afternoon, as the conference was beginning to get under way, Helfrich in Lembang received more intelligence from his own air patrols in the Java Sea to the northeast of Surabaja. They had spotted thirty transports escorted by two cruisers and four destroyers moving southwest (course 245 degrees) at 10 knots around midday. On this basis Helfrich (CZM) sent a message to Doorman (as EC) that was copied to Collins (CCCF) and Glassford (COMSOW-ESPAC); it read: "Striking force is to proceed to sea in order to attack enemy after dark. After attack striking force is to proceed towards Tandjong Priok."[63] More reports confirming enemy convoys moving down toward the northeast coast of Java filtered in to Helfrich's HQ throughout the day and evening. Yet locating the Japanese proved maddeningly difficult; accurate intelligence about the exact whereabouts of the convoy and its support forces would continue to elude Doorman and the CSF after they sortied.

During this final meeting with his subordinates Rear Admiral Doorman had given other verbal orders in his "careful English" according to Parker.[64] He went over destinations for the ships should they become separated or after action was joined, along with details regarding night recognition signals. He said that any disabled Allied ships would have to "be left to the mercy of the enemy" and that other CSF vessels were not to stand by for rescue attempts.[65] This would have been in keeping with the general conception of the operation as a "Hit and Run" affair, which it was hoped would prove to be the case.[66] At about 1800 hours Doorman concluded the meeting. He wished all the officers in the striking force good luck in the coming operation.[67] The men filed out of the conference room, exchanging more hopeful expressions as they went, and were taken to waiting automobiles, which then drove them back to the gloomy, smoky harbor and their ships. It was to prove the last time that many of these brave men saw one another alive.

As for Karel "Tank" Doorman, he and his force were being driven to their fate as inexorably as cattle led into an abattoir. Whether they heard the gate "clang" behind them or not, the metaphor was an apt one—not directed by choice or even circumstances beyond their control, however, but through the sheer obstinacy of Lt. Adm. C. E. L. Helfrich. Members of the RNN staff in Surabaja as well as his own men said that Doorman wanted nothing to do with the coming battle against the Japanese.[68] Instead he had continued to hope that his ships might be permitted to withdraw to ports of safety—like those of the Americans and the British—in Australia or India and from there continue the war. This was something that Helfrich would not countenance, especially once air reports began to arrive showing the enemy bearing down on Java. Conrad Helfrich, with his firm—if naive—belief that the enemy transports were vulnerable, was going to have his naval confrontation with the Japanese in *his* waters, no matter the consequences.

Accordingly, between 1830 and 1900 hours, Doorman's CSF put out to sea from Surabaja in search of the enemy they suspected had now come within striking distance. It was a final parting both melancholy and portentous. Extra yard hands were so scarce that in some cases the lines were cast off by local family members who had gathered to say their farewells to the sailors they expected never to see again. The wife of an RNN officer actually handled the mooring lines as one of the Dutch destroyers prepared to go back out to sea. And even then, in these final hours, ill luck clung to the ships. As she emerged from the harbor, *De Ruyter* managed to ram a tug towing a string of water barges, some carrying yard workers. At least one sank, leaving dozens of men swimming in the murky waters of Tandjong Perak. A small number had to be taken aboard the flagship and were thus compelled through another accident to share in her fate.[69]

When the ships emerged from the minefields and headed out into the open sea, a bugler on one of the ships—thought to have been a Dutch cruiser—blew the "close all watertight doors" signal for his ship. To the Americans on *Houston* it sounded just like "A-hunting We Will Go" (as popularized in the Bugs Bunny cartoons) and under the grim circumstances, when levity was highly prized, struck them as both spirited and humorous. But as we will see, for these young men there would be precious little to really smile about over the next few days.

• • •

Before departing Surabaja on the twenty-sixth, *Houston* had flown off her remaining operable SOC, with Tommy Payne piloting the biplane. It was felt that in view of the impending night action, the floatplane would not be of any value, but leaving it behind at Surabaja might preserve it for future use. Payne had left the cruiser in his machine during one of the morning air raids, taxiing the SOC into an inconspicuous hiding place, described as "a bug-infested swamp" along the shoreline.[70] Later Captain Rooks instructed the flier to take the Seagull to the Dutch naval air base at Morokrembangan and await further orders there. Payne, who admired and respected Rooks greatly—calling him "thoroughly competent," and "a gentleman of good bearing" who never lost his temper—did as instructed.[71] Although he would be advised by Captain Wagner of PatWing 10 two days later to obtain a seat in one of the last departing PBYS as an evacuee, Payne declined to do so, telling Wagner that he had been given his orders and he would follow them.

Air reconnaissance was to again prove critical during the impending engagement, as would the absence of any useful air cover for the CSF.[72] Dutch and American sighting reports on the twenty-sixth as the enemy's eastern Java convoys descended on the island from the Makassar Strait were being sent to the Commander Naval Base Surabaja (CMR) before being routed to Helfrich at his headquarters in the mountains at Bandoeng. As one might expect, this added time delays and potential garbling to the messages that were then forwarded to Doorman. Consequently neither the shore organizations nor those forces at sea could acquire a coherent picture of the enemy's location throughout most of the twenty-sixth and much of the twenty-seventh. Astonishingly, the RAF intelligence officer for two squadrons then available on Java was not asked to provide any liaison personnel to the Dutch HQ at Batavia until Friday, February 27. This belated request shows, if nothing else, the wretched state of cooperation between the Western allies even as the Japanese invaders were bearing down on the island.

Although there would be a smattering of Allied aircraft over the fleets, and very few Imperial Navy planes—just the floatplanes launched by their cruisers, in fact—the Japanese did a better job. Doorman would never feel as if he had a firm grasp on the enemy convoy's whereabouts. The Japanese, by contrast, had a clear enough picture of the size and location of the Allied fleet from morning until night. And in the preradar period of naval combat in the Pacific, the sharp-eyed and well-trained Imperial Navy often came away with the upper hand in nighttime encounters.

Led by the three British and two Dutch destroyers, Doorman's five cruisers were followed by four rather than five flushdeckers in this sortie. Welford Blinn's *Pope* had been compelled to remain in Surabaja to work on a poor weld that had left the ship with a badly leaking hot well. The problem had become so severe that the boilers were in danger of having to use salt water, which in turn could have caused very serious damage. Native yard laborers were increasingly difficult to find at Surabaja, and those who would work would do so only under the cover of darkness. After some delays due to unfamiliarity with the harbor, *Pope* found her way to a dock next to an electrical welding shop in the navy yard. Although at first dubious about the chances for locating capable welders, *Pope's* engineering officer, Lt. "Red" Bassett, was quite surprised to find the next morning that the Javanese workers had done a remarkably fine job—better in fact, Bassett said, than anything that might have been achieved at Cavite, even under unhurried conditions.[73]

That evening, as the striking force crept east along the northern coastline of Madura Island (where the Dutch had anticipated initial landings would be made by the enemy) another sighting report came in—and quite belatedly, as it had been made around midday—from the Dutch flying boat X-28: "3 cruisers—5 destroyers—24 transports bearing 315 . . . estimate course 245."[74] It is not entirely clear whether Doorman ever received all these sightings; if so they would have done little to clarify matters for him and could have just as easily added to his confusion.

About three hours after the above report was made, another Dutch Catalina, Y-59, returning to Surabaja from an attack against Kema in the northern Celebes, stumbled on several dark shapes northeast of the Kangean island group. These were mistaken at first for small islets. Soon enough, though, they were perceived to be enemy warships steaming west; two big cruisers and a pair of destroyers. They were at that time far off to the east, over 150 miles away from the convoy sightings. It is fairly certain that this information never reached Doorman at sea, but even if it had, his orders from Helfrich (which had been sent two hours after the CSF departed Surabaja) would have remained unchanged: "You must continue attacks until enemy is destroyed."[75] Through the long night, with men at action stations, the weary ships and their exhausted crews steamed eastward along Madura and beyond, from Sapoedi Island, where they reversed course, and then back west for two hundred miles all the way to Rembang. What meager air reports that did arrive were of no help in pinpointing the enemy convoy or its support forces.

By the same token, early on the morning of the twenty-seventh, efficient enemy air reconnaissance found the Combined Striking Force off Surabaja, and it came as something of a nasty surprise to the Japanese. There had been speculation that Allied naval assets were more seriously reduced following the bombing attacks of February 4 in the so-called Battle of the Flores Sea; it was therefore a shock to spot five cruisers and a large number of destroyers at sea again north of Surabaja during the forenoon of February 27—all the more so given the relatively light covering forces of the East Java convoys—only the two destroyer squadrons of Rear Admirals Nishimura (DesRon 4) and Tanaka (DesRon 2) were close enough to engage the Allies' CSF at that time.

Rear Adm. Takagi Takeo's unit, made up of Sentai 5 in *Nachi* (F) and *Haguro*, plus two destroyers—the first section of DesDiv 7, *Ushio* and *Sazanami*—was still a couple of hours away. These ships had been steaming in a rectangular box north of Bawean Island in their distant support role. By early afternoon on the twenty-sixth, they were approximately one hundred miles northeast of the island and moving west, with the Annie Florence Rock between them and Bawean's Mount Besar. They would continue in this holding pattern for the next twenty hours and be on the southerly leg of its western side when the location and movements of Doorman's flotilla were finally ascertained just after midday on February 27.

A few B-17s flying out of Malang made desultory attacks that morning on Tanaka's squadron, but their bombs landed well away from the destroyer *Yukikaze* and were ineffective. To one of the Japanese skippers in another destroyer nearby (*Amatsukaze*), this seemed folly. The "sluggish" transports in the convoy appeared such defenseless targets.[76] Forty-one Japanese ships arrayed in two elongated columns 600 meters apart that stretched out for some 12 kilometers were moving slowly to the south and had then reached a position roughly 50 miles northwest of Bawean Island. At about the same time, before midday, a new air report came in from a land-based Eleventh Air Fleet plane: "Five enemy cruisers and six destroyers are steaming at a speed of 12 knots, course 80 degrees, 63 miles and 310 degrees off Surabaja."[77] This placed Allied surface units within 60 nautical miles of the convoy and about 120 miles away from Takagi's heavy ships.

Over the next hour Takagi launched a scout plane from *Nachi*, as did Nishimura from *Naka*, to keep tabs on the enemy flotilla. Other Sentai 5 reconnaissance units were being readied. However, on the day prior *Haguro* had damaged one of her planes, a Type O (a three-seater with good range later called a JAKE) as it was being recovered from the sea after encountering an enemy flying boat. One pilot, a chief petty officer (*jōtōheisō*) named Kameda, had received minor head injuries when he was thrown into the water and swept into the screws' whirlpool as the cruiser suddenly picked up speed. The ship retained another biplane aboard—the smaller Type 95 DAVE and used primarily for spotting purposes—that was available, and it was pressed into service. *Haguro*'s air group commander, Lt. Utsunomiya Michio, had adequate time that afternoon to brief his crews on their mission. Meanwhile, the Type O from *Nachi* was transmitting a stream of accurate sighting reports on the contradictory movements of Doorman's flotilla.

Well removed from events, Takagi was of two minds regarding the CSF's intentions. He first thought the striking force was coming out to intercept the convoy but then believed it was withdrawing back to Surabaja. This ambiguous reaction was understandable as Doorman's CSF zigzagged its way east and west, reversing course and altering speeds frequently as it went. At the same time, the Allied force was now paying the price of having no air reconnaissance.[78] Not one of the five cruisers was able to get a scout plane into the air that day; this deficiency would have dire ramifications on February 27. To have placed themselves in such an informational blind spot would have seemed unthinkable just eight or nine months later in the Pacific War. They were within sixty miles of the enemy and yet could not determine his location.[79] Unable to get good intelligence on the exact whereabouts of the Japanese convoy, Doorman—who had already informed Helfrich that his crews had reached and exceeded the limits of endurance—began to swing back toward Surabaja. His smaller ships were burning up oil quickly as they strove to keep up with the more robust cruisers; he told Helfrich that the destroyers would have to fuel again by the twenty-eighth.

Observing that Doorman had indeed reversed course and was leading the CSF back to Java, his movements were carefully recorded by a stalker in the sky. *Nachi*'s floatplane made a series of precise and accurate reports back to Takagi and his commanders: "At 1405 [Tokyo/IJN time; or 1235 for the Allied force] the enemy fleet consists of two heavy cruisers, three light cruisers, and nine destroyers at a speed of 24 knots, course 180 degrees, 45 miles and 194 degrees from the [Japanese] fleets." This was soon followed by: "At 1425 the enemy seems to be heading to Surabaja." And then: "At 1455 they are sailing into Surabaja port."[80]

It would have been these sighting reports that allowed Takagi to imagine Doorman's force was retreating to Surabaja and that the convoys could again move south to the jumping-off point north of Kragan. No more than thirty minutes passed, however, before additional messages from *Nachi*'s plane came in that threw all the Japanese plans into upheaval once more. The Allied flotilla was seen to have altered course to 60 degrees at a speed of 18 knots; then, over the next hour, it completely reversed course through several turns so that by 1518 hours the ships of the CSF were steaming on course 315 degrees at 22 knots.

Over those confusing hours Takagi struggled with his multiple responsibilities, that of protecting his precious convoy and the disposition of his covering forces along with that of a demanding timetable for landings. At first he became somewhat alarmed and ordered Nishimura in *Naka* and Tanaka in *Jintsū* to prepare to rendezvous with his force. Nishimura accordingly turned over direct control of the convoy—which had reached a position within a few miles to the northwest of Bawean island—to the commander of *Wakataka*, an outdated old destroyer now used only for escort duty. The convoy duly altered its assigned course for the Kragan landing points and moved away from Bawean. *Naka* then increased speed to 21 knots as she steamed off to meet Tanaka, Takagi, and come to grips with the Allied fleet. Within ninety minutes—and after the *Nachi* plane's message—the exasperated Takagi seems to have recognized that his support forces would have to make contact with the Allied ships and exert every effort to "annihilate" them.

Given these evolving alterations to plans, it is hardly surprising that the convoy was reduced to "chaos" as one IJN veteran destroyerman described the scene. "The transports turned around and fanned out. Their movement was painfully slow. They were mostly requisitioned merchant ships and their crews were untrained. It was distressing to watch their disarray. Many were baffled at the repeatedly changing orders and they were unable to respond quickly."[81] It took an hour or so to restore order to the jumbled columns of transports; eventually they resumed their places and moved away from the waters in which the impending combat would soon take place. Thus, as the Combined Striking Force under Doorman was steaming at high speed in the direction of the invasion convoy, and with Rear Admiral Takagi's support forces divided up into three separate groups, the stage had messily been set on that clear, mild afternoon for what would soon become known as the Battle of the Java Sea.

. . .

On the Allied side, for exhausted officers and men, with bodies screaming for sleep, eyes bleary and brains "like hot porridge," the time had come at last to confront the enemy fleet—an enemy fleet they had been seeking for so long that it had become a kind of phantom.[82] Over the next few hours many more reports would stream in, but until the three-pronged Japanese covering units collided with the Allies' Combined Striking Force late in the afternoon, the fog of war would still maintain dominance over Doorman and his ships.

And while some of the other Allied skippers and officers were critical of Doorman's tactics, others understood the impossible position he had been thrust into through no fault of his own. Lt. Harlan G. Kirkpatrick on *Houston* remembered feeling sympathetic to Doorman, with the unfamiliar and hodgepodge fleet he had inherited and been compelled to use "right away." Kirkpatrick and others understood that Doorman himself did not create the situation. In spite of the confusion and disorder, the Dutch admiral was, as one of the flushdecker officers on *John D. Edwards* remembered, quite well regarded, especially in contrast to Helfrich.[83] Similarly, Helfrich's own adjutant and secretary at headquarters in Lembang during the two men's final meeting saw a Karel Doorman who, in their eyes, was in poor health by late February and utterly exhausted.[84]

Although a multitude of transports was known to be descending on Java, the exact location and composition of the Japanese covering forces remained something of a mystery. Air reconnaissance on the morning of the twenty-seventh finally got an accurate picture of the convoy and its screen when it spotted what was reported as a "great fleet consisting two cruisers 6 destroyers and 25 Transports position 20 miles west of Bawean course south. One cruiser four destroyers proceed south full speed transports stay behind."[85] This report from the Dutch Catalina Y-45 (sent at 0620 Z) was routed through the usual inefficient channels, but it seemed to galvanize some attempted activity in air groups and submarines.[86] As with so much else in this jumbled defense, air efforts were piecemeal, haphazard, and ineffective.

Within minutes CZM (Helfrich) messaged the following to COMSOWESPAC (Glassford) and CCCF (Collins): "Confirming oral instructions, request you interpose all submarines possible on East-West line between enemy reported 0620 Z position and North coast of Java."[87] Rather than showing that the Allies had an effective strategy mapped out ahead of time, these orders—given as they were far too late—reveal how disorganized and ill-prepared the air and sea forces defending Java remained.

In the meantime, and despite the beautiful, clear day, Doorman's CSF had found nothing. On the flushdeckers of Cdr. Thomas Binford's DesDiv 58 occasional messages came in via the British destroyers that mystified the Americans. HMS *Jupiter* would report air contacts that were said to be as much as seventy-five miles distant. To the unenlightened flushdecker sailors—who knew nothing of *Jupiter*'s air search radar—this was baffling in itself. "We were wondering who on that ship had those marvelous eyes!" wrote Lt. Cdr. E. N. "Butch" Parker years later.[88] On this fateful day neither radar, reconnaissance planes, attack planes, nor submarines would be of any real help for the Combined Striking Force.

The crews of Doorman's ships, at action stations for prolonged periods, with many having had no sleep for two nights, were obviously worn out. The sweeps along Java's northern coast also meant that his ships were beginning to run low on fuel. Therefore, he decided to reenter Surabaja—although whether this was in the hope of getting his men some rest or simply to refuel, we do not know.[89]

However, Helfrich remained troubled by the communications problems he felt were inhibiting Doorman's actions. He was quite certain—as verified in his postwar *Memoires*—that there was "a technical defect of his [Doorman's] receiving equipment" that prevented the timely transmission of what Helfrich was to term "good messages."[90] And Helfrich was not especially helpful in adding reports such as a submarine sighting of three cruisers and three destroyers southeast of Sepandjang (in the eastern Kangean Archipelago) moving south toward Lombok Strait at 15 knots. This pointless communication was sent to Doorman just as he and the CSF steamed off in the opposite direction to the west, along the northern side of Madura that morning. Its only real significance was the suggestion—but not the confirmation—that the enemy was closing off the eastern exits from the Java Sea around Bali and Lombok.

Around midday Doorman decided to bring the CSF back to Surabaja. The Allied column once more approached the extensive minefields off the Westervaarwater. After passing through the minefields they were to anchor in the harbor and resume the daily struggle to obtain a sufficient amount of bunker oil. It was only after the ships had already entered the minefields, with the Dutch destroyers leading, that Doorman finally received confirmation—based on the 0620 Z message by Catalina Y-45—of the Japanese fleet's location. Upon getting the latest reconnaissance information, which was precise and appeared reliable, he gave orders to his ships to turn about and head out to sea again: "Am proceeding to intercept enemy units. Follow me. Details later." *De Ruyter*, *Exeter*, *Houston*, *Perth*, and *Java* duly reversed course in the cleared channel—a tricky and dangerous business that took some fifteen minutes to execute—and pointed their bows toward the enemy forces now thought to be no more than an hour or two away.[91] The time was 1445 hours.

At about that point Doorman very sensibly requested air cover as well. Although Helfrich subsequently claimed in his *Memoires* that Doorman's calls for air cover were "in vain," he does acknowledge the attacks made by U.S. Army Air Force A-24 dive-bombers later against the Japanese transports.[92] In truth Helfrich's complaint in this respect, too, remains an unsettling one. Unknown to Helfrich—or Doorman—both American and Dutch fighter pilots had been instructed by Java Air Command (JAC) to provide support to the CSF during its sortie.[93] Augmenting this air cover was the decision to attack Japanese convoys with a few dive-bombers. This plan, such as it was, may be seen as representative of the puny resources and frail means left to the Allies as they sought to defend the island. Three A-24s of the Ninety-First Bomb Squadron flying out of Singosari were to make an attack on the enemy transports, escorted by all operational P-40s and Brewster Buffaloes. The fighters were then to "clear the sky of any Japanese aircraft in the expected area of action between the two naval forces."[94] An American air force officer had come to Ngoro after discussing the plans for this mission with Rear Admiral Koenraad, the Royal Netherlands Navy officer in charge at in Surabaja. Maddeningly, it seems *none* of this was known to Helfrich at HQ in Bandoeng or to the exhausted Doorman and his CSF at sea.[95]

Anticipation of imminent action produced different reactions. Aboard *Haguro* the inexperienced flight crews subsequently claimed that the atmosphere in their division was much the same as in peacetime maneuvers prior to the battle, but the nature of their conversations might indicate otherwise. While they were having a few beers in their wardroom before the fleets clashed, there was quite a bit of talk among various *chui* and *taii* about the proper way to conduct themselves in case their ship was sunk. After discussion of the chances for being rescued by one of their own destroyers, the subject of being picked up by the enemy naturally arose. Some of the men felt that it was undignified to bob up and down in the water shouting, "Glory to our emperor!" ("Banzai") and thought it preferable to die while still on deck. When one of the junior men suggested he would drown himself by "diving," another replied that even so, they would nonetheless float back up soon enough. Others claimed to carry small knives in their underclothes with which to commit suicide. None seemed to have felt that becoming "a shameful prisoner" was an acceptable alternative. Finally, a heated exchange broke out over the proper term to call Hirohito when yelling, "Banzai." When one young officer asked whether he should be called "Our Great Marshal"—as he had heard him called at Hirohito's birthday celebration—or "Our Emperor," an exasperated senior officer rebuked him: "You idiot, it is the same."[96]

Steaming into battle, the flight commander of *Haguro*'s air squadron—Lt. Utsunomiya Michio—was on the cruiser's bridge with the commanding officer, Capt. Mori Tomoichi. Both men were perturbed over the damage to their Type O (JAKE) in the previous day's accident, which the captain saw now as having led to a missed opportunity. Each man realized only too fully that the plane was sorely needed as Sentai 5 searched for the whereabouts of Doorman's striking force. Lieutenant Utsonomiya wrote later that these oblique yet clearly critical remarks from his skipper, as the two men stood on the bridge peering off to the south for Doorman's ships, caused him to break out in a heavy sweat at that time.[97]

· · ·

Under almost ideal weather conditions—a mild day of few clouds and a light breeze, with good visibility on the sea and in the skies overhead—the CSF headed out into the Java Sea, increasing speed from 18 to 22 knots as the ships steamed to the northwest. The Japanese were no more than an hour or two away. On board the Allied ships the weary sailors and officers drew on their penultimate reserves of strength once again. Worn-out machinery and exhausted men had to face the test for which they had been designed and trained, although now under far from optimal circumstances. Doorman's CSF had operated together a grand total of two days, with a tatty hodge-podge of communications systems augmented by liaison personnel who had not worked together previously. They had been given no chance for exercising tactically as a unit; there was simply no time for that. The fourteen Allied ships may have appeared at first glance to be a formidable force, but overwork and material wear had already taken their toll.

Capt. Albert Rooks's big cruiser was a case in point. *Houston*'s 5-inch-gun crews were especially fatigued, having been at general quarters for two nights straight in addition to having endured several air raids on Surabaja while in port. It was known that her Mark 19 AA directors were susceptible to numerous failings. Her primary searchlight battery had only two operational lights, one on each side. The other two had never been repaired after being disabled in the February 4 bombing in the Flores Sea action. Turret 3 remained out of commission, but most if not all of her 8-inch projectiles that had been subjected to flooding after the February 4 attack were still usable. As she steamed into action on February 27, the ship would have possessed almost all of her official allotment of nine hundred rounds of main battery ammunition. Unfortunately one-third of these—three hundred rounds, along with their powder cans—were still in her aft magazines.

Her communications division had been expanded by the addition of two Dutch RNN liaison personnel: Lt. Jacobus C. van Leur and Machinist Mate Petrus J. A. Stoopman. It appears from surviving records that Van Leur and Stoopman operated an ultrashortwave set (using the 5100 kc/s band) that had been installed in the direction-finder shack. They had direct communications via telephones with the conning tower, main radio, flag plot, after signal station, battle 2 and radio 2.[98] When messages were received from De Ruyter, they would then be transmitted directly to the various stations on Houston after being copied, deciphered, and translated by Van Leur and Stoopman. Houston was also responsible for transmitting messages on to the four flushdeckers of Cdr. Thomas Binford and Cdr. Henry Eccles, but as may be imagined the system was both laborious and frail, involving TBS, flashing lights, and flag hoists. As Commander Maher on Houston later wrote in his action report, due to the communications snarl, "orders had to be few and brief. As a result there was always doubt in the minds of all regarding the tactical situation and the action expected from each ship."[99] The testy Eccles wrote caustically that only crystal balls could determine Doorman's actual intentions throughout the battle.

Four U.S. Navy signal personnel were on board De Ruyter as well. They were Lt. Otto Kolb (USNA 1936)—from the staff of DesRon 29, who was fluent in Dutch and had been on the flagship since late December—and three young seamen: Marvin Sholar from Black Hawk, Jack Penhollow from Black Hawk, and Dan Rafalovich, detached from Houston.[100] British liaison personnel, too, had been sent to both De Ruyter (Lieutenant Jackson, RNVR) and Java (Lt. Gerry Jenkins). Sholar, while serving on De Ruyter, remembered operating several different types of equipment, from the shortwave radio to signal lights to hand-carried Aldis lamps. Finally, when the radio and lights were all knocked out, he was reduced to using flags before darkness closed in. After nightfall only the handheld lamps were used.

On their northwestern course—310° T.—the CSF steamed, its column over a dozen miles in length, with De Ruyter leading the other cruisers: Exeter, Houston, Perth, and Java, each separated by about six hundred yards. They were followed at a distance of several more miles by the four 1,200-tonners of Binford, Edwards, Alden, John D. Ford, and Paul Jones. Some five miles ahead of the cruisers were the three most experienced and capable destroyers, Jupiter, Electra,

CHAOS AND NIGHT

and *Encounter*, spread out across a ten-mile span. Off the cruisers' port quarter were *Witte de With* and *Kortenaer*; the latter soon struggled to keep station as she was suffering from boiler troubles that limited her top speed to 24 knots.

Naturally the initial contacts were made by the vanguard ships, which were British, but at that time a few bombs were dropped from planes overhead—assumed wrongly to be enemy—which disrupted the CSF slightly. At 1530 hours the four American destroyers went to general quarters when "enemy bombers attack[ed] this formation," at which point the flushdeckers all scattered.[101] These attacks were actually by American B-17 bombers, apparently mistaking the Allied destroyers for enemy ships, with the nearest misses landing in the vicinity of *Jupiter*. It took about fifteen minutes to regroup and rejoin the formation. The ships resumed a course of 315° T. and increased speed to 25 knots. Being positioned at the rear of the Striking Force meant that the flushdeckers had a quite limited view of the battle in its initial stages, which was restricted all the more by their very low profiles.[102] On *John D. Ford*, the recently transferred radioman striker from *Stewart*, "Elly" Ellsworth, when not on duty in the radio room, helped man the number 1 4-inch gun on the foc's'le. His view of the battle would be typical for the destroyermen: uncertain of events in the distance but all-too-clear and terrifying at close-range.

Unlike the four-pipers, however, *Houston*'s visibility was much less restricted. Sited atop the foremast, the cruiser's main battery director towered almost 120 feet over the water. This was 40 feet higher than the crow's nest on the U.S. destroyers and with a range of vision correspondingly greater. Swaying in the enclosed steel box of control 1 (just below the Mark 24 director) Cdr. Arthur Maher, the gunnery officer, along with Elmo Bush, AOM3/c, acting as supervisor of the lookouts (who included Gene Crispi, Y3/c, Wayne Johnson, S2/c, and others) were all straining for a first glimpse of enemy ships. Above them Lt. Bruce D. Skidmore and his men trained their scopes off the starboard bow as well. Down on *Houston*'s crowded signal bridge, talkers in their headsets transmitted updated information as needed to the ship's various departments. With no scout plane to fly, Lt. (j.g.) Walt "Windy" Winslow took up station there as well. Captain Rooks, tall and florid-faced, was on the flying bridge, an exposed position with good all-around visibility that wrapped around the front of the bridge structure itself. In sky forward, Lt. Lee Rogers and his men had been aware that two or three Japanese floatplanes were spying on them but were reluctant to waste more ammunition on these snoopers, since they had remained off at good distance.

But as it happened, one of the Japanese floatplanes had already taken it upon itself to lead the forces of Takagi to the Allied fleet. It signaled, "Will guide you to the enemy" and then, rocking its wings in emphasis, flew off in the direction of Doorman's ships.[103]

Many of the men topside were about to be treated to a spectacular view that afternoon of one of the first major sea engagements since the Battle of Jutland in 1916. In *Houston*'s spotting top and forward AA director, as on those of *De Ruyter*, *Exeter*, *Perth*, and *Java*, fatigued men continued to strain their tired eyes through binoculars and telescopes, scouring the horizon for signs of the enemy. Visibility was quite good that day, perhaps as much as thirty-five thousand to forty thousand yards. No more than a few dozen miles away, just over the horizon and closing rapidly, was the flagship *Nachi*. One of her officers recalled: "The sky was clear and deep blue, the sea was ultramarine. . . . There was nothing to obstruct our vision all around. Moving at high speed, waves were breaking at the bow of each ship, and its wake etched a brilliant white streak across the shining mirror-like ocean."[104]

. . .

It fell to *Electra*, the northeastern-most ship, to first spot the enemy's presence: "At three minutes past four [1603 hours] our lookouts detected against the prevailing powder-blue of the sky a faintly darker streak; well over to the north-east, on our starboard bow. By five minutes past four the streak had widened, revealing itself as smoke." *Electra* then sent the first contact message to Doorman: "Enemy fleet in sight."[105] What the British destroyer had spotted first was Rear Admiral Tanaka's Second Squadron, steaming at high speed to the southwest.

However, turning to the south with her destroyers, Tanaka's flagship *Jintsū* (one of the 5,500-tonners Japan had constructed in the early twenties) had already spotted the CSF at 1609. The superstructure of one of Doorman's cruiser's— probably it was the tower of *De Ruyter* itself—became visible at some 29,000 meters (31,600 yards). Toward this contact Tanaka led a division of his destroyers. Just behind Tanaka's ships, from a more northerly direction, came Nishimura's Fourth Squadron, while off to the northeast—still some eight kilometers (about five miles) away but steaming fast—was Rear Admiral Takagi's Fifth Cruiser Squadron (Sentai 5), with *Nachi* leading *Haguro*.

Making precise identifications among the numerous masts appearing over the horizon was quite difficult for the Allies, and errors naturally resulted. One of the initial reports sent to Doorman stated that the enemy force contained "two battleships" in addition to the light cruisers and destroyers. This message was relayed to Doorman and disseminated throughout the flotilla, much to the horror of all who received it. On *Houston*'s bridge the two heavy cruisers of Takagi were also misidentified first as battleships by Chief Signalman Kenneth Blair. This sent a chill through her men, who believed that battleships could have remained beyond the range of the cruiser's guns and decimated Doorman's ships at will. Soon, however, this report was corrected to read "two heavy cruisers" as Takagi's *Nachi* and *Haguro* appeared on the horizon at a distance of over thirty thousand yards, though looking like nothing more than a pair of small dots at first.[106] Lt. (j.g.) Leon "Buck" Rogers could just make out the tops of masts in the distance through his binoculars as he sat on the roof of *Houston*'s forward Mark 19 director; he then climbed back down into the steel cubicle, with only his head poking out through its open hatch on top.

On *Exeter* Lt. Cdr. George Tyndale Cooper, her first lieutenant (or "Number 1"), was acting as close-range AA officer in her Air Defense section, in charge of the multiple pom-poms carried by the cruiser. He was stationed at the rear of the bridge but could look out through his binoculars, too, for a first sight of the enemy. About two thousand yards off *Exeter*'s starboard bow—and directly in their line of vision—steamed Commander May's *Electra*. From his position on the starboard side of the cruiser's bridge, Cooper would never forget "seeing the large, squatty tops of the . . . Japanese cruisers coming over the horizon."[107]

At this point Doorman's CSF was moving to the northwest at about 26 knots and building up speed. The British destroyers in the van made a T at the head of the column, followed by the five cruisers in line, and trailed by the "stinger" in the tail: Binford's four flushdeckers. To the port, or disengaged, quarter of the cruiser column was the pair of Dutch destroyers, with *Kortenaer* struggling somewhat to keep pace as the other ships accelerated. The Japanese forces— all three elements—were in a position to cross ahead of the CSF, which would put the ships of Doorman at a marked disadvantage, for most of the enemy's guns could be brought to bear broadside against their far more limited forward arcs of fire. Seeing, or at least sensing this, Doorman turned his force slightly to the left, altering course from about 315 degrees to 285 degrees "by column movement." At the rear of the CSF, Binford's destroyers began to bunch up as they maintained station on the disengaged sided, too, and were briefly forced to reduce speed to 15 knots to conform to Doorman's alterations.

In the meantime Tanaka in *Jintsū* led his Sixteenth Destroyer Division (*Yukikaze*, *Tokitsukaze*, *Amatsukaze*, and *Hatsukaze*) aggressively toward the British vanguard of *Electra*, *Encounter*, and *Jupiter*. At about 1615, while steaming at 30 knots on a course of 230° T., *Jintsū* opened fire against *Electra*, then distant some 16,800 meters (a little more than 18,000 yards).[108] Most of her first shells fell short, but the range closed very quickly. With her heavier 5.5-inch main batteries the enemy light cruiser was soon able to find the distance, and shells began landing with uncomfortable proximity around *Electra*. The long-anticipated sea battle for Java had now begun in deadly earnest. May's destroyermen termed the Japanese shooting "good—extremely good" in the opening phase of the engagement.[109] Within three minutes at the most, *Electra*'s batteries replied, with her "four-point-seven's cracking away like whips," according to one of her officers.[110] Japanese records show that one of the CSF cruisers—probably *Exeter*—then loosed a dozen or so salvos at Tanaka's ship, driving it off, before opening fire at bigger game that soon appeared.[111] Steaming at 32 knots, throwing enormous white bow waves over their long, low forecastles, Rear Adm. Takagi Takeo's Sentai 5 had reached the field of battle.

At 1617 hours, at the extreme limits of gun range, Takagi's flagship, *Nachi*, and consort *Haguro* commenced fire. *Nachi* made her target Doorman's flagship, *De Ruyter*, as she fired a full ten-gun salvo, which all landed well short. *Haguro* fired initially at *Electra*, though, from a range of 20,000 meters (22,000 yards). She got off four salvos expending 33 rounds of 8-inch before quickly turning her attention to *De Ruyter*. Similarly, within three minutes *Nachi* switched her focus to *Exeter* and began raining shells on the British cruiser at ranges from 23,700 meters (26,000 yards) to 26,300 meters (28,900 yards). The flagship of Rear Admiral Takagi fired no less than twenty-six salvos, expending 255 main battery shells in a matter of minutes, claiming seven straddles, and made an unforgettable impression on her adversary. Captain Gordon and his officers would all remember the marvelously tight Japanese salvos falling in groups around their ship, certain that such precise firing was controlled by radar.

Hoping to outrange their opponents and adhering to IJN doctrine for heavy cruisers, *Nachi* and *Haguro* continued to fire at extreme range.[112] Doorman was in the process of turning his column at the same time, and as soon as it was set on a more westerly course, Cdr. Al Maher in *Houston*'s foretop unleashed the main battery of the Asiatic Fleet's last flagship. In sheets of white flame and billowing mushrooms of ochre-colored smoke, the old cruiser's 8-inch guns erupted in anger for the first time in her long career. After first firing two or three salvos with *Exeter* against *Jintsū*, Rooks's heavy cruiser shifted to the two big Myōkō-class sisters on the edge of the horizon. At an estimated 30,500 yards, firing at her tiny target approximately 20 degrees off her starboard bow—this was initially *Haguro* ("the right hand ship"), not *Nachi*—the number 1 and 2 turrets of *Houston* got down to business. Junior officers on the Japanese ships had watched Doorman's approach with a mixture of fascination and anxiety, describing the CSF cruisers as "monsters." Ironically, it was the flagship *De Ruyter* with her pocket-battleship-style bridge structure that caught their eye.[113] Fifteen miles away, on *Nachi*, a tense young lieutenant commander named Tanaka Tsuneji recorded seeing that first flash and then another, as *Houston* opened fire. Moments later he saw *Exeter* following suit, as she fired her forward guns. *Nachi* and *Haguro* were soon both returning fire as well. At this stage it was still a matter of getting the range with slow, deliberate firing until a straddle was achieved; then the guns would go into rapid salvos.

In the massive control tower of *Haguro*, Ens. Candidate Kimura Hachiro (Sixty-Ninth *ki*), an assistant torpedo officer, recalled the men's demeanor as they waited for the enemy shells to arrive: "We stood there, stiff, silent, nervous."[114] At such a distance the projectiles would take about a minute to reach them. As these missed, the men could exhale and prepare themselves for the next salvo. Simultaneously there were numerous errors in spotting with many excited— and erroneous—reports of "Hit!" in the tension and confusion that followed.

On *Nachi*—her battery directed by Commander Inoue, her gunnery officer— Tanaka described the concussion of his own guns. He felt "giddy ... [and] a shock as though being hit hard with a big rubber ball."[115] On *De Ruyter* one of the Dutch sailors in an exposed position said that when all the guns went off together it was as if someone had punched him in his side, adding, "You felt very small at that moment."[116] On the bridge of *Houston* CSM Kenneth Blair recalled that all the men soon learned to get down and take cover in sitting positions on the far side of the bridge when the guns fired. Although many of the men took the wise precaution of stuffing cotton in their ears prior to action, this measure would ultimately offer little useful protection as the battle reached full ferocity. Experiencing shellfire on a heavy cruiser moving at high speed elsewhere in the war, an American reporter described it in even more graphic terms: "The guns turn loose all at once with a brain-jolting slap and your diaphragm caves in.... Continuous concussion caves in your stomach.... Cotton in your ears is small comfort now." This "sickening roar of the main battery" also produced what one of *Houston's* gunners called "a vacuum-cleaner effect" in which one's clothes might be ripped off by residual blast effects.[117] For those in exposed positions topside it was much worse than for the gun crews within the main battery gunhouses themselves.

At the outset of the battle both *Nachi* and *Haguro* concentrated their fire against *De Ruyter* and *Exeter*, which allowed *Houston* a brief but invaluable period of undisturbed time to concentrate on her long-range firing.[118] Like her Imperial Navy counterparts, *Houston's* opening salvos were short by two to three thousand yards but quickly ranged in. On her sixth salvo Lt. Bruce Skid-more reported, "Straddle!" and the cruiser's batteries settled into a steady pace in their firing. Throughout the engagement *Houston* employed director fire with control 1, director 1, and spot 1 in control. Although her well-trained fire-control and gunnery personnel functioned ideally, her aged construction and the severe stress placed on her systems led to mechanical and electrical prob-lems. In one such instance only the extraordinary performance of her turret crew enabled others to overcome a mechanical breakdown for an extended period while repairs were made.

Eyewitness reports by men at the head of Doorman's column and on the tail end are notable for their similarities. On the signaling bridge of *De Ruyter*, liaison man Dan Rafalovich from *Houston* at first saw distant mast tops on the horizon but had trouble determining the types and numbers of ships beneath them: "I couldn't visualize what they were;" he recalled. "And then I'd see a puff of smoke, and a flash." At that point the reality of the engagement pene-trated the baffled young seaman's consciousness: "I said, 'My God, they're try-ing to sink us!'"[119] Well away from the cruisers—"a long way behind the Allied cruisers, and to the lee of the firing"—men on the bridge of Lieutenant Com-mander Kroese's destroyer *Kortenaer* watched in fascination. "Terrific flashes were visible every time one of our cruisers fired a salvo and a dense cloud of yellow-brown smoke rose up."[120]

At the rear of the formation, Marion "Elly" Ellsworth was still up on *Ford*'s forecastle helping man the number 1 4-inch gun and like others straining his eyes to the north for a sight of the enemy. In the distance, across the deep blue waters of the Java Sea, Ellsworth briefly glimpsed "matchsticks" poking up over the horizon, followed shortly by small bursts of smoke.[121] A minute or so later shells began landing at the head of the CSF column near the cruisers. Within another two or three minutes the Allied cruisers were already "engag-ing in heavy firing" (according to the log book of *Paul Jones*) against the enemy cruiser line as Doorman led his ships on a westerly heading, from a course of about 260° for perhaps ten minutes before then settling on course 275° T. This avoided having his T crossed and brought his ships' main batteries into action more fully, although the distance still remained too great for effective fire from any of the light cruisers.

On the bridge of *Perth*, Capt. "Hec" Waller quickly became annoyed by this long-range slugging match—more befitting a conventional heavy battle line than the action at hand—but it is an error to imagine that his ship did no firing in this period. At about 1625 hours *Perth* commenced fire with her 6-inch guns against the advancing Japanese destroyers of Nishimura and Tanaka. Waller had every need to do so. It was then, or very soon thereafter, that Rear Adm. Nishimura Shōji in *Naka* led a contingent of his DesRon 4 destroyers in the boldest—some would say the most foolhardy—attack made during the opening phase of the battle. Steaming down from the north at 30 knots Nishimura had brought his force pall-mall across the bows of both Takagi's cruisers and the ships of Tanaka's squadron and taken it directly at Doorman's column like an arrow.

To observers such as Al Maher in *Houston's* foretop it appeared that the Japanese came in "as one group"—comprising two cruisers and twelve destroyers—firing furiously before they launched their torpedoes.[122] IJN records show that Nishimura's ships launched twenty-seven torpedoes between 1633 and 1645 hours at distances from 16,350 down to 13,625 yards, then "left the scene with a smokescreen."[123] Not to be outdone, Tanaka's *Jintsū* also launched four Type 93 "Long Lance" weapons from what must have been uselessly long distance—over 30,000 yards—at the same time. The light cruiser's torpedo officer, Cdr. Toyama Yasumi (who was also Tanaka's senior staff officer), was in charge of these attacks. Paradoxically, he was said to be fond of an old Japanese martial saying: "If the enemy cuts skin, you cut meat; if enemy cuts meat, you cut bone."[124] Such graphic aphorisms notwithstanding, these long-range attacks "cut" nothing, although they did cause Doorman to turn his cruisers away. The ships altered in order to "comb the tracks" of the Japanese torpedoes, but it proved to be an unnecessary maneuver by and large.

This was the case because a significant number of these Type 93s exploded prematurely well before reaching the CSF battle line, a fact that mystified both the Japanese and the Allied commanders and sailors on the scene. Even the aerial observers such as Lt. Utsonomiya Michio in one of the Type 95 DAVE spotting planes from *Haguro* flying six thousand feet above the Java Sea saw these premature explosions and recognized that something was amiss. Many thought that submarines were present among the fleets, and there *were* a number of submarines on patrol in the Java Sea that day, but none were nearby or attacking the fleets at this time. Others misread the explosions to be either hits—there were none from this group—or the results of an unknown minefield. It turned out to be a technical problem with the Type 93 detonator when the torpedo was calibrated to run at its shallow depth setting, and one that was soon rectified by the Japanese. At that moment both sides were left baffled. For many years it was thought that Japanese submarines played a role in this long, drawn-out battle, but this, too, was an error.

Doorman's ships had turned slightly away from the Japanese during these gunnery exchanges and the torpedo attacks and then resumed a northwesterly course. At that time the ships of both Nishimura and Takagi were on roughly parallel courses, although separated from each other by several miles. The CSF light cruisers were firing on Nishimura's force while the heavy cruisers were still dueling at long distance; neither Takagi nor Doorman showed much inclination to close the range. Steaming at 32 knots ahead of Takagi and located between his ships and those of Nishimura was Rear Adm. Tanaka Raizo's four-funneled light cruiser *Jintsū* with her six DesRon 2 tin cans: all four destroyers of DesDiv 16 and one section (two ships) of DesDiv 24. The guns on the destroyers, however, refrained from firing due to the extreme range. Tanaka's ship was shooting throughout this period at Doorman's force when she could, expending 137 of her 5.5-inch shells, but she had also been under the "concentrated fire of two or three enemy cruisers," which battered his flagship with no less than thirty-one straddles and near misses, some of which shook the cruiser quite severely.[125] These, along with the Japanese torpedoes' inadvertent detonations, also appear to have impacted Tanaka's visual judgment.

Looking out through what seemed a multicolored forest of gigantic shell splashes from *Exeter*, *Perth*, and *Houston*, Tanaka and his men in *Jintsū* saw what they wanted to see: their torpedoes hitting and sinking enemy ships. The commander of DesRon 2 reported to Takagi that a pair of destroyers or cruisers had been "sunk instantly" by his torpedo attack. Spotters on *Nachi* had a better vantage point, however. Although under considerable fire from *Houston* and *Exeter*, they had a clearer picture of the actual situation. They could see through their big binoculars that five enemy cruisers remained afloat—and more to the point were still returning fire. So, as one young IJN officer later phrased it, *Jintsū* had expended four precious torpedoes at twenty-eight thousand meters merely to have "surprised schools of fish for nothing."[126]

At this stage things did not seem to have gone too unfavorably for the Allies. In his gunnery director tower on HMS *Encounter*, Lt. Sam Falle noted, "*Houston*'s shells showed bright colours when they hit the water. . . . I could see her straddling the enemy."[127] Meanwhile, to the rear of Doorman's column Cdr. Thomas Binford and his quartet of flushdeckers steamed on gamely, pushing their venerable machinery through the waters of the Java Sea with as much urgency as they dared. Binford had also seen the cruisers firing at long range and the enemy splashes over and short, but he received no messages at all from Doorman. His ships' ability to gather accurate information visually was limited by the time of day (afternoon was giving way to evening), their position (at the far end of the CSF formation), haze and smoke from the cruisers' gunnery duels, and the low silhouettes of the four-piper destroyer. On *John D. Ford* Lt. (j.g.) J. F. Harmon, spotting in the crow's nest, offered an excited (and probably embellished) running commentary on the action—such as he could see of it. Harmon stated that he could glimpse enemy battleships beyond their cruiser line, while Lieutenant Mack, the gunnery officer, observing *Houston*'s spirited shellfire claimed she got "off two for every one of the other ships, and [was] straddling every time with the electric flashes of hits among the waterspouts."[128]

It is debatable whether Lieutenant Mack saw *any* of *Houston*'s shells strike the cruisers of Takagi's Sentai 5 from his perspective, yet evidence from both sides does suggest that several near misses, if not actual hits, were made during that time frame. In fact, on the old *Galloping Ghost* herself, Ens. John B. "Lord" Nelson reacted as if she had inflicted serious damage on one of the Japanese cruisers at that time. Nelson was spotting for the main battery through spot 2, the auxiliary director set-up aft (just below sky aft's Mark 19 director), when he saw what he definitely believed were hits on the second enemy ship (*Haguro*). At that point Nelson—who had a tendency to become animated—let out a wild whoop and erupted into what was described as "an Indian war dance" around the aft director, yelling, "We got the sonuvabitch!"[129] Nelson's superior officer, Commander Maher in the foretop appears to have confirmed this as well when he recorded in one of his action reports that "by 1655 the target was aflame both forward and amidship. The target ceased firing and fell out of column under the cover of the smoke from the fires and from her own funnel."[130]

IJN records in JACAR for Sentai 5 show *Haguro* laying a smokescreen in this period, but there is no concrete evidence that she suffered any direct hits or material damages. The written memoir of an officer serving on *Nachi* observed that *Haguro*, "which was steaming astern took a heavy list to starboard and in a second she was covered with dense smoke. We watched her with a start." In the next moment, however, he saw the big cruiser "steaming astern as though nothing had happened. She [had] only dodged the enemy shells and applied full rudder and listed heavily."[131] Although this officer claimed elsewhere that it was not IJN doctrine to "chase salvos" as the Allied ships were clearly doing—since the Japanese believed this threw off their gunnery too much—it seems that being under heavy fire from *Exeter* and *Houston* may have proved intolerable. Along with her sister, *Nachi*, the 15,000-ton cruiser continued to slug it out with Doorman's ships, and her contribution was anything but a negligible one.

In these opening minutes the opposing cruiser lines remained engaged in long-range—and largely ineffectual—firing. *Haguro*'s chief gunnery officer, Captain Nakajima, admired the accuracy of *Exeter* and *Houston*'s shooting at such long range without the aid of any spotting planes.[132] Distances continued to fluctuate from a little over 28,000 yards down to about 19,500 yards but rarely less than that. Takagi's two cruisers seem to have felt that "outranging" tactics were justified by the superior number of Allied cruisers.

On the bridge and spotting top of *Nachi* this ongoing tension manifested itself in the exchanges between her gunnery officer, Lieutenant Commander Inoue, and the senior staff officer, Captain Nagasawa, the former directing her gunfire and the latter her movements. With a wave of his hand as he stood at the gyrocompass—left for port, right for starboard—Nagasawa directed the ship's course in and out of the battle line. When the gunnery officer became exasperated and barked at him, the senior staff officer waved left, shouting, "Toh-ri, kah-ji!" ("Left rudder"), and the great ship closed the distance between herself and the Allied cruisers: 25,000 meters then 23,000, then 21,000, 19,000, 18,000 . . . As *Nachi*'s gunnery seemed to improve, so too came the inevitable reply from Doorman's ships: "The sharp sounds of enemy shells tore the air, followed by the shooting up of numerous red geysers." After a few nerve-racking minutes of this, the senior staff officer again " waved his hand to the right irritably," ordering, "Omoh-kah-ji" ("Right rudder"), and the ship began listing as she turned away at high speed. Following a momentary respite Lieutenant Commander Inoue then became infuriated again—he especially disliked the abrupt maneuvering that caused the cruiser to list when she turned—and he once more yelled at the senior staff officer, resuming the entire cat-and-mouse routine. Soon enough the sharp sounds of shells came back "as though tearing a piece of silk cloth," and in the clear sky clusters of shells could be seen with the naked eye, like a group of ducks or geese falling toward one's ship from a great height, always as though about to land directly on target but only rarely doing so.[133]

Within each of the two forward main battery turrets of *Houston*, her gun crews put long months of relentless drill into practice: an almost identical process was taking place as the men loaded, fired, and loaded each salvo again. The entire sequence, so central to the existence of a warship, is worth describing in some detail. At the outset it is important to understand that the turret captain—who was usually a chief or a petty officer first class—was the real honcho in each gunhouse. The turret officer had other duties and was less directly involved. For the most part he remained sealed off during combat within his turret officer's booth—a small armored compartment with a heavy, shatterproof glass porthole through which he could observe the interior of the gunhouse.

First, in order to start the loading cycle, a sailor known as the pointer spun a wheel that lowered the three huge guns to a horizontal level—they were in a common cradle, or slide, in the Northampton-cruiser type, so that they elevated and depressed together. As they reached the proper loading angle, each gun captain pressed a button that opened the breech of his gun through compressed air. This also unmasked four nozzles that "sent powerful jets of compressed air hissing into the gun barrel, blowing out, one hoped, any burning remnants of powder or bags and any gases which might ignite behind the breech and kill the gun crew."[134] Behind the breech of each gun were stationed two sailors, called the first and second tray-men. They stood next to a jointed bronze trough, highly polished and roughly eight inches in width; this was the tray, and it was kept in its folded, upward orientation until the breech opened. Once the breech opened and was clear, these men lowered the tray, unfolding it to extend into the breech itself. What followed was a critical, indeed mortal, moment in the gun-loading evolution: the first tray man bent down and with his head level to the tray quickly peered into the breach down the bore of the gun. It was "a matter of life and death" in the most literal sense that no flames, smoke, or obstruction be seen in the thirty-six-foot length of the barrel. The first tray man had the lives of every person in the gunhouse in his hands at that instant, so he had to be an attentive, alert individual. Turret officers made sure that "no dull-witted, shiftless or unimaginative man was ever given the job."[135]

Assuming the first tray man found nothing untoward in the barrel, he called out, "Bore clear!"[136] Once the turret captain heard the cry "Bore clear!" from each of his three first tray-men, he screamed, "Load!" Not before that order was given could any powder be exposed in the part of the gunhouse containing the breeches of the main battery guns. At that point the teams of gunners began their evolutions. At the rear of the gunhouse sat three rammer men, each operating by lever their fifteen-foot-long electric-hydraulic chain drive for inserting the shells into the breach of their respective guns. This device was referred to jokingly as the "mechanical rattlesnake." Eight-inch shells came up from below in "a near-vertical hoist which tilted its cargo out onto a slightly hollowed bench beside the tray." The shell man next pushed the 260-pound greased projectile out of this hollow and rolled it sideways into the bronze tray in front of the rammer. The "mechanical rattlesnake" then went into operation: with the rammer man pushing his lever forward, its chains rumbled, clanked, and thumped as it shoved the projectile along the tray into position within the bore, where it settled with a final jarring "clunk" that shook the entire gunhouse. At that, "the Rammer-man pulled his lever rearwards, and the monster rattled back over the tray, to coil obediently in waiting, its electric motor humming purposefully (and a little malevolently) in repose." As one might envision, it was gravely important that the first tray man had not taken too long to examine the bore of his gun, and that the rammer man timed his actions properly, because it was "obvious that a carelessly handled rammer could remove the head of the tray man."[137] Once the rammer had been withdrawn, another shell came up the hoist, beginning the next loading cycle.

With these evolutions the powder was ready to come into the system. On port and starboard sides of the gunhouse—sealed off from the guns with a flameproof door—were small, claustrophobic enclosures known as the "'upper powder handling room" (also called the "powder flap" or "powder box"). The men working in these spaces, who were called powder men or flap men, were often sailors of small stature whose flexibility and size permitted them to do their job within the restricted area. The opening into the enclosure was not much more than a foot and a half across and a very tight squeeze for even the most diminutive individual.

At the forward end of the powder flap was the opening to the top of the powder hoist, which was also a steel, flameproof door (or "scuttle"), in which silk bags of propellant, each weighing forty-five pounds, came up from the lower powder handling room situated one deck below the turret's floor. The powder man did not have his scuttle opened until the "load" signal was given. At that point three bags of powder came out of the hoist: two went to the gun immediately next to the flap man, while the third was passed through a separate aperture over the tray to the center gun, which received its propellant bags from each powder flap. This required "a good shove" because of the distance it needed to travel.[138] So simultaneously as the "mechanical rattlesnake" withdrew after ramming the projectile into the breach, "out came the powder, and into the tray to be pushed into the breach by the powder-men and tray-men."[139] All these actions were taking place in a coordinated and remarkably swift series of movements taking up no more than a matter of seconds.

Slightly above and forward of the center rammer man was a small metal seat for the turret captain, who oversaw the highly organized chaos of these critical operations in the gunhouse. He had a switch next to his seat for turning on the "ready light" in the turret officer's booth, which he activated once he had received the correct verbal and visual signals from his three gun captains. ("Right ready!" "Center ready!" "Left ready!") At the same time the turret captain told the officer over his phones that the next salvo—giving its number—was ready to be fired ("Ready six!"). The turret officer then informed the gunnery officer through his phone, "Turret One ready!" as "he turned on his own 'ready light' switch which flashed a small light at the control stations." Once "Control" had lights from the turrets and from plot (the below-decks computer room), "a button was pressed and the ship staggered from the discharge of a . . . main-battery broadside. Twenty seconds had elapsed since the previous one."[140]

In the Battle of the Java Sea the cruiser's forward turrets initially fired several dozen salvos—over a period of roughly twenty minutes—without checking fire. That they were able to do this in the teeth of a significant mechanical breakdown in one gunhouse is a testament not only to their endurance but to their fine training as well. None of the *Galloping Ghost*'s gunnery officers who survived the war ever forgot what those young sailors did that afternoon, and we owe it to ourselves and to their memory to understand what this entailed.

In *Houston*'s turret 1 the well-trained crew led by veteran William Rhodes, TC1/c (Turret Captain First Class), found themselves faced with a severe test very early on. After one of the first salvos, the right rammer motor was jarred off the bulkhead and short-circuited the "mechanical rattlesnake," which sent the shell into the breech. At that the men were compelled to either slow the pace of their salvos or hand-ram that particular 8-inch gun themselves.[141] These young American sailors met the test and crushed it. Turret Captain Rhodes, his right gun captain, Leo Rody, GM3/c, along with his first tray man, George T. Rocque, S1/c, and another seaman first class named Richard J. Herman (who would have been the second tray man on that gun) did what was considered impossible in peacetime training: they hand-rammed "without rest or without loss of firing time to the main battery," about sixty salvos until repairs could be affected.[142]

Below in the powder circle, Bosun's Mate First Class Shelton H. "Red" Clymer and his men worked furiously to keep the guns supplied with propellant. Among those laboring there under appalling conditions of extreme heat and inadequate ventilation were two young sailors: a gangling Texan, Thomas Eugene "Punchy" Parham, S1/c, one of the boxers on the ship, and his pal, William E. "Bill" Darling, S1/c. "Punchy" Parham operated the portside powder hoist, which brought bags of propellant up to the powder box above—in this instance manned by Wilford E. Logan, S1/c.

Beneath these men another group of sailors manned the shell deck. This station was also a tight, confined, and poorly ventilated space, not more than ten or eleven feet in diameter, around the deck of which rows of the projectiles stood, with an additional row stacked on steel shelving along the bulkhead above the others. It was the job of these sailors to manhandle the greased 260-pound shells by chains into hoists that brought them up to the gunhouse. This was usually the station of a young seaman second class from New Jersey named Otto Carl Schwarz. His would be the one of the least well-informed positions during battle, but this did not keep Schwarz, like his shell-deck ship-mates, from wondering how the engagement was progressing.

Before the war during training exercises, Schwarz and others in his inexperienced magazine crew had asked some of the "old-timers" on the ship how they would ever be able to get those big projectiles off the shelves during a battle once the rows of shells stacked around the deck had been expended. The veterans merely shrugged off their questions by stating that with all the power and technology of modern naval gunnery, sea battles could never possibly last more than a few minutes. As Otto Schwarz—a man with a sense of irony if there ever was one—enjoyed recalling time and again in later years, after being told that the average naval battle would be over in fifteen minutes, the fight in the Java Sea would then go on for some ten hours.

Eventually the odds caught up and a few shells did strike what they were aimed at, even at such great ranges. At some point in the first forty-five minutes, De Ruyter was struck by a Japanese shell that penetrated but did not explode. In this she was as lucky as Houston would also be when she, too, was struck by enemy duds. The projectile hit Rear Admiral Doorman's light cruiser in her forward superstructure tower, went through the diesel room, and ended up in her double bottom. A small number of men were killed outright, however, by the shell's entrance and path through the ship's interior. What damages that did result appear to have been quickly repaired or controlled, and De Ruyter lost no steaming power.

At this time the two lines of cruisers were on more or less parallel courses, steaming to the west and firing at long range as visibility permitted. Binford's four flushdeckers were still struggling at the rear of the CSF formation to keep up; they began altering course some seven or eight minutes later to stay on the cruisers' disengaged port quarter. At that time the smokescreen laid earlier by Nishimura's attacking destroyers was dissipating, and Takagi could see the Allied ships angling toward him on a slightly northwestern course. He would promptly attempt to take advantage of that course change.

At the same time that Takagi's patience with his own forces' gunnery was beginning to dwindle along with their supply of shells, a decision was made to prepare for an attack with torpedoes. Nachi and Haguro were then slightly ahead of Doorman's cruisers, which were bearing 170 degrees to the south, so the firing solution was not unfavorable. The two big cruisers swung their quadruple torpedo tubes to port in anticipation of firing. While Haguro was prepared to fire, flagship Nachi's torpedo men under Lieutenant Horie experienced an embarrassing snafu. It seems that an unnerved or maladroit sailor had turned the stop-valve wheel the wrong way. In his confused state he thought the wheel itself was jammed and could not be opened, but as one officer later wrote: "When things let up a little, after investigating the shut-off valve, they found that it had been fully open. No matter how hard you might try, you could not open a fully open valve any further." With no more time to waste, the senior staff officer on *Nachi*, who was by then fully irritated, gave the orders: "Commence firing torpedoes!" At 1652 to 1655 *Haguro* fired all eight Type 93s from her port battery and "the white and shiny torpedoes jumped into the deep blue water." Sentai 5 track charts show the range at this time to have been about 22,000 meters (24,200 yards), and the Japanese cruisers steaming on a course of 250 degrees after which they altered away to 300 degrees. With the loss of compressed air due to the open stop-valve, *Nachi* was not able at that time to launch her torpedoes, and it was said that her torpedo officer, Lieutenant Horie, suffered a considerable loss of face.[143]

Doorman appears to have suspected the torpedo launchings also, as he had his column alter away to 250 degrees at 1700 hours. By then the Japanese torpedoes would have traveled perhaps seven thousand yards toward the Allied cruisers. However, before the Japanese torpedoes reached Doorman's line, a single shell from one of Takagi's heavy cruisers altered the course of the battle.

At approximately 1714 hours, after numerous straddles (according to the report submitted by CCCF Collins later), Capt. O. L. Gordon's *Exeter* was struck in a starboard twin 4-inch mount by a 20 cm shell from one of the Japanese cruisers, almost certainly *Haguro*.[144] The projectile went through the shield on the right side of the mount—leaving the four men there dead yet sparing the crew of the left gun—and penetrated into a boiler room where, it broke up in a low-order detonation as it entered the boiler. This explosion killed all ten men of that watch and knocked power out of six of her eight boilers. Within moments *Exeter*'s speed fell from 27 knots down to about 11 knots. Unable to maintain station, the cruiser was forced out of her position in the CSF line. Because she had to turn away very suddenly, the cruisers of Doorman's patchwork force were thrown into disorder. Immediately astern were *Houston*, *Perth*, and *Java*, and all had to maneuver rather abruptly. *Houston* at first thought that the British ship was taking evasive action and turned with her. *Perth* appears to have been well aware of the damage—*Exeter* had signaled *Perth* that she had taken a shell in her boiler room, and in any event she was emitting clouds of white steam and black funnel smoke as she slowed—so "Hec" Waller swung his ship around to try to screen the British cruiser. This he did "with funnel smoke and all available smoke floats."[145]

Ahead the men of *De Ruyter* was momentarily oblivious of what was taking place to the rear—as any ship might be—and continued on their course, but they soon realized that the CSF battle line had been shattered. Spotting the British ship as she hauled out of line, Doorman exclaimed to Captain Lacomblé that something was amiss. Doorman then ordered the ships again to follow him, but *Perth* stayed close to *Exeter*. Seeing this, and as his flagship rounded back into position—most of the ships were now on a southerly course—Doorman radioed *Exeter*: "What is wrong with you?"[146] This message was copied by radiomen on *Houston* and forwarded by TBS to *John D. Ford*. Waller then managed to inform Doorman of the damage to *Exeter* and was again ordered to follow *De Ruyter*, which he did as the entire force wobbled off to the south to eventually settle on a course to the southeast. At about 1715 the deck log of *Paul Jones* also noted that the ships were then "running through torpedo water course approximately south. All ships paralleling torpedoes."[147]

Unfortunately, not *all* the CSF ships managed to parallel the eight "Long Lances" of *Haguro* in the chaotic turnaround following *Exeter*'s hit. A number of the Japanese torpedoes were spotted, since many were running close to the surface; some even exploded prematurely or at the end of their runs. Ships made alterations to course and speed to try to resume some semblance of order in their formation at the same time that they were suddenly aware of these torpedoes in their midst. About seven or eight hundred yards off the starboard bow of Commander Binford's *John D. Edwards*, the Dutch destroyer *Kortenaer* was seen turning as well but not swiftly or sharply enough. It may have been that the spectacle of *Exeter*'s abrupt change of course had briefly distracted the RNN ship. (The British cruiser was then wreathed in clouds of smoke and steam.) For no sooner had Binford's flushdecker received a flashing light signal from Commander May's destroyers alerting him to enemy torpedoes than *Kortenaer* was struck amidships by one of *Haguro*'s torpedoes. The Type 93 lived up to its subsequent nickname—"Long Lance"—by traveling upwards of twenty kilometers in eighteen minutes. And with its thunderous arrival the fighting career of Lt. Cdr. Antonie Kroese's *Kortenaer* came to an abrupt and terrifying end.[148]

The destruction of *Kortenaer* was also clearly visible to the men on *Perth* and *Houston*. It was a sight few were ever able forget. Barely 1,500–2,000 yards from *Houston*—where it had reached a point broad off the cruiser's starboard bow—an immense column of water and whitish smoke erupted alongside what Walt Winslow called the "little grey and green-painted destroyer."[149] She was then completely obscured from sight. After the column collapsed back on itself, a pillar of black smoke and rubbish rose into the sky. As the wind blew this cloud away, the Dutch destroyer capsized and then jackknifed. Her keel having been snapped, the ship quickly upended with bow and stern vertical above the waves and both funnels pointing inward.

From the bridge of *Kortenaer*, the torpedo's detonation came with brutal and unanticipated violence. Wrote one sailor stationed on the bridge: "Suddenly, as we were watching the *Exeter*, we were thrown all in a heap by a terrific explosion." All the stunned personnel there struggled to untangle themselves, as the stricken ship promptly heeled over on her beam ends. Those who could fought clear of debris, scrambling over the steel windscreen, which was even then beginning to close over their heads like the lid of a coffin. Then, within a handful of short minutes, "the bows of the ship rose up with a heavy snorting sound and the bridge disappeared under water."[150]

To others on board the destroyer it was "an impossible explosion." One survivor said, "You can't imagine a bang like that." And another veteran flatly stated that the ship "broke like a biscuit."[151] On the bridge of *Kortenaer*, Lieutenant Commander Kroese had been able to disengage himself from the others and then tumbled into the sea. An equally fortunate young sailor manning a gun amidships named W. H. H. Peeters also found himself tossed into the water and ended up quite close to the skipper. Peeters watched as the bow and stern remained floating for a few brief minutes, with men sliding off the split hull, while others floundered in the water among debris, searching for any flotsam or rafts that might have survived the explosion. The ship's two big screws were still revolving slowly, and legend has it that *Kortenaer*'s doctor had climbed down to perch on one.[152] It was also believed that the shock of the torpedo had set off her mist-making apparatus on the aft part of the ship, and forlorn clouds of white chemical smoke were seen pouring up into the sky.

The ships of the CSF had no chance to render effective aid but continued on to the southeast at speed. Observers on *Houston* and *Perth* could see survivors of *Kortenaer* in the water, and some men had clung to the shattered stern before it, too, sank. Able seaman Gregory "Darky" Oliver on the 4-inch gun deck of *Perth* remembered, "Way aft on the stern part we saw about half a dozen blokes—then they dropped off into the water."[153] From *Houston* a small number of life preservers and rings were quickly tossed to the Dutchmen as the cruiser steamed past. In those unnerving moments, on the bridge of *John D. Edwards*, Cdr. Thomas Binford was certain that his Dutch friend "Cruiser" Kroese, who with his wife and daughters had just entertained Binford and Butch Parker at his Surabaja home a few hours earlier, was now dead. At that instant it seemed fantastic that *anybody* could have survived the explosion. A few of the RNN sailors in the water may have waved at the ships as they passed, but whether signaling for rescue or encouraging the others to keep up the fight, we will never know with certainty. What we do know is that while fifty-six men were lost in the sinking of *Kortenaer*, about one hundred officers and enlisted men had lived and were eventually rescued, although not before more remarkable adventures in the warm waters of the Java Sea.

. . .

As the cruisers of the CSF continued on, raggedly resuming their battle line—while *Exeter* began to steam off alone to the south licking her wounds and leaving the survivors of *Kortenaer* to an uncertain fate—Cdr. Thomas Binford's flushdeckers received their first direct communications of the battle from Doorman.[154] A signal was sent for the old destroyers to make smoke, and Binford's ships did so. In fact, they made a great deal of it. Soon thereafter they were given orders to cease making smoke. At this time visibility was becoming fairly well obscured. This was the result of shellfire, *Perth*'s smokescreen around *Exeter*, the destruction of *Kortenaer*, and also the heavy screen laid by Binford's ships.[155]

To the rear of the now-scattered Allied formation, Cdr. C. W. May's three Royal Navy destroyers were compelled to face the advancing Japanese ships alone. They received orders to make a counterattack against the pursuing Japanese, to help cover the escape of *Exeter* and allow Doorman to re-form his disordered CSF battle line. Although the three British destroyers were too widely dispersed to make a unified attack, *Electra* and *Encounter* went back knowing full well that the enemy ships were waiting for them on the other side of that smoky haze.

Sam Falle on *Encounter* remembered hearing the orders, too, even as his skipper, Lt. Cdr. E. V. "Rattler" Morgan began turning the ship to charge the Japanese head-on at 30 knots. The British destroyers emerged from the smoke, firing all the while, and closed to within effective torpedo range—about four thousand yards in this instance—before unloading their fish. Then, under heavy shellfire from the enemy, they made more smoke, and it was time, as Falle put it, to "get the hell out of there."[156] His ship was profoundly lucky to have escaped unscathed. Imperial Japanese Navy track charts show that these gunnery exchanges in what had clearly become a melee were at close range, perhaps as little as three thousand meters. Her consort, *Electra*—which was seen by the enemy to be the second destroyer to emerge from the smoke—was not so fortunate. By then the Japanese destroyers were fully alert.

On *Electra* Lt. T. J. Cain recalled hearing May's plans over the ship's phones:

"The Japanese are mounting a strong torpedo attack against the *Exeter*. So we are going through the smoke to counterattack." As Lieutenant Cain correctly observed: "*Electra*'s hour had come."[157] The plucky ship with H-27 painted on the side of her hull (in letters large enough to be read by the Japanese spotters) and her crew of 173 men entered the smoke, trailing *Encounter*, and swiftly cleared it. She was met with a withering fusillade from a pair of aggressive Japanese destroyers of the Ninth Destroyer Division, *Asagumo* and *Minegumo*. *Asagumo* had already expended her torpedoes at a range of six thousand meters as the Japanese ships pursued Doorman's forces. However, *Minegumo*, which had placed herself in danger of being hit by friendly torpedoes, was unable to launch hers.[158] In the same exchanges *Minegumo* likewise received hits that damaged her and caused some casualties. Tanaka's DesRon 2 flagship, the light cruiser *Jintsū*, was involved in these gunnery duels as well. Although outnumbered at least three or more to one, *Electra* fired with skill and tenacity at her assailants and succeeded in hitting *Asagumo*—the British gunners saw several flashes as their shells struck home—before the odds took over. "Near misses rocked [*Electra*] and the stench of Nip explosives swept down on her with the falling spray. But her guns were still firing furiously, still aiming at the leading enemy; their crews, undistracted by the tumult that raged around them. The pedals snapped down, the guns recoiled, brass cylinders, smoking, empty, rolled from the mounts to end up on the deck. Splashes rose around the Nips, corrections were made, and breeches clanged shut again. Then two more hits sparked along the enemy's hull; two hits."[159]

At that time, by making emergency repairs *Exeter* had managed to work back up to 14 or 15 knots and was then heading for Surabaja on a course of about 150° T. The cruiser's engineering force had also restored electrical power and brought her 8-inch main battery back online. When *Jintsū* broke through the murk firing at *Electra*, the wounded British cruiser caught sight of the dark gray, four-funneled ship in the distance and prepared to unleash a few salvos at Rear Admiral Tanaka's DesRon 2 flagship. Captain Gordon on *Exeter* thought the enemy cruiser was as much as eight nautical miles to his north.[160] Unfortunately her fire was fouled briefly by the counterattacking *Electra* before the destroyer altered course enough to allow Gordon's ship to deliver a handful of salvos at *Jintsū*. Tanaka's light cruiser turned away once more. At the same instant Tanaka's destroyers were being shelled effectively by Hec Waller in *Perth* as the Australian cruiser maneuvered to regain her position in Doorman's cruiser line. Some of these shells from *Perth* may well have added to *Asagumo*'s injuries.

Nonetheless, *Electra* soon received a number of direct hits herself: one to the bridge cut off communications and part of her gunnery control; a second struck her electrical switchboard, which disabled more electrical power forward; the third, which came on the port side, was mortal, as it took out her aft boiler room and steering gear. May's ship soon coasted to a stop. At that point the "prepare to abandon ship" orders were given. Dead in the water she was quickly riddled by the enemy gunners firing on her from different bearings. Even though *Asagumo* had received damage serious enough to knock out her electrical power, she could and did return fire for some time. And despite *Minegumo* having also been damaged by gunfire, the pair still managed with numerous direct hits to disable and finally sink *Electra*.

This entire exchange between the Japanese and the British destroyers had come at dusk; as May's men began abandoning their mortally stricken ship, the night fell "soft as an English summer's evening." *Asagumo* and *Minegumo* then ceased firing to attend to their own wounds and left the battered destroyer to meet her fate unmolested. It was over by 1824, when the veteran British tin can that had rescued the only three survivors of HMS *Hood* after the Battle of Denmark Strait listed to port and sank by the bow swiftly and silently into the Java Sea, her stern and propellers "silhouetted against the stars."[161]

As *Electra* was fighting her lonely final action, Doorman's forces moved away to the southeast. In that interim *De Ruyter*'s bridge personnel could see that at least one enemy destroyer was dead in the water. The Dutch rear admiral also managed to get signals to Lieutenant Commander Schotel's *Witte de With* to escort the crippled *Exeter* back to Surabaja. The remaining RNN destroyer had helped lay smokescreens during the re-formation of the cruiser line. *Witte de With* evidently believed she was engaging submarines during the battle; in this misapprehension she was by no means alone. Numerous fanciful reports of submarines were made by almost all of Doorman's ships. In any case, as she screened *Exeter* during its retirement to the south, *Witte de With* was also taken under fire by some of the Japanese ships as they poked their bows through the Allied wall of smoke. The Dutchmen could see the winking of enemy gunfire in the hazy distance, and they replied in kind with eight salvos of their own.

It has been suggested that some of the damage suffered by *Asagumo* or *Minegumo* may have come from *Witte de With*'s gunnery. This is entirely possible since *Witte de With*'s second gunnery officer, Lieutenant Van der Moer—who had been transferred from *Banckert* after leaving *Van Ghent*—was helping direct her fire for his destroyer's four 4.7-inch guns, and claimed that he "saw [their] first salvo score a hit." But the Japanese destroyers knew how to shoot, too. "The enemy returned fire immediately with great accuracy," wrote the young officer. "We heard and saw some shells passing and exploding in the water, but we did not sustain any more damage than a shot-down antenna." In the course of this short and sharp exchange with the enemy destroyers, the Dutch ship had maneuvered so wildly that two live depth charges had fallen overboard, where they exploded much too close to the hull. Those blasts and some low-angle firing from the ship's guns over the stern seem to have affected *Witte de With*'s starboard propeller shaft, which began vibrating badly. However, the destroyer was able to carry on escorting *Exeter*, still limping at less than half speed, and both ships reached Surabaja safely in the middle of the night.[162]

Immediately following this confused period of the guns-and-torpedo brawl (from about 1745 to 1810 hours) between *Electra*, *Asagumo*, and *Minegumo* to the west and the sporadic long-range gunnery duels among the cruisers, Commander Binford's four destroyers were to make their one and only torpedo attack against the enemy battle line. This, too, came through the initiative of Cdr. Thomas Binford rather than direct orders from Doorman. And it came in the wake of fresh dangers that threatened the men of Binford's division, in particular those sailors and officers on "Jocko" Cooper's *John D. Ford*.

At 1805 hours on *Ford*, a man on the number 4 4-inch gun (above the aft deckhouse), suddenly reported a torpedo approaching the destroyer on its port quarter about two hundred yards distant. This would most likely have been from the Japanese forces' third series of torpedo attacks, primarily fired at extreme range by Nishimura's DesRon 4.[163] From his position on the number 1 (bow) 4-inch gun, Marion Ellsworth saw it too. As he recalled this seventy years later, Ellsworth's breathless syntax revealed as much as the actual details:

> Nothing to do at that time [the gunners were not firing] so all of us were just watching and waiting when we spotted a torpedo headed for us and we were right below the bridge so we all started yelling at the bridge to change course, had a man on sound powered phone that was supposed to be in contact with bridge and he was desperately trying to warn them and gradually we came parallel to the torpedo and I leaned over the port side and actually seen the torpedo go on past us and I think we had to be going about 35 knots.[164]

As this angle was not in Cooper's field of vision, control was given to the gunnery officer, Lt. William Mack. He conned the ship for several minutes as the big torpedo gained on *Ford*. It was on a converging course, and any radical movement by the destroyer might have swung her stern into the torpedo's path. With the enormous weapon speeding no more than four or five feet below the surface of the sea, it was highly visible to the unnerved crew watching from the destroyer's port side. Another *Ford* sailor who saw it—and with more sangfroid—also recalled the scene vividly decades later: "With the deep blue water of the Java See and that long silver cylinder of the torpedo with the little crystal waters splashing over it . . . it was the prettiest damned thing I'd ever seen in my life."[165] Still running at more than 30 knots, the sinister weapon gradually sidled up to within perhaps twenty-five feet of the destroyer's thin hull before Lieutenant Mack was able to edge the ship away. After several more excruciating moments, the torpedo finally curved off to the left and *Ford* pulled away safely to the right.

At that time the CSF cruisers were only firing against their opposite numbers intermittently.[166] There were two reasons for this: poor visibility, and the fact that *Houston* was beginning to run out of 8-inch ammunition for her forward turrets. Rooks sent a message to Doorman (via *Perth*) informing him that his 8-inch ammo was getting low. To this EC had replied that the American cruiser should be "very careful" with its main battery firing.[167] As a result of another long-range torpedo attack by the Japanese destroyer squadrons, there were seemingly random explosions in the water that again convinced the Allies that they were in a "nest" of enemy submarines.[168] During the same period Doorman received reports from his destroyers on remaining oil stocks. The message from DesDiv 58 evidently informed the EC that the U.S. ships were quite low on fuel by then.[169]

For a brief interval *Nachi* and *Haguro* were once more glimpsed through a break in the smoke, far astern, and a few salvos were exchanged, with the range then at least twenty-one thousand yards (according to Waller's report.) However, the Japanese gunners could still see their adversaries well enough. At this great distance *Houston* was struck by an 8-inch shell from one of the Japanese cruisers that went through her narrow forecastle without exploding. It hit ("with a high angle of fall") on the port side and exited out the starboard side of the hull between frames 14 and 15, leaving a pair of neat openings.[170] Such a hit was negligible in terms of damaging the ship's ability to steam and fight, but it did create problems. The exit hole was close enough to the waterline—below second deck level, and perhaps ten feet or less from the waterline—to allow seawater to enter, flooding the ship's stores compartments there.

As the Japanese heavy cruisers then appeared to be on an opposite course and drawing astern quickly, *Houston*—lacking her aft turret—had to make sharp right and left course alterations in order to load before being able to shoot. This meant both of her forward turrets were firing aft as far as they could be brought to bear, and this caused considerable superficial damage to her interior compartments as well as to lighter fittings near her bridge. While stationed there Walter Winslow was thrown back against the bulkhead with his tin helmet ripped off his head by the concussion from the cruiser's big guns as they fired on extreme after bearings. Meanwhile, in the course of this zigzagging *Perth* had passed ahead of *Houston* in the cruiser line.

During the first phase of the battle, *Houston*'s forward turrets had each fired about seventy salvos; in this second period—in which the action was more confused and firing less regular—she expended another thirty or so salvos. Her ammunition for turrets 1 and 2 was therefore being rapidly depleted, and all available sailors—from the 5-inch ammo party and repair parties—were soon detailed to start moving the remaining shells and powder cans from turret 3's magazines forward.

While this arduous business began, some of the men in the forward turrets and magazines recognized both mechanical and human signs of the toll being exacted on the ship's main battery. Below turret 1 in the powder circle, Eugene "Punchy" Parham could distinguish a difference in the sound now made by the overworked heavy guns with each salvo. It was "a dull jarring sound" that he attributed to poor recoil resulting from leaks and a loss of lubricant.[171] Due to the many cases of exhaustion among personnel in the magazines, O. C. McManus, PTR2/c, had been reassigned from his previous repair party duty to the shell deck of turret 1. There he helped manhandle the 8-inch projectiles into hoists that took them up to the guns. Survivors would later tell of multiple instances of men passing out from the intense physical labor under conditions of severe heat and lack of ventilation within these tightly enclosed steel compartments.

In the interval of firing off against her adversaries aft between zigzags, *Houston* received her second direct hit of the battle. This was another dud 8-inch shell from one of the Japanese heavy cruisers that struck her on her port quarter at about frame 115 just above the waterline, near compartment D-304. *Houston*'s senior survivor, Commander Maher, recorded that the hit "buckled the deck of this compartment and started leaks in the outer shell of tank C-9, and flooded D-12-A. The oil tanks involved were pumped down to avoid leaving an oil track."[172]

For the officer and sailors on *Houston*'s bridge and forward superstructure, it would prove a severely taxing point in the battle. The men inside the lightly built forward Mark 19 director suffered in this interval especially. Its door was repeatedly blown in by the concussion of the main battery firing, much to the consternation of the crewmen inside, and the director's floor plating was loosened. It finally dropped out of place entirely until, as Seaman First Class George Stoddard later remembered, "We were just standing on the angle-irons."[173]

Concurrently, as he moved up on the battle line, Binford received three successive signals—at this point all by signal lights—from Doorman.[174] The first was to counterattack, but this was quickly rescinded by another: "Negat— Make smoke" and followed by "Cover my retirement." Binford's division duly made smoke but only for seven minutes (from 1812 to 1819 hours according to the log of *Paul Jones*), while the American destroyer commander made up his mind about taking decisive action on his own. Binford gave and canceled several signals, too, based on Doorman's uncertain instructions. As he did so, the main body of CSF was making a series of wobbling movements generally to the south and east.

There has always been a dearth of clear documentation regarding communications received by the U.S. ships—in this case, the flushdeckers of CDD 58— during the battle from EC (Doorman), but most accounts do agree on one thing: this next-to-last signal from Doorman merely said to cover his retirement.[175] This order Binford interpreted (in agreement with Eccles, the skipper of *Edwards*) to mean that an attack with torpedoes would be the most effective action his ships could take for covering the cruisers' retirement. In later reports Binford said he was puzzled by Doorman's series of movements after the hit on *Exeter* had broken up the battle line: "I had no idea what he was doing. After the mêlée, some ships were not there. I didn't know what had happened."[176]

Baffled as he was, Cdr. Thomas Binford was neither an officer to disregard orders from a superior nor the weak-kneed type. The EC's message to "cover [his] retirement" came at about 1815 hours. At that time the commander of DesDiv 58 revealed his true mettle—one might imagine this pudgy Mississippian having led a cavalry charge for the Confederacy during the Civil War in one of the South's many forlorn battles against greater odds—and he formed his four destroyers into a column once more. They were then between the CSF cruisers and the enemy heavy ships to the north. The tactical plan, as Binford saw it, was to fire a "straight broadside, short spread" from his starboard torpedo batteries, then reverse course by column movement and fire the port torpedoes, after which the ships would make smoke and retire to the disengaged side of the battle line. Yet little had gone smoothly for the CSF that afternoon, or indeed throughout much of the Java campaign, and one further difficulty would interfere with Binford's scheme in the following minutes.

On the leading tin can's bridge, Cdr. Henry Eccles prepared *John D. Edwards* for her first torpedo salvo. The omnipresent gremlins of the Java campaign, however, would now sow more discord between Eccles and his immediate superior. While Eccles instructed his signalmen to get out the appropriate flag hoists—for maneuvering the ships into formation for a "curved fire ahead" salvo—Binford suddenly asked him, "What are you going to do?" Eccles replied that he was ordering the necessary "victor turn" signal that would direct the ships into an echelon for the attack. To this he was told by Binford, "You can't do that." Eccles, by now feeling nonplussed, asked him why not, and Binford replied that the torpedoes were already "set for 'broadside fire.'" (Once set in this way, the torpedoes' gyros could not be altered quickly for "curved fire ahead." They could, however, if set for "curved fire" still be fired broadside.) "In other words," as Eccles recalled with evident unease some eighteen years later, "just as we started the attack I suddenly realized that I had failed to insure that the torpedoes in all the ships in this hastily thrown together division were set in the same way."[177]

It had not occurred to Eccles that each division within DesRon 29 might have had its own method of making a torpedo attack. Falling back on his previous experiences, he had adhered to the doctrine of his old unit, DesDiv 57, in which the "curved fire ahead" method was routinely employed. That there had been no prewar exercises among the squadron's three divisions to iron out such tactical matters now caught up with the four-pipers in one of the most challenging moments they had yet faced. It was the ABDA/Combined Striking Force's bête noire once again in a nutshell.

It took a few moments for the two men to decide that the ships would fire "straight broadside" independently steaming in column. Eccles understood perfectly well that this meant getting much nearer to the enemy than they would if employing the "curved fire ahead" method. When employing an echelon formation for "curved fire ahead" attack, the ships could approach at high speed, unload their torpedoes in less than a minute, and retire before actual damage from enemy shellfire might be received. Not so with the "broadside fire" method. This entailed what Eccles called a "cumbersome" series of column movements and could take five or six times as long to execute, perhaps as much as three to four minutes. All the while a division would be under the guns of enemy secondary batteries and susceptible to serious damage. No one had any great desire to close the Japanese ships, which had already proved their prowess with torpedoes and gunfire, but Eccles was in no position or mood to quarrel with Commander Binford, whose displeasure he had already incurred.[178] They would just have to undertake the type of attack "that [they] were forced by circumstances to use" and make the best of the situation.[179]

As Doorman and the cruisers moved off to the south and east, Binford wheeled his four destroyers around and headed for the Japanese ships, which were in at least two groups. They were then as much as eight to ten miles distant. Binford's plan was to steam for the pursuing Japanese cruisers "head on" so as to bring his column's torpedo broadsides to bear and fire straight salvos with short spreads. At 1820 hours Binford had the signalman make the flag signal, and the ships—*Edwards, Alden, Ford,* and *Paul Jones* in column—maneuvered to make a division torpedo attack.[180] They were soon between the two Japanese cruiser lines. As best we can reconstruct this most chaotic of periods in the Battle of the Java Sea, to their north were elements of the enemy destroyer squadrons led by one or two of the light cruisers, and to the northwest were Takagi's two heavy cruisers, misidentified in some American track charts as battleships. Binford's division was steaming at about 28 knots, the old ships "straining every rivet" to maintain station, with their power plants only holding together through the remarkable efforts of their respective black gangs.

For the men on board the flushdeckers it was an exhilarating (if not terrifying) interval.[181] It was also one of marked confusion. On *John D. Ford* a sailor named Audrey Clark, F2/c, was on deck helping with one of the 4-inch guns, and his recollections were of shells tearing overhead, caroming off the waves, and ricocheting across the Java Sea in enormous whomps, with the Japanese ships seemingly everywhere: "They'd be in front of us and they'd be in back of us." His shipmate, Henry Fox, S1/c—a .50 cal. machine gunner on the portside of the galley deckhouse—expressed the same sense of spatial disorientation that gripped many: "Enemy starboard, enemy port, enemy dead ahead, enemy overhead. I said, 'Where are our friends out here?'"[182] Another gunner on *Ford,* J. Daniel Mullin, compared the role of the destroyers with that of the ill-fated British cavalrymen of the Crimean War celebrated in Tennyson's great poem "The Charge of the Light Brigade."[183] However, it fell to an unnamed sailor on the bridge of *Alden* to utter what became the most justly appropriate comment—and one which quickly became legendary—when he deadpanned, "I always knew these old four-pipers would have to go in and save the day." According to his captain's action report written later, this quintessential Asiatic Fleet drollery "called forth a laugh from all hands." It is not hard to envision the need for laughter at such a tense moment.[184]

For a five-minute period fortune favored the old ships of Binford and his men in the declining light. Japanese shooting was neither concentrated nor accurate. For whatever reasons—their small profile, smoke and haze, distance—the low-lying flushdeckers seem not to have attracted the attention of their enemies. At between fourteen thousand and fifteen thousand yards, the four destroyers went in against the Japanese and fired torpedoes from their starboard batteries first. This was probably twice the range they needed to be firing from if they had any realistic expectation of making hits on the enemy line, and both Binford and Eccles knew it.

*Alden* and *John D. Ford* expended six torpedoes each. *Edwards* launched only three fish since she had gone into the engagement with only half of her full allotment. *Paul Jones* expended five torpedoes because she experienced a primer misfire on her number 3 tube. Despite three attempts to fire it by "emergency percussion firing" (applying the hammer, that is) and replacing the impulse charge and primer, her torpedo battery captain could not get the weapon off in time for that first spread. Therefore twenty (rather than twenty-four) vintage Mark 8–Mod. 3 torpedoes went into the water on the first run toward the enemy. These all appeared to run normally. Binford then had the ships execute a course reversal "by column movement" in order to fire their port torpedoes. During this approach all twenty-one torpedoes from the port batteries were expended properly with no malfunctions. Japanese shells were by then falling but in no alarming proximity. One of the U.S. track charts displays these enemy salvos as "landing 1,500 yards short."[185]

Unknown to Binford or his skippers, Rear Adm. Karel Doorman had not only seen the destroyers turn to make their attack but had understood and appreciated the spirit behind this action. On the bridge of *De Ruyter*, as he witnessed the four old flushdeckers go in for their attack, the Striking Force commander moved over to liaison signalman Marvin Sholar and said, "Good! He needs no orders." (This remark confirms that Doorman had *not* given DesDiv 58 direct orders to attack.) Seeing the Japanese ships in the distance coming toward Binford's division, Doorman went on: "He'll die if they don't turn." He then added, "They are so low on fuel, he [Binford] doubts he will make it to Surabaja, but he is not going to get sunk with a full division of destroyers lying dead in the water with no fuel."[186] Whether or not the rotund Mississippian Binford actually had thoughts of such fatalistic gallantry in mind himself, Doorman's remarks at least indicate how the Dutch commander personally viewed the situation.[187]

By 1828 hours the four-pipers had finished delivering their torpedo attack. They then laid a thick smokescreen to cover their withdrawal. In the distance some of the U.S. sailors thought they saw both enemy heavy cruisers turn away to the north, but all doubted any hits were possible.[188] Heading back onto a northeast by north course of approximately 30 degrees, the four ships of Binford's division swung behind Doorman's cruiser line and steamed hard to take up position astern on the disengaged side. At this time the CSF was moving at speed, first to the east and then northeast. At 1831 hours Doorman had signaled the other ships: FOLLOW ME. Binford contacted the EC, sending a message by signal light to *De Ruyter*: "All torpedoes expended," which was apparently acknowledged by Doorman. Fittingly these final communications came with the sun descending into the sea.[189] Doorman then led his force to the northeast for ten minutes or so before altering to the northwest. He had no clear idea where the transports were, but he *did* have a very clear directive from his superior—Helfrich—to continue his attacks until the enemy was destroyed.

In any case, as Tom Binford and others later recorded, these were the last messages received from Karel Doorman. Flag signals were not possible after dark, and flashing lights were not used for fear of revealing the ships' positions. In this transition from daylight to dusk and the onset of night, *Houston*'s TBS set also failed, purportedly knocked out by the concussion of her extended main-battery firings. For Binford and his destroyers—just as for the rest of Doorman's CSF—the remainder of the engagement would be undertaken "in the dark" in almost every sense of the term. Although the American four-pipers would tag along, burning up more precious fuel oil for another indecisive ninety minutes or so, their active role in the Battle of the Java Sea was over.

*De Ruyter* remained then at the head of the column, followed by *Perth*, *Houston*, and *Java*. Trailing as best they could were the remaining six destroyers: *Jupiter*, *Encounter*, and Binford's quartet of flushdeckers. The CSF in its first two hours of battle had been reduced from fourteen to ten units. The Japanese, apart from the damage to *Minegumo* and *Asagumo*, were unaffected. Doorman was evidently still hoping to work his way around the enemy covering force to locate the transports.[190] It was a vain hope, of course. The forty-one lumbering transports had been withdrawn well to the north and were in no peril with Doorman and the CSF now reduced to literally groping in the dark. Paradoxically, due to darkness and reduced visibility, the Japanese were likewise suffering from an equal degree of uncertainty and doubt at this juncture.

As he attempted to contain Doorman's force and keep it from approaching the convoy, Rear Admiral Takagi of the Fifth Cruiser Division was becoming more concerned with the proximity of his forces to possible Dutch minefields laid along the northern coast of Java. His navigators had estimated that the Japanese ships might be no more than twenty miles from Cape Awarawar (northwest of Toeban) at one time. This worried him because, like most of the Japanese commanders at sea, Takagi seems to have always retained a healthy respect for Allied minefields. The haze from gunfire, exploding or damaged ships, and various smokescreens along with the fading light were combining to render visibility problematic as well. Sunset came at 1820 hours that evening.[191] Adding to Takagi's apprehension were distant sightings of explosions in the sea that the Japanese feared might indeed have been mines. (These were apparently the Type 93 Long Lances exploding prematurely, or at the end of their runs.) With such considerations in mind—along with concerns about the enormous number of shells and torpedoes already expended by his ships—Takagi chose at 1830 to cease fire and reorganize his own forces.

This decision was also influenced by the messages he had received from the Ranin Butai commander, Vice Adm. Takahashi Ibō in *Ashigara*, who was hurrying to the scene with *Myōkō* at their best speed. Takahashi's ships—known as Main Force—were at that time somewhere to the northwest of Kangean Island, well off to the east but steaming for the Java Sea at 20 knots. He thought (too optimistically, as it turned out) they might reach the battle area within four or five hours. Messages from Takagi and others already seemed to have impressed on Vice Admiral Takahashi the urgency of the situation. That afternoon at midday Takahashi had sent a polite request—"fuel status and other situations permitting"—to the light cruiser *Kinu* to split off from a convoy bound for Bali with the light cruiser *Nagara* and half of DesDiv 8 (*Asashio* and *Arashio*) and proceed westward into the Java Sea.[192] *Nagara* remained with the Bali group—they were north of Lombok that morning—as the other three broke away. Having reached the area where Takagi and Tanaka's forces were operating, the destroyers would then come under the command of Nishimura's DesRon 4.

With direct escort of the convoy *his* responsibility, Rear Adm. Nishimura Shōji in DesRon 4 flagship *Naka* had grown increasingly worried about the transports. Therefore, at 1845, or fifteen minutes after Takagi decided to break off action, Nishimura ordered the convoy to reverse course and move back to the north at its best speed. In the case of the plodding marus this was all of about 8 knots. The head of DesRon 4 had little patience with the sluggish manner in which his orders were carried out, and at 1904 and 1905 hours he sent two more peremptory orders to the convoy commander, emphasizing the imminent approach of Doorman's force. Yet there can be little question that Nishimura had the debacle suffered by his convoy at Balikpapan in late January in mind as well. He would have been in no mood to allow any slackness in the transports' course or their protection.

These impatient communications were largely dictated by the tracking of Doorman and the Combined Striking Force through spotting planes overhead. In particular the floatplane of *Jintsū* was regularly reporting Doorman's movements back to the Japanese commanders. It would also begin dropping markers to pinpoint the location of the CSF.[193] Clusters of eerie green parachute flares were seen by many of the Allied ships falling into their wakes after dark over the next hour, giving an uneasy sense that despite being unable to find their opponents, the enemy knew right where Doorman's force was.

At 1846 hours CSF was found to be on a course of 310 degrees at an estimated speed of 20 knots—which could lead the Allied force to the Japanese convoy—and it was this information that had so alarmed Nishimura. Sadly, for Doorman it was never exactly clear where the Japanese covering forces were, still less the elusive transports. It seemed to the Allied force that the enemy had enough foreknowledge of its movements to block every move its ships made to get at the transports. The flares also had the distinct psychological effect of making those men on the upper decks and bridges of the CSF ships feel exposed and vulnerable.

At the same time that *Nachi* and *Haguro* began preparing for a night battle, they ordered their planes to return. In this Takagi made an error in judgment that might have cost him dearly. Beginning at 1857 hours the cruisers began recovering their spotting planes. *Haguro*'s plane under Lieutenant Utsunomiya had landed on the sea's calm surface as the big cruiser made a large turn to face the wind before recovery. While the last plane was preparing to be hoisted aboard, at 1922 hours an enemy ship was seen approaching. The Type 95 of *Haguro* was being lifted from the sea a few minutes later when star shells burst in the night sky and giant splashes from a salvo of heavy shells landed much too close for comfort. These came from *Perth* and *Houston,* which had been steaming north with the CSF column when at least one of Takagi's ships was spotted in the dim moonlight.[194]

*Perth* had sighted and reported four enemy ships off the port beam at 1927 hours, range estimated to be nine thousand yards. At that moment more parachute flares were dropped on the CSF ships. By 1933 hours both Allied cruisers had opened fire with star shell (which failed to illuminate the enemy) and a few salvos before turning away into the darkness, fearing a torpedo attack. Startled, Takagi's two cruisers swung off under a smokescreen, gathering power for 28 knots. It took them twelve minutes to reverse course and put themselves in a position to resume firing against the Allied ships.[195]

However, as it turns out the return fire when it did happen came not from *Nachi* and *Haguro* but from *Jintsū*. The DesRon 2 flagship had returned at high speed on seeing the pyrotechnics falling—evidently alerted by her own spotter— and interposed herself between Sentai 5 and the Allied ships. At 1936 hours Rear Admiral Tanaka's undetected light cruiser fired on *Perth* and *Houston* from a range of nineteen thousand meters. Both Australian and American survivors later reported near misses, although such memories are not always to be taken at face value.[196] It is now also known that *Jintsū* had indeed launched four more torpedoes (at 1936 hours), so Doorman's turn away was a wise precaution. But on that fateful night he would not be so fortunate when he again encountered Takagi's ships under similar circumstances.

. . .

With yet another missed opportunity by the luckless CSF, the second part of the battle may be said to have ended.[197] Over the next quarter of an hour the four cruisers and six destroyers of Doorman's force steamed more or less east before heading due south for a protracted period lasting well over an hour. Between 1957 and 2009 hours more flares were dropped on Doorman's column by one or more of the Japanese floatplanes flying above, unseen but audible in the darkness. One may only speculate about the intentions of the exhausted Doorman beyond this point. Within ten minutes of 2000 he ordered the CSF south; the ships were soon heading on a course of about 180 degrees at 27 knots. In the rear Cdr. Thomas Binford's four flushdeckers still labored to keep Doorman's cruisers in sight. At that point Binford and Eccles were utterly mystified about Doorman's intentions—Eccles making the acerbic observation in his action report that "the crystal ball was [their] only method of anticipating the intentions of Commander Combined Striking Force"—and with Binford even imagining that perhaps Doorman was taking the ships back into Surabaja.[198]

This was not the case, however. Rear Adm. Karel Doorman had returned once too often from previous sorties under circumstances that appeared premature and questionable, and he knew it. His superior, Lieutenant Admiral Helfrich, had exhorted him repeatedly over the past days to seek out the enemy and destroy his forces. Anything less was going to be considered yet another unacceptable failure.[199] Some of the surviving CSF commanders thought that Doorman was trying to ascertain if the convoy had slipped south of his ships, while others speculated that he wanted to work his way around to the transports via another course. Communications regarding the location of the convoy were sporadic and vague; it is not even known how many messages were received—or in what form—by Doorman that night.[200]

The CSF then proceeded south at 22 knots back toward the coast of Java. Binford had no clue regarding Doorman's plans; he could only play "Tail-End Charlie," tagging along as best as possible with the cruisers barely visible a mile or two off in the night. With no enemy ships visible on the horizon, it was nonetheless an extended period of pronounced tension. On board *Houston* Walter Winslow would note the ominous silence as the cruiser's "bow knifed through the somber sea. . . . How beautiful was the covering darkness, but how terrifying to think that the enemy was aware of our every move, and was merely biding his time to strike."[201] Even "Hec" Waller in *Perth* could not help but admire the work of the enemy reconnaissance planes: "During this whole period the Allied force was being superbly shadowed by Japanese aircraft," his report noted. Lines of brightly burning "calcium flares" fell into the water at right angles to the ships as they steamed south. "This happened every time we steered a new course and it was soon obvious that our every move in the moonlight was being reported."[202] Many of the exhausted men found these "weird floating lights" that bobbed in the sea "lining [their] track . . . like ghoulish jack-o-lanterns" highly unsettling, and they were certain the enemy must have known precisely where the Allied ships were at all times.[203]

For an hour Doorman led the ships south until "the island's dark mountains were seen silhouetted against the moonlit sky," at which point the sea depth became quite a bit shallower.[204] The ships were at that time approaching the coast near Toeban—roughly between Cape Awarawar to the west and Pangkah Point to the east—at a fairly high rate of speed. Some of the ships' commanders felt that Doorman was taking a risk getting in so close to the shore, where there was known to be newly laid Dutch minefields.

On *Houston* the men aft suddenly began to notice that the cruiser's "wake was getting very broad, indicating shoal water." Piling up on both sides of the fantail, it resembled "a solid wall of water following the ship" ten to twelve feet high.[205] Olen Minton, s1/c, a rammer man on one of the "flight deck" 5-inch guns likened it to a "power boat wake."[206] This fact was quickly reported to the navigating bridge by both Chief Signalman Kenneth Blair and Lieutenant Commander Galbraith (among others). At the conn, the helmsman simultaneously remarked that the wheel was becoming difficult to handle, while also noting that the ship was vibrating badly and seemed to be losing speed. Rooks instantly understood these as signs of dangerously shallow water and yanked his cruiser away from the coastline. Within a few moments *De Ruyter* also turned sharply, making a 60-degree alteration. She continued "to the westward, keeping about four miles from the coast."[207] *Houston* rejoined the column shortly as did the remaining destroyers, *Encounter* and *Jupiter*, both of which were then steaming astern of *Java*.

At that point—and there is no agreement on the exact time, as the U.S. destroyers' logs are not very precise in these events—Commander Binford decided that he had endured enough. His ships were short on fuel, out of torpedoes, and being continually tracked by airplanes above and submarines below.

According to *Alden*'s dead-reckoning track kept during the engagement, the destroyers broke off from the CSF at 2111 hours and altered course to the east for Surabaja.[208] They were then some fifty miles from the port. As Binford later recounted, "At 930 pm [2130 hours] saw that fuel was low. Could be of no further service. I decided to return to Surabaja where I could get oil. Tried to communicate . . . couldn't. Sent out radio [message] to shore station. Told them I was returning to Surabaja for fuel."[209]

Nearly an hour later, as the four flushdeckers entered the outer minefields off Surabaja, a message from Doorman finally reached Binford. It had been routed through the shore station and instructed CDD58 to take his destroyers and "proceed to Batavia and replenish with fuel, and orders as to obtaining new torpedoes." With his ships inside the minefields, an hour or less from the docks, almost out of fuel and lacking torpedoes, Binford held a hurried conference with his commanders by TBS. "We weighed the matter," said Binford, "and decided it would be suicide to go to Priok [Batavia]. It meant a daylight run. . . . [We] might encounter Jap destroyers and cruisers, and there were no torpedoes in Priok anyway." Adding that he believed "it was in the general interest not to go," Binford told his skippers that he wanted to proceed in to Surabaja and "fuel to capacity and clear the docks by daylight." He did, however, ask the captains for comments or suggestions. All replied in plain English that they "agreed 100%" with his plan.[210] And that was that. Cdr. Thomas Binford had made the first of several decisions that would eventually lead to the salvation of his Six Hundred. Yet, for the remainder of the CSF still at sea off Toeban on that moonlit night, more and deadlier perils awaited.

. . .

After Doorman had altered course again to the north, extricating the column from shoal water, the last ship in line suddenly exploded with great violence at about 2125 hours. This was the British destroyer HMS *Jupiter* (under Lt. Cdr. Norman Thew). Her only message—transmitted by blinker tube—stated that she had been "torpedoed" but this was a preliminary assumption and an error. She had in fact suffered the misfortune to run upon a Dutch mine laid out of position in the shallows off Toeban Bay on the night of the twenty-sixth/twenty-seventh by the RNN minelayer *Gouden Leeuw*. Even though Doorman had been informed of the plans to lay this minefield (in the Surabaja conference on the twenty-sixth), the captain of *Gouden Leeuw* clearly failed to lay his mines accurately within the prescribed area. Thus, due to his poorly executed actions the Allies lost yet another vessel.[211] As previously the ABDA allies were often their own worst enemies, and in the fate of *Jupiter* we see this same ill luck manifesting itself again.

The blast had hit on her starboard side near the forward bulkhead of the after engine spaces, and damage was severe. The stricken British destroyer was then less than ten miles offshore from Toeban. Although she came to an abrupt halt, due to her size and more robust construction *Jupiter* did not sink promptly. (This class of ship was about 10 percent longer and displaced as much as 20 percent more than the Dutch destroyers—and *far* more than the old four-pipers of the Asiatic Fleet.) Nonetheless, her men seem to have abandoned her with some swiftness. A survivor later wrote: "Before I realized the seriousness of the situation, the port motorboat was jammed to its gunwales with people. The whaler on the starboard side had pulled away full of people, including one dying casualty, who I later learned, was buried ashore. I went over the side, down a scrambling net, and onto a Carley float; there were 10 of us on it."[212]

Since it took nearly four hours for the destroyer to founder, most of her crew was able to get off safely, and a large number made it to shore in boats and Carley floats. Some groups of men were in the water for up to thirty hours before making it to land, and as always, there was no rhyme or reason to who survived, who perished, who made landfall, and who was captured at sea.[213] Caught up in the tricky currents prevailing in that part of the Java Sea, quite a few were not able to get to the coastline quickly and would meet their naval adversaries in person over the next couple of days.

This alarming event was seen, although misinterpreted, by other ships in the CSF. "Hec" Waller of *Perth* later wrote in his report that "one of the American destroyers blew up with a tremendous explosion and sank." (This suggests, if nothing else, that Waller was not yet aware that Binford had withdrawn his division.) Walter Winslow on *Houston* claimed that the ship blew up "in a burst of flames" before being "left to sink unattended."[214] There was no question of remaining behind to try to aid the damaged ship; the CSF had to keep moving if it was to avoid a similar fate. Satisfied that an enemy landing was not in progress near Toeban, Doorman led his ships back to the north.

By this point the CSF had suffered attrition to the extent of reducing its numbers by more than half; what had started out as a force of fourteen ships was now five. Additionally, their fuel was dwindling, and both *Perth* and *Houston* had fired a significant percentage of their main-battery ammunition already. Be that as it may, the doomed persistence of Karel Doorman was going to bring results. He was still determined to make the maximum effort to come to grips with the invaders if possible. In the end he did this and paid the ultimate price for his efforts. Yet, to debate whether "that Dutchman [had] more guts than brains"—as one of the destroyer commanders was alleged to have remarked when the CSF moved into those perilous shallows off Toeban—is to miss the point.[215] Doorman's courage was beyond question, and it was of a higher species than that of a reckless individual behaving irresponsibly. It was that courage of a man of experience and intelligence who *knew better* but was fulfilling an overarching imperative: that of duty to his service and his country.

As the ships headed north, away from Toeban and the disabled *Jupiter* and with their force then reduced to *De Ruyter, Perth, Houston, Java,* and *Encounter,* overhead in the darkness returned the ominous whine of Japanese floatplanes. These scouts—from light cruisers *Naka* and *Jintsū*—continued to mark the track of Doorman's force with flares and report back to their commanders. By this time Takagi's ships had all moved off well to the north of Bawean Island. On the bridge of *Jintsū* Rear Admiral Tanaka was still receiving reports from his sole floatplane above the enemy column, which it marked with flares from time to time. Although no one could then have possibly foreseen it, this observation plane from *Jintsū* was fated to set into motion a snowball of events later that would result in more tragedy, producing one of the campaign's most intractable mysteries.[216]

About 2200 hours or shortly thereafter, the four CSF cruisers ran through a large mass of men in the sea; many were blowing whistles, while others shouted in what to the Australians and Americans sounded like a foreign tongue. It was too dark at that time for more than a few on the cruisers to make them out distinctly. Chief Signal Man Blair on *Houston's* bridge could hear then "shouting in unison.... Soon [they] could make out men in the water to port of the formation."[217] One of the cruiser's bridge talkers, Gene Wilkinson, S2/c, recalled the event but also the sense of dread and uncertainty that precluded any thought of rescuing those men: "To stop and help them would be almost suicide . . . as far as we knew at that point . . . because we never knew where the torpedoes came from."[218]

As for the RNN sailors in the water, it had seemed nothing short of miraculous that a hundred men or more had lived through the terrific destruction of *Kortenaer.* They had tied their life rafts and floats together; some of these that had been damaged were lashed to bamboo poles that were brought on board the ship for just such an eventuality. *Kortenaer's* officers seem to have made efforts to group the survivors together; others helped keep spirits up during the time they were in the sea by encouraging the sailors to sing songs. Inevitably a few of the badly wounded on the floats died, and their bodies were slipped gently into the sea to make room for others. After some four hours adrift in the inky darkness, an officer recalled: "Suddenly we heard a drone." Looking to the south, toward the coast, he could make out a familiar shape: "It was the *De Ruyter* approaching." Another survivor was alarmed; he saw that the cruiser was "coming right at [them]." He recalled, "I thought, 'My God, we're going to get mashed up in the propellers!'" To the amazement of all, the cruisers sped through their midst at high speed, not slackening in the least. Rafts were overturned and "rammed on all sides by the bow waves" but it is not known if any of the men in the water were killed by the passing ships.[219] On *De Ruyter* the presence of the men in the water was not ignored, however. Presumably because he understood the destroyer was low on fuel oil, Doorman gave orders at around 2215 hours to "Rattler" Morgan in *Encounter* to pick up the survivors and return to Surabaja with them.[220] Although this order seemed to be in contradiction to his verbal instructions given at the afternoon conference on February 26 concerning disabled ships—that they were to be "left to the mercy of the enemy" as Doorman had stated—it is fair to assume the EC understood that Morgan's destroyer was also low on fuel and would need to return to Surabaja very shortly anyway.

*Kortenaer*'s men then saw the British destroyer approach them. As *Encounter* did so, its crew began tossing nets and lines over her side. Although grasping anything was, as one Dutch survivor put it, "pure luck [since] you couldn't see a thing," some 113 RNN sailors were picked up from the Java Sea that night.[221] They were—all things considered in this most unlucky of Allied naval battles—extraordinarily fortunate. The British offered rum and lemonade to the survivors, and the destroyer's doctor attempted to tend the wounded. However, not everyone rescued by *Encounter* was as well favored by fate. A badly injured young Dutch seaman named B. H. Hagendijk somehow managed to pull himself up to the deck of the destroyer, but his wounds were so severe that the twenty-one year-old sailor expired before Morgan's ship reached Surabaja.

The Allied crews were of course not the only exhausted men serving in men-of-war on the Java Sea that night. On board *Haguro* a profoundly weary Lt. Utsunomiya Michio had been debriefed by the captain after his hours in the Type 95 DAVE over the battle that afternoon and evening. He then spent a few moments speaking with *Haguro*'s gunnery officer, Captain Nakajima, about his performance. When the flier asked if he had given good information for spotting, Nakajima responded that his reports were "very precise." The gunnery officer expostulated that the reason the cruiser had not made more hits was because "the bridge"—meaning *Haguro*'s skipper, Capt. Mori Tomoichi, presumably—had "never turned toward the enemy." He also opined, and with reasonable justification, that the captain was reluctant to close the gap before having expended his Type 93 torpedoes. (The Japanese were always alert, with good reason, to the potential dangers of carrying such highly volatile and lethal weapons on board their ships.)[222] After that exchange Utsunomiya went down to the cruiser's upper deck. There he located a folding chair, sat down, and realizing he had no immediate duties before the next morning, "immediately" dropped off into a sound sleep.[223] If Utsunomiya's memoir is to be believed, this was a severely sleep-deprived young pilot indeed, for he would not reawaken until the battle had reached its cruel and explosive climax.

During this same period, as his ships transited the channels off the Westervaarwater, Cdr. Thomas Binford sent out a reply to Doorman (copied to CCCF/Collins and CZM/Helfrich) via Surabaja at 2155 hours: "Re your message. 1403. [This would correspond to 2133 hours that night.] Followed by aircraft and enemy force(s). With disposition of enemy force(s) considered impossible to reach Batavia tonight. Now in channel(s) Sourabaya. Will fuel immediately. Will proceed to as directed. . . . Entire communication with e.c. and Houston lost at dark. All torpedoes fired."[224] Binford had made his choice; with all his four-pipers low on fuel and out of torpedoes, he was not about to turn his ships around and try to make the long, perilous run to Batavia that night.

Ten minute later they passed Slempit Point Light to port a mile off; in another twelve minutes the destroyers secured from general quarters. About an hour later—at just past 0200 hours—they anchored in the outer harbor of Surabaja. Tugs were soon ready to tow them into the fuel dock at Holland Pier. Binford and his skippers all had one thing in mind: to fuel to capacity and prepare for maneuvering in the harbor when the air raids they knew would come arrived at dawn. As Lt. Cdr. Lewis Coley, the captain of *Alden*, began to take his ship into the fuel dock, he informed the others of his plan. Like siblings competing for food at an overcrowded family table, Lt. Cdr. J. J. Hourihan on *Paul Jones* responded in kind: "What Lew does, I'm going to do."[225] Within another hour, by 0302 hours, *Jones* was being towed into Holland Pier, where she moored to the port side of *John D. Edwards* at 0430 and began receiving fuel twenty minutes later.

At sea Doorman led the CSF north for another fifteen or twenty minutes after passing through the survivors of *Kortenaer*, his column then completely denuded of its destroyer screen. Within forty minutes both *Houston* and *Perth* spotted a pair of large ships to the northwest; they were visible in the moonlight on an opposite course. *Houston*'s 5-inch battery fired a few salvos of star shell set for 10,000 yards. Although they could be seen as two cruisers, these shells did not illuminate the enemy ships properly. *De Ruyter* and *Perth* began firing at more or less the same time against the Japanese ships, which accurately returned fire, although at a slower pace.[226] The next 5-inch projectiles fired from *Houston* were set for maximum star-shell range—14,500 yards—but these, too, failed to reveal the enemy ships. *Houston*'s turret 2 then unleashed a single 8-inch salvo at 15,000 yards. But Captain Rooks was unwilling to expend any more main-battery shells unnecessarily, and Commander Maher quickly checked fire.

The two Imperial Navy cruisers—*Nachi* and *Haguro*—would likewise expend only a handful of shells at their foes, knowing their own inventories were dangerously low. Heading south on a course of 180° T. they had sighted Doorman's column at 2303 hours; the Allied ships were ahead of them at 152° and about fifteen thousand meters distant. A Japanese lookout on *Nachi* reported: "Presumably four enemy ships, port 30 degrees, one five zero [or, fifteen thousand meters]." The bugler sounded, "All hands, general quarters, man your battle stations!" and the order went out, "Prepare for simultaneous gun and torpedo attacks!"[227] Although their 8-inch ammunition had been almost exhausted, the two big cruisers still had a number of torpedoes left, and Takagi intended to use these in the night engagement if possible.

Making a sharp right turn, *Nachi* led *Haguro* around at 2310 hours to come on to a course paralleling Doorman's column although still well ahead of it. The Japanese ships increased speed to 33 knots at the same time. This gave Takagi the chance to execute what has been an unrecognized piece of tactical excellence: his maneuvers would have made it appear to the Allied ships that they were fleeing when in reality it put the Sentai 5 cruisers slightly ahead of their adversaries and in an excellent position to make a torpedo attack.

After steadying on her new course *Nachi* opened fire from a range of 13,300 meters (14,500 yards); *Haguro* followed immediately thereafter at 12,000 meters (13,100 yards). They fired a limited number of main-battery projectiles during this encounter with the CSF which was "clearly visible in the dark . . . under the dim moonlight." Nonetheless, the slow pace of Japanese gunnery was in effect a ruse; their torpedo men were working furiously to prepare their remaining Type 93 fish for another test. On board *Nachi* their torpedo officer, Lieutenant Horie, embarrassed earlier in the battle, had been granted a chance to redeem himself and his men. *Nachi*'s skipper advised him to "calm down, take good aim, and then fire."[228] Horie and his men took full advantage of this second opportunity. He and his fire-control teams did fine work, obtaining a textbook firing solution against the CSF column to the southeast. On the other hand, Rear Adm. Karel Doorman had taken a chance too many with his Striking Force. This final one would end in catastrophe.

26. The Japanese heavy cruiser *Haguro*—shown here in the 1930s—was bigger, faster, and more heavily armed than her Western adversaries in the East Indies. She expended an immense number of main battery shells in the Battle of the Java Sea and the engagement off Cape Puting. Official U.S. Navy photograph, NH 73017.

27. This beautiful full-length image of the battleship *Kirishima* (taken off Tsukomo Bay in 1937) gives an indication of her speed and power. She operated as a member of Vice Adm. Mikawa Gunichi's Sentai 3 accompanying Vice Adm. Nagumo Chuichi's Kidō Butai during the East Indies campaign and was involved in the pursuit and sinking of *Edsall* on March 1, 1942. Wikipedia; Shizuo Fukui-Kure Maritime Museum, *Japanese Naval Warship Photo Album: Battleships and Battle Cruisers*, edited by Kazushige Todaka (White Diamond, 2005), 124.

28. The Japanese destroyer *Asashio*, which performed superbly in the chaotic Battle of Badoeng Strait. Wikipedia; Shizuo Fukui-Kure Maritime Museum, *Japanese Naval Warship Photo Album: Destroyers*, edited by Kazushige Todaka (White Diamond, 2005), 84.

29. *Ikazuchi* the Sprinter. An Akatsuki-class destroyer of 1932, she was powerful and extremely fast but also a notorious oil-guzzler, which restricted her operational range. Few other IJN tin cans' whereabouts have been harder to document in the East Indies campaign—largely due to the paucity of primary source records. Wikipedia; Shizuo Fukui-Kure Maritime Museum, *Japanese Naval Warship Photo Album: Destroyers*, edited by Kazushige Todaka (White Diamond, 2005), 72.

30. Symbol of overmatched U.S. air forces in the East Indies: Japanese military personnel on March 10, 1942, examining the wreck of 1st Lt. J. L. "Duke" DuFrane's B-17-E (41-2459) lost at Kendari II airfield in January after a mission in which it was damaged, force-landed at KII, and then wrecked by enemy strafing. Roger Pineau Collection, NHHC Photo Archives, Naval History and Heritage Command, Washington DC, courtesy of J. Michael Wenger.

31. Seen from *Marblehead* as she reaches Tjilatjap on February 6, 1942, *Houston*'s crew congregate topside to cheer their injured sister cruiser into port. Some of the battle damage to *Houston*'s third turret may be seen in this image. Official U.S. Navy photograph, U.S. Naval Historical Center, NH 82480, from *Marblehead* files, via Robert Stern.

32. A widely reproduced photo of the old light cruiser *Marblehead* licking her wounds at Tjilatjap, Java, after suffering severe bomb damage on February 4, 1942. What has not been recognized previously is that the individual atop the turret is believed to be her Royal Netherlands Navy liaison officer, Lt. Ted Luxemburg. Official U.S. Navy photograph, 80-G-237439.

33. (*opposite top*) The Japanese invasion convoy's formation in its anchorage at Balikpapan, Borneo, when attacked by the old four-pipers of Cdr. Paul Talbot on January 24, 1942. This official chart shows the positions of IJN patrol boats, subchasers, and minesweepers, as well as the destroyers of DesDiv 2, 9, and 24. Japan Center for Asian Historical Records, ref. C08030109800, p. 56, National Institute for Defense Studies, Japan.

34. (*opposite bottom*) Asiatic Fleet seaplane tender USS *Langley* at Darwin during her service there in early 1942. On her reduced flight deck are some of the remaining planes of the Asiatic Fleet's Utility unit, including O2U Kingfishers and SOC Seagulls. Also visible are .50 cal. machine-gun mounts atop her bridge and 3-inch/50 cal. AA weapons on her flight deck. Author's collection via Otto Schwarz / USS *Houston* Survivors Association.

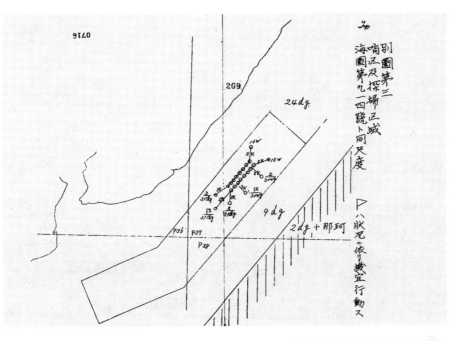

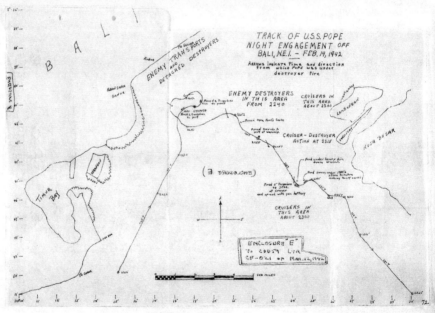

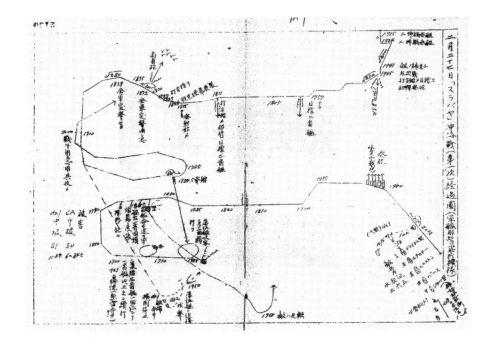

35. (*opposite top*) USS *Peary* perishes at Darwin, February 19, 1942. Her four funnels swathed in smoke, the old destroyer sinks at her moorings after being hit by at least five Japanese bombs. To the right is the Australian hospital ship *Manunda*. Australian War Memorial, Canberra, P05303.013.

36. (*opposite bottom*) The chaotic track of *Pope* and *John D. Ford* in the Battle of Badoeng Strait. Following *De Ruyter*, *Java*, and *Piet Hein*, they did most of their fighting with torpedoes and fired very few 4-inch at all. *Asashio* and *Ōshio* literally ran rings around them, and both four-pipers were lucky to escape serious damages. Fold3 by Ancestry, Historical Military Records, at www.fold3.com.

37. (*above*) Track chart of Rear Admiral Takagi's Fifth Squadron (Sentai 5) in the opening phase of the Battle of the Java Sea. This chart shows the initial IJN long-range gunnery and torpedo attacks against Doorman's Striking Force over a two-and-a-half-hour period. The damaged *Exeter* is shown turning away after being hit and retiring under a smokescreen at 6 to 8 knots. Japan Center for Asian Historical Records, ref. C0803004260, p. 58, National Institute for Defense Studies, Japan.

## Details of *Nachi* fire control for Battle of the Java Sea, February 27–28

| Date | Target | Time | No. of salvos | No. of rounds fired | Length of time of firing | Avg. rounds fired per min. | Max. range* | Min. range* | Straddles | Over | Under | Not known |
|---|---|---|---|---|---|---|---|---|---|---|---|---|
| 2/27 | De Ruyter | 1747.5 | 1 | 10 | — | — | — | — | 1 | — | — | — |
| 2/27 | Exeter | (1750) 1750.5 | 26 | 255 | 11'-52" | 22.5 | 263 | 237 | 7 | 12 | 4 | 3 |
| 2/27 | Houston | (1805) | 9 | 88 | 5'-30" | 16 | 278 | 253 | 3 | 0 | 5 | 1 |
| 2/27 | Houston | (1813) | 31 | 262 | 14'-00" | 18.7 | 210 | 154 | 1 | 18 | 9 | 3 |
| 2/27 | DeRuyter | (1829) | 26 | 140 | 15'-40" | 8.9 | 276 | 192 | 3 | 12 | 10 | 1 |
| 2/27 | Houston | (1914) | 14 | 110 | 12'-10" | 9 | 252 | 210 | 2 | 2 | 10 | 0 |
| 2/28 | Houston | 0052 | 4 | 19 | 2'-10" | 9.4 | 148 | 133 | 0 | 0 | 0 | 4 |

* Ranges given in hectometers. Multiply by 100 for range in meters.

Source: Adapted from Sentai 5 gunnery table in the Japan Center for Asian Historical Records by Kan Sugahara and Donald M. Kehn Jr.

別紙第

## 那智 射撃 指揮 関係 （2月27.28日）

| 月 | 日 目標 | 初彈発砲時刻（打チ始メ） | 斉射回数 | 発射彈数 | 射撃時間 | 平均毎分発射彈数 | 彈着距離 max | mean | 遠近斉射回数 | | 近 | 不明 |
|---|---|---|---|---|---|---|---|---|---|---|---|---|
| | デュミクテル | 17:41.5 | 1 | 10 | | | | | 1 | 0 | 0 | 0 |
| 27 | エンビター | (17:50) 17:50.5 | 26 | 255 | 11'-53" | 22.5 | 263 | 237 | 7 | 12 | 4 | 3 |
| | ヒューストン | (15:-5) | 5 | 55 | 5'-30" | 16 | 278 | 253 | 3 | 0 | 5 | 1 |
| | 同上 | (18/3) | 31 | 262 | 14'-0" | 18.7 | 210 | 154 | 1 | 18 | 9 | 3 |
| | デロイテル | (18:25) | 26 | 140 | 15'-40" | 8.9 | 276 | 172 | 3 | 12 | 10 | 1 |
| | ヒューストン | (9/4) | 14 | 110 | 18'-10" | 9 | 252 | 210 | 2 | 2 | 10 | 0 |
| 28 | 同 | 00:52 | '' | 19 | 2'-10" | 9.4 | 148 | 133 | 0 | 0 | 6 | 4 |

38. This chart from *Nachi*'s official wartime records details the cruiser's 20 cm/8-inch gunnery against Doorman's Striking Force during the Battle of the Java Sea. Japan Center for Asian Historical Records, National Institute for Defense Studies, Japan.

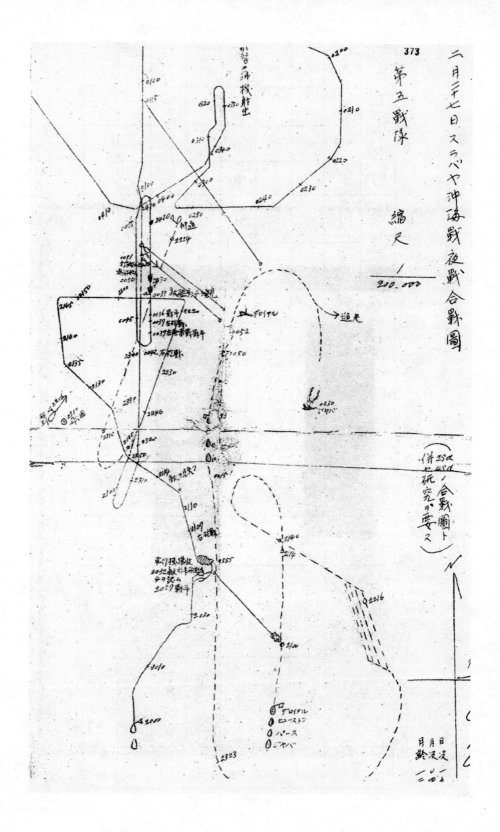

373

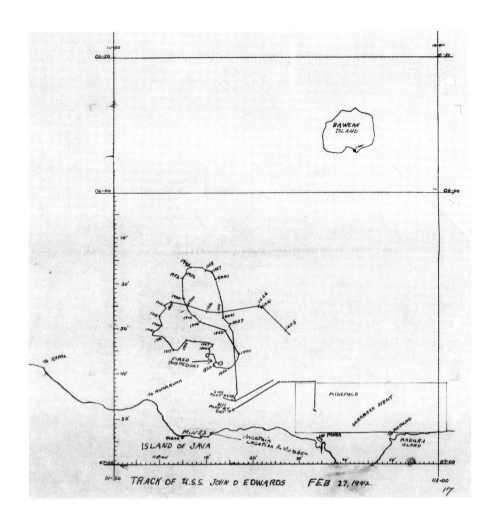

TRACK OF U.S.S. JOHN D EDWARDS    FEB 27, 1942.

*17*

39. (*opposite*) This IJN chart from the official records of Sentai 5 shows
clearly the position from which Rear Admiral Takagi's cruisers *Nachi*
and *Haguro* fired the final, and fatal, torpedo salvo that sank *Java* and
*De Ruyter*. Both Japanese cruisers had remained well to the northwest
of the CSF column, thereby providing a favorable firing angle for their
superb Type 93 weapons. Japan Center for Asian Historical Records,
ref. C0803004260, p. 64, National Institute for Defense Studies, Japan.

40. (*above*) This chart of the Battle of the Java Sea was taken from the
USS *John D. Edwards* Action Report and shows the general course
of the battle from first contact with the Japanese up to Binford's
withdrawal of the American tin cans. It is useful for showing the two
loops made by the destroyers during their torpedo attacks. Fold3 by
Ancestry, Historical Military Records, at www.fold3.com.

41. Unknown before now, the purpose-built Japanese hydrographic survey vessel *Tsukushi* (seen here under air attack at Rabaul later in the war) was operating with the destroyers of DesDiv 21 in Bali Strait on the night that Binford's quartet of four-pipers slipped through. Her formidable lines gave her the look of a Japanese tin can to the U.S. destroyermen, but her unusually low speed betrayed the survey vessel's true identity. Official U.S. Army Air Forces photograph, Jack Heyn Collection via Daryl Ford.

42. (*opposite top*) Fifteen survivors of *Houston* and one Lost Battalion survivor (named Houston) meet postwar. Many recollections by these men appear in the book. Author's collection via Otto Schwarz.

43. (*opposite bottom*) Track chart from Action Report of USS *Alden* for the Battle of the Java Sea. National Archives and Records Administration, Archives II, College Park, Maryland.

1) Olen Minton 2) ——— 3) Frank Cambell 4) Archie Tern
5) Elmo Bush 6) Walter Winslow 7) Johan Pelascher 8) Al
Neitch 9) Fred Jenkins 10) Tony Maresca 11) O.C.
McManus 12) Lanson Harris 13) Henry Thew 14) Houston
"Slug" Wright (LB) 15) Valdon Roberts 16) Milt Russell

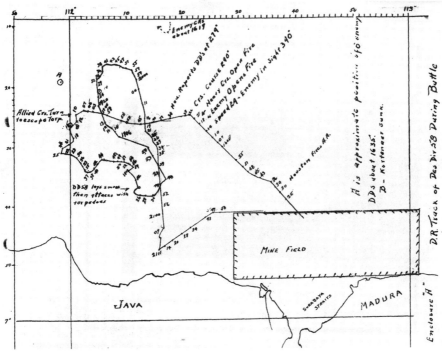

THESE HONORED DEAD

## *Donald Donaldson, Who Died in March Off Java—*

# Mother Thought He'd Come Through

### *—Now, She Says, the Others Will Carry On*

*Young men of Des Moines already have given their lives in the battle for freedom. They leave to their country the task of making certain that they have not died in vain. This is the fourth of a series telling the stories of these men, and the stories of those who continue to fight, even though they have not their sons. Many of these facts could not be printed before because of the necessity for secrecy at the time the deaths were announced.*

**DONALD G. DONALDSON,** 20, fireman first class, navy destroyer Edsall, lost early in March, 1942, near Java.

**NEXT OF KIN:** Mrs. Pansy Burgett, and step-father, Jim Burgett, a car loading company freight checker, of 23 Park ave.; brother, Jack Donaldson, 23, Des Moines; two half-sisters, Mrs. Imogene Martin, Des Moines, and Betty Burgett, 15, and a half-brother, Jimmy, Burgett, 6.

### The Story

Donald Donaldson was born Apr. 2, 1921, in Des Moines. Ever since he was just a youngster, listening to children's adventure programs on the radio, he wanted to join the navy.

He liked to listen to the Jack Armstrong radio serial and dreamed that he, too, was having those exciting adventures among the Moros in the Philippines.

One summer he worked with a circus as a mess tent waiter; he toured the United States and Canada.

### To Great Lakes.

At 16, while a Lincoln High schooler, Donald joined the navy. He had to wait until his

Donald Donaldson's mother, Mrs. Jim Burgett, still cherishes hopes that her son may be [illegible] although his ship has been lost. She is shown with (left to right) Donald's brother, Jack 22; his half-brother, Jimmy, 6; his half-sister, Betty, 15; and his step-father, Mr. Burgett.

stroyer Edsall, would miss the action in the early part of the war.

**Notification came by telegraph on Mar. 20.** The Edsall, a four-stacker world war I destroyer, with 145 officers and men, was lost near Java.

Mrs. Burgett has not reconciled herself to the thought that her son is dead.

"Some days I think he is, and then, on others, I still have hope," she said.

After the Edsall was lost a card and a letter arrived. On the card Donald said, "I am well. A letter follows at first opportunity."

On Apr. 2, Donald's birthday—

the fourth anniversary of his entrance into the navy, another of his letters reached his mother.

It had been mailed as airmail Dec. 18, with 80 cents worth of postage.

"Just a couple of lines," he had written, "to let you know that everything is Okay. I'm well and happy. . . . I've heard numerous rumors to the effect that the Japanese had announced in the states that the Asiatic fleet had been annihilated.

"I can't say yes or no or otherwise, except don't believe anything until it is officially confirmed. . .

"Please don't worry about anything because I am not."

Mrs. Burgett has utmost faith

that the men who are [illegible] on the fight will win in the [illegible] She thinks things will be [illegible] —much worse; but then, [illegible] will be better, too.

### Views on Japanese.

As for the Japanese, she [illegible] "I don't see how they can [illegible] so mean, when they are supposed to be educated. I think [illegible] are just plain heathens. We [illegible] done nothing to cause them to [illegible] what they have done.

"When this is over, something must be done with the Japanese and the Germans so [illegible] this will never happen again. Their countries should be [illegible] ed up some way. . .

"Unless something is done [illegible] will happen every generation."

## TWO IN MELEE ARE IMPROVED

The condition of two men injured in a melee Saturday night at Mike's Tavern, E. Twenty-third

## Carnation Day Nets $575 for Veterans

A total of $575.55 was raised [illegible] the Spanish American War Veterans auxiliary in its annual Carnation day drive Saturday in

## TAXI DRIVER ROBBED OF $8

1618 Des Moines at., was held up and robbed of $8.15 about 3:30

44. The disappearance of Donald G. Donaldson, MM3/c, USS *Edsall*, was but one of countless family tragedies recorded in local newspapers across America throughout the war. Of note here is the reproduction in the news article of Don's final message sent home from the doomed destroyer: "I've heard numerous rumors to the effect that the Japanese had announced that the Asiatic fleet had been annihilated. . . . Don't believe anything until it is officially confirmed." Author's collection via the Donaldson family.

# County Boy, Survivor of Langley, is Home

## William Warnes, Jr., Escapes Hail of Death in Java Sea

**By EDGAR D. RACINE**

Fresh from the hail of death Jap bombers rained on the U.S. Aircraft Tender Langley, and the oil tanker Pecos, William Warnes, Jr., 24, radioman second class aboard the Langley, at home in Macomb county today would reveal only meager details of his thrilling escape from death.

One of less than 200 Langley crew members to survive the twin Jap attacks, Warnes is enjoying a two-week furlough at the farm home of his father at 1545 Davis road, one and one-half miles north of the village of Davis, near Mount Clemens.

Virtually all of the crew escaped death Feb. 27 when 16 Jap bombers destroyed the Langley, Warnes recalled, "but weren't so fortunate two days later when 27 bombers dropped their eggs on the Pecos."

**FLY AT 15,000 FEET**

The Japs sighted the Langley and her escorting destroyers early on the morning of Feb. 27 in the combat zone of the Indian Ocean north of Australia and south of Java, Warnes said. Flying at 15,000 feet, the planes were mere specks against a sky freckled with dark puffs of bursting anti-aircraft shells.

The second Jap salvo virtually destroyed the Langley, Warnes recalled. "I swam with others of the crew a distance of 50 yards to the destroyer. There was nothing to it."

**EVADE BOMBERS**

Attempts to bomb the destroyer proved fruitless and the survivors were soon transferred to the Pecos, Warnes continued, adding "we weren't so fortunate when the Pecos went to the bottom."

Jap bombs smashed virtually all life boats aboard the Pecos, and the survivors fought giant waves with only lifebelts for protection.

"The waves were so high by the time a destroyer picked us up seven hours later that we were swept to a height level with the deck. Three and one-half weeks later we reached Los Angeles after escaping any further bombing."

**LAUDS CREW**

Warnes doesn't remember details of the bombing "because I was busy at my station." He did describe the crew of the destroyer as "the bravest men I've ever known" and wished "they could have had a rest too."

He laughed at the Jap claims that the Langley had been sunk on the first day of the war, on the third day and later at Johnston's Island. "We hadn't even seen a Jap plane before that attack."

**500 KILLED**

Warnes escaped the attacks without a scratch even though 500 fellow crew members were killed in the raids. He notified his parents on April 2 that he was en route home, but "red tape kept me from arriving until two days ago."

Another survivor is his boss, Charles Snay, now visiting his parents, Mr. and Mrs. Frank Snay at 8248 Jackson, Baseline.

Warnes enlisted in the navy only two weeks after he graduated from Romeo High school in June of 1936. He had planned to leave the navy when his second hitch expires in July of this year, but that's out of the question now.

Warnes father, William, Sr., served 14 months overseas during World War 1. His younger brother, Bob, would like to fight for Uncle Sam too, but he failed to pass an Army physical examination.

Warnes won't work on his father's farm while he's home and he hasn't any heart interest in the neighborood. He predicts that much of his time will go to "neighbors who want to know more than I've told you."

## Escapes Death

**WILLIAM WARNES, JR., 24** year old Macomb county sailor, who was aboard both the U. S. S. Langley and the oil tanker Pecos when each went to the bottom of the Java sea under a merciless hail of Jap bombs. He is now on a two-week shore leave visiting his parents at their home, near Meade north of Mount Clemens.

Mr. and Mrs. William Warnes, of Washington, R 1, look for their son, who has arrived in San Francisco and is expected home soon. He had been radio operator on the Langely.

The war is beginning to register in Macomb County homes. Mr. and Mrs. Wm. Warnes, of Davis, are eagerly looking for the return of their son William, Jr., from whom they have received a cable saying he had escaped death, a survivor of the aircraft tender Langly, sunk last week by the Japanese. ■

## Twice Periled Sailor Impatient on Leave

MT. CLEMENS, Mich., April 21.

William Warnes Jr. 23 years old, radioman 2/c who survived the sinkings of the Aircraft Tender, Langley and Oil Tanker, Pecos in the Java sea is anxious to to return to Naval duty to "settle with those Japs". He is on leave

45. Local Michigan newspapers told of Bill Warnes's great good fortune in surviving the sinkings of *Langley* and *Pecos*. Warnes was interviewed several times by the author and proved a wellspring of knowledge regarding the old Asiatic Fleet. Paul St. Pierre, *USS Langley CV-1 AV-3: America's First Aircraft Carrier* (Self-published, 1988), 451, via Henryetta Cokor.

46. Warrant Officer Machinist Floyd E. Butts of *Langley* (shown with his wife, Margaret, in December 1936 after he became a warrant officer) was a pillar of strength in the tender's final ordeal—first in damage control efforts on *Langley* and later helping men in the water as *Pecos* sank. He was not among those rescued by *Whipple*. Butts was a close family friend of *Langley*'s chief machinist mate, Adam H. Mummey, and has been described as a true hero by Mummey's daughter, Henryetta. Author's collection via Henryetta Cokor.

47. Dan Rafalovich, s1/c, had his life changed forever by the flip of a coin when he volunteered as a liaison signalman. Here he is shown in late 1996 at a screening in Los Angeles of Dutch director Niek Koppen's documentary *De slag in de Javazee*. Dan was interviewed in that film and told his story of going to the cruiser *De Ruyter* and surviving the sinking. Eventually he ended up in Japan as a POW during the war. Author's collection via Otto Schwarz / USS *Houston* Survivors Association.

48. Two old USS *Stewart* shipmates: Marion "Elly" Ellsworth and Capt. Wick Alford (author of *Playing for Time*) at the 1997 Asiatic Fleet reunion. Ellsworth evacuated Java on the four-stacker *John D. Ford*, while Alford escaped on board the converted yacht *Isabel*. Author's collection via M. Ellsworth.

49. Admirals Page Smith, William Mack, and E. N. "Butch" Parker at the U.S. Asiatic Fleet 4-Stacker Destroyers Reunion, Norfolk, Virginia, May 1989. Author's collection via M. Ellsworth.

50. Overlooked heroes: Rear Adm. E. Paul
Abernethy, the dogged skipper of *Pecos* who
fought his oiler to the bitter end, and former
crewmember Bob Foley at a mid-1980s navy
reunion in California, not long before Abernethy
passed away. Author's collection via Bob Foley.

Beginning at 2323 hours a total of twelve torpedoes from *Nachi* and *Haguro* leaped into the Java Sea. The two cruisers had pulled well ahead of Doorman's ships and were firing back at a favorable angle.[229] Sentai 5 track charts show the torpedoes launched with an angle of roughly 130° T. Time of impact was calculated at ten to fifteen minutes. From the point to the northwest at which they launched their torpedo spreads, the Japanese cruisers had executed a potentially lethal attack. No matter whether the CSF ships turned away or not, the Japanese firing solutions were favorable for hits.

In the interim, despite having slowed to 28 knots, the Japanese still opened the range slightly. Takagi's cruisers fired a few final 8-inch rounds at the Allied ships to maintain the illusion and conceal their torpedo launches. *Nachi* loosed four salvos at *Houston* over a two-minute period; firing nineteen shells. *Haguro* expended three last salvos of twenty-seven projectiles herself. On *Houston* Lieutenant Commander Galbraith saw no more enemy gunfire himself, but enormous splashes were still landing in proximity to his ship from time to time. These seemed to Galbraith much larger than the shell splashes they had seen earlier. He and a few others on the American cruiser suspected that their ship was being bombed from the air, but of course these splashes were the results of nothing but surface shelling.

By that time Doorman had either seen something suggesting torpedoes or wanted to elude the precise IJN gunnery—there was thought to have been a shell hit on his flagship's quarterdeck in this exchange—and he began a turn to starboard in *De Ruyter*. Waller, too, claimed later that he suspected Doorman had spotted torpedoes, and he turned *Perth* in the wake of the Dutch cruiser. *Houston* then followed suit. Three hours earlier Doorman had executed a long, looping turn after exchanging gunfire with Takagi when *Nachi* and *Haguro* had been surprised taking aboard their floatplanes. It is likely he was repeating such a maneuver. Trailing the formation was the elderly *Java*, but she made the turn as well. It might have been better for her men had she not.

At 2336 hours a colossal blast erupted on *Java*'s stern. From five miles away observers on *Nachi*, who had been anxiously waiting for their torpedoes to arrive, saw "a flash . . . followed by big red flames shooting up."[230] Other Japanese witnesses in Sentai 5 wrote of "a huge explosion that lit up the sky."[231] To the southwest about six kilometers away, men of Tanaka's DesRon 2 also observed explosions in the distance. On the bridge of DesDiv 16's flagship, *Yukikaze*, Capt. Shibuya Shiro and the ship's skipper, Tobita Kenjiro, saw the fire burst with their own eyes. Much closer, a mere nine hundred yards away, men on *Houston* were stunned. "There was one hell of an explosion; the aft part of the ship seemed covered in flames, and explosion followed explosion in rapid succession, with each one sending a tower of flame and debris a hundred feet in the air while the old Java just rocked and bucked."[232]

A single Long Lance had struck the Dutch cruiser aft on the port side.[233] The one-thousand-pound warhead's detonation and subsequent explosions— the torpedo appears to have set off a magazine, possibly *Java*'s hold of depth charges—severed the ship's stern. On the bridge an RNN officer heard the helmsman exclaim, "She's out of control!" as he spun the ship's wheel around with no results. As men came down off the bridge, it was soon apparent that the ship was mortally damaged. With her stern blown off to gun number 7, the cruiser was already beginning to settle with a pronounced list.[234]

*Java* was an old ship, well advanced in years, and her water-tight integrity was poor. Capt. P. B. M. van Staelen and his officers immediately saw that she would not last long. Orders to abandon ship were given, but for the crew this only led to a rush toward life-vest stations amid considerable panic. The ship had lost electrical power, and none of her boats could be lowered. A number of men were physically injured during the scramble for vests; others were thought to have been crushed by heavy life rafts being dropped without warning on top of them in the water after they went overboard. To add to the danger *Java*'s ruptured oil tanks created a heavy sheen of bunker oil around the ship, some of which caught fire, hindering attempts to get away from the doomed ship. The swiftness of her destruction and the absence of a destroyer screen, along with the dense blanket of flaming fuel oil, combined to ensure a highly lethal result. Out of her crew of 528 men there would be fewer than 40 survivors, and several of these men would not last the war in Japanese captivity.[235] Watching in the water as the cruiser upended and slid vertically into the Java Sea, her executive officer, Beckering-Vinkers, led the men in a brave, if forlorn, cheer: "Long live the Queen! Hip-hip hooray, hip-hip hooray, hip-hip hooray!"[236]

When he witnessed the blasts, Captain Shibuya of DesDiv 16 had immediately ordered his division to up speed and make a turn toward the burning enemy. Before they had completed their alteration to the northeast, another explosion and a pillar of fire appeared in the distance. However, *Yukikaze*'s chief engineer soon advised against a quick advance. He told Shibuya that they "must be cautious, as they had only half their fuel remaining" after the high-speed maneuvering during the afternoon engagements.[237] Reluctantly the division commander instructed his ships to reduce speed. On the bridge of another DesDiv 16 destroyer, *Amatsukaze*, Cdr. Hara Tameichi also eyed the distant flames in the darkness, feeling both its personal and historical significance: "This one battle meant more to me than all the hundreds of practice maneuvers in which I had participated."[238]

Much farther away the effects of this final deadly encounter were soon noticed as well by Vice Admiral Takahashi's Main Force—*Ashigara* and *Myōkō* with three destroyers—as they hurried to the scene. After being informed around midnight that contact could be expected within the hour, all five ships were steaming hard, excitement mounting in anticipation of action. A few hours earlier cooks began distributing late-night meals of hard biscuits and *shiruko* (a sweet, red bean-paste soup) to the hungry Japanese sailors, many of whom had been at action stations for almost twenty-four hours. For the five ships of Main Force steaming down from Makassar, the Java Sea was smooth and silent: "The Southern Cross was shining in the night sky as usual. Only the waves created by the bows of swiftly steaming cruisers and destroyers made white gleaming scars on the surface of the dark sea."[239]

The first sighting of battle had come from the destroyer *Ikazuchi*, when Petty Officer Yamaguchi calmly reported seeing a bright flash in the distance off the port bow, followed by a glow in the distant night: "The battle is in full swing. The horizon looks all red." Then the high-pitched voice of the ship's navigator was heard: "Forward 30,000 [meters]. Sea battle is in progress."[240] The men found themselves trembling in anticipation as they retied their sweat-soaked *hachimaki* (traditional headbands). They made awkward jokes and tried to focus on their duties as action appeared imminent, but their excitement was premature. Although all five ships were closed up at battle stations, they would not arrive in time to take part in the fighting. This was in part because they first ran into their own somewhat disordered convoy of forty-plus transports with its escort vessels—including light cruisers *Naka* and *Kinu*, eight destroyers, multiple subchasers, minesweepers, patrol boats, and even an auxiliary gunboat—milling about in some confusion north of the battle. This unanticipated run-in with their own forces hindered their advance just enough; by the time they reached the battle scene (between 0100 and 0130 hours), *Java* had long since disappeared, and both *Perth* and *Houston* had escaped to the west. A few patches of burning oil and a number of dead bodies floating in the sea marked the area. However, they did find one shattered, smoking hulk drifting in the night. This wreck was Rear Adm. Karel Doorman's flagship, *De Ruyter*.

While everyone's attention was directed on the doomed *Java* after she had been torpedoed, they heard and felt yet another terrific thump. Not more than two to four minutes had elapsed since the first explosion on *Java*.[241] Standing at one of *Houston*'s 5-inch guns, Bill Weissinger turned and saw a ball of fire billow up from *De Ruyter* and sweep along the ship, spreading out into an "orange Christmas tree" of flames. To one more eyewitness on the U.S. ship, Lt. Harold Hamlin, the explosion had the crisp abruptness of a cigarette lighter's flame snapping on in the black night.[242] Within moments the sky was illuminated by fireworks as the 40 mm ammunition from the Dutch cruiser's Bofors AA battery cooked off with murderous violence. Soon the entire after half of the ship became robed in flames.

On *De Ruyter's* bridge the tremendous explosion jarred men off their feet, injuring some; others saw instantly that the ship had been seriously damaged. Like *Java* she lost electrical power at once, with her backup systems knocked out. The torpedo—or torpedoes, for it is not certain that she was not hit simultaneously by two Long Lances—struck on her starboard side near the aft engine room, directly above the AA station.[243] Sheets of fire swept up over the AA platform and ignited the 40 mm ready ammo boxes. Sailors and marines jumped overboard to escape the inferno, undoubtedly fearing that such intense fires would cause a catastrophic explosion in one of the cruiser's 5.9-inch gun turrets. Very few men emerged alive from her aft engine room or the reduction gear compartment adjacent to it.

Yet, despite the horrific damage sustained and the fierce conflagration then destroying the ship, *De Ruyter* remained afloat for about three hours before finally sinking. The loss of electrical power made launching her boats impossible, although one sloop was manually lowered. This, however, was done badly, and through either clumsiness or panic one of its falls was cut, which let the heavy wooden hull drop into the water with a murderous smack, injuring more men in the water below if not killing them outright. Through pools of fiery oil the men paddled away from the cruiser as it burned in the night. A number of overcrowded life rafts were eventually lashed together and then tied up behind the lone sloop.

As with the sinking of *Java* the death toll on *De Ruyter* was extremely heavy; some 345 men, including Rear Adm. Karel Doorman, the CSF commander—remembered by Butch Parker as a "fine man"—and the cruiser's skipper, Captain Lacomblé, along with her gunnery officer, Paulus de Gelder, all perished.[244] The USN signal liaison officer, Lt. Otto Kolb, did not survive, but the trio of enlisted men serving with him—Marvin Sholar, Dan Rafalovich, and Jack Penhollow—made it off the ship and into the water successfully. These three sailors would have their own adventures, and not without some controversy. In the end two would be rescued by Allied forces, while one would be captured at sea by the enemy and made a prisoner of war.

Over the next hour or so the Japanese forces made continued efforts to locate any remaining Allied ships without success. Rear Admiral Tanaka's DesRon 2 ships had altered course in the direction of tracers—the gunfire between Sentai 5 and the CSF—seen to the north. Then the second blast (on *De Ruyter*)—what they called "a huge fire column"—unfolded in the distance at 2338 hours, lighting up the night sky. They started off on a course of 45° T. at 2350 hours, altered to 90° ten minutes later, but found nothing.[245] At this time Takagi, who had lost sight of the Allied ships at 2355, radioed both of his subordinate commanders to exercise caution in their pursuit, so as to avoid "misjudging friendly forces and the enemy," noting, "We expect that *Ashigara* and *Myōkō* will join us shortly."[246] Twenty minutes later, at 0015 hours, Takagi prudently launched another floatplane from his flagship *Nachi* to look for the enemy; at 0030 he turned his cruisers to the southwest in search for the enemy ships, "but he could not find them."[247] During the confusion and excitement following the torpedoing of *Java* and *De Ruyter*, as the Japanese lookouts concentrated on the pair of blazing cruisers, both *Perth* and *Houston* vanished into the darkness.

Even with these mournful losses—over eight hundred Dutch sailors lost their lives on the two RNN cruisers alone that moonlit night—the climactic and horrendous weekend for the Allied naval forces was not yet over by any means. After the sinkings of *Kortenaer*, *Electra*, *Jupiter*, *Java*, and *De Ruyter*, with all their casualties, the next night and following day would bring more tragedy and an even greater loss of life for the Allies in the Java Sea.

Up until the morning of Saturday, February 28, at the time he learned more in detail about the losses to Doorman's CSF, Glassford could maintain the facade of wholehearted cooperation. After he got a better understanding of the Java Sea encounters during the afternoon and evening of February 27—on top of the *Langley* disaster—the complexion of the campaign deteriorated quickly. As those scales fell away, the grim determination to resist (despite the odds) became the inescapable recognition that there was *no* realistic hope of victory at all.

At that juncture a tipping point was reached, beyond which both the American and the British commanders refocused their attention on saving as many lives as possible. And although much has been made of Dutch determination to continue fighting to the bitter end—primarily though the self-exculpatory writings later of Helfrich—it is evident that they, too, understood that Java was lost. Most of the naval operations and engagements that took place after February 28 should be seen in the light of a general effort to get ships and personnel away from the East Indies. In truth this motive may be said to have effected almost all the events at sea in one form or another over the ensuing week. However, as the fate of *Langley*'s survivors and the men of *Pecos* and *Edsall* show, the fact that many hundreds of men were still fated to perish was primarily a by-product of last-minute confusion and staggeringly bad luck rather than incompetence.

When reconsidering the debacle that befell on the Allied forces in the Netherlands East Indies in early 1942, it is hard not to feel as if one is viewing a colossal tragedy that *no* Western military commanders might have eluded, let alone overcome. There one must concede that ABDAFLOAT's limited naval forces would have produced no better results in the final analysis, whether commanded by Bill Halsey, Raymond Spruance, Frank Jack Fletcher, James Somerville, or Andrew Cunningham.

# TWELVE

## A Death So Valiant and True

### *The Last Fight of* Perth *and* Houston

After the spectacular destruction of *Java*—bathed in ghastly blue and white flames, her afterdeck shorn off—and with *De Ruyter* last seen spewing pink and red streamers into the night in all directions as explosion after explosion racked Rear Admiral Doorman's flagship, *Perth* and *Houston* made a feint in the direction of the enemy before swinging their bows around and heading west to Batavia.[1] Like so much else in the battle, this, too, was very nearly a disaster, for as they avoided the stricken Dutch ships, they narrowly missed colliding. *Houston*'s clipper bow barely cleared the stern of *Perth*, according to some eyewitnesses by no more than twenty yards. *Houston* had to back down sharply in this maneuver with *Perth* splitting off in the opposite direction. In the darkness and confusion the two ships became separated for a brief period before rejoining. For a number of hours the Allied cruisers were able to elude the enemy and make their way toward Batavia's Tandjong Priok on the western end of Java. *Nachi* and *Haguro* continued north and then northeast as Takagi sensibly judged the protection of the eastern invasion convoy his foremost priority.

*Perth* signaled *Houston* by blinker light, "FOLLOW ME," as the ships formed up. They went at high speed, with *Perth* taking the lead—Waller was the senior officer present afloat—and both ships were "zigzagging without plan."[2] This was in compliance with prebattle instructions to proceed after night action to Tandjong Priok, as well as the final message from Rear Admiral Doorman to *not* stand by for survivors but make for Batavia.[3] When *Perth* changed station and moved ahead of *Houston*, she signaled for a speed of 30 knots. This drew a grim chuckle from officers on *Houston*'s flag bridge, as that ship was already making revolutions for 28 knots. Their laughter would have caught in their throats, however, when *Perth* very nearly smacked into *Houston* (yet again) as the two ships switched positions. Running off *Houston*'s port quarter the light cruiser sped up and began to cross ahead of *Houston* before the larger ship had slowed or altered away and another near collision was avoided. This clumsy ship handling may have been attributable to exhaustion and stress or possibly to a recurrence of *Houston*'s steering difficulties.[4] At around the same time Waller sent an ominous message to CCCF/Collins: "RETURNING TO BATAVIA. DERUYTER AND JAVA BOTH DISABLED BY HEAVY EXPLOSIONS IN POSITION 006 DEGREES SOUTH 112 DEGREES EAST."[5]

In his *Memoires* published after the war, Lieutenant Admiral Helfrich (CZM)—with his proclivity for meddling with the facts extending into postwar accounts—would be unable to refrain from more acerbic remarks about the actions of *Perth* and *Houston* following the torpedoing of the two Dutch cruisers. He stated that they had acted in accordance with neither his instructions nor his wishes. Their lives would have been "sold at a greater cost to the enemy" (or so he argued in language echoing his colonialist heritage) had they remained to contend with Rear Admiral Takagi's ships north of Surabaja after the Battle of the Java Sea.[6] Helfrich, protesting too much to the last, even went so far in his *Memoires* as to express reservations about *Perth* and *Houston*'s subsequent conduct at the Battle of Sunda Strait. To such rather startling charges and more we will return later in the narrative.

On that Saturday, after so much prolonged exertion and stress aboard *Houston*, it was a small mercy that during the trip to Batavia, "the balance of the night was uneventful."[7] The ship seems to have experienced no further steering issues, and control was shifted back to the pilot house, but the electricians were never altogether successful in repairing the selsyn motors in the conning tower wheel, which had caused problems earlier in the evening. Meanwhile, there was a "constant stream of signal traffic [between the two cruisers] mainly to do with alterations to course and speed in order to thwart submarines," wrote a signalman serving on the flag deck of *Perth*.[8] Several submarine sightings were apparently reported by unnerved or bone-weary lookouts, but no attacks materialized. As for the weather, it was mixed, with intermittent rainfall and poor visibility.

Among other communications, an "urgent" message from Vice Admiral Glassford (COMSOUWESPAC) at Bandoeng went to the cruiser that morning (at 0045Z) informing both warships that enemy forces had been spotted some 150 miles south of Tjilatjap. These appeared to be "TWO CR TWO LARGE VESSELS POSSIBLE COURSE WEST X HOUSTON PERTH PROCEED TOGETHER TO RENDEZVOUS LAT FIFTEEN ZERO SOUTH LONG ONE THIRTEEN EAST TO AWAIT ARRIVAL OF ALLIED SMALL SHIPS ENROUTE TJILATJAP TO

A DEATH SO VALIANT AND TRUE

EXMOUTH GULF X AVOID ENEMY FORCE X PASS THIS TO PERTH AS ACTION AS ORIGINATING FROM CCCF."[9]

After the campaign Glassford himself penciled in across the bottom of the message: "Did the Houston get this? Doubtful."[10] This confirms that Glassford's original intention was for the two cruisers to act as a covering force for Allied vessels attempting to escape from Tjilatjap through the enemy-infested waters of the Indian Ocean to the relative sanctuary of western Australia. It also makes clear that he had no desire to engage units of the Imperial Navy again; the emphasis was on saving American and British lives, not squandering more.

At the time, of course, the catastrophe suffered by Rear Admiral Doorman's Combined Striking Force in the Java Sea had set off a blizzard of messages among the various commands: *Which* ships had survived the battle and *how many* of these were still combat-worthy? *Where* were these surviving vessels licking their wounds? The truth is that these questions—to the extent they pertained to Allied offensive capabilities—no longer mattered in the least; the remnants of the variegated fleet had been shattered, scattered, and neutralized as decisively as Humpty Dumpty. Helfrich's complaints notwithstanding, the vessels still afloat were intent on one thing at that stage and only one: escaping the East Indies slaughterhouse.[11] And nothing would ever put the Allies' naval striking force back together again.

It was known early on from messages by Commander Binford (COMDESDIV 58) at Surabaja that *De Ruyter* and *Java* were both badly damaged in an unknown position, probably lost. Later it was discovered that the hospital ship *Op Ten Noort* had been seized, when the Dutch flying boat x-28 flew over the captured vessel on the afternoon of the twenty-eighth as it was being herded to Makassar by two enemy destroyers, both of which had fired on the plane. It was understood that the American submarine s-37 had given about sixty survivors of *De Ruyter* in open boats enough food and water for five days. Also that her sister, s-38, had picked up over fifty survivors from HMS *Electra* and was returning to Surabaja with them on board.[12]

Glassford, moreover, knew that *Stewart* remained capsized in her dry dock, wrecked beyond anything short of a lengthy salvage. A team of men under Lt. Francis Clark had been dispensed to the old four-piper on February 25 to ensure that all sensitive materials were removed, her ECM coding devices destroyed, and her stores and useful ordnance (from small arms to torpedoes) redistributed. The men from *Stewart* were reassigned to *Pecos, Edsall, Pillsbury, Isabel,* and *Parrott,* among other Asiatic Fleet ships. In every instance it was the luck of the draw. One sailor from *Stewart* wanted to be with his friends on *Pillsbury* but drew *Parrott* instead. At the time he felt disappointed, but after the campaign he fully realized the blessings of his fortune. Many men would lose their lives in last-moment sailings from Java when they were ambushed by Japanese forces prowling the Indian Ocean.

In the early morning hours *Perth* sent another short message to CCCF/Collins in Batavia: "ETA BATAVIA WITH US CRUISER HOUSTON 1215 GH 28TH FEBRUARY 50% FUEL STOCKS REMAINING."[13] Yet, even as the ships made their way to the western end of Java that Saturday morning in the aftermath of the Java Sea battle and what they knew was an Allied defeat, the British high command was preparing to withdraw from the doomed island. CCCF/Collins at Batavia sent a message that day declaring that in view of the "redisposition" of his forces, *his* headquarters would close at Batavia on the morning of March 2 and relocate to Tjilatjap in HMS *Anking*. There are no indications in *any* messages from Collins that the Royal Navy was contemplating the reconstitution of a striking force.

What remained of the administrative section of Glassford's command, which had already moved to Tjilatjap—under Capt. Lester Hudson, USN—was likewise struggling to organize the navy's final communications systems aboard ships still in harbor. This appears to have been in clear anticipation of leaving the island, with its shore-based installations. The TBA (high-frequency) and TBK (low-frequency) transmitters in use were diesel-powered, but they and their receivers were in the process of being dismantled; others could not be reassembled due to a lack of blueprints for either the diesels or the transmitters. And not all the available U.S. vessels had the capability to operate as a communications hub. *Pillsbury* could; *Parrott* could not. It was felt that *Isabel*—formerly the alternate flagship of the Asiatic Fleet—might be able to function in that capacity to a limited degree. She is known to have possessed a TAZ, which was a low-power, high/medium-frequency transmitter-receiver that could use a battery pack, hand-cranked power supply, or gasoline-powered generator.[14] All these decisions absorbed time and created delays. Clifford Teer, a radioman second class on *Parrott*, thought that his ship was held at Tjilatjap in order to pick up radio equipment belonging to the Dutch, but it is more likely that he was recalling these various American pieces.[15]

Thus, like the sizable portion of USN staff at HQ in Lembang's Grand Hotel who had already decamped, very few if any Americans had remained in Tandjong Priok on the other side of the island. (At this time Glassford and his small staff were still in Bandoeng.) Their absence that afternoon at Allied HQ in Batavia would prove disastrous in another cascade of intelligence failures.

. . .

What the Dutch were *really* contemplating, though, is almost as much a mystery today as it was seventy years ago. On February 28 at 0947 hours (GH) the commander of Dutch naval forces, Lieutenant Admiral Helfrich (CZM)—who had also moved his HQ from Lembang to Bandoeng—sent the following message to his lone remaining Western Striking Force destroyer, HNLMS *Evertsen*: "LEDENVOND VERTREKKEN VAN PRIOK NAAR T TJILATJAP DOOR STR SOENDA STOP ZOOVEEL MODELIJK GELIGKTIJHIG MET IN NABIJHEID HOUSTON EN PERTH" (Head from Priok for Tjilatjap via Sunda Strait X As much as possible remain vicinity *Houston* and *Perth*). This message went to *Evertsen*—a confused ship if ever there was one—in a timely manner and was copied to COMSOUWESPAC and CCCF.[16] Allegedly the destroyer had become separated from the others in Howden's force in a rainsquall as they exited Sunda Strait bound for Ceylon, and she then went *back* to Batavia.

In this confusion or reluctance she resembles HNLMS *Witte de With* at Surabaja the same Saturday; *that* destroyer was to have accompanied the *Exeter* group but found reason to remain in port, there to be sunk at anchor the following day.[17] (A "mechanical problem" was mentioned in some narratives about *Witte de With*, which may or may not have been a damaged stern, a vibrating shaft, or a nicked propeller, but in view of *Exeter*'s damage, as well as the poor condition of *Pope*, this seems rather unconvincing.) In any event *Evertsen* was not the only vessel in proximity that declined confronting the invading Japanese forces, in spite of Lieutenant Admiral Helfrich's clamoring for a naval Götterdämmerung.[18]

. . .

Around ten that morning *Perth* and *Houston* realized that they had been detected by enemy air patrols and another request for air cover went out from the cruisers.[19] The spotty weather hampered attempts to provide it. A lone Dutch Brewster had been unable to locate the two ships earlier that morning despite searching one hundred kilometers out to sea. Five Hurricanes of 242/605 Squadron were then scrambled from western Java's Tjililitan field and arrived to give high cover.[20] Even so aboard *Houston* Lt. (j.g.) Walter Winslow and others noted that they were rarely alone: enemy float planes hovered on the horizon well beyond gun range, avoiding the RAAF fighters. The implications of this situation produced a distinct uneasiness among the cruiser's deck personnel who had little doubt that the enemy was tracking their movements.

These snoopers in the air were from the light cruiser *Yura*, which had first sighted the two ships, mistaking them for a cruiser and a destroyer. Rear Adm. Kurita Takeo then ordered another pair of scout planes into the air from his section of Sentai 7 (*Kumano* and *Suzuya*) to keep tabs on the enemy vessels. At 1117 these planes spotted the ships steaming west at 28 knots; at 1230 "one Glasgow class and one light cruiser" were sighted stationary some ten miles from Tandjong Priok.[21] Two hours later the plane from *Kumano* reported back to Kurita on the types and number of ships inside and outside the harbor.

With ineffective air cover over Priok at least one C5M (BABS) Type 98 reconnaissance plane from the Imperial Navy's Twenty-Second Kōkusentai had also penetrated Allied airspace and reported the presence of two flying boats and fourteen merchantmen in the harbor.[22] Floatplanes from enemy cruisers offshore were also still making reconnaissance flights over Priok throughout the afternoon to ascertain the whereabouts of remaining Allied warships during the slow, inexorable advance of the Japanese invasion convoy. No evidence exists among primary IJN sources to suggest that the Japanese realized *which* two ships were heading for Tandjong Priok, or once there, that they were preparing to sortie for Sunda Strait.

· · ·

Nor were any alerts regarding these two Allied units provided at that time for the western Java invasion convoy or its screening forces of the Third Escort Group under Rear Adm. Hara Kenzaburo of the Fifth Destroyer Squadron (DesRon 5) in light cruiser *Natori* and the four Mogami-class heavy cruisers of the Seventh Cruiser Squadron (Sentai 7) led by Rear Adm. Kurita Takeo, with his flag in *Kumano*. Already behind schedule, the staffs of these covering forces had become embroiled in an absurd stalemate the previous day, one that threatened the Ranin Butai timetable for invasion again even as the Combined Striking Force under Rear Adm. Karel Doorman was being destroyed piecemeal at the other extremity of the Java Sea.[23] A recapitulation of these movements and internal disputes among the Japanese is necessary to grasp the situation in which *Perth*, *Houston*, and *Evertsen* later found themselves.

Japanese records state that "at 0530 on February 27, the West Java invasion force reached a pre-determined point about 140 miles to the north of Batavia; detached the convoy as planned, and proceeded to the standby point for the landing." But four hours later one of the four floatplanes launched by Kurita spotted one Allied heavy cruiser, two light cruisers, and two destroyers thirty-five miles northwest of Batavia steaming south at 20 knots.[24] This was the so-

A DEATH SO VALIANT AND TRUE

called Western Striking Force; a weak group consisting of *Perth*'s sister ship, the light cruiser HMAS *Hobart* under Capt. Harry Howden, RAN, with the obsolete D-class light cruisers HMS *Danae* and HMS *Dragon*, accompanied by two small World War I–era destroyers, HMS *Tenedos* and HMS *Scout*. Unbeknown to Howden, his frail striking force was only eighty-five miles away from the powerful cruisers and big destroyers of Kurita.

The Japanese were not exactly unaware of these Allied vessels, having kept their reconnaissance eyes on them for several days. But they seem to have lost track of them or perhaps felt that they had left Batavia. Described in air patrol reports by Twenty-Second Kōku at 1005 (JST) on the morning of the twenty-fifth as "one heavy cruiser, two light cruisers and five destroyers in Batavia Harbor," they were undoubtedly (if unnecessarily) causing the Japanese some worries.[25] Fortunately for Howden and his command, the Japanese heavy cruisers were led by an officer never known for his aggressiveness and who displayed none on that or subsequent days.[26] In the end this was a life-saving boon to Howden's ships; all of them managed to escape the East Indies.

*Hobart* was herself especially fortunate as she *should* have been included in the Combined Striking Force then assembling under Rear Admiral Doorman at Surabaja, but she had in fact been delayed in refueling at Tandjong Priok on the twenty-fifth and missed her chance. Tied up to the oil tanker RFA *War Sirdar*, the two vessels were attacked by enemy bombers and narrowly escaped destruction. *War Sirdar* was damaged when "a huge bomb was dropped on [the ship, and] went clean through it," exploding underwater alongside the vessel. Lifted bodily out of the water by the blast, *Hobart* had her "funnels . . . riddled with shrapnel and deck fittings . . . scarred."[27] The cargo was then removed from *War Sirdar* and transferred to RFA *Francol*, and these ships left Batavia on the twenty-seventh in a final convoy along with depot ship HMS *Anking* (which was loaded with Australian troops) and the motor minesweeper MMS 51. They were escorted by HMAS *Yarra* and the Indian sloop HMIS *Jumna*. *Hobart* remained in Priok with the other fighting ships, ordered by CCCF/Collins to make an attempt—of a precisely *de*limited nature—to confront the invaders. The British knew that the Japanese convoy was somewhere approaching Bangka Island, off the eastern coast of Sumatra.

Howden's striking force had departed Tandjong Priok on the evening of the twenty-sixth "and steamed north for about 90 miles until 3 a.m., when [it] reversed course."[28] Thorough searching with the intent to engage was not theirs; they understood their lack of strength. Howden waited until a dawn reconnaissance reported no enemy forces—large or small—south of Bangka. This relieved him of any implicit need to risk an aggressive display. He returned his units to port, although not before being attacked again by air and suffering casualties to his own flagship when it was straddled by bombs from eight land-based Kanoya Kū G4M Type 1 Rikko (BETTY) a few miles from shore.[29] By midafternoon of February 27, the ships of Western Striking Force—a grandiose appellation out of all proportion to their fighting abilities—were back in the oily waters of Priok, where a tangible air of gloom and impending collapse hung over all.

. . .

Yet, ironically, the weakness of Howden's group during its perfunctory sweep off Batavia on the twenty-seventh was not recognized by the Japanese, and this "powerful enemy surface force" of five cruisers and destroyers was sufficient to alarm IJN commanders on the scene. Even though an instance of not knowing what the enemy was *actually* capable of doing but rather what he *appeared* to be capable of doing, the Japanese reacted prudently. Rear Admiral Hara on *Natori*, mindful of the fiasco off Balikpapan in January, chose to reverse his convoy. He then took his light cruiser, along with DesDiv 11 (*Fubuki, Shirayuki, Hatsuyuki*) and one section of DesDiv 12 (*Murakumo, Shirakumo*), and turned to interpose these vessels between the enemy warships and the transports. At the same time he alerted Rear Adm. Kurita Takeo in *Kumano* and the Seventh Cruiser Division (Sentai 7) of this development—which along with DesDiv 19 (*Isonami, Uranami,* and *Shikinami*) were some thirty miles to the south of his group—and "requested" that Kurita move his big cruisers down to destroy the Allied force.

This "request" was not only disregarded by Rear Admiral Kurita—with whom no formal chain of command existed, since CruDiv 7 had been detached from Malaya Butai and tacked on as an afterthought to the NEI operation the previous afternoon—but never even acknowledged. As Kurita's ships steamed away to the north, as if avoiding action, he simply had *Mikuma* and *Mogami* (the Second Section of CruDiv 7) launch another pair of floatplanes to maintain visual contact with the Allied ships.[30] To say that such extraordinary behavior led to consternation on the bridge of *Natori* would be an understatement. It is recorded that the restless Hara, a salty officer of the type called *kurumahiki*—that is, a tough and earthy *rikisha*-puller—"was walking around on the bridge with the veins standing out on his forehead, and grinding his teeth," as this unsettling situation unfolded.[31]

His chief of staff, Cdr. Yoshikawa Shukichi (Fifty-First *ki*), and the skipper of *Natori*, Capt. Sasaki Seigo (Forty-Fifth *ki*), also appear to have harbored feelings of resentment against CruDiv 7, which was considered an elite unit field-ing four of the navy's most modern and powerful cruisers. By the same token it was undeniably felt that CruDiv 7 viewed Rear Admiral Hara as presumptu-ous, and they may have had "a tendency to belittle the Commander of a unit [DesRon 5] temporarily and hurriedly organized in war time with an aged light cruiser and 'surplus' destroyer divisions."[32]

In reality, though, the cautious Kurita had no desire to bring his cruisers down into the waters near Sunda Strait or close to the harbor of Batavia, fear-ing these to be both a submarine stalking area and mined. He stated, "We shall operate near the Convoy. Should the enemy move up to the north, then we would exterminate it."[33] At about this time (0948 hours) he had received yet another contact report from *Kumano*'s floatplane, and the news it brought was not heartening, stating, "[The ship] in the van is a very large vessel, and there are fears that she is a BB. Although we confirmed at a distance of 4,000 meters, it is still questionable."[34] Discretion being the better part of valor, and with the situation hardly clarified, Kurita kept his ships headed north, much to the dismay of Rear Admiral Hara and staff aboard *Natori*. At this juncture Hara decided to reverse his convoy, reconfigure the screen, and begin assem-bling his offensive surface units to deal with what he perceived as an immedi-ate threat, with or without the aid of Kurita and Sentai 7.

For his part Kurita had chosen to put more floatplanes from his cruisers in the air to keep tabs on Howden's "fleet." Two Type O (JAKE) floatplanes were launched by the second section of Sentai 7, *Mikuma* and *Mogami*, and airborne by 1024 hours; within less than an hour they were sending reports back to Kurita. Their identification abilities were far better; they accurately described the enemy's strength as "one Glasgow class, two Danae class, and two DDS" at 1115 hours. Twelve minutes later *Mogami*'s plane reported that the Allied fleet was "without a BB and CV," news that should have relieved both Kurita and Hara.[35] The Allies had no such respite; a solitary Hudson flying in bad weather that day located at least part of the invasion force as it turned back to the north-east, approximately fifty miles from Bangka Island. This sighting was consid-ered inconclusive, however, and the precise whereabouts or composition of the western invasion fleet remained uncertain.

· · ·

Howden's anemic force made a final, rather halfhearted search north of Bata-via in the early hours of the twenty-eighth. With the Dutch destroyer *Evertsen* now included, they went out briefly before turning and making for Sunda Strait at a brisk 24 knots, which was the best speed the older ships could manage. Once through the strait, they steamed to Padang, Sumatra, to fuel and evacuate troops and refugees; *Hobart* took aboard 512 persons herself. They then proceeded to Trincomalee.[36] All, that is, except *Evertsen*. Lt. Cdr. W. M. DeVries's wayward little DD had become separated from the others in a rainsquall "and was not seen after about 4 a.m. on the 28th." She had, in fact, eventually turned back for Tandjong Priok, arrived sometime before *Perth* and *Houston*, and in so doing ensured her crew a very different fate.[37]

. . .

Although the Japanese operational plans had anticipated possible delays in "H" and "L" days—the coded landing days for the Sixteenth Army's Second Division and Shoji Detachment on the island's western end at Merak and Bantam, and for the eastern force's Forty-Eighth Division near Kragan respectively— weeks of screening the transports while eluding Allied submarines and air patrols had left the navy's commanders understandably on edge. Their army counterparts seem to have been less concerned, and although a number of veterans later recalled the convoy's progress southward as being uneventful, the timetable for invasion had been moved up with the unexpectedly rapid fall of Singapore on February 15.

Despite enjoying substantial advantages in the air—Japanese records after the war claimed that they allocated roughly 180 army planes plus another 240 navy machines to the overall operation to capture Java—several of the commanders on the scene remained tense. Intelligence had (correctly) indicated that Java's ground forces were weak, with not more than about thirteen infantry battalions believed involved—and these unlikely to fight very well—but the ongoing problems on Luzon as well as the complications in seizing Palembang's oilfields were in the forefront of many Japanese minds.[38] And as always, behind their operations the twin concerns of time and fuel consumption exerted relentless pressure of their own. Understandably, internecine bickering could not be permitted to continue.

By midafternoon on the twenty-seventh, Yamamoto's Combined Fleet headquarters had heard enough of the squabbling between Hara and Kurita. "Having seen the telegrams going back and forth between Sentai 7 and DesRon 5 since that morning, the fleet HQs became unable to stand it any longer and issued the instructions . . ." These originated from Rear Adm. Ugaki Matome, Adm. Yamamoto Isoroku's chief of staff, and read: "Considering the enemy situation in the Batavia area, this HQs finds it appropriate that Commander of

A DEATH SO VALIANT AND TRUE

the 7th Sentai should take unified control over the various units in that area." Later that evening as the Japanese continued to dither over how best to neutralize Howden's deceptive striking force, Vice Adm. Kondō Nobutake (commander of Nam'po Butai) and Vice Adm. Takahashi Ibō (commander of Ranin Butai) issued further orders by telegram at 1850 hours specifying that (1) Kurita's Sentai 7 and Ryūjō's small force—the Fourth Air Flotilla, including her destroyers—would "be incorporated into the invasion forces," and (2) that "with regard to the operation" Rear Adm. Kurita Takeo would assume overall command of the Batavia invasion forces himself. Kurita then notified Lieutenant General Imamura of the Sixteenth Army of plans to delay the landings by one day, and to this he received a reply of no objection. Kurita did not wish to postpone operations beyond this single day primarily due to fuel considerations.[39] His cruisers and destroyers would have to withdraw from their covering positions off the landing zones to replenish fuel oil from tankers that could not approach the area—or in some cases they might even have to return all the way to the port of Bandjermasin on Borneo's southern coast.

. . .

After some delay in accessing local harbor pilots and the tricky maneuverings required in getting through the Dutch minefields and various sunken hulks, *Perth* and *Houston* reached Batavia's port of Tandjong Priok around 1330 hours. An hour or so later they were tied up at dockside and began efforts to fuel. Native yard workers at the harbor had disappeared by this time, having fled in terror after Japanese bombs were dropped three days previously. But it seems that preparations for abandoning the port had already begun. Few warships of any size remained; a few auxiliary patrol vessels and motor launches were there, along with the restive Dutch destroyer *Evertsen*.

A sailor aboard *Perth* later wrote, "The place was strangely hushed and deserted. The exhausted ship's company were [*sic*] infinitely depressed by the lack of spirit there."[40] Masts and upper works of sunken vessels studded the harbor's oily waters, over which "black smoke, drifting across the harbor, touched everything with the suggestion of impending disaster."[41] This grimy pall of smoke, noted by a number of *Perth* and *Houston* survivors, came from oil storage tanks bombed several days earlier that continued to smolder near the shattered wharves. And, to be fair, it was also true that Tandjong Priok's fueling facilities had been damaged by recent bombings just as at Surabaja. In conjunction with an almost complete absence of local labor this would have contributed to the replenishment problems facing the two ships that afternoon.

Regarding fuel the Dutch remained intractable to the last, refusing to move any of the abundant fuel oil (tens of thousands of tons) available at Surabaja to either Batavia or Tjilatjap. Now, in the crunch, it appeared they wanted to save as much fuel as possible for their own vessels. At Priok *Houston*'s chief engineer, Lt. Cdr. "Shorty" Gingras, and his assistant engineering officer, Lt. Bob Fulton, had both gone ashore to secure fuel but found disorder and lack of cooperation from the local Dutch authorities in the harbor office. No one seemed to know what was going on, or if so willing to divulge any information to their allies. Neither the commander of the Dutch naval air station at Priok nor the port captain would say much beyond the fact that they were awaiting word from their superiors to destroy both the air base, port facilities, and all shipping that remained in the harbor.[42] In the end, after more haggling, *Houston* got some fifty tons, a negligible amount.[43]

The relative freedom from enemy action during the first half of the twenty-eighth allowed the physically debilitated men of *Houston* a chance to recover a little strength after their superhuman efforts of the previous afternoon and evening. Not only had the men in the engineering spaces suffered from the tremendous heat and poor air-circulation, but also the old ship's ventilation system for her shell decks, powder circles, powder pockets, transfer rooms, handling rooms, and magazines had proved utterly inadequate. In fact *every man* in the shell deck of turret 1 had passed out from exhaustion at one time or another. Replacements for these men came from the forward repair party during the battle. Upward of six dozen men in all were treated for heat prostration, according to one officer. An accumulation of water, perspiration, and urine one inch deep in both powder circles of the forward turrets made not merely the footing treacherous but wetted trays and contributed as well to dampened powder.

Yet, given the ship's age and material condition, the men and machinery of *Houston*'s main battery had performed splendidly. Even with its electrical malfunctions, turret 1 under Lieutenant (j.g.) Hamlin had fired ninety-seven salvos, with nine misfires; turret 2 under Ensign Smith had gotten off one hundred salvos, with four misfires.[44] Wear on the 8-inch rifles had been extreme, though—with "liner creep" as much as one inch being recorded—and the barrels needed to be replaced soon. At least one survivor later recalled that ship-fitters addressed the liner creep problem that afternoon at Tandjong Priok by cutting off the protruding steel.

At the same time *Houston*'s men—with the exception of 5-inch gun crews and engineering watches—continued, in spite of their fatigue, to work transferring about three hundred 8-inch projectiles and upward of eight hundred service charges by hand from the previously flooded aft magazines to the forward magazines.[45] This was an "all hands" process on which the ship's very existence might depend, and every sailor knew it. The heavy (260-pound) projectiles were put into jerry-rigged slings made of canvas and wood, carried by parties of four men each, then attached to dollies and manhandled with great physical effort almost the full length of the ship. Negotiating passageways and ladders and making turns around tight corners made this task exceptionally difficult. Sometimes more than four sailors were needed to maneuver one projectile in such circumstances, and it was always dangerous work. However, human flesh, blood, and bone are never cheaper than in wartime.

A stocky Brooklyn native, Seaman Second Class James T. Bergen, whose battle station was below deck supplying ammunition to the cruiser's eight 5-inch/25 cal. AA guns—which, among other things, involved taking the protective safety covering off the heads of the shells with a pair of pliers and then setting the timing mechanism before passing them to one of the hoists—was caught up in this process like many others. Unluckily, while helping muscle an 8-inch projectile up a two-and-a-half-foot-wide ladder to the main deck, one of the wood supports in the sling snapped and Bergen's little finger on his left hand took the blow. Caught between the deadweight of the shell and the steel ladder, his hand was "squashed" and the finger broken like a twig.

In the ship's compact little infirmary, Houston's chief medical officer, Cdr. William "Doc" Epstein, didn't waste much time as he prepared to remove the finger by giving Bergen an injection of Novocain. When he was questioned by his assistant, Pharmacist Mate 2/c Raymond Day, if the amputation was *really* necessary, Epstein only muttered, "Can't save it." Then he popped the mangled finger off and sewed up the wound. As the dazed but dutiful sailor started to return to his shell-carrying detail, the doctor told him to get to bed. Remarkably, James Bergen's pinky finger was the sole casualty aboard Houston in the lengthy Battle of the Java Sea. The remainder of that afternoon Bergen, thoroughly exhausted like so many others, fell into a deep sleep in one of the dozen beds in Houston's sick bay. Later he would receive a terrifying wake-up call. But while he slept the relocation of Houston's main and secondary battery ammunition continued. And rows of stacked ammo were still in place in the forward mess hall when the ship began her last engagement a few hours later.

After their tireless work helping the 5-inch ammunition supply party in all previous actions, the engineering auxiliary crew also worked night and day at this spine-snapping task.[46] As Houston's gunnery officer, Cdr. Arthur Maher, later wrote, "Although this ammunition had been subjected to flooding in connection with the casualty to Turret III, it was necessary to replenish the depleted magazines of the forward turrets in order to be prepared for future contacts with enemy forces." According to Walter Winslow this occupied no less than twenty-two out of the last twenty-four hours of the ship's life, and most survivors later recalled the tremendous efforts made by worn-out sailors who understood only too well the necessity for this backbreaking work. Maher's report verified that "a small amount of this ammunition was yet to be transferred when work had to be stopped at about 1730."[47] The two forward turrets then had approximately three hundred rounds between them, or enough for some fifty salvos, as the ship prepared to weigh anchor and get under way from Tandjong Priok.

As Seaman Bergen slept, the "extremely conscientious" Doc Epstein continued with his usual attentiveness and dedication.[48] And as noted, at least seventy men needed some type of treatment for heat exhaustion. A condition 3 watch was set in port, with one-quarter of the guns manned. This allowed a fair number of the off-duty men to get a shower, change of clothes, and some well-deserved rest.

Much the same occurred aboard HMAS *Perth* on the way to Batavia. Ready ammunition lockers were refilled, and after many grueling hours what passed for a decent meal was served as well. Some off-duty personnel were given the chance to sleep for the first time in days. The light cruiser's men were able to determine that she had about 55 percent of her main battery ammunition left, the ship having expended upward of 1,400 rounds of 6-inch ammunition in its off-and-on engagements with the enemy on Friday.

Upon reaching Tandjong Priok, where she was met at the dock by Commodore Collins (CCCF), the Australian cruiser—like *Houston*—found little fuel and ammo. It is recorded that she received about three hundred tons of oil (which brought her to roughly one-half capacity) and some additional 4-inch rounds.[49] Her officers allowed her crew to set a minimal watch, utilizing "only those absolutely necessary," while many of the rest, who were "dirty, hungry, and tired, hardly knew what to do with themselves . . . just dropped where they were and sank into a bottomless sleep."[50] Others were able to get a shower and cleaned up, but *all* recognized that they were far from real security; they knew the enemy was near and that his forces were moving in great strength toward Java.

Plentiful nonessential items for ABDA had been abandoned throughout port warehouses, many of them filled to capacity and more by vessels that were diverted from Singapore. Due to enemy air attacks base organization was almost nonexistent. As the captain of HMS *Exeter* had noted after visiting the port several times earlier in the month, "Tandjong Priok [had been] under almost continuous air attacks which also upset any organization for distributing the supplies. Docks, warehouses, and roads were filled to overflowing with equipment of every kind, and there it seemed to stay."[51] It was believed that British demolition teams were preparing to destroy these shore installations. The Tommy sappers cheerfully told *Perth's* men to help themselves to whatever remained in the soon-to-be-blown canteen store. The canny Australians knew better than to look a gift horse in the mouth. They had already helped themselves at Singapore and had retained their expropriation skills.

As one survivor later artfully phrased it: "Opportunity was taken to embark stores which were marked Victualling Officer, Singapore."[52] Tens of thousands of Woodbine cigarettes were "liberated" by *Perth's* men along with nonregulation cases of liquor, but the more significant finds in bomb-damaged or abandoned godowns near the wharves were stacks of small life rafts—wood and copper floats—intended for East Indian faithful traveling to Mecca aboard regional transports, plus a pair of wheeled fire-fighting pumps ready for use. With consummate foresight two dozen rafts were taken aboard by Commander Martin, *Perth's* executive officer, in addition to the fire tenders. From the vantage point of *Houston* the sailors working along the deck of *Perth* resembled nothing so much as a line of industrious white-clad ants laboring double-time to bring aboard and stow these supplies.

On *Houston* the ship's interior was not a comforting sight. The heavy and prolonged main-battery firing on extreme aft bearings during the Java Sea actions had reduced officers' country, located below and just aft of the forward turrets, to a shambles of shattered glass, dislodged soundproofing, and overturned furniture. Elsewhere clothing and storage lockers were emptied of their contents, clocks broken, and fans spun on their cords as they revolved aimlessly. The two hundred or so 8-inch salvos fired the previous day and night had indeed put the cruiser's light construction through the mill. In the words of another survivor, the ship then seemed to be "falling apart."[53]

In truth the structure of *Houston* had never fully recovered from the bone-rattling near misses of the February 4 bombing in the Flores Sea. A number of hull plates had been sprung, with a multitude of small leaks developing; by late February engineering personnel had noticed from time to time a suspicious noise in one of the shafts. It was nothing too alarming, but it was enough to get the attention of Lieutenant Fulton and some of his men.[54] As things stood, available yard facilities and time were both nonexistent anyway, so there was little point in worrying about it. The men still believed they were about to escape the East Indies and that a refit at Pearl Harbor or on the West Coast would naturally follow.

But such hopeful thinking was offset by distasteful realities. Survivors recalled that following the bombing on February 4, the smell of death had never left the ship's aft area. No matter how hard they tried steam cleaning and hosing out compartments, the stench of scorched and mangled human beings would *not* go away. Pfc. Hampton Cray of the Marines remembered that "the horrible odor of burnt human flesh [and] men roasted alive" stayed on the ship until she sank.[55] Other survivors remembered making gruesome discoveries of body parts wedged in various fittings and even obstructing machinery within the ship for days afterward.

• • •

Meanwhile, Capt. Albert H. Rooks went ashore with "Hec" Waller to get some semblance of a clear picture of the situation regarding intelligence and any new operational orders. It must be mentioned that the British naval headquarters there were in the process of being closed; Collins and his staff were to move south to Tjilatjap over the next couple of days. There seems little doubt that at just this fatal juncture the "fog of war" had moved ashore. Rooks and Waller were taken to the British Naval Liaison Office in Batavia, where they were told recent air reconnaissance of the Sunda Strait area showed it free of enemy activity.[56] Enemy convoys and escorting vessels had been spotted by at least one lone patrol plane, but they were believed to be to the northeast and moving eastward of Tandjong Priok, thus posing no immediate threat to the cruisers' projected course. On the basis of this late-afternoon report—which was wholly and disastrously inaccurate as it turned out—the captains felt they might yet escape the Batavian bottleneck.

But in an even more stunning irony (if true), another, more up-to-date contact report (said to have been from about 1700 hours) contained far different information, and more accurate information at that. This aerial reconnaissance (which appears to have been two inadvertent sightings from an RAAF Blenheim on a bombing mission against Palembang) reported some fifty troopships and transports with screening vessels, including what appeared to be an aircraft carrier, about 150 kilometers north of St. Nicholas Point at the entrance to Sunda Strait and moving south at a speed that would have them arriving around 2200 hours. However—and preposterously—neither Hec Waller nor Albert Rooks were made aware of this report. It remained unprocessed and useless at Batavia in the Dutch headquarters of Maj. Gen. Wijbrandus Schilling, the commander of First KNIL Infantry Division. As fateful irony would have it, Schilling's HQ was in the very same building as the British Naval Liaison Office. Schilling later (in March 1944, as a POW) admitted that he had this information at hand but—as fantastic as it seems—knew *nothing* of the captains' whereabouts or even of the ships' presence in Tandjong Priok.

What remained of the Java Air Command's reconnaissance force had in fact made several sightings of the western invasion fleet and fully expected a landing somewhere near Bantam that night or the next day. Although only about half a dozen Dutch flying boats were still serviceable for recon flights, until midday on February 28, the Japanese convoy had not been located. Then elements of the convoy and its screening force were spotted from a Catalina of the Dutch Naval Air Force (MLD), while the crews of three British Blenheim bombers flying to attack Palembang—an attack that never materialized due to bad weather conditions over the target—saw a much larger convoy as they flew west to Sumatra as well as on their return flight. More sightings were reported during the course of the afternoon. However, in the general chaos of an imploding Allied command, none of these reports made clear to Waller and Rooks the proximity or estimated point of arrival of the Japanese fleet.[57]

. . .

At the silent, grim harbor Lt. Harlan G. Kirkpatrick had remained aboard *Houston*. Without the captain aboard, the weary lookouts on *Houston* appear to have been less vigilant than they should have been, even in a condition 3 watch. Sometime later in the afternoon a solitary biplane glided in from seaward at low speed and, before anyone realized it was an enemy intruder, abruptly pounced on the ships. It "dropped a few light bombs in the vicinity of the *Evertsen*, doing no damage, but causing much confusion in the harbor."[58] *Evertsen* responded with AA fire as did the local shore batteries. After releasing a few harmless bursts as a parting gesture to *Perth*, which had also opened fire belatedly, it flew away unscathed, but the men were further unnerved by this failure to remain alert.

Most had been told to expect Tommy Payne's SOC, inbound from Surabaja, and had relaxed their guard as the Japanese biplane from one of the cruisers—which seems to have been a Mitsubishi F1M2 Type O (later codenamed PETE)—approached.[59] Accordingly, when Payne's floatplane arrived some time later, he was greeted by angry and accurate antiaircraft fire from the nervous Dutch shore battery and British 40 mm Bofors guns. This forced him to turn back and land well beyond the breakwater, where his identity was confirmed by a Dutch patrol boat that kept its machine gun trained on his weary plane. As Quentin

Madson of *Houston* later recorded in his diary: "We were expecting one of our planes to return from a reconnaissance flight and we saw what it was apparently, but the *Perth* opened fire. As the plane sheered [*sic*] off we could see the red spots under her wings. They have a plane copied exactly from our S.O.C. Our plane returned about 15 minutes later but landed in the middle of the bay and taxied alongside to be picked up."[60] This may be considered yet one more example of the deplorable IFF (identification friend or foe) problems that dogged the Allies throughout the entire ABDA campaign.

To make IFF matters even more ironic, before departing Lieutenant Kirkpatrick had visited that very evening with a pair of RAF pilots who had come aboard the ship. He chatted with the two men in *Houston*'s wardroom. They told him they had been out over Sunda Strait and seen nothing but two "British cruisers" that afternoon, and these ships had nervously fired on them.[61] This hitherto unrecorded encounter speaks ill yet again of Allied identification abilities. Those cruisers assumed to be British were in fact the ships of Kurita's Seventh Sentai, whose combat reports stated that at 1720 hours [1550 USN time], "[We] drove away enemy flying boat that was tracking us. It headed for the Patrol Force."[62] Here, too, the reconnaissance skills of the Allied forces, whether through incompetence or exhaustion, were conspiring to produce a tragedy.

After his rude welcome off Tandjong Priok, Lt. Tom Payne maneuvered the SOC—its wings holed by several shells—alongside the cruiser at sunset and was hoisted aboard, muttering several angry remarks. Captain Rooks then returned to the ship, and Payne reported having seen at least one cruiser and a merchant vessel to the east of Batavia, the former not more than seventy-five miles distant. He also recognized that the snooping Japanese intruder was probably a cruiser floatplane and *that* meant an enemy warship was in some proximity to the two surviving cruisers. Rooks appears to have disregarded this information, relying instead on Dutch air recon patrol reports, augmented by more than a little of his own wishful thinking.

*Perth*'s black gang wisely kept steam up in anticipation of a prompt departure. On the other hand, after much waiting *Houston* received considerably less oil than her counterpart once her men commandeered fuel lines on their own initiative. These hoses were then hurriedly snaked all over the cruiser's decks, yet even this essential task was torturous: at one point a fuel line burst, hemorrhaging more precious bunker oil into the gunky waters of the harbor.

Without doubt the aura of impending doom hanging over Priok was also a factor. ABDA had already shown itself to consist of allies who usually preferred to "let the other guy do it."[63] In view of these difficulties it is all the more bitterly ironic that the last Dutch naval vessel of any useful size at Tandjong Priok, the destroyer *Evertsen*—one of the vessels for which the tightfisted Dutch were ostensibly husbanding that valuable black gold—should have found a way to avoid going to sea in the company of the two bigger warships that evening. In any case the men of *Houston* believed—or perhaps *hoped*—that more fuel was available in Tjilatjap. But there was never any question of reconstituting a naval fighting force from Batavia's Tandjong Priok. *Sauve qui peut* was again the order of the day for all concerned.

· · ·

On *Houston* some of the officers may have also reflected on the fate of their Dutch naval compatriots under Rear Adm. Karel Doorman, that big, genial sailor of whom it was said: "There was nothing devious or subtle about him. Everyone liked him."[64] Now Doorman was gone, along with over eight hundred Royal Netherlands Navy officers and sailors, their sacrifice rendered all the more tragic by its futility. The Japanese landings were hampered at most by a single day; their losses had been minimal. The East Indies campaign would still conclude well ahead of schedule with the swift capitulation of Allied ground and air forces on Java a mere eight days later, after what must be considered a feeble, token resistance.

Subsequently Lt. Harlan Kirkpatrick *did* recall having heard scuttlebutt that the cruiser was to be sent to Tjilatjap "to assist in evacuations" there.[65] Another sailor assigned to the 5-inch guns, Olen Minton, s1/c, said that *he* had heard rumors that the ship was to go to "Flapjack" (the nickname for Tjilatjap) to pick up American troops and get them off Java.[66] These rumors underscore the fact that conflicting command arrangements and priorities still existed among the remnants of ABDA. Surviving messages *do* show that Glassford was preoccupied with getting adequate escorts to screen Allied ships departing from Tjilatjap.[67] However, Kirkpatrick later remarked that he did not believe *Houston* could have made it safely to Australia even if she had transited Sunda Strait successfully.[68] In this skepticism he was neither unreasonable nor alone.

A number of the other veterans were equally apprehensive: Chief Carpenter "Chips" Biechlin, his mood perhaps darkened by the somber burial duties he had already been compelled to face, bet Chief Warrant Officer Gillet that the ship would *never* make Australia. Gillet took the wager. Two or three days earlier, Aviation Ordnance Mechanic Elmo Bush had offered to bet another sailor on the ship one hundred dollars that *Houston* would not escape Surabaja. Upon arriving at Tandjong Priok he was relieved that the man had refused his offer.

Elsewhere groups of sailors congregated and talked over the previous days' events, while others hoped to get ashore. "Tang Juan Priok! What a heck of a name for a town," recalled Clarence Nixon Day, s1/c. "Typical of small Oriental towns . . . beautiful . . . only a shame we [couldn't] enjoy it."[69] Day was right about that; no one was getting off the ship to make liberty on February 28. However, in general the crew's morale, considering what the men had been put through, remained positive. Many sailors, knowing far less than the officers, were optimistic; they believed they had weathered the worst already and that they still stood a fair chance to get out of Java alive.[70]

Sailors such as Charley Davis, a first-class machinist mate in the forward engine room, began to imagine they might yet escape the Java trap. Davis remembered that there had been a feeling of "optimism" among some of the men—if not among the officers—in the short interim at Tandjong Priok. As throughout history the thoughts of young men who have narrowly eluded death are swiftly turned by biological drives to procreation. Davis and his two close blackgang friends, John Stanczak, mm2/c, and Albert Waldschmidt Jr., mm2/c, were no different. They dreamed of young women they had known or hoped yet to know. For his part Davis was just "exuberant" about the prospects for getting away to Australia and then on to the States.[71]

Yet other men exhibited more serious effects from the prolonged stress of recent weeks. Warrant Officer (Machinist) E. V. May—in charge of the midship (also called number 3) damage control party—was said to have behaved in a markedly eccentric manner. One surviving officer interviewed after the war would describe the big, carrot-headed chief, who was called the Red Torpedo by his shipmates, as "suffering from shell shock" at the time.[72] Another junior officer used less polite language in postwar interviews to describe May's behavior.

May himself later gave a different view of things, as one might expect, reminding an interviewer almost two decades later that his duties *had* in fact changed after the February 4 bombing attacks. He had been attempting to "acclimate" himself to his new responsibilities in a new station on the ship—the upper deck—and readily admitted that his actions may have appeared unusual. A second-class fireman named John Ferguson reiterated this, having heard tales of May not being at his old station but rather topside. Ferguson was not so critical of May's behavior, though, feeling it had an understandable basis.

May was frank in acknowledging the impact of losing several close friends on February 4, including Chief Warrant Officer Joseph Bienert, with whom he had shared a cabin for three years aboard *Houston*. May also nursed the old superstition of sailors who felt that it was unlucky to remain aboard any one ship for too long; he had served on *Houston* for several years then, as had Bienert. And as if these factors weren't enough, in the Battle of the Java Sea a dud 8-inch shell from one of the Japanese heavy cruisers that struck *Houston*'s foc's'le had actually penetrated May's sleeping berth and gone through his pillow as through a bull's eye. Any serviceman could be forgiven for being disconcerted by such a piercing reminder of the unpredictable yet ubiquitous proximity of death in wartime.[73] In this it must in fairness be said that he was not alone.

The outlook of *Houston*'s skipper, Capt. Albert H. Rooks, as befitting a leader, was not as dour. In his final conversation by phone with Glassford, we know his mood was elevated. (Glassford noted the captain's upbeat frame of mind when he wrote to Rooks's widow, Edith, some weeks later.) Glassford said Rooks sounded pleased that he had engaged and probably damaged the enemy, that the men fought the ship well, and that they had survived without personnel casualties.[74] Another officer who served under Rooks later wrote: "In action he . . . proved imperturbable; cold as ice, solid as a rock."[75] The former faculty aide to Adm. Thomas Hart at the Naval Academy—and one who had been "good at that" as Hart noted—had proved himself to be proficient "as a hairy-chested sailor."[76] Under the circumstances one could ask no more of Albert Rooks.

While Waller and Rooks sought information that afternoon, the following signal was made to *Perth* and repeated to both *Houston* and *Evertsen* from CCCF/Collins (and copied to CZM/Helfrich) at 1747/GH hours: "TAKE HOUSTON AND EVERTSEN UNDER YOUR ORDERS AND PROCEED IN COMPANY TO TJILATJAP LEAVING PRIOK AS SOON AS CONVENIENT AFTER DARK."[77] This order suggests that by that point the British and the American naval commanders were going to call the shots for their own forces. A number of air commanders, whose actions would have controversial ramifications later, had also made this decision.[78]

On the basis of this message the subsequent report by Waller of the Battle of the Java Sea and its aftermath must be considered. It is also recorded that when Waller returned to the ship at Priok, he chanced to meet Cdr. P. O. L. "Polo" Owen. Owen was an officer destined for HMAS *Hobart* (sister to HMAS *Perth*) who would never reach that cruiser. He described the port as looking "like a nautical cemetery" when he wrote of this meeting some thirty years after: "[Waller] had prepared his report of the Battle, written a letter to his wife, insisted I should also send a letter to my wife and handed them to the Staff Officer who departed with them all in a hurry for Batavia. 'Polo, we're sailing for

Tjilatjap. Are you coming with us or going ashore to become a prisoner of the Japs?' 'I'm coming with you.' I never saw him again."[79]

A commander of a warship is responsible for the morale of his crew, and another indication of Capt. Albert H. Rooks's positive outlook could be found in the repair parties at work during the few hours the cruiser spent at Tandjong Priok on February 28. One of the three dud Japanese cruiser shells that struck *Houston* had penetrated her forecastle deck "with high angle of fall" (due to the extreme range at which it hit), leaving a neat eight-inch diameter entry hole "about six feet to port of the centerline at Frame 14 [that] passed out about three feet below second deck at Frame 15."[80] This was the hit that maimed Warrant Officer May's sleeping berth. The exit hole, which had been close enough to the waterline to allow some flooding in the ship's service stores compartment, had to be replaced and patched by shipfitters after the water was pumped out. Much to the displeasure of their chiefs, the men were forced to consume or give away many items damaged by seawater, including candy, cigarettes, and toiletries. Any sailors who ambled past the compartments during this process were liable to be handed free candy bars by the repair crew. Lt. (j.g.) Leon Rogers remembered that Captain Rooks ordered the excised plate to be saved as a souvenir of the battle. This suggests that the skipper fully expected the ship to survive, *and* that he understood the historical nature of the Battle of the Java Sea only hours after the fact.

While at Priok the cruiser shifted oil from her starboard to port tanks to facilitate work on the damaged areas. Another patch was welded over the plate that the other dud had struck at the midships waterline. It penetrated the petty officer's head, leaving an eighteen-by-thirty-two-inch hole, wrecking laundry machinery as well as nicking oil tanks. This damage had caused the cruiser to lose precious fuel. Men were lowered over the side of the ship on stages to complete these repairs.

At least a few of the men later speculated that had she not been required to put in to Batavia to repair that damage, *Houston* might have made it through Sunda Strait on February 28 and steamed safely on to the south coast of Java. This, at any rate, was the opinion after the war of several survivors, including John Harrell, the communications yeoman, and two marines, Jimmy Gee and Marvin Robinson. The two jarheads had worked their hands raw handling 5-inch shells—each weighing some sixty-seven pounds—in the claustrophobic, sweltering aft magazine's ammo rooms.[81] Above the cruiser's bridge Aviation Mechanic Elmo Bush saw men once more working on the forward Mark 19 antiaircraft director, which was acting up again.[82] A pair of first class fire-control men, Henry Thew and Charles Peters, finally solved the latest problem, but not before a message had gone out to COMSOWESPAC stating that the forward director was inoperable.

Although Bush had complained since Mare Island in 1940 that the new directors' rangefinders were never properly aligned, few had listened. In his opinion this problem had been a primary cause for poor shooting by the secondaries throughout the campaign, and Bush had even taunted the 5-inch crews that they would never hit anything, but other veterans had their own explanations.[83] The 5-inch/25 cal. weapons were old, short-barreled, and fired antiquated, often defective rounds. But in the final analysis, what would be of greater significance was the efficiency of her personnel in getting ammunition from the magazines along the transfer line to the guns themselves. As we will see, her men—despite their fine training—were not in the optimal readiness condition for this duty when her last action began.

At 1942 hours the ships got under way, with Waller sending a final message in exasperation to his superiors: "I CANNOT PERSUADE EVERTSEN TO COME WITH ME AM PROCEEDING."[84] The cruisers had wasted enough time already in the forlorn harbor of Tandjong Priok. As later reported by *Perth*'s navigator, Lt. Cdr. John Harper: "The examination vessel was passed at 2100 and course set for Sunda Strait along the searched channel at 22 knots. Zigzag no. 10 was started."[85] They kept their speed down, expecting the recalcitrant *Evertsen* to catch up with them, but she never did.

After nearly thirty-six straight hours at action stations, Captain Rooks decided that his exhausted crew now merited and required a break. The transit through Sunda Strait was not expected to be contested by enemy surface forces. Therefore condition 2 was the order: half of the 8-inch main battery ("Turret One manned and powder train filled," wrote Commander Maher in his action report) and 5-inch battery fully manned. In reality this meant that 5-inch gun crews were relaxing or sleeping by their respective guns, and only gun captains, pointers, and trainers were on duty. Available ammunition, though, was solely that which was already stored in the ready service boxes. The men in the ammo supply train for the 5-inch batteries were not at action stations.

The 5-inch battery had been split by Maher and Galbraith to deal with a nighttime surface engagement. Flight-deck guns would be controlled by the crew of battery control officer Lt. (j.g.) Leon Rogers in sky forward, and the boat-deck guns controlled by the men of sky aft, where Lieutenant Commander Galbraith himself, along with his assistants, Lt. Russell Roosevelt Ross, and Captain Ramsey of the marines were stationed. The after battery on the boat deck was also to be used for illuminating targets—as required—with star shells. Accordingly four ready boxes there were filled with these shells. All other boxes on the flight deck and boat deck contained common shell. Therefore, contrary to a number of allegations in different versions of *Houston's* end, the facts show that although worn, battered, and with an insufficient number of 8-inch projectiles left, the cruiser did *not* steam into her final action short of 5-inch ammunition.

The extra hours expended at Tandjong Priok ensured that what she was truly without was simply luck. But it did not appear so to her crew at the time. Dutiful cooks and mess attendants saw that hot coffee and cold roast beef sandwiches were distributed to those who had enough residual energy to eat. Then tired young men lugged cot, mattress, or blanket topside in a fog of exhaustion and fell into unconsciousness. A few others remained on edge, apprehensive, and could not sleep; they fidgeted next to the guns, chatting with fellow sailors and chiefs about their odds of escaping the Java rattrap. The worst *seemed* to be over, and the young or more naive men felt they would make it out of the campaign safely. *Houston's* officers offered them little hard news—they knew so little themselves. It was not the time to give false hope *or* to cause excessive anxieties, but in general morale remained quite high.

Ensign Herb Levitt, OOD that evening, had mustered available communications personnel as the ship stood out to sea and asked if there were enough life jackets for all the men in "C" (Communications) Division. The men came up about eight or nine vests short. Levitt then left the bridge to see what, if anything, he could scrounge. The first persons he found nearby were Lt. (j.g.) J. F. Woodruff chatting with Ens. Fred Mallory, a tall, angular young member of one of the cruiser's gunnery divisions. When Levitt asked the two officers if they had any extra jackets, a crusty chief bosun's mate named Archibald "Red" Dutton sauntered over and asked Levitt if he expected the ship to be sunk. The ensign replied that he did not expect to be sunk but that the jackets offered some warmth as well as protection against small splinters. Red Dutton, a twenty-year veteran, was described by survivors as "a sourpuss" and fond of responding to almost any suggestion with, "The navy has been doing it this way since Christ was a carpenter's mate, and now you want to change!"[86] In this instance, though, he proved as helpful as he had shown himself after the bombing on February 4, and Levitt got his extra life jackets.

Before falling into fatigue-saturated sleep, John Harrell, Y3/c, had time to talk with his "C" Division shipmate, Barnard Kaiser, Y2/c. Kaiser had traveled out to Australia with Harrell on the old *Chaumont* in the so-called Pensacola Convoy and helped persuade him to strike for a spot in the Communications Division. As they were chatting, the ship's chaplain, Cdr. George S. Rentz walked up. The pair of youngsters asked "if they were going to get out alive?" Rentz quietly replied yes, he thought they would, and then moved on. Of the three men, one would survive and return to the United States; the second would be swallowed up by oblivion; and the third would pass into legend.[87]

Other survivors of *Houston* later thought that most if not all of the remaining 8-inch ammo had finally been moved forward as the ship steamed for the island's westernmost exit. One of these was Donald C. Brain, s2/c, who told of having had some time to recover from this "heavy job" with other sailors on the detail, including Jim Kenney, "Swampy" Dethloff, and the Ebaugh brothers, Elmer and Forest. They were not on watch but "relaxing" as best they could, on the main deck's port side just off the carpenter's shop, shooting the breeze and discussing probable next moves. They figured that the ship would go back to the states, although some men had heard she would be overhauled in Australia, perhaps in Perth (wherever *that* was—no one seemed to actually know). Brain and friends thought that once stateside, the ship would have the old, less effective 5-inch/25 cal. guns removed and more up-to-date 5-inch/38 cal. mounts installed. Some men also expressed uninformed opinions on the new 40 mm antiaircraft weapons, although none had actually operated them.

Jack Dale Smith, s1/c, who had helped save the ship on February 4 by his prompt actions in compartment D-411-M, was now without an assigned battle station. After the conflagration in the Flores Sea, Smith had been assisting the 5-inch ammo handling details like many other men; he had done so in the mid-February action with the Timor Convoy and at the Battle of the Java Sea. On this night he was to keep shells supplied to 5-inch guns number 6 and 8 on the boat deck, port side aft. Worn out by the almost constant alarms and actions of the past two and a half days, he, too, had gone topside, where he fell asleep on the fantail along with other weary sailors beneath the trio of huge 8-inch gun barrels looming silently out of fire-gutted turret 3.

Elsewhere, Theodore "Itch" Schram, Bkr2/c, an old China hand, was sleeping on his cot outside the galley, worn out by his efforts in the unsuccessful attempts to bake bread and brew coffee during the previous day and night's battle. Schram had been working with head baker William Tisdale, sc1/c, and Tisdale's assistant, Raymond Klymazewski, sc2/c. The concussion of the ship's main batteries had knocked loose the blue cover over the galley's battle lights almost at once. In exasperation Schram finally punched them off himself between handling the hot pans filled with fragile bread dough that would not rise—due to the inferior Dutch yeast the men had been forced to use and the heavy jarring from *Houston*'s guns—as he tried at the same time to keep the harsh Dutch coffee from tasting as if dirty socks had been thrown in with the grounds. Every time he put the bread dough in the pans and into the ovens, a salvo would go off and the dough, its $CO_2$ released, would then collapse. There had been a lot of "bitching" that night and the next day about this, according to Schram, and remarks from hungry sailors such as "What the *hell* did you do to this bread?" were not uncommon.[88] Working overtime, the harried cooks threw together sandwiches of dry, leathery roast beef on the temperamental bread, with green apples for dessert, all washed down by that imperfect coffee.

Some of the men who had established friendly relations with the Chinese mess attendants (by sharing their own "goodies," especially pastries and sweets) had benefited from this earlier in the campaign by receiving surreptitious leftovers filched from the officers' mess. By now there was little time for such small kindnesses. Yet compared to the food they would receive (if they were lucky) over the following three and a half years, even this meager fare would have seemed delectable.

• • •

Less than three hours later, as Don Brain, Jim Kenney, Swampy Dethloff, and the Ebaugh brothers shared opinions and weighed probabilities based on inadequate information, the ship began its approach to Sunda Strait under a moonlit night sky. On *Houston*'s bridge at least some of her officers for the first time allowed themselves the "rash hope" they might yet escape. Ens. Herb Levitt was only just then beginning to permit such thoughts to enter his mind following his search for more life jackets. *Houston*'s pay clerk, Ens. Preston Clark, had been assigned the somewhat unusual task of recording conversation in general on the bridge during action and that of the captain in particular, if possible.[89] He had found the flag bridge so crowded with talkers during the Battle of the Java Sea that this was not feasible. Ensign Clark, a meticulous fellow, had contented himself with keeping an accurate record, however, of the ship's speeds and course changes in action, while also noting the proximity of the Japanese salvos as they fell. Clark would recall in later years their extremely tight grouping, remarking that if one enemy shell hit, it was quite probable others would arrive in the same area as well.

During this time, above the bridge in sky forward, the director's officer, Lt. (j.g.) Leon Rogers and his marine counterpart, 2nd Lt. Frank "Ned" Gallagher Jr., were chatting in the cool evening. At that height above the water, the breeze generated by the ship's speed had persuaded Rogers to keep his life jacket

A DEATH SO VALIANT AND TRUE

on for warmth. The two young officers' views on the conflict were divergent, although not incompatible: Rogers, a stolid and dependable Tennessean from Knoxville raised in Washington DC (his father was an executive with the Interstate Commerce Commission), was thinking of the "horrors of war" soon to be visited on the women and children of Java by the enemy invaders; in this he was imagining a sustained bombing campaign—perhaps influenced by Japanese actions in Shanghai, Nanking, Chungking, Manila, and Singapore—taking many innocent civilian lives.[90] The crisp, prepossessing Gallagher—who alternated watches with Rogers as the battery control officer in sky forward—replied that such tragedies did not upset him. As a marine he had signed up to fight, and this was his profession. The young USMC lieutenant would not allow himself to be distracted by what were, after all, the inevitable corollaries of war.

All along the length of the great ship's upper deck, *Houston's* sleep-deprived and drained men were catching what rest they could. On the foc's'le, alongside the massive bulk of turret 1, an exhausted Eugene "Punchy" Parham, S1/c, was asleep on the deck. The gangling Texan's battle station was number 1 powder hoist operator inside the mount, but since the blowers there didn't offer much relief, he preferred the open air, as did most sailors.

One of those who did not was a youngster from Illinois named Bill Ingram—only seventeen years old—stationed in the starboard powder box. Although he frequently lounged around outside the turret on deck when not in condition 1, Bill had slept inside the gunhouse for most of his brief tour on board *Houston*. Ingram was a small individual and could squeeze through the foot-and-a-half-square hatch into the powder flap without too much difficulty; once inside he had space enough to throw down his blanket and grab what sleep he could. His assigned bunk and locker below deck were like a foreign country to Ingram; spending so much time at general quarters, he rarely got a chance to go there.

A few feet aft, one level above on the communication deck—the same level as the main communication and radio stations, both located behind turret 2—Jim Ballinger and John Harrell of the radio gang also lay on blankets with their life vests as pillows. Having exhausted himself moving ammo, Harrell was completely addled with fatigue. He had managed to get some warm food in his stomach at Tandjong Priok after his talk with Chaplain Rentz and was feeling "full and sleepy." Yeoman Harrell slept so soundly as the ship departed that he retained no recollection later of having left the port.[91]

About 150 feet aft, dozing on a blanket on the quarterdeck, was the assistant engineering officer, Lt. Robert B. Fulton, who found that location more comfortable than his stifling stateroom. One of his second-class water tenders in the forward engine room, Jack Leroy Smith, was also sleeping on the quarter-deck that night. Smith had joined the ship after suffering an appendicitis attack that resulted in his being hospitalized at Cavite's Canacao Naval Hospital just before war broke out. He felt fortunate to have escaped the Philippines before Japan tightened the noose around the islands, but after this night his idea of luck would change. Another sailor—one who knew something about hospitals—Griff Douglas, HA1/c, had come up from the sick bay and with blanket and pillow likewise slumbered nearby on the deck.

Overhead through a few clouds could be seen a brilliant moon, almost full; visibility was good, and the temperature mild. Looking off the port side of the ship to the south, one could see a thick black line against the sea's horizon. This was the low-lying, "much indented" coast of Java, with its "ranges of undulating hills backed by imposing mountains."[92] Small islands dotted the waters offshore through this stretch of the Java Sea, and the men were well aware of its navigational obstacles. The threat of enemy vessels being concealed among the many tiny islets offshore had not escaped the men, and such possibilities occupied the attention of those on *Houston*'s bridge.

A half mile ahead in the darkness, next to the conning position on the bridge of *Perth*, another officer sought respite: Hec Waller had placed a camp stretcher nearby, and there he lay down for a well-needed rest, having "barely left the bridge for the past three days." He told the officer of the watch, Lieutenant Gay, "Kick me if anything breaks."[93] For a brief period Waller did sleep, but soon enough he was up again, and by roughly half past ten back at his post. Within another few minutes things would indeed begin to break apart.

*Perth* and *Houston* were then several miles slightly north and east of Babi Island—which itself lies ten miles northeast of Pandjang Island, at the top of Bantam Bay—and zigzagging at over 20 knots. They had *not* swung north of the Thousand Islands but instead paralleled the coastline in a familiar shipping lane and were now about five miles from shore on a southwesterly course heading between 230 degrees to 240 degrees. The two ships were probably not much more than thirty minutes from the strait's entrance.

They had been duly warned to be alert for Dutch patrol vessels or RAN corvettes in the Bantam Bay and Sunda Strait areas. The Dutch vessels were the small Gouvermentsmarine craft pressed into service as the so-called Sunda Straits Auxiliary Patrol only a few days earlier: HNMLS *Fazant*, *Bellatrix*, *Sirius*, *Reiger*, and *Merel*. After a few days these five were joined by four Australian Bathurst-class corvettes of the Twenty-First Minesweeping Flotilla: HMAS *Maryborough* (flotilla leader), HMAS *Goulburn*, HMAS *Burnie*, and HMAS *Bendigo*.

A DEATH SO VALIANT AND TRUE

These RAN ships operated primarily out of Merak on the eastern side of Sunda Strait, where they received a number of unwelcome visits from enemy planes.

The Auxiliary Patrol also included several antiquated coal-burning British steamers from Singapore pressed into service—and crewed by survivors of HMS *Repulse* for the most part—as well as a few British motor launches that had also escaped from Singapore two weeks earlier. As for the Dutch boats, they were both there and in Bantam Bay. They were patrolling at night and remaining anchored by day, hoping to avoid the attention of the ever-present and deadly Japanese planes. A number of merchant ships and assorted auxiliaries were still attempting to escape Sumatra and western Java, and these small patrol vessels were also being pressed into escort duty.[94]

As fate would have it that night, the 600-ton Dutch patrol boat *Reiger* was unlucky enough to first greet the new masters of Java on their arrival. What usefulness she may have offered as a picket was quickly shown to be utterly negligible. She was neither prepared, capable, nor willing to offer much resistance when (to her crew's evident terror) they encountered the Japanese convoy as the long columns of nearly three dozen transports lumbered into their designated anchorage between Pandjang Island and the mainland below St. Nicholas Point. "By the glimmering light of the hazy moon, the mountains of Java silently cast their deep shadows," wrote an army officer on the Imperial Japanese Army command vessel, *Shinshu Maru*.[95] The convoy, with its transports carrying the men and matériel of the Sato Detachment, was led into the anchorage by the minesweepers of Minesweeper Division One (W-1, W-2, W-3, and W-4) and the destroyers *Fubuki* and *Harukaze*.[96] The minesweepers had completed their work several hours earlier in the afternoon as they swept the northwest passage into the landing areas.[97] Struggling to maintain station in the powerful, eddying currents off Bantam Bay, the old, small Kamikaze-class destroyers of DesDiv 5 (*Harukaze*, *Hatakaze*, and *Asakaze*) had become spread out and separated. *Fubuki* then moved out seaward to patrol the area to the north and east around Babi Island, beyond the bay itself.

The next screening destroyer into the area was *Harukaze* under Cdr. Koeu Keiji (Fifty-Seventh *ki*), and her sharp lookouts soon made out the small Dutch patrol boat against the shore.[98] The Japanese ship quickly illuminated *Reiger*, which was desperately trying to raise her anchor—the time was about eleven o'clock—and then opened fire on the luckless patrol boat with her 4.7-inch/50 cal. main battery.

Aboard Major General Imamura's ungainly flagship, the specialized landing ship *Shinshu Maru*, which was still several thousand meters to the northwest, Imperial Army staff officers were bemoaning the dullness of their landing operations when distant rumblings of shellfire disturbed the quiet night.[99] The first wave of the Sato Detachment had just been sent ashore successfully to its appropriate area (District C) in an undisturbed landing. Having received a signal to this effect, the next wave was preparing to disembark. At that time Major General Imamura, his chief of staff, and a lieutenant colonel in the army were roused at the sound of the gunfire exchange. The lieutenant colonel, who described himself as dispirited by the lack of Allied resistance, recorded his experiences: "About this time the faint sound of gunfire was heard to the south of the anchorage, so I went up on deck and looked out with my binoculars.... A naval staff officer who had boarded the same boat reported that the destroyers were engaged in firing in front of the anchorage."[100]

As *Harukaze* held the startled patrol boat in her searchlights, *Reiger* went to full speed—maybe 16 knots—in the midst of shell splashes while returning fire with her single 75 mm gun against her larger antagonist. The fleeing patrol boat's skipper sought shelter in the lee of a small islet in Bantam Bay and then ran the ship hard aground on its coral reef. "The crew abandoned ship after having destroyed the secret documents and swam to the Java coast. The captain and the telegrapher swam a long way along the coast and were eventually captured by natives.... *Reiger* lost two officers and an unknown number of natives NCO's and crewmen."[101] Following this brief excitement *Harukaze* swung east and north around Pandjang Island and began proceeding to her patrol area immediately north of Bantam Bay proper. *Hatakaze*, in the meantime, was closer to the convoy's anchorage on the northwest side of Pandjang with *Asakaze* somewhere behind both, closer to the headland that terminated in St. Nicholas Point.

Onboard *Shinshu Maru* the army officer noted, "The sound of guns ceased after a while. According to the report from the convoy fleet, our leading destroyer attacked and destroyed the enemy gunboat, which was prowling in front of the anchorage."[102] He then returned below decks to his cabin, as he was not yet scheduled to go ashore. There he resumed his attempt to finish reading a book he had started during the journey south. He enjoyed only a brief interval of peace and quiet, however. On *this* night he would get little further reading accomplished but *all* the excitement he could have possibly imagined. Within little more than an hour, two very formidable warships would approach the convoy.

Although visibility was said to be as much as twelve thousand to fourteen thousand yards, the lookouts aboard *Perth* and *Houston* were either too fatigued or concentrating too intently on the entrance to the strait to notice yet the shadowing vessel off to seaward. But that shadower had certainly seen them.

A DEATH SO VALIANT AND TRUE

Roughly two miles west of Babi Island, and well-concealed in the darkness, lurked the namesake of a revolutionary class of modern warships: the Tokugata ("Special Type") destroyer *Fubuki* of DesDiv 11.[103] After the encounter earlier with the Dutch patrol boat, *her* well-trained lookouts were nothing if not alert. And it was now the turn of the Japanese to be startled, for there on the moonlit sea to the east, bearing about 85 degrees and ten thousand meters distant, they saw two large shapes approaching—shapes soon to become silhouettes far larger and swifter than any patrol boats. At nine minutes past midnight—Tokyo time—*Fubuki* sent *Natori* an urgent message: "Sighted two objects that appear to be enemy—northeast of Babi Island. 0009."[104]

. . .

Aboard DesRon 5's flagship the communications officer donned his headphones and spoke to the radio shack: "'Sesa [Senior Staff Officer], was *Fubuki* assigned to the easternmost patrol area?" Commander Yukawa, senior staff officer, who was working on the chart table, replied to the commander in a loud voice from the chart room, which was separated by drapes from the bridge: "No, Sir, she was assigned to the west of Babi Island, Area 3."[105] This news would have been disconcerting; the unidentified ships were much too near the invasion convoy if they were already that close to Babi Island. But less than ten minutes later, as *Natori's* officers mulled over the contact report, another message came from *Fubuki*. She had skillfully maintained visual contact, working her way around and behind the enemy ships: "They are two enemy cruisers. Our position two miles west of Babi Island. Enemy heading 240°, 0018 [2248]." At that moment, the real possibility of Allied surface units successfully penetrating the invasion convoy's anchorage—with the potential for a repeat of the Balikpapan disaster or worse—threw the command personnel of *Natori* into "an uproar."[106] Shouted orders from officers mixed with messages from other units on the TBS now turned up to full volume, and these, along with excited screams from lookouts, all quickly and sharply reverberated through the bridge.

Nonetheless, Rear Admiral Hara, the veteran torpedo man, kept his composure as he ordered the ship to "number 5 battle speed." This was followed by Captain Sasaki's notification to Hara that he was changing the ship's heading to 90 degrees. The navigator confirmed this with both senior officers, and the ship swung to the west, already picking up speed. *Natori* was then almost directly north of St. Nicholas Point, some eight miles offshore; with her were the remaining two destroyers of DesDiv 11, *Shirayuki* and *Hatsuyuki*. Simultaneously another report was received, this one from *Harukaze*: "Sighted two enemy cruisers at 060°. Distance 8,000. Our heading 310°, 0029 [2259]."[107] And now she, too, had been sighted by the Allied cruisers.[108]

After twenty minutes of being shadowed undetected by big *Fubuki*, it was the low-lying little *Harukaze* that lookouts on *Perth* and *Houston* first spotted. They initially mistook her for a Dutch patrol boat or an Australian corvette, as they had been led to expect. Seen first at 2306 hours and from a distance of some five miles—and promptly challenged on Waller's orders by *Perth*'s chief yeoman, Bert Hartwell—the Japanese destroyer replied with an incomprehensible signal in a pale green light.[109] When the ship turned, away exposing her distinctive profile, experienced eyes aboard the Australian cruiser had seen enough, and Waller wasted no time ordering the forward turrets to open fire. At that moment *Harukaze* fired a reddish-colored warning rocket—as she also began making smoke—and for all intents and purposes the Battle of Sunda Strait began. For over 1,700 American and Australian officers, sailors, and marines—a great number of whom believed they were on the verge of salvation—the sands of freedom had at last run out.

What would follow over the ensuing two hours of that dark night would be one of the war's epic naval encounters, and one in which every imaginable element was present: violent gunnery at close range, repeated torpedo attacks, wild and remarkable ship handling, devastating friendly fire accidents, with terror and extraordinary heroism on every quarter. Yet through its very chaos and the number of participants involved, it would remain one of the least understood and misrepresented of all sea battles during the Pacific War and for many decades afterward.[110]

*Perth* sent out at least one contact message, and it may have been copied by her sister, HMAS *Hobart*, then well off to the northwest on her way to India from Sumatra with her evacuees. On *Houston* Cdr. Arthur Maher later wrote that "upon contact with the enemy a contact report was transmitted stating 'Enemy forces engaged'" and that this message was addressed to COMSOWESPAC/Glassford for action and to NPO (Rear Admiral Rockwell's COM 16, or "Radio Corregidor") and CNO (Admiral Stark in Washington DC) for information, but no copy of this message exists in the files that Glassford preserved from his command at Bandoeng.[111] On the other hand, another surviving officer from *Houston* (Galbraith) flatly stated that "no coded messages were sent during the night battle."[112] Commander Maher noted that battle damage to *Houston*'s radio antennae and transmitters soon ruled out any further messages. For the two Allied cruisers, operating on the far side of the globe in obscure waters under conditions of primitive communications, it was as if they had steamed headlong off the edge of a hand-colored medieval map and plummeted into the depths of *mare incognita*.

Following undetected, *Fubuki* had waited until 0043 [2313] and then fired a spread of nine torpedoes at the two cruisers from a distance of less than three thousand yards. She mistakenly claimed two hits on *Houston*'s stern, but there were none at that time. Her presence given away, *Fubuki* was taken under fire at once by the Allied ships and responded in kind for two minutes with sixteen rounds of searchlight-directed gunfire from her 5-inch main battery. She noted that *Perth*'s return fire was especially intense and accurate. And it must have been, for the veteran Japanese destroyer kept heading north and away from the battle, where she would find more excitement elsewhere later that night.

Aboard *Houston* and *Perth* the men only knew that all hell had broken loose again with a vengeance. On *Houston* Ens. Charles D. Smith, turret officer for turret 2, had gone below earlier to try to get some rest in his stateroom. (In the condition 2 watch his mount was secured and only Hamlin's turret 1 fully manned.) At about 2315 hours he was awakened from an exhausted sleep by the call to general quarters. As he stumbled up and out through ladders and hatchways onto the main deck, Hamlin's turret 1 got off its first salvo of the night, which very nearly knocked Smith overboard. After he reached his armored turret officer's booth, Smith's mount quickly joined in the firing within another minute or two at most.

While the Japanese considered natural lighting conditions good that night—with an almost-full moon over head—the Americans, especially those officers associated with gunnery duties, felt that visibility was dreadful. For much of the next hour the two sides lunged wildly and blindly at each other, and in this sense the engagement was akin to a violent yet clumsy fistfight among drunks in a darkened bar or pool hall.

Just a few miles off to the north, anchored in the shallows near the shore, Japanese army officers, soldiers, and civilian war correspondents no longer felt bored or sleepy as they began to hear and feel the deep, booming salvos in the distance. Soon, across the black water, on a moonlit horizon, flashes, then star shells, multicolored flares, and tracers became visible to those still on troopships in the anchorage or in open boats and landing-craft being ferried to shore.[113] To the untrained ears of even senior commanders, such as Lieutenant General Imamura himself, these ominous thunderclaps were the work of enemy battleships threatening the landing operations. And to many those great, ragged blasts were soon growing louder and closer, or so it seemed. Writing for the Japanese public in marvelous hyperbole worthy of an action film (or cartoon)—

and with every syllable tightly controlled by official navy censors—Nakayama Hideo would speak for the powerless viewers on the transports: "Staring at this terrible but swift action, we stood on the bridge and gripped the steel rails until our fingernails cracked under the tension of the moment. Our whole being was concentrated in our vision as we saw this mighty scene. We forgot the dangers surrounding us in the midst of this battle, and at times we were so carried away by the action that we felt we were seeing a motion picture of sea warfare."[114]

Rear Admiral Hara then moved as swiftly as possible to arrange his scattered forces. He ordered the immediate screening ships (DesDiv 5's three destroyers, *Harukaze*, *Asakaze*, and *Hatakaze*), which were then beginning to come under fire, to attack the enemy. At the same time he sent out a request to the second section of Sentai 7—heavy cruisers *Mikuma* and *Mogami*—along with their destroyer, *Shikinami*, to prepare for battle. However, it seems they had intercepted *Fubuki*'s initial contact report, for by then they were already increasing speed to come south for the battlefield. Within a matter of minutes Hara also radioed orders to the DesDiv 12 destroyers patrolling the upper reaches of Sunda Strait, *Shirakumo* and *Murakumo*, to join up with his forces and attack the enemy as well. Therefore, in not more than fifteen minutes, the Japanese were able to marshal about a dozen cruisers and destroyers to counterattack the pair of Allied intruders menacing the troopships. By then the enormity of their predicament would have sunk in on the Allied ships' crews as they realized they were to be in for the fight of their lives.

Throughout *Houston* hundreds of sleeping and dozing men all sprang or staggered up as general quarters sounded, some half dazed but others instantly alert as they made their way to action stations as quickly as possible under the chaotic circumstances. Water Tender Jack Leroy Smith, asleep on the quarterdeck, ran below to his station in the forward (number 1) engine room under Chief Water Tender Archie Terry. Nearby, Terry's superior, Lt. Bob Fulton, the assistant engineer officer who was in charge of the forward engine room, was also awakened by the call to GQ and dashed down to his station. There he had Terry, Smith, and others fire up all remaining boilers; within five to ten minutes the ship began producing full power. Chief Gunners Mate Anton "Tony" Manista was dozing in his bunk in the lower chief's quarters aft when he heard the alarm sound around 2315 hours; he went forward to his battle station overseeing the 5-inch ammo supply train. Rammer man Robert Martin, s1/c, of the Fourth Division, was sleeping near 5-inch gun mount number 7—on the starboard side boat deck—but his assigned station was at gun number 3 under Jim Kenney, BM2/c. That gun was on the flight deck forward, and Martin scurried up the access ladder to his position as swiftly as he could.[115] Because of the condition 2 watch that had been established and the initial confusion caused by the sudden, unexpected appearance of the enemy, only a few of the 5-inch guns were fully manned by their usual crews. Quite a few men arrived at their stations only to find that other sailors had already taken their places due to the speed with which *Houston's* 5-inch batteries had begun firing.

At the same time Cdr. Arthur Maher, like "Hec" Waller, soon spotted the enemy destroyers emerging from the darkness as they formed up coming out of Bantam Bay. *Perth* reacted to these developments by altering course. *Houston* followed as the Australian cruiser made a turn to the north, but as soon as this was done, Maher observed nine more hostile ships to seaward. After the course change Maher thought there appeared to be at least "two or three enemy heavy ships" off the cruiser's port side.[116] These may have been the destroyers of DesDiv 5, but it is quite possible that Maher was recalling the appearance of DesDiv 11 destroyers—much larger vessels—a little later. As *Houston's* "Gun Boss" would describe the battle in general, "enemy attacks consisted of destroyers attacking in groups of three or four with the leading destroyer smoking and turning away under the severe fire directed on it by all batteries of the *Houston*."[117] As we will see, this was indeed a fairly accurate representation of the fighting that night.

Both Allied cruisers were firing from their main and secondary batteries within a few minutes, with *Houston* utilizing fire control from spot 1 and director 1. Her main battery and aft (boat-deck) 5-inch guns were operating together, that is, with the aft secondaries providing illumination—when possible—for the main battery. As noted the forward (flight-deck) 5-inch guns were being controlled by the forward AA director under Lt. Lee Rogers. They were ordered to engage targets on the opposite side. To their horror the men quickly realized that enemy ships were around them on all bearings. Maher later wrote, "The fight developed into a mêlée with the *Houston* engaging targets on all sides at various ranges."[118]

On *Perth* Waller's veteran gunners were firing as fast as their guns could be served. It was surely the Australian light cruiser that poured fire into *Fubuki*, *Harukaze*, and *Hatakaze* in the initial minutes of the fighting. On *Perth's* darkened bridge Waller called out course changes and questions in a steady monotone to the officers and sailors around him. They included his gunnery officer (Hancox), navigator (Harper), assistant navigator (Burgess), first lieutenant (Johnson), officer-of-the-watch (Gay), torpedo officer (Clarke), chief yeoman (Hartwell), RAAF flying officer (McDonough), and midshipman paymaster (Tranby-White), among others. These men were all experienced and tough, but they were also physically exhausted by the excessive hours spent at action stations in recent days.

After her torpedo attack and brief exchange of gunfire, *Fubuki* had continued away from the battle to the north, where she was needed to maintain a patrol to the east of Babi island. By this time the Sixteenth Army's troop ships had drawn the attention of at least one of the Allied cruisers as they turned west and then north above Bantam Bay. It appears that *Perth* was the first to fire on the transports in their anchorage. This shelling was reported by the captain of *Harukaze*, and it naturally caused the Japanese naval commanders great anxiety. *Harukaze* and her DesDiv 5 sisters, *Hatakaze* and *Asakaze*, had yet to make their presence strongly felt, but it was up to these three small and elderly destroyers to take the fight to the enemy ships until more powerful forces could arrive. Although clumsily executed, thanks to *Perth*'s and *Houston*'s energetic return fire, their torpedo attacks would display considerable courage and determination.

*Harukaze* had laid what she felt was an effective smokescreen upon first contact, which temporarily protected her and the vulnerable convoy. But the ships of DesDiv 5 were still separated and struggled to form up for the torpedo attacks ordered by Hara. *Hatakaze* soon sailed out from the Bantam Bay area and at a point west-northwest of Pandjang island began searchlight-directed gunfire by herself on the cruisers from a range of 3,500 meters (3,800 yards) with her 4.7-inch battery. For her audacity she was subjected to heavy gunfire from *Perth* ("the first ship") and turned away in order to rejoin *Harukaze* and *Asakaze*. The three destroyers regrouped about six miles north of St. Nicholas Point at 2332 hours and prepared for their torpedo attacks.

In the meantime two more destroyers of DesDiv 11 had appeared, and within another ten minutes made a concerted torpedo attack on the Allied cruisers. Running on a parallel course to the north, *Shirayuki* and *Hatsuyuki* each discharged nine starboard Type 90 torpedoes at *Houston* from a distance of 3,500–3,800 meters at 2330 hours.[119] There were no hits by these eighteen torpedoes, but the cruiser returned fire using star shells for illumination and both 5-inch and 8-inch batteries to telling effect. *Shirayuki* in particular received a ferocious barrage from *Houston* and suffered damage to her upper works with three men killed and six wounded. *Shirayuki* and *Hatsuyuki* both turned away under a smokescreen after the attacks. They would join up with *Fubuki* in another half hour or so to the northwest of the battle area.

Off to the north the men of the cruisers *Mikuma* and *Mogami* could also see the firing in the distance, and greatly concerned that the transports' landing operations were being endangered, they altered course southward at best speed.

In this brief but hectic period before the heavy cruisers of Sentai 7 arrived, the trio of elderly Japanese destroyers comprising DesDiv 5—*Harukaze, Hatakaze,* and *Asakaze*—reassembled and turned back toward the enemy cruisers. They did so with some trepidation since they had already witnessed the aggressive firing of *Perth* and *Houston* and had no illusions about their chances in a gunnery exchange against such heavily armed warships. Their attack did not go off without a few glitches either. By then the Allied cruisers had executed a large turn back toward Bantam Bay, and the situation was rapidly becoming one of scarcely controlled chaos, with the Japanese commanders deeply unnerved by not only enemy gunfire but also the awareness of so many torpedoes being loosed within such a tightly congested area.

On the bridge of *Harukaze,* it was the biter's turn to be bit. Cdr. Koeu Kenji, and his men now felt "very uneasy" as they went in to attack.[120] This was not the same business at all as shooting up a frightened and lightly armed Dutch patrol boat in the shallows off Bantam Bay, but they had been given direct orders from Rear Admiral Hara. With *Hatakaze* and *Asakaze* trailing behind division flagship *Harukaze,* the three small DDs steamed dutifully at *Perth* and *Houston.* Overhead, flares lit up the night sky in chartreuse and silver; searchlights snapped on for a few moments waving ghostly beams of light across the black water; drifting haze from gunfire and smokescreens masked some Japanese ships' locations while other ships blended in against the dark coastline. One might think that the larger, light-colored hulls of *Perth* and *Houston* would have stood out against the sea beneath the nearly full moon, but the Japanese had to exercise great care not to fire on their own vessels.[121] Under what soon became severe gunfire, the trio of DesDiv 5 destroyers tried to position themselves as advantageously as possible for the launching of their fish.

For these older Japanese ships, none of which had been really frontline units, the attack went badly from start to finish. First, *Harukaze's* torpedo officer miscalculated the correct moment to launch her torpedoes—which were old World War 1–era weapons of limited range and slower speed—and missed his opportunity. The ship next in line, *Hatakaze,* was then taken under such accurate gunfire that her vision was blocked by enormous shell splashes—probably from *Houston's* main and secondary batteries—and she, too, was unable to launch her torpedoes. Only the third unit, *Asakaze,* expended all six of her Sixth Year Model torpedoes against *Perth* ("the first ship") at 2343 hours from a distance of 3,700 meters, after which she and *Hatakaze* wrapped themselves in a smokescreen and sped off to the north, away from the Allied cruisers' sharp gunnery.[122]

On *Houston's* so-called flight deck atop the cruiser's scout-plane hangar and abreast the second funnel, the augmented forward 5-inch gun battery had been sited during the 1940 King Board upgrades at Mare Island. This comprised an additional quartet of 5-inch/25 cal. guns, numbered 1 through 4, odd numbers to starboard, even numbers to port. A USMC crew under Sgt. Charley Pryor was normally assigned to one of the mounts. And like the good leathernecks they were, this group would quickly be ready to shoot at anything and everything that came within range that night.

Gun captain Pryor was a tall, no-nonsense Texan who had been in the Far East since March 1940, when he had been sent to the flagship USS *Augusta* (CA-31). When that cruiser was relieved by *Houston*, Pryor came to CA-30 as part of Admiral Hart's flag allowance. He had often been given duty as the skipper's orderly on the bridge, but at GQ he was a gun captain. On this fateful night Pryor had been spared duty until the following morning. He recalled, "For the first time in a month I went down below, got my mattress, brought it back up onto the gun deck, spread it out and took off my outer clothing. For the first time in ten days, I was actually going to get some sleep."[123]

Pryor did not get much rest as events transpired, nor was he in charge of his usual gun number 8. In the barely controlled pandemonium that followed initial contact with the enemy, Pryor ended up at gun number 4, atop the "flight deck"—fifty feet above the waterline. He and his men ran to their regular mount, as previously, but found that it had been manned by a navy crew that was already firing at enemy targets. Always a consummate professional, the formidable six-foot-one-inch Texan and his gun crew made their presence felt nonetheless at gun number 4. In interviews conducted fifteen years after the war, Pryor remembered how his men fired on a trio of enemy destroyers laying a smokescreen as they attacked *Houston* on her port bow. Another marine on his gun crew, Pvt. Fred "Pinky" King, recalled the Japanese ships turning on their searchlights as they fearlessly bored right in.

Commander Koeu's *Harukaze* had remained behind to make up for what he saw as a gaffe by his torpedo officer and he wheeled his ship around in a 360-degree turn "for another try." The results of this determined effort were predictable enough. As Koeu states in his memoir, "The enemy gunfire concentrated on us and we had a hard time of it." Main, secondary, and tertiary batteries from *Houston* and *Perth* savaged the twenty-year-old destroyer as she pressed in for the attack. Many years later Koeu recalled those harrowing moments under fire at close range: "We were even machine-gunned. . . . Soon a fire broke out aft of the bridge. MG tracers caused it. In addition near miss shells hitting the surface of the water exploded one after another, and their fragments scattered all around and rained on us."[124] A number of these fragments flew into *Harukaze*'s bride, where her assistant communications officer stood among the other men. He was struck by a ricochet that tore so much flesh from his buttocks that he died of blood loss before the night was over. Two or three other enlisted men were killed, and five more suffered nonfatal wounds in these near misses. Another salvo from *Perth* resulted in a dud 6-inch shell embedded in the starboard side of *Harukaze*'s thin hull. This shell eventually fell out due to the high-speed steaming of the destroyer and led to some flooding, but that was the extent of her structural damage.[125] Despite such opposition Koeu's ship did finally make her attack, firing all six of her torpedoes at *Perth* at 2356 before reversing course back to the north and away from the battle. No less determined, her division mate *Hatakaze* then also returned and unloaded six old torpedoes at the enemy from a range of 4,200 yards at 2358 in an almost bow-on approach. She then turned away to the northwest.[126] Although it had been a frightening half-hour for the ships of DesDiv 5, for them the night's action was now largely completed.

Naturally very few of these events in the engagement took place in isolation. As DesDiv 5's three destroyers were occupied with their strikes, Rear Admiral Hara Kenzaburo brought his flagship, *Natori*, into action. The destroyers of Koeu were occasionally between him and the enemy, so he opened fire first with the light cruiser's 5.5-inch battery at 2343 hours before making his torpedo attack. As soon as the destroyers cleared the range sufficiently, *Natori* launched four vintage Eighth Year Type torpedoes at 2344 hours to starboard against her adversaries before retiring under a smokescreen herself. These "fish" hit nothing either.

At this point in the fighting the Japanese had already expended over forty torpedoes at *Perth* and *Houston* and achieved no hits. Fine ship handling by Waller and Rooks may be credited with keeping their ships intact for as long as they did, but the stress and uncertainty of night fighting in general and of making torpedo attacks under heavy gunfire were equal factors. Commander Koeu, the skipper of *Harukaze*, spoke frankly in his memoirs, stating, "What you practice in training cannot always be applicable to an actual battle. First of all, you lose your composure. . . . If you get closer to the enemy, you will be in more danger. So, you will launch your torpedoes when you think you are close enough. You will follow your instinctive reaction." The similarities between his experiences and those of Binford's old flushdeckers at the Battle of the Java Sea were obvious. Koeu went on to recall, "At any rate, [you] launch the torpedoes as soon as possible and run away like the devil before you are hit. It may not be fear, but you get impatient to finish your duties sooner. Then you will launch the torpedoes at 4,000 meters where you should [launch] at 3,000."[127] There is no question that Lieutenant Commander Koeu was a brave and dedicated captain, but his candor and complete lack of bluster reveal another side of his character—one that had no desire to squander his men's lives pointlessly.

Next came the turn of the 1,300-ton veteran minelayer *Shirataka*, the smallest adversary to engage the Allied cruisers that night. She was then positioned directly off St. Nicholas Point, northwest of the convoy's anchorage; at 2346 she began steaming gamely toward the fighting. Displaying considerable temerity, she made a resolute approach, advancing, and at 0005 hours opened fire with her 4.7-inch battery. It is not known if the two beset cruisers took any notice of this aged ship's impertinence, for at that time they had other and larger opponents to contend with.[128]

At about 2340 hours the destroyers of DesDiv 12's subsection, *Shirakumo* and *Murakumo*, then farther out to sea north of St. Nicholas Point and steaming due east, spotted the enemy cruisers to starboard in the distance about fourteen thousand yards away. This would have been at the extreme limits of visibility that night and again speaks well of the vision of Japanese lookouts. *Shirakumo*'s navigator, Lt. Ishihara Takenori, helped direct the ships toward their opposition. The two big destroyers had been pushing themselves hard for over forty-five minutes coming from the upper Sunda Strait area, and they made no attempt at subtlety as they sped into action. *Murakumo* began searchlight-directed gunfire and then followed it with a salvo of torpedoes; *Shirakumo* followed suit before checking fire at 0005. The two destroyers of DesDiv 12 then turned away, no doubt influenced by the return fire they had provoked.

It was during this phase of the fighting that Lieutenant Commander Galbraith of *Houston*'s secondary battery got one of the only direct orders he would receive that night when he was told to counter-illuminate the enemy destroyers. Here doom was tapping *Houston* ominously on the shoulder, reminding the cruiser that when she had been forced to leave Cavite at the end of November with her new uninstalled searchlights still on the dock, she was tempting fate. Now that very fate had appeared. For two minutes the cruiser's dubious old searchlights came into play, but then Conn ordered the shutters closed, as they were not helping light up enemy ships but were instead making the six-hundred-foot-long *Houston* a better target. It is interesting—and galling—to realize that Japanese accounts after the battle would make special note of the weakness of Allied searchlights.

As Galbraith later told interviewers, for at least the first half hour of this bat-

A DEATH SO VALIANT AND TRUE

tle *Houston* was basically firing all its batteries more or less constantly. He had instructed his 1.1-inch battery to fire on any enemy ships using searchlights. The 5-inch guns were both illuminating for the main battery and firing against attacking destroyers when possible. (The order from Rooks to illuminate with star shells was the only other direct order Galbraith received that night. In post-war accounts Galbraith characterized communications with Conn and Control as being "very poor.") Yet the 5-inch batteries were not using star shells to illuminate their own shooting—Lt. Leon Rogers in the forward Mark 19 director simply tried to follow his own "tracers" for spotting—but continued to attempt (unsuccessfully) to place their shells over the enemy ships for the main battery. At length the aft AA director had its guns "firing at maximum range on eight-inch tracer bearings," but all these efforts were for nothing; the cruiser was making so many turns in her radical maneuvers that it was all but impossible to get good illumination over the main battery's targets.[129] As for the men stationed topside, most remember the ear-splitting din of so many weapons firing at once, but as the minutes ticked by, and the ship began to receive more hits, something more unsettling emerged: a terrible *diminishing* of sound, as one by one *Houston*'s guns were silenced.

Simultaneously, the second section of Sentai 7—heavy cruisers *Mikuma* and *Mogami*, with their escorting destroyer, *Shikinami*—had arrived from the north, effectively trapping *Perth* and *Houston* between the coast and the various divisions of Japanese fighting ships offshore, which enveloped them "on all bearings." The IJN cruisers were still warily trailing their paravanes in case of mines and these threw up enormous sheets of white water along their bows as they cut through the black waters of the Java Sea at 26 knots. Capt. Sakiyama Shakao of *Mikuma* had seen evidence of the battle in the distance at around 2334 hours, with red tracers, flares, and machine-gun bullets showing up against the smoke hanging over the water, but "the exact location of the enemy was still unclear."[130] Although the Japanese captain was frustrated at this time because he was in an unfavorable position to launch one of his floatplanes due to the wind direction, the fighting quickly assumed an urgent and deadly character.

At 2340 the Japanese ships sighted *Perth* ("Unit No. 1") and *Houston* ("Unit No. 2") to the south about two kilometers above Pandjang island and began paralleling their course. Within less than ten minutes, Sakiyama's big cruiser was close enough to launch her first "Long Lance," and here, she too, like the destroyers of DesDiv 5 (and her fellow cruisers in the Battle of the Java Sea the day before), encountered technical problems on this opening torpedo salvo. *Mikuma* had intended to fire a full salvo of three, but one of the torpedoes "slipped down and landed on the second torpedo" and only one weapon could be launched from that mount. This minor fiasco was offset then by a favorable shift in the wind, and *Mikuma* launched one reconnaissance plane, yet even this had consequences. The powder charge for the launch seemed to have caught the attention of the Allied cruisers—or so Captain Sakiyama believed—for much to his annoyance his ship was fired upon before she loosed a salvo of six Type 93 torpedoes at *Perth* ("Unit No. 1") a few minutes later from a range of about 10,000 yards.[131] *Mogami* also fired the same number of torpedoes at *Perth* at 2349 hours. On the advice of his navigator Sakiyama then turned away and reversed course as the two Japanese cruisers were then heading directly for Babi Island at high speed. Three minutes later both *Mikuma* and *Mogami* opened searchlight-directed gunfire against the second enemy ship, *Houston* at a distance of 12,300 yards. This finally gave the two Allied ships a chance to shoot back at their antagonists, and they made the most of the opportunity. *Mikuma* was the first to feel the effects of their return fire.

At 2355 the cruiser *Mikuma* was struck, and her "electrical wiring was damaged."[132] Both of her main battery guns and searchlights suddenly lost power. Clearly the ship had been hit at that point, either directly or by fragments, for it is also recorded that she lost six men killed along with nine more wounded in the battle. At the same time Sakiyama ordered *Mogami* to illuminate the enemy cruisers, while his repair parties worked to fix the damaged electrical circuits. Her sister cruiser did as instructed. Then, at 2357 hours, as if trying to protect her division mate, *Mogami* fired another half-dozen "fish" to port at *Houston*. Although these Type 93 torpedoes all missed the American ship, they wrought truly remarkable damage elsewhere, for these were the torpedoes that reached the transport anchorage along the shoreline.

It is difficult to reconstruct *exactly* which Japanese ship was responsible for the initial torpedo hits against "Hec" Waller's *Perth*, as she had been targeted by no less than three other torpedo attacks—more or less at the same time—after she turned back to the northwest and began heading for Sunda Strait again. All these attacks were from IJN units to the west, between *Perth* and the strait's northern entrance, and all fired their torpedoes on angles that sent their "fish" eastward. Only *Mogami*'s Long Lance torpedoes were traveling to the south-southwest; and while these may or may not have impacted the Australian cruiser, they certainly found their mark among Imamura's anchored convoy. At approximately midnight four Japanese transports, along with the minesweeper *w-2*, were torpedoed in the anchorage; all were sunk.[133] Most ironically this included the command ship *Shinshu Maru*, which was carrying Lieutenant General Imamura and members of his Sixteenth Army staff among others.[134]

Waller's ship was still making at least 20–25 knots when the first torpedo struck her. *Perth* had by that time already been hit by several Japanese projectiles, all of which were recorded by one of her men in the plot, Schoolmaster "Tiger" Lyons. He meticulously noted the first hit at 2326 hours; it went through her forward funnel "with a burst of steam like a locomotive going off"; a second at 2332 hit in the vicinity of the flag deck, with another at 2350 along the waterline, detonating in her ordinary seaman's mess.[135] The first two were most likely the work of destroyer shells, but the last might well have been from one of Sentai 7's heavy cruisers. In any case there does not appear to have been any really crippling damage to Waller's ship prior to the first torpedo hit.

According to Lyons, this devastating hit came at 0005 hours, striking the ship between the forward "A" boiler room and engine room on the starboard side.[136] The "shattering blast" seemed to lift the entire ship bodily out of the sea. All the men in this space were thought to have been killed outright by this explosion. In "B" boiler room, the crew under Chief Stoker Reece continued to monitor their machinery, although most had been knocked down by the explosion. A different survivor from *Perth* later wrote of Engineer Lt. Frank Gillan's experiences in his space: "The boilers began to scream and blow off at their safety valves. He grabbed the phone to the engine room: it was dead; he tried to call damage control: dead; he called the bridge: dead; he tried to ring the telegraph to the engine room: the telegraph was jammed." Suddenly the men realized the ship was already listing to starboard at almost fifteen degrees, and that although the boiler-room diesel generator was still functioning, it was time to get out. They shut down the boilers and cut off the oil fuel lines to prevent explosion and fire, and then everyone went up the stokehold ladders. Gillan recalled the sense of pride he felt serving with these calm, sensible men as they abandoned their station and went up to the uncertainty and violence of the upper decks.[137]

A damage report allegedly reached Waller of this hit and the reduction in speed, but within a minute or two *Perth* was struck again by another torpedo. This weapon appears to have detonated closer to the bridge of the cruiser, abreast the forward 6-inch turret. This second torpedo hit was definitive for many of the officers and sailors of *Perth*, men such as Harold Hill, who was stationed in the 4-inch gunnery control room. Hill had been debating whether to join his shipmates as they abandoned ship—feeling reluctant, as did many men, to leave his familiar station, although his instruments had been put out of operation by the concussion and all phone lines were useless—when he abruptly found himself knocked down by the "spine-jarring force" as the decks slammed up beneath his feet. At that point Hill scrambled out through the bulkhead door and climbed up for the "open air of the quarterdeck."[138]

There was little question that the light cruiser was doomed. *Perth* was still being mangled by shellfire, and flames had broken out along her upper decks, while the numerous hits among gun, signal, and searchlight parties cut down men singly and in clusters. An experienced veteran of many actions, Waller understood what the second torpedo hit meant only too well. He had first ordered either "prepare to abandon ship" or "abandon ship"—various accounts differ—but when the second torpedo exploded he simply said, "Christ, that's torn it." Waller then told his people to get off the bridge in a "clear and hard" voice. When last seen alive, Hector Macdonald Laws Waller had refused to leave his position. He was standing alone on the bridge with his arms on the steel windshield, "looking down at the silent turrets."[139]

A third torpedo struck the cruiser again as the men were trying to get off her; this hit well aft on the starboard side. A fourth torpedo detonated on her port side a few minutes later at 0015 as the ship was dead in the water. This last hit must have caused tremendous damage for it appeared to right the ship almost immediately. Her topsides were still being raked by shellfire and fragments, causing many casualties among men in exposed positions in addition to near misses in the water, which delivered rib-crushing jolts to survivors already in the water. Within no more than fifteen or twenty minutes after the first torpedo, HMAS *Perth* twisted onto her side and sank by the bow some four miles north-northwest of Pandjang Island.[140] Roughly half of *Perth*'s men would be lost in the sinking of their gallant cruiser—a ship they called "The Demon of the Sea"—and which had fought with as much tenacity as any warship of its size in the Second World War.[141] Slightly less than one-third of her crew of 682 would ever live to see their homes and families again after over three years of relentlessly brutal captivity under the Japanese.

• • •

South of *Perth*'s final location, the heavy cruiser *Houston*—last flagship of the Asiatic Fleet, President Franklin Roosevelt's "Little White House" at sea during the prewar years, and a ship fondly dubbed the *Huey Maru* by her own men—now found herself alone in the midst of unnumbered enemies. Survivors of the Australian cruiser, who were by then floating in the currents off Sunda Strait, could make out searchlights, tracers, and explosions in the distance as the Japanese then concentrated all their fury on the lone Allied warship.[142] For her part

　　　　　　　　A DEATH SO VALIANT AND TRUE

*Houston* had been unable to readily follow the Australian cruiser's movements for some time due to gunfire flashes that obscured vision as she fought off her own assailants. Maher believed *Perth* was last seen dead in the water "in a sinking condition about 2345."[143] And while he had more than enough to keep his attention focused elsewhere, the Gun Boss noted that until *Perth* was stopped, the enemy seemed to have trouble singling *Houston* out among the welter of ships present. The sinking of *Perth* may or may not have helped the Japanese fire-control crews, but it surely simplified *Houston*'s IFF problems. *Everything* her gunners spotted from that point was assumed to be enemy and was fired on.

Although *Perth* actually sank a little later (but certainly by 0025 hours), *Houston* had then taken the first of several highly destructive hits from the enemy. The first came just before midnight when a salvo of heavy shells (or possibly a small torpedo) struck the ship on the port side near the after (number 2) engine room. The explosion and escaping steam obliterated the black gang there, which would have been made up of about two dozen men under Lt. Cdr. Richard Gingras, the cruiser's fine engineer officer along with Chief Warrant Machinist J. R. Cravens and First Class Machinist Mate Albert Waldschmidt.[144] For Jack Leroy Smith, WT2/c, in the forward (number 1) engine room, steam and exhaust poured into his space through blowers but was quickly dissipated. Up until that point things were running quite smoothly in Smith's engine room—this is also confirmed by Lt. Bob Fulton, who remembered that his turbines were still making full power—and Smith had even been able to take down the hourly oil consumption reading at twelve o'clock sharp. This devastating explosion in the number 2 engine room cut the cruiser's speed to 15 knots briefly, but a maximum of 23–24 knots was soon achieved from the remaining power generated in the forward room. Although they knew a catastrophic event had taken place in the aft engine spaces—all communications were lost after the hit, with the phone lines suddenly mute—these forward engines continued to function normally under Fulton and his men.

More seriously for her gunnery, hot steam vented topside, which caused the aft Mark 19 AA director (sky aft, under Lieutenant Commander Galbraith) and secondary conn (battle 2) to be temporarily abandoned, along with most of her boat-deck 5-inch guns. To Floyd Arnold in the number 4 1.1-inch mount, these men were engulfed in clouds of escaping steam that looked like "a big blanket of smoke."[145] For many the decks underfoot became too hot for them to remain at their stations. And even when some of the 5-inch gun crews later returned to their mounts, they found the steam continued to obscure their vision, making sighting—already tremendously difficult—all the more problematic.

Below, several other sailors each received different impressions from the engine room hit. For Ted "Itch" Schramm, the baker who doubled as a 5-inch ammo handler on the mess deck, the blast produced the odor of human flesh being cooked. Another sailor, Jack D. Smith—no longer required in the magazine spaces aft—was also in the mess-deck detail handling 5-inch shells. He had been running them up to gun mounts six and eight on the boat deck's portside in the first wave of fighting. A short time later, as Smith was handling star shells in the mess hall, he heard and felt the explosion below. The entire ship trembled, and an ominous *keening* sound—as of air escaping under great pressure—became noticeable, as did a tremendous pressure on the engine room hatches. Although according to Smith these unnerving effects lasted only about one minute, in essence the ship had received a mortal wound.

*Houston*'s after damage repair party under Ens. A. F. Nethken struggled to seal off steam lines but had only minimal success. Fireman Albert Elmo Kennedy and Machinist Mates Phil "Joe" Gans and J. O. Burge worked with others to close valves, but no more than a few were managed and these "with great difficulty."[146] Gans recalled manhandling a giant six-foot-long "crow's foot" wrench with other sailors in the damage repair party as they tried to close several valves that would have stopped the steam escaping topside but achieved nothing.[147]

Over the next half hour the cruiser would slowly and inexorably be shot full of holes as her hull was blasted open by at least three or four torpedoes. In that bloody process scores of men would die as a result. Yet in the end far more would perish in the treacherous currents around Bantam Bay and Sunda Strait after they escaped their doomed vessel. By contrast the Japanese found the engagement extremely nerve-racking for other reasons: friendly fire near misses. In the relatively confined waters off Bantam Bay, over seven dozen Japanese torpedoes went into the sea, and only eight struck their targets. Four had already terminated the career of HMAS *Perth*, and *Houston* is suspected to have been hit by at least one by then. The courageous old cruiser would take three more torpedoes before the dark waters closed at last over her riddled hull. Yet a great number of these lethal weapons sped through the sea, endangering Japanese ships as well. After the battle Rear Admiral Hara Kenzaburo freely acknowledged this peril in his detailed action report: "At the Batavia Battle our destroyers experienced quite a few torpedo near-misses, fired from our [own] cruisers. We felt very much in danger. . . . So many destroyers were involved in a small area."[148]

For a little less than half an hour after *Perth* sank, *Houston* fought on alone against her adversaries. By twenty minutes after midnight she had come within effective gun range of the two heavy cruisers of Sentai 7 as they steamed south at

165 degrees from the location of *Perth*'s destruction. *Mikuma* and *Mogami* were then clipping along at almost 32 knots, led by the destroyer *Shikinami*. After noting the lack of return fire from *Houston*—apart from machine guns—the cruisers' guns were briefly blocked by *Shikinami*. They ordered her aside so that their big search-lights could pin down the slowing American ship. Once *Shikinami* had done so, the cruisers opened fire with their main batteries at 6,500 meters (7,150 yards) and quickly achieved hits. Soon her enemies wrought a dreadful spectacle on *Houston*.

As Ens. C. D. Smith's men in turret 2 were preparing for another salvo—their twenty-eighth of the night—with shells in the upper chamber and powder bags ready, a Japanese projectile struck the left side of the turret's 2.5-inch faceplate. Above the gunhouse in sky forward, Lee Rogers suddenly heard a tremendous metallic clang, followed by a blinding shower of sparks as at a fireworks display. A very brief interval of silence followed, then up from the turret flew a roaring sheet of flame like a blowtorch. Inside the gunhouse Ensign Smith only heard the hit—there was no explosion—followed by a hissing sound like escaping steam. Then brilliant red particles believed to be unburned powder began fly-ing through the interior, striking the wall of the turret officer's booth with tre-mendous force before setting the silk propellant bags on fire. Smith had time to glance into the gunhouse through the porthole in his flameproof enclosure as he triggered the sprinkler system. All he could see was a reddish fog in which the fiery particles flew violently in all directions. Within ten to fifteen seconds these flying bits of powder shattered the glass porthole, and Smith narrowly escaped, tumbling out with the rangefinder operator and the booth talker. By then the gunhouse was an inferno, with the forty-five-pound bags of powder burning to death thirteen members of the turret on the spot; a fourteenth man died of shrapnel wounds. Twenty-seven others escaped that hell unhurt or with burns only to die in the water later; none were known to have made it to shore alive. Out of all of the Second Division men working turret 2 that night, only eight besides Ens. Charles Donovan Smith got off the ship and negotiated the treacherous Sunda Strait currents safely to the coast of Java.[149]

The intensity of the fire in the turret meanwhile drove officers and talkers, including Captain Rooks, Commander Hollowell, the navigator, and Lieu-tenant Hodge, communication officer, from *Houston*'s armored conning tower located just aft of the gunhouse. By this time the ship was slowing rapidly, and steering had been lost. The ship was filling with hundreds of tons of seawater from dozens of shell holes and at least three torpedo hits. Her plotting room had been taken out of action, so that remaining guns had to go to local con-trol. She had begun slowly circling back to the east in a large arc. From the Japanese ships the enormous "fire pillar" was clearly observed, and propaganda artists later created a suitably dramatic image of this climactic moment. Unseen to their eyes (if not imaginations) within *Houston* hundreds of life-and-death dramas were being enacted.

At this time some survivors reported conversations between the captain and his senior officers that they believe suggested he meant to try to ground the ship on Pandjang Island, which was then no more than two miles to the south. Other surviving officers have flatly, not to say emphatically, ridiculed such claims. What *does* appear to have happened was some hesitation and confusion regarding the first abandon ship order. Eventually communications broke down between the bridge and various other fire control stations.

In Hamlin's turret 1 the men had persevered against increasing damage. As he was to later describe it in a postwar paper on gunnery, "Local control assumed the turret was entirely cut off, and operating on its own. The turret officer really came to life for this business. He had to—he was the whole works." Since all the turret officer had to work with was his own guns and rangefinder, "plot was located under his hat."[150]

Hamlin's postwar account gives a better view of what the men were really facing that night. And the very first thing a turret officer (TO) in local control had to do was pick a target and get the trainer to swing the turret in that direction. All Hamlin could see to target was an enemy searchlight in the distance. In reality this was probably from either Sentai 7 or its escorting destroyer, *Shikinami*. "Train left! Target is a searchlight way around to the left! . . . Keep coming you've still got 40 degrees to go!" This was shouted while the TO alternately looked out through his periscope sticking through the top of the gunhouse and eyeballed its indicator dial inside his booth. "Keep coming! Easy now you're almost there. Mark! You just went past it!!! Train right! That's it! *Mark!* Keep on it." At that point he had to get a range from the rangefinder. "Gimme a range to the searchlight, rangefinder!" This was met with silence. "*Range!*" Then the worst response: "Rangefinder out of commission, sir. Left window smashed." As Hamlin drily put it, "Faced with this deviation from standard procedure [I] had to get a range [myself] by estimating it through the periscope."[151] At the same time the TO was noting the turret slowly training right or left as it tried to stay on target.

A very rough, one-eyed guess was the best he could do under the circumstances: "Set range 4,000 . . . deflection left 10." He was firing in the dark in every sense but had no other options. The sight-setter then replied "Set!" and the TO gave the order: "Shoot!" after which he peered through his periscope trying to spot the fall of shot. Hamlin later observed, "That's all there is to local control, but it partakes of the nature of [a] rifleman in [a] rocking boat shooting at [a] running deer."[152]

Around the time that Hamlin's turret had fired some twenty-nine salvos, disaster struck Ens. C. D. Smith's number 2 turret just aft and above. What then followed in the wake of that conflagration was more confusion. Before Hamlin and his junior turret officer, Ens. Coleman Sellers, knew precisely what was occurring, Commander Maher had ordered flooding of the magazines of turrets 1 and 2 as well as a small-arms magazine between the two. To make matters worse, sprinklers were turned on by mistake in the upper powder hoist and powder circle, which eliminated several other rounds that might have been fired. This left Hamlin's turret with only the shells and powder at the guns already; these they then loaded and fired. The result of this final salvo was not observed as *Houston* was then slowing down, afire in multiple places, and enemy gunners had found a killing range. Within moments, and as Hamlin listened to Maher's futile attempts to contact the bridge through his phones, the Gun Boss went ahead and ordered abandon ship.

No sooner had Hamlin passed this information to his crews below over his turret phone and the men began emerging from the decks below than the cruiser took another torpedo or shell salvo on her starboard side forward. This killed and wounded a number of men, including some of the sailors attempting to get out of the magazine spaces. And in this battle—as in all battles—life and death walked a meaningless razor's edge. In that explosion Eugene "Punchy" Parham and his close buddy, Bill Darling, in the powder circle would suffer two horribly dissimilar fates. "Punchy" Parham made it up into the gunhouse chamber all right, but Darling was severely injured from the blast. When last seen by Parham, Darling lay helpless on the powder circle deck below, his back broken. As if this grim scene was not haunting enough, as Parham came up into the gunhouse his ears were assaulted by horrors of another nature: the ugly sounds of shells tearing his beloved ship apart. These he recalled as "an awful, ripping, shredding noise."[153]

Except for the two officers, almost all the other men had evacuated the lower chambers and gunhouse, led by their chief, Bosun's Mate "Red" Clymer, and were huddled beneath the turret outside. This group included "Little Bill" Ingram, who had wriggled out of his starboard powder box and out onto the upper deck. Bill then climbed up into the gunhouse overhang and wrapped a mattress around himself for protection against splinters. Inside the turret Parham and his pal, Wilford Logan—the flap man in the port powder box—had paused briefly before getting out, gathering their thoughts. At just that time the sprinkler system was activated. The two sailors stood side by side and quickly recited the Lord's Prayer together, water streaming down their faces.[154] When they came out, they were the final sailors to emerge from the turret alive, although officers Sellers and Hamlin were the last to leave.

Outside the gunhouse, under searchlights and occasional flares that reminded some men of a Fourth of July celebration, shells and fragments were still screaming into the ship—with most of the enemy firing coming from the port side—and the men briefly sought shelter in the lee of the turrets. After noting the disappearance of all the life rafts lashed to the exterior of the turret, which had been blown away by fragments leaving only "several burning pieces of bulk balsa wood" lying around, Hamlin looked up and to his astonishment saw a very much alive Ens. C. D. Smith standing atop turret 2's smoking roof with a fire hose. He later recalled, "I had written him off when I heard that his turret had blown up, but he was quite unharmed." Smith then yelled down to Hamlin to get himself and his crew back into the turret, "Don't leave your station. We haven't been ordered to abandon ship."[155] Evidently Smith had been told orally by the navigator, Commander Hollowell, that the abandon ship order was rescinded.[156] There was a reason for this: Capt. Albert H. Rooks had been killed just minutes after giving the order.

The intense fire from turret 2 drove the men out of the armored conning tower, and at that stage Rooks and the senior officers with whom he still had direct or phone contact chose to issue the abandon ship order. Eyewitnesses state that Rooks had come out of the conning tower and down a ladder to a passageway abaft the main radio station, located on the communication deck. On his way he passed several officers and men with whom he shook hands, telling them good-bye and good luck. Based on this, it was believed that he had made a decision to stay with the ship. As he came down the ladder to the communication deck, other desperate sailors were abandoning the ship from the depths of her fire rooms and engines spaces. A few sailors were from as far below as central station and plot, very close to the bottom of the ship. Some would emerge up and out onto the communication deck just in time to see the captain killed.

One of the luckiest survivors was Jack Leroy Smith, WT2/c, who had escaped from his station in number 1 boiler room along with four or five other men via a convoluted and at times terrifying path in darkness, flames, and smoke. Serving under Chief Archie Terry, Smith verified that the first abandon ship order came well after midnight because he had already taken the hourly oil consumption readings at twelve, despite the battle. A few minutes later a message blared

A DEATH SO VALIANT AND TRUE

out over the PA speakers. Terry turned to Smith, asking, "Did he say abandon ship?" When Smith affirmed that that was indeed the order, Terry made no bones about it: "Let's get out of here!" He then cut fires beneath the boilers and secured the oil lines; Smith shut off the oil pumps. They and a handful of others began to leave the boiler room when Jack Smith remembered the blowers were still running; he rushed back to turn those off. Afterward he and others would recall that they left their stations as if on a drill. Smith rejoined a few men who left via a claustrophobic climb into the port air lock, up ladders and through hatches, from the first platform and the second deck—where Smith realized he was at the USMC compartment (which was darkened and empty)— past a blazing mess hall up to the blower rooms abaft the captain and admiral's cabins before reaching a hatch at the communication deck. There they found the starboard door to the deck next to the radio shack and opened it.[157]

In the dark passageway behind the radio shack, away from the Japanese searchlights, huddled a cluster of officers and sailors, including Ens. Herb Levitt and Pay Clerk Kenneth Shaw of the marines. At least two of the Chinese mess attendants were also present. Some men were flat on the deck taking shelter from flying steel fragments. One of these sailors was radioman David Flynn, who had escaped successfully from plot, deep in the belly of the ship. Flynn had made a fantastic voyage to get out, climbing up tight vertical trunks and even entering the foremast's leg to scale its rungs in pitch blackness, frightened beyond all imagining yet always keeping in mind his basic orientation by noting the directional sounds of shellfire outside.[158] The young sailor had emerged onto the communication deck and was on his stomach not far from Jack Leroy Smith and the others just up from the boiler room. At that instant voices rang out at the starboard number 1 pom-pom mount not more than fifteen feet away. Smith looked over to the gun tub and heard someone exclaim, "Here they come!"[159] It was the last thing anybody in that mount ever said.

From fine on the starboard bow the Japanese had come in and attacked yet again, pouring more gunfire into the big ship at short range—now illuminated by a large fire on her forecastle and bridge area, making her a far less difficult target. This shell made a direct hit on the starboard pom-pom mount, resulting in what Smith termed a very large explosion that killed the entire gun crew there outright, leaving nothing but "wreckage [and] shambles."[160] Deadly fragments blew through the passageway, cutting down several standing men and wounding others who were prone. David Flynn had his calf shredded by shrapnel, but in this he had been lucky.

Just then as Captain Rooks was coming down off the ladder from the signal-bridge level, he was struck by multiple shards in the head and chest. Fatally injured, he managed to stagger across to the communication deck's port side, where he collapsed. Other men lay slumped nearby. Pay Clerk Shaw was still alive but bleeding profusely, suffering from multiple wounds. When Levitt examined him, Shaw told the young ensign to see to the others. To port Levitt then noticed a figure on the deck in the darkness. He went over and found that this individual was Captain Rooks, with clearly mortal wounds. Levitt called over Ens. C. D. Smith; together they attempted to help Rooks, "but he was too far gone to talk to [them]." Knowing that it was merely a matter of time, Smith injected his captain with two tubes of morphine from the emergency first aid pack on his belt. Capt. Albert Harold Rooks (USNA 1914), the last commanding officer of *Houston*, then expired in the presence of Smith, Levitt, and Shaw. Rooks's body was covered with a blanket, and his death made known to Commander Maher and Commander David Roberts, the executive officer. A veteran Chinese steward named Tai Chi Fat (nicknamed "Buda"), well known for his loyalty, remained with the body of his slain captain until the end.[161]

Hamlin informed Smith that his magazines had been flooded, and there was nothing more he could do; turret 1 was out of action. His men continued to mill around, some finding life jackets, others helping Ensign Sellers put out the stubborn fire on the forecastle. Shellfire and fragments hitting the ship continued to reap exposed sailors on the foredeck. A number of these wounded were aided—to the extent this was possible—by Hamlin and his men. For many this aid amounted to nothing more than a morphine injection. Over the next few minutes, with *Houston*'s starboard list increasing, several score of unwounded men put rafts overboard and slid along the canting hull or jumped into the black waters off Bantam Bay. The swift currents carried them aft quickly, and a great many of these men were never seen again.

With the ship heeling over to starboard more and more—first at 15 then 20, 25 degrees—most of the sailors and officers knew they must get off or run the risk of being taken down with the six-hundred-foot-long cruiser when she went under. All throughout this period the ship continued to take considerable damage from enemy gunfire. Yet shells are small relative to such a huge structure, and quite a few sailors got off the ship unscathed, though most witnessed the dead or wounded, or worse. A number of men who had taken shelter in the hangar or were tending wounded there would be killed when it was hit by a salvo of Japanese shells. Not all the projectiles exploded; many went clear through the thin plating, leaving bright red rings glowing around the entrance and exit holes in the blackness.

A DEATH SO VALIANT AND TRUE

One of the men wounded (only slightly) was Jack Feliz, MM1/c, a towering, hard-nosed veteran. He was coming up from his forward repair party station after the men ran out of fire extinguishers and bumped into a group of sailors leaving fire room number 1. He asked what they were doing and got the response: "Didn't you hear it?" meaning the abandon ship order. He had not, and since he did not have a life jacket, he proceeded topside and encountered an old machinist mate he only knew as "Sherman" (Raymond Shireman, MM1/c), who told him there were more life jackets in the hangar. Feliz made his way aft to the hangar and went inside, where he grabbed a life jacket just in time to see a Japanese shell blast through the hull with a burst of sparks like a Roman candle. Numerous tiny pieces of metal peppered his legs, but he was not seriously injured.[162] Just outside the hangars, quite a few men were also cut down by machine-gun bursts that raked the quarterdeck.

Yet even with such carnage and horrors—the mangled bodies and severed limbs amid pools and gouts of blood; men in flames, blinded, who leaped off the communication deck onto the main deck when turret 2 was hit; entire gun crews lying dead around at least two of the 5-inch mounts—were instances of farcical truth stranger than fiction. At the first abandon ship order, Walter Schneck, Mus2/c, left his position as first loader for the number 2 pom-pom mount (portside forward) and moved back to his abandon ship station. This was next to the forward funnel, where a number of life rafts were secured. There he encountered a fellow band mate who also worked the pom-poms, a tall trombone player named Severyn Dymanowski, Mus1/c. Dazed and uncertain of their next move, the two musicians sat down together. They had just lit cigarettes when a voice from the darkness suddenly barked, "The smoking lamp's out!" Walter Schneck thought this a fairly odd command, since, as he put it, "the ship was on fire from stem to stern."[163]

Up on the bow the First Division's bosun, Shelton "Red" Clymer, went around the base of the forward turret, yelling, "Anybody here? Anybody here? Get off, abandon ship!" A frightened Bill Ingram emerged from beneath the overhang still clinging to his mattress. Clymer told him, "Come on, let's go. We're going over the side." When Ingram replied that he didn't have a life jacket yet, Clymer went back and grabbed a spare life ring, which he handed to the young sailor. Not far away "Punchy" Parham prepared to go over the side, too. While Ingram hesitated briefly, he saw that Red Clymer was still trying to tie his life jacket properly. As the veteran bosun went over the side, Parham heard him say, "I can't swim a lick, but I'm going to give it hell!"[164] On their haunches these men slid down the slanting port bow over the bulbous forefoot and into the dark water.

After he had made it into the sea, Bill Ingram swam like the devil to get free of any undertow that the sinking ship might generate. Clymer had been with him briefly as they hit the water, but when he looked back he realized that the older man had simply disappeared into the black night. What Ingram then saw scared him enough to keep him moving away. The huge ship had gone over so far on her starboard side that two enormous holes in her hull were visible, through which flames sprouted into the night: "You could still see the ship out there, but it was all fire."[165]

Not long before this, musician Walt Schneck had made it into the sea; glancing back he could clearly see one of the marine's .50 cal. machine guns still firing from the foremast. It kept on firing to the last moment, he recalled, even as the old ship went down illuminated in the enemy searchlights.[166] Numerous other survivors in the water reported seeing the same thing, as did the Japanese for that matter. It was, of course, the veteran leatherneck, Walter "Gunny" Standish, doing exactly what he had long said he would do: return fire to the bitter end, making no effort to save himself.

Standish had shrugged off pleas from his remaining gunner, Pfc. Bob Charles, as well as from Commander Maher—then coming down from spot 1—both of whom asked the hard-bitten sergeant to come with him and get off the ship. Standish refused; he was too old, too heavy, and he couldn't swim anyway. He told Charles good-bye calmly just before the younger man went down the rungs to the deck below. Once in the oily water Bob Charles looked back as he drifted away from *Houston*: "The ship was down by the bow, sinking slowly, majestically, stern and screws in the air, flag fluttering in the glare of searchlights."[167] The ship rolled onto her starboard side and slowly sank by the head; her slim bow almost severed by the final torpedo launched by *Shikinami* in a down-the-throat shot. Only then did the darkness and sea claim *Houston* at last. The location was, and is, north of Pandjang Island, with the ship pointing east on a bearing of about 80 degrees. The time according to Japanese records was 0036 hours.[168]

*Houston* and crew had fought as stubbornly and valiantly against a superior enemy as Sir Richard Grenville's famed *Revenge* facing the Spanish four centuries earlier. It would be many years before they found any voice to rival that of Sir Walter Raleigh—one of *the* very greatest Elizabethans, after all—to sing their praises in the dramatic scope and richness befitting what they had done. And while precise facts regarding her loss were not known during the war, there was no doubt she had been sunk and many of her crew captured. The sinking of a ship as famous as *Houston*—with her history of chauffeuring FDR on presiden-

　　　　　　　　　A DEATH SO VALIANT AND TRUE

tial cruises throughout the thirties, and the Asiatic Fleet flagship to boot—was not a military victory that Japanese propaganda could afford to ignore or fail to exploit. Therefore, predictably, within weeks Japanese publications in English gave notice of Houston's sinking, along with other Allied ships. A quite precise total number of her survivors and those of an ill-fated national guard unit, the Second Battalion/131st Field Artillery (known as "The Lost Battalion") who were left behind to be captured and imprisoned with the cruiser's survivors, became available in Japanese publications on Java at that time.

From the 1,060-odd men crewing Houston that last night, hundreds abandoned ship successfully, but fewer than 400 negotiated the deadly currents of Sunda Strait to reach Java's emerald (but no longer friendly) shores and become prisoners of the Japanese. For most of the men, their greatest ordeal was just beginning. Three years and five months later fewer than 300 men would return from the jungles of Southeast Asia, the mines and factories of Japan, or hidden POW camps in desolate Manchuria to their families and friends in the States. There they were recognized as authentic heroes among their own, though all but forgotten by the war-weary public at large. And like so many other survivors of this great and scarifying ordeal, they preferred anonymity, showing little appetite for reliving the past with its dark memories. Yet even as they met and married good women, found new careers, fathered children, and got on with life, they did not allow the past to fade altogether from memory. For veterans of the old Asiatic Fleet, the saying "Lest We Forget" is one that is taken with the utmost seriousness by these men and their families.

. . .

As for the surprised Japanese units off Bantam Bay, they had their own duties to return to after Perth and Houston sank, and the night was not over. Ninety minutes after the two Allied interlopers had disappeared into the sea, destroyers Fubuki, Shirayuki, and Hatsuyuki encountered another luckless Allied vessel, what they described as "a medium-sized tanker." It, too, was attempting to elude the Japanese dragnet then being tightened from Batavia to Sunda Strait. Located northeast of Pandjang Island and close to Babi Island, the solitary ship, whose identity has never been firmly established, was illuminated and riddled by seventeen main battery rounds from Fubuki and another forty-seven from Hatsuyuki.[169]

This tanker was not the only other Allied victim that night either. Along with smaller Dutch ships in the vicinity that made no attempt to aid Perth and Houston was the last RNN destroyer in the Batavia area, Evertsen. She had managed to avoid departing with the cruisers in spite of her orders—or because of them, depending on whose story one accepts—but she was never far away while *Perth* and *Houston* were engaged and battling for their lives. As a final absurdity, *Evertsen* even reported the fight, which Helfrich then passed on ("EVERTSEN REPORTS SEA BATTLE IN PROGRESS OFF ST NICOLAS PT AT 1555 ZED X IF ANY OF ADDRESSEES ARE ENGAGED WITH ENEMY OTHERS REN-DER ASSISTANCE AS POSSIBLE X") to *Houston, Perth,* and *Evertsen* and forwarded to Collins and Glassford.[170]

One of her surviving officers—Lt. Cdr. H. Volten—as a POW later wrote an explanation for his ship's actions (or nonactions) aided by Ens. Herb Levitt from *Houston.* In order to avoid detection ("without disclosing [their] presence to the enemy"), *Evertsen's* boilers were not all lit off as she steamed around the chaos off Bantam Bay. Taking a course north and then west, she managed to skirt the battle and enter the upper end of Sunda Strait. According to Volten, "As we headed south along the Sumatra coast we could see the action was still raging fiercely. The multicolored tracers made a beautiful pyrotechnic display." Her luck holding, *Evertsen* then passed Merak, and she noted a large number of ships lying off that small port. Soon the Dutch destroyer entered a rainsquall, and, Volten maintained, "When we emerged we no longer saw nor heard any firing."[171]

However, within an hour—at approximately 0130—when west of Thwartway Island, *Evertsen's* lookouts spotted what appeared to be two cruisers on her beam about ten thousand yards off. At that time her crew's lack of experience and what little luck *Evertsen* had been running on finally ran out. Thinking the ships were *Perth* and *Houston,* the captain decided to challenge them "as a precautionary measure." These were actually the destroyers *Shirakumo* and *Murakumo,* which after the battle returned to their patrol station and were then heading on an opposite course. *They* at least were fully alert and replied to the challenge by instantly opening fire. The first Japanese salvo scored two hits on *Evertsen's* forecastle and wardroom. Within a short period another shell struck the ship's fire control equipment, wrecking it and inflicting casualties. With her men now slapped into full recognition of her predicament, the Dutch destroyer then made a run for her life, but she could not escape the larger and faster Japanese destroyers. More hits followed, putting her aft 4.7-inch gun out of action, holing the hull, and starting several fires. Seeing that he would be sunk no matter what, *Evertsen's* captain chose to drive the ship aground on coral reefs near Seboekoe Island off the southern tip of Sumatra. His choice may or may not have preserved lives—there were quite a few men lost as it turned out—but it did keep the ship out of enemy hands. At 0300 hours on March 1, *Evertsen* was abandoned and her internal fires, unchecked, gradually progressed over the ensuing day into the aft magazine. Japanese records recorded that the ship violently exploded later that afternoon. Volten's report simply declared: "The ship eventually blew up."[172]

# THIRTEEN

## They Fled to Bliss or Woe

### *The End of the Game*

In Surabaja the Allied command was in the process of disintegrating over that weekend. Around 0800 on February 28, Cdr. Thomas Binford left *Edwards* and went ashore, where he spoke with Rear Admiral Koenraad at the Dutch navy HQ. Although Binford—like his officers and crews—was exhausted and the destroyers were all in dire need of repairs, he knew he had to act decisively. *Only* that could save his ships and men from imminent destruction. Meanwhile, Dutch headquarters at Surabaja had had no communications from Doorman or the CSF since about 0100 that morning, and they wanted Binford's story. He informed them of what he knew and of his proposal to take his ships out to Australia. Rear Admiral Koenraad raised no objection. Then the weary American commander phoned COMSOWESPAC headquarters on the other end of the island via the secure "green" line. He had already sent a message to HQ in midmorning giving such information as he had: "EDWARDS ALDEN PAUL JONES FORD POPE NOW SURABAYA X ALL SHIPS FUELED READY TO SAIL X POPE ELEVEN TORPEDOES PAUL JONES ONE OTHERS NONE X . . . RETIREMENT FROM HERE URGENT TO NORTH AND WESTWARD NOT SAFE X UNDERSTAND LOMBOK AND BALI STRAIT BEING GUARDED X SHOULD HAVE AIR RECONNAISSANCE FOR DEPARTURE AND DEFINITE INFORMATION X WOULD LIKE USE BALI STRAIT IF POSSIBLE AND RETIRE TO AUSTRALIA AND NIGHT AIR RECONNAISSANCE FROM CHINA POINT UNTIL CLEAR BALI STRAIT."[1] This message got through but was delayed for many hours in the miserable communications tangle that defined so much of the ABDA period.

Some of that delay is understandable, as COMSOWESPAC HQ had its hands very full at the moment, simultaneously weighing the losses and dispersal of Allied forces in the Java Sea and trying to get a handle on the rapidly deteriorating situation in the Indian Ocean to the south. When Binford finally spoke with Glassford's operations officer in Bandoeng, he made it clear that he wanted to get his ships away promptly. In one of his finest moments, Binford told him: "I want to get out of here to go to Australia. I have no torpedoes. I have four ships and 700 officers and men. The bottom's dropped out of everything. I don't think it's right to sacrifice them. If we stay 24 hours our ships will be gone." HQ asked about *Houston* and *Perth*; Binford told him that he knew nothing of their fate. He did, however, inform COMSOWESPAC that *Exeter* was in Surabaja, and that she had had casualties. When asked about the fuel situation, Binford said that he had some but was not fully replenished. The harried operations officer replied, "I'll tell the boss and let you know."[2] At that Binford returned to *John D. Edwards*, where he had lunch while awaiting news.

When 1300 hours came, Binford had still received no instructions from COMSOWESPAC. Time was everything; the sands were running out for the Allied forces on Java, and everyone knew it. Binford, to his eternal credit, knew and *felt* it. "By 1:30 [1330] couldn't stand it and I went back ashore. I called [on the] Green Line: 'What's the dope?'" True to form, communications were still jumbled and delayed. He was told, "We sent you a signal." At this Binford reacted sharply: "What in hell did it say?" The overburdened staffer replied, "We told you to go to Australia on your own." Binford started to breathe easier, but then the officer continued, "But *Pope* has to stay to escort the *Exeter*, since she still has her torpedoes." The commander expostulated, "If she stays, she's gone!" He was met with a firm and unequivocal reply: "That's too bad. She *has* to escort the *Exeter*." The cards had been dealt; Binford's four ships drew a winning hand; Willie Blinn's *Pope* did not.[3]

Before leaving Surabaja for the last time, Binford had a final talk with Rear Admiral Koenraad at Dutch naval HQ. "I told the Dutch CO what I had in mind doing. We would get underway at sundown through the East Channel, through Bali Strait, and then to Fremantle." Koenraad asked if he had enough fuel, and Binford said that he thought so. Then the American commander expressed what must have been on a lot of minds at that time: "I'm not running away because I'm scared. I'm leaving to save four ships and 700 men. They'll all be lost if we stay." To his credit, the Dutch officer said that he understood.[4]

That evening Binford began a complicated ruse to try to throw off Japanese aerial surveillance, as there had been enemy planes over Surabaja intermittently since morning. There were some four separate bombing attacks on the harbor and shore installations over the course of that day, which wrecked piers and shore installations but did not damage any of the warships present. Enemy snoopers (primarily from Denpasar on Bali) had been overhead as well. Binford had therefore wanted the ships to depart in two groups, *Edwards* and *Ford* at 1630 hours and *Alden* with *Paul Jones* at 1700. But Asiatic Fleet officers were not above sticking their necks out on behalf of their ships and crews if the circumstances warranted the risk. The skipper of *Alden*, Lt. Cdr. Lewis Coley, did just that. As *Edwards* began to depart, Coley started to get *Alden* under way. Binford got on the TBS and told him to remain at anchor and follow orders. Coley took the plunge, replying, "No. We'll all go together."[5] The commander of DesDiv 58 relented; the ships would get under way at short intervals appearing to head in different directions, then form up in column as they headed past Madura and down into the narrow Bali Strait.[6]

*Edwards* and *Alden* left at 1654, heading for the eastern channel; eight minutes later *Ford* departed for the western channel. And at 1718 *Paul Jones* got her anchor up and steamed for the eastern channel. Then, at 1720 hours, *Ford* reversed course and sped up to rejoin the other three destroyers as they all went out through the eastern channel. At 1755 the ships formed up in column, *Edwards* leading *Alden*, *Ford*, and *Paul Jones* at 12.5 knots. For the next five hours they steamed slowly to conserve fuel. A couple of hours before midnight they cut in the remaining boilers for full power. At 2305 they cleared the minefields spread between Cape Patjenan and Madura, passing a small Dutch patrol vessel, then altered course gradually to the southeast and increased to 22 knots. At midnight the crews went to general quarters. They wanted to be able to exit the Bali Narrows at speed—where the hourglass-shaped strait pinched tight to no more than a mile and half of water between eastern Java and Bali—and sprint out past any Japanese naval pickets in the vicinity.

Vague word from Dutch naval HQs had reached Binford's ships during the afternoon of Allied sinkings in the strait by enemy destroyers and cruisers, and they expected to be spotted at some point. Requests for air reconnaissance came to naught; neither Captain Peterson of PatWing 10 nor Tommy Payne of *Houston* had any useful recon info. About all that Binford's skippers knew was that at least one and maybe two Allied ships had been attacked and sunk in the Bali Straits by enemy warships that day. As contact was felt to be inevitable, the men in the four small and weakly armed destroyers—now denuded of their primary offensive assets, torpedoes—set about doing what they could to make themselves appear more formidable. As "Butch" Parker put it: "Without torpedoes our old 4-Stackers weren't a match for very much, so we tried to do everything that might give us a chance."[7]

The officers knew this activity would serve a dual purpose; it both kept the men busy and helped morale. They had the torpedo gangs put black powder

THEY FLED TO BLISS OR WOE

in the empty tubes so that these "pseudo booster charges" could be fired as if launching fish at the enemy. Alone among the others, *Paul Jones* had actually retained one torpedo. With their 4-inch/50 cal. main batteries on the flushdeckers laid out so that only three guns could bear on a side, they arranged to have their 3-inch/23 cal. "peashooter" AA gun on the fantail "fire in unison with the 4[-inch], so it would look as if [they] were firing 4 gun salvos, and therefore might be more powerful ships."[8]

After clearing the narrows at 22 knots, the destroyers increased speed to 25 knots at 0054 hours for the most dangerous part of their transit. This was just below the tightest stretch, where the four ships would hug the western side of the strait along the coastline of Java's southeastern tip. All the men understood that escape would require expert ship handling, steady nerves, and a great deal of luck. The lead ship, *Edwards*, had an experienced navigator in Lt. William Giles Jr., and as the skipper (Cdr. Henry Eccles) later wrote, Giles "did an outstanding piece of navigation in taking the division through Bali Strait under the conditions we encountered."[9] The conditions encountered by Binford's division that night were about as challenging as can be imagined: excellent visibility, a narrow and shallow waterway through calm seas, and enemy ships known to be nearby. The officers and crews of Binford's destroyers all expected trouble but prayed they might elude the worst of it.

Overhead on the starboard beam of the division hung a fat moon. A few clouds obscured its silver disc from time to time.[10] Lookouts were straining their eyes to the east toward Bali in search of enemy units, while other men— including the watchful navigation teams—could clearly see waves breaking on the beach in the moonlight. The Java shoreline was only a few hundred yards to starboard, and from it bearings could be taken as the ships began to skirt a line of reefs wrapped around the island's southeastern tip.

At 0210 hours the ships increased speed to 29 knots, which was about the maximum power their timeworn boilers and turbines could be expected to produce. Simultaneously *Edwards* and *John D. Ford* spotted a solitary vessel some seven thousand yards to the east. Creeping along very slowly, it at first moved away from the Americans. ComDesDiv 58 Binford in *Edwards* then alerted the others at 0212; he told his ships by TBS not to open fire first, but "if they shoot return fire immediately."[11] Closely monitoring their fathometers, navigators and quartermasters called out depth readings as they helped conn the four-stackers along the shoals.

On *John D. Ford* that night, Elly Ellsworth was not in the radio shack but instead helping man the forward (number 1) 4-inch gun. He, like others, saw breakers on the Java shore to his right and the Japanese ships to his left. He recalled, "I saw this Jap destroyer very clear on the port side just barely moving, practically no wake and like everybody else was wondering what was going on, as I remember two of us had already gone by [it]"—meaning *Edwards* in the lead, followed by *Alden*—"and we were coming up almost even with [it], their ships were so much bigger than ours and looked almost like a cruiser."[12] Within moments the other U.S. lookouts also spotted enemy destroyers, slightly further off and at a different angle. The entire Japanese force was moving in the opposite direction but soon turned together, forming a column. These destroyers then altered course to parallel the four-pipers but quickly began to fall aft of the American ships, which had a speed advantage of at least 15 or more knots.

But the enemy had seen them by then. The destroyers of DesDiv 21 (*Wakaba*, *Hatsushimo*, *Hatsuharu*, and *Nenohi*) were responsible for patrolling the waters off Bali Strait that night for just such fleeing Allied ships. It was only the second day back in combat operations for *Hatsuharu*, which had been damaged six weeks earlier off Staring Bay. For reasons that have remained somewhat obscure until now, the Japanese destroyers had allowed over ten minutes to pass before they opened fire.[13] By this time they were following in line on the Americans' port quarter. Then, as Ellsworth on *Ford* recalled, "All hell broke loose." Enemy salvos rang out, and the first splashes bracketed both *Ford* and *Alden*. The Americans replied instantly in kind.

At an estimated range of six thousand yards *Ford* began firing with ranging ladders rocking at five-hundred- to one-thousand-yard intervals.[14] The American ships were steaming at high speed while zigzagging to escape the enemy shells. Blinded by their own gun flashes, the gun crews on *Ford* were unable to range and spot their salvos as they were trained to do. Instead they fired as swiftly as possible in rocking ladders and hoped their speed advantage might get them out of range. Meanwhile, the black gang monitored boilers and turbines, alternating curses with prayers that the elderly machinery would hold together. Although the first Japanese salvo or two landed close enough to splash water on *Ford*, subsequent salvos were well off. On the lead destroyer, *John D. Edwards*, navigator Lt. Bill Giles was proving to be the "cool expert ship handler" his skipper took him to be as he led the division through the gauntlet. With at times no more than twenty feet of water under their thin hulls, the four tin cans shot past the reefs and shoal water. After several minutes the shooting stopped. *Paul Jones* checked fire last. It was 0240; her number 4 gun fired in local control until its gun captain got word to cease fire from the after steering station.[15] That ship had fired forty rounds of 4-inch in four heart-stopping minutes. Of the others *Alden* expended thirty-one rounds, and *John D. Ford* fired thirty-three 4-inch plus twenty rounds from her fantail 3-inch gun. For whatever they were worth, the fake torpedo booster charges had been utilized as well.

At the same time at least one of the flushdeckers had started to make smoke, but this was countermanded quickly as it was believed it could make it easier for the enemy—now well astern—to pinpoint their location. As Parker later wrote, "Neither side illuminated and no hits were observed or believed made by either side."[16] Binford wanted to make a feint toward Tjilatjap and had the division alter course first to 205° T. and then to 210° for the remainder of the night. Tail-end Charlie *Paul Jones* poured on the steam and got 391 revolutions out of her power plant, good for 30 knots, for the next ten minutes. She had the sense not to push her luck though and eventually cut back to 29.5 knots before settling in at 27 knots with the rest of Binford's destroyers.

Over thirty minutes went by and then far astern in the black night, gunfire again commenced. An enemy ship appeared to be firing, but not in the direction of Binford's division. This outburst lasted less than five minutes, ending at 0325 hours. Some of the men thought that the Japanese were attempting to lure the Americans into giving away their position by drawing their fire. Others suspected they were finishing off another luckless Allied vessel that had crossed their path. None of the flushdeckers responded. "We hauled away from there," said Binford years later, and they all held course south by southwest at 27 to 29 knots.[17] Fantastically, or miraculously, they had eluded—at least for the time being—their antagonists. To put the maximum distance between enemy land-based planes as well as any lurking surface craft, Binford had the division run at full power until daylight. But to their immense relief the day broke clear of enemy ships trailing behind them or snooping planes overhead.

However, at about 0720 hours a strange aircraft was spotted, and all the ships scattered. This turned out to be a low-flying PBY that passed them by and kept on going. An hour later *Paul Jones* suffered the ill effects of prolonged high-speed steaming. An engine casualty slowed her to 15 knots for about half an hour while her black gang worked to repair a nipple on the main feed pump. Within a matter of minutes she worked back up to 20 knots and then to 29, sprinting to catch up with the formation. At noon the division altered course to due south at 180° T. and lowered its speed to 22 knots.

Engineers were busy making fuel calculations, and all soon realized it would be a near-run thing to make Australia. With this in mind Binford had the ships lower their speed to 15 knots just after 1800 hours. Throughout the night they steamed at this speed, anxiously on the alert for possible enemy units and dread-ing the approach of dawn. They still hoped for storms and cloud cover, but March 1 had offered none of any appreciable measure. The engine rooms secured half the boilers—with the remaining two on one half-hour's notice—to give the black gangs some rest. Cooks on *Ford* were able to fix what approximated regular meals for the first time in several days; the hungry, weary men devoured steak and eggs, soup and stew, coleslaw with raisins.[18] This was a unique and short-lived luxury, though. Other ships had not been able to replenish provisions so well. *Edwards* was quite low on fresh food when she left Java and according to Binford "had only hard provisions left."[19]

Yet each hour steaming south put more sea between the four battered destroyers and the air patrols of the enemy on Bali. By the end of that Black Sunday, with its bloody tragedies to the west entirely unknown to Binford's division, the ships had run several hundred miles closer to Australia. Luck rode with the four tin cans, even as it had clearly deserted so many other Allied vessels leaving the doomed East Indies. Engineering casualties continued to occur but were not overly serious. *Alden* suffered condenser and boiler tube failures; *Edwards* even lost the use of two boilers entirely due to tube failures. Still they were able to steam doggedly south.

Monday morning, March 2, broke free of enemy contacts but with worsening weather. The ships were hit briefly by the giant swells, high seas, and wind for which the Indian Ocean is notorious. For the destroyers such rough weather was a blessing in the existential sense even if it made the sailors' lives miserably anxious again. Marion "Elly" Ellsworth on *Ford* recalled this interval as a very unnerving period indeed: "The ship would go over a big wave and then . . . would plunge down with a terrible noise; I was sure that it would break in two or that it would break all of the firebricks in the burners and we would lose power; [it was] very frightening to me . . . [and] more scary than the battles."[20]

Around midday on Tuesday, March 3, the ships sighted land; a lighthouse was spotted seventeen miles off their port side. The men all cheered and were promptly met with warnings from officers that the Japanese task force was still at sea and might well be between them and Fremantle (the original destination of Exmouth Gulf had been changed). They were not quite out of the woods yet. So for a short period the ships sped up again to 22 knots as they maintained their southerly course. On the same day Binford detached *Ford* and *Paul Jones* to locate and escort their DesRon 29 "mother hen" *Black Hawk*—also heading south from Exmouth Gulf—due to enemy submarine sightings, but no contact with the tender was made, and the two tin cans rejoined *Edwards* and *Alden* the next morning. Eventually a "friendly patrol plane" was sighted in the early afternoon. During the day the quartet had slowed gradually to 15 knots and then to 10–12 knots as the gravity of their fuel situation became more apparent.

No more noteworthy incidents occurred from there on, but the ships did pair off and spread out at one point to search for possible survivors of sunken vessels. Apparently some floating debris was encountered, but no survivors—or dead bodies—were found. As the ships also possessed an insufficient number of charts, Binford had seen that a chart was transferred to one ship in each pair so that they could navigate together. This worked well enough, and around 1600 hours on Wednesday, March 4, all ships reached the Australian port of Fremantle at last. Records show they had used up almost 90 percent of their fuel. At 1652 hours *Ford*'s log recorded that the ship was anchored off Fremantle. In the baseball vernacular of Lt. Cdr. "Jocko" Cooper, they had "come from behind" and won the game after all, against tremendous adversity. But for other veteran Asiatic Fleet units—*Pecos, Edsall, Pillsbury, Asheville, Pope*—the odds caught up and payment in full was extracted in blood.

A few hours later the good shepherd *Whipple* reached port, her oil bunkers also very nearly empty. *Whipple*'s helmsman was aided by Walt Frumerie and McConnell from *Langley* as the destroyer came into the harbor. In retrospect that evening must have seemed a conclusion to the most hellish week imaginable for McConnell, Abernethy, Crouch, Karpe, and their men. The case of *Whipple* in particular now seems especially fantastic.

From departing Tjilatjap the previous Thursday afternoon (February 26) on the *Langley* mission (along with their ill-starred sister *Edsall*) until finally reaching Fremantle several thousand miles away on Wednesday (March 4), Eugene Karpe's *Whipple* had been through one of the Pacific War's most implausible and horrendous odysseys. But even if they were heroes worthy of an epic poem, these men had no epic poets to speak or write for them. Therefore, no one would be surprised to learn of Walt Frumerie's melancholy recollection of the final leg on that long journey south to Fremantle. He remembered that it had been "very hard on Karpe."[21]

. . .

After limping back into Surabaja at 5 knots early on Saturday, February 28, the damaged *Exeter* anchored and made preparations for burying her casualties, while her engineers and artificers labored to get as much of her damaged power plant back into commission as possible. By midafternoon these emergency repairs were successful to the extent that the ship's engineers thought she could make 15–16 knots later that night using two boilers. And it was believed she might steam at 24 knots on the following day if by then four boilers could be operated. Captain Gordon told Palliser in Bandoeng as much when he called from Dutch naval HQ at Surabaja. There was absolutely no question that *Exeter* needed to leave promptly if she was to have any chance at all of escaping.

In the afternoon Gordon also sent a message regarding the Japanese shooting to Collins, who then relayed it on to London and Ceylon: "JAP 8 INCH GUN CRUISERS GUNFIRE EXTREMELY ACCURATE AT 28,000 YARDS X APPARANTLY [*sic*] RDF CONTROLLED X VERY SMALL SPREAD EXCELLENT." Two and a half hours later Collins informed Helfrich and the Admiralty that "in view of redisposition of remaining ships of China Force," he would close down his office at Batavia on the morning of March 2 and transfer to the depot ship HMS *Anking* at Tjilatjap.[22] As it turned out, he had to move quicker than that.

By late afternoon the plans at Surabaja were laid: HMS *Encounter* and USS *Pope* would go with *Exeter* as her escorts. The Dutch destroyer *Witte de With* was also to accompany the force, although she would depart about two hours later than the others. She was expected to join up shortly after midnight, and with this understanding her navigator was given information on the anticipated courses and speeds by *Exeter*. However, this Royal Netherlands Navy vessel never left Surabaja to join the others, and no explanation or information reached the *Exeter* group regarding her failure to do so. Whatever the cause, in the end she remained behind and was destroyed at her moorings the following day by one of the many Japanese bombing raids on Surabaja. All her crew had gone ashore to shelter in bombproof bunkers during these air attacks. They later emerged unharmed only to find their ship on the bottom of the harbor.

Not surprisingly, the hastily made plans for the *Exeter* group's breakout were of the same wishful (and wrongheaded) thinking that characterized so much of ABDA's disorderly life. The course chosen for this sortie by *Exeter* and her two escorts was as foolhardy as any involved in the *Langley* fiasco. Nonetheless, the brutal truth is that by retiring to Surabaja the British cruiser was left in an impossible position. She was considered too large, her draft too deep, to transit Bali Strait—unlike Binford's division of four-pipers—and Lombok Strait to the east was believed to be covered by enemy surface and air units. Under the circumstances the ships were ordered by Collins (CCCF)—via instructions from Helfrich—to depart Surabaja and steam some twenty miles east along the upper coast of Madura Island, then turn north and pass to the east of Bawean Island before steering northwest.[23] This route would take the trio on a course parallel to the southern coast of Borneo for a couple of hundred miles after which they would—if undetected—alter course for Sunda Strait, which lay well to the southwest. Had *Exeter* been able to do this successfully, her orders were then to proceed to the British naval base at Colombo, Ceylon.

In terms of realistic possibilities, though, Collins, Palliser, and Helfrich might just as well have asked the trio of weary ships to steam overland across Java's mountains to reach the Indian Ocean. Above the Java Sea on all quadrants—to the north, west, south, and east—operated enemy air forces—from Kendari to the northeast, from southern Borneo to the northwest, from Bali and Timor to the east, from Sumatra to the west. And in those vectors not adequately patrolled by land-based aircraft had been situated a thick web of shipborne planes from cruisers, carriers, and auxiliaries. Japanese naval units were heavily invested in the waters from Sumatra to the eastern Celebes. They were working earnestly and efficiently to cover landings from Merak, Bantam Bay, and Eretanwatan (Patrol) on Java's western end to Kragan on the northeast coast. Below the island in the Indian Ocean, streaming many hundreds of miles to the south, were the dual Japanese task groups of Kondō and Nagumo. Under such conditions the ultimate fate of *Exeter* and company were truly as foregone a conclusion as anyone might have envisioned. It only remained to be seen how the final, inevitable results would be played out.

*Pope*, doomed to this fateful duty because she still carried eleven of her torpedoes, received her orders from COMOWESPAC at about 1700 hours. An hour later the skipper, Lieutenant Commander Blinn, and his communications officer, Lt. Bill Spears, went together to *Exeter* to receive their instructions on courses, station keeping, and communications. They soon returned to the four-piper and informed the other officers of their mission. A general cursing of the Dutchman responsible for issuing such orders was the predictable result, followed by oaths directed against the torpedoes themselves, the tender *Black Hawk* for supplying them in the first place, and "on general principles," as *Pope*'s first lieutenant, Jack Michel, later drily recalled.[24] When asked by a bosun's mate about their chances, Michel nonetheless replied disingenuously. He told him that escape was "a cinch" because contact with the Japanese was to be avoided, and the enemy would be too preoccupied with his landing operations in any event.[25]

For those on board *Pope*'s opposite number, the British destroyer HMS *Encounter*, reactions were perhaps less overt, but explanations no less absurd. Her skipper (Commander Morgan) outlined the plan to his officers, offering the same rather strained rationalization that the Japanese covering forces would be so busy protecting the landings on Java that the Allied trio could slip away undetected behind them. The Royal Navy, too, of course produced its fair share of optimists and pessimists, the gullible and the wary. Some of the young men apparently believed they would get away from the East Indies to Ceylon. Others, like a gunner named John Lieper, had for some time—at least since the fall of Singapore—expressed more gloomy (if realistic) sentiments. He was heard to mutter repeatedly, "This bastard's going down under me." As the ship's gunnery control officer, Sam Falle, expressed it years later: "The mind boggles, once more, at the idiocy of man, particularly the asinine admiral concerned. The captain, [Morgan] of course, understood what was happening only too well, but the rest of us did not realize that we were going to our execution, and our ill-based optimism held."[26]

As darkness settled in following a beautiful sunset, the three ships got under way from Surabaja's quiet, deserted harbor. It was 1900 hours on Saturday, February 28. They steamed until clear of the northeastern channel and minefield; then the destroyers took their screening positions ahead of *Exeter*. *Encounter* moved off to port, while *Pope* took up station on the cruiser's starboard bow some 1,500 yards away. The Java Sea was tranquil, as it often was, but the bright moon on that lovely tropical night gave more illumination than the ships' men would have preferred.

For Bill Penninger, MM2/c, on *Pope*, the night unfolded quietly, as it did for Jack Michel. Penninger was able to sleep a little before his 0400–0800 shift in the engine room. Michel, likewise, turned in "to get as much rest as possible before [his] midwatch."[27] Above, on the after deckhouse, Joe Sam Sisk was at one of *Pope*'s .50 cal. mounts, wearing his steel helmet and talker's phones.

On *Encounter* Sam Falle remembered, "Slowly we sailed on through that glorious night. For a long time we saw nothing and everything seemed peaceful."[28] The ships were not making much speed at that point, perhaps 12 knots at first, then working up to 16, as the engineers continued to labor on *Exeter*'s boilers. Captain Gordon likewise noted that "the first part of the night . . . passed without incident."[29] They crept east for some time along the upper coast of Madura Island, then turned north at midnight, altering course to 000 degrees in order to pass approximately twenty-five miles east of Bawean Island. Two hours later the force changed course—"veering to the northwest" as Penninger recalled—to 345 degrees as *Exeter* increased her steaming capacity to 23 knots.[30]

The issue of whether this force received any messages regarding the fate of *Perth* and *Houston* at Bantam Bay remains a somewhat conjectural matter. At least one account states unequivocally that some communication had been intercepted indicating the battle off Sunda Strait, but Captain Gordon later wrote that absolutely no such reports ever reached his force. So the three ships

THEY FLED TO BLISS OR WOE

steamed on peacefully in the dark. Dawn brought a sunny, clear day and with it a very harsh awakening.

In those final hours of tranquility, with the ships zigzagging at slightly over 20 knots, Jack Michel took over as OOD on *Pope* for the midwatch (midnight until four o'clock). Off to starboard Michel spotted what he thought were either ships or possibly islands in the darkness. He woke up Lieutenant Commander Blinn, who was sleeping on the bridge at that hour, and the two men pondered what it was they were seeing. On the bridge of *Exeter*, Captain Gordon had also been alerted to objects seen "in the light of the setting moon" by his look-outs.[31] These were soon identified as three ships: two large merchant vessels and a small cruiser or destroyer. They were several miles away, steaming to the southwest, and passing west of Bawean Island. With no desire for any type of encounter, Gordon turned *Exeter* away, her stern to the enemy ships, and in so doing lost *Pope* in the night.

As he discussed possible identities with Blinn on the four-piper's bridge, Jack Michel looked back to check the position of Gordon's cruiser. She was nowhere to be seen. Momentarily alarmed, he told Blinn, and the unperturbed skipper simply had him reverse course. Within a few more minutes "the *Exeter* appeared out of the gloom ahead of [them] on a similar course."[32] Formation was rejoined just as his relief, Lt. "Red" Bassett, came up to the bridge. Relieved in more ways than one, Michel then went below to his minuscule cabin and enjoyed a few hours' sleep before breakfast.

Gordon in *Exeter* had taken the ships around to the north before resuming a course of 345 degrees again at about 0430 hours. An hour and a half later she altered to 290 degrees. The day emerged brilliant, sunny, and clear with extreme visibility. Although many had anticipated finding themselves ringed by enemy surface ships, daybreak brought nothing of the sort at all. In the words of Sam Falle on *Encounter*, they found "only a wide horizon, an empty sea."[33]

On both destroyers men were able to eat breakfast, or at least some of it, before the inevitable occurred. For Falle this last meal consisted of one duck egg, a "chunk of bread" and the ubiquitous cup of tea.[34] It is unlikely that *Pope's* crew enjoyed much finer cuisine that morning themselves; the destroyer had been low on provisions since her last real replenishment in late January. Lieutenant (j.g.) Michel had just finished his breakfast, such as it was—Bill Penninger was midway through his—when the first enemy units appeared over the horizon's flat rim.

The mast tops of what appeared to be two enemy cruisers were spotted by the crow's nest lookout on *Exeter* at some time just after 0730 hours. These big ships were seen almost dead ahead, hull down and steering to the north-

northeast. Gordon swiftly turned his ships away on a reverse heading, hoping that they had not been spotted. Although he suspected they had seen his force, the two vessels—Rear Adm. Takagi Takeo's Sentai 5, *Nachi* and *Haguro*, along with two accompanying destroyers, *Kawakaze* and *Yamakaze*—were intent on their patrol route and indeed failed to spy the three Allied ships to the west.

To the north Gordon's group would soon be confronted by the Japanese group known as Main Force. This was made up of the two other heavy cruisers of Sentai 5, *Ashigara*—the Third Fleet flagship, with Vice Adm. Takahashi Ibō and staff embarked—and her sister, *Myōkō*. The latter warship had only very recently returned to combat following repairs to damage inflicted by U.S. B-17s in the Philippines in early January. These big, sinuous cruisers—each over 640 feet long and well over 14,000 tons displacement—were screened by two modern destroyers, *Akebono* and *Inazuma*.

All the Japanese ships had other priorities that morning. Takagi's group was providing offshore support for the eastern convoy's landings at Kragan. During the night, as they patrolled, these warships had passed through a concentration of Allied sailors drifting in the water. The men were survivors from the Dutch light cruiser *Java*, and they called out to the Japanese. At 0150 hours the destroyer *Kawakaze* took aboard thirty-seven survivors of *Java*. The four officers and thirty-three enlisted men were all then transferred to *Nachi* later that morning and remained aboard the cruiser for several (no doubt exciting, or terrifying) days before finally being sent ashore to become POWs at Makassar.

The overall commander of Ranin Butai, Vice Admiral Takahashi Ibō in Main Force was himself preoccupied that morning with the dilemma presented by the seizure of a Dutch hospital ship, the *Op ten Noort*. That large vessel had been sent out from Surabaja by Rear Admiral Koenraad after news of the probable sinkings of *Java* and *De Ruyter* reached Dutch naval HQ in the early hours of February 28. It was hoped she could rescue as many survivors from the cruisers as possible. She was directed to head for the spot of the sinkings, thought to be southwest of Bawean Island. In assigning *Op ten Noort* this mission, the Dutch seem to have rather naively assumed that her neutrality would be respected, but this was not the case.

Steaming at 0600 hours that morning, she received further instruction from a Dutch patrol vessel to be on the lookout "north of the lightship for an American submarine, reported to have on board 30 survivors of a Dutch destroyer."[35] She did not encounter this submarine, which was undoubtedly Lt. Cdr. H. C. Munson's pigboat S-38, then crammed with over four dozen survivors of HMS *Electra*.

In the afternoon at approximately 1400 hours, while still some ten or fifteen miles from the reported position of the *Java* and *De Ruyter* sinkings, the hospital ship stumbled into the Japanese eastern invasion convoy heading south. Several escorting screen vessels immediately detached themselves from the mass of transports and steamed straight for *Op ten Noort*. A DesRon 4 destroyer, *Murasame*, was the first to reach her, hoisting flag signals. "YOU SHOULD STOP" was then followed by "YOU SHOULD NOT OPERATE YOUR WIRELESS."[36] *Op ten Noort* did as she was instructed. And at that moment the ship became a kind of unwitting pawn that would exert considerable influence on a series of subsequent events. Rear Admiral Nishimura had quickly ordered *Murasame* back to her position screening the all-important convoy and informed Rear Admiral Tanaka of DesRon 2 in *Jintsū* to take charge of the enemy ship. This led to even more convoluted movements by the Japanese. When he learned of the hospital ship's whereabouts that morning, Vice Admiral Takahashi detached *Akebono* from Main Force to race ahead and take *Op ten Noort* in to Bandjarmasin. *Akebono* was hurrying along on this new assignment when she ran smack into the *Exeter* group.

Sam Falle remembered that on *Encounter* the men had been "piped to defence stations [after the brief 0730 sightings] which gave the ship's company a brief break with half the crew members standing down."[37] Then at about 0935 hours as the ships were on a course of 260 degrees, *Exeter* suddenly sighted more mast tops appearing over the horizon. These appeared to the south and were seen to be two large cruisers moving west. The ships were Takagi's *Nachi* and *Haguro*, and as they were very low on ammunition following their lavish gunnery in the Battle of the Java Sea, they preferred to "help" Takahashi by waiting for his units to arrive. In the meantime they launched two observation planes between 0947 and 0958 to keep tabs on the Allied force. Inside another ten minutes Takagi had communicated with the Eleventh Air Squadron's seaplane tender *Chitose*, and that ship launched two planes "for the purpose of attacking the enemy cruiser."[38] Immediately Gordon had his group alter to 320 degrees, but the enemy ships turned toward the Allied squadron, although they did not close. It was while on this northwest heading, trying to evade the two southernmost Japanese cruisers of Takagi's Sentai 5, that the *Exeter* group ran headlong into solitary *Akebono*.

At first mistaken for a light cruiser by the Gordon-led force, at 1010 hours she spotted the Allied ships. At 1013 *Akebono* radioed, "Sighted one enemy cruiser and two destroyers that appear to be enemy. Bearing from us 120 degrees." The intrepid Japanese DD continued to head directly toward the enemy group. For this temerity she received a warm welcome: 8-inch gunfire erupted from *Exeter* at a range of some twenty thousand yards. *Akebono* then sent another message immediately after her contact report: "We are engaging with enemy."[39] Both Allied destroyers also opened fire, too, with ranges going down to twelve thousand to fourteen thousand yards, as confirmed in Welford Blinn's account. After twelve salvos *Encounter* checked fire from her 4.7-inch battery. And while *Akebono*'s return fire was predictably sharp, with her salvos landing "splashes . . . close about the *Pope*," she was being attacked by three adversaries and understood the better part of valor.[40] She made smoke, then wheeled and turned away to the west. Of course the Japanese destroyer knew she had two big siblings nearby, and these soon made their presence known.

As Gordon wrote: "Almost simultaneously [as *Akebono* turned away] two more large cruisers were sighted bearing approximately 330 degrees and these at once turned towards."[41] Unwittingly but predictably, the three Allied ships had been caught between the jaws of the most powerful Japanese covering forces in the eastern Java Sea. Gordon then altered course east on a 90-degree heading, and what would become a long, lethal stern chase developed.

The paired cruisers to the north were Vice Admiral Takahashi of Main Force in his flagship, *Ashigara*, and her sister, *Myōkō*. They had a single destroyer still in company with them, *Inazuma*. Coming up from the south was Rear Admiral Takagi of Sentai 5 with *Nachi* and *Haguro*, accompanied by the destroyers *Kawakaze* and *Yamakaze*. It was well understood that Takagi's Fifth Sentai had already expended a huge amount of ordnance during the previous day and night against Doorman's CSF, so herding Gordon's ships into the maw of Takahashi's force made sense. Accordingly, even though at greater distance, it was Vice Admiral Takahashi who took the fight to Gordon's ships.

At 1020 hours the two heavy cruisers of Main Force opened 8-inch gunfire at a range of 23,500 meters (almost 26,000 yards).[42] *Exeter* was then making 23 knots and heading due east with *Encounter* ahead to the north (port) and *Pope* to the south (starboard). As the action commenced, Gordon received word from his engineer officer that within the hour another boiler in B boiler room might be connected, giving the ship another knot or two of speed. Gordon gave orders to do so, and as events played out the connections were made even quicker than estimated. Within thirty minutes *Exeter* had worked up to 25 knots, with Gordon later noting, "Before the end the ship was steaming at 26 knots."[43] As they all zigzagged east, with enemy salvos beginning to land dangerously near *Exeter*, the three Allied ships started making smoke from both funnels and smoke floats.

For roughly forty-five minutes *Exeter* gave a gallant account of herself, showing the mettle that had won the British cruiser acclaim off Montevideo in December

1939 against the German *Panzerschiffe Graf Spee*. But at that time she had two other consorts, *Achilles* and *Ajax*, with which to team up against the more heavily armed but slower Kriegsmarine warship. Now the tables were turned; she was the fox, and the hounds were more numerous as well as larger and faster. It is improbable that the men on the Allied ships that midday southwest of Cape Putting had many thoughts of winning glory in those last desperate hours.

In the battle's opening phase *Exeter*'s primary difficulty lay in avoiding enemy salvos while simultaneously trying to open her firing arcs to shell those ships pursuing astern and off her quarters. Course alterations—as recalled by Gordon—varied between 70 degrees and 0 degrees as he dodged the Japanese splashes and returned fire. The wear and tear of gunfire shock impacted the old British cruiser as well. Early on, her fire control table in the transmitting station suffered a mechanical breakdown. It was never completely repaired, and the crew improvised with a clock and Dumaresque for the rest of the action.[44]

Chief Ordnance Artificer W. E. Johns recalled that the aft main battery "Y" turret had several serious problems. These included a failure of the compressed air system for clearing cordite fumes and a potentially deadly hang-fire in the right-hand 8-inch gun. Luckily a cool-headed sailor in the loading seat, Able Seaman Jock Lindsay, kept his wits during the latter and prevented a devastating explosion in the turret by *not* forcing open the breech at the wrong time.[45]

Physical exhaustion likewise took its toll. For example, another of the ship's ordnance artificers, a Scotsman named Doug Grant, who was a member of a damage repair party, recalled long, tense minutes waiting in a closed compartment during the battle's opening phase. After a period he was sent back to work on a jammed 8-inch shell hoist that served "Y" turret. At length he did get the hoist functioning again, but these repairs had consumed precious time. His efforts in the hot, stifling shell room also left him utterly drained, and he, too, ended up sprawled atop the big projectiles in exhaustion. As he realized, this failure in the hoist meant that at least one of *Exeter*'s aft 8-inch guns was not firing for a good part of the engagement. The Japanese themselves would verify this, too, before all was finished.

The smokescreens laid by Gordon's ships did help conceal them for a time. Welford Blinn recalled later that *Exeter*'s spotting crew said they could actually see over the smoke and still direct fire against Takahashi's ships, and this may have compelled the Japanese to close the range. In any event *Pope* struggled to maintain station during the next phase as Gordon swung his ship slightly south then back to the east, avoiding the enemy salvos from the north. *Pope* then found herself on *Exeter*'s engaged side, and as Blinn wrote, "At this time

*Pope* was about 3,000 yards on the port quarter of *Exeter* and it took considerable time to reach our station on the port bow."[46] The flushdecker pushed her wheezing power plant to the limit and achieved 29 knots during this shift in position. Nonetheless, the more powerful Japanese destroyers *Akebono* and *Inazuma* had closed right in, working their way first aft and then to the starboard quarter of the Allied force. Their superior speed would have allowed them to press in at will, but all three enemy ships were still returning fire energetically, and greater risks were simply unnecessary. The three Allied ships weren't going to escape under *any* circumstances.

With the Japanese pressing in, *Pope* fired a brace of torpedoes "at the oncoming destroyers at a torpedo range of about 7,000 yards." It may have been these firings that compelled *Akebono* and *Inazuma* to slide around again to the south of Gordon's ships, narrowing the range as they did so. Below decks in *Pope's* broiling after engine room—with temperatures of 115° F—throttle-man Bill Penninger, MM2/c, labored with the other black gang members to squeeze every ounce of power from the old ship's boilers and turbines. They had lashed down the boiler safety valves "so that they wouldn't pop, in an effort to gain more speed, in an attempt to outrun them." At the same time, like many others, Penninger admitted, "I would pray to the Good Lord silently to protect the crew from injury and to protect the ship from destruction."[47] Throughout the battle the stalwart machinist mate and his fellow throttle man—two were assigned to each throttle during action stations—would be allowed to take turns at fifteen minute intervals to run up to the main deck for a gulp of fresh air. He could then also glance out at the sky and sea to get a snapshot impression of the action. Doing this Penninger recalled that *Pope* had even dropped some of her remaining depth charges in an effort to lighten the ship and perhaps make better speed.

Japanese shells *were* landing at times near *Pope*, if only infrequently. Her initial taste of enemy 8-inch gunfire came just after she laid her first thick smokescreen around *Exeter*. This apparently got the attention of the Japanese, and in response Takahashi's ships walked a few salvos to within a few hundred yards of *Pope*. Fortunately Blinn was able to maneuver his small ship through them, but as Lieutenant (j.g.) Michel—acting as spotter in the crow's nest—understood, such luck was unlikely to go on indefinitely. And all through this phase *Pope* was unable to return fire herself, this, as Michel noted, "for the excellent reason that our guns could not reach the enemy cruisers."[48]

Soon enough, though, the Japanese destroyers forged ahead and came up on the starboard beam of the Allied ships, firing salvos in tightly grouped patterns as they did so. *Exeter* replied with her 4-inch secondaries, while *Encounter* fired away with her 4.7-inch battery as well. The many splashes falling around the enemy ships made Michel's already difficult spotting job on *Pope* no easier. To compensate he "walked [their] salvos across the target a number of times to make sure that what [he] judged to be straddles were not all shorts."[49] So far as is known, however, the Allied shooting was not particularly accurate and they made no known hits against Takahashi's ships at that point. The patience of the Japanese, and their willingness to keep their ships at arm's length, just beyond the limits of the Allied destroyer guns' effective range, may have added to the ragged return fire from Gordon's force.

After firing her first two torpedoes to port at Takahashi's cruisers, *Pope* and the others next found the situation going from bad to worse: two more large, heavy cruisers and two big destroyers suddenly appeared from the south. These, too, were soon engaged in the battle. The cruisers were Rear Admiral Takagi's fully blooded sisters *Nachi* and *Haguro*, which had now caught up with the action. They were screened by destroyers *Kawakaze* and *Yamakaze*, which were several thousand yards closer to the Allied ships. *Nachi* and *Haguro* moved to within some 17,600-19,800 yards before opening fire at about 1055 hours. Their two destroyers were soon paralleling Gordon's force a few points forward of *Pope's* beam at 12,000 yards and firing as they ran eastward.

Within another ten minutes or so, *Exeter* fired torpedoes herself at the northern pair of cruisers, *Ashigara* and *Myōkō*. Welford Blinn in *Pope* took that as a cue and expended four more torpedoes a few minutes later at the same enemy cruisers—with the range estimated at 6,500 yards. None of these hit, but it was believed, and hoped, that they may have caused the Japanese to turn away briefly. *Pope's* forecastle gun—number 1—had by this time expended her ammunition, and rate of fire was slowed while the men shifted more 4-inch rounds from the after magazines. The flushdecker coaxed a few more knots from her engines and swung ahead of *Exeter*. After moving to starboard Blinn had his torpedo men fire five more fish "in a regular spread, all that remained" at the nearest ships of Takagi's force, then perhaps ten thousand to twelve thousand yards to the south.[50]

It made little enough difference. Gordon's three ships were now being fired on by four destroyers and four heavy cruisers of greater speed, armed with a total of twenty-four 5-inch guns and forty 8-inch guns. And each of these ships carried the powerful Japanese 24-inch torpedoes (although not all were of the Type 93 Long Lance oxygen-fueled model). The weight of enemy gunnery began to tell with many straddles falling closely around *Exeter* for the next ten or fifteen minutes before inexorable fate caught up with the British cruiser.

The time was roughly 1120 hours when a single 8-inch projectile struck her operational "A" boiler room fair and square. As Lt. Cdr. George Tyndale Cooper remembered, "It was a one in a million shot as it cut our one remaining main steam pipe." Without question this was a killing hit. "The ship just came to a stop in all departments. The main engines stopped through lack of steam. The dynamos stopped. The turrets were motionless on different bearings. The steering failed. The inside became full of smoke as escaping fuel oil in the forward boiler room burst into flames."[51]

On *Pope* Welford Blinn and Jack Michel both knew *Exeter* was hit, although they had seen little visible effects at first. The cruiser then slowed down radically, began "emitting heavy gray smoke," and lost maneuverability. Soon her guns ceased firing altogether. *Exeter* was still being hit by shellfire during this period as the Japanese ships closed from all quarters. As the Japanese propaganda magazine *Asahigraph* that appeared soon after the campaign ended put it: "Although she was flying a battle-flag, she was panting for breath. Her turrets were destroyed, engine room shot through, and speed was greatly reduced." The less flowery language of Sentai 5's action report noted, "Around 1124 a large fire was observed aboard the cruiser and her speed dropped dramatically, until almost a total stop. Her fighting ability seemed to be seriously impaired: the forward turrets were trained aft and one gun of the aft turret was pointing skywards at maximum elevation. . . . At 1128 the cruiser developed a perceptible list."[52]

*Encounter* made a valiant but futile attempt to conceal her wounded consort by steaming around the slowing cruiser and dropping smoke floats. She then received a signal from Gordon informing her that *Exeter* was being abandoned and that she should "proceed independently." However, "Rattler" Morgan turned a blind Nelsonian eye to this message. For this loyalty his destroyer came under the guns of the enemy ships between 1128 and 1130 hours. Still she did not leave the stricken cruiser but continued to make smoke. Before long *Encounter*, too, began taking near misses and direct hits. An 8-inch salvo from *Ashigara* hamstrung the British destroyer, lifting her bodily from the water. Then came the inevitable end. *Yamakaze* and *Kawakaze* were also ordered to join in the shelling of *Encounter*. Within another ten minutes at the most "Rattler" Morgan's steadfast ship, too, was dead in the water, ablaze and with a pronounced list.[53]

At about this time most of the Japanese ships were ordered to make torpedo attacks and finish sinking the cruiser. First Takagi's ships launched a total of fourteen torpedoes from the south at ranges varying from seven thousand to ten thousand yards. These did not hit either *Exeter* or *Encounter*. A few minutes later the northern cruisers—or at least *Ashigara*—fired torpedoes as well.

Although they hit nothing, they may have helped scare Takagi's force briefly when at 1143 *Yamakaze* spotted a torpedo "fired from the north side of the enemy" approaching. (Some IJN accounts stated that these were "recognized" to be Japanese torpedoes, but it is also possible they were among the last spread fired by *Pope*.) In any case, operating off *Nachi*'s port bow, the Japanese tin can reported: "Enemy torpedo[es] passing below me," and the two Sentai 5 cruisers had to take "sharp evasive maneuver[s]."[54]

It then fell to *Inazuma* to give the coup de grâce to *Exeter*, as the cruiser had by then slowed from 5 knots to nothing, wallowing in the flat seas with a list to port. Coming first to 6,100 yards off the starboard beam, the destroyer fired two 24-inch torpedoes, which missed. *Exeter*'s guns were completely silent, her men clear of the sinking ship, so the IJN destroyer closed to within 3,700 yards and fired another pair of fish. These did the job. The British cruiser was dead in the water, listing heavily, when one or both of the torpedoes fired by *Inazuma* struck her hull flush on the starboard side, and a tremendous blast resulted. Overhead, a Japanese floatplane carried a skilled photographer who captured a series of images of *Exeter*'s death that would rapidly find their way into numerous propaganda publications, including *Asahigraph*.

According to other witnesses, the torpedo (or torpedoes) must have opened her up like a zipper because *Exeter* "shuddered a bit . . . then went right over to starboard until her funnel and masts were horizontal." As he had prepared to abandon ship a few minutes earlier, Lieutenant Commander Cooper tossed aside his excellent pair of large Barr and Stroud binoculars, which he felt was an awful waste, "yet a bagatelle compared to the loss of a fine 8-inch cruiser with a score that included the Graf Spee off the River Plate." Watching at a safe distance in the water as he drifted astern, he later wrote in his memoir: "The old dear seemed to shudder. . . . Then, heaving herself up in a final act of defiance, she disappeared in a swirl of water, smoke and steam."[55] It was high noon according to surviving records from the Japanese ships.

Not too far off to starboard was the settling ruin of *Encounter*, and her men also witnessed *Exeter*'s end. On the shattered British destroyer Sam Falle did not need to toss away his binoculars. As he and the captain were climbing into the destroyer's motorboat a small-caliber projectile struck and rendered the small craft useless. "At the same time a shell splinter took away my binoculars which were hanging around my neck," Falle reported.[56] The officers got into the water posthaste and there endured the uncomfortably intense shelling of *Encounter*'s hulk until she also "rolled over and sank." It was about 1215 hours. Falle and the surviving crew then gave three cheers for "Rattler" Morgan.

A couple of miles away the men of *Exeter* also gave three cheers for their old ship as she went under. "You could hear the faint cheers rippling over the water," remembered Cooper.[57] Then, suddenly a Welsh voice yelled out: "It's Saint David's Day!"[58] And so it was.

But of Welford Blinn's four-stacker *Pope* there was no sign.

Concealed beneath a screen of dense black funnel smoke, *Pope* had not lingered but sped off. After "Willie" Blinn saw that both *Exeter* and *Encounter* had "slowed radically and cease[d] firing," he swung his ship's bow away to the east-northeast. A couple of dark squall lines appeared ahead of the U.S. destroyer, and Blinn urged the ship toward them at top speed.

As soon as the flushdecker entered the first squall, she stopped making smoke. This all-too-brief concealment allowed the harried U.S. destroyermen to take stock of their predicament. In no sense was the situation to their liking, but engineers looked to their machinery, gunners to their weapons, and perhaps most amazing of all, her cooks carried on with preparing a noontime meal for the crew. Jack Michel would later see this food in the galley before he left the ship, and he had not regretted missing lunch: Vienna sausage and sauerkraut.

As for the ship's combat status, there appeared little cause for optimism. After some 140 salvos from her 4-inch main battery—firing 345 rounds in the process—the number 3 boiler's firewall bricks gave up the ghost due to gunfire concussion and crumbled inside the boiler. That boiler was secured, and a few steam and water-pipe leaks were repaired—so much for her power plant. It was then found that the ship had but twenty rounds of main-battery ammunition left, and her torpedoes had all been expended by that point. This left the ship with little firepower apart from her .50 cal. and .30 cal. machine guns. Double-checking instruments in the hopes of getting a navigational sight a few minutes later showed "that [her] chronometers were greatly in error as a result of shock of continuous gunfire." This would have made efforts to follow plans by Blinn and his navigator, Lt. Richard Antrim, "to skirt the southern coast of Borneo and retire south of the barrier through Lombok Strait during darkness"—then approximately seven hundred miles distant—more than a little problematic.[59]

Well above all these unpleasant realizations, Jack Michel remained at his spot 1 post in the tiny crow's nest. As the destroyer drew inside the mantle of the heavy rains—with visibility limited briefly to no more than fifty yards—he abruptly felt something novel: "I realized that I was scared."[60] He was not alone in that fear. Far beneath Mr. Michel's cramped metal box were those other sailors also encaged within a world of steel, steam, and noise. Bill Penninger's role

THEY FLED TO BLISS OR WOE

as throttle man had not spared him the terrors of battle: "At each firing of the 4-inch guns, the reverberations would be transmitted throughout the ship. The quarter-inch steel plates and half-inch gratings that comprise[d] the deck of the engine rooms, would raise about an inch or two and then drop back in place (most of the time), which gave one the feeling the ship had been hit."[61]

With his duties on the throttle wheel routine for prolonged periods, Bill's mind had time to torment him with other anxieties: "Many was the times [sic] I would look at the 3/8-inch steel plate that was the skin or bulkhead of the ship, expecting at any moment to see a shell penetrating it. If it had of course, I would never have lived to tell about it." Then, as the ship found a brief refuge in the rainstorms for some thirty minutes, Bill Penninger could also reflect on those men above decks. "My thoughts turned to the men that were topside, that were more directly engaged in the battle, the gun crews, ammunition handlers, gun loaders, machine gunners, torpedo-men, the officers directing the firing and those involved in directing the ship. They had their hands full and like those of us below decks were sweating keeping up the pace." And because he had faith in the "well-trained crew giving it their all" despite the heat and stress, he also believed they had found the time "to say a few prayers of their own."[62] For by then all the men, officers and enlisted, surely understood—each in his own way, whether by rational analysis or gut instinct—that it was only going to be through a series of miracles that they might yet escape.

As they passed through one rainsquall, then another, Blinn altered course to 60 degrees with the ship still maintaining high speed. With the second squall cleared, the course was changed to roughly 40 degrees, which angled the ship toward the southern coast of Borneo. Within another few minutes, after emerging into brilliant sunlight, the ship found herself trailed again by several enemy floatplanes. These were the cruiser planes, and soon there were six of them. At first they milled around indecisively at a distance, as though testing the destroyer's AA fire.

Takagi's Sentai 5 cruisers had expended so much ammunition in the Java Sea battle and against *Exeter* that it was now hoped they would not have to use up more. *Nachi* and *Haguro* had fired 1,271 shells on February 27–28, and another 288 against the three ships on March 1. Similarly, both *Kawakaze* and *Yamakaze* were decidedly low on fuel and needed to be replenished. With this in mind Vice Admiral Takahashi at 1223 hours ordered Takagi's ships to suspend combat and make for Bandjarmasin to the northeast. There they could refuel and deal with the survivors from *Exeter* they had rescued before proceeding on to Kendari.[63] Meanwhile, Vice Admiral Takahashi would see to the errant tin can that had temporarily escaped. As it turned out, the leader of Main Force had some additional support from the sky.

Well to the west, a solitary light carrier, the *Ryūjō* (of Carrier Division 4), had been attached to the support forces covering Lt. Gen. Imamura's Western Invasion landings. On this day she was alerted to the breakout of the *Exeter* group earlier in midmorning. At 1130 hours she flew off six Type 97 *kanko* (KATE) level bombers all armed with 250 kg weapons. An hour and a half later they would reach the floundering *Pope*, but by then their efforts were largely unnecessary.

For some time *Pope*'s 3-inch "peashooter" on the fantail was still firing at the hovering cruiser floatplanes when it could; this briefly held them at bay. Even the 4-inch guns, which had almost no real AA capabilities, were fired intermittently. This was good for the gun crew's spirits, if nothing else. Soon enough, however, the scout planes recognized the old destroyer's lack of defensive firepower and swung around to approach the ship from head-on, thereby negating the stern-mounted 3-inch gun's firing arcs.

They made twelve glide-bombing attacks—two by each plane—dropping their 60 kg bombs singly as they came in from the starboard bow. *Pope* was only able to fire on these flights with two of her .50 cal. machine guns and with three 1918-vintage Lewis guns as Blinn directed evasive action. Joe Sam Sisk recalled Lieutenant Antrim lying "flat on his back" on the deck looking up through his binoculars during attacks, doing what he could to help Blinn conn the ship. Nonetheless, the Japanese pilots were determined, and the ship's weak AA defenses made her an easy target. The third attacker placed a bomb "close aboard off the port bow," which peppered topside personnel with shards, wounding two men on gun number 1.[64] This bomb also sent a fragment through the rangefinder, tearing a four-inch hole in it. Other explosions were of very low order and caused almost no real damage but left chunks of metal strewn over the upper deck. On the next-to-last attack, however, *Pope*'s luck finally ran out.

On this, the eleventh attack, the biplane dropped its bomb accurately enough. The near miss hit abreast the number four torpedo mount (to port aft) where it exploded underwater. The blast cracked the hull like an eggshell, springing plates "for a considerable length and threw the port shaft seriously out of line necessitating the stopping of the forward (port) engine because of the severe vibration set up at once." Below in the fire room, Bill Penninger was rattled by this explosion like the others stationed in the engine spaces. With the alarming vibrations soon worsening due to the high RPMs the turbines were producing, the men realized that "it was literally shaking the ship to pieces. The decision was quickly determined to secure the port turbine."[65] However, the loss in speed only

THEY FLED TO BLISS OR WOE

increased the ocean's ingress. Water then began pouring into the living spaces aft through the torn shaft alley. Despite all efforts, which included stuffing mattresses into the holed compartment and starting all bilge pumps and any auxiliary pumps that could be jury-rigged, this flooding could not be contained.

The ship was now moving sluggishly with an odd fishtailing motion. Her stern 3-inch/23 cal. AA gun was silent. The "peashooter" had at last expired like a good warrior with the stubby barrel literally falling out of its slide onto the deck. *Pope* had also taken on a definite list, although to starboard, the result of a radical turn to avoid the last glide-bombing attack. In making that hard turn the ship had heeled over to starboard, and as Jack Michel recalled, "There we remained."[66] *Pope* never righted herself. In this precarious orientation she continued for some time, losing momentum and attempting clumsily on one engine to elude what came next: the level bombing attacks from *Ryūjō*'s Type 97 *kanko* (KATES).

At 1335 hours the six *kanko* spotted *Pope* on the horizon and took up their attack positions. Within another fifteen minutes their attacks had ended, and the observer from *Chitose*'s number 1 plane reported back: "Enemy destroyer has become unable to make way by the bombing of friendly medium attack bombers."[67] The planes from *Ryūjō* were not very accurate in their bombing runs, but they were thorough. They made four separate attacks on *Pope*, dropping all their 60 kg bombs. Fortunately none of them hit or came very near the ship, for by that time Blinn and his officers had seen the futility of prolonging the odds against them. He conferred with Antrim and others and made the difficult but sensible choice.

What came next was still a surprise to Michel, high up in the crow's nest—bruised and half-deafened by gunfire after being whipped around in his steel box on the mast like a mouse in a coffee can—to find the ship slowing, canted over in a list, and his phones suddenly dead. Michel called through the auxiliary voice pipe and received a startling reply: "Spot 1, bridge. Come on down, we are abandoning ship."[68]

Although the official order had not yet been given, the men were getting three cork life rafts and a damaged wherry over the side, while the wounded were being placed in the remaining motor whaleboat. Blinn and his XO, Lieutenant Antrim, knew they probably had little time before the enemy cruisers would reach the scene. And Welford Blinn wanted above all to give his men as good chance as he could to get away with their lives. It also happened that the enemy planes were now making sporadic strafing runs on the destroyer, no doubt angered by the return fire that several gunners on *Pope* had kept up.

Following the third level bombing attack, which was no more accurate than any of the others, and as preparations for abandoning ship continued, Blinn had the remaining starboard engine stopped. At that time the motor whaleboat was lowered into the water, and word was passed to abandon ship.[69] The sea was calm, the battered old four-stacker was virtually dead in the water, and the men were able to get off in as orderly a fashion as possible, with some extra encouragement from Antrim. Coming down from his .50 cal. mount on the after deckhouse, Joe Sam Sisk took off his headphones, threw away his steel helmet, and left from the fantail. Meanwhile, with *Pope*'s stern under water and the sea lapping at her weather deck, Blinn had already decided to take steps to ensure the destruction of sensitive materials and his crew's safety as they left the ship. The remaining depth charges were set on safe and dropped overboard. Also a smaller demolition charge was detonated in the sound room to destroy the four-piper's QCL gear. As a result of this explosion *Pope* suffered her only death during the entire action. One of the captain's bridge talkers, a yeoman second class named Howard Davis, was taking shelter face down on the deck. However, the demolition charge in the sound room—which had been installed as standard procedure at Cavite before the war—was more powerful than expected. A shard of metal blew through the deck, striking the yeoman in the chest and killing him instantly.

Bill Penninger had then climbed up out of the engine spaces, after helping secure the fire rooms and engines (with fires under the boilers extinguished and valves shut off), and soon found himself ducking for cover from the strafing enemy planes. While he huddled beneath an empty torpedo mount, a 7.7 mm bullet grazed his right knee. "There was no pain connected with it," he recalled. "It was more like someone had touched it with a hot iron, luckily it did not hit bone."[70] He remembered that others were not as fortunate and received more serious wounds during the strafing.

Next, as the men all started to "hit the water," an officer approached looking for help in a dangerous task. "Mr. Antrim, the executive officer appeared on the fantail and asked, 'Who's going to volunteer to help me blow up the ship?'"[71] Blinn had decided that time required the men assure the more rapid sinking of the ship, so that she would not be boarded by the enemy and run the risk of being salvaged or have any confidential documents recovered. Wounded knee or not, Penninger followed Antrim and another sailor named Donald A. Matthews, MM2/C, and helped ready the charges. Penninger then left the ship himself and began swimming away through the warm Java Sea.

After his crew got off the ship, Blinn and several other officers remained behind to make certain all procedures were followed correctly. Satisfied with this final step, Blinn was one of the very last men to get away from the settling destroyer. Gunnery officer Lt. Bill Wilson and Donald Matthews went below to set off the final demolition charge in the forward engine room. It blew a negligible hole in the portside hull barely above the waterline; a little burst of smoke plopped out of a stack. Watching from the water as he swam clear, Jack Michel recalled feeling disappointed with this "seemingly ineffective demolition," but he could see the ship was clearly going under by then.[72] Lieutenant Wilson and Matthews at last left the destroyer. Then all the men tried to put as much distance as possible between themselves and *Pope*, knowing the ship would only attract trouble. They were correct.

A few Japanese planes were still circling overhead and occasionally diving toward the ship and the men in the water. (Most of the strafing had ceased after a testy U.S. sailor in the whaleboat firing back at the planes with a BAR came to his senses and stopped shooting.) Suddenly from the west two long, dark shapes appeared on the horizon, moving closer. This was Takahashi's flagship *Ashigara* and her sister, *Myōkō*. When they came to within about four miles of the sinking four-piper, the big cruisers opened fire again with their main batteries.[73] They were shooting from astern, and *Pope*'s narrow beam probably made her an even slimmer target. Tightly grouped shell splashes began landing around the flush-decker, although most fell well over at first. Survivors in the water were located several hundred yards off the destroyer's port and starboard quarter and not greatly endangered by these salvos, but all the men paddled and swam quickly to get out of the line of fire. Fortunately the inaccuracy of the 8-inch batteries of *Ashigara* and *Myōkō* did not bring any errant projectiles into their midst.

Although the two Japanese ships had already expended a vast amount of ordnance that day themselves—over 1,100 shells—they made no attempt to close the range. No direct hits were made until, as Bill Penninger observed, "the stern of the ship was completely under water and the bow pointing to the sky."[74] At that time a final 8-inch salvo struck the destroyer's upended hull "at the waterline which tended to speed up her sinking." Within moments the battered four-piper slid under the waves, "leaving only swirling water to indicate where she had been."[75] For Jack Michel a sense of relief came over him; he felt that the cause for all of the shooting and bombing was now gone. To Bill Penninger a different emotion emerged: "We regretfully realized we had lost not only a fighting ship, but our home away from home. With saddened hearts we knew we would never walk the decks of the *Pope* again."[76]

Indeed they would not. Another of the aged, sacrificial flushdeckers of Des-Ron 29 had gone to the bottom forever. The time was 1410 hours, and according to Japanese sources, USS *Pope* sank about thirty miles offshore, bearing 160 degrees from Cape Puting, Borneo. Having fulfilled her duty as an escort and paid the price for it, her lonely wreck would remain unidentified for some sixty-five years, her grave on the seabed even more obscure than the details of her final, lopsided engagement.[77]

Over the next three days most of the survivors from *Exeter*, *Encounter*, and *Pope* would be picked up from the Java Sea by various IJN warships. By and large they were well treated at first by their navy captors. Not until they reached the port of Makassar and were turned over to the SNLF troops there would real abuse and cruelty begin in earnest. In the Makassar area were numerous camps, both prisoner-of-war and civilian internment camps, for captured military, Dutch residents, and locals considered untrustworthy. As in all other areas of the East Indies following the capitulation of the Dutch, the Japanese preparations for housing and feeding prisoners were utterly inadequate. Over the course of the war they would not improve. Administration fell under the aegis of whichever service branch controlled that particular region—as the Imperial Army and Navy had divvied up the conquered areas between themselves with their usual lack of cooperation and jealous hoarding of resources—and both branches employed their lowest ranks to carry out the actual work in POW camps. This meant that Japanese enlisted men of particular energy and viciousness often controlled life in the camps, and many of these individuals were little more than professional sadists. Such arrangements were designed of course to inflict maximum damage to their Western prisoners of war—who were regarded as embarrassments to their families by the harsh standards of the Japanese military ethos—as well as to shield enemy officers and higher echelon commanders from direct responsibility. As a rough rule of thumb, one might say that the further from large urban areas or homeland Japan, the worse the treatment. To those Allied prisoners who ended up in the obscure outposts of the East Indies, remote Philippine islands, or in the jungles of Burma and Siam, imprisonment under the Japanese often meant a living hell that would have taxed the imagination of Dante in his descriptions of the Inferno.

Of the 151 men who survived *Pope*'s sinking, 124 would make it through the war; 27 of her sailors perished as POWs from a variety of causes, ranging from disease to malnutrition to the effects of physical maltreatment. In this their fate was statistically similar to those survivors of *Houston*. Both ships lost about 20 percent of their survivors as POWs under the Japanese, a far greater percentage than Allied personnel captured by the Germans in the ETO for example. *Pope*'s officers—Welford "Willie" Blinn, John J. A. "Jack" Michel, Richard "Bull" Ant-

THEY FLED TO BLISS OR WOE

rim, Bill Wilson, Jack Fisher, Bill Lowndes, and "Red" Bassett—all survived the war and captivity. Most of them ended up in Japan or Manchuria, but the bulk of the destroyer's enlisted personnel remained at Makassar.

. . .

The last remaining Asiatic Fleet destroyers operating out of Tjilatjap—both being held there to the last minute—were *Parrott* and *Pillsbury*. Surviving communications from COMSOWESPAC on Saturday, February 28, stated that "SPEED OF BOTH MATERIALLY REDUCED DUE TO NEEDED ENGINEER- ING REPAIRS." They, along with the patrol yacht *Isabel*, were busy escorting various vessels in and out of the port, taking on as much radio gear as possible before the Americans shut down their headquarters in the hope that commu- nications could be maintained at sea as they dissolved the Java command and retreated to Australia. Neither ship was especially suited for offensive action; *Parrott* by this time had but a single torpedo left, and *Pillsbury* only three.

*Parrott* screened USS *Pecos* as she left Tjilatjap for India and was detached on the twenty-seventh when the oiler was ordered south to Christmas Island to pick up the survivors of *Langley*. *Parrott* would then return to escort another vessel into port from *Langley*'s convoy (MS-5), the C2 cargo ship SS *Sea Witch*— also screened briefly by *Pillsbury*—carrying twenty-seven crated P-40E fighter planes into Tjilatjap on February 28. *Sea Witch* unloaded her valuable matériel with as much speed as possible.[78] She immediately put to sea the next night (midnight of March 1–2) wrapped in the cloak of a dense rainsquall. Her reluc- tant escort would be *Isabel*. The little armed patrol yacht had also been held back at Tjilatjap to pick up some of the navy's tail-end stragglers, along with parts of various radio systems in the hope she might be able to provide com- munications as Glassford's command left Java for Australia.

*Pillsbury* and *Parrott* departed Tjilatjap late on the afternoon of Sunday, March 1, 1942, within an hour of each other. Almost thirty members of the aban- doned *Stewart* had transferred to *Pillsbury*. Unknown to these men, the assign- ment to Lt. Cdr. Harold Pound's flushdecker—as for those who had been sent to Lt. J. J. Nix's *Edsall*—would prove a death warrant. The flight from the East Indies by remaining Allied forces was nothing if not a "crapshoot," and those who survived did so largely on the basis of sheer luck rather than skill or wiles.

. . .

Pound's destroyer, nearly ruined at the outset of the war in the bombing at Cavite, had made a gritty comeback and contributed her part during the campaign. Her fight at Badoeng Strait ten days earlier when she had helped cripple *Michishio* had been one of the only ABDA highlights in that unfortunate operation. Like the other tin cans in DesRon 29 she had a tough, determined crew and capable officers, and these men surely hoped to slip through the enemy dragnet they well knew was closing in around Java from all quarters. Yet even most of those who managed to get away successfully on other ships would not understand for decades the narrowness of their escapes. What became of a pair of radio operators from *Stewart*—Marion "Elly" Ellsworth and Wilbur Lauridsen—is a cardinal example of this dice roll.

As we saw, after *Stewart* was abandoned in Surabaja, the crew was at first divvied up among *Parrott*, *Pillsbury*, and *John D. Edwards*. These were temporary assignments initially, and the orders came down so suddenly (at 1330 hours on Sunday, February 22) that *Stewart*'s crew had little time to gather up all their belongings. Both men—Lauridsen, a third class radioman, and Ellsworth, a seaman striker for that rating—were ordered to *Pillsbury*. They had started for that ship, walking together along the docks, with Lauridsen even carrying some of Ellsworth's gear as they went, when at the last moment Ellsworth's orders were changed: he was to join *John D. Edwards* after which he would be sent on to *John D. Ford*, whose radioman John Darby—that sole seriously wounded casualty from the Balikpapan strike of a month before—had been unable to resume his duties. In the haste and confusion of the moment Ellsworth turned around, while Lauridsen went ahead and boarded *Pillsbury* per his orders, still lugging some of his pal's belongings. Elly Ellsworth would never see his gear or Wilbur Lauridsen again in this world.

· · ·

For Allied ships, on the other hand, the choice to "clear the region" had come not a moment too soon. But only the luckiest would safely make the transit to Australia or Ceylon. Many men later wrote that these were the most trying moments of the entire war. Lt. (j.g.) Wick Alford aboard *Isabel* described his feelings in a journal as the little vessel steamed away from Java on March 2: "Have hell of a gauntlet to run. . . . Running for our lives and at dawn a bare 75 miles from the coast."[79] All the men knew that Japanese air, submarine, and surface forces were operating in the Indian Ocean, and that many vessels had already been lost. "Have never been so scared in my life," Alford wrote. "All afternoon we lived in mortal fear and dread of bombers and warships. . . . There followed until darkness the most awful, terror-filled hours of my whole life, before or since. . . . Darkness came as a reprieve."[80]

THEY FLED TO BLISS OR WOE

By that time *Pillsbury* had also left Tjilatjap, Australia-bound. She departed the port at 1507 hours on Sunday, March 1, 1942.[81] Her sister, *Parrott*, departed about forty-five minutes later. There can be little doubt that the men on the overcrowded *Pillsbury* would have felt much the same as Wick Alford in *Isabel*, even if they had more weapons to fight with should they encounter the enemy. For the veteran *Pillsbury*, however, the cover of night would bring no real sanctuary. Although she was then free from the ubiquitous daylight Japanese air patrols, in that deceptive darkness there still lurked deadly predators.

As we have seen, the invasion of Bali, along with the seizure of airfields near Palembang on Sumatra, had given the Japanese a considerable increase in range for the overall scope of their operations, especially in their ability to bomb targets in Java and to spot and interdict reinforcements coming to the beleaguered island by either sea or air from India or northern Australia. As soon as the Japanese landed and secured Denpasar airfield on February 20, the Imperial Navy began bringing in fighters of the Tainan Kōkusentai. Reconnaissance planes and twin-engine bombers would soon follow; these could range great distances across the Indian Ocean.

For the first twenty-one hours of her escape attempt, *Pillsbury* led a charmed life. Yet sometime before midday on Tuesday, March 2, her fortunes (and their "charm") shifted. At 1210 hours she was spotted by an Eleventh Air Fleet reconnaissance plane flying out of Denpasar's newly won airfield, which forwarded the contact information to Vice Admiral Kondō's Main Body: "Sighted an enemy light cruiser fleeing on a course of 130° at 24 knots, bearing 197° 300 miles from the airfield on Bali Island."[82] Kondō in his flagship *Atago* decided to try to intercept the "light cruiser." This misidentification stemmed from the four-piper destroyer's profile resembling that of the Omaha-class cruiser USS *Marblehead*, long known as a fixture in the Asiatic Fleet. Kondō then ordered *Atago's* sister cruiser from Sentai 4, *Takao*, to form a search line to the south of his ship at 1439 hours. The two big vessels increased speed to 26 knots and began the long run southeast for the hoped-for interdiction. At 1530 hours they estimated the enemy was about 180 miles away.

Five hours later, well after nightfall, the Japanese lookouts were astonished to spot a small ship in the distance moving across their path. Some 18,000 meters away, "under the bright moon light," steaming from left to right ahead of the two cruisers was a four-funneled vessel. Sharp-eyed lookouts aboard *Atago*, the closest ship, spotted her first: at 2038 the flagship ordered *Takao* to join up. It was "Froggy" Pound's venerable destroyer moving at a standard 14 knots. An anonymous writer (*shicho*) on *Takao* later wrote: "The enemy light cruiser came into view . . . as though it had been drawn by the invisible thread of fate." At 2043 *Takao* saw that "the enemy ship did not notice that [they] were approaching her."[83] Like her sister flushdecker, USS *Edsall*, which also lacked radar, *Pillsbury* would steam headlong into her fate.

Three minutes passed while the Japanese watched undisturbed as the American ship crossed their bows, but at 2046, the Japanese records indicate, "the enemy ship changed course. She seemed to have noticed us." To the amazement of the Imperial Navy crews, *Pillsbury* was not turning away. "Since we outnumbered the enemy, we took it for granted that she would run away," their records noted at 2047. "We were totally wrong. We thought she would run away, but she did not! What was she up to? She was dashing directly toward us. Her bow became clearly visible minute by minute."[84] We will never know with absolute certainty, but the physical resemblance between *Atago* and the American light cruiser USS *Phoenix*, ordered to that very area, may well have deceived *Pillsbury's* unwary and fatigued crew.[85]

As the destroyer closed to within eight thousand meters, the Japanese account exclaimed, "The time was ripe to open up!" Still they held off firing, as if mesmerized themselves. Another seven full minutes passed as *Pillsbury* unwittingly approached her executioners like a lamb to the slaughter. Events then moved with terrible rapidity, as bloody and absolute as the annihilation of the luckless British armored cruiser HMS *Black Prince* at Jutland. Then, a quarter century earlier, on a darkened sea at midnight, the bumbling Royal Navy cruiser had "in all ignorance . . . wandered into the path of the High Seas Fleet," only to be savagely dismembered under a horrific steel tornado of 11- and 12-inch German battleship shells at short range in what scholars of the battle have called, "an episode of staggering futility."[86]

At 2054 1/2 hours, with the range only six thousand meters, *Atago* split the darkness by illuminating the little destroyer with her powerful searchlights. In another few moments *Takao* opened the shutters on her lights, revealing in stark clarity the tin can, which had slowed to less than 10 knots. One hesitates to imagine the reaction of those tense, worn sailors aboard *Pillsbury* when they found themselves bathed in that dazzling light from two enormous warships now looming far too close. For ninety agonizing seconds the flushdecker transmitted frantic recognition codes—"CU" or "UC" then "CM" or "MC" and perhaps "COT"—from her white signal lights near the bridge. At 2056 hours the big enemy cruisers had seen enough; it was time to begin the killing: they opened main-battery fire at the point-blank range of 5,200 meters.[87]

Both cruisers' first salvos hit the destroyer squarely, and in an instant "a fire broke out in her forward section." Shells poured into and around the hapless vessel. In a span of 340 seconds no fewer than 170 8-inch projectiles were fired at *Pillsbury*, one shell every two seconds. The destroyer sheered away to starboard in desperate evasion from her tormentors; as she turned the Japanese could see in their brilliant searchlights "a large flag on her foremast." Before *Takao* could unleash her second salvo, however, the old flushdecker returned fire herself in the final act of an aging warrior: "We observed one aft gun of the enemy cruiser [*sic*] open up admirably. . . . It was the only gun showing the fighting spirit of the United States Navy." For a few moments the crew of gun number 4, atop the aft deckhouse, acquitted itself valiantly. The men got off three rounds before being killed or incapacitated: "One of them landed near the aft of *Atago*, a second between *Atago* and *Takao*, and a third far from *Takao*, respectively."[88]

And then the Japanese resumed the execution. The *shicho* on *Takao* recorded: "Geysers of the second salvo completely enveloped the enemy ship, and [steam] vapor was emitted violently from near the smokestacks." Another projectile or fragment appears to have ignited the 4-inch ready-service ammunition stored beneath *Pillsbury's* bridge, for the IJN accounts stated that a "fire also broke out under the forward bridge." Although the destroyer had then turned away from her assailants, they could not determine whether this was an "emergency evasive maneuver" or steering damage. "She must have become uncontrollable due to the damage to her machinery," recorded the Japanese, as she staggered under multiple hits and near misses. *Pillsbury* was briefly stern-on to the two cruisers, although this did not keep them from pouring more shells into her narrow width: "The enemy ship's aft mast snapped off and flew away. Her fire control director seemed to have been destroyed. . . . Our near-misses seemed to have opened many holes near her waterline."[89]

At 2101, after some five minutes of firing from 4,200 meters, *Takao* checked main battery fire and commenced firing with her 12.7 cm/5-inch AA guns. The cruiser expended only fifteen of these against the dying four-piper. It was unnecessary; the destroyer's slim hull had been shattered, and she began to sink very swiftly. As Takao's *shicho* described it, "The enemy had listed to the starboard side, and began going down, showing her upper deck to us. Our last salvo pierced through her upper deck." A penultimate glimpse of the ship showed that her "aft turret" (gun number 4) was turned to port, pointing skyward as she heeled over. And then, not more than six minutes after *Atago* and *Takao* had opened fire, "the enemy ship raised her stern with her bow in the water, and rapidly went down to the bottom. . . . It took only five seconds until she completely disappeared."[90]

The cruisers' searchlights shut off, darkness once more fell on the sea with only the bright moonlight as illumination, and the two big warships turned and headed back to take up station again with their sister ships for another day of hunting on the Indian Ocean. Whether out of caution or callousness, the Japanese made no attempt to pick up survivors. Their records simply show that the "enemy light cruiser of *Marblehead* class" they attacked that night and sank at 2102 hours disappeared in Lat. 15° 39' S, Long. 113° 27' E.[91]

In the bitterest of ironies, and unknown for over six decades, the location of her destruction is in fact more or less where she had been instructed to meet with other Allied ships fleeing Java, per orders from COMSOUWESPAC (Glassford) on March 1: "PROCEED EAST ALONG THE COAST UNTIL DARK X PROCEED SEPARATELY TO RENDEZVOUS LAT FIFTEEN SOUTH LONG ONE ONE THREE EAST TO REMAIN THAT VICINITY UNTIL SHIPS JOINED UP THEN PROCEED TO EXMOUTH GULF X." This suggests that *Pillsbury* may have anticipated meeting up with other Allied warships—particularly of the *Phoenix* type—when she noticed the two huge shapes looming fine off her starboard bow. Such an expectation would perfectly explain *Pillsbury's* otherwise puzzling pace and response, but it renders her tragic end no less disturbing.[92]

• • •

A number of the other, small Asiatic Fleet ships did manage to escape—the gunboat *Tulsa*, the destroyer *Parrott*, the patrol vessel *Isabel*, the minesweepers *Lark* and *Whippoorwill*, and Kemp Tolley's little converted yacht *Lanikai*—and were fortunate to have done so, as they all well understood. In some instances they were shielded, it seems, by inclement weather, which was as capricious as ever in the Indian Ocean that week.[93] In others their smallness might have been a factor—*Lanikai* was after all nothing but a pint-sized auxiliary schooner, twenty-seven years old, and less than ninety feet long—but everyone recognized the role played by sheer luck in their survival. It may have also been that the overenthusiastic destruction of their fellow ships aided them, that is, the cases of *Edsall*, *Stronghold*, and *Asheville*, in which huge amounts of ordnance were expended by too many Japanese ships on what were essentially targets of negligible value. The enemy ships and planes devoted to those actions were that many fewer to be used to spot (or engage) other fleeing vessels. This meant that on certain days the Japanese forces were scurrying around like spiders with an overabundance of helpless flies in their web, while on others the hours passed monotonously, with a noticeable dearth of targets.

Finally we come to the story of *Asheville's* loss. That she left but one survivor who provided a few scant details of her end, and all of those recorded sec-ondhand, does not mean we have *that much* clearer a picture of her sinking. The single sailor who was rescued from the Indian Ocean—a young fireman from her engineering force—left no written record, and he died before the end of the war in a POW camp on Celebes, another victim of neglect, disease, and brutality.[94] Thus there still remain several aspects of her final days that are not well understood, but at this stage it seems questionable whether they will ever be fully clarified. As in the cases of *Edsall* and *Pillsbury*, the gunboat *Asheville* perished alone at the hands of far superior foes, and like them, she took with her a significant number of trained navy personnel and officers into the pro-found oblivion of the Indian Ocean.

For the bulk of the campaign *Asheville* and *Tulsa* operated as harbor patrol vessels with (and under the operational control of) the Dutch at Surabaja and later at Tjilatjap. This suited their advanced age and limited combat capabil-ities. That they were employed on Java for such improvised duties, however, illustrates again the central failing of the entire ABDA organization: that of too few assets. For such aged and offensively useless ships to have been necessary shows just how desperate and unprepared the Allies were at that stage of the war. The Dutch navy simply did not possess enough ships to effectively man-age their larger, more critical ports—Batavia, Surabaja, Tjilatjap—and into the breach were pressed the old gunboats *Asheville* and *Tulsa*, along with other undersized anomalies such as the converted yacht *Isabel*.

The gunboats were mechanically unreliable and weakly armed vessels and had spent long profligate years on the Asiatic Station, but their crews were all regular navy as were many of their officers. *Tulsa* and *Asheville* had even man-aged to rig up improvised depth-charge racks on their sterns after scrounging a few surplus depth charges left by American destroyers in Java. Armament oth-erwise consisted of old 4-inch weapons and possibly a 3-inch/23 cal. AA gun, augmented by a few machine guns, at least one of which was a .50 cal. mount. Yet against just one of the older Japanese destroyers—let alone a large mod-ern type—*Tulsa* or *Asheville* would have had no more chance of survival than an elderly armadillo wandering across a busy interstate.

The two gunboats had departed Tjilatjap on March 1. It is believed they may have skirted the southern shore of Java for some time, hoping to avoid enemy air patrols, before altering course to the south. *Asheville*, under Lt. Cdr. Jacob Britt (USNA 1929), seems to have been suffering from characteristic mechani-cal difficulties that kept her from attaining full speed; it was said that she could make no more than 10 knots.[95] This problem would have only added to the anxiety and gloom being experienced by her crew, who already felt that she was too slow to outrun enemy predators and too weakly armed to defend herself if confronted.[96] However brutal, in this dark fatalism they were being perfectly honest.

On the following morning the two U.S. ships were spotted by a Japanese reconnaissance plane well south of Java. Alarmed by this sighting, they decided to split up, believing this might increase their odds of survival. Lt. Cdr. J. B. Berkley's *Tulsa* could make slightly better speed—perhaps 12 or 13 knots— and she must have been one of the last Allied vessels to see *Asheville*. Berkley later reported: "At dawn [on March 2] I sighted the *Asheville* two points on my starboard bow, hull down proceeding on a southeasterly course. I changed my course to south and by 1000 I had lost sight of the *Asheville*." He then altered course periodically over the rest of that day and night to try to avoid enemy contact. But on the morning of March 3 "at 0903 . . . [he] intercepted a radio distress signal from the *Asheville* on 500 kcs [the distress frequency]—'RRRR RRRR RRRR ASHEVILLE ATTACKED 12-33S 111-35E.'" Then, nothing.[97]

The minesweeper *Whippoorwill* also intercepted a brief message from *Asheville* stating that the ship had been intercepted by a "raider." It was followed by silence. Lt. Cdr. Charles A. Ferriter, skipper of *Whippoorwill*, realized he was not more than ninety miles from the last position given by *Asheville*, so he altered course toward that location in a very natural impulse to aid a stricken comrade. However, common sense returned to Ferriter just as swiftly. Thinking it over, he soon realized that anything that might have overpowered the 1,300-ton *Asheville* would make mincemeat of his lightly armed little 850-ton sweeper. He then changed course away from *Asheville*'s estimated location and resumed *Whippoorwill*'s long, agonizing creep toward Australia. The minesweeper would arrive on March 9, one of the very last U.S. ships to have escaped calamity in the East Indies. But for *Asheville* the predators would soon arrive in force.

As feared the enemy air patrol of the previous day had sighted not only *Asheville* and *Tulsa* but also the straggling *Yarra* convoy. The air forces and ships of the Imperial Navy were still doing their best to carry out their directives to intercept and destroy any and all Allied shipping. Many of these Japanese ships, despite nearly three months at war, had seen no combat; all were hopeful they might yet come to grips with the despised Anglo-Saxons at sea and give the white men an unforgettable display of the skill and might of the emperor's navy.

Vice Adm. Kondō Nobutake's Main Body was hunting in the area to the east of 110 degrees, and its men were eager for more "victories" such as they had experienced in the preceding days.[98] One of the Sentai 4 heavy cruisers, the 15,000-ton *Maya*, and two destroyers, *Arashi* and *Nowaki* of DesDiv 4, were sent

THEY FLED TO BLISS OR WOE

to try to intercept these fleeing Allied ships.[99] On the morning of the third, as they steamed on a westerly course, the two Imperial Navy destroyers *Arashi* and *Nowaki*, which were "in the vanguard" ahead of *Maya*, sighted the high stack of *Asheville* in the distance. The time was about half past eight, and they were then 160 miles southwest of Bali, bearing some 196 degrees from the island.

Japanese accounts provide the bulk of our information regarding the engagement, which was brief and violent. *Maya* remained aloof from the action and took no part in the fight. There are several valid explanations for that; a primary one would have been to conserve ammunition for targets of more value. Also, she may have then been taking aboard some fifty prisoners of *Stronghold* from the captured Dutch steamer *Bintoehan*, which had rescued these men just after daybreak that morning after the destroyer was sunk the previous night. The men—and a number more, according to survivors later—were in Carley floats and in the process of being picked up by *Bintoehan* when *Maya* appeared on the scene and halted the rescue.[100] It would have been at just around this time that *Asheville* was first spotted by the enemy ships.

Unleashed from their screening duties like a pair of hunting hounds, *Arashi* and *Nowaki* increased speed to 32 knots to overhaul the "enemy ship with a tall funnel" from astern.[101] Enjoying a 20-knot speed advantage, the Japanese closed the distance with chilling swiftness. For *Asheville* it was the very trap her men had long anticipated and dreaded. They could neither outrun nor outgun their adversaries. No choice remained but to try to give a good account of themselves against overwhelming odds. The most they could hope for was a lucky hit against one of the enemy ships. As the range narrowed to 8,500 meters— roughly 9,300 yards—the pair of big destroyers opened fire against the American gunboat. To the Japanese Britt's vessel appeared to be painted in a three-tone camouflage scheme. The time was 0906 hours.

For a few minutes the venerable gunboat "gamely returned fire" with one or more of her 4-inch guns, before the telling weight of enemy shells tore her topsides to shreds and decimated the gun crews and bridge personnel. *Arashi* claimed to have scored a hit with her first salvo, which "blew off the enemy's forward gun."[102] The enemy destroyers rapidly closed to within 4,500 meters and paralleled *Asheville* as they fired. Soon they registered more hits on the forward part of the U.S. ship, and flames could be seen breaking out. The bridge area and forecastle were badly damaged, and many men topside seem to have been killed. *Nowaki* then made repeated hits on the gunboat's aft section, and before long *Asheville* went dead in the water, listing to port.

By that time *Asheville's* personnel began going overboard to escape the dying gunboat's death throes. Shortly thereafter the gunboat's "stern rose high in the air" as she began her final slide into the Indian Ocean.[103] It was 0938 hours when the battered *Asheville* disappeared at last beneath the waves. Thirty-two minutes of murderous combat ended her long, faithful, and colorful career in the Far East. Knowing that the odds were stacked against them in every sense, the men of *Asheville* had still performed their duties and made every effort to carry their own weight. It appears that only the short supply of Allied patrol vessels in the Dutch Javanese ports had demanded their retention in the East Indies. The oppressive sense of doom under which her officers and men had lived in the final weeks of the Java campaign had come to its inevitable end. At least 160 Americans, Filipinos, and Chinese were lost with *Asheville*.

For their part the Japanese expended a large number of 5-inch projectiles in this sinking. *Nowaki* fired 143 and *Arashi* 233 rounds. This was, however, consistent with most other sinkings in the Java campaign by Japanese destroyers and cruisers. No matter what the target—tanker, freighter, man o' war—they *all* required far too many shells.

Afterward, the two IJN destroyers moved in warily to the area of the sinking. There were a number of men in the water who had survived the action, but they were widely scattered, having probably abandoned *Asheville* in some haste. The Japanese appear to have asked for officers but allegedly found none to rescue. It is most unlikely that they made a purposive effort to save many survivors; they had urgent reasons to get elsewhere.[104] Only one destroyer, *Arashi*, which had closed to within a hundred meters of the sinking, threw a line over its side to an American sailor, and from the ocean they would pull only one individual. The moonfaced young man with "Roy Roger eyes" they rescued was not an officer at all. He was a member of *Asheville*'s black gang, a fireman second class from Indiana named Fred Louis Brown.[105]

He was held aboard the destroyer for four more days, at which time *Arashi* and the other Main Body ships under Vice Admiral Kondō returned to their advance base in the East Indies at Staring Bay on March 7. *Arashi* accompanied Kondō and his triumphant cruisers to Makassar for an "inspection tour" on March 18. There Fred L. Brown was transferred to the Dutch hospital ship *Op Ten Noort*. He was finally incarcerated in a Makassar POW camp with several hundred other Allied prisoners who had been captured or rescued at sea during the conclusion of the Java operations. With the sinking of *Asheville*, the last surface vessel of the old Asiatic Fleet still in the East Indies had been disposed of by the victorious Japanese.

On the same day enemy destroyers also managed to damage Lt. Cdr. David

THEY FLED TO BLISS OR WOE

Hurt's submarine *Perch* (ss-176) in the Java Sea. The boat was scuttled by Hurt and his men, and the IJN destroyer *Ushio* later captured the entire crew. As the American sailors who had escaped *Perch* watched their boat sink out of sight beneath the water, *Ushio* left its formation and headed for them. Two electrician's mates floating together discussed what was coming.

Jessie Robison, EM2/c, asked his companion, Ernest Plantz, EM3/c, "Kid, do you know what your next meal will be?" The young sailor answered, "No."

"Rice," said Robison.

Plantz then gave a reply that was not soon forgotten by the men of *Perch*.

"Not me. I can't eat rice unless it has cream and sugar on it."

He would soon learn otherwise.[106]

The butcher's bill for the campaign was especially high on ships long associated with the Asiatic Fleet: *Houston, Pope, Pillsbury, Peary, Perch, s-36, Edsall, Stewart, Asheville, Langley,* and *Pecos* were lost. Upward of 1,800 Americans gave their lives. The majority of these deaths occurred under Helfrich's command, which troubled Hart, King, and others. Hart alluded to these casualties in his postwar "Supplementary Narrative," comparing them to U.S. casualties at Tarawa, which (unlike the navy's losses) had received extensive, and heartbreaking, press coverage. In this comparison Hart understood that the Java campaign's travails were similar to those suffered later by the USMC at Tarawa.

Those losses marked the end of the Java campaign for the forces of the U.S. Navy. On the ground there was a fair amount of rather confused maneuvering by the Allied forces but only marginal resistance. At no time was the Japanese assault seriously threatened in the ground fighting. The campaign to take the seven-hundred-mile-long island went advantageously for the Japanese and their losses were minimal.[107] Over March 8–9, 1942, the Dutch capitulated, forcing their British, Australian, and American allies to lay down their weapons, and thousands of Allied service personnel became POWs.

Of the small American contingent known as "the Lost Battalion" (Second Battalion/131st F. A. Regiment), but one soldier was killed on the ground—ironically by mishandling his own rifle. Pvt. Bruce Rhodes shot himself accidently on March 7 (near Bandoeng) and died.[108] Over five hundred members of this Texas National Guard unit then went into Japanese captivity along with their fellow Allied servicemen. They were brave soldiers who were willing enough to fight, but mismanagement and confusion saw them thrown away in the campaign to no useful purpose.

# FOURTEEN

## Post Diem

*In the Highest Degree Tragic*

Despite postwar claims by surviving officers and men from ABDA's warships, Japanese losses in action against the Allied striking forces were slight. Other than merchant ships, one submarine (*I-60*), and the friendly-fire sinkings at Sunda Strait, only the little patrol boat hit by three U.S. torpedoes at Balikpapan was sunk in a surface engagement.[1] Indeed, from December until April the Japanese Imperial Navy lost nothing larger than a destroyer. That the Japanese considered their merchant sinkings problematic was really a comment on the paucity of those shipping bottoms, *not* on Allied efficiency. For the loss of a handful of destroyers, submarines, merchant ships, and smaller craft, the Imperial Japanese war machine had conquered and seized not one but three Western empires in the Far East.

As soon as Java surrendered, the Japanese began a vast reorganization, with a series of administrative changes both civil and military. On March 9 a liaison conference was held in Tokyo to determine the allocation of valuable strategic materials seized in the East Indies. New programs and laws were then enacted almost immediately to deal with the recently acquired resource areas in the south. The IJN restructured its forces in the East Indies and began establishing governing bodies—particularly in Southern Borneo, the Celebes, and the Lesser Sundas—that were ostensibly civilian but in actuality controlled by the Imperial Navy. For the next six weeks or so, the Japanese were permitted to bask in the delusional glow of success. But on April 18, 1942, with the Doolittle raid, their sense of invulnerability and divine righteousness would be punctured. Within another two months, following reversals in the Coral Sea in May and at Midway in June, the Imperial Navy's offensive bolt would be shot. Yet even so it would remain a deadly and determined adversary for the next two years.

But the heady victories of early 1942 would prove to be a catastrophic conquest in the end. A scant three and a half years later the home islands would lie in ashes and rubble, its people starving, and the once-mighty Japanese military forces reduced to impotence. It may therefore be argued that in at least one very real sense the sacrifice of the old U.S. Asiatic Fleet in the dismal Java campaign had permanent value: we had learned more, and better, from our defeats than our enemies had from their victories.

Many of the Asiatic Fleet officers who escaped Java rose to positions of considerable responsibility. Admiral Thomas C. Hart returned to the General Board in 1942, then became involved in the Pearl Harbor Attack Hearings and chaired his own board of investigation. In May 1942 Roosevelt had applied a conciliatory salve to Hart's wounded pride when he presented the admiral with a "Gold Star in lieu of the Second Distinguished Service Medal . . . for exceptionally meritorious service as the Commander-in-Chief, United States Asiatic Fleet." The award stated that Hart's conduct of operations in the Southwest Pacific "during January and February 1942 was characterized by unfailing judgment and sound decision coupled with marked moral courage in the face of discouraging surroundings and complex associations." Later Hart served as a senator from Connecticut from 1945 to 1947. The man who loved to frustrate his physicians by being so fit at an advanced age—in his sixties his doctor told him that "it would take an axe to kill [him]"—lived another quarter century before dying at ninety-four on July 4, 1971.

American survivors of the East Indies campaign meanwhile went on to fill out divisions in newly commissioned ships or leaven existing ones, with their experiences always useful (and often inspirational to those who knew of them). Edward "Butch" Parker had other important destroyer commands, including that of *Cushing* in the Naval Battle of Guadalcanal, while Jacob "Jocko" Cooper became xo of the battleship *Iowa*. J. J. Hourihan of *Paul Jones* commanded an attack transport later in the war. Thomas Binford became skipper of the light cruiser uss *Miami* (cl-89) in 1945 and, as a rear admiral, commanded the so-called Taiwan Patrol Force from the heavy cruiser uss *Saint Paul* (ca-73) at the start of the Korean conflict; he would retire in the fifties as a vice admiral. Henry Eccles rose to the rank of rear admiral and helped revolutionize naval thinking about logistics. Former pby pilot Lt. Tom Moorer of PatWing 10 would reach the apex of navy leadership as Adm. Thomas H. Moorer, head of the Joint Chiefs of Staff in the seventies.[2]

Of surviving Asiatic sailors, their fortunes were just as diverse, but nearly all continued in the war. Bob Foley went to the light cruiser uss *Columbia* (cl-56) and saw action again at the Battle of Empress Augusta Bay in late 1943. Lowell Barty ended up on the destroyer uss *Gainard* (dd-706) and had experiences that he told me were far more frightening than the *Langley* fiasco when his ship endured terrifying kamikaze attacks at Okinawa. Bill Kohl found himself on the destroyer escort USS *Dempsey* (DE-26), where he learned how to get the ornery 1.1-inch quad machine cannon to operate more efficiently. After he reached Fremantle, Ted Luxemburg was assigned as a signals officer working on code breaking, then traveled back by merchant vessel to England via Ceylon and Bombay (contracting dengue fever in the process), before finishing up on a subtender at war's end. After being plucked from the Java Sea, Jack Penhollow made five patrols with the submarine that had rescued him, the old pigboat S-37.

In the postwar period these men rarely spoke of their wartime careers, for a variety of reasons. Many Java campaign veterans felt that they were not the "winners" after all and more than a few believed that they had long since been relegated to the scrap heap of history. After all, textbooks and best sellers ignored them then as they continue to do so today. Whenever they encountered a younger person who knew much of *anything* about their service in the Southwest Pacific in early 1942, they could be openly appreciative. But by and large they remained modest men who were content to live outside the spotlight and alone with their memories. Only in the company of their former shipmates would they allow themselves any emotional displays, although even then these were rare enough. In advanced age, as in their younger years, these men remained reserved and taciturn, having been raised during the tough, unsentimental years of the Great Depression.

Nonetheless, it is my belief—and has been for decades—that they still deserve more fundamental recognition for their sacrifices. This book has been an attempt to provide that. The men of the old Asiatic Fleet more than fulfilled their contract with America as members of the armed forces. Perhaps it is time for their country to keep its contract with them by remembering those sacrifices. A step in that direction, at the very least, would be to incorporate their story into standard history textbooks today. I believe that for future generations to know more about and hopefully *learn* in some detail the sacrifices these young Americans made in 1941–42 would best honor their memory.

# ACKNOWLEDGMENTS

My first and deepest thanks go to Anthony P. Tully, with whom a collaborative project on the NEI campaign was initially conceived even before my first book was released. That project, sadly, never came to fruition, but Tony and I continued to exchange information—principally IJN-related—and bounce ideas off each other concerning a number of problematic naval mysteries in the East Indies. For seven years I have been able to rely on Tony for impeccable fact checking, superb research and analysis, and as importantly, for friendship.

I wish to again thank my agent, James D. Hornfischer, for his labor in securing a publisher. I must also thank the editors and staff at the University of Nebraska Press and Potomac who have been involved in the long process of turning a large, sprawling manuscript into a published work.

Principal among contributors of original material as well as memories of prewar life in the Philippines is Henryetta Cokor, daughter of Adam Mummey, CMM, who perished on *Langley*. She has been a consistent joy to communicate with over the years and has given selflessly of her own time and materials repeatedly. It is only through such living participants that a dedicated historian can hope to begin to approach a fully honest reconstruction of the past. Written archival sources are one thing, but living memories and impressions are of another—often higher—order altogether. In my view to overlook or leave out such human sources often reduces a historical work to the level of mere accounting.

Additional thanks goes to Bill Wills, son of Clarence Wills, who generously supplied a large collection of *China Gunboatman* and the USS *Trinity (AO-13) Newsletter*. These were of paramount value in fleshing out and illuminating—often with vivid humor—the lives of Asiatic Fleet sailors in the late thirties and early forties.

The Asiatic Fleet veterans I interviewed without exception deserve special recognition. These included Bill Kohl (*Houston*), Clarence Wills (*Trinity*), Ray

Kester (*Houston/Marblehead*), Clifford Teer (*Parrott*), Benton Potter (*Tulsa/* USMC), Bill Warnes (*Langley*), Walt Frumerie (*Langley*), Lowell Barty (*Langley*), Paul Johnson (*Whipple/J. D. Edwards*), Joe McDevitt (*Whipple*), Ted Luxemburg (*Marblehead/Whipple*), Bob Foley (*Pecos*), Jack Penhollow (*De Ruyter*), and Elly Ellsworth (*Stewart/J. D. Ford*). All were modest, forthright, and helpful, and each man had a unique perspective and memories of this critical but half-forgotten campaign in World War II.

The men from *Houston* whom I have known and enjoyed friendships with over the past quarter century are too numerous to list here, but Rear Adm. Bob Fulton, Howard Brooks, David Flynn, and Bill Ingram were of particular help in this book's creation. It goes without saying that their passing has affected me, but I am also strengthened by their example and my desire to tell their stories.

From the family of Otto C. Schwarz, founder of the USS *Houston* (CA-30) Survivors Association, I inherited a bounty of material that enriched this work immeasurably. Trudy and John, your old historian thanks you from the depths of his heart, as always. The rest of the board and *all* the members of the *Houston* Survivors Association over many years have my gratitude as well. In particular I want to thank Matt Johnson, Val and Max Poss, Sharron Long, Sue Kreutzer, Dana Charles, and Pam Foster. Similarly, my fellow officers and members of the Naval Order of the United States, Texas Commandery, deserve thanks for their support and friendship. It has been a delight and a privilege to serve as the historian for the Texas Commandery.

My "amigo" and translator, Kan Sugahara—a member of the Seventy-Seventh *ki* at Etajima in 1945, respected researcher, fluent in Spanish as well as English, and a published author in his own right—once again performed admirably and added insights from the Japanese perspective. For eleven years now we have worked together, and I have only the highest regard for Sugahara-*san*. In every instance he has been a commendable and tireless colleague.

Another academic historian from Japan, Professor Munehiro Miwa of Kyushu University, also helped with his own insights, a deep understanding predicated on the many invaluable relationships he established and important interviews he conducted as a young man with leading officers of the Imperial Japanese Navy in the Shōwa period.

My wonderful Dutch East Indian friends, Fred Hekking and Bernice Harapat, both helped with translations as well as their own family memories and personal recollections of the long-past world of Java and the East Indies before World War II. I have enjoyed every moment we have spent together over the years and hope there will be more still to come.

Quite a few colleagues and correspondents from a variety of institutions, associations, and websites likewise deserve special mention: the late Luca Ruffato; Daryl Ford; Sam Cox; Kevin Denlay; Bill Bartsch; Vic Campbell; Jim Nix; Sean Frey; Vincent O'Hara; Bob Alford; Mike Wenger; Tom Womack; Klemen Lužar; Jan Visser; Osamu Tagaya; the Special Collections staff at University of Houston's M. D. Anderson Library, especially Julie Grob—and of course Valerie Prilop (who processed the Milner Collection); Dick Lillie; Mark Weber at the Navy Memorial in Washington DC; and Pat Osborn at NARA II *all* merit acknowledgment.

Finally, the dedication of the book to the U.S. Army historian Samuel Milner (1910–2000) is simply my small way of thanking a giant, one on whose shoulders I have been able to stand to obtain a larger and more comprehensive overall perspective of the Asiatic Fleet in the Java campaign. One of the army's *Green Book* authors, Sam labored on his own USS *Houston*/Lost Battalion project for over forty years, long before the Internet, and accumulated an extraordinary amount of data as well as scores of in-depth firsthand interviews conducted between 1959 and 1964. That his ambitious project was never published should not obscure the greatness of his efforts. My research and understanding have been enriched a hundredfold by exposure to Samuel Milner's work. Unsung no longer, Sam!

# NOTES

### Introduction

1. Adm. Thomas C. Hart, "Supplementary of Narrative, 1946–47," National Archives and Records Administration, Archives II, College Park MD (archive hereafter cited as NARA II). Fabius Maximus: Roman military leader famed for the evasive strategy he employed against Hannibal in the Punic Wars but called Cunctator—the Delayer—by domestic opponents.

2. Vice Adm. William Glassford, USN (ret.), "Supplementary Narrative, 1939–1942," May 1950, 45–46, NARA II.

3. These remarks by Billy E. Green can be found at http://archiver.rootsweb.ancestry.com/th/read/ROOTS/1996-12/19809.

4. Joe McDevitt's comments are taken from a conversation with the author, summer 2012.

### 1. Prewar

1. Leutze, *Different Kind of Victory*, 116. For his part, Hart considered FDR "liberal, even radical" and did not favor the administration's pro-labor policies.

2. Leutze, *Different Kind of Victory*, 140–41.

3. Morison, *Rising Sun in the Pacific*, 151.

4. Hart was made a full (four-star) admiral as CINCAF. Hart referred to his "lone wolf tactics" in at least one diary entry.

5. Forrestel, *Admiral Raymond A. Spruance*, 7. Forrestel here also included the dry understatement: "Many non-regulation practices were unofficially but customarily accepted in the Asiatic Fleet."

6. *Naval History* 13, no. 5 (September–October 1999): 14.

7. Never one to bandy words, Yarnell would later incur the displeasure of FDR, Harry Hopkins, and the British when he wrote an article for *Colliers* magazine criticizing the Royal Air Force's effectiveness. (Roosevelt, *FDR, His Personal Letters*, 2:1236.)

8. Quoted in Tolley, *Yangtze Patrol*, 271.

9. Rhodes Farmer, *Shanghai Harvest*, quoted in Wakeman, *Policing Shanghai 1927–1937*, 277–80.

10. Tuchman, *Stillwell and the American Experience*, 169.

11. Chungking was bombed regularly as well, and there, too, a number of Asiatic units were present. Near Nanking on December 12, 1937, the Japanese bombed and sank the U.S. gunboat *Panay*. These unprovoked attacks on the Yangtze were certainly not forgotten by the Americans or the British.

12. The convoluted situation regarding American oil firms in the Far East, U.S. foreign policy, and Japan's unceasing belligerence and law breaking are worth a new work. The best book to date on the subject remains Anderson, *Standard-Vacuum Oil Company*.

13. A prime example of such doublespeak is Tokyo's handling of U.S. oil firms' claims in Manchukuo regarding a proposed Japanese oil monopoly there. Foreign Minister Hirota Koki released a polite dis-

avowal on November 5, 1934, which infuriated Secretary of State Cordell Hull. Hirota simply denied that the matter concerned the imperial government at all. He stated that it was "not within the knowledge or concern of the Imperial Government and the Imperial Government [was] not in a position to give an explanation with regard to it" (Hull, *Memoirs*, 1:275). He claimed that Manchukuo was a separate nation and conducted its own affairs. Such bland and transparently false statements were a standard Japanese response throughout the thirties.

14. Leutze, *Different Kind of Victory*, 151.

15. Hart, private diary, July 25, 1939, copy on microfilm in the Samuel Milner Papers, M. D. Anderson Library, Special Collections, University of Houston, Houston TX (hereafter cited as Milner Papers; subsequent citations of Hart's diary appear as Hart, diary).

16. Kemp Tolley—the Asiatic Fleet veteran and historian—characterized Hart's feelings for FDR as "pure bile" (*China Gunboatman*, issue and page unavailable).

17. Wohlstetter, *Pearl Harbor*, 130. See also Ickes, *Secret Diary*, vol. 3.

18. Throughout 1939 and into 1940 Hart's personal diary records his dissatisfaction with the Asiatic Station as well as with Washington's diplomacy in the Far East. After Hitler's Wehrmacht and Luftwaffe overran Europe in the spring of 1940, more signs of weariness and wariness appear in Hart's diary. May and June show this in particular, when he seems especially concerned about the demise of the British following the fall of Belgium, Holland, and France. Hart's birthday entry in late June 1940, when he turned sixty-three, was a particularly gloomy meditation and frankly questioned his ability to handle the CIN-CAF position.

19. Hart, diary, July 20, 1939.

20. Adm. Thomas C. Hart, "Narrative of Events, Asiatic Fleet, Leading Up to War and from 8 December 1941 to 15 February 1942," 5–7, Fold3 by Ancestry, Historical Military Records, at www.fold3.com. Totals vary—some say twenty-eight, others twenty-nine—but the figure of thirty PBYs used here comes from "The History of Fleet Air Wing 10" (www.fold3.com). The wing was made up of two squadrons, VP-101 and VP-102. Tenders *Preston* and *Childs* arrived after *Langley*, but *Heron*—whose responsibility was the Utility Squadron's smaller aircraft—had been on the Asiatic Station since the twenties.

21. Navy Department, *Annual Report*, 4.

22. At this time Shanghai consisted of Chinese city sections and the International Settlement, which was an extraterritorial enclave based on treaties dating back almost a century. The settlement was governed by a municipal council with members elected by the United States, Great Britain, France, and Japan, which also policed it. The French Concession was separate.

23. Danklefsen, *Navy I Remember*, 85–88. A popular Asiatic Fleet saying ("Chefoo by the sea, Chefoo by the smell") referred to the Chinese practice of using human waste ("night soil") as fertilizer.

24. *China Gunboatman*, March 2001.

25. Danklefsen, *Navy I Remember*, 87–88.

26. One of the best studies is L. Young, *Japan's Total Empire. Manchurian Legacy* by Kuramoto gives the perspective of a Japanese family in Manchukuo.

27. Leutze, *Different Kind of Victory*, 152–53. Also, the so-called Tientsin Crisis (1938–39) led to secret talks between USN and Royal Navy leaders and may have contributed to FDR's fateful decision to retain the Pacific Fleet at Pearl Harbor the following year.

28. James T. Nix, grandson of an Asiatic Fleet officer lost in action during the Java campaign (Lt. J. J. Nix, skipper of *Edsall*), has saved many reels of 8 mm film taken in 1938–40 by his grandfather and grandmother on the Asiatic Station. These include scenes filmed at locations from Hong Kong to Chefoo and also across the Philippine islands.

29. Shimbunsha, *Shiryō Meiji Hyakunen* (Documents for the Meiji centennial), 495–96. Quoted in Lu, *Japan, A Documentary History*, 2:418–19.

30. These were two IJN officers who happened to be brothers-in-law: Capt. Nakahara Yoshimasa (who may or may not have been called "The King of the South Seas") and the Machiavellian extrem-

ist Cdr. Ishikawa Shingo, a disciple of Katō Kanji, mentored by Oka Takazumi, and friend to Matsuoka Yōsuke. Both Nakahara and Ishikawa would later find themselves assigned to military posts in the East Indies during World War II.

31. See L. Young, *Japan's Total Empire*, pt. 3, 183–241 in particular. Also, with Chiang Kai-shek preoccupied with his internal wars against Communist forces in 1935, Japan militarists began their plans to detach five of China's northern provinces with the aim of establishing Manchukuo-like puppet states. This was not entirely successful but gained for the imperial military a foothold that enabled subsequent aggression to spread and led, finally, to the Marco Polo Bridge Incident. For numerous contemporary accounts, see Johnsen, *Chinese-Japanese War, 1937–*.

32. Deacon, *History of the Japanese Secret Service*, 142. It is indisputable that the Japanese viewed the Foreign Settlements in those treaty ports as problematic. A section of their 1941 prewar plans also determined that the "hostile foreign Settlements" would be seized "at appropriate times" (Japanese Monograph no. 147, "Outline of Developments in Political Diplomatic and Military Affairs during 1941," 27–28, http://ibiblio.org/hyperwar/Japan/Monos/).

33. Wasserstein, *Secret War in Shanghai*, 6.

34. Wasserstein, *Secret War in Shanghai*, 1.

35. The Chinese lost 130,000 men by mid-October (out of roughly 500,000 assembled by Chiang for the siege of Shanghai), but overall Japanese forces had risen from some 5,000 in early August to as many as 200,000 by the middle of September 1937 (Dreyer, *China at War*, 216–19).

36. Wasserstein, *Secret War in Shanghai*, 22.

37. British Documents on Foreign Affairs, part 2, series E, *Asia, 1914–1939*, 17:335.

38. These oil figures are drawn from Worth, *No Choice but War*, chapter 8 ("The Petroleum Supply Crisis of 1941") and are derived from USSBS statistics. Japan was then getting approximately 10 percent of her oil from the East Indies.

39. Simpson, *Admiral Harold R. Stark*, chapters 5–6. Plan DOG—so named for the fourth option ("D") offered by Stark in November 1940—referred to the decision to focus on the European theater rather than the Pacific. It was predicated on a "defeat the Nazis first" strategy, and it reversed much prewar U.S. thinking. As Stark and others then reasoned, defeat of Hitler was absolutely necessary to preserve Europe and the West, while Japan, regardless of its power then, would offer no such ultimate existential threat. This plan was formalized in the March 1941 "ABC-1" talks with the British, which then formed the basis of America's RAINBOW 5 war plans. Stark sent a completed RAINBOW 5 plan to all his fleet commanders—including Hart—in late May "with instructions to prepare their own fleet operating plans in accordance with it" (Simpson, *Admiral Harold R. Stark*, 101).

40. Thorpe, *East Wind, Rain*, 44.

41. "Tommy Hart Speaks Out."

42. By the spring of 1941, caution in Washington seems to have ruled out any thoughts of sending more cruisers or destroyers to Hart. Along with assurances of Royal Navy backing, fears in the State Department of provoking the volatile Japanese won out at that time (Simpson, *Admiral Harold R. Stark*, 103). It was also still believed—at least in theory—that Kimmel and the Pacific Fleet would steam to relieve the Philippines, although it is difficult to see much evidence of Hart's faith in that aspect of the navy's old plans.

43. Morley, *Fateful Choice*, 138.

44. The Japanese economic missions to Java in 1940–41 under Kobayashi and Yoshizawa are, unfortunately, beyond the scope of this book.

45. The anemic Philippine treasury could not have possibly equipped and maintained a force large enough to resist armies as huge and well disciplined as those fielded by Japan in that period.

46. Hart, diary, November 5, 1940.

47. Ens. Herb Levitt of *Houston* described the slender Glassford as "easy-going . . . amiable . . . [a] dandy," who was nicknamed "Tubby." Others referred to Glassford as "a drawing-room admiral" (Herb Levitt interview with Samuel Milner, ca.1959/1960, Milner Papers).

48. This included navy ministers such as Shimada Shigetarō and heads of the navy general staff, Prince Fushimi and Adm. Nagano Osami, along with high-ranking subordinates such as Navy Vice Minister Toyoda Teijirō, among others. Often these leaders were poorly served by pliant upper-echelon naval officers. Admiral Nagano appears to have been particularly susceptible to pressure from middle-echelon hawks and jingoists. The insidious phenomenon that Irving Janis later defined and analyzed as "Groupthink" was clearly at work as well.

49. Anderson, *Standard-Vacuum Oil Company*, 74–75.

50. Nakahara was a member of the Japanese delegation sent to Batavia in 1940 for the economic talks. Additionally, many insights into these Japanese officers were provided in conversations with Professor Miwa Munehiro of Kyushu University in Japan during his annual research trips to the United States. Miwa-*sensei* interviewed and communicated with a number of important IJN commanders as a student himself over thirty years ago.

51. Ishikawa Shingo (1894–1964) was a member of the Navy Ministry's Dai Ichi Iinkai (The First Committee), involved in policy and war plans in 1941 during a series of brutal turf wars with the rival planning committee. Ishikawa had been personally involved at many of the cardinal junctures in the occult decision-making processes within the military and civilian regime, proving time and again that his reputation as a dangerous extremist was no exaggeration. In early 1943 a tipsy Rear Admiral Ishikawa would brag to staff officers during his tenure as CO of the Twenty-Third Kōkusentai at Kendari, Celebes, that *he* was responsible for bringing Japan into the Great East Asia War. Sadly, Ishikawa's grotesque boast contained more than a little truth.

52. Morley, *Fateful Choice*, 248.

53. This nickname appears to be a play on *fukidasu*, meaning to blow (wind), gush out, or erupt. "Blowhard" might also apply.

54. Hart, diary, October 16, 1940.

55. Hart, diary, October 18, 1940.

56. Hart, diary, October 21, 1940.

57. Hart, diary, February 1942.

58. From Cdr. Ted Drag, USN (ret.), in the USS *Trinity Newsletter*, Winter 2005, 11. Copies of newsletters courtesy of the family of Clarence Wills.

59. Drag, USS *Trinity Newsletter*, Winter 2005, 11.

60. Drag, USS *Trinity Newsletter*, Winter 2005, 11.

61. Drag, USS *Trinity Newsletter*, Winter 2005, 11.

62. USS *Trinity Newsletter*, Summer 2001, 12–13.

63. Anecdotes about Gobidas, Hiller, Chesnutt, and Chief Birchmire are taken from the USS *Trinity Newsletter*, Summer 2001, 12–14.

64. USS *Trinity Newsletter*, Summer 2001, 12–14.

65. USS *Trinity Newsletter*, Summer 2001, 12–14.

66. Carl Hiller reminiscences taken from the USS *Trinity Newsletter*, Spring 2000 and Summer 2009 issues.

67. With his shipmates on "The Mighty T," Clarence Wills survived his Asiatic adventure and ended up at war's end on the staff of Adm. Thomas Kinkaid. His "accidental" posting to the Far East appeared in issues of the *China Gunboatman* and the USS *Trinity Newsletter*, plus interviews with the author, January 2012.

68. Hart, diary, November 28, 1939.

69. Hart, diary, September 25, 1941.

70. Matloff and Snell, *Strategic Planning for Coalition Warfare*, 46–47.

71. Purnell, "Summarized Report of Conversations Held by Chief of Staff, with Netherlands East Indies Naval Authorities at Batavia, 10–14 January 1941," Milner Papers.

72. Hart, diary, January 13, 1941.

73. McCrea was given his orders by Stark in mid-November 1940, but due to a series of problems the trip itself took from December 13 to January 6.

74. Hart, diary, April 18–19, 1941.

75. From a June 1960 memorandum written by H. E. Eccles for John Toland, Milner Papers.

76. Holmes, *Underseas Victory*, 1:67.

77. Holmes, *Underseas Victory*, 1:67.

78. The USN submarine torpedo scandal has been well covered in other PacWar texts and need not be revisited in this narrative.

79. This was the memory of Rear Adm. Edward N. Parker in a 1960 letter to John Toland. Before the war, Parker had commanded USS *Parrott* (DD-218) (Milner Papers).

80. Eccles memorandum for Toland, June 1960, Milner Papers.

81. Hart was tasked by Washington at this time to find an appropriate southern Philippines anchorage that could be transformed into another U.S. naval base, and he had chosen Tutu Bay.

82. Walter Schneck interview with Samuel Milner, August 1959, series 1, box 2, folder 71, Milner Papers.

83. A native of Mississippi, Binford was made commander in July 1940, then replacing Cdr. Charles E. Coney as ComDesDiv 58. In the end Binford did not get to test his social skills after all. A few days before the Army-Navy game, his ship was sent south with other units to Tarakan, Borneo.

84. Alford, *Playing for Time*, 43–44.

85. Goodhart, *Fifty Ships That Saved the World*, 195.

86. Ships lost in the Java campaign are indicated by an asterisk (*). DesRon 29's thirteen destroyers were all constructed by Cramp of Philadelphia in 1919–20—and were, by 1941, completely unsuited to extended operations at sea far from adequate base and repair facilities. Captain Wiley commanded from *Black Hawk* during the campaign.

87. This move coincided with the German invasion of Russia, an action that exacerbated the tense situation in the Far East. Additional personnel for fleet HQ at Manila were drawn at this time by volunteers from other ships, some of whom were captured when the Philippines fell.

88. Survivors from *Houston*'s Communications Division, including Ens. Herb Levitt and David Flynn, RM2/c, both recalled friction with the flag staff, in particular with Cdr. H. B. Slocum, Hart's assistant chief of staff and operations officer.

89. From personal reminiscences of Cdr. Thomas Binford, ComDesDiv 58, recorded in an interview with John Toland in 1960 (Milner Papers).

90. *Stewart*, for example, had not been in the Dewey dry dock for a proper overhaul since February 1941.

91. Hart, diary, July 17, 1941.

92. Hart's diary details his ongoing problems with Cavite. He found the personnel not only dim-witted but addicted to spending excesses. All this plus Bemis's attempted suicide and problems with Rockwell's predecessor, Rear Admiral Smeallie, in late 1940 had left Hart feeling depressed. At one point a vexed Hart wrote that Cavite had probably *never* been very well run.

93. Levitt interview with Milner.

94. See Hart, diary. Eventually the army was to control the minefields. These mines remained a serious problem even when the USN went back into Manila in 1945.

95. Hart, diary, July 6, 1941.

96. Elmo "Joe" Bush interview with Samuel Milner, August 1960, series 1, box 2, folder 50, Milner Papers, and Merritt Eddy, "Autobiography," 38, in the author's collection (a gift from Eddy's daughter, Sandra Swanson).

97. Hart, diary, September 15, 1941.

98. *China Gunboatman*, December 1994, 20.

99. Details of this incident drawn from reminiscences of Carl Hiller in the USS *Trinity Newsletter* of Fall 2000 and Fall 2006.

100. Sailors are perennially fond of such nicknames. The prewar skipper of USS *Alden* was called "Madman Haight" (Lt. Cdr. Stanley Martin Haight, 1935–38) for his habit of steaming across Manila Bay at over 30 knots, scaring his crew out of their wits with his high-speed approaches to the docks at Cavite.

In 1938 Haight had lived up to his nickname by behaving impetuously during the notorious *President Hoover* grounding incident (Bill Warnes interviews with the author, 2010–11).

101. This was CNO's secret message 272337 drafted by Rear Adm. Richmond Kelly Turner, director of war plans: "This despatch is to be considered a war warning. Negotiations with Japan looking toward stabilization of conditions in the Pacific have ceased and an aggressive move by Japan is expected within the next few days.... Execute an appropriate defensive deployment preparatory to carrying out the tasks assigned in WPL 46" (*Pearl Harbor Attack Hearings*, pt. 5, 2124–25).

102. Glassford, "Supplementary Narrative," 36, NARA II.

103. Glassford, "Supplementary Narrative," 41, NARA II.

104. Recorded in Leutze, *Different Kind of Victory*, 225, and Hart's own narrative of events.

105. Glassford, "Supplementary Narrative," 39–40, NARA II.

## 2. As Is

1. Hart was awakened in his quarters by his duty officer, Lieutenant Colonel Clement, USMC, who gave him the news. Hart's message was copied and logged on *John D. Ford*—part of *Marblehead*'s group in Tarakan, Dutch Borneo—at 0329 hours. Some historians have faulted Washington for its tardy response to Hart's earlier request (November 20) to alter his war plans—which were denied by Secretary of the Navy Knox—and claimed that this delay led to the number of vulnerable ships still in the Manila Bay area on December 8. Much merchant shipping remained in Manila's harbor at that time also.

2. Letter from Bill Mack to John Toland, ca. 1960, subseries 10, box 5, folder 32, Milner Papers. In Washington DC, Roosevelt's cabinet had reacted similarly. Navy Secretary Frank Knox blurted out, "My God, this can't be true! This must mean the Philippines," when Stark delivered the first reports from Admiral Kimmel that afternoon. It is possible confusion resulted, too, from Hart's message about four hours later—at 0745—stating, "AIR ATTACK HAS BEEN MADE ON DAVAO." These were in fact raids by thirteen B5N (KATE) bombers escorted by nine A5M4 (CLAUDE) fighters flying from the light carrier *Ryūjō* directed against U.S. PBY Catalinas stationed there at Malalag Bay along with their tender USS *Preston*. Two PBYs were destroyed, but the tender—a converted four-piper destroyer—was not damaged and managed to escape.

3. Tolley, *Cruise of the Lanikai*. Tolley would later become as fine a memoirist as the old Asiatic Fleet ever produced, but his anti-FDR bias and Pearl Harbor conspiracy-theory obsessions mar an otherwise superb body of work.

4. Hart, diary, December 8, 1941.

5. Walt Frumerie interview with the author, July 15, 2012.

6. Michel, *Mr. Michel's War*, 31.

7. These recollections are taken from a series of letters written late in life by William "Texas Bill" Penninger to a relative and were provided to the author by the historian Anthony P. Tully, who collected many of Penninger's letters and notes (Penninger Papers).

8. Penninger letters, undated.

9. USS *Trinity Newsletter*, date unknown.

10. Details derived from copies of USS *Trinity Newsletter*, from my interviews with veterans, and above all from numerous talks over several years with Henryetta Cokor, daughter of Adam H. "Hank" Mummey, CMM (PA) of *Langley*, whose family lived at Long Beach and Cavite in the prewar years. Henryetta also generously supplied me with much rare, period archival material from Manila and Cavite.

11. Hart, "Supplementary of Narrative, 1946–47," 8.

12. These figures are taken from Japanese Monograph no. 80, "Operational Situation of the Japanese Navy in the Philippines Invasion Operations, December, 1941," copy in subseries 5, box 13, folder 40, Milner Papers.

13. American and Filipino forces then resisted with great fortitude for several months, proving the wisdom of Thomas De Quincey's observation after the Battle of Navarino (October 1827): "[Regarding]... the length and severity of the resistance... we are obliged to recollect, that absolute desperation is a for-

midable quality, even when possessing an undisciplined force" (De Quincey, *New Essays by De Quincey*, 186). Such desperation was rarely evident in the NEI ground campaign.

14. USS *Paul Jones* was the "extra" flushdecker in the baker's dozen of DesRon 29 and the designated squadron flagship. Before World War II, *Paul Jones* had usually been attached to DesDiv 59. Once fighting began, she operated with various divisions, few of which were able to maintain the precise organization established in the prewar Asiatic Fleet. *Marblehead* had departed Manila on the morning of November 24 and met the destroyers en route.

15. Germany's 1936 agreement with Rumania gave it access to important installations there, but wartime use began depleting these swiftly, and Hitler soon became obsessed with seizing the great Russian oilfields on the Black Sea.

16. Rear Adm. Edward N. Parker interview with John Toland, ca. 1960, Milner Papers.

17. Alford, *Playing for Time*, 37.

18. Ray Kester, RM2/c, *Marblehead*, email to the author.

19. Capt. Albert H. Rooks, "Estimate of the Situation, Far East Area, November 18, 1941," NARA II.

20. Details from Parker interview with Toland, Milner Papers.

21. Raised as an orphan, Bill Kale was a young signalman who had enlisted in 1935 as a teenager. He kept a private diary during the war's opening months detailing his experiences on *Stewart*. Bill survived the Java campaign, escaping on the *John. D. Edwards*. He transcribed and printed his diary in February 1985, making copies available to his shipmates. Author's hardcopy came from Marion "Elly" Ellsworth, a radioman on *Stewart* (hereafter cited as Kale, diary).

22. From PatWing 10's "Information concerning Naval Campaign in Orient, 1941–1942," Fold3 by Ancestry, Historical Military Records, at www.fold3.com.

23. Adm. Thomas C. Hart, "Narrative of Events, Asiatic Fleet, Leading Up to War and from 8 December 1941 to 15 February 1942," Fold3 by Ancestry, Historical Military Records, at www.fold3.com. Phillips then had four destroyers in Singapore—HMS *Express*, HMS *Electra*, HMS *Tenedos*, and HMAS *Vampire*—at his disposal for the sortie with *Prince of Wales* and *Repulse* in Force Z.

24. Years later Churchill argued, rather implausibly, that schemes had been considered for sending the big ships to hide in the numberless obscure islands to the south. There was also talk of having *Prince of Wales* and *Repulse* steam to Hawaii to reinforce the weakened U.S. Pacific Fleet. Neither one seems very realistic, given the admiralty's dominant concerns at that time.

25. Capt. J. M. Creighton, USN, "Singapore-Java-West Australia: July 17, 1941–April 19, 1942," Fold3 by Ancestry, Historical Military Records, at www.fold3.com.

26. Lt. Cdr. J. S. Mosher, USNR, "Report on Malaya, Java and Australia—March 2, 1941 to March 10, 1942," 6, Fold3 by Ancestry, Historical Military Records, at www.fold3.com.

27. Hart, diary, December 9, 1941.

28. From a letter of Adm. Thomas Hart, CINCAF, to Chief BuShips, dated December 6, 1941. Hart also noted that as soon as new paint became available to his fleet, the ships would be repainted in Measure 11 (*Warship International* 38, no. 3 (2001): 217).

29. Funding, as always throughout the thirties, was problematic, too, as was getting the guns, their mounts, shields, and directors to Mare Island. Some were as far away as the Brooklyn Navy Yard; others appear to have been in Puget Sound Navy Yard (Miscellaneous, subseries 11, box 5, folder 60, Milner Papers).

30. Friedman, *U.S. Cruisers*, 136–37. This was done in the other *Northampton*-class cruisers when they were also upgraded, but not in the case of *Houston* because of her early loss in the war.

31. Fulton recollections in conversation with the author, ca. 2006.

32. Letter from Lt. Bob Fulton to his parents, December 5, 1941, Cruiser *Houston* Collection, M. D. Anderson Library, Special Collections, University of Houston, Houston TX (hereafter cited as Cruiser *Houston* Collection).

33. Glassford, "Supplementary Narrative," 42, NARA II.

34. Blair, *Silent Victory*, 132.

35. The big Dewey dry dock had been towed from its traditional location at Olongapo to Mariveles in July.

36. E. M. Perry, *Ghosts of Canopus*, 57–58. According to Japanese records this was actually a small attack of seven medium bombers on Clark Field that night.

37. Perry, *Ghosts of Canopus*, 58

38. Mullin, *Another Six-Hundred,* 35.

39. Joe Sam Sisk memories taken from a filmed interview made on May 9, 2007, at his home in Greenville, Texas, by Texas A&M University at Commerce, http://dmc.tamuc.edu/cdm/singleitem/collection/uw/id/4191/rec/13.

40. Hart, diary, December 10, 1941.

41. Japanese Monograph no. 80, "Operational Situation of the Japanese Navy in the Philippines Invasion Operations, December, 1941" (available online at http://ibiblio.org/hyperwar/Japan/Monos/) states that fifty-four bombers—divided into two groups of twenty-seven each—were utilized in these attacks concentrating on Cavite and ships in Manila Bay.

42. *Peary* Deck Log for December 10, 1941.

43. Mullin, *Another Six-Hundred*, 38.

44. Mullin, *Another Six-Hundred,* 41.

45. Hart, diary, January 3, 1942

46. Bulkeley, *At Close Quarters*, 1–28. After helping evacuate President Manuel Quezon and members of his family, staff, and the cabinet, Bulkeley would extricate General MacArthur from Corregidor in early March. The general was then flown from Mindanao to Australia on March 17. Bulkeley would himself be flown out from Mindanao on April 13.

47. Hornfischer, *Ship of Ghosts*, 32.

### 3. Manila Abandoned

1. Tolley, *Cruise of the Lanikai*, 311.

2. *Trinity* could carry roughly 275,000 gallons of avgas in addition to some 65,000 barrels of fuel oil and about 4,500 barrels of diesel.

3. Wilbur Bingham's reminiscences are taken from the Fall 2007 issue of the *USS Trinity Newsletter*, 11–18. Copies of newsletters courtesy of the family of Clarence Wills.

4. Lieutenant Miropol had been ordered to report "without delay" just two days earlier, after *Trinity's* medical officer, Dr. Charles Dwyer, himself a patient, was admitted to the Naval Hospital.

5. Of the Standard Vacuum Oil Company but administered at Oeban by a Dutch East Indies subsidiary.

6. These men were not all that *Trinity* left behind when she departed Manila. The oiler had also left her new evaporators, generators, and ice machines on the wharf at Cavite.

7. Letters by Dr. Harold S. Miropol reprinted in the Summer 1997 and Winter 2002 issues of the *USS Trinity Newsletter.*

8. Reminiscences of AMM3/c Bill Kletter, in St. Pierre, *USS Langley CV-1 AV-3*, 253–55.

9. Messimer, *Pawns of War*, 12.

10. The Japanese moved swiftly to seize oil installations on British Borneo at Miri, Seria, and Lutong during December. Despite demolition schemes these installations were repaired quickly. By September 1944 they were the primary Japanese production facilities for most of the crude oil sent back to the home islands.

11. Rose, *Islands of the Sulu Sea*, 184. SOPA would have been Cdr. Felix D. Stump—relieved by Cdr. Robert McConnell a few weeks later.

12. At war's outbreak *Boise* was at sea, en route to Cebu off Negros Island, thus in proximity to *Houston*.

13. Mullin, *Another Six-Hundred*, 25–34.

14. MacDonald, *Navy Retread*, 72.

15. The journey consumed 134 hours (almost six entire days) and 1,311 miles before the convoy reached the Dutch oil port of Balikpapan on December 14, 1941.

16. E. Paul Abernethy of *Pecos* would become a commander on January 7, 1942, while at Darwin.

17. USS *Boise* (CL-47) War Diary, December 19, Fold3 by Ancestry, Historical Military Records, at www.fold3.com.

18. Mullin, *Another Six-Hundred*, 50–65.

19. Winslow, *Fleet the Gods Forgot*, 259–63.

20. Rear Adm. Edward N. Parker interview with John Toland, ca. 1960, Milner Papers.

21. Parker's account from his interview with Toland, Milner Papers; Lt. Cdr. H. Page Smith's recollections from *China Gunboatman*, July 1995, 15.

22. Parker interview with Toland, Milner Papers.

23. St. Pierre, USS *Langley* CV-1 AV-3, 382.

24. Lowell Barty interview with the author, July 15, 2012.

25. Glassford had asked Rooks to act as his chief of staff when he first went to *Houston*, and Rooks had agreed to his request.

26. Glassford, "Supplementary Narrative," 51–52, NARA II.

27. Glassford, "Confidential War Diary, November 29, 1941 to March 15, 1942," 6, NARA II.

28. The Asiatic Fleet staff sent ashore at this time included Rear Admiral Purnell and six officers from various units.

29. Letter from Lt. Robert B. Fulton to Mr. and Mrs. W. L. Fulton, December 18, 1941, Cruiser *Houston* Collection.

30. These areas of operational responsibility would be codified soon afterward in the formation of ABDA as three regional groups, with the British dominating the West, the Dutch the Central, and the Americans the East.

31. Glassford, "Supplementary Narrative," 52, NARA II.

32. *Gold Star* was caught loading coal on the southern coast of Mindanao at Malangas—a small port on Dumanquilas Bay—at the time of the Pearl Harbor attacks. Ordered to Manila, she had come within seventy-five miles of her destination when she was rerouted to Balikpapan, Borneo. She reversed course and reached the Dutch oil port via the Sulu Sea on December 14.

### 4. A Nasty, Brutish, and Short Life

1. In early variants this command was called ADBU, for Australian–Dutch–British–United States forces, but Secretary Stimson refused to permit *U* to be used as the abbreviation for U.S.A.

2. However, few of its participants, especially the leaders, cared to revisit that period later in their careers. Most appeared to see it as a less-than-admirable episode.

3. Matloff and Snell, *Strategic Planning for Coalition Warfare*, 123.

4. Letter from Brig. Gen. Elliott R. Thorpe to Samuel Milner, January 23, 1964: "In retrospect it would have been better had the Dutch been told they were strictly on their own." By this Thorpe meant he felt that repeated assurances of reinforcements to the NEI misled the public and disappointed the Dutch in particular (Milner Papers).

5. Brink was the U.S. military observer in Singapore and attended the conferences on coalition strategy held there December 18–20, 1941 (Matloff and Snell, *Strategic Planning for Coalition Warfare*, 86–87).

6. The Dutch naturally wanted to control naval forces in NEI waters with which their commanders were already familiar. The Australians were alarmed that the ABDA theater as initially mapped did not include Australia proper. The separate issue of Australian troops and ships squandered in the ABDA campaign is valid enough, but no more so than similar claims by the United States or Britain.

7. Buell, *Master of Sea Power*, 152. Also, on December 29 King suggested creating another committee to provide direct consultation with Dutch and Australian officials, but this was altered to place ABDA's CinC (Wavell) directly under the joint British-American Chiefs of Staff Committee in Washington. After Churchill and Roosevelt both decided this was acceptable, the arrangement was agreed to on December

31 in the seventh meeting of the joint staff talks. Neither the Dutch government in exile in London nor the Australians had yet accepted this revision, however (Matloff and Snell, *Strategic Planning for Coalition Warfare*, 125–26).

8. See Kok, "Knickerbocker Weekly."

9. Lt. Gen. George Brett appears to have fallen into the former category, while Col. Albert Searle—who left instructions that his name *not* be included in any histories of the "Lost Battalion," for example—seems to have belonged to the latter.

10. Hart, diary, February 16, 1942, as he departed Java for India on HMS *Durban*.

11. Hart had originally asked for Rear Admiral Van Staveren of the RNN as his chief of staff, but Helfrich blocked this request. Vice Admiral Layton then left for Ceylon, and Capt. John Collins, RAN, promoted to commodore in mid-January, eventually took charge of Royal Navy units in the ABDA area under the title of CCCF (commodore commanding China Force) on January 20 (Gill, *Royal Australian Navy*, 516–17).

12. *Shark* embarked an extra sixty-six passengers in addition to her crew. Hart's departure from the Philippines had been approved by Stark on December 17 (Tolley, *Cruise of the Lanikai*, 311).

## 5. Overtures in Blood and Oil

1. It should be noted that this date preceded the declaration of war by Japan against the Netherlands by four days.

2. This group was also known as the Western Invasion Convoy, with its counterpart, the Eastern Convoy, splitting off south of Davao for Menado, Kendari, and Ambon.

3. From Geoffrey Tebbut, "Treasure Island of Oil Threatened by Japanese," *Courier Mail of Brisbane*, January 9, 1942.

4. Dr. Colijn was in fact the son of Holland's five-term prime minister, Hendrik Colijn. The family had long, deep ties to BPM (the East Indian subsidiary of Royal Dutch Shell). Colijn's heroics deservedly became the stuff of legend, and he was awarded the Cross for Meritorious Service and promoted to major. His wife remained incarcerated for the duration, while Colijn was eventually recaptured with two of his daughters on Sumatra after the sinking of the *Poelau Bras* (March 7) and died in prison on Bangka Island on March 11, 1945. His wife and all three daughters survived the war. The oldest of the girls, Helen, published a memorable book on her experiences in 1995, titled *Song of Survival*, which became the basis for the 20th Century Fox film *Paradise Road*.

5. Fabricius, *East Indies Episode*, 36.

6. Southern approaches were mined by the 1,300-ton Dutch minelayer *Prins van Oranje*. She attempted to escape on the night of the eleventh but was caught and sunk, with heavy casualties, by the Japanese destroyer *Yamakaze* and patrol boat *P-38* (Van Oosten, *Battle of the Java Sea*, 18).

7. There were fifty-three Japanese survivors, according to BKS/*Senshi Sōsho*, vol. 26, *Naval Operations in the Dutch East Indies*.

8. The Dutch officers executed included Capt. J. W. Storm van Leeuwen, in charge of the Peningki Battery, which did not fire, and reserve Lt. J. P. A. van Adrichem, a South African who commanded the fatefully accurate Karoengan Battery.

9. Postwar Dutch investigations produced ample source materials, but these shed only imperfect light for historians. There is confusion whether *all* the POWs were slain at sea or if a number were executed on land. At least a few of the Dutch documents indicated the latter—one in particular, written by a son of one of the victims, carried considerable weight—and they account for this reading (Monument Tarakan website, www.mobe.nl/tarakan).

10. Hart, diary, January 10, 1942. The rest of Hart's diary entry for that "momentous day"—he was in Batavia to meet with Layton, Helfrich, and Wavell, among others—speaks of official events with high-ranking ABDA commanders and also the pressing requests that he was even then receiving from Manila to help keep MacArthur's forces supplied during their struggle.

11. Wendell Bedford, S1/c, *Houston*, interview with Samuel Milner, Milner Papers.

12. The translations from Helfrich's *Memoires* used here were done by a Mrs. De Vogel and made for John Toland's research for his 1961 book, *But Not in Shame* (Milner Papers).

13. See Brown, *From Suez to Singapore*, 508, for Van Mook's admission of his own scheming on behalf of Helfrich to replace Hart: "It took me a month and a half of argument in Washington to get Admiral Helfrich appointed to succeed Admiral Hart."

14. Glassford, "Confidential War Diary," 23, NARA II. "Holo" is Jolo, in the southern Philippines. It is not clear why Helfrich assumed at this early juncture that U.S. submarines would operate solely out of Darwin. Helfrich's letter after the campaign to Fürstner stated that Hart's forces should have operated out of Tarakan initially and targeted Japanese forces then massing at Davao because, in his opinion, there was "no Japanese air" at Davao then. This was utterly incorrect—there were certainly IJN air units present in and around Davao—and again shows how poorly informed, or obtuse, Helfrich was.

15. By contrast Hart found the British to be "fair and open" and "square," even if preoccupied with imperial territory. Hart also noted that Helfrich "wanted to do all the talking" during their first meetings in Java (diary, January 4, 1942).

16. It was not Brett's intention to have this battalion—which was embarked without full ammunition allotment or mechanized transportation—sent into Java at all. The decision by his predecessor, Brig. Gen. Henry B. Clagett, to ship them to Darwin on *Bloemfontein* was made before Brett could halt the plans. Brett's private diary sharply recorded his exasperation with Clagett (Milner Papers).

17. Letter from Lt. Bob Fulton to his parents, December 29, 1941, Cruiser *Houston* Collection.

18. Only the lone Dutch vessel, *Riegel*, which had both minesweeping and laying capabilities and was equipped with ASDIC, was available for patrol operations off Surabaja in the first week of January. It was due to this shortage that Hart had retained two American destroyers there.

19. Craven and Cates, *Army Air Forces in World War II*, 1:377–78.

20. Morison, *Rising Sun in the Pacific*, 281.

21. From Commander Talbot's prebattle instructions to his destroyer captains, in Mullin, *Another Six-Hundred*, 123.

22. Colijn, *Song of Survival*, 2–5.

23. Fabricius, *East Indies Episode*, 38–40.

24. To no one's surprise, the Japanese version of the Colijn affair was quite different. Japanese Monograph no. 29, "Balikpapan Invasion Operations Record" (Milner Papers) states that an unnamed former manager of the "Borneo Petroleum Manufacture Company agreed to work for the Japanese Army on the condition they would employ him in repairing the wrecked oil fields in Tarakan." He and a "captured officer [Reinderhoff]" were then to be sent to Balikpapan as emissaries to deliver a message to the commander of Dutch forces there "demanding that the oil refinery equipment be handed over to the Japanese Army without being damaged." These two men and three Japanese interpreters left Tarakan on the sixteenth, were transported "on a captured Dutch ship" (*Parsifal*), and arrived off the coast of Samboaja, where a Dutch flying boat "took them aboard" and flew them to Balikpapan. There they gave the ultimatum to the garrison commander. "The Commander refused the demands and the three Japanese interpreters were returned to their unit on 23 January. The two foreigners [Colijn and Reinderhoff] did not return."

25. See the Monument Tarakan website (www.mobe.nl/tarakan) for details of Reinderhoff's career, including the Balikpapan adventure with Anton Colijn.

26. Sources include the Monument Tarakan website (www.mobe.nl/tarakan); Klemen Luzar's NEI website articles on Tarakan and Balikpapan; Fabricius, *East Indies Episode*; Colijn, *Song of Survival*; McDougall, *Six Bells off Java*; and Japanese Monograph no. 29, "Balikpapan Invasion Operations Record," Milner Papers.

27. Japanese Monograph no. 29, "Balikpapan Invasion Operations Record," 6, Milner Papers.

28. BKS/*Senshi Sōsho*, 26:194. Translated by Kan Sugahara.

29. This force, under Major Kaneuji, comprised the Second Battalion/146th Regiment, with two companies of engineers and a radio platoon.

30. Fabricius, *East Indies Episode*, 46.

31. Fabricius, *East Indies Episode*, 46.

32. Fabricius, *East Indies Episode*, 46–53.

33. Fabricius, *East Indies Episode*, 49.

34. Fabricius, *East Indies Episode*, 48.

35. *Pike* patrol report, Historical Naval Ships Association, at www.hnsa.org.

36. Perry and Leighton, *Where Away*, 69.

37. Mullin, *Another Six-Hundred*, 115.

38. Perry and Leighton, *Where Away*, 76–81.

39. Perry and Leighton, *Where Away*, 74–77.

40. Perry and Leighton, *Where Away*, 78.

41. Michel, *Mr. Michel's War*, 42.

42. Holmes, *Underseas Victory*, 1:99.

43. Holmes, *Underseas Victory*, 1:85.

44. Mullin, *Another Six-Hundred*, 116.

45. John Harrell, Y3/c, *Houston*, interview with Samuel Milner, June 1960, Milner Papers.

46. Harrell interview with Milner.

47. Rooks's ship handling and natives from interview with John Harrell, Y3/c, *Houston*, June 1960, Milner Papers.

48. Stewart anecdote from USS *Trinity Newsletter*, Winter 2002, and USS *Houston* Deck Log, copies in author's possession.

49. Most of these mundane operational details are from the *Confidential War Diary* of Rear Admiral Glassford.

50. AOC Harry L. Keneman, USN (ret.), "Career Is Born," 45. Keneman served as an AOM3/c aboard USS *Memphis* (CL-13), one of *Marblehead*'s sisters, in 1938–40.

51. Keneman, "Career Is Born," 51.

52. Glassford, "Confidential War Diary" (NARA II) on January 19 states that he recommended withdrawal of Base Force ships from Darwin to southwest Australia (presumably Fremantle) because he believed the enemy was on the verge of assaulting Timor "in order to cut [Allied] lines of communication between Torres Strait and the island of Java." But this movement—a month prior to Nagumo's carrier attack on Darwin and Japanese operations to seize Timor—was not at all to Hart's liking, and he had ships moved *forward* to Tjilatjap at the beginning of February. Some were then sent out of the theater to India and the Persian Gulf, however.

53. Mullin, *Another Six-Hundred*, 116. It was also on January 20 that HMS *Jupiter*, patrolling Sunda Strait, detected and engaged a Japanese submarine—the *I-60*—which it destroyed.

54. Adm. Thomas C. Hart, "Events and Circumstances concerning the 'Striking Force,' Feb. 6–17," 2, NARA II.

55. Unlike the four destroyers, neither of these warships' fuel tanks was full. *Marblehead* was 36 percent filled and *Bulmer* 67 percent.

56. Bell, *Condition Red*, 70. Bell was at that time a lieutenant serving on *Boise*.

57. Perry and Leighton, *Where Away*, 94. The rhetorical swagger expressed by Perry and Leighton in 1944 should be contrasted with the account written by one of *Pope*'s officers then who recalled, "Everyone on board the Pope was glum. . . . We felt let down from being ready to go into action and having the attack called off" (Michel, *Mr. Michel's War*, 42).

58. Mullin, *Another Six-Hundred*, 118.

59. W. C. Blinn, "The Story of the USS *Pope* (DD-225)," subseries 10, box 5, folder 28, Milner Papers, is a personal reminiscence written by the skipper of that ship after the war (hereafter cited as "Story of *Pope*"). Also USS *Pope* (DD-225) Action Report, "Night Destroyer Attack off Balikpapan, January 24, Netherlands East Indies Area," January 25, 1942, NARA II.

60. Leighton and Perry, *Where Away*, 94.

61. Rear Adm. E. N. Parker interview with John Toland, ca. 1960, Milner Papers.

62. Frost, *On a Destroyer's Bridge*, 113.

63. USS *Pope* (DD-225) Action Report, January 25, 1942, 1.

64. USS *Parrott* (DD-218), "Report of Attack on Japanese Force off Balik Papan on January 24, 1942," Enclosure C, Fold3 by Ancestry, Historical Military Records, at www.fold3.com.

65. Pratt, "One Destroyer," 187.

66. Mullin, *Another Six-Hundred*, 120–21.

67. Blinn, "Story of *Pope*," 6.

68. Pratt, "One Destroyer," 187. These little ships had long been known for excessive rolling, particularly when light.

69. Technical papers today say between 2,500 and 2,800 psi on World War II–era torpedoes; the figure of "up to 3,000 psi" comes from Dan Mullin on *Ford*.

70. Mullin, *Another Six-Hundred*, 120–21. The Mark 8 torpedo was slow, prone to erratic runs at shallow depth settings due to its sensitive gyro—which required launching on an even keel—and had a small warhead.

71. Bill Slagle, letter, *China Gunboatman*, December 1994, 8–9.

72. Blinn, "Story of *Pope*," 6.

73. Pratt, "One Destroyer," 187.

74. Messimer, *In the Hands of Fate*, 217.

75. USS *Pope* (DD-225) Action Report, January 25, 1942, 1.

76. Michel, *Mr. Michel's War*, 44.

77. Pratt, "One Destroyer," 187.

78. BKS/*Senshi Sōsho*, 26:195.

79. Mullin, *Another Six-Hundred*, 120.

80. "Special A.A.P. Correspondent," Batavia, *Morning Herald* (Sydney), February 4, 1942.

81. Kato Shizuo, *Anokoro no Omoide* (Reminiscences of those days), a memoir by the captain of *Tsuruga Maru*, privately translated, ca. 2007. Additionally, on January 24, eight B-17s from Malang took off at 0615 hours to bomb the transports at Balikpapan. Six B-17Es of the Seventh Bomber Group BG and two from the Nineteenth Bomber Group BG were involved.

82. Details of *Tsuruga Maru*'s loss in Kato, *Anokoro no Omoide*.

83. Kato, *Anokoro no Omoide*, 2.

84. Kato, *Anokoro no Omoide*, 2.

85. Kato, *Anokoro no Omoide*, 2.

86. The track-charts in vol. 26 of BKS/*Senshi Sōsho* indicate that the two groups of IJN destroyers to the east may have been six to nine miles distant when Talbot's four-pipers penetrated the anchorage.

87. Most details of *Parrott*'s part in the battle are taken from Enclosure C of her Action Report, written by the destroyer's captain and executive officer. Those of *Paul Jones* are from her Action Report, "Report of Action off Balikpapan, Borneo, Jan. 24, 1942," Fold3 by Ancestry, Historical Military Records, at www.fold3.com.

88. Mullin, *Another Six-Hundred*, 125.

89. Pratt, "One Destroyer," 188.

90. *Parrott*, Enclosure C.

91. Aboard *Pope*, executive officer Lt. Richard Antrim noted the same ship exploding and thought the flames went up "about 500 feet" (USS *Pope* [DD-225] Action Report, "Night Destroyer Attack off Balikpapan, January 24, 1942," Enclosure A, 5, NARA II).

92. Michel, *Mr. Michel's War*, 45.

93. Kato, *Anokoro no Omoide*.

94. *K-XVIII* suffered for her efforts, being heavily attacked by Japanese escorts. As she made her way

back gingerly to Surabaja on the morning of January 25, she was also attacked by an enemy flying boat but suffered no further damage.

95. Michel, *Mr. Michel's War*, 45.

96. Mullin, *Another Six-Hundred*, 126.

97. Mullin, *Another Six-Hundred*, 137.

98. Mullin, *Another Six-Hundred*, 137–38.

99. *Parrott*, Enclosure C, in the destroyer's Action Report of January 26, 1942; BKS/*Senshi Sōsho*, vol. 26; Vincent P. O'Hara, "Battle of Balikpapan," in *U.S. Navy against the Axis*, 21–26.

100. Mullin, *Another Six-Hundred*, 134–48. Commander Talbot was in poor physical condition, suffering from a variety of medical problems and would suffer a near heart attack on the return voyage. At Surabaja he was hospitalized after Hart visited him and realized the seriousness of his condition. Subsequently, Talbot was flown out of Java to Australia before returning to the States for convalescence.

101. Michel, *Mr. Michel's War*, 46.

102. Mullin, *Another Six-Hundred*, 138–39.

103. Misidentified as the "hospital ship" *Asahi Maru* in some records, but it was definitely *Asahisan Maru*, an entirely different ship.

104. According to TROMS at www.combinedfleet.com, *Kuretake Maru* was also hit by torpedoes and gunfire from *John D. Ford*, although later in the action it seems.

105. Newcomb, *U.S. Destroyers of the World Wars*, 127.

106. USS *Paul Jones* (DD-230) Action Report, "Report of Action off Balikpapan, Borneo, Jan. 24, 1942," Fold3 by Ancestry, Historical Military Records, at www.fold3.com.

107. Mullin, *Another Six-Hundred*, 139.

108. BKS/*Senshi Sōsho*, 26:198–201. Translated by Kan Sugahara.

109. Mullin, *Another Six-Hundred*, 146.

110. Report of Executive Officer, Lt. Richard N. Antrim, U.S. Navy, USS *Pope* (DD-225) Action Report, "Night Destroyer Attack off Balikpapan, January 24, Netherlands East Indies Area," January 25, 1942, Enclosure A, 5, NARA II.

111. Mullin, *Another Six-Hundred*, 146.

112. Mullin, *Another Six-Hundred*, 144–47.

113. Mullin, *Another Six-Hundred*, 152.

114. Aloysius Mondschein interview with John Toland, undated, Milner Papers.

115. Capt. John S. Slaughter, letter, *China Gunboatman*, December 2000, 15.

116. Hart, diary, January 25, 1942.

117. Mullin, *Another Six-Hundred*, 153.

118. Hart, diary, January 26, 1942.

119. Aloysius Mondschein interview with John Toland, Milner Papers.

120. Slagle, letter, *China Gunboatman*. This letter was in memory of Vice Admiral Parker's passing. "One of the best captains the Navy had ever produced," Slagle wrote. Parker died, aged eighty-five, in October 1989, and Slagle attended the admiral's funeral.

121. Slagle, letter, *China Gunboatman*. Also the skipper of *Amatsukaze* (Hara Tameichi) in an interview with John Toland admitted that "Commander Tarubot [Talbot] made a smart attack" (Milner Papers).

122. As described elsewhere, the Mark 8 torpedoes, which the flushdeckers carried, were small, slow, and not known for their accuracy. A 1926 BuOrd document gave their specs as 13,500 yards at 27 knots. Their warhead had an explosive charge inferior in size to torpedoes used in other navies during World War II.

123. *Life*, February 9, 1942, 34.

124. Michel, *Mr. Michel's War*, 50–51.

125. Mullin, *Another Six-Hundred*, 155.

### 6. First Sortie of the Striking Force

1. Also Washington had decided to reorganize the Asiatic Fleet, causing Hart more administrative headaches at the least useful time. Therefore, at the end of January Rear Admiral Glassford was put in charge of "U.S. Naval Forces in the Southwest Pacific." His command was known as COMSOWESPAC, and the U.S. Asiatic Fleet ceased to exist. Led by Lt. Cdr. Egusa Takeshige, planes of Vice Admiral Nagumo's Second Carrier Division, *Hiryū* and *Sōryū*, attacked Ambon on January 23–24. This alerted the Allies that the small, miserably unprepared Australian/Dutch force there was living on borrowed time. It fell within another week after minimal fighting.

2. Mendenhall, *Submarine Diary, the Silent Stalking of Japan*, 34.

3. The message with the words "You can be certain you are not forgotten men" was actually from Gen. Henry "Hap" Arnold to Lt. Gen. George Brett, dated February 13, and was to be distributed to every army air force officer on Java, ostensibly to boost morale (Bartsch, *Every Day a Nightmare*, 104).

4. Adm. Thomas C. Hart, "Narrative of Events, Asiatic Fleet, Leading Up to War and from 8 December 1941 to 15 February 1942," 68, Fold3 by Ancestry, Historical Military Records, at www.fold3.com.

5. In the meantime Kendari to the east and its valuable airfield had been seized on January 24 by Japanese amphibious forces. Its Staring Bay anchorage would then become *the* critical advance location for forthcoming Japanese naval operations over the next two months. USS *Childs* had a narrow escape from the Japanese invaders at that time. See Messimer, *In the Hands of Fate*, 211–16.

6. Also see Hornfischer, *Ship of Ghosts*, 42, for Helfrich's sometimes less-than-candid dealings with Hart.

7. Kale, diary, 20.

8. Hart, diary, January 31, 1942. Throughout January Wavell's chief of staff, Lt. Gen. Henry R. Pownall, whose attitude toward the Americans was condescending at best, recorded a number of scathing opinions about Hart in his own diary.

9. Quote from Hart, diary, February 1, 1942.

10. Hart, diary, January 28, 1942.

11. Hart, diary, January 28, 1942.

12. Hart, diary, January 28, 1942.

13. This observation in his diary by Hart is notable because it came just as Bill Glassford celebrated his promotion to COMSOWESPAC—something Glassford later claimed he'd had to fight for against some resistance from Hart.

14. Hart had also just been informed of the Pacific Fleet's "punishing raid on the Marshall Islands" (diary, February 1, 1942).

15. They were spotted by IJN bombers and heavily attacked but escaped without serious damage.

16. As in Europe and China, the prewar mixture of fiscal frugality and strategic timidity by the Allies was as lethal a combination as anything the Japanese could have concocted by themselves.

17. There are several detailed studies of the NEI air campaign. The following are recommended: Shores, Cull, and Izawa, *Bloody Shambles*, vol. 2; Bartsch, *Every Day a Nightmare*; Boer, *Loss of Java*.

18. W. Jackson Galbraith interview with Samuel Milner, June 1959, Milner Papers. The remark about Oldendorf as "a big, good-natured Swede" came from personal conversations in 1998 between the author and Al Kopp, PHM2/c, *Houston*.

19. Galbraith interview with Milner.

20. Details on *Houston*'s USMC personnel and G/Sgt. Standish from Milner's interview with PFC Marvin E. Robinson, July 20, 1959. Of Russian descent, "Gunny" Standish was a barrel-chested individual of the classic leatherneck type: a six-foot, 240-pound, cigar-chomping soldier who, when off-duty, was said to be an inveterate card shark, as fond of poker as his food and whiskey. Standish—who had changed his given Russian name some years prior—was not a young man when the war started, being over forty then. Jim Slocum was an "outlaw, bad man breed" from Oklahoma with a history of disciplinary troubles. Robinson believed Slocum, like Standish, would also have fired his weapon to the bitter end.

21. Schultz, *Last Battle Station*, 15; and Milner's interviews with Galbraith, Leon Rogers (August 1960), and Elmo Bush, Milner Papers.

22. Ted Luxemburg interviews with the author, summer 2013.

23. Beuford Grant Gabriel, "Narrative of Attack on the U.S.S. Marblehead by Japanese Aircraft on February 4, 1942," Fold3 by Ancestry, Historical Military Records, at www.fold3.com.

24. Remarks by Dan Rafalovich and Gene Wilkinson (filmed 1993–94) are taken from the Dutch film *De slag in de Javazee*.

25. Clearly Doorman issued the operational plans. And no matter the precise route chosen—an excuse Helfrich often used after the fact—the CSF was going to be vulnerable to air interdiction.

26. Perry and Leighton, *Where Away*, 109. At the same time that morning—as reported later by John Harrell, Y3/c—*Houston's* division officers called a meeting to inform their men of the imminent action against the enemy. It was never concluded because twenty minutes later the first enemy planes began appearing in the distance (Harrell interviews, June 1960, Milner Papers).

27. Galbraith interview with Milner, Milner Papers.

28. In interviews after the war, Bush claimed to have designed a mount for handling twin .30 cal. machine guns in the SOCs that had been adopted by other scout planes of the Asiatic Fleet, including those of the fleet Utility unit.

29. Pneumercators were apparatus for measuring the depth and volume of the contents of various tanks and reservoirs in the ship. See Schultz, *Last Battle Station*, 92.

30. In interviews with Milner (May 1960) *Houston's* turret 1 officer, Hamlin, recalled that the first stick of Japanese bombs on February 4 "unnerved the men badly" and that the ship's vulnerability, as soon revealed by the disaster in turret 3, came as a profound shock (Milner Papers).

31. Winslow, *Ghost That Died at Sunda Strait*, 89.

32. Cdr. A. Maher, CONFIDENTIAL "Action Report of the USS *Houston* (CA-30) against Enemy Aircraft," November 15, 1945, NARA II.

33. Lee Rogers interview with Samuel Milner, August 1960, Milner Papers; and numerous conversations between Rogers, Stoddard, and the author, from 1992 through 2005.

34. Cdr. A. L. Maher, "Action Report—USS *Houston* (CA-30) 4 February 1942 against Enemy Aircraft," November 15, 1945, 2, NARA II.

35. Kale, diary, 21.

36. Maher, "Action Report—USS *Houston* (CA-30) 4 February 1942 against Enemy Aircraft," NARA II.

37. Dale Johnson, included in Hay, "Little Known Facts," 25.

38. Details of the bombing here are from Johnson, in Hay, "Little Known Facts"; and from Perry and Leighton, *Where Away*.

39. Karig and Kelley, *Battle Report*, 188.

40. Karig and Kelley, *Battle Report*, 190.

41. Gabriel, "Narrative of Attack," 2, Fold3 by Ancestry, Historical Military Records, at www.fold3.com.

42. Memories of Captain Ramsey taken from Charley Pryor interview with Samuel Milner, ca. 1960, Milner Papers.

43. Firing against the enemy aircraft had been on both engaged and disengaged sides and as close to the superstructure as the 5-inch batteries were allowed by their newly installed safety systems. These were the cutout cams designed to prevent the guns firing into the ship itself. They were tested to their limits in this engagement and operated perfectly.

44. Snyder conversations with the author, 1992–94.

45. Maher, "Action Report—USS *Houston* (CA-30) 4 February 1942 against Enemy Aircraft," NARA II.

46. Galbraith interview with Milner, Milner Papers.

47. Floyd V. Arnold interview with Samuel Milner, May 1960, Milner Papers.

48. Samuel Milner interviews with James McCone, August 1960, and with T. J. McFarland, September 1959, Milner Papers.

49. Marvin Robinson interview with Samuel Milner, July 20, 1959, Milner Papers.

50. This is according to a Leonard W. "Dutch" Kooper interview with Samuel Milner, Milner Papers.

51. The lengthy postbattle CINCPAC report on Midway in June reiterated the navy's belief in this defensive method.

52. Lieutenant (j.g.) Hamlin said he sought to reassure the gun crews in his turret by telling them to relax because "you never hear the one that gets you," but the men (understandably) remained tense and uncomfortable (interview with Samuel Milner, May 1960, Milner Papers).

53. Schultz, *Last Battle Station*, 100. Bill Kohl interviews with the author, September–October 2009. It appears that only ten men from Third Division in the turret and powder train survived the bomb hit.

54. Louis E. Biechlin interview with Samuel Milner, August 1960, Milner Papers.

55. Dr. Clement Burroughs interview with Samuel Milner, undated, Milner Papers.

56. Elmo Bush interview with Samuel Milner, August 1960, Milner Papers.

57. Winslow, *Ghost That Died at Sunda Strait*, 92.

58. Details on John Ranger and Russell Shelton taken from meetings and conversations between the author and Ranger himself (1992–2000), and Ranger's son, Jerry, and daughter, Jolene, in 2010–13.

59. Bush interview with Milner, Milner Papers.

60. For his fearless work in putting out the fires, Ranger would eventually be awarded the Silver Star. In this same action Lt. (j.g.) Walter Winslow won the Silver Star, and Cdr. Arthur Maher was awarded the Navy Cross. John Ranger, who engaged in ten SOC flights during the campaign, later also won the Air Medal: "For distinguishing himself by meritorious action while participating in aerial flight as a radio-gunner."

61. Letter from Jack Smith to Val Poss, undated. Copy in USS *Houston* (CA-30) Survivors Association Archives, privately stored.

62. Biechlin interview with Milner, Milner Papers.

63. Neitsch told Samuel Milner in his interview on August 2, 1960, that Joe Bienert was a "nice, clean-cut individual" and that the two men often visited over cups of coffee in the compartment housing the ice-machine compressor, where Neitsch usually worked.

64. James "Red" Reynolds interview with Samuel Milner, August 1960, Milner Papers.

65. Theodore "Itch" Schram interview with Samuel Milner, July 1960, Milner Papers.

66. From "Autobiography of Merritt Volney Eddy," 58, courtesy of Eddy's daughter, Sandra Swanson.

67. Floyd Arnold interview with Samuel Milner, May 1960, Milner Papers.

68. Bush interview with Milner, Milner Papers.

69. Luidenga and Guns, "Tjilatjap 1942," page numbers unavailable.

70. Hampton Cray interview with Samuel Milner, July 1960, Milner Papers.

71. Biechlin interview with Milner, 1960, and Eddy, "Autobiography," 60.

72. Hart, diary, February 5, 1942. Of course there is much more to the story of Hart's replacement than space allows here, but FDR also displayed a politician's flair for telling a dishonest truth and maintaining plausible deniability. Thus his message to Churchill on February 7: "Admiral Hart has asked to be relieved because of ill health" (Kimball, *Churchill and Roosevelt*, 1:348).

73. Mullin, *Another Six-Hundred*, 167.

74. Details on the wartime experiences of N. E. "Ted" Luxemburg via letter, emails, and phone interviews with the author, spring 2013, arranged by Luxemburg's son, Nick.

75. The man who became known as "Doc" Wassell was a navy reserve lieutenant recently arrived on Java. At Surabaja he had been put to work going through medical supplies when he chanced upon a crate marked IODINE. When opened, it was found to contain torpedo warheads. While attempting to inform his commanding officer, he was told he was desperately needed to act as the liaison officer for several dozen wounded sailors from the two American cruisers then approaching Tjilatjap. The next thing Wassell knew, he was being flown to that port on the other end of the island (Hilton, *Story of Dr. Wassell*, 7).

76. Letter from Maurice Hurd to Samuel Milner, March 25, 1960, Milner Papers.

77. Harold Hamlin Jr. interview with Samuel Milner, May 1960, Milner Papers.

78. Sessions and Perry, *Where Away*, 184.

79. Sessions and Perry, *Where Away*, 186.

80. "Steps Taken to Make USS *Marblehead* Seaworthy following Action with Japanese Planes in Java Sea. Feb. 4, 1942," May 4, 1942, 4, Fold3 by Ancestry, Historical Military Records, at www.fold3.com.

81. From Capt. A. G. Robinson, "Report of Action with Japanese Planes, February 4, 1942," May 4, 1942, Fold3 by Ancestry, Historical Military Records, at www.fold3.com.

## 7. Abortive Efforts East and West

1. Hart, diary, February 8, 1942

2. Hart, diary, February 8–9, 1942.

3. Page 3 of Cdr. A. L. Maher, "Action Report—USS *Houston* (CA-30) 4 February 1942 against Enemy Aircraft," November 15, 1945 (NARA II), on *Houston*'s fight against enemy aircraft on February 4, contains a good description of the forward AA director's malfunction and the steps taken to correct it.

4. The details of this fateful series of events are taken from W. Jackson Galbraith interview with Samuel Milner at the Naval Gun Factory, June 1959, Milner Papers.

5. Cdr. H. H. Keith, USN, "Narrative: Philippine Invasion" (recorded August 6, 1943), 5, Fold3 by Ancestry, Historical Military Records, at www.fold3.com.

6. In later years Hamlin, one of the cruiser's more outspoken surviving officers, would argue that the ship's gunhouses had enough structural steel to hold heavier armor, but as a result of politics—and the navy's threadbare budget during the prewar era—these vital improvements were never made. No evidence has been found to support this claim. In reality no U.S. cruiser afloat in 1941 had turret armor heavy enough to resist a 250 kg bomb.

7. Letter from Lt. Robert Fulton to his parents, February 10, 1942, Cruiser *Houston* Collection.

8. This information derived from Coxswain Q. Madson's diary (courtesy of Matt Johnson); also Lee Rogers interview with Samuel Milner, August 1960; and Donald Brain interview with Ron Marcello of North Texas State University, 1981, Milner Papers.

9. Hart's remarks are taken from his report of February 6 and 17, 1942, titled "Events and Circumstances concerning the 'Striking Force,'" 6–7, NARA II.

10. Some USN personnel thought that *Whipple* had then been lost for the duration, but her damages were repaired sufficiently in the Tjilatjap dry dock to get her back to sea.

11. Kale, diary, February 14, 1942, 24–25.

12. To Air Ministry Whitehall from Peirse, February 10, 1942, signed by Group Capt. L. Darval, Milner Papers.

13. Tankers sent to Palembang, located some fifty miles from the coast up the Moesi River, could not load fully due to the bar and shallow water at the mouth of the river. They would then be sent to another terminal (such as Miri in northwest Borneo) for the balance of their cargo before proceeding to their ultimate destination.

14. Takushirō Hattori, *The Complete History of Greater East Asia War*, 4 vols. (Masu Shobō, 1953), 2:83–86, microfilm, series 7, box 17, Milner Papers.

15. Shores, Cull, and Izawa, *Bloody Shambles*, vol. 2, chap. 2, "The Fall of Sumatra," 89–126.

16. Kelly, *Nine Lives of a Fighter Pilot*, 72.

17. Shores, Cull, and Izawa, *Bloody Shambles*, 89–126; and Japanese Monograph no. 69, "Air Operations in the Invasion of the NEI," http://ibiblio.org/hyperwar/Japan/Monos/.

18. Findlay, *Directory for Navigation*, 228.

19. Van der Moer, "He Who Sees First Lives Longest."

20. *Banckert* rescued the entire crew of *Van Ghent*, and these men then all returned to Java.

21. June 1960 memorandum written by H. E. Eccles for John Toland, Milner Papers.

22. Kale, diary, February 16, 1942.

23. USS *Parrott* (DD-218) Deck Log for February 15, 1942, NARA II.

24. Newcomb, *U.S. Destroyers of the World Wars*, 139.

25. Shores, Cull, and Izawa, *Bloody Shambles*, 2:124.

26. Kale, diary, February 16, 1942, 27. Within another day or so, Bill Kale and others would learn of the British defeat at Singapore. *Stewart*'s skipper, Lt. Cdr. H. P. Smith, told his men that the Japanese cruisers they had hoped to engage had in fact returned to Singapore, "expecting the British to pull another Dunkirk" (Kale, diary, February 16, 1942, 2).

27. Harris's recollections of Hart from Mullin, *Another Six-Hundred*, 167.

28. Hart, diary, February 16, 1942.

29. Leutze, *Different Kind of Victory*, 270.

30. *Houston*'s ten wounded—too badly injured to remain with the ship—were sent by Dutch military hospital train to Jogjakarta, about one hundred miles to the east. They went into the Petronella (today Bethesda) Hospital and eventually came under the care of Lt. Cdr. Corydon Wassell. Wassell was later to be instrumental in safely evacuating a number of wounded Asiatic Fleet sailors from Java to Australia on a small Dutch vessel, *Janssens*. For his devotion to his men and his sense of duty, Wassell was awarded the Navy Cross.

31. George Hedrick, "War Cruise of the USS *Houston*," 3, courtesy of Matt Johnson.

32. Exact figures on the number of projectiles may never be known, given the loss of *Houston* and her damage report sent on *Pecos*. However, a (speculative) solution might be this: *Houston*'s allotment at war's outbreak was apparently 2,400 5-inch shells (300 x 8). In the first major bombing action of February 4, she fired approximately 386 projectiles at the attacking planes. On February 15–16 *Houston* expended another 933 rounds of AA ammo. On February 26 Rooks reported to COMSOWESPAC that the ship still had 1,571 rounds—all of them from the defective batch. On the basis of these known values the following numbers may be derived: 2,400 - 386 = 2,014; 2,014 - 933 = 1,081; 1,571 - 1,081 = 490. This seems to indicate that Quinn Madson's diary entry and Walter Winslow's recollection of *Houston* being "able to load five hundred of them before getting underway for Darwin" were both fairly accurate. See Winslow, *Ghost That Died At Sunda Strait*, 100.

33. Hedrick, "War Cruise of the USS *Houston*," 3.

34. Details of the Darwin "battle of the bands" taken from Lt. Cdr. Harold P. Smith, formerly EM1/c on *Houston*, interview with Samuel Milner, October 1, 1960, Milner Papers.

35. Gill, *Royal Australian Navy*, 581. Gill notes that Lieutenant General Sturdee, the Australian chief of general staff, opposed the sending of the Pioneer Battalion to Timor, believing it could not help save the island from a determined assault. In this negative assessment he was of course correct.

36. Winslow, *Ghost That Died at Sunda Strait*, 101.

37. Capt. Wm. J. Galbraith narrative, "The Air Attack off Darwin," June 1959, Milner Papers.

38. Piper, *Hidden Chapters*, 68–75.

39. Hedrick, "War Cruise of the USS *Houston*," 3; and Winslow, *Ghost That Died at Sunda Strait*, 101.

40. As recounted in Piper, *Hidden Chapters*, five crewmen in the MAVIS survived the shoot-down and clambered into a life raft. They drifted for several days to the east and ended up on the southern shore of Melville Island, where, more dead than alive, they were eventually captured. However, Buel's own family knew nothing specific until fifty years after the encounter, when the memoirs of Takehara Marekuni appeared in a Japanese magazine (*Eimuzu*) and were later translated into English.

41. Letter from Lt. Bob Fulton to his parents, February 17, 1942, Cruiser *Houston* Collection.

## 8. Surprisals and Terrifications

1. By this time there were some vague rumors among ABDA personnel that Timor was being built up as yet another "fortress" along the lines of Corregidor, presumably. This was untrue but shows the type of thinking then prevalent.

2. The memoirs of several Western journalists—including William MacDougall, George Weller, Bill Dunn, and especially Harold Guard—who were caught up in the Far East war record the lunatic mind-

set that prevailed at Singapore during these final weeks. Guard at one point was detained and questioned by what he called "a military tribunal" of British officers in charge of censorship who accused him of revealing sensitive information about the situation at Singapore—which was certainly already far gone by then—when he wrote an article for United Press describing a typical day in the besieged city. In this article he described scrounging and cooking a "right leg of pork." To these officers Guard had committed the grave transgression of seeking to evade military censorship by "conveying subtle nuances" about the "leg of pork"–shaped island of Singapore. See Guard, *Pacific War Censored*, 81–83.

3. For the sake of comparison it will be useful to bear in mind that the 1,200-ton Clemson-class flush-decked destroyers of the Asiatic Fleet had been constructed around 1919–20. Although once capable of 35 knots—when new—by 1941 they had to strain to make 28 or 30 knots. They were armed with four 4-inch/50 cal. guns and twelve 21-inch torpedoes of World War I–vintage also. They had a crew of roughly 150 men in the latter stages of the Java campaign, but most went into the war considerably under strength.

4. "Report of Third War Patrol," USS S-37, 10, www.hnsa.org.

5. Adverse comments on such omissions from combat by RNN ships are scrupulously avoided by Helfrich in his *Memoires*, but he freely censures American vessels for any failure—real or imagined—to engage the enemy during the NEI campaign.

6. Rear Admiral Glassford, who was in Batavia and Bandoeng at the time, had decided to move his administrative offices from Surabaja to Tjilatjap. This was done February 17–18. The Badoeng Strait mission was rightly termed "helter skelter improvisations" by Lt. Cdr. H. E. Eccles of *John D. Edwards* afterward. Eccles also presciently noted: "It is fantastic to assume that the enemy can, in this war, ever again be surprised as he was at Balikpapan" (USS *John D. Edwards* [DD-216], "Report of Engagement of Badoeng Straits," February 20, 1942, 2, Fold3 by Ancestry, Historical Military Records, at www.fold3.com).

7. Helfrich, *Memoires*, 2:361.

8. Helfrich, *Memoires*, 2:362.

9. Cdr. Thomas Binford interview with John Toland, ca. 1960, Milner Papers.

10. The eighteenth-century Scottish novelist and naval surgeon Tobias Smollett.

11. Mullin, *Another Six-Hundred*, 171.

12. From Tjilatjap to Denpasar by air is about 930 kilometers.

13. Watanabe, *Bali Island Battle*, a self-published memoir, provided to the author by Klemen Lužar and translated by Akio Oka, ca. 2006.

14. There was a ninety-minute difference between the time used by the Asiatic Fleet vessels and those of the Imperial Japanese Navy. Thus, 0200 JST time equals 0030 hours in USN (Z-7.5) records.

15. HMS *Truant* (N68) was one of the Royal Navy's modern boats, launched in May 1939. Although her patrol off Bali in early 1942 was not a success, she had an admirable wartime career. On February 24 she did attack Rear Admiral Kubo in *Nagara*, hitting the light cruiser with two torpedoes from a spread of six, but both proved to be duds. It seems that not only U.S. torpedoes had problems early in the Pacific War.

16. *Seawolf* and S-37 patrol reports for February 18–20, 1942, at hnsa.org.

17. *Seawolf* and S-37 patrol reports.

18. Watanabe, *Bali Island Battle*.

19. Watanabe, *Bali Island Battle*.

20. Japanese Monograph no. 101, "Netherlands East Indies Naval Invasion Operations," 4, NARA II, allowing for time conversion to USN/Z-7.5 hours. The first bombing attacks were carried out by B-17s of the Nineteenth Bombardment Group (H) flying out of Malang in eastern Java; there were several other sorties that day by midafternoon. AAF data kindly supplied by Bob Alford.

21. Womack, "Naval Duel off Bali," 53.

22. Alford, *Playing for Time*, 128–29. Lt. (j.g.) Lodwick Alford (USNA 1938) was first lieutenant on USS *Stewart* at this time.

23. Blinn, "Story of *Pope*," 6. These same concerns were voiced by Alford on *Stewart*.

24. Some of the American commanders apparently thought that *Tromp* would be informed by radio

during the engagement, which appears to be borne out in remarks made by the Dutch officers after the engagement, but *how* this was to be done is unclear.

25. Michel, *Mr. Michel's War*, 61.

26. Blinn, "Story of *Pope*."

27. Alford, *Playing for Time*, 133.

28. Michel, *Mr. Michel's War*, 61.

29. "Nest of submarines" is taken from a Japanese propaganda broadcast noting the battle a few days later.

30. Yoshida, "*Ōshio*'s Total Victory off Bali Island." Translated by Kan Sugahara.

31. Pratt, "One Destroyer," 187.

32. BKS/*Senshi Sōsho*, 26:328–31.

33. A number of Western accounts say this hit took place in a later phase of the engagement, but official Japanese sources state that it occurred early, and from one of the first—i.e., Dutch—ships firing on *Asashio*.

34. Japanese sources for this phase of the engagements that made up the Battle of Badoeng Strait— and which are called "Sea Battle off Bali Island" in their literature—are from *Naval Operations in the Dutch East Indies*, vol. 26 of BKS/*Senshi Sōsho*, and were translated by Kan Sugahara.

35. BKS/*Senshi Sōsho*, 26:328–331.

36. There has long been speculation about *Piet Hein*'s smokescreen that night, and various sources allege (not very convincingly) that she *accidentally* started her chemical smoke generator (*nevelapparaat*) and betrayed her position to the enemy.

37. *Michishio*, like many IJN units, had begun extremely arduous training in January 1941, which lasted through November of that year. These exercises were conducted at dawn, early morning, and night, and included live firing drills often held in harsh weather conditions at sea off Tosa. Several Japanese sailors lost their lives during these tough training exercises (Watanabe, *Bali Island Battle*).

38. Mullin, *Another Six-Hundred*, 173.

39. Mullin, "Badoeng Strait," 27. At the time of the engagement in Badoeng Strait, Mullin served as a GM1/c on USS *John D. Ford*.

40. Binford interview with Toland, Milner Papers.

41. According to BKS/*Senshi Sōsho*, vol. 26, this order was at 0145 hours.

42. Lt. Cdr. Welford Blinn, Action Report USS *Pope* (DD-225), "Night Raid on Enemy Forces off Bali Island, Combined U.S. and Dutch Forces, February 19–20, 1942," February 20, 1942, NARA II (hereafter cited as Blinn Report).

43. Blinn Report.

44. Pratt, "One Destroyer," 190.

45. Michel, *Mr. Michel's War*, 62.

46. Yoshida, "*Ōshio*'s Total Victory off Bali Island."

47. Blinn Report, 2. Also, just before the battle started, *Pope* suffered a casualty in one of her torpedo tubes when a fish "ran hot" and had to be fired astern as a precaution. She therefore began the fight with eleven torpedoes.

48. Mullin, "Badoeng Strait," 27.

49. Mullin, *Another Six-Hundred*, 173–74.

50. Rear Adm. Edward N. Parker, "The Fortunes of War," undated memoir, 2, Milner Papers.

51. Mullin, *Another Six-Hundred*, 174.

52. Mullin, *Another Six-Hundred*, 175

53. Blinn Report, 2.

54. Mullin, *Another Six Hundred*, 175. Several other flushdeckers also experienced problems with their torpedo launch systems that night, and these included difficulties with the electrical firing mechanisms.

55. Blinn Report, 2.

56. Michel, *Mr. Michel's War*, 62.

57. BKS/*Senshi Sōsho*, 26:328.

58. See Mullin, *Another Six-Hundred*, 175, for Parker's state of mind as the American ships left the strait.

59. Mullin, *Another Six-Hundred*, 176.

60. Blinn Report.

61. These were the men who came across *Ford*'s floating boat and *Pope*'s jettisoned gasoline. Parker used the term "fortuitous" to describe this event when he wrote John Toland.

62. Alford, *Playing for Time*, 133.

63. Binford interview with Toland, Milner Papers.

64. Mullin, *Another Six-Hundred*, 177. *Ford*'s radio had been damaged by the shock of her gunfire. Her TAD adapter was inoperative, and she could not transmit to COMSOWESPAC or ComDesDiv 58 at all. Apparently her TBS was working, though.

65. This was the firing heard by men on *Stewart* and others below Tafel Hoek as they made their approach.

66. Alford, *Playing for Time*, 44. Binford's own account to Toland (1960 interview, in Milner Papers) describes his clothing.

67. Then, as now, such multiple duties would have been standard on small ships such as destroyers.

68. These details taken from interviews and emails between the author and Marion "Elly" Ellsworth, RM1/c, December 2012 to March 2013.

69. Alford, *Playing for Time*, 134.

70. It is again important to note that *Pillsbury* had only two sets of triple tubes, rather than her original four, as a consequence of damage she received on December 10, 1941, during the Japanese bombing of Cavite.

71. Alford, *Playing for Time*, 135.

72. As shown in the *Nachi* documents, IJN practice regarding the use of searchlights was specific, conservative, and probably became more conservative as the war progressed. Searchlights were to be used only when visibility was limited; "strict precautions" were to be used to avoid illuminating friendly ships or giving away the position of their own force if possible; searchlight beams—"cones of light"— were always to be kept tightly focused. If the enemy was successfully illuminating the IJN ships—as at Badoeng Strait—then counterillumination for firing was perfectly acceptable. Copies of these documents generously provided to the author by W. David Dickson.

73. Email from Elly Ellsworth to the author, 2013.

74. There appear to have been no specific arrangements made for communications between Dutch and American ships that night, so this seems a rather odd remark.

75. Kale, diary, 30.

76. Binford interview with Toland, Milner Papers.

77. Alford, *Playing for Time*, 134–37.

78. Alford, *Playing for Time*, 137.

79. Kale, diary, 30.

80. Binford interview with Toland, Milner Papers.

81. USS *Pillsbury* (DD-227) Action Report, "Report of Enemy Action during the Night of 19–20 February 1942," Fold3 by Ancestry, Historical Military Records, at www.fold3.com.

82. Lenton, *Royal Netherlands Navy*, 12.

83. Kale, diary, 30.

84. Mullin, *Another Six-Hundred*, 185.

85. BKS/*Senshi Sōsho*, 26:328–31. After temporary repairs to her damage in Makassar, the destroyer returned to Japan, where she was under refit until nearly the end of 1942.

86. BKS/*Senshi Sōsho*, 26:330.

87. Watanabe, *Bali Island Battle*, 6. At this point it is necessary to note that while the times of IJN and USN primary records do tally reasonably well in this battle, for this very confused and chaotic phase of the fighting the times are approximate at best. In general terms one would do well to understand that the action here lasted only about ten minutes, from roughly 0215 hours to 0225.

88. USS *Parrott* (DD-218) Action Report, "Report of Night Attack on Japanese Forces in Badoeng

Strait, Southeast Coast of Bali, N.E. I., on February 20, 1942," February 21, 1942, 3, Fold3 by Ancestry, Historical Military Records, at www.fold3.com.

89. Watanabe, *Bali Island Battle*, 7.

90. Alford, *Playing for Time*, 139.

91. Watanabe, *Bali Island Battle*.

92. BKS/*Senshi Sōsho*, vol. 26, states that *Michishio*'s casualties amounted to a total of sixty-four men.

93. Watanabe, *Bali Island Battle*, 7.

94. Miraculously, Padgett made safely it to shore. In company with other Dutch survivors he crossed over to Java and reported back on board *Parrott* in time to escape when the island fell.

95. Mullin, *Another Six-Hundred*, 181.

96. Mullin, *Another Six-Hundred*, 181–82.

97. Binford interview with Toland, Milner papers.

98. Kale, diary, 31.

99. Elly Ellsworth email to the author, 2013.

100. Japanese navy fighters were operating out of Denpasar field on February 20 and medium bombers by the twenty-third.

### 9. Disaster at Darwin

1. Walter Winslow wrote later that his ship learned of the attacks on Darwin while at sea steaming back to Tjilatjap and heard again Japanese claims—via Tokyo Rose—to have sunk the *Galloping Ghost* at her moorings. Unknown to Winslow or the other men of *Houston* at that time, they had narrowly avoided what could have been a fatal encounter with superior Imperial Navy covering forces—including the heavy cruisers *Nachi* and *Haguro*—off Timor during the invasion of that island.

2. Mullin, *Another Six-Hundred*, 54–55.

3. The material damage to *Peary* was quite extensive, although it had not affected her hull's structural integrity. Per official navy accounts she lost her radio receivers, sound gear, torpedo exploders, and warheads, with both torpedo directors badly damaged; all charts, chronometers, sextants, and navigational equipment destroyed; her gun director and rangefinder were both wrecked; the girdle of the degaussing cable was severed; one boiler drum was dented by fragments, and there were thirty-five perforations of the well deck over number 1 fire room; her mainmast was blown into three pieces; her radio antennae were ruined; twenty-six holes were left in her four funnels. Clearly she was a badly wounded vessel, and the fact that she survived for two more months is another remarkable example of the grit and determination of Asiatic Fleet personnel making do under conditions of extreme adversity.

4. Hoyt, *Lonely Ships*, 183.

5. Mullin, *Another Six-Hundred*, 80–100.

6. Details of this final meeting with Koivisto from Rear Admiral Fulton's conversations with the author, September 2006.

7. "A Brief History of the USS *Wm. B. Preston*, June 1940 to Oct. 1945," 4, Fold3 by Ancestry, Historical Military Records, at www.fold3.com.

8. Messimer, *In the Hands of Fate*, 248.

9. Muzzell remarks from a 1983 interview in Bradford, *In the Highest Traditions*, 43–44.

10. Letter from Butch Parker to John Toland on errors in S. E. Morison, 1960, Milner Papers.

11. Curtis Ewing diary, quoted in Mullin, *Another Six-Hundred*, 196. Ewing was an army soldier recently arrived at the port.

### 10. Six Days to Oblivion

1. Helfrich, *Memoires*, 2:426.

2. On February 13 the military attaché in Washington, Colonel Weijerman, sent a message to Governor-General Van Stachouwer in Buitzenzorg, Java, noting these promises by Hopkins to Van Mook. Not to

be outmaneuvered without a word, both General Marshall and Admiral King of the Joint Chiefs of Staff had quickly commented (in their conferences on February 10) that the Munitions Assignments Board had "initiated" this promise without consulting them first. But it was recognized that any reversal then "however informal, would cause considerable embarrassment." Therefore the shipment was approved— with the Dutch informing Hopkins they would provide the shipping bottoms (another assurance they never fulfilled) and with the Joint Chiefs of Staff agreeing to review further requests in two weeks. By then Java was clearly beyond help (Notes of JCS Conferences, Fold3 by Ancestry, Historical Military Records, at www.fold3.com).

3. This should not be misconstrued as a complete lack of Allied fighters. Dutch and British air units did have a number of planes available—Brewster Buffaloes, Curtiss-Wright Demons, and Hawker Hurricanes— but these were of course being whittled down rapidly by Japanese army and navy fighters, which were of higher quality, flown by more experienced pilots, and in greater numbers.

4. *Ku* is an abbreviation for *kōkutai*, which means air squadron or air group; these were generally organized as either bomber or fighter *kōkutai*. Several such squadrons would make up a *kōkusentai*, or air flotilla; a number of these in turn would compose a *kōkukantai*, or air fleet.

5. Shores, Cull, and Izawa, *Bloody Shambles*, 2:163; Bartsch, *Every Day a Nightmare*, 125–31.

6. Bartsch, *Every Day a Nightmare*, 125–31.

7. ABDA technically included the Philippines, in the main because the only possible reinforcements to MacArthur's command would have to come through the ABDA region, but it was clear to all involved that operational matters in the Philippines per se would be little affected by Wavell's HQ.

8. Admiralty War Diary, entry for Tuesday, January 3, 1942, mentions this request in a message (1836A/3) from the First Sea Lord (Pound) to Washington, Fold3 by Ancestry, Historical Military Records, at www.fold3.com.

9. Tolley, *Cruise of the Lanikai*, 36; and Leutze, *Different Kind of Victory*, 217.

10. Hart kept "a detailed narrative" among his private papers that scrupulously recorded his dealings with MacArthur, in anticipation of that general's predilection for finding scapegoats and the army's well-known hostility to its rival service branch (Leutze, *Different Kind of Victory*, 253).

11. Hart, diary, January 10, 1942. It would not be the only such mission conducted by a sub from the Asiatic Fleet; several operations of this type took place. Before Corregidor fell in early May 1942, *Permit*, *Spearfish*, *Snapper*, *Seawolf*, *Seadragon*, and *Trout* all made voyages to the Rock.

12. Leutze's biography records the first meeting between Hart and King after the former returned from Java in early March. King was said to be "still angry with the Dutch about their behavior regarding Hart" and reassured him that he had fully understood that Hart was neither too ill nor too decrepit to do the job at ABDA (Leutze, *Different Kind of Victory*, 286).

13. Marshall and Eisenhower were driven to attempt their own measures to circumvent what they saw as Hart's intransigence by concocting a secret mission ("Plan X"). This was undertaken by army officers along with Patrick J. Hurley, former secretary of war in the Hoover administration, in which large funds (said to be as much as 10–12 million U.S. dollars) were made available to charter individual ships as blockade runners to the Philippines in early 1942. But by mid to late February the mission was failing. No more ships could be sent from Australia. As a last measure Hurley, then given the rank of brigadier general, and an aide flew to Java to argue with Wavell about ships destined for the Philippines that were being held up at Surabaja. When Hurley appeared unannounced at Bandoeng HQ in mid-February, Hart seemed mystified, having no real idea why he was there. Clearly Hart was *still* not being fully informed by Washington. Hurley, while making no mention of his actual mission, only noted the possibility of the Dutch surrendering the East Indies. This made little difference in the long run, Hart felt; the Japanese were going to take the NEI regardless (Hart, diary, February 15–16, 1942).

14. King and Whitehill, *Fleet Admiral King*, 368, footnotes that King was "disturbed over the behavior of the Dutch," and although he later encountered Helfrich in Washington DC during the war, King reacted with coolness, and "his enthusiasm for the Dutch continued to be measured."

15. Matloff and Snell, *Strategic Planning for Coalition Warfare*, 133n.

16. Brett recorded "Question of Allocation of P-40's and Expense of Reserves for U.S. Squadrons Being Examined," Milner Papers.

17. Maj. Gen. Julian Barnes, commanding USAFIA as of late January, had been notified by Wavell on February 7 to begin preparations for shipping planes to Java by sea. The Australian government had sought to retain the AAF planes for defense at Darwin, but this request was denied.

18. Craven and Cate, *Army Air Forces in World War II*, 1:395.

19. Bill Warnes, RM2/c, *Langley*, interviews with the author, 2010–11; conversation and emails between Ray Kester, RM2/c, *Marblehead*, and the author, 2011–12.

20. Adm. Thomas C. Hart, "Supplementary of Narrative," written in the winter of 1946–47, 26, NARA II. The Brett diaries record quite similar complaints.

21. The operational PBY-4 Catalinas of PatWing 10 patrolled northward in the direction of the Moluccas and Ambon; these planes and the remaining J2Fs had been withdrawn from Ambon to Darwin in the second week of January.

22. See Kehn, *Blue Sea of Blood*, 101–6.

23. Lt. Gen. George Brett, diary, January 2, 1942, Milner Papers. At this time he also stated his displeasure with Claggett's performance.

24. See Dwight R. Messimer, *Pawns of War*. Messimer's is still the best single-volume account of this confused operation and its aftermath.

25. As it transpired, *Athene* was neither part of convoy MS.5, nor would she return to Java. Instead, she was recalled on March 4 and steamed back to Australia.

26. Romanus and Sunderland, *China-Burma-India Theater*, 92.

27. Hart, diary, February 14, 1942.

28. Brett Papers in Milner Papers; and Bartsch, *Every Day a Nightmare*, 198.

29. Wavell's message went out on February 21. Rear Admiral Palliser, ABDAFLOAT chief of staff, was tasked earlier with replying to the Admiralty regarding *Indomitable* on February 16 (Brett Papers, subseries 6, box 13, folder 6, Milner Papers).

30. Matloff and Snell, *Strategic Planning for Coalition Warfare*, 134–36.

31. After ravaging Darwin—and had they been required—the four First Air Fleet carriers under Vice Admiral Nagumo could have mustered approximately 250 additional combat planes for operations against Java.

32. In two unrelated matters—naval operations at sea (without air cover) and the loyalty of East Indian local populations—Helfrich remained astonishingly obtuse. His postcampaign writings, in the 1942 letter to Admiral Fürstner and his *Memoires* of 1950, which continued to argue that strikes at sea against Japanese targets (at Davao, Menado, Kema, and Ambon) would have succeeded, are the stuff of fantasy. And his rationalizations concerning the local population were equal parts delusion ("without exception, demonstrated a rare solidarity when confronted with the danger, and also after that") and finger-pointing ("Otherwise, the . . . Indonesians . . . know very well that the supreme command of the warfare in their own territory, was neither assigned to the Dutch nor to the Indonesians, but to the British and the Americans") (letter from Lt. Adm. C. E. L. Helfrich to Adm. J. T. Fürstner, March 1942, "Correspondentie met Fürstner, 1941–1944," no page numbers, 2.12.44, I.C. de Regt, 1998, Nationaal Archief, The Hague, Netherlands).

33. From two hard-bound volumes titled *Bandoeng*, in the Glassford Papers, RG 24, box 370, NARA II (hereafter cited as Glassford, *Bandoeng* volumes). Further evidence of the disconnect between Washington and the Far East about *Langley* and MS.5 is revealed by remarks made in the third week of February by Adm. Ernest King to the other joint chiefs. King said that he was "distressed" to learn that *Phoenix* had been delayed for some two weeks in Melbourne "in spite of his instructions allocating her to the ABDA area." Notes of JCS Conferences, Fold3 by Ancestry, Historical Military Records, at www.fold3.com.

34. War Diary of USS *Phoenix*, Fold3 by Ancestry, Historical Military Records, at www.fold3.com.

35. Notes of JCS Conferences, Fold3 by Ancestry, Historical Military Records, at www.fold3.com.

36. Matloff and Snell, *Strategic Planning for Coalition Warfare*, 135.

37. St. Pierre, USS *Langley* CV-1 AV-3, 20.

38. St. Pierre, USS *Langley* CV-1 AV-3, 19–20.

39. St. Pierre, USS *Langley* CV-1 AV-3, 23

40. Bartsch, *Every Day a Nightmare*, 260.

41. This crew chief was Sgt. Jack Ellwood (St. Pierre, USS *Langley* CV-1 AV-3, 20).

42. St. Pierre, USS *Langley* CV-1 AV-3, 27.

43. St. Pierre, USS *Langley* CV-1 AV-3, 21.

44. The skipper of *Sea Witch* had reported to *Langley* for his orders in Fremantle and not learned of the plan for leaving the convoy and going up to Java until the morning of February 22. A day had been lost in conversations between USAFIA HQ and Royal Australian Navy representatives in Melbourne, which saw more confusion about the convoy's destination. On the twenty-first it had been once more revised to a vague destination in "the Burma area" (Messimer, *Pawns of War*, 34). It also appears that the captain of *Phoenix* may have received his instructions belatedly, as he, too, went aboard *Langley* on the morning of February 21 from 1030 hours until 1110 for "an official call" (CL-46 Deck Log).

45. Helfrich, *Memoires*, 2:425. Conversely, British Admiralty War Diary entries show that there *were* concerns, based on reported sightings—although quickly disproved—as early as the first week in February of a Japanese carrier or carriers operating south of Java, possibly in the Andaman Sea.

46. On February 25, for example, in Glassford's COMSOWESPAC/Bandoeng files, NARA II, we find that an IJN submarine was reported at "13.53 South, 119.09 East, course 185°."

47. Japanese Monograph no. 102, "Submarine Operations, December 1941–April, 1942," NARA II; and Boyd and Yoshida, *Japanese Submarine Force*, have details of the cooperation between Group "C" and Kondō's Southern Force and Nagumo's Kidō Butai during the Second (Java) and Third (Indian Ocean) Mobile Operations respectively.

48. Boyd and Yoshida, *Japanese Submarine Force*, 72–75. The three other boats—*I-1, I-2,* and *I-3*—moved to positions some three hundred nautical miles off the northwest cape of Australia. The second pair patrolled southward along the west coast of Australia toward Shark Bay and Fremantle. By early March these boats were recalled to the sub base at Penang, Malaya, and arrived about the middle of that month.

49. Lamb narrative in St. Pierre, USS *Langley* CV-1 AV-3, 21–23.

50. War Diary of USS *Phoenix* (CL-46), February 22, 1942, Fold3 by Ancestry, Historical Military Records, at www.fold3.com.

51. Walt Frumerie interview with the author, July 2012.

52. Lowell Barty interview with the author, July 15, 2012.

53. Messimer, *Pawns of War*, 41; St. Pierre, USS *Langley* CV-1 AV-3, 252.

54. Bill Warnes conversation with the author, July 2011.

55. Helfrich, *Memoires*, 2:426.

56. Glassford, *Bandoeng* volumes.

57. Glassford, *Bandoeng* volumes.

58. Report by Cdr. R. P. McConnell, commanding USS *Langley* (AV-3), Action Report, "Operations, Action and Sinking of USS *Langley*, period from February 22 to March 5, 1942," NARA II (hereafter cited as McConnell Report).

59. On the night of February 27, Dutch merchant vessels were ordered to depart Tjilatjap steaming south into the Indian Ocean, there to adopt a holding pattern some four hundred kilometers offshore to await further instructions. The U.S. Navy was also attempting to get smaller noncombatant vessels away, just as were the British, who had sent a final convoy out of Batavia that day for Tjilatjap and southward. It was apparently these departing ships that Glassford hoped to escort with *Whipple* and *Edsall*.

60. McConnell Report.

61. Hata, Izawa, and Shores, *Japanese Naval Air Force Fighter Units*, 20. According to original records in

the Japan Center for Asian Historical Records (hereafter cited as JACAR) found and translated by Luca Ruffato, the Takao Kū Rikko unit began operations at Denpasar on February 23, 1942.

62. McConnell Report, 2.

63. See Bartsch, *Every Day a Nightmare*, 423n2. Thanks also to Peter Boer for these additional details on the Dutch command.

64. Messimer, *Pawns of War*, 1.

65. Several details of the IJN air operations against *Langley* are from official IJNAF records accessed for the author by Luca Ruffato of Italy, ca. 2011. Luca Ruffato's early death from cancer in 2013 was a great loss for the community of Pacific War researchers, especially those focusing on Japanese naval air operations.

66. Messimer, *Pawns of War*, remains, after over thirty years, far and away the finest, most accurate history of the entire operation. Many of these details are drawn from chapter 6, 40–60.

67. *Langley* was built originally in 1912 as the coal collier USS *Jupiter* (AC-3), an early experiment in turbine-electric propulsion; in 1920–22 *Jupiter* was converted into the navy's first aircraft carrier, renamed and commissioned USS *Langley* (CV-1). In 1937 she was once again reconstructed; with much of her flight deck removed, *Langley* then became a seaplane tender (AV-3).

68. Frumerie interview with the author.

69. Messimer, *Pawns of War*, 40–60. As it turned out, these planes came under attack, too, and one was severely shot up, losing an engine, but both made it safely back to Tjilatjap.

70. McConnell Report.

71. McConnell Report.

72. *Los Angeles Examiner*, April 4, 1942.

73. Details of the wounding of Lieutenant Bailey are from Messimer, *Pawns of War*, 50; Dr. Robert Blackwell's official medical report in St. Pierre, USS *Langley CV-1 AV-3*, 67; and Lowell Barty phone interview with the author, July 2012.

74. Dr. Blackwell's report stated that Lieutenant Bailey was brought in about thirty minutes after the first attack suffering from "mortal shrapnel wound of the left chest penetrating the left lung and pericardium. He died the following day after transferring to the USS *Edsall*" (St. Pierre, USS *Langley CV-1 AV-3*, 67).

75. McConnell Report, 4.

76. McConnell Report.

77. McConnell Report, 4.

78. St. Pierre, USS *Langley CV-1 AV-3*, 382.

79. From USS *Parrott* (DD-218) Deck Log, February 1942, NARA II.

80. Glassford, *Bandoeng* volumes.

81. Abernethy actually had taken only a small number of these passengers on board; records compiled after the "disaster" show that *Pecos* carried seven wounded men in all, including Ens. C. H. Coburn from *Marblehead* and three men (K. B. George, Vince Koenig, and Samuel Marsh) from *Houston*. Lt. Archibald Stone of USS *Stewart* was not a "passenger" at all—he had not been wounded—but had been reassigned to *Pecos* after *Stewart* was lost at Surabaja.

82. USS *Pecos* Action Report, March 7, 1942, 1, NARA II; and Messimer, *Pawns of War*, 94.

83. This 270545 message was in fact copied by *Langley*'s intrepid radiomen and logged at 1329 hours immediately prior to abandoning ship.

84. McConnell Report, handwritten addendum ("Fifth Endorsement") of May 14, 1942.

85. McConnell Report.

86. Cdr. Edwin M. Crouch, ComDesDiv 57, "USS *Edsall*, Record of Known Activities between 26 February, 1942 and 1 March, 1942," May 21, 1942, Fold3 by Ancestry, Historical Military Records, at www.fold3.com.

87. USS *Langley* Action Report, "Operations, Action and Sinking of USS *Langley*, period from February 22 to March 5, 1942."

88. Crouch, "USS *Edsall*, Record of Known Activities between 26 February, 1942 and 1 March, 1942," www.fold3.com.

89. Barty interview with the author.

90. Frumerie interview with the author.

91. *Whipple* rescued 308 survivors from *Langley*, while *Edsall* took 177 men.

92. The preservation of the ship's money and records was the responsibility of *Langley*'s paymaster, Ens. Jay Martin. He was one of the last men to leave *Langley*. Yet because a number of bags had opened in the water and their contents spilled into the ocean, Martin was held responsible "for every cent of this money. . . . The Navy takes a very dim view of any money lost by a Paymaster no matter under what circumstances" (St. Pierre, USS *Langley* CV-1 AV-3, 277). Some of the recovered, water-soaked money was later laid out on the upper deck of *Whipple* in a roped-off area—under guard—to dry in the sun. See Messimer, *Pawns of War*; St. Pierre, USS *Langley* CV-1 AV-3.

93. Messimer, *Pawns of War*, 86; and St. Pierre, USS *Langley* CV-1 AV-3, 251.

94. Although Butler would be lost with the entire complement of *Edsall*, Commander Blackwell, after transfer to *Pecos*, was rescued by *Whipple* and later learned the fate of Bailey through other survivors.

95. Warnes phone interview with the author, July 11, 2010; and St. Pierre, USS *Langley* CV-1 AV-3, 451.

96. McConnell Report, Addendum, "Fifth Endorsement."

97. McConnell Report, Addendum, "Fifth Endorsement."

98. McConnell Report, Addendum, "Fifth Endorsement"; and Log Book of USS *Whipple* (DD-217), NARA II.

99. COMSOWESPAC dispatch 270903, in Glassford, *Bandoeng* volumes.

100. Glassford, *Bandoeng* volumes.

101. COMSOWESPAC dispatch 270840, in Glassford, *Bandoeng* volumes.

102. A British merchant vessel, *City of Manchester* (8,917 tons), was sunk much closer to Tjilatjap around this time by a Japanese sub, the *I-53*, which torpedoed and gunned the freighter, killing nine. It may have seized half a dozen POWs as well. Fortunately, 126 crewmen, 17 gunners, and 13 naval signalmen were quickly rescued early on February 28 by the minesweepers USS *Whippoorwill* (AM-35) and USS *Lark* (AM-21). Ten injured survivors of the British ship were then transferred to the gunboat USS *Tulsa* (PG-22) for medical treatment.

103. The message from CSAF (Commander Submarines Asiatic Fleet), dispatch 271525, went to *S-39* early on the morning of February 28. Further details of the mission are found in both Roscoe's semiofficial *U.S. Submarine Operations in WWII*; Gugliotta, *Pigboat 39*, 143–46.

104. Glassford, *Bandoeng* volumes.

105. Glassford, *Bandoeng* volumes.

106. The true value of these pursuit planes—in contrast with the lives expended to get them to Java—is still open to debate. Although most of them were unloaded and quite a few uncrated and eventually transported by rail to Dutch airfields, they made no useful contribution to the defense of Java and only appear in Japanese propaganda photos of captured matériel later.

107. Virtually all the remaining communications over the final days show that Glassford and staff were really trying to preserve lives. Postcampaign accounts by surviving commanders—especially by Helfrich and Glassford—are misleading to the extent that they suggest there were more efforts for organized resistance at sea than actually existed.

108. It should be remembered that these groups had been preceded by the Vanguard Force of IJN submarines, which entered the Indian Ocean several days earlier.

109. The Tjilatjap raid—carried out by 149 planes from all four carriers on March 5—has always remained a rather mysterious operation, as it was originally scheduled to take place earlier that week, but the lack of worthwhile shipping targets seems to have permitted a delay of two or three days. First Air Fleet was apparently given some flexibility in determining when to make the strikes, and later events

would show that Nagumo may indeed have been biding his time hoping for the arrival at Tjilatjap of more substantial Allied naval forces to attack.

110. Source Document 7 (as part of Exhibit no. 8) used in Record of Proceedings, Volume 13 of the *Joint Congressional Investigation of the Attack on Pearl Harbor*, 513–24. "Captured Japanese Document, Op-16-fe, Translation No. 290, 25 July 1945," NARA II (hereafter cited as Kuramoti, "Southern Cross").

111. Kuramoti, "Southern Cross," 7.

112. In pencil on the original message Glassford wrote, "Unable possible"—referring to the sentence that he underlined himself—and this shows that he was already unhappy with the decisions made by McConnell and Crouch (Glassford, *Bandoeng* volumes).

113. *Eidsvold* had been torpedoed on January 20, 1942, by the Japanese submarine *I-59* while lying-to off Flying Fish Cove.

114. Donovan, "Ordeal to Forget."

115. Messimer, *Pawns of War*, 97–99.

116. Donovan, "Ordeal to Forget."

117. Japanese air squadron records (*kōdōchōsho*) for the Takao Kū that day merely stated that they bombed Christmas Island and "missed a transport." Takao Kōkusentai combat reports, or *kōdōchōsho*, at JACAR. Generously provided and translated by Luca Ruffato.

118. The island would be bombarded by the battleships *Kongō* and *Haruna* with their destroyers later the next week. Then on March 31, 1942, came Operation X ("X Sakusen"), which was a sizable amphibious landing undertaken by the Japanese to capture the island. At that time Lieutenant Commander Donovan was made prisoner and returned to Batavia as a guest on one of the IJN light cruisers supporting the invasion forces. From Tandjong Priok he was transshipped to Makassar, Celebes, and entered the large Allied POW camp there, where he met Jack Michel from *Pope*, among others.

119. Crouch Report, USS *Edsall*, "Record of Known Activities between 26 February, 1942 and 1 March, 1942," Fold3 by Ancestry, Historical Military Records, at www.fold3.com.

120. Crouch Report.

121. To a certain extent one is reminded of the Doctor Wassell episode in this regard. In a number of other instances we find Asiatic Fleet personnel, enlisted men as well as officers, exhibiting the same marked wariness of running afoul of navy regulations, to say nothing of *any* failure to follow orders explicitly.

122. Glassford, *Bandoeng* volumes.

123. Dr. Blackwell's Report, in St. Pierre, USS *Langley* CV-1 AV-3, 67–68.

124. Messimer, *Pawns of War*, 100–101.

125. These details are derived from Commander Abernethy's Action Report, "Action and Sinking of USS *Pecos* 1 March 1942," March 7, 1942, written on board USS *Mount Vernon* while returning to the States; the Log Book of USS *Whipple* (DD-217); and *Whipple*'s Action Report, "Activities between 26 February and 4 March 1942," written March 4, 1942, by her skipper, Lt. Cdr. Eugene S. Karpe, all in NARA II.

126. Glassford, *Bandoeng* volumes.

127. Glassford, *Bandoeng* volumes.

128. The men of *Black Hawk* in particular are known to have tangled in shoreside brawls with the crew of *Phoenix* at Fremantle when "the resentment aroused by the sight of this many-gunned cruiser sitting by the dock while their friends and shipmates up north were being slaughtered, had finally exploded" (Mullin, *Another Six-Hundred*, 254). Liberty parties were apparently canceled for the men of *Phoenix* as a result.

129. *Whipple*'s Action Report, "Activities between 26 February and 4 March 1942," NARA II.

130. Unless otherwise noted, Japanese contact reports and messages are from the original Message Log of DesRon 1 flagship *Abukuma*, March 1942 in JACAR. These were provided by Anthony P. Tully and translated by Kan Sugahara. The BatDiv 3 War Diary and CruDiv 8 Detailed Engagement Report and Log Book in JACAR are utilized here as well for the IJN side of events on March 1, 1942. Those translations also by Kan Sugahara.

131. Both Sentai 8 cruisers had each launched one recon plane (Type O, JAKE) at 0700 hours that morning. These planes headed west to the vicinity of Christmas Island to search for Allied shipping. Both JAKES later returned to their respective ships at about 1400 hours.

132. Kehn, *Blue Sea of Blood*, 212n53.

133. Message Log of DesRon 1 flagship *Abukuma*, March 1942, JACAR.

134. Message Log of DesRon 1 flagship *Abukuma*, March 1942.

135. Messimer, *Pawns of War*, 102.

136. The IJN records (*kōdōchōsho*) for the Kaga air group claimed to have left the ship in a sinking condition. The direction of the attacks comes from Lieutenant Commander Abernethy, Action Report, "Action and Sinking of USS *Pecos* 1 March 1942," 3, NARA II.

137. Abernethy quoted in "Smothered with Bombs, They Go Down Fighting," *Los Angeles Examiner*, April 4, 1942.

138. Abernethy, "Action and Sinking of USS *Pecos*," 4, NARA II. Abernethy wrote this document on March 7 as he returned home on USS *Mount Vernon*.

139. Dr. Blackwell's Report in St. Pierre, USS *Langley* CV-1 AV-3, 67–68. Crotty never recovered. He was last seen unconscious and believed lost when the ship sank.

140. Abernethy, "*Pecos* Died Hard," 75–83.

141. Abernethy, "*Pecos* Died Hard," 80.

142. Bob Foley interview with the author, September 2012.

143. Capt. Lawrence E. Divoll, USN (ret.), "Langley's Last Voyage," *Shipmate*, January–February 1981, reproduced in St. Pierre, USS *Langley* CV-1 AV-3, 121–22; Messimer, *Pawns of War*, 117, 170.

144. Messimer, *Pawns of War*, 116–17; Abernethy, "*Pecos* Died Hard," 80.

145. Abernethy, "Action and Sinking of USS *Pecos*," NARA II.

146. Messimer, *Pawns of War*, 121–22.

147. Messimer, *Pawns of War*, 122–23; and St. Pierre, USS *Langley* CV-1 AV-3, 382–83.

148. Both Bob Foley and Jim Long survived the *Pecos* sinking (Foley interview with the author).

149. Creal Gibson, "Fight for Life!," in St. Pierre, USS *Langley* CV-1 AV-3, 201–5.

150. Barty interview with the author.

151. Bill Warnes interviews with the author, 2010–12. Bill Warnes was in fact a technician who maintained the radio equipment and not an operator at that time.

152. Chief Petty Officer Gustave Peluso interview with John Toland, ca. 1960, Milner Papers; Messimer, *Pawns of War*, 129–39.

153. St. Pierre, USS *Langley* CV-1 AV-3, 168. Also Frumerie interview with the author.

154. St. Pierre, USS *Langley* CV-1 AV-3, 204.

155. Gibson, "Fight for Life!"

156. Foley interview with the author.

157. All IJN messages are from records of "1st Torpedo Squadron" (DesRon 1) in JACAR and were found by Anthony Tully and translated by Kan Sugahara.

158. Records of "1st Torpedo Squadron" (DesRon 1) in JACAR.

159. Messimer, *Pawns of War*, 136–37.

160. Peluso interview with Toland, Milner Papers.

161. Peluso interview with Toland.

162. Kuramoti, "Southern Cross," 8.

163. Sentai 3 Detailed Engagement Report (DER) in JACAR states explicitly that three planes from *Sōryū* were overhead as CAP at that time. However, *Sōryū kōdōchōsho* suggest that she had flown off CAP in the morning and early evening.

164. Bezemer, *Geschiedenis van de Nederlandse Koopvaardij*, 734. Translation courtesy of Jan Visser.

165. We now know that *Edsall* had left Tjilatjap with nine torpedoes still in her tubes.

166. The most extensive published account of *Edsall*'s last fight is in Kehn, *Blue Sea of Blood*, 136–65.

Figures here on survivors are from CruDiv 8's DER, and Wartime Logbook entries for the engagement as found in JACAR. Other details are taken from the BatDiv 3 Action Report in JACAR. Quotation is from BKS/*Senshi Sōsho*, vol. 26.

167. Kuramoti, "Southern Cross," 8.

168. Kuramoti, "Southern Cross," 8.

169. BKS/*Senshi Sōsho*, vol. 26.

170. Peluso interview with Toland, Milner Papers. It should be emphasized that Toland's interview with Gustave Peluso from *Langley* as copied by Sam Milner is jumbled, confused, and at first glance highly suspect; Milner's chaotic handwriting is also a complicating factor. However, I found that after several closer readings, aided by a knowledge of the events of the day and the ships involved, Peluso's account began to yield many fascinating details.

171. Kuramoti, "Southern Cross," 8.

172. DesRon 1 Message Log in JACAR.

173. From "KdB Secret Telegram No. 63, Outline of the After Action Report No. 7" sent by Vice Admiral Nagumo to Admiral Yamamoto, Admiral Nagano, and Vice Admiral Kondō in JACAR. Around this time Nagumo was also informed of the Dutch surrender on Java.

174. Vice Admiral Kondō with the ships of Main Body had already returned to Staring Bay on March 7, 1942.

175. See "Postscript: The Revelations of Dr. Haraguchi" in Kehn, *Blue Sea of Blood*, 234–44, for a more detailed memoir by one of the IJN officers on *Chikuma* who helped rescue *Edsall*'s survivors and then later turned them over to the Sasebo SNLF troops at Kendari, Celebes.

176. Barty interview with the author, July 2012.

177. St. Pierre, USS *Langley* CV-1 AV-3, 205.

178. *Whipple* details from her Action Report, "USS *Whipple*—Activities between 26 February and 4 March 1942," 5; Peluso interview with Toland, Milner Papers.

179. Karpe, *Whipple*'s Action Report.

180. Abernethy, "*Pecos* Died Hard," 82.

181. In early Renaissance emblems, Fortune—or "that Bald Madam, Opportunity"—was often represented as a blindfolded female with a single, long forelock of hair, perched atop a revolving globe.

182. Gibson, "Fight for Life!," 201–5.

183. Foley interview with the author.

184. Frumerie interview with the author.

185. Karpe, *Whipple*'s Action Report; and Barty interview with the author.

186. Karpe, *Whipple*'s Action Report.

187. Karpe, *Whipple*'s Action Report

188. Quotes from Karpe, *Whipple*'s Action Report; Messimer, *Pawns of War*, 147.

189. Commander Abernethy's Action Report (dated March 7, 1942) recorded a total of 220 men rescued by *Whipple*. These were broken down as follows: from *Pecos* 8 officers and 63 enlisted men for a total of 71; and from *Langley* 9 USN, 2 USAAC, 138 EM for a total of 149. He wrote that records of the latest changes to personnel were put aboard *Pillsbury* and *Parrott* before *Pecos* sailed, and that the final muster list was mailed to BuNav, but admitted that due to the loss of the oiler's executive officer (McPeake) and her yeomen, "an accurate list of those missing cannot be submitted." The report of *Whipple*'s skipper, Lieutenant Commander Karpe, of March 4 gave the exact number rescued as 231.

### 11. Chaos and Night

1. Very few of these factors were permitted by censors and propaganda organs to exert a negative effect in the press; there was the same official and semiofficial verbiage about "the impregnable Preanger Plateau" (around Bandoeng), and—per Churchill's favorite species of rhetoric—absolutely no surrender, and fighting to the last man, last shell, last bullet, and so on. Nothing could have been further from the truth when the time came.

2. Mullin, *Another Six-Hundred*, 187; Michel, *Mr. Michel's War*, 64–65.

3. Whiting, *Ship of Courage*, 52.

4. Whiting, *Ship of Courage*, 52

5. They would escort *Black Hawk* and *Holland* on their journey to Australia.

6. Gill, *Royal Australian Navy*, 599.

7. See COMSUBAF document, "War Activities of Submarines U.S. Asiatic Fleet, 12/1/41 to 4/1/42," Fold3 by Ancestry, Historical Military Records, at www.fold3.com.

8. These World War I–design "D-class" cruisers were of 4,650 tons, 471 x 46 x 15 feet with six 6-inch guns, twelve 21-inch torpedoes, and lacked radar or upgraded AA capabilities; the "S-class" destroyers were even smaller and weaker than their Asiatic Fleet contemporaries, being but 276 feet in length with a beam of 26 feet and displacing only about 1,000 tons. For many years both classes had been considered unsuitable for fleet duties and were often relegated to coastal commands. All were well worn if not decrepit by December 1941.

9. Hart, diary, February 18, 1942.

10. Churchill, *Hinge of Fate*, 139–40.

11. Churchill, *Hinge of Fate*, 140–43.

12. Churchill, *Hinge of Fate*, 165. On the Japanese side all thoughts of invading Australia proper ended a few weeks later, in early March. This of course had no effect on the turbulence that had brewed up in Australia, where months of political and military squabbling would continue well into MacArthur's arrival. These conflicts often centered on issues related more intimately to Australia's internal politics than any actual threats from the Japanese. For a full-length examination of this unsavory subject, see Burns, *Brisbane Line Controversy*.

13. See Takushirō, *Complete History of Greater East Asia War*, 2:260. Col. Takushirō Hattori argues in this extensive history—published in four volumes—that the enveloping strategy was a compromise made between IJA and IJN planners before the war. Each service branch had devised its own operational plans independently for the southern advance, with a compromise agreement leading to the hybrid plan actually utilized when war started.

14. For purposes of deception this important vessel was deliberately misidentified as *Ryujo Maru* in messages and in many Japanese accounts. As a result of this intentional deceit, the wrong name has passed into a number of Western histories of the campaign over the years.

15. As always, the need to undertake and conclude these operations speedily was driven first and foremost by concerns with fuel (heavy oil but more significantly gasoline) stocks.

16. Japanese Monograph no. 101, "Netherlands East Indies Naval Invasion Operations," 4, NARA II.

17. Details on the planning for the Java Invasion are here taken from vol. 26 of BKS/*Senshi Sōsho*, 374–78, and Japanese Monograph no. 66, "Invasion of Java: Operations of the 16th Army," NARA II.

18. This small but critical group of ships in which Vice Adm. Takahashi Ibō sailed was known as Main Force and is so designated throughout this section of our narrative. His destroyers occasionally changed, but *Ashigara* remained the flagship of the Third Fleet and Main Force throughout the campaign.

19. Japanese Monograph no. 101, "Netherlands East Indies Naval Invasion Operations," 3, NARA II.

20. According to vol. 26 of BKS/*Senshi Sōsho*, the seizure of Timor was but one of four parallel operations originally scheduled per the Manila Agreement of late January 1942 between the Imperial Army and Navy. The other operations were the East and West Java invasion landings and the capture of Bali. All had initially been planned for February 21–23.

21. BKS/*Senshi Sōsho*, 26:45–46.

22. Michel, *Mr. Michel's War*, 65.

23. Mullin, *Another Six-Hundred*, 187–88.

24. Letter from J. W. Gelvin, Y1/c, *John D. Ford*, to John Toland, February 1960, Milner Papers.

25. Whiting, *Ship of Courage*, 52–53. These U.S. ships then proceeded to Exmouth Gulf, Australia, arriving there at 1151 hours on February 26.

26. The flushdeckers only encountered what they thought was a Dutch patrol vessel as they passed through. For his part Waller was alerted to the presence of an Australian corvette there, HMAS *Maryborough*.

27. Mullin, *Another Six-Hundred*, 188; Michel, *Mr. Michel's War*, 66.

28. Mullin, *Another Six-Hundred*, 202.

29. Japanese naval records are replete with accounts of their warships having to riddle Allied merchant ships with hundreds of shells in order to sink them. The Imperial Navy, quite naturally, was appalled at this heavy, and wasteful, expenditure of ordnance.

30. Kale, diary, February 19, 1942, 29.

31. "Destruction of USS STEWART." CONFIDENTIAL report dated March 12, 1942, from Lt. F. E. Clark to COMSOWESPAC (Glassford), NARA II. Clark would later escape—very luckily—on the small Dutch steamer *Generaal Verspijck*, out of Tjilatjap, along with a *Houston* sailor named Thomas Borghetti Jr., FC1/c, who had been wounded on February 4 and sent to Jogjakarta's Petronella Hospital.

32. Relegated to duty as a floating AA battery, *Soerabaja* had been attacked a week earlier, at which time a single Japanese bomb hit her, penetrating through the ship and exploding beneath the hull, killing and wounding almost two dozen men She then settled on the shallow bed of the harbor with her machine guns still operable, and there she remained (Royal Netherlands Navy Warships of World War II, at www.netherlandsnavy.nl).

33. Michel, *Mr. Michel's War*, 71. As for the hospital ship *Op Ten Noort*, she had been attacked while in the Western Channel near Surabaja on February 21 by Japanese bombers. Three near misses wounded over twenty persons and killed three others. As a result "the ship incurred severe material damage." IMTFE document no. 8471-A, "Report Regarding the Adventures of the Netherlands Military Hospital Ship *Op ten Noort*," May 8, 1946, NARA II.

34. Messimer, *In the Hands of Fate*, 245–57.

35. Boer, *Loss of Java*, 180, reveals the astonishing fact that at this critical moment there were only two out of ten Dutch recon flying boats capable of operations.

36. Glassford's narrative states that by this time the harbor was operating at about 5 percent efficiency due to the disappearance of labor.

37. Binford narrative, April 11, 1942, Fold3 by Ancestry, Historical Military Records, at www.fold3.com.

38. The extensive oil installations at Tjepoe (Cepu today) would have been a primary reason for the selection of Kragan as the landing point for the Imperial Japanese Army's East Java invasion forces.

39. Bezemer, *Geschiedenis van de Nederlandse Koopvaardij in de Tweede Wereldoorlog*, 721.

40. Winslow, *Ghost That Died at Sunda Strait*, 106–8; Shultz, *Last Battle Station*, 129–30.

41. Albert Elmo Kennedy interview with Samuel Milner, September 1959, Milner Papers.

42. Jack Leroy Smith interview with Samuel Milner, August 9, 1960, Milner Papers.

43. Winslow, *Ghost That Died at Sunda Strait*, 108. Hornfischer, *Ship of Ghosts*, 57.

44. Smith interview with Milner, August 9, 1960, Milner Papers.

45. Confirmed in interviews by Samuel Milner with Sgt. Charley Pryor, USMC, September 1959, and Lt. Harlan G. Kirkpatrick, September 1961, Milner Papers.

46. Warrant Officer Carpenter Louis E. Biechlin interview with Samuel Milner, August 1960, Milner Papers.

47. Winslow, *Ghost That Died at Sunda Strait*, 110.

48. Admiralty Messages, ADM 199/2067.

49. These appear to have been from sightings by two U.S. PatWing 10 PBYS—early on the twenty-fourth and twenty-fifth—both of which were shot down by Japanese fighters. See Messimer, *In the Hands of Fate*, 258–61.

50. It was through the clockwork regularity of these bombing attacks by the Japanese that they began to be called the "Pepsi boys" by some sailors on *Houston* because they seemingly showed up at 10, 2, and 4 every day.

51. For the spotting aid given by *Paul Jones* during this seventy-minute action, Ens. Herb Levitt of

*Houston* stated that he and others felt that Lieutenant Commander Hourihan deserved an official commendation (Levitt interview with Samuel Milner, Milner Papers).

52. From the Glassford messages in *Bandoeng* volumes.

53. This is not to suggest that the Americans meekly acquiesced to their fate; they did not. Many of the sailors and officers never lost their sense of optimism or of humor. The wisecrack about the sound of "the gate clanging shut behind us" is indicative of the hard-boiled wit these tough individuals maintained throughout the campaign and afterward as POWS.

54. Hamlin, *Shipmate*, May 1946, 10.

55. Cain and Sellwood, HMS *Electra*, 212.

56. Report by Capt. Oliver Gordon, CO of HMS *Exeter*, October 1945, Milner Papers.

57. Thomas, *Battle of the Java Sea*, 156.

58. Mullin, *Another Six-Hundred*, 206–9; and Rear Adm. E. N. Parker interview with John Toland, ca. 1960, Milner Papers.

59. Mullin, *Another Six-Hundred*, 208.

60. Mullin, *Another Six-Hundred*, 207.

61. Tandjong Priok was chosen by Helfrich with the clear notion of continuing sweeps against any Western invasion forces from that port, with the option of sending his remaining Striking Force units down through Sunda Strait to Tjilatjap, which was still free at that time from enemy air attacks. He expected Surabaja to suffer increasingly heavy bombing attacks in the meantime.

62. Details from Vice Adm. Edward N. Parker, "Conference in Surabaja," in Mullin, *Another Six-Hundred*, 206–9. Binford recollections from his "Report of Action with Japanese on February 27, 1942; Events Before and After," March 4, 1942, NARA II, courtesy Jim Hornfischer.

63. Admiralty Messages, ADM 199/2067.

64. Parker interview with Toland.

65. Van Oosten, *Battle of the Java Sea*, 74. This remark by Doorman is also quoted verbatim in CCCF/Collin's Report of March 17, 1942, and reproduced in McKie, *Survivors* (AKA *Proud Echo*), in appendix 1.

66. This is one of the relatively few useful, and explicit, statements in Helfrich's *Memoires*, 2:398.

67. It has been asserted (by members of Dutch HQ) that Doorman suffered from a variety of tropical maladies and that his health was not good at the time of the final naval operations in defense of Java.

68. In Niek Koppen's 1995 documentary, *De Slag in de Javazee*.

69. A Dutch source noted that only two or three were actually picked up and went to sea aboard *De Ruyter*. Additionally, Butch Parker later wrote that the water barge had probably been the same one he had been waiting to use that afternoon. With his old ship's very high consumption of water due to leaks, he had taken every opportunity to get as much freshwater into her tanks as possible before each sortie.

70. Schultz, *Last Battle Station*, 142.

71. Details on Captain Rooks from Tom Payne interview with John Toland, ca. 1960, Milner Papers.

72. This brings up the sometimes contentious matter of Allied air cover over the CSF during the battle, a subject on which others—such as Dr. Peter Boer—have produced entire books—and with which I am not in perfect agreement. Here, and to be clear, I am pointing up the lack of "effective" air cover for the CSF of Rear Admiral Doorman and not simply debating the mere presence of Allied or Japanese aircraft overhead.

73. Michel, *Mr. Michel's War*, 70–71. This seems to confirm other remarks about the quality of personnel at Cavite Navy Yard.

74. Admiralty Messages, ADM 199/2067.

75. Helfrich, *Memoires*, 2:398.

76. Hara, Saito and Pineau, *Japanese Destroyer Captain*, 73–77.

77. Utsonomiya (commander of *Harugo* Flight Squadron), "Haguro Suitei," 12. Translated by Kan Sugahara.

78. It is just possible to see in the surface actions off Java in the February 27–March 1 period a fore-

taste of the coming catastrophe at Savo Island off Guadalcanal in August, that is, in terms of both failed aerial recon and reporting and surface fighting at night in which radar played little or no role.

79. The very same type of blindness would have equally disastrous and bloody consequences in the Indian Ocean south of Java, as fleeing Allied ships blundered across the paths of two separate Japanese task groups.

80. BKS/Senshi Sōsho, 26:448–49. Translation by Akio Oka.

81. Hara, Saito, and Pineau, Japanese Destroyer Captain, 77.

82. McKie, Survivors, 45.

83. "Everyone liked him [Doorman]. Same was not true of Helfrich. Most sea-going people didn't have much use for him" (Lt. Bill Giles, the XO and navigator from John D. Edwards, interview with John Toland, Milner Papers).

84. This is confirmed explicitly in their interviews in the 1995 Dutch documentary De Slag in de Javazee.

85. Miscellaneous pages from British Admiralty records, ADM 199, in USS Houston (CA-30) Survivors Association Archives.

86. Boer, Loss of Java, 188–89.

87. Miscellaneous pages from British Admiralty records, ADM 199, in USS Houston (CA-30) Survivors Association Archives.

88. Letter from Rear Adm. Edward N. Parker to John Toland, July 7, 1960, critiquing Samuel Eliot Morison's The Rising Sun in the Pacific (Milner Papers).

89. According to Helfrich's Memoires, 2:402, when he learned that Doorman had brought the CSF back to the Western Channel, he sent a message, "ATTACK IMMEDIATELY." However, Helfrich states that Doorman had already turned the ships around and was heading back out to sea by the time this message was transmitted.

90. Helfrich, Memoires, 2:399–400.

91. Electra recorded receiving a simpler signal: "Follow me. The enemy is ninety miles away." In Cain and Sellwood, HMS Electra, 218.

92. Helfrich, Memoires, 2:403–10.

93. According to Bartsch, Dutch pilots flying Brewsters out of Ngoro field were under instructions that morning to "fly two-ship protective patrols above the CSF . . . on the lookout for any Japanese reconnaissance planes," as Doorman's force steamed back and forth along the north coast of Java (Bartsch, Every Day A Nightmare, 294–95).

94. Bartsch, Every Day A Nightmare, 295. The A-24 was the AAF variant of the navy's famed SBD Dauntless machine, but it was an altogether inferior model, lacking the speed and maneuverability of its naval counterpart.

95. Bartsch, Every Day A Nightmare, 295. That these Allied planes were in the air over the CSF both before and during the Battle of the Java Sea meant next to nothing in terms of effectively disrupting the Japanese operations. Helfrich's Memoires appear exceptionally misleading—even by his standards—on this matter and contain what must be read as numerous contradictions. The central question remains how Rear Admiral Koenraad could have known of the missions being flown over the Java Sea that morning and afternoon, yet Vice Admiral Helfrich did not. What Doorman did or did not know is, at this juncture, a less relevant point.

96. Utsonomiya, "Haguro Suitei," 393–94.

97. Utsonomiya, "Haguro Suitei," 396.

98. Statement by K. S. Blair, CSM, USS Houston, "Action off Surabaja, 27 February," Milner Papers.

99. Capt. A. L. Maher, "Action Report of the USS Houston (CA-30) in the Battle of the Java Sea, 27 February 1942," November 16, 1945, 2.

100. Penhollow had come from a circuitous series of transfers from Chaumont to Pensacola to Marblehead and finally De Ruyter. According to Sholar—as recounted in Lieutenant Commander Kroese's 1945 book, The Dutch Navy at War—the men were stationed on the Dutch cruiser's signaling deck, where Lieutenant Kolb took photographs of the action during lulls in his communication duties.

101. Deck Log for uss *Paul Jones* (DD-230), February 27, 1942.

102. With her crow's nest some seventy-four feet above the water, a typical flushdecker would have had visibility of about twelve miles to the horizon under clear conditions.

103. From an account by the AA officer on *Nachi*, Lieutenant Commander Tanaka, "Decisive Battle in the Java Sea," 204–28. Translated by Kan Sugahara.

104. Tanaka, "Decisive Battle in the Java Sea."

105. Cain and Sellwood, *HMS Electra*, 219–20.

106. It is worth noting that the Japanese *Nachi*-class heavy cruisers were enormous vessels in their day, with an overall length in excess of 660 feet, and would have been longer than many of the older American battleships, thus much bigger than any U.S. heavy cruisers of contemporary design.

107. Letter from Lt. Cdr. George Tyndale Cooper to John Toland, July 1960, Milner Papers.

108. BKS/*Senshi Sōsho*, 26:452. This is more or less consistent with IJN gunnery doctrine for cruisers at that time.

109. Cain and Sellwood, *HMS Electra*, 221.

110. Cain and Sellwood, *HMS Electra*, 222.

111. Japanese eyewitness accounts agree that *Jintsū* opened fire first and was the first to be fired on—and severely at that—in return. Capt. O. L. Gordon confirmed in postwar accounts that *Exeter* had indeed opened fire at extreme range on *Jintsū* (described as a four-funneled light cruiser) with her A and B turrets and found hitting range within about a dozen salvos. The enemy then turned away under cover of a smokescreen, which is precisely what Japanese records state as well. Capt. "Hec" Waller's Action Report states that *Exeter* opened fire one minute before *Houston*.

112. Extant IJN documents on "Cruiser Gunnery Doctrine in Day Action" stated that "standard opening ranges for heavy cruisers" when firing against other heavy cruisers would be "23,000 meters (without spotting planes)" and 25,000 meters if planes were utilized. Document in the author's collection courtesy of W. David Dickson.

113. Ironically, because the Dutch flagship was hardly more than a German K-class light cruiser, similar to the Kriegsmarine vessels *Köln*, *Karlsruhe*, and *Königsburg*.

114. Kimura Hachiro interview with John Toland, Milner Papers.

115. Tanaka, "Decisive Battle in the Java Sea."

116. From an interview with an unidentified RNN survivor of *De Ruyter* in Niek Koppen's documentary *De Slag in de Javazee*.

117. Casey, *Torpedo Junction*, 147–49. The "vacuum-cleaner effect" was noted by *Houston* gunner Bill Kohl in interviews with the author.

118. Tanaka, "Decisive Battle in the Java Sea." This is seen in *Houston* survivors' accounts, some of which stated—although purely from memory—that the ship was able to fire undisturbed for some fifteen minutes. Indeed, IJN records in JACAR indicate that *Nachi* did not fire on *Houston* for almost eighteen minutes.

119. Rafalovich quote from Niek Koppen's documentary *De Slag in de Javazee*.

120. Kroese, *Dutch Navy at War*, 85.

121. Marion "Elly" Ellsworth interviews with the author, summer 2013.

122. Maher, "Action Report of the uss *Houston* (CA-30) in the Battle of the Java Sea, 27 February 1942," November 16, 1945, 3.

123. BKS/*Senshi Sōsho*, 26:452. Van Oosten, *Battle of the Java Sea*, contains an appendix that states the Japanese ships—*Naka* with her destroyers *Asagumo*, *Minegumo*, *Murasame*, *Samidare*, *Harusame*, and *Yudachi* expended a total of thirty-one fish at this time.

124. Cdr. Toyama Yasumi interview with John Toland for *But Not in Shame*, Milner Papers. However, talk was one thing, and braving enemy shellfire another. After the battle Toyama's tactics would be sharply criticized by officers in Takagi's squadron as wasteful, while the long-range shooting of *Nachi* and *Haguro* would receive the same criticism from others in the Imperial Navy—both by fellow participants and also IJN shore commands assigned to make post-action analyses of Japanese gunnery.

125. Tanaka, "Decisive Battle in the Java Sea."

126. Tanaka, "Decisive Battle in the Java Sea." As for the multicolored splashes, Cdr. Toyama Yasumi on *Jintsū* claimed to John Toland to have seen splashes colored red, yellow, and green. We know *Houston* used red dye in her shells, but the other shades noted by Toyama might have been made by the particular explosives in the shells themselves rather than dye coloring. It is not believed any of the other cruisers employed dye-loaded shells.

127. Falle, *My Lucky Life*, 32–33.

128. Pratt, "One Destroyer."

129. Nelson's "war dance" was witnessed by a crewman on the cruiser's number 1 (starboard) 5-inch gun, Bill Weissinger, s1/c, who acted as the trainer on that gun. Weissinger was extensively interviewed in the summer of 1959 by Sam Milner, who said that the *Houston* sailor possessed a "phenomenal eye for detail and a power for total recall beyond anything I have ever seen" (Milner Papers).

130. Maher, "Action Report of the USS *Houston* (CA-30) in the Battle of the Java Sea, 27 February 1942," November 16, 1945, 3.

131. Tanaka, "Decisive Battle in the Java Sea."

132. Utsonimya, "Haguro Suitei," 399.

133. Tanaka, "Decisive Battle in the Java Sea." There were other IJN accounts by men present claiming that Commander Nagasawa was frightened, clutching the compass in fear as Allied shells whistled over the cruiser.

134. "8-Inch 3-Gun 'Turret'—Gun Mount—Loading" and "Control of Naval Gun Batteries, circa 1942," by Capt. Harold Hamlin, former turret captain for turret 1 on *Houston*, Milner Papers.

135. Hamlin, "8-Inch 3-Gun 'Turret.'"

136. On the other hand, if he happened to notice something that displeased him, his cry was "Silence!" This word was "chosen because it had a ringing, incisive sound which cut through the clangor of the turret's operations." It was a term that "caused every man to freeze, and brought everything to a halt . . . [for] it signaled genuine peril" (Hamlin, "8-Inch 3-Gun 'Turret'").

137. Hamlin, "8-Inch 3-Gun 'Turret.'"

138. "With a good shove" comes from conversations between Bill Ingram—who served the right-hand (i.e., starboard) flap man in turret 1 on *Houston*—and the author, summer 2013.

139. Hamlin, "8-Inch 3-Gun 'Turret.'"

140. Hamlin, "8-Inch 3-Gun 'Turret'" and "Control of Naval Gun Batteries, circa 1942."

141. Each of the three guns had a 7.5 horsepower ramming motor, and it was the motor on the right-hand gun in turret 1 that malfunctioned. Propellant charges for the main battery weighed ninety pounds and came in two bags (forty-five pounds each). These were pushed into the breech manually by the tray man and the powder man.

142. "Main Battery Log, USS *Houston*, 27 February off Surabaja" (a reconstructed log written by survivors after the sinking; copy in the Milner Papers). See also Winslow, *Ghost That Died at Sunda Strait*, 115. As a note of interest, after being captured, Leo Rody, GM3/c, was struck by his Japanese interrogators when he tried to tell them that *Houston* carried a 6-inch main battery. They knew perfectly well that she was a heavy cruiser with 8-inch guns (Jack Dale Smith interview with Samuel Milner, August 1960, Milner Papers).

143. Tanaka, "Decisive Battle in the Java Sea." See also Van Oosten, *Battle of the Java Sea*, appendix 14, 116. The distressed Lieutenant Horie was able to redeem himself later that night when one of *Haguro*'s torpedoes helped sink a Dutch cruiser. The Japanese Detailed Engagement Report and Wartime Log of Sentai 5 in JACAR show the torpedo launchings at 1655 hours (1825 IJN/Tokyo time); more interestingly Sentai 5's official records actually show that the ship was indeed laying smoke at just this time and that the two cruisers were also making 30-degree course alterations in an effort to elude CSF shelling.

144. Regarding the accuracy of Collins's report, as always in a battle as lengthy and confusing as this one, such factual details cannot be said to match up perfectly in every instance. The radio log of *John D.*

*Ford* seems to indicate that *Exeter* may have been struck as early as 1710 hours, but this evidence is far from conclusive. Sentai 5 gunnery tables in JACAR show that *Haguro* straddled *Exeter* a dozen times in this period, with twenty-three shells falling over and six short. *Haguro* was the only heavy cruiser then firing on the British ship.

145. Waller Report, in Thomas, *Battle of the Java Sea*, 245.

146. Log of radio messages in USS *John D. Ford* (DD-228) Action Report, "Report of Action of Allied Naval Forces with Japanese Forces off Soerabaja, Java, NEI, February 27, 1942," March 4, 1942, hyperwar.com.

147. Deck Log for USS *Paul Jones* (DD-230), February 27, 1942.

148. If these figures are approximately accurate, the striking Long Lance would have given a very formidable performance by any standard. At that range its speed would have approached 42 knots to hit *Kortenaer* at such a time.

149. Winslow, *Ghost That Died at Sunda Strait*, 118.

150. Kroese, *Dutch Navy at War*, 86.

151. These remarks from *Kortenaer* survivors are taken from Niek Koppen's 1995 documentary film, *De Slag in de Javazee*. The fate of Lt. Cdr. A. Kroese and Peeters are recorded in Mullin, *Another Six-Hundred*, 215–16.

152. This clearly makes little sense but may be perhaps a misremembered impression, although it is possible that a man or men had climbed down onto the rudder as the ship sank.

153. Parkin, *Out of the Smoke*, 233–34.

154. About ten minutes after his query to *Exeter* regarding her status, Doorman sent a message to the British cruiser to "Proceed Soerabaja"—this was his final communication with the ship.

155. Japanese track charts for Sentai 5 in JACAR show almost all the CSF ships making smoke in this period.

156. This remark by Sam Falle on *Encounter*'s torpedo attack was taken from Niek Koppen's 1995 documentary film, *De Slag in de Javazee*.

157. Cain and Sellwood, HMS *Electra*, 229.

158. Japanese records show *Asagumo* launching four torpedoes at 1937 (1807 Allied time) at a range of seven thousand meters. One minute later—at 1938/1808—*Asagumo* received the first of the shell hits that would incapacitate her. *Minegumo*'s "lost chance" to fire torpedoes is covered in BKS/*Senshi Sōsho*, 26:455.

159. Cain and Sellwood, HMS *Electra*, 232.

160. This seems more or less confirmed by *Jintsū*'s recorded firing of four torpedoes at 1754 from 18,000 meters (19,600 yards); see BKS/*Senshi Sōsho*, 26:454.

161. BKS/*Senshi Sōsho*, 26:454; quotations from Cain and Sellwood, HMS *Electra*, 235–40. Commander May waved to his men in the water from his position on the bridge as they yelled at him to get off, but he made no attempt to save himself. For the survivors floating in the oil film on the surface of the sea, it was the beginning of a fantastic ordeal. For many this would involve great good fortune in being rescued at all but be followed by the bitterest setback later for those who, as they were being transported to Ceylon from Australia via the steamer *Nankin*, found themselves intercepted in the Indian Ocean by the German raider *Thor*. They were promptly seized and then put aboard a *Kriegsmarine* support ship, the *Regensburg*, and taken *back* to the East Indies as prisoners of war. A number of these men ended up perishing in Japanese POW camps before war's end.

162. Van der Moer, "He Who Sees First Lives Longest."

163. There were a series of Japanese torpedo attacks in the 1750 to 1807 period, during which over seven dozen weapons launched.

164. Email from Marion Ellsworth to the author, January 2013.

165. From *De Slag in de Javazee*.

166. Japanese records for Sentai 5 in JACAR show *Nachi* firing 14 20 cm salvos against *Houston* in a twelve-minute period between 1744 and 1756, expending 110 rounds at ranges of twenty-one thousand to twenty-five thousand meters.

167. Quoted by Kenneth Blair, CSM of USS *Houston* (CA-30), in his postwar "Statement: Action off Soerabaya, 27 February 1942," NARA II, given at Calcutta in September 1945 after his liberation.

168. There are more than a few anecdotal reports of enemy submarines in the sea that were blown up and large pieces of metal were hurled into the air. It is quite likely these were in fact the detonations of the big Type 93 weapons at the end of their runs or in premature explosions.

169. Mullin, *Another Six-Hundred*, 226.

170. Maher, "Action Report of the USS *Houston* (CA-30) in the Battle of the Java Sea, 27 February 1942," 3.

171. Interview with Eugene Parham by Samuel Milner, September 30, 1959, Milner Papers.

172. Cdr. Arthur Maher, "Action Report—USS HOUSTON (CA30) on the Battle of Sunda Strait, 28 February 1942," November 13, 1945, 2, NARA II.

173. George Stoddard's remarks came from conversations with the author between 1992 and 2004 at various USS *Houston* (CA-30) Survivors Association annual reunions. The affable, mild-mannered Stoddard was well known to have been yelling expletives almost nonstop during the battle in his frustration with the AA director's flimsy doors, which were being blown open by each salvo from the main battery. He and the forward director officer, Leon Rogers, were regular attendees of survivor reunions for many years.

174. Deck logs of the flushdeckers show that the ships were heading very nearly due south at this point. Binford's Action Report states explicitly that all these orders were by lights, although some other sources mention flag signals.

175. CDD58 in messages stood for Commander Destroyer Division 58, sometimes also shown as ComDesDiv 58.

176. Cdr. Thomas Binford interview with John Toland, ca. 1960, Milner Papers.

177. Capt. H. E. Eccles, "Memorandum on Java Sea Campaign," June 1960, Milner Papers. This is a nine-page typewritten document prepared by Eccles, although for whose use is not clear. The date suggests that it was written for John Toland during his research for *But Not in Shame*. And while not as heated or personal, perhaps, as the exchange between Captain Nolan and Lord Lucan on the Balaklava plains in 1854, it is worth understanding, since the confusion between Binford and Eccles also helped dictate how the attack of "another six-hundred" would unfold.

178. Binford was upset with Eccles's outburst at Doorman during an earlier conference at Surabaja on Saturday, February 22. He informed John Toland that he told his junior commander to "shut up and let me talk." In the same interview Binford termed Eccles a "blowhard" and "an alarmist." Still, it is hard not to sympathize with Eccles during the Java Sea debacle.

179. Eccles, "Memorandum on Java Sea Campaign," Milner Papers.

180. Here, again, sources differ on whether the ships fired their torpedoes in unison. Most of the evidence suggests rather strongly the latter that they did not. Binford and Eccles reported that the ships made their attacks and turns in column, but one DesDiv 58 survivor, J. W. Gelvin, Y1/c—a bridge talker on *John D. Ford*—stated in an interview with John Toland in February 1960 that the destroyers went in "abreast" to made their torpedo attack, and that he was fairly certain "each ship acted independently" (Milner Papers).

181. The great diversity in written accounts and track charts purporting to show DesDiv 58's gallant but almost suicidal charge against the enemy forces that evening all agree on one aspect: spatial disorientation. Virtually none of these documents are in agreement as to the course DesDiv 58 had taken, the manner in which Binford's destroyers attacked, or where exactly the enemy ships were located when the torpedo salvos were fired.

182. Quotes by Clark and Fox taken from interviews in *De Slag in de Javazee*. Clark was also unusually frank in his interview about the pervasive fear that gripped all of the destroyermen during the battle.

183. Dan Mullin's memoir of the Fifty-Ninth Destroyer Division, in which he served—and easily one of the most valuable documents ever produced about the Asiatic Fleet's role in the war—is titled *Another Six-Hundred*, clearly referencing Tennyson's poem.

184. Action Report, USS *Alden* (DD-211), DD211/A16–3, "Engagement with the Enemy 'Battle of the Java Sea.' February 27, 1942," March 7, 1942, RG 38, Office of CNO, NARA II.

185. From Enclosure A, p. 25, one in a series of nine "diagrammatic sketches of various phases of battle" in Cdr. Henry E. Eccles, Commanding Officer USS *John D. Edwards* (DD-216), "Battle of Bawean Islands, Report of Action; Events Prior and Subsequent Thereto," March 4, 1942, Fold3 by Ancestry, Historical Military Records, at www.fold3.com.

186. Mullin, *Another Six-Hundred*, 226–28. This account of events was taken from a talk by signalman Marvin Sholar given to the officers, chiefs, and first class petty officers of *John D. Ford* in that destroyer's wardroom at Fremantle, Australia, after the ship reached port safely in the first week of March 1942.

187. In them one may also be reminded of one of the most famous torpedo attacks by an American destroyer in the entire Pacific War. It came some thirty-two months later in the Battle of Leyte Gulf, off Samar, and involved the destroyer USS *Johnston* (DD-557) as she faced an overwhelming Japanese fleet bent on sinking the escort carriers she was shepherding. *Johnston*'s skipper in late October 1944 was Cdr. Ernest E. Evans, former XO of the Asiatic Fleet four-piper *Alden*. Evans never forgot the humiliating defeat of Allied forces under ABDA and their retreat to Australia—or the men and officers squandered in that campaign—and he had made clear his intention of never again retreating from an enemy force. At Samar, as he prepared to take *Johnston* into her torpedo attacks on the giant warships of Vice Adm. Kurita Takeo, Evans was heard to remark: "We can't go down with our fish still aboard" (McDonald, *Tin Can Sailors Save the Day!*, 1).

188. Lewis Coley, Henry Eccles, and Tom Binford all frankly expressed skepticism about the effectiveness of their torpedo attacks. Eccles felt it was a complete failure, while the other officers believed it was possible that the Japanese did turn away fearing torpedoes. No one seems to have really believed they made any hits, however.

189. Binford would later state that he "had an understanding with Doorman" that once his torpedoes were expended and the ships low on fuel, his force could "retire at will" (interview with John Toland, ca. 1960, Milner Papers).

190. This was the supposition of several surviving American officers after the battle. The air defense officer of *Houston* (Galbraith) and CDD58 (Binford) later recorded being baffled by Doorman's tactics at that stage in this so-called turn away. Both imagined he might have wanted to avoid action in the twilight and to instead work his way around Takagi's screening forces to get at the transports under the cover of darkness. Some of these guesses were based on the remarks of a USN survivor from *De Ruyter*, signalman Marvin Sholar, who recalled Doorman speaking in English to the liaison personnel on the bridge of his flagship during lulls in the battle, remarking on the effectiveness of Japanese spotting planes. It was Sholar who claimed that Doorman was heard at least once to curse softly under his breath at the omnipresent IJN floatplanes (Mullin, *Another Six-Hundred*, 219–26).

191. This, however, was followed by a twilight period of roughly forty minutes before darkness fully closed.

192. Message Log for Sentai 5 for February 27, 1942, specifically as contained in "Report of the Progress of the Support Force," Sentai 5 Action Reports and DERS, JACAR.

193. The floatplane of *Jintsū* would set into motion another series of events over the next two days that have not been understood correctly for over seventy years. After detaching that night (following her last drop of seven parachute flares), *Jintsū*'s plane was directed to fly north to a rendezvous point off the mouth of a river near Bandjermasin. She was there to be met by the torpedo boat *Tomozuru*, which was to either refuel her or—if not practical—pick up the crew and abandon the plane. However, *Tomozuru* could not locate the plane and wasted the night in futile searching while the hapless plane and its crew were forced to spend an uncomfortable night adrift, using up more fuel by running the engine when necessary to keep from being washed ashore. Following the delays caused by this mission, *Tomozuru* was sent south from Bandjermasin to Java on March 1.

194. BKS/*Senshi Sōsho*, 26:456. See also Utsonomiya, "Haguro Suitei," 393–94.

195. Both the Waller Report and *Senshi Sōsho* are in fairly close agreement on the details of this brief exchange.

196. The maximum range of the 5.5-inch guns of *Jintsū* would have been slightly less than twenty thou-

sand meters, and straddles or even near misses on *Perth* or *Houston* at nineteen thousand meters *at night* would have been phenomenally good shooting with or without radar.

197. This very brief action was yet one more pivot point on which the course of the battle might have shifted. Had the ships of Doorman been able to capitalize on encountering Takagi's two heavy cruisers in their vulnerable and unprepared condition recovering floatplanes, the contest might well have turned—if only temporarily—in the Allies' favor. Disabling or sinking *Nachi* and *Haguro* would have represented a major setback to the convoy's covering forces, and one may well question whether the two scattered destroyer squadrons under Tanaka and Nishimura could have kept the CSF away from the transports. That such a limited success against Takagi's covering forces would not have altered Japanese invasion plans to any substantial or ultimate degree is indisputable, however.

198. Cdr. Henry E. Eccles, Commanding Officer USS *John D. Edwards* (DD-216), "Battle of Bawean Islands, Report of Action; Events Prior and Subsequent Thereto," March 4, 1942, Fold3 by Ancestry, Historical Military Records, at www.fold3.com.

199. Lieutenant Admiral Helfrich's subsequent views on the battle and the performance of the CSF under Doorman were neither charitable nor altogether honest. It was a pattern the admiral had started before the conflict reached Java and never greatly altered. In his letter of mid-March to his superior, Admiral Fürstner, in which he blames everybody but himself, Helfrich refers to Van Straelen and Doorman rather coldly as "poor guys" (*arme kerels*) yet still manages to find fault with the manner in which Doorman operated. Helfrich goes on to make some unconvincing remarks to the effect that Doorman's CSF should have been handled more aggressively on the night of the twenty-sixth and sought out the enemy at that point: "Then there would have been a chance (no certainty however) that he could have partially beaten the Japs." This self-serving criticism of course makes not the least sense if one understands that (1) the Japanese could not be turned away from Java by being "partially beaten," and (2) in any case no further Allied reinforcements of any substance were going to reach Java, the Allied high command at that juncture having recognized the folly of throwing away more valuable assets on what was clearly a lost cause. Letter from Lt. Adm. C. E. L. Helfrich to Adm. J. T. Fürstner, March 1942, "Correspondentie met Fürstner, 1941–1944," no page numbers, 2.12.44, I.C. de Regt, 1998, Nationaal Archief, The Hague, Netherlands. Letter provided to the author by John Waller, who found it at the Dutch archive. Translation courtesy of Bernice Harapat.

200. Boer, *Loss of Java*, 197, contains a number of pertinent comments on the poor atmospheric conditions prevailing that day and night, as well as Japanese jamming of several important radio frequencies used by the Allies. Dunn, *Pacific Microphone*, 122, mentions "eccentric atmospherics" causing "additional headaches" for radio broadcasters that week as well.

201. Winslow, *Ghost That Died at Sunda Strait*, 122.

202. Waller Report, in Thomas, *Battle of the Java Sea*, appendix C, 243.

203. Winslow, *Ghost That Died at Sunda Strait*, 123.

204. Winslow, *Ghost That Died at Sunda Strait*, 122.

205. H. P. Smith, EM1/c, interview with Samuel Milner, 1960, Milner Papers.

206. Olen Minton interview with Samuel Milner, Milner Papers.

207. Collins (CCCF) Report of March 17, 1942, to Commander-in-Chief, Eastern Fleet, in Thomas, *Battle of the Java Sea*, appendix C, 237.

208. For an example of this disparity in primary sources, Binford's March 4 Action Report states that Doorman turned the CSF west along the coast at 2140 hours.

209. Binford interview with John Toland, Milner Papers.

210. Binford interview with Toland.

211. Both Helfrich and Van Oosten went to some lengths attempting to explain this disaster. And to be fair, they made no great efforts to excuse or rationalize what the *Gouden Leeuw* had done, and done badly. The fact that Koenraad in Dutch naval HQ at Surabaja, Helfrich in Lembang, and EC/Doorman—as well as the Dutch submarines *O-19* and *K VIII*—had all been informed of the mine-laying action and its

location seems to prove rather conclusively that *Gouden Leeuw* had failed to place her mines accurately within the allotted area.

212. *By Golly-By George*, a privately published memoir written by George Squance, a former crew-member of *Jupiter*, 8, Royal Canadian Naval Association, at http://hqrcna.com/files/ByGollyBy Georgechg1.pdf.

213. Reliable figures concerning casualties, prisoners, and missing have not been determined for *Jupiter*, and there remains a surprising degree of uncertainty even after more than seventy years. As of late 2010 at least one credible researcher stated that 94 men were MIA, 1 died of wounds, 97 became POWs, and some 75 survived. This would place her complement in the range of +260 men, which seems inexplicably high. Normal complement on the "J" class destroyers was about 183 with flotilla leaders enlarged to carry roughly 218.

214. Winslow, *Ghost That Died at Sunda Strait*, 122.

215. Quote attributed to Binford in Thomas, *Battle of the Java Sea*, 207.

216. This plane was not recovered that night but had been instructed to fly to a point off the southern coast of Borneo where it was to be picked up the following day. In the course of those events *Jintsū's* floatplane became integral to the discovery and seizure of the Dutch M/V *Augustina*.

217. Statement by K.S. Blair, CSM, USS *Houston*, "Action Off Surabaja, 27 February," Milner Papers.

218. Gene Wilkinson remarks transcribed from *De Slag in de Javazee*.

219. These quotes are also taken from the filmed interviews with the survivors of *Kortenaer* in *De Slag in de Javazee*.

220. The radio log of *John D. Ford* shows the message from EC that was sent at 2220 hours as addressed to "British ships"; it read, "Pick up survivors we just passed in a boat" (USS *John D. Ford* [DD-228] Action Report, "Action in Java Sea between combined Dutch, British, American Naval Forces and Japanese Forces on 27 February, 1942; engagement between U.S. Destroyers and Japanese Forces in Bali Straits on March 1, 1942," 6, Fold3 by Ancestry, Historical Military Records, at www.fold3.com).

221. Quotation from unidentified survivor of *Kortenaer* in *De Slag in de Javazee*.

222. A number of Japanese warships, including destroyers and cruisers, would succumb during the war as a result of what in Japanese accounts are termed "induced explosions" (*yubaku*) among their torpedo batteries.

223. Account and quotes from Utsonomiya, "Haguro Suitei," 399.

224. Glassford, *Bandoeng* volumes, vol. 2.

225. Binford interview with Toland, Milner Papers.

226. Waller's Report notes this as "very slow."

227. BKS/*Senshi Sōsho*, 26:457; Tanaka, "Decisive Battle in the Java Sea."

228. Tanaka, "Decisive Battle in the Java Sea."

229. Japanese records for Sentai 5 in JACAR show the torpedoes were launched at an 80-degree "target angle"—this is *not* a bearing; the Japanese naval term is *hohi kaku*—and a range of 9,500 meters (10,400 yards). The disparity between the gun ranges and torpedo ranges is also instructive for understanding the angle(s) from which the Sentai 5 torpedoes were launched.

230. Tanaka, "Decisive Battle in the Java Sea."

231. Sentai 5 DER, JACAR.

232. Quentin Madson, coxswain, quoted in Schultz, *Last Battle Station*, 160.

233. That *Java* took her first—and presumably only—torpedo from port tallies with the IJN track chart of the action, which shows the IJN ships expending their torpedoes at CSF from well to the northwest. Doorman's was column arcing slightly to the northeast in a large turn when torpedoes were launched.

234. When located by divers sixty years later, the wreck of *Java* would reveal this massive damage to her stern, with the severed aft section resting on the seabed nearly three hundred meters from the hull of the old cruiser.

235. One of the few officers to make it alive through the ordeal was Sub-Lieutenant Gerry Jenkins of

the Royal Navy—formerly with *Exeter*—who had been attached to *Java* as the British signals liaison officer. He later became the camp librarian at Makassar when the survivors were made POWs.

236. As recorded by one of her survivors in *De slag in de Javazee*.

237. As Hashimoto, "Commentaries on the Sea Battles Fought by Tokugata Destroyer *Ikazuchi*" (hereafter cited as *Ikazuchi* document).

238. Hara, Saito, and Pineau, *Japanese Destroyer Captain*, 85.

239. *Ikazuchi* document.

240. *Ikazuchi* document.

241. Japanese records in BKS/*Senshi Sōsho*, vol. 26, record the explosions as occurring at 0106 (2336) and 0108 (2338) hours.

242. Hornfischer, *Ship of Ghosts*, 92.

243. Anecdotal evidence suggest that lookouts on *De Ruyter* may have reported the torpedo approaching from a relative bearing of 135 degrees—which conforms to the location of the Japanese ships after *De Ruyter* had reversed course: approximately 315 degrees or well off the northwest.

244. Parker interview with John Toland, Milner Papers. There is no general consensus regarding the fate of these three important officers on *De Ruyter*. Some survivors stated they saw the three men alive, getting into a life raft after the battle, while others reported that they witnessed Doorman and Lacomblé reentering their cabins on the ship, despite the raging fires, where it was believed they then shot themselves. A veteran of *De Ruyter* in prison camp later heard from fellow crew members that as the last sailors got off the sinking cruiser, Captain Lacomblé allegedly remarked that it was time for the officers to get their revolvers, which suggested suicide.

245. At that point *Perth* and *Houston* had both turned away to the west for Batavia.

246. BKS/*Senshi Sōsho*, 26:457.

247. BKS/*Senshi Sōsho*, 26:457.

### 12. A Death So Valiant and True

1. In October 1930 the *Houston Post Dispatch* newspaper wrote on the occasion of the first visit to her homeport by the new scout cruiser USS *Houston*: "But if the defense of our country makes it necessary to clear the decks for action, we are convinced that the vessel which bears our name will cover herself in glory" (subseries 7, box 4, folder 58, Milner Papers).

2. Declassified document: Cdr. Arthur Maher, "Action Report—USS HOUSTON (CA30) on the Battle of Sunda Strait, 28 February 1942," November 13, 1945, 1, NARA II. Other accounts note that radical evasive maneuvering when *Java* was torpedoed led *Houston* into a near collision with *Perth* at her stern or port quarter. It has not been previously recognized that *Houston* was suffering from steering control issues as well.

3. Message from CZM/Helfrich on the morning of February 26 to Rear Admiral Doorman at Surabaja, CCCF/Collins in Batavia, and COMSOWESPAC/Glassford at Bandoeng: "STRIKING FORCE IS TO PROCEED TO SEA IN ORDER TO ATTACK ENEMY AFTER DARK. AFTER ATTACK STRIKING FORCE IS TO PROCEED TOWARDS TANDJONG PRIOK" (Glassford, *Bandoeng* volumes). As soon as the two surviving Allied cruisers left *Java* and *De Ruyter*, Helfrich sent a message (at 0021 Z/28) to the British Naval Office in Batavia stating the ships were on their way and would arrive about 1000 Z/28, with a need for necessary arrangements, including harbor pilots.

4. Lt. Cdr. Harold P. Smith, interview with Samuel Milner, October 1, 1960, Milner Papers; Smith was an EM1/c aboard *Houston*. Smith told Milner that he spent about forty minutes on the evening of February 27–28 in the conning tower attempting to repair an electrical problem with the cruiser's steering wheel.

5. Glassford, *Bandoeng* volumes.

6. Gill, *Royal Australian Navy*, 616.

7. Herb Levitt interview with Samuel Milner, ca.1959–60, Milner Papers.

8. Bee, *All Men Back*, 18.

9. Glassford, *Bandoeng* volumes.

10. Glassford, *Bandoeng* volumes, vol. 2, RG 24.

11. Helfrich was still asking for the elusive cruiser USS *Phoenix* at this time, but that valuable vessel was not going to be squandered in a losing cause after the *Langley* catastrophe.

12. S-37 had also taken aboard the two American signalmen from *De Ruyter* in this group of survivors, Marvin Sholar and Jack Penhollow.

13. Glassford, *Bandoeng* volumes.

14. These arrangements were spelled out in one of the final USN messages from Tjilatjap before the station shut down there. See Glassford, *Bandoeng* volumes. I am most grateful for the kind expertise of Ray Kester, formerly a radioman on USS *Marblehead*—and an ex-crew member of *Houston*—who helped explain the arcana of these communications systems during the research for this chapter. Mr. Kester later served as president of the Asiatic Fleet Association.

15. From Clifford Teer interview with the author, July 2012.

16. This message—from Glassford's *Bandoeng* volumes—has no specific time zone designation, and if the 0947 was Z rather than local (GH), then it still would have reached the RNN destroyer at Tandjong Priok late in the afternoon of February 28, at 1717 hours. That was more than two hours before *Perth* and *Houston* departed.

17. Reasons for the failure of *Witte de With* to go to sea are confused. One account stated the ship was damaged and needed repairs, although she had just taken part in the Battle of the Java Sea and had not received any combat damage from the enemy. Some accounts say that *Witte de With* received damage to a prop or her stern when one or more of her own depth charges fell overboard during the battle. Another records that the destroyer's captain had granted shore leave to his crew on returning to Surabaja because the ship was expected to enter a dry dock the following day, which seems utterly fantastic, given the circumstances. The Dutch destroyer did not accompany the *Exeter* group but remained in Surabaja and was duly sunk by an enemy air raid on March 1; her crew had left the ship for the safety of shelters ashore.

18. After the war, in his *Memoires* of 1950 (2:430), Lieutenant Admiral Helfrich elides and eludes the matter, saying merely that "due to a misunderstanding the *Evertsen* did not go at the same time." This is an extraordinarily feeble explanation in view of his persistent nitpicking at the failure of British, American, and Australian ships to follow his instructions to the very letter.

19. CZM/Helfrich did send out another message that morning as the ships were steaming for Batavia that air cover and harbor pilots were requested: "HOUSTON and PERTH retiring to Batavia arrive about 1000 tomorrow [*sic*] Request pilots and air protection if available" (CZM to COMSOWESPAC, T.O.O. 0555z/28, T.O.R. 0556, Records of the British Admiralty, ADM 199/2067, 175, copy in author's personal collection). Records of the Fifth Destroyer Squadron in JACAR show that the two Allied ships were spotted by IJN air at 1135 JST.

20. Boer, *Loss of Java*, 202.

21. Battle Report of Sentai 7 (CruDiv 7), Milner Papers.

22. Shores, Cull, and Izawa, *Bloody Shambles*, 2:247; Boer, *Loss of Java*, 203, states that at least two British fighters were over Batavia all afternoon on February 28.

23. Earlier, around midday on February 22, a postponement request went out from the Third Fleet to the army due to a sighting of several Allied cruisers and destroyers in the Java Sea; the Western convoy reversed course at 1400 hours and steamed north-northwest for about twenty-four hours before reversing course again on February 23 and heading back in a southerly direction toward Java. At this time some of the escorts took the opportunity to fuel from the accompanying oiler, *Tsurumi*. See Japanese Monograph no. 66, "Invasion of the Netherlands East Indies, 16th Army," 22, NARA II; and BKS/*Senshi Sōsho*, vol. 26.

24. According to BKS/*Senshi Sōsho*, 26:435, map no. 43, Kurita's force launched a single plane each from *Kumano*, *Mikuma*, *Suzuya*, and *Mogami* in a west-to-east fan at about 0800 hours the morning of February 27 to search southward. Quotation from *Ikazuchi* document.

25. Battle Report of Sentai 7 (CruDiv 7), Milner Papers.

26. It seems that Rear Adm. (later Vice Adm.) Kurita Takeo was not highly respected within the Imperial Navy, and his actions at Midway, in the Solomons, and at Leyte Gulf displayed what was seen as a lack of aggressiveness. After his sea commands he was appointed president of the Naval Academy late in the war, but this was an appointment *not* given by the emperor and so considered of little prestige.

27. Anonymous article in the Melbourne newspaper *Barrier Miner*, April 10, 1942: "Hobart's Men Tell of Narrow Escapes" (http://nla.gov.au/nla.news-title53).

28. Gill, *Royal Australian Navy*, 608

29. Per official *kodōchōshō*, eight Mitsubishi Type 1 Rikko (BETTYS) of 3 Chutai were airborne from Base 366 at 1257 JST armed with a total of 1 x 250 kg plus 49 x 60 kg bombs. They sighted the Allied fleet at 1430 JST fifteen miles off Batavia bearing 28 degrees. At 1438 JST they made the attack. At 1556 the eight Rikko returned to Base 366. Thanks to the late Luca G. A. Ruffato for this info from IJN records in JACAR.

30. This was consistent with Kurita's procedure during the previous days; on the twenty-sixth, for example, he had launched one plane each from *Kumano*, *Suzuya*, and *Mogami* at 0800 that morning for recon patrols toward Batavia.

31. *Ikazuchi* document.

32. *Ikazuchi* document. One should bear in mind the fact that although Hara Kenzaburo was senior in *ki* (Thirty-Seventh) to Kurita (Thirty-Eighth), the latter had been promoted to rear admiral a year before the former.

33. BKS/*Senshi Sōsho*, 26:430.

34. *Ikazuchi* document.

35. BKS/*Senshi Sōsho*, 26:431.

36. Although not without some adventures; HMS *Dragon* ended up towing the drifting HMS *Kedah* into Ceylon, for example.

37. Helfrich (CZM) sent very clear orders showing that *Evertsen* had been assigned to the Western Striking Force early on the twenty-seventh: "EVERTSEN from this moment under command Western Striking Force for action" (0227–0724, Telegram no. 2848, copies of messages in author's collection courtesy of Otto Schwarz; original source unknown).

38. The capture of the oilfields at Palembang was costly: the American-owned refinery received damage that required about six months to be repaired; the Dutch refining complex was more heavily damaged, with fully one quarter of its oil storage facilities destroyed by fire. However, oil drilling equipment, transportation, and shipping facilities were intact. See Japanese Monograph no. 185, "Sumatra Operations Record, 25th Army," Milner Papers.

39. BKS/*Senshi Sōsho*, 26:433–34. One of the first things Kurita did on February 27, when he was given command of the entire operation, was to make a request to Vice Admiral Kondō for additional supply vessels.

40. Parkin, *Out of the Smoke*, 243.

41. Hill, *Wind Tracks on the Waters*, 68–69.

42. Of the few remaining naval ships present in Tandjong Priok at that time were two British coal-burning merchant steamers converted for use as minesweepers: HMS *Rahman* and HMS *Sin Aik Lee*. These small, 200-ton vessels were some of the last to escape from Singapore. In Batavia they became part of the Sunda Strait Auxiliary Patrol force. Their crews were mainly men who had survived the sinking of HMS *Repulse*. Also in Tandjong Priok was the British motor launch HDL 1063. Most were caught by Japanese warships the following night when they attempted to escape.

43. Hornfischer, *Ship of Ghosts*, 98, 466.

44. "Main Battery Log: USS *Houston*, 27 February off Surabaja," Milner Papers.

45. "Main Battery Log: USS *Houston*, 27 February off Surabaja," Milner Papers.

46. Letter from Chief Gunner's Mate Anton Manista of *Houston* to Cdr. W. Jackson Galbraith, November 5, 1945, Milner Papers.

47. Declassified document: Maher, "Action Report," November 13, 1945, 1.

48. Ens. Herb Levitt interview with Samuel Milner, Milner Papers.

49. Hill, *Wind Tracks on the Water*, 68–69.

50. Parkin, *Out of the Smoke*, 243–44.

51. Gordon, *Fight It Out*, 117.

52. Parkin, *Out of the Smoke*, 244.

53. Elmo Bush, AOM 3/C, interview with Samuel Milner, undated, Milner Papers.

54. Bob Fulton interview with the author, January, 2010

55. Hampton Cray interview with Samuel Milner, July 31, 1960, Milner Papers.

56. At least one account declared that the commanding officers went to the office of the Naval Base Commander, Commander Van der Lindt of the RNN. This version came from Ens. Herb Levitt's postwar narrative (Milner Papers).

57. Apologists for General Schilling have stated that since his was a Dutch army command, there was no reason why he, or his staff, should have paid the least attention to any of this naval intelligence anyway. This seems a singularly unconvincing argument. Herb Levitt of *Houston* thought an absence of U.S. personnel at Batavia's HQ was a contributing (negative) factor.

58. Postwar narrative written by Ens. Herb Levitt, 8, USS *Houston* Survivors Association Archives.

59. According to the records of Sentai 7 in JACAR this was the number 1 plane from *Suzuya*, which "bombed gunboat on patrol at north Batavia harbor."

60. "The Wartime Cruise of the USS *Houston*," by Quentin Madson, a coxswain on *Houston*. Document in author's collection; also available at http://ibiblio.org/hyperwar.

61. Harlan G. Kirkpatrick interview with Samuel Milner, September 18, 1961, Milner Papers.

62. See Battle Report of Sentai 7 (CruDiv 7), Milner Papers.

63. See Mosher and Creighton reports on the disorganization and general lack of cooperation at ABDA naval HQ. Capt. J. M. Creighton, USN, "Singapore-Java-West Australia: July 17, 1941–April 19, 1942," Milner Papers; and Lt. Cdr. J. S. Mosher, USNR, "Report on Malaya, Java and Australia—March 2, 1941 to March 10, 1942," Milner Papers.

64. Lt. William J. Giles, XO and navigator of USS *John D. Edwards* (DD-216), interview with John Toland, undated, Milner Papers. Giles described Doorman as "bluff . . . cordial . . . hospitable." And he added: "Same was not true of Helfrich. Most seagoing people didn't have much use for him."

65. Kirkpatrick interview with Milner, September 18, 1961.

66. Olen Minton interview with Samuel Milner, August 3, 1960, Milner Papers. This remark is one of the very few by a survivor of *Houston*'s crew that indicate *any* awareness of U.S. troops on the ground in Java. However, RAN sailors did record similar thoughts of evacuating Aussie troops from Tjilatjap.

67. This is made quite clear in references to the last mission of USS *Edsall*, among others.

68. The "Confidential Diary" of Vice Adm. William A. Glassford, 40, NARA II, states that he ordered *Houston* to Australia on February 28 from his HQ in Bandoeng.

69. Day, *Hodio*, 23.

70. H. P. Smith interview with Samuel Milner, October 1, 1960, Milner Papers.

71. C. B. Smith interview with Samuel Milner, August 15, 1960, Milner Papers.

72. Commander Maher would later record that the ship's morale was "excellent" with "spirit throughout the ship . . . maintained at an incomparably high level," but he admitted that "the physical condition of both officers and men was poor" (Cdr. Arthur Maher, "Action Report—USS HOUSTON [CA-30] on the Battle of Sunda Strait, 28 February 1942," November 13, 1945, 2, NARA II).

73. John Ferguson, F2/C, no. 4 fire room, survived the battle and the war, and in an April 1960 interview with Milner he made this very observation himself, saying he thought that the Red Torpedo had been unnerved by the direct hit on his bunk (Milner Papers).

74. Hornfischer, *Ship of Ghosts*, 96

75. Lt. (j.g.) Harold S. Hamlin interview with Samuel Milner, May 1960, Milner Papers. Hamlin was the turret officer for turret 1.

76. See Hart, diary, August 23, 1941, and comments on the arrival of Rooks to take command of *Houston*.

77. Glassford, *Bandoeng* volumes.

78. Principally the U.S. air commanders who began evacuating their men without direct communications with their Dutch counterparts. Ugly controversy later brewed up over these actions after the campaign.

79. Cdr. P. O. L. Owen, *Naval Historical Review*, August 1972. Owen did join *Perth*, of course, and survived her final battle, but "Hec" Waller did not.

80. Maher, "Action Report," November 13, 1945, 2. Many experts consider this one of the longest hits made at sea during World War II, and it was certainly one that took place at a very great distance—perhaps in the 22,000–24,000-meter range. This is also the hit that skewered Chief May's bunk.

81. Marvin Robinson (June 20, 1959), Jimmy Gee (no date ), John Harrell (June 1960) interviews with Samuel Milner, Milner Papers. Harrell told Milner that "Hec" Waller wanted to get in and out of Batavia quickly, but Rooks felt he needed to have the repairs made before proceeding. It is also suggested that Rooks thought the stop in Tandjong Priok might give his weary crew a brief but necessary respite.

82. On February 4 in the Flores Sea, as previously described, the mount had been knocked off its roller path by concussion from Japanese aerial bombs near-missing the ship.

83. Elmo "Joe" Bush, AOM2/c, interview with Samuel Milner, August 1960, in Tulsa, Oklahoma, Milner Papers. An old-timer who had enlisted in 1934, the voluble Bush was almost thirty when the ship sank. His critical remarks about the ship's material condition should *not* be confused with his estimate of the crew. He felt *Houston* had one of the finest crews he had ever served with in the navy.

84. Glassford, *Bandoeng* volumes.

85. Lt. Cdr. John Harper, "Official Report on the Battle of Sunda Strait," October 1, 1945, Milner Papers. This report is also reproduced in McKie, *Survivors*, 219.

86. "Sourpuss" description from Marvin Robinson interview with Samuel Milner, July 20, 1951, Milner Papers. Levitt's details are from his interviews with Milner.

87. John Harrell interviews with Samuel Milner, June and July 1960, Milner Papers.

88. Theodore Schram interview with Samuel Milner, July 24, 1960, Milner Papers. Schram died in 1966—not an elderly man at all—probably as a result of ill health exacerbated by his wartime experiences. He told Milner that he had left a Chinese wife and daughter (b. 1938) at Shanghai in late 1940 when the cruiser went back to the Philippines for the last time. Milner's personal interview notes contain several remarks concerning Schram's behavior and health at the time.

89. Ensign Clark was in "C" Division, and his original action station was in the coding room. A paucity of such coded messages led to the decision to have him record the captain's conversations on the bridge. This rather unusual duty was inspired—so Clark believed—by British Royal Navy practice.

90. Lee Rogers interview with Samuel Milner, August 1960, Milner Papers.

91. Harrell interview with Milner, June 1960.

92. Forbes, *Unbeaten Tracks*, 33.

93. Whiting, *Ship of Courage*, 90.

94. The combat value of these vessels was clearly nil, and at no time did they attempt to engage the enemy. Evasion was their only chance for self-preservation. In functional terms they would have been the naval equivalents of canaries in a coal mine.

95. Allied Translator and Interpreter Section (ATIS) Report no. 32, August 11, 1943, "Account of the Netherlands East Indies Operation Feb–Mar '42," 3, derived from *Osaka Mainichi*.

96. Other Japanese records claim that the destroyer *Usanami* was also involved in the attacks on *Reiger* with *Harukaze*, but this is unlikely and has not been confirmed. The so-called Sato Detachment was part of the Second Division of the Sixteenth Army, named for Col. Sato Hanshichi of the Imperial Army and commander of the Twenty-Ninth Infantry Regiment, comprising the Twenty-Ninth Infantry Regiment, the Second Tank Regiment, the First Coy of the Second Artillery Regiment, and Second Engineer Regiment less the Second Coy of that organization.

97. Japanese records state that this was accomplished by early afternoon—1530 hours JST—and that

there were then no loose mines to endanger the transports. This would have been about the time *Perth* and *Houston* reached Tandjong Priok.

98. Additional details of *Harukaze's* action that night are taken from an article by her captain, Cdr. Koeu Keiji, "Friendly Fire," 275–79, in the Kancho-tachino anthology (a series of pieces by former IJN destroyer captains). Translated by Kan Sugahara.

99. A Japanese reporter traveling with the Imperial Army, Nakayama Hideo, described the scene in more idealized terms: "In a precise line-ahead formation the convoy reached its destination a few hours after night had fallen. Two beacon-lights winked peacefully on the extreme tips of two islands near the mouth of the bay. The full February moon was just beginning to rise and was painting a broad stripe across the side of Mt. Karang, which seemed to jut out into the sea ahead of our ships. The wind had died and the waves were less turbulent. Presently the sound of a launch put-putted faintly over the dark waters. Landing operations had begun! Then, from the dark shores across the waters a signal-lamp blinked the terse but pregnant message, 'Landing operations completed.' Not even a rifle shot broke the silence of the night" (*Osaka Mainichi*, April 1942, in ATIS Report no. 32, 3, Milner Papers).

100. ATIS Report no. 32, 3.

101. Thanks to Jan Visser of Netherlandsnavy.nl.com for these details from Dutch records, accessed January 2009. *Reiger's* Lt. Willem Van Der Jagt would end up in the infamous Serang movie-house jail several days later with American survivors from *Houston*.

102. ATIS Report no. 32, 3. Other Imperial Navy records show that the action with *Reiger* was over at 2253 hours (JST) or approximately one hour before the convoy safely entered its anchorage off Bantam Bay.

103. Almost all the surviving first generation of Special Type destroyers—*Fubuki, Shirayuki, Hatsuyuki, Murakumo,* and *Shirakumo*—would end up participating in the fighting at Sunda Strait that night.

104. This would correspond to 2239 hours on the Allied ships.

105. *Ikazuchi* document.

106. *Ikazuchi* document.

107. *Ikazuchi* document.

108. On the Japanese troopship reporter Nakayama noticed, "A destroyer which had been stationed just off our right bow suddenly kicked forward and cutting deeply into the water drove headlong towards the enemy force moving in from east of Babi Island." He then added the obligatory propaganda garnish his article needed if it was going to pass the official navy censors: "We were witnessing a death-defying assault by a unit of the Imperial Navy" (from *Osaka Mainichi*, April 1942, ATIS Report no. 32, 3).

109. Parkin, *Out of the Smoke*, 248, quoting navigator John Harper's official report; and McKie, *Survivors*, 64–65.

110. As for useful technical facts and lessons learned, the battle reiterated the obvious conclusions that should have been drawn from the Balikpapan strike in January: naval gunfire alone from cruisers and destroyers was rarely if ever adequate to sink other warships or even transports. Torpedoes were by far the most effective means for getting hulls under the water; that much was painfully obvious. But this fact also undercuts almost every criticism written later about the action by Helfrich in his 1950 *Memoires*, 2:430–35. His cavils against *Perth* and *Houston* (but not *Evertsen*) regarding the engagement in which the two cruisers are criticized for "steaming on" past the Japanese transports as if they had ignored them while running away is both a falsehood and a delusion. The cruisers had no knowledge of the transports' positions until *after* the battle had begun, not before, and both were by that time fighting for their very lives against overwhelming Japanese covering forces that attacked them from all bearings. Even Helfrich must have known that only *Perth* carried torpedoes—*Houston* removed her tubes in the midthirties—and that these eight weapons would scarcely have had the ability to seriously disrupt the enemy landings. Also, we know from a document written later by the commanding officer of *Evertsen* (in an attempt to justify his actions) that the Dutch destroyer had deliberately sought to *avoid* contact with the enemy that night.

111. For the message allegedly sent by *Houston*, see Maher, "Action Report," November 13, 1945, 15.

112. W. Jackson Galbraith interview with Samuel Milner, June 1959, Milner Papers.

113. Reporter Nakayama's account also recorded the battle's first moments: "A solitary time-shell executed a wide rose-colored arc in the clear Java skies. Then a flare-bomb exploded with a clear, penetrating brilliance to bathe the sea in a ghastly pale light. On all sides shells crashed into the waves and threw up huge pillars of water that fell back with a resounding splash. . . . There was a terrible beauty of the scene on that night of February 28, 1942" (from *Osaka Mainichi*, April 1942, in ATIS Report no. 32, 3).

114. Nakayama Hideo, "The Landing on Java," in *Osaka Mainichi* and *Tokyo Nichinichi*, April 1942, Milner Papers.

115. Memories here all derived from Bob Fulton (interview with John Toland, no date), Jack Leroy Smith (August 9, 1960), Anton Manista (August 6, 1960), and Robert Martin (no date) interviews with Samuel Milner, Milner Papers.

116. Maher, "Action Report," November 13, 1945, 4.

117. Maher, "Action Report," November 13, 1945. 5.

118. Maher, "Action Report, November 13, 1945, 4.

119. Type 93 Long Lance torpedoes were carried only by the two heavy cruisers of Sentai 7 that night. Type 90 torpedoes were quite powerful in their own right, though, but with a slightly smaller warhead and considerably less range than the monstrous Type 93 weapons.

120. Koeu, "Friendly Fire."

121. The strange camouflage scheme worn by *Perth* at that time may also have made identification puzzling. She was painted in a dazzle pattern on her starboard side while her port side had been painted a solid gray color.

122. BKS/*Senshi Sōsho*, 26:485.

123. Schultz, *Last Battle Station*, 173.

124. Koeu, "Friendly Fire."

125. Koeu Kenji's memoir explicitly repudiates the *Senshi Sōsho* account that *Harukaze* suffered any damage to her propellers or rudder in the battle or lost steering, which caused her torpedo attack malfunction. It looks as though the large circle made by *Harukaze* to regroup before going in a second time for her torpedo attack was mistaken for rudder damage.

126. BKS/*Senshi Sōsho*, 26:483–87, "The Third Phase of the Battle."

127. Koeu, "Friendly Fire," 275–79275–79.

128. BKS/*Senshi Sōsho* states that *Shirataka*'s gunfire "hit the enemy," but there is no way to determine this given the remarkable volume of fire then being directed against *Perth* and *Houston*. If her attack is noteworthy at all, it is because old *Shirataka* was the sole Imperial Navy ship to attack *Houston* and *Perth* with gunfire alone that night. All the other Japanese ships fired torpedoes eventually. Ironically, *Shirataka* would encounter *Perth* and *Houston* again later but not as surface units.

129. W. Jackson Galbraith interview with Milner, June 1959, at the Naval Gun Factory, Milner Papers. In personal talks with Capt. Lee Rogers in the early nineties, I asked about visibility in the engagement. Rogers responded candidly, saying that he "couldn't see a thing" in the black night at Sunda Strait, only an occasional puff of smoke or gun flash.

130. BKS/*Senshi Sōsho*, 26:483–87; "Sea Battle off Batavia."

131. BKS/*Senshi Sōsho*, 26:483–87, "Battle Report" sent by Captain Sakiyama to Rear Admiral Hara later.

132. Captain Sakiyama's Battle Report, in BKS/*Senshi Sōsho*, 26:483–93.

133. Four transports were lost (*Maru Tatsuno, Maru Horai, Maru Sakura,* and *Maru Shinshu*), but two were refloated and put back into service. Subsequent repairs at Singapore revealed their extensive structural damage could only have been caused by the huge warheads of the Type 93s fired by *Mogami*. Given a firing time of 2357 hours and the hits in the transport line recorded at 0005 hours, the torpedoes would have probably traveled between 9,700 and 11,300 yards. This certainly appears consistent with the ranges at which the action was then occurring. *W-2* was split in half, losing thirty-four enlisted men and one officer killed, with seven enlisted men and two officers wounded.

134. The commanding general of the Sixteenth Army was forced to spend some three hours swimming

in his life vest in the oily waters off Bantam Bay before being rescued at approximately 0300 hours. The next day Imamura would have a spirited face-to-face interview with *Houston*'s senior pilot, Lt. Tommy Payne, who later wrote of this encounter and the apoplectic anger of the IJA general.

135. McKie, *Survivors*, 67. The detailed track charts in *Senshi Sōsho* show that this torpedo salvo by the IJN cruiser was surely the one that produced the hits on Imamura's transports in their anchorage. However, a close examination of the charts indicates that *Perth* may well have been first struck by one or two of *Hatakaze*'s torpedoes.

136. IJN records from DesRon 5 show that *Murakumo* ceased her firing at this time because *Perth* was seen to be in a sinking condition.

137. Whiting, *Ship of Courage*, 94.

138. Hill, *Wind Tracks on the Water*, 73.

139. Hill, *Wind Tracks on the Water*, 85–86.

140. Adjusted for the zone time kept by the Allied ships, the records of the IJN give the time of *Perth*'s sinking as 0012 hours. The cruiser's assistant navigator, Lt. Lloyd Burgess, is said to have looked at his own watch when the ship went down, and it read 12:25 a.m., or 0025 hours. See Carlton, *Cruiser*, 458.

141. Able Seaman L. J. Golding of HMAS *Perth* wrote a lengthy poem as a POW titled "The *Perth*'s Last Stand."

142. Carlton, *Cruiser*, 457.

143. Maher, "Action Report," November 13, 1945.

144. A survivor, Ens. J. M. Hamill (USNA 40), declared that the destructive hit on *Houston*'s engine room was from gunfire. Lieutenant Commander Gingras, the engineer officer, was favorably regarded by all who served with him. A highly capable officer known as a strict disciplinarian, Gingras was *always* spoken of in the very highest terms by his chief subordinate, Lt. Bob Fulton.

145. Floyd Arnold interview with Samuel Milner, May 1960, Milner Papers.

146. Albert E. Kennedy interview with Samuel Milner, September 1959, Milner Papers.

147. Schultz, *Last Battle Station*, 184.

148. From chapter 7 of BKS/*Senshi Sōsho*, vol. 26. Translated by Akio Oka, 2006.

149. These narrow escapes from death in Smith's turret led to a variety of fates for survivors subsequently. Bill Stewart, who had been very severely burned, made it ashore to Java east of St. Nicholas Point, floating between the two lines of anchored enemy transports. Ray Goodson, unharmed, floated all the way down into Sunda Strait, where he ended up on Topper's Island in midstrait with Doc Epstein and others. They managed to hold out there until late March before giving themselves up.

150. Capt. Harold Hamlin, "Control of Naval Gun Batteries," Milner Papers.

151. Hamlin, "Control of Naval Gun Batteries."

152. Hamlin, "Control of Naval Gun Batteries."

153. Thomas Eugene Parham interview with Samuel Milner, September 30, 1959, Milner Papers.

154. Parham interview with Milner.

155. Lt. (j.g.) H. S. Hamlin Jr., narrative, "USS *Houston* in Battle of the Java Sea," September 14, 1945, 7, NARA II.

156. A fair amount of confusion has always surrounded the two abandon ship orders. Some surviving officers later speculated that the first order was indeed a mistake based on talk overheard by *Houston*'s gunnery officer Maher, who had more than one phone circuit open. Others thought that there might have been a difference of opinion between Rooks, Maher, and Roberts, who presumably wanted to fight the ship to the bitter end, and Commander Hollowell, the navigator, who was thought to be more concerned with giving as many men as possible a chance to get off the ship alive.

157. Jack L. Smith interview with Samuel Milner, August 9, 1960, Milner Papers.

158. Hornfischer, *Ship of Ghosts*, 130–31.

159. J. L. Smith interview with Milner.

160. J. L. Smith interview with Milner.

161. Quotations from narrative of Ens. Charles D. Smith, USN, USS *Houston* (CA-30), September 18, 1945, 12. The hit on pom-pom mount number 1 and the death of Captain Rooks are taken from narratives and interviews by both Smiths, from the Levitt account, and recollections by other survivors. Despite his wounds, pay clerk Kenneth Shaw of the marines actually survived the sinking of *Houston* and imprisonment. Another Chinese mess attendant, identity not known, had been wounded according to Levitt, given a life jacket, and helped over the side. Clarifying the correct identities and fates of all of *Houston*'s Chinese mess attendants and stewards has been problematic for many years due to the numerous incorrect names recorded by the USN at the time. Some information regarding the Chinese men serving on *Houston* was derived from a February 27, 1994, article in the *Houston Chronicle* newspaper titled "Unexpected Alliance," by Bob Tutt.

162. Feliz, *Saga of Sailor Jack*, 38.

163. Walter K. Schneck, Mus2/c, *Houston*, interview with Samuel Milner, August 1959, Milner Papers.

164. Parham interview with Milner, Milner Papers.

165. From an oral history interview with William Ingram Jr. conducted by Floyd Cox of the National Museum of the Pacific War (the Nimitz Museum) in Fredericksburg, Texas, on March 1, 2002. Transcription in the author's collection.

166. Walter Schneck interview with Samuel Milner, August 1959, Milner Papers. Severyn Dymanowski was not among the survivors.

167. Charles, *Last Man Out*, 36.

168. As the IJN track chart in BKS/*Senshi Sōsho*, vol. 26, shows, and as verified by an official USN track chart kept by the USS *Houston* (SSN-713) in 1993, the cruiser sank north-northeast of Pandjang Island. She lies on her starboard side on an incline, with her fractured bow in some 120 feet of water and her stern in 80 feet.

169. Current research suggests this may have been the Dutch auxiliary tanker *TAN 1* (formerly *Paula*), which had been believed "scuttled off Tandjong Priok" on March 1, 1942. It is also quite possible that the ship returned to the port in a damaged condition after her encounter with the IJN destroyers and foundered there.

170. Message in Glassford's *Bandoeng* volumes. 1555 Zed = 2325 local, or 11:25 p.m.

171. "Report on the Movements of RNS *Evertsen*," written by Lt. Cdr. H. Volten, RNN, and translated by Ens. Herb Levitt Jr., USNR, Milner Papers.

172. "Report on the Movements of RNS *Evertsen*."

## 13. They Fled to Bliss or Woe

The chapter title is taken from Samuel Taylor Coleridge's "Rime of the Ancient Mariner."

1. Glassford, *Bandoeng* volumes.

2. Cdr. Thomas Binford interview with John Toland, ca. 1960, Milner Papers. Binford's postcampaign Action Report was written more circumspectly: "I advised him [Glassford's operations officer] of the engagement the day and night before and also of the vital necessity of leaving Sourabaya that day and no day later. The enemy was closing in on all sides of Java and each exit through the Barrier was being guarded by air and surface ships."

3. Binford interview with Toland.

4. Binford interview with Toland.

5. Binford interview with Toland.

6. Binford's four destroyers were spotted leaving the Eastern Channel by several Dutch motor torpedo boats under Lt. H. C. Jorissen that were heading in the opposite direction. Four of the Dutch MTBs were spotted at sea outside of Surabaja at 1125 hours (JST) by *Naka*'s floatplane.

7. Letter from Rear Adm. Edward N. Parker, USN, to John Toland, July 7, 1960, Milner Papers.

8. Letter from Rear Adm. Edward N. Parker to John Toland, July 7, 1960, Milner Papers.

9. Cdr. Henry E. Eccles, Commanding Officer USS *John D. Edwards* (DD-216), "Battle of Bawean Islands—Report of Action; Events Prior and Subsequent Thereto," March 4, 1942, Fold3 by Ancestry, Historical Military Records, at www.fold3.com.

10. Butch Parker later wrote: "The night was clear with brilliant moonlight, sea smooth, visibility about five to six miles" (USS *John D. Ford* [DD-228] Action Report, "Action in Java Sea between combined Dutch, British, American Naval Forces and Japanese Forces on 27 February, 1942; engagement between U.S. Destroyers and Japanese Forces in Bali Straits on March 1, 1942," 6, Fold3 by Ancestry, Historical Military Records, at www.fold3.com).

11. Binford interview with Toland.

12. Email from Marion Ellsworth to the author, January 2013.

13. New research has uncovered a most intriguing fact. The four ships of DesDiv 21 tasked with guarding Bali Strait were not alone that night. They were in company with the 1,400-ton Japanese hydrographic survey vessel *Tsukushi*, a highly specialized auxiliary built to penetrate enemy waters and take soundings of potential landing zones in anticipation of amphibious operations. She had echo sounding gear as well as an array of five fathometers of three different types. It is possible that either *Tsukushi* herself was the first enemy ship spotted by Binford's division or that the destroyers of DesDiv 21 were preoccupied by *Tsukushi*'s mission at that moment and had become distracted. The fact that the first Japanese ship appeared to be almost stopped or moving quite slowly suggests it may have been the survey vessel, which had special turbines for very low-speed cruising. The sluggish initial response and failure to illuminate also seem to imply it was *not* one of the destroyers. All participants agree that it was a night of good visibility with a large moon. (The presence of *Tsukushi* with DesDiv 21 comes from BKS/*Senshi Sōsho*, 26:479, item no. 16. I am indebted to Osamu Tagaya and Kan Sugahara for their kind help with this information.)

14. Mullin, *Another Six-Hundred*, 241–42.

15. Mullin, *Another Six-Hundred*, 243.

16. Rear Adm. Edward N. Parker, USS *John D. Ford* (DD-228), "Report on Engagement between U.S. Destroyers and Japanese Forces in Bali Straits on March 1, 1942," Fold3 by Ancestry, Historical Military Records, at www.fold3.com.

17. Binford interview with Toland.

18. Mullin, *Another Six-Hundred*, 245–46.

19. Binford interview with Toland.

20. Email from Elly Ellsworth to the author, January 2013, and phone conversation, January 2014.

21. Walt Frumerie interview with the author, July 14, 2012.

22. These messages by Collins are from Glassford, *Bandoeng* volumes, vol. 2.

23. Helfrich's *Memoires*, vol. 2, chap. 24, has his account of the *Exeter* group's designated route.

24. Michel, *Mr. Michel's War*, 73.

25. Michel, *Mr. Michel's War*, 73.

26. Falle, *My Lucky Life*, 30–39.

27. Michel, *Mr. Michel's War*, 73.

28. Falle, *My Lucky Life*, 34.

29. Gordon Report, October 1945, 29, Milner Papers.

30. Penninger letter.

31. Gordon Report, October 1945, 13.

32. Michel, *Mr. Michel's War*, 73–74.

33. Falle, *My Lucky Life*, 35.

34. Falle, *My Lucky Life*, 35.

35. From a report by former medical orderly first class of the *Op ten Noort* A. W. Mellema, RNN, dated May 8, 1946, at Surabaja and prepared in IMTFE documents, exhibit 2065, document no. 8471-A.

36. IMTFE document no. 8471-A, "Report regarding the Adventures of the Netherlands Military Hospital Ship 'Op ten Noort,'" May 8, 1946, NARA II.

37. Falle, *My Lucky Life*, 35.

38. Sentai 5 Message Log, JACAR.

39. Sentai 5 Message Log, JACAR.

40. Blinn narrative, USS *Pope* (DD-225) Java Sea Battle, p. 37, Fold3 by Ancestry, Historical Military Records, at www.fold3.com.

41. Gordon Report, October 1945, 14.

42. BKS/*Senshi Sōsho*, vol. 26, chap. 7, "Annihilation of the Surviving Enemy Fleet," 461–63.

43. Gordon Report, October 1945, 14.

44. Johns and Kelly, *No Surrender*, 64.

45. Johns and Kelly, *No Surrender*, 64–65.

46. Blinn narrative, 37.

47. Penninger letters.

48. Michel, *Mr. Michel's War*, 75.

49. Michel, *Mr. Michel's War*, 76.

50. George Cooper, *Never Forget, nor Forgive*, at http://ww2today.com/1st-march-1942-hms-exeters-final-battle.

51. Cooper, *Never Forget, nor Forgive*.

52. Detailed Action Report (DAR) for Sentai 5, March 1, 1942, with times adjusted to match Allied records. This document is from the JD reels, not JACAR, and is courtesy of Anthony Tully.

53. Details of this final action are taken from Captain Gordon's report later published in the *London Gazette*, July 1948; from BKS/*Senshi Sōsho*, 26:461–64; from the March 1, 1942, DER of Sentai 5 in JACAR; from the April 15, 1942, issue of *Asahigraph* magazine; from Falle, *My Lucky Life*; from Cooper, *Never Forget, nor Forgive*; as well as from Blinn Report and Blinn's narrative; from Michel, *Mr. Michel's War*; the Bill Penninger letters; and a television interview with Joe Sam Sisk recorded in 2007 by Texas A&M University. Quotation from Falle, *My Lucky Life*, 37.

54. DAR for Sentai 5, March 1, 1942.

55. Cooper, *Never Forget, nor Forgive*.

56. Falle, *My Lucky Life*, 38–39.

57. Cooper, *Never Forget, nor Forgive*.

58. From a poem written later ("Java Sea 1942") by an *Exeter* survivor named Gwynne Hodge, at https://sites.google.com/site/ahistoryofmumbles/recollections-of-a-japanese-prisoner-of-war-by-gwynne-hodge.

59. USS *Pope* (DD-225) Action Report, March 1, 1942, NARA II.

60. Michel, *Mr. Michel's War*, 77.

61. Penninger letter.

62. Penninger Papers.

63. A majority of survivors from *Exeter* and *Encounter* were picked up by the Japanese in the immediate aftermath of the battle and over the ensuing days. The chronology and details of these rescues are quite complicated, falling well outside the scope of this work, however. Far and away the best and most complete research yet done on the subject has been by Anthony P. Tully.

64. USS *Pope* (DD-225) Action Report, March 1, 1942, NARA II.

65. Penninger, "The USS *Pope*'s Last Action," 7, Penninger Papers.

66. Michel, *Mr. Michel's War*, 79.

67. Sentai 5 Message Log, JACAR.

68. Michel, *Mr. Michel's War*, 9.

69. Narrative by Capt. Welford C. Blinn, USN, "USS POPE, DD 225, Java Sea Battle and Prison Experiences," 9, Fold3 by Ancestry, Historical Military Records, at www.fold3.com.

70. Penninger Papers.

71. Penninger Papers.

72. Penninger Papers.

73. Some sources say they closed to within four thousand yards, while others state that the cruisers remained at about eight thousand yards.

74. Penninger Papers.

75. Michel, *Mr. Michel's War*, 82.

76. Penninger Papers.

77. In late 2008 professional divers located the remains of *Pope*. Being closer to the coast of Borneo meant that *Pope's* wreck—in relatively shallow waters—had already been significantly degraded. By that time there was little left of her other than the deteriorated framing of her hull, enshrouded within a webbing of fisherman's nets. *Pope* is situated within fifteen nautical miles of a far more enigmatic wreck, that of an intact tanker resting upright on the bottom. When examined in 2007 this vessel was found to be the Dutch oil tanker *Augustina*, also believed lost on March 1, 1942. The full history of *Augustina's* end is one of obscure and fantastic improbability but must be reserved for another work. Credit for the best, most convincing research into the *Augustina* mystery goes to Anthony P. Tully.

78. Here a peculiar lapse seems to occur in Glassford's narratives, as he claimed to have supervised the unloading of *Sea Witch* himself at Tjilatjap, yet his other accounts state he was then at Bandoeng with Helfrich, Palliser, and other high-echelon members of what had been the ABDA HQ there. He elsewhere stated that after his final meeting with these admirals on the morning of March 1, during which the combined command was dissolved, he then left Bandoeng by automobile for Tjilatjap. His secret war diary makes no mention of any trips between Tjilatjap and Bandoeng during the final days other than his departure on March 1, when the command ended.

79. Alford, *Playing for Time*, 237.

80. Alford, *Playing for Time*, 237.

81. Again, there would have been a one-and-a-half-hour difference (ninety minutes) between USN and IJN times that day; 1200 hours USN = 1330 hours JST time. *Pillsbury's* departure time (1507) is taken from the Deck Log of USS *Parrott* (DD-218).

82. *Takao* report ("*Takao* Weekly") in JACAR.

83. Japanese primary source records are all from JACAR. The *Takao* weekly newsletter (C08030743600) depicts the destruction of *Pillsbury* and is reproduced in its entirety in JACAR. *Atago's* detailed engagement report (C0803074550) has the same raw data.

84. *Takao* weekly in JACAR.

85. The story of *Phoenix's* participation in the operations south of Java during the conclusion of the Java campaign is worthy of a study itself. This modern cruiser, armed with fifteen 6-inch rifles, was highly coveted by Lieutenant Admiral Helfrich, who insisted that the ship be diverted to his fleet. It is still not clear what her real status was at the time, since Adm. Ernest King also appears to have believed she would go to Java, although she was clearly marked for escort duty then with convoy MS.5 (which included *Langley* and *Sea Witch*). At the time of *Pillsbury's* loss, *Phoenix* was roughly 100–150 miles west-northwest and steaming to the east at a standard speed. Even if she had steamed through the very waters in which Pound's ship and crew were lost, given the sea conditions at that time it is extraordinarily unlikely that survivors could have been rescued—assuming there were any.

86. Steel and Hart, *Jutland, 1916*.

87. The Japanese 20 cm/8-inch naval gun of the type used on these cruisers had a maximum range in excess of thirty thousand meters.

88. *Takao* report ("*Takao* Weekly") in JACAR.

89. *Takao* report ("*Takao* Weekly") in JACAR.

90. *Takao* report ("*Takao* Weekly") in JACAR.

91. *Takao* report ("*Takao* Weekly") in JACAR.

92. Also see COMSOUWESPAC message to *Phoenix* at 0306 hours on March 1: "PROCEED TO POSITION LAT FIFTEEN EAST LONG ONE ONE THREE SOUTH TO REMAIN THAT VICINITY TO ASSIST SMALL ALLIED SHIPS ASSEMBLING THERE X" (Glassford, *Bandoeng* volumes, vol. 2, NARA II).

93. A number of survivors recorded encountering severe storms, or at least very heavy seas, during the March 1–5 period. This was noted by the men on *Pecos*, *Whipple*, and *Edsall*, as well as by those in *Lanikai*, and also by the destroyermen who escaped through Bali Strait. Australian crews in the corvettes of

the Twenty-First Minesweeping Flotilla made similar observations on their return voyage to Fremantle at the same time.

94. He died in March 1945 from the cumulative effects of dysentery, pellagra, and a severe beating at the Makassar POW camp, in which a number of survivors of *Pope, Perch, Exeter, Encounter, Stronghold, Francol,* and *Anking* were also imprisoned.

95. The "*Ash-can Maru*" was a well-worn vessel with "a long history of failures in her engineering systems" dating back to her shakedown cruise in 1920 (Tom Dorton article [untitled], *China Gunboatman,* March 2000, 18–20). That she was able to perform her wartime duties as well as she did is another testimonial to the resourcefulness and skill of her crew.

96. This dark mood was noted by one of the last men to have served on *Asheville* who survived the war, Ens. Paul L. Mansell Jr., D-V (G), USNR. He went to the gunboat from the submarine *Stingray* after suffering a noncombat injury to his knee while working ashore with a provisioning party at Surabaja in early February. After being hospitalized briefly, he was finally allowed to leave and ordered at first to *Marblehead,* which was then repairing her bomb damage at Tjilatjap. However, the cruiser departed before Mansell could get to the port, and he was reassigned to *Asheville,* which was then under Dutch operational control at Tjilatjap and going nowhere. He arrived after a bone-jarring twelve-hour train ride on the evening of February 14. Mansell's knee gradually worsened, though, and he was again told he should leave Java—as he could not stand his watches on *Asheville.* He departed (via verbal orders) on a Dutch ship, *Tjitjalengka,* on February 22, before the island fell, and made it safely to Australia in the first week of March. His story comes from "Asheville Luck," *China Gunboatman,* September 1993, 3–7.

97. Berkley's report in *China Gunboatman,* June 2006, 13.

98. *Arashi* and *Nowaki* were exceptionally busy in this period. They sank the British minesweeper *Scott Harley,* along with the Dutch merchant ship *Parigi* on March 1. The Dutch vessel *Tomohon* was set afire by their shelling on March 2 with six from the merchantman's crew killed; three boats made it into the water, of which two reached Java and the third was picked up by *Zaandam.* Then, aided by *Maya,* they sank the small World War I–era Royal Navy destroyer HMS *Stronghold* on the evening of March 2 after an enormous expenditure of ammunition.

99. Their other two sisters from that division, *Hagikaze* and *Maikaze,* were both attached to Vice Admiral Nagumo's Kidō Butai with its nucleus of four fleet carriers, for the Second Mobile Operation south of Java.

100. This is the story as given by one of *Stronghold*'s survivors, a New Zealand rating, Able Seaman John F. Murphy.

101. Japanese accounts of this engagement are taken primarily from Lacroix and Wells, *Japanese Cruisers of the Pacific War,* and from the U.S. Navy Historical Center (microfilmed Japanese war records) [n.d.], JD 204 Tabular Records of Movement and Action Reports of Japanese Destroyers (*Akatsuki-Kasumi*) and from Kimata Jiro's history of IJN destroyers (provided by Anthony Tully). These have been matched up with the message received by *Whippoorwill* and secondhand reports from Joe Sam Sisk of USS *Pope,* who knew Fred L. Brown at Makassar, available at http://toto.lib.unca.edu/findingaids/mss/ashe_walter /jpeg_ashe_scrapbook_1/ashv1/ashv1p034.jpg.

102. Kimata Jiro's history of IJN destroyers, no page numbers.

103. Berkley's report in *China Gunboatman,* June 2006, 13.

104. One good reason for their impatience was the *Yarra* convoy. They wanted to also intercept this larger group of vessels. And they were able to do just that on the following morning of March 4—unfortunately and tragically for the Allied ships under the protection of the Australian sloop.

105. Although Fred Brown had endured the violent sinking of his ship to become a prisoner, he would not survive the war. He died in March 1945 at Makassar's POW camp, the victim of multiple deficiency diseases and the effects of a severe beating by his captors over a trivial infraction. The account of *Asheville*'s end by Brown, which has passed down to posterity, came through a fellow POW named Joe Sam Sisk, a survivor of *Pope.* According to the Japanese history, this division (*Maya, Arashi,* and *Nowaki*) continued "to prowl the area for the rest of the day" but found no more Allied ships to attack. On the follow-

ing morning, though, these ships would have more excitement, as they rejoined Vice Admiral Kondō's group (the flagship *Atago* and her sister, *Takao*), then discovered and ruthlessly destroyed the small British convoy of *Francol*, *Anking*, and *MMS-51*, which had been screened by the Australian sloop, HMAS *Yarra*, another small, lightly armed warship of much the same size, displacement, and strength as *Asheville*.

106. Jessie H. Robison, "The Last Days of the *Perch*," 7 (Milner Papers).

107. This should be contrasted with the battle for Bataan and Corregidor, USMC fighting on Wake Island, or Japanese resistance on several small Pacific atolls later in the war such as Tarawa, Peleliu, or tiny Iwo Jima—all a fraction the size of Java—for any who have questions about what really determined defensive fighting looked like.

108. According to an interview with Samuel Milner, this shooting ("accidental discharge of his service rifle") was witnessed by Pfc. Egbert T. Hudson of HQ Battery. It was also recorded in the private diary of Maj. Winthrop Rogers, November 1941 to November 1942 (in author's possession).

## 14. Post Diem

The chapter subtitle is taken from Lt. Adm. C. E. L. Helfrich's letter to Adm. J. T. Fürstner, March 13, 1942, in "Correspondentie met Fürstner, 1941–1944," 2.12.44, I.C. de Regt, 1998, Nationaal Archeif, The Hague, Netherlands. Translated by Bernice Harapat.

1. Obviously this does not include the losses of the Japanese destroyer *Shinonome* (off northern Borneo) to aerial bombing and several minesweepers (at Tarakan and Ambon) to mines and shore battery fire, or the sinking of the destroyer *Natsushio* by S-37.

2. In the summer of 2000 I met Tom Moorer in Fredericksburg, Texas, when he spoke at a Nimitz Foundation Pacific War symposium, and I can attest that even at age eighty-eight he remained a formidable figure.

# BIBLIOGRAPHY

### Archival Sources

Ibiblio, The Public's Library and Digital Archive, University of North Carolina at Chapel Hill.

M. D. Anderson Library, Special Collections, University of Houston, Houston TX.

    Cruiser *Houston* Collection.

    Milner Papers.

Nationaal Archief, The Hague, Netherlands.

National Archives and Records Administration, Archives II, College Park MD.

U.S. Navy Historical Center, Washington DC.

    Records of the Japanese Navy.

### Published Sources

Abe, Zenji, with J. Michael Wenger and Naomi Shin. *The Emperor's Sea Eagle.* [Honolulu] Hawaii: Arizona Museum Memorial Association, 2006.

Abernethy, Rear Adm. E. P., USN (ret.). "The *Pecos* Died Hard." *USNI Proceedings*, December 1969, 74–83.

Akashi, Yoji, and Mako Yoshimura, eds. *New Perspectives on the Japanese Occupation of Malaya and Singapore, 1941–1945.* Singapore: NUS Press, 2008.

Alford, Lodwick H. *Playing for Time: War on an Asiatic Fleet Destroyer.* Bennington VT: Merriam Press, 2006.

Anderson, Irvine. *The Standard-Vacuum Oil Company and United States East Asian Policy, 1933–1941.* Princeton NJ: Princeton University Press, 1975.

Barnhart, Michael A. *Japan and the World since 1868.* London: Edward Arnold, 1995.

———. *Japan Prepares for Total War.* Ithaca NY: Cornell University Press, 1987.

Bartsch, William H. *December 8, 1941: MacArthur's Pearl Harbor.* College Station: Texas A&M University Press, 2003.

———. *Every Day a Nightmare: American Pursuit Pilots in the Defense of Java, 1941–1942.* College Station: Texas A&M University Press, 2010.

Bee, W. A. (Bill). *All Men Back—All One Big Mistake.* Carlisle WA: Hesperian Press, 1998.

Bell, Capt. Fredrick J., USN. *Condition Red: Destroyer Action in the South Pacific.* New York: Longmans, Green, 1944.

Best, Antony, ed. *Imperial Japan and the World, 1931–1945.* Vol. 3, *Economics and Finance, 1931–1945.* Critical Concepts in Asian Studies. London: Routledge, 2011.

Bezemer, K. W. *Geschiedenis van de Nederlandse Koopvaardij in de Tweede Wereldoorlog* (History of the Dutch Merchant Marine in World War II). 2 vols. Amsterdam: Elsevier, 1987.

BKS/*Senshi Sōsho*. Vol. 26, *Naval Operations in the Dutch East Indies and Bay of Bengal* [in Japanese]. Tokyo: Asahi Shimbunsha, 1969.

Blair, Clay. *Silent Victory*. New York: J. B. Lippincott, 1975.

Bland, Larry I., and Sherry R. Stevens, eds. *The Papers of George Catlett Marshall*. Vol. 3. Baltimore: Johns Hopkins University Press, 1991.

Boer, P. C. *The Loss of Java*. Singapore: NUS Press, 2011.

Boyd, Carl, and Akihiko Yoshida. *The Japanese Submarine Force and World War II*. Annapolis MD: U.S. Naval Institute Press, 1995.

Borneman, Walter R. *The Admirals*. New York: Back Bay Books, 2013.

Bradford, John. *In the Highest Traditions . . . RAN Heroism Darwin 19 February 1942*. Henley Beach, Australia: Seaview Press, 2000.

Brereton, Lt. Gen. Lewis H. *The Brereton Diaries: The War in the Air in the Pacific, Middle East, and Europe, 3 October 1941–8 May 1945*. New York: William Morrow, 1946.

*British Documents on Foreign Affairs: Reports and Papers from the Foreign Office Confidential Print*. General editors: Kenneth Bourne, D. Cameron Watt, Paul Preston, and Michael Partridge. Part 2: *From the First to the Second World War*. Series E: *Asia, 1914–1939*. Vol. 17, *Japan, Jan. 1938–Dec. 1938*. Frederick MD: University Publications of America, 1990–97.

———. Part 3: *From 1940 through 1945*. Vol. 3, *Far Eastern Affairs, January 1941–June 1941*. Frederick MD: University Publications of America, 1997.

———. Part 3: *From 1940 through 1945*. Vol. 6, *Far Eastern Affairs, October 1942–June 1943*. Frederick MD: University Publications of America, 1997.

Brown, Cecil. *Suez to Singapore*. New York: Random House, 1942.

Buell, Thomas. *Master of Sea Power: A Biography of Fleet Admiral Ernest J. King*. Annapolis MD: U.S. Naval Institute Press, 1980.

Bulkeley, Capt. Robert J., Jr., USNR (ret.). *At Close Quarters: PT Boats in the United States Navy*. Washington DC: USGPO, 1962.

Burns, Paul. *The Brisbane Line Controversy*. St. Leonards, Australia: Allen & Unwin, 1998.

Butler, J. R. M., ed. *Grand Strategy*. Part 1, vol. 3, *June 1941–August 1942*. London: HM Stationary's Office, 1964.

Cain, T. J., and Arthur V. Sellwood. *HMS Electra*. London: Futura, 1976.

Carlton, Mike. *Cruiser: The Life and Loss of HMAS Perth and Her Crew*. Sydney: William Heinemann, 2010.

Casey, Robert J. *Torpedo Junction*. Halcyon House, 1944.

Charles, H. Robert. *Last Man Out*. Austin TX: Eaking Press, 1988.

Churchill, Winston S. *The Hinge of Fate*. Vol. 4 of *The Second World War*. Boston: Houghton Mifflin, 1950.

Colijn, Helen. *Song of Survival*. London: Headline, 1995.

Craigie, Sir Robert. *Behind the Japanese Mask*. London: Hutchinson, 1945.

Craven, Wesley F., and James L. Cate, eds. *The Army Air Forces in World War II, Volume 1: Plans and Early Operations January 1939 to August 1942*. Chicago: University of Chicago Press, 1948.

Danklefsen, Ralph W. *The Navy I Remember*. Xlibris, 2000.

Day, Clarence Nixon. *Hodio: Tales of an American POW*. Merrillville IN: ICS Books, 1984.

Deacon, Richard. *A History of the Japanese Secret Service*. London: Frederick Muller, 1982.

DePalma, Arthur R. "Japanese Naval Nightmare." *World War II*, February 2001, 50–56.

De Quincey, Thomas. *New Essays by De Quincey: His Contributions to the Edinburgh Saturday Post and the Edinburgh Evening Post*. Edited by Stuart M. Tave. Princeton NJ: Princeton University Press, 1966.

*De slag in de Javazee*. Directed by Niek Koppen. Odusseia Documentaries, 1995, 138 minutes.

*Documents on German Foreign Policy, 1918–1945*. Series D, vol. 10, *The War Years, 1940*. Washington DC: USGPO, 1957.

———. Series D, vol. 11, *The War Years, 1940–41*. Washington DC: USGPO, 1960.

Donovan, Thomas A. "An Ordeal to Forget." *Naval History* 14, no. 3 (June 2000).

Dreyer, Edward L. *China at War, 1901–1949*. London: Longman, 1995.

Dull, Paul S. *A Battle History of the Imperial Japanese Navy, 1941–1945*. Annapolis MD: U.S. Naval Institute Press, 1978.

Dunn, William J. *Pacific Microphone*. College Station TX: Texas A&M University Press, 1988.

Evans, David C., and Mark R. Peattie. *Kaigun: Strategy, Tactics, and Technology in the Imperial Japanese Navy, 1887–1941*. Annapolis MD: U.S. Naval Institute Press, 1997.

Fabricius, Johann. *East Indies Episode*. London: Shell Petroleum, 1949.

Falle, Sam. *My Lucky Life: In War, Revolution, Peace and Diplomacy*. Lewes, England: Book Guild, 1996.

Feis, Herbert. *The Road to Pearl Harbor*. Princeton NJ: Princeton University Press, 1950.

Feliz, Jack. *The Saga of Sailor Jack*. San Jose CA: Writer's Club Press, 2001.

Ferrell, Robert H., ed. *The Eisenhower Diaries*. New York: W. W. Norton, 1981.

Findlay, Sir Alexander G. *A Directory for Navigation in the Indian Archipelago, China, and Japan . . .* London: Richard Holmes Laurie, 1878.

Forbes, Anna. *Unbeaten Tracks in Islands of the Far East: Experiences of a Naturalist's Wife in the 1880s*. New York: Oxford University Press, USA, 1987.

*Foreign Relations of the United States: Diplomatic Papers, 1941*. Vols. 4 and 5, *The Far East*. Washington DC: USGPO, 1956.

Forrestal, Emmet Peter. *Admiral Raymond A. Spruance, USN: A Study in Command*. Washington DC: USGPO, 1956.

Friedman, Norman. *U.S. Cruisers: An Illustrated Design History*. Annapolis MD: U.S. Naval Institute Press, 1984.

———. *U.S. Destroyers: An Illustrated Design History*. Annapolis MD: U.S. Naval Institute Press, 1982.

Frost, Cdr. Holloway H., USN. *On a Destroyer's Bridge*. Annapolis MD: USNI, 1930.

Gamble, Bruce. *Darkest Hour: The True Story of Lark Force at Rabaul*. St. Paul MN: Zenith Press, 2006.

Gill, G. Hermon. *Royal Australian Navy, 1939–1942*. Canberra: Australian War Memorial, 1957.

Goldstein, Donald M., and Katherine V. Dillon. *The Pacific War Papers: Japanese Documents of World War II*. Washington DC: Potomac Books, 2004.

Goodhart, Philip. *Fifty Ships That Changed the World*. Garden City NY: Doubleday, 1965.

Gordon, Capt. Oliver L. *Fight It Out*. London: William Kimber, 1957.

Grose, Peter. *An Awkward Truth: The Bombing of Darwin February 1942*. Crows Nest, Australia: Allen & Unwin, 2009.

Guard, Harold. *The Pacific War Uncensored*. Edited by John Tring. Philadelphia: Casemate, 2011.

Gugliotta, Bobette. *Pigboat 39*. Annapolis MD: U.S. Naval Institute Press, 1984.

Hara, Tameichi, with Fred Saito and Roger Pineau. *Japanese Destroyer Captain*. Annapolis MD: U.S. Naval Institute Press, 1961.

Hashimoto, Mamoru. "Commentaries on the Sea Battles Fought by Tokugata Destroyer *Ikazuchi*." *Kojinsha*, December 1999.

Hata Ikuhiko, Izawa Yasuho, and Don Cyril Gorham. *Japanese Naval Air Force Fighter Units and Their Aces 1932–1945*. Annapolis MD: U.S. Naval Institute Press, 1989.

Hay, Capt. Richard R., USN (ret.). "Little Known Facts." *U.S. Navy Cruiser Sailors Association* 9, no. 1 (Winter 2000): 25.

Helfrich, Lt. Adm. C. E. L. *Memoires van C. E. L. Helfrich*. Tweede Deel: *Glorie en Tragedie*. Amsterdam: Elsevier, 1950. English translations by Mrs. De Vogel for John Toland and by Bert Schwab for the USS *Houston* (CA-30) Survivors Association.

Hezlet, Sir Arthur, VADM, KBE, CB, DSO, DSC. *The Electron and Sea Power*. London: Peter Davies, 1975.

Hill, Harold J. *Wind Tracks on the Waters*. Self-published, 1992.

Hilton, James. *The Story of Dr. Wassell*. Boston: Little, Brown, 1943.

Holmes, W. J. *Underseas Victory*. Vol. 1, *1941–1943: Against the Odds*. 1966; repr., New York: Zebra Books, 1980.

Hornfischer, James D. *Ship of Ghosts*. New York: Bantam, 2006.

Howse, Derek. *Radar at Sea: The Royal Navy in World War 2*. Annapolis MD: U.S. Naval Institute Press, 1993.

Hoyt, Edwin P. *The Lonely Ships: The Life and Death of the U.S. Asiatic Fleet.* Abridged and rev. ed. New York: Jove Books, 1989.

Hull, Cordell. *The Memoirs of Cordell Hull.* 2 vols. New York: Macmillan, 1948.

Ickes, Harold. *The Secret Diary of Harold L. Ickes.* Vol. 3, *The Lowering Clouds, 1939–1941.* New York: Simon & Schuster, 1954.

Ike, Nobutake. *Japan's Decision for War.* Stanford CA: Stanford University Press, 1967.

Ishikawa, Shingo. *Shinjuwan made no Keii Kaisen no Shinsō* [Circumstances Leading to Pearl Harbor: The Truth about the Commencement of the War]. Tokyo: Jiji Tsūshinsha, 1960.

Janis, Irvin L. *Victims of Groupthink: A Psychological Study of Foreign-Policy Decisions and Fiascoes.* Boston: Houghton Mifflin, 1972.

Johns, W. E., and R. A. Kelly. *No Surrender.* 1969; repr., London: W. H. Allen, 1989.

Johnsen, Julia E., compiler. *Chinese-Japanese War, 1937–.* New York: H. W. Wilson, 1938.

Karig, Cdr. Walter, USNR, and Lt. Welbourn Kelley, USNR. *Battle Report: Pearl Harbor to Coral Sea.* New York: Farrar & Rinehart, 1944.

Kehn, Donald M., Jr. *A Blue Sea of Blood.* Minneapolis: Zenith Press, 2008.

———. "Old Ships Turn the Tide." *America in World War II*, October 2014, 14–23.

Kehn, Donald M., Jr., with Anthony P. Tully. "Drowned in Mystery." *America in World War II*, August 2013, 24–31.

Kelly, Terence. *Nine Lives of a Fighter Pilot.* Shrewsbury, England: Airlife Publishing, 2003.

Keneman, AOC Harry L., USN (ret.). "A Career is Born." *U.S. Navy Cruiser Sailors Association Magazine* 16, no. 1 (Winter 2007): 45–46.

Kimble, Warren F., ed. *Churchill and Roosevelt: The Complete Correspondence.* Vol. 1, *Alliance Emerging, October 1933–November 1942.* Princeton NJ: Princeton University Press, 1984.

King, Ernest J., and Walter Muir Whitehill. *Fleet Admiral King: A Naval Record.* New York: W. W. Norton, 1952.

Klar, John W. "USS *Stewart* (DD-224), Design and Construction." *Warship International*, no. 4 (1988): 376–98.

———. "World War II Operational History of USS *Stewart* (DD-224)." *Warship International*, no. 2 (1989): 139–67.

Koeu, Keiji. "Friendly Fire—Participation in the Battle off Batavia." In *Kancho tachino Taiheiyo Sensō*, edited by Sato Kazumasa, 275–79. Tokyo: Kojinsha, 1993.

Kok, Charlotte. "The Knickerbocker Weekly and the Netherlands Information Bureau: A Public Diplomacy Cooperation during the 1941–1947 Era." MA thesis, American Studies Program, Utrecht University, 2011.

Kroese, A. *The Dutch Navy at War.* London: Allen & Unwin, 1945.

Kudō Akira, Tajima Nobuo, and Erich Pauer, eds. *Japan and Germany: Two Latecomers to the World Stage, 1890–1945.* Vol. 2. Folkestone, England: Global Oriental, 2009.

Kuramoto, Kazuko. *Manchurian Legacy: Memoirs of a Japanese Colonist.* East Lansing: Michigan State University Press, 1999.

Lacroix, Eric, and Linton Wells II. *Japanese Cruisers of the Pacific War.* Annapolis MD: U.S. Naval Institute Press, 1997.

Langer, William, and S. Gleason. *The Undeclared War, 1940–1941.* New York: Harper & Bros., 1953.

Lebra, Joyce C., ed. *Japan's Greater East Asia Co-Prosperity Sphere in World War II: Selected Readings and Documents.* New York: Oxford University Press, 1975.

Lenton, H. T. *British Fleet and Escort Destroyers.* Vol. 1. Navies of the Second World War. Garden City NY: Doubleday, 1970.

———. *British Fleet and Escort Destroyers.* Vol. 2. Navies of the Second World War. London: MacDonald, 1970.

———. *British Submarines.* Navies of the Second World War. Garden City NY: Doubleday, 1972.

———. *Royal Netherlands Navy.* Navies of the Second World War. Garden City NY: Doubleday, 1968.

Leutze, James. *A Different Kind of Victory: A Biography of Admiral Thomas C. Hart.* Annapolis MD: U.S. Naval Institute Press, 1981.

Liu, F. F. *A Military History of Modern China: 1924–1949.* Princeton NJ: Princeton University Press, 1956.

Lu, David J. *Agony of Choice: Matsuoka Yōsuke and the Rise and Fall of the Japanese Empire, 1880–1946.* Lanham MD: Lexington Books, 2002.

———. *Japan, A Documentary History.* Vol. 2, *The Late Tokugawa Period to the Present.* London: M. E. Sharpe, 1997.

Luidenga, Frans, and Nico Guns. "Tjilatjap 1942: The Drama after the Battle of the Java Sea." *Marineblad,* 2002.

MacDonald, Jack. *Navy Retread.* Tallahassee FL: Dura-Print, 1969.

Maddox, Robert F. "Senator Harley M. Kilgore and Japan's World War II Business Practices." *West Virginia History Journal* 55 (1996): 127–42.

*Maru Special: Japanese Naval Operations in WWII,* no. 95 (January 1985).

Matloff, Maurice, and Edwin Snell. *Strategic Planning for Coalition Warfare, 1941–1942.* Washington DC: USGPO, 1953.

McDonald, Kevin. *Tin Can Sailors Save the Day! The USS Johnston and the Battle off Samar.* Ashland OR: Paloma Press, 2010.

McDougall, William H., Jr. *Six Bells off Java.* New York: Scribner's & Sons, 1948.

McEwan, James. *The Remorseless Road: Singapore to Nagasaki.* Shrewsbury, England: Airlife, 1997.

McKenna, Richard. *The Sand Pebbles.* New York: Harper & Row, 1962.

McKie, Ronald. *The Survivors (AKA Proud Echo).* New York: Bobbs-Merrill, 1953.

Mendenhall, Corwin Guy, Jr., *Submarine Diary: The Silent Stalking of Japan.* Annapolis MD: U.S. Naval Institute Press, 1991.

Mendl, Wolf, ed. *Japan and South East Asia.* Vol. 1, *From the Meiji Restoration to 1945.* London: Routledge, 2001.

Messimer, Dwight R. *In the Hands of Fate: The Story of Patrol Wing Ten.* Annapolis MD: U.S. Naval Institute Press, 1985.

———. *Pawns of War: The Loss of the USS Langley and the USS Pecos.* Annapolis MD: U.S. Naval Institute Press, 1983.

Michel, John J. A. *Mr. Michel's War.* Novato CA: Presidio Press, 1998.

Middlebrook, Martin, and Patrick Mahoney. *Battleship: The Sinking of the Prince of Wales and the Repulse.* New York: Chas. Scribner's & Sons, 1977.

Mimura, Janis. *Planning for Empire: Reform Bureaucrats and the Japanese Wartime State.* Ithaca NY: Cornell University Press, 2011.

Morison, S. E. *The Rising Sun in the Pacific, 1931–April 1942.* Vol. 3 of *History of United States Naval Operations in World War II.* Boston: Little, Brown, 1948.

Morley, James W., ed. *The Fateful Choice: Japan's Advance into Southeast Asia, 1939–1941.* Selected translations from *Taiheiyō sensō e no michi: Kaisen gaikō shi.* New York: Columbia University Press, 1980.

Morley, James W., ed. *The Final Confrontation: Japan's Negotiations with the United States, 1941.* Translated by David A. Titus. New York: Columbia University Press, 1994.

Mullin, J. Daniel. *Another Six-Hundred.* Self-published, 1984.

———. "Badoeng Strait." *Shipmate,* January–February 1989, 26–29.

Nakayama, Hideo. "The Landing on Java." *Osaka Mainichi,* April 29, 1942.

Navy Department. *Annual Report of the Navy Department for the Fiscal Year 1928.* Washington DC: USGPO, 1929.

Newcomb, Richard F. *U.S. Destroyers of the World Wars.* Paducah KY: Turner, 1994.

O'Hara, Vincent P. *The U.S. Navy against the Axis.* Annapolis MD: U.S. Naval Institute Press, 2007.

Palmer, Russell. "Economics of Tanker Speed." *World Petroleum Journal* 8 (April 1937).

Parkin, Ray. *Out of the Smoke.* New York: William Morrow, 1960.

*Pearl Harbor Attack Hearings.* Parts 2, 5, 13, and 38. Washington DC: USGPO, 1946.

Perry, Everett Marion. *Ghosts of Canopus: The War Diary of a Lucky Old Lady.* Boise ID: Riverside Press, 2010.

Perry, George Sessions, and Isabel Leighton. *Where Away: A Modern Odyssey.* New York: Whittlesey House, 1944.

Piper, Robert. *The Hidden Chapters: Untold Stories of Australians at War in the Pacific.* Carlton, Australia: Pagemasters, 1995.

Pogue, Forrest C., L. Bland, J. Bland, and S. R. Stevens, eds. *George C. Marshall Interviews and Reminiscences for Forrest C. Pogue.* Lexington VA: Geo. C. Marshall Research Foundation, 1991.

Pratt, Fletcher. "Campaign in the Java Sea." Americans in Battle, no. 1. *Harper's,* November 1942, 561–754.

———. "One Destroyer." Americans in Battle, no. 8. *Harper's,* January 1944, 183–92.

Record, Jeffrey. *A War It Was Always Going to Lose: Why Japan Attacked America, 1941.* Washington DC: Potomac Books, 2011.

Reynolds, Quentin. *Officially Dead: The Story of Cdr. C. D. Smith.* New York: Random House, 1945.

Romanus, Charles, and Riley Sunderland. *China-Burma-India Theater: Stillwell's Mission to China.* U.S. Army in World War II. Washington DC: Office of the Chief of Military History, Department of the Army, 1953.

Roosevelt, Franklin D. *FDR, His Personal Letters.* Vol. 2. Edited by Elliott Roosevelt. New York: Duell, Sloan & Pearce, 1950.

Roscoe, Theodore. *United States Submarine Operations in World War II.* Written for the Bureau of Naval Personnel from material prepared by R. G. Voge [and others]. Designed and illustrated by Fred Freeman. Photographs by the U.S. Navy. Annapolis MD: U.S. Naval Institute, 1949.

Rose, Kurt. *The Islands of the Sulu Sea.* Palo Alto CA: Glencannon Press, 1993.

Ross, Al. *The Destroyer Campbeltown.* Anatomy of the Ship. London: Conway Maritime Press, 2004.

Samuels, Richard J. *Rich Nation, Strong Army: National Security and the Technological Transformation of Japan.* Ithaca NY: Cornell University Press, 1994.

Sato, Kazumasa, ed. *Kancho tachino Taiheiyo Sensō.* Tokyo: Kojinsha, FN, 1993.

Schultz, Duane. *The Last Battle Station.* New York: St. Martin's Press, 1985.

Sheehan, Ed. *One Sunday Morning.* Illustrated by Robert McCall. Honolulu: Island Heritage, 1971.

Shimer, Barbara, and Gary Hobbs, trans. *The Kenpeitai in Java and Sumatra: Selections* from the Authentic History of the Kenpeitai *(Nihon Kenpei Seishi).* Ithaca NY: Cornell Modern Indonesia Project, 1986.

Shores, Christopher, and Brian Cull with Isuho Izawa. *Bloody Shambles.* Vol. 1. London: Grub Street, 1992.

———. *Bloody Shambles.* Vol. 2. London: Grub Street, 1993.

Simpson, B. Mitchell, III. *Admiral Harold R. Stark: Architect of Victory, 1939–1945.* Columbia: University of South Carolina Press, 1989.

Smith, Peter C. *Fist from the Sky: Japan's Dive-Bomber Ace of WWII.* Mechanicsburg PA: Stackpole Books, 2006.

Spang, C. W., and R. H. Wippich, eds. *Japanese-German Relations, 1895–1945.* London: Routledge, 2006.

Spence, Jonathan. *To Change China: Western Advisers in China, 1620–1960.* Boston: Little, Brown, 1969.

Stafford, David. *Roosevelt and Churchill, Men of Secrets.* Woodstock NY: Overlook Press, 1999.

Steel, Nigel, and Peter Hart. *Jutland, 1916: Death in the Grey Wastes.* London: Cassell Military, 2003.

St. Pierre, Paul A. *USS Langley CV-1 AV-3: America's First Aircraft Carrier.* Self-published, 1988.

Takushirō, Hattori. *The Complete History of Greater East Asia War.* Tokyo: Masu, 1953.

Tanaka, Tsuneji. "The Decisive Battle in the Java Sea" (Java kai no Kessen). In *Jitsuroku Taiheiyō Senso,* edited by Itō Masanori et al., 1:204–28. Tokyo: Chuokoron, 1960.

Tarling, Nicholas. *Britain, Southeast Asia and the Onset of the Pacific War.* Cambridge: Cambridge University Press, 1996.

Thomas, David A. *The Battle of the Java Sea.* New York: Stein & Day, 1968.

Thorpe, Brig. Gen. Elliott R. *East Wind, Rain.* Boston: Gambit, 1969.

Toland, John. *But Not in Shame: The Six Months after Pearl Harbor.* New York: Random House, 1961.

Tolley, Kemp. *Cruise of the Lanikai*. Annapolis MD: U.S. Naval Institute Press, 1973.

———. *Yangtze Patrol: The U.S. Navy in China*. Annapolis MD: U.S. Naval Institute Press, 1971.

"Tommy Hart Speaks Out." *Time*, October 12, 1942.

Totten, George O., ed. *Democracy in Prewar Japan: Groundwork or Façade?* Boston: D. C. Heath, 1965.

Tuchman, Barbara W. *Stillwell and the American Experience in China, 1911–45*. New York: Macmillan, 1970.

Utsonomiya, Michio. "Haguro Suitei—Aerial Surveillance over Surabaja Sea Battle." In *Maru Bessatsu—Sensho no Hibi*, edited by Noriki Deguchi, 393–94. Tokyo: Ushio Shobo, 1988.

Van der Moer, Lt. Abraham. "He Who Sees First Lives Longest." *Naval History*, August 1994, 35–40.

Van Oosten, F. C. *The Battle of the Java Sea*. Sea Battles in Close-Up. Annapolis MD: U.S. Naval Institute Press, 1976.

Wakeman, Frederic, Jr. *Policing Shanghai, 1927–1937*. Berkeley: University of California Press/Philip E. Lilienthal Books, 1996.

Ward, Ian. *The Killer They Called a God*. Singapore: Media Masters, 1992.

Wasserstein, Bernard. *Secret War in Shanghai: An Untold Story of Espionage*. Boston and New York: Houghton Mifflin, 1999.

Watanabe, Daiji, *Bali Island Battle by Michishio of the 8th Destroyer Division* [in Japanese]. Privately published, 1988.

Weintraub, Stanley. *Pearl Harbor Christmas*. Cambridge MA: Da Capo Press, 2011.

Whiting, Brendan. *Ship of Courage: The Epic Story of HMAS Perth and Her Crew*. St. Leonards, Australia: Allen & Unwin, 1994.

Wigmore, Lionel. *The Japanese Thrust*. Canberra: Australian War Memorial, 1957.

Wilmott, H. P. *The Barrier and the Javelin: Japanese and Allied Pacific Strategies, February to June 1942*. Annapolis MD: U.S. Naval Institute Press, 1983.

———. *Empires in the Balance: Japanese and Allied Pacific Strategies to April 1942*. Annapolis MD: U.S. Naval Institute Press, 1982.

———. *The Second World War in the Far East*. Washington DC: Smithsonian Books, 1999.

Winslow, Walter. *The Fleet the Gods Forgot*. Annapolis MD: U.S. Naval Institute Press, 1982.

———. *The Ghost That Died at Sunda Strait*. Annapolis MD: U.S. Naval Institute Press, 1984.

Wohlstetter, Roberta. *Pearl Harbor: Warning and Decision*. Stanford CA: Stanford University Press, 1962.

Womack, Tom. "Naval Duel off Bali." *World War II*, February 1996, 50–56.

Worth, Roland H., Jr. *No Choice but War: The United States Embargo against Japan and the Eruption of War in the Pacific*. Jefferson NC: McFarland, 1995.

Yoshida, Toshio. "*Ōshio's* Total Victory off Bali Island." *Rekisha to Tabi: The 300th Commemorative Issue* 5 (September 1993): 84–87.

———. "Study of 'Combinations' by Examples: Commanders and Their Staff Officers." *Maru Special*, no. 13 (February 1995): 172–77.

Young, Donald J. *First 24 Hours of War in the Pacific*. Shippensburg PA: Burd Street Press, 1998.

Young, Louise. *Japan's Total Empire: Manchuria and the Culture of Wartime Imperialism*. Berkeley: University of California Press, 1998.

# INDEX

tions and status of ships at, 36–48; prewar personnel unreadiness of, 1, 18–22, 31, 441n92

Charles, Bob, 388

Chestnut, Orville, 20

Chiang Kai-shek, 3, 349n31

Chihaya Takehiko, 246

*Chikuma*, 232, 240–41, 251–53

*Childs*, 7, 36, 58, 438n20, 451n5

China, 2–16, 33

Chisholm, J. K., 133

*Chitose*, 405, 415

*Chōkai*, 149

Christensen, Robert "Chris," 244

Christmas Island, 199, 229–41, 254, 259, 261–63, 268–69, 273, 419, 465nn117–18

Chupak, John, 186

Churchill, Winston, 67–70, 112, 264, 443n24, 445n7, 453n72, 467n1

*City of Manchester*, 464n102

Claggett, Henry B., 203, 461n23

Clark, Audrey, 316

Clark, Francis E., 181, 186, 270, 337, 469n31, 475n182

Clark, Preston, 360, 483n89

Clark Field, 32, 40, 444n36

Clymer, Shelton H. "Red," 303, 383, 387–88

Coburn, C. H., 463n81

Coe, Red, 230–31

Coley, Lewis E., 327, 394, 476n188

Colijn, Aaltje, 79–81, 446n4

Colijn, Anton, 73, 79–82, 88, 446n4, 447n24

Collings, Charles, 130, 134

Collins, John: and ABDA formation, 446n11; and Battle of Flores Sea, 110; and Battle of Java Sea, 275, 279, 286, 305, 327, 473n144; and Battle of Sunda Strait, 336, 338, 341, 348, 350, 355; and conferences with American and Dutch commanders, 64–65; and *Langley* episode, 211, 237–38; and retreat from Java, 400–401; and sinking of *Perth* and *Houston*, 390

Combined Striking Force (CSF), 114–15, 120, 155, 225, 242, 275–98, 304–8, 312–33, 337, 340–41, 392, 452n25, 470n72, 471n89, 471n93, 471n95, 473n143, 474n155, 477n197, 477n199, 477n208, 478n233

Combs, E. Cecil, 78

convoy MS.5, 202–14, 238, 461n25, 461n33, 490n85

Cooper, J. E. "Jocko," 97–99, 102–3, 157, 172–73, 188, 268, 311, 399, 410–12, 431

Craigie, Robert, 11

Cravens, J. R., 379

Cray, Hampton, 350

Creighton, John, 45

Cresap, J. B., 248, 250, 260

Crispi, Gene, 291

Crotty, W. J., 243, 466n139

Crouch, Edwin M., 29, 43–45, 63, 218, 225–26, 229–30, 233–39, 258, 399, 465n112

CSF. *See* Combined Striking Force (CSF)

*Danae*, 263, 276, 341

Daniels, Theodore Duane, 138

Darby, John T., 100, 106, 420

Darling, William E. "Bill," 303, 383

Davis, Charley, 354

Davis, George E., Jr., 129, 134–35, 139

Davis, Howard, 416

Day, Clarence Nixon, 354

Day, Raymond "Rainy," 135, 347

de Gelder, J. A., 114

de Gelder, Paulus, 332

de Meester, J. B., 126, 159, 174

*Dempsey*, 432

Dempsey, J. C., 156, 160–61

*De Ruyter*: and Bangka Strait sortie, 141–44, 147–48; and Battle of Bandoeng Strait, 155–58, 164–67, 172–74; and Battle of Flores Sea, 114, 119, 123; and Battle of Java Sea, 275–80, 287, 290, 292–96, 304–6, 310, 317–18, 322, 325–33, 471n100; and Battle of Tarakan, 77–78; and *Langley* episode, 216; sinking of, 337, 404–5; at war's outbreak, 64

Destroyer Division 1, ABDA (DesDiv 1), 114

Destroyer Division 2, IJN (DesDiv 2), 97

Destroyer Division 4, IJN (DesDiv 4), 426

Destroyer Division 5, IJN (DesDiv 5), 363, 368–71, 373, 375

Destroyer Division 7, IJN (DesDiv 7), 283

Destroyer Division 8, IJN (DesDiv 8), 155–56, 175, 182, 319

Destroyer Division 9, IJN (DesDiv 9), 97

Destroyer Division 11, IJN (DesDiv 11), 342, 365, 369–70

Destroyer Division 12, IJN (DesDiv 12), 342, 368, 374

Destroyer Division 16, IJN (DesDiv 16), 298, 329–30

Destroyer Division 17, IJN (DesDiv 17), 250, 254

Destroyer Division 18, IJN (DesDiv 18), 240–41

Destroyer Division 19, IJN (DesDiv 19), 342

Destroyer Division 21, IJN (DesDiv 21), 156, 396, 488n13

Destroyer Division 24, IJN (DesDiv 24), 94, 298

Destroyer Division 57, U.S. (DesDiv 57), 43–45, 63, 216, 227, 315

Destroyer Division 58, U.S. (DesDiv 58), 27, 41, 54, 114, 143–44, 157–59, 277, 287, 312, 314, 317, 394–95, 441n83, 458n64, 475n180

Destroyer Division 59, U.S. (DesDiv 59), 29, 41, 59, 61, 90, 157, 164, 443n14

Destroyer Squadron 29, U.S. (DesRon 29), 26–29, 36, 261, 290, 398, 417, 420, 441n86, 443n14

Mack, William P., Jr., 36, 92, 101, 105, 170–71, 270–71, 299, 311–12

*Macon*, 28

Madson, Quentin, 351

Maher, Arthur: and Bangka Strait sortie, 142; and Battle of Flores Sea, 117, 122, 124, 132, 453n60; and Battle of Java Sea, 290–91, 294, 297, 299, 313, 328; and Battle of Sunda Strait, 347–48, 357, 366, 369, 379, 383, 386, 388, 482n72, 486n156

*Maikaze*, 491n99

Makassar POW camp, 404, 418–19, 428, 479n235, 491n94, 491n105

Maki Yukio, 219

Mallory, Fred, 358

Manchukuo, 9–11, 437n13, 439n31

Manchuria, 2, 10, 13, 389, 419

Manila Agreement, 265

Manista, Anton "Tony," 368

Mansell, Paul L., Jr., 491n96

*Marblehead*: and Bangka Strait sortie, 141, 143; and Battle of Balikpapan, 83–90, 103–4, 448n55; and Battle of Flores Sea, 111, 114, 116, 118–19, 123–27, 135–40; and Battle of Tarakan, 77; prewar locations and status of, 6–7; at war's outbreak, 41–42, 54–55, 60, 63, 443n14

Marco Polo Bridge Incident, 3

Marsh, Samuel, 463n81

Marshall, George, 68–70, 200, 205, 207, 460n2

Martin, Jay, 464n92

Martin, Robert, 128, 368

*Maryborough*, 362

Masano Yutaro, 184–85

Matsunaga Sadaichi, 44

Matsuoka Yōsuke, 16, 439n30

Matthews, Donald A., 416–17

*Mauna Loa*, 152

May, C. W., 293–94, 306, 308–10, 474n161

May, E. V., 354–55

*Maya*, 232, 426–27, 491n98

McCall, F. B., 242, 248, 250, 256, 260

McClune, Donald, 180

McCone, James "Packrat," 128–29

McConnell, Robert, 202, 215, 219–23, 225–29, 233, 242, 248–49, 256, 258–60, 399, 444n11, 465n112

McCrea, John L., 24, 440n73

McDonald, J. N., 65

McElroy, Ivan, 209

McManus, O. C., 313

McNabb, Roy "Breezy," 248–49

McPeake, Lawrence, 245, 248, 467n189

*Meigs*, 152

*Merel*, 362

Michel, John J. A. "Jack": and Battle of Balikpapan, 85, 93–94, 98–99, 101, 108; and Battle of Bandoeng Strait, 165, 170, 172; and Battle of Java Sea, 268–71; and sinking of *Pope*, 401–3, 408–12, 415, 417–18, 465n118; at war's outbreak, 38

*Michishio*, 155, 159, 162–63, 165, 169, 175, 182–86, 188, 420, 457n37

Mikawa Gun'ichi, 240, 252–54

*Mikuma*, 342–43, 368, 370, 375–76, 381, 480n24

Miller, Carl W. "Ace," 31

Mills, Reginald, 257–58

*Minegumo*, 309–11, 318, 472n123, 474n158

Minton, Olen, 122, 128, 322, 353

Miropol, Harold S., 57, 444n4

*Mizuho*, 267

*Modjokerto*, 240–41, 253–55

*Mogami*, 342–43, 368, 370, 375–76, 381, 480n24, 481n30, 485n133

Mondschein, Aloysius, 105–6

Moorer, Tom, 431, 492n2

Morgan, E. V. "Rattler," 308, 326, 401–2, 410–11

Morison, Samuel Eliot, 1

Morita Kan'ichi, 16

Mori Tomoichi, 289, 326

Mosher, J. S., 45, 260

*Mount Vernon*, 260

Mowrey, Cliff, 32

Moyers, Robert, 150

Muckley, Dwight, 198

Mullin, Daniel J., 84, 91, 101–2, 105, 171–72, 192, 316, 457n39, 475n183

*Murakumo*, 342, 368, 374, 390, 484n103, 486n136

*Murasame*, 405, 472n123

Muzzell, Norman, 194

*Myōkō*, 319, 331, 333, 404, 406, 409, 417

*Nachi*: and Asian Fleet's retreat from Java, 404–6, 409–13; and Battle of Bandoeng Strait, 458n72; and Battle of Java Sea, 266–67, 283–85, 292–95, 298–300, 304–5, 312, 320, 328–29, 333, 335, 472n106, 472n118, 472n124, 474n166; and encounter with *Houston* off Timor, 459n1

*Nagara*, 156, 188, 319, 456n15

Nagumo Chuichi, 125, 200, 211, 232, 239–42, 246, 249, 251–54, 256, 259, 401, 461n31, 465n109, 467n173

*Naka*, 74, 81, 95, 101–3, 266, 284–85, 297, 319, 325, 331, 472n123

Nakahara Yoshimasa, 16, 438n30

Nakayama Hideo, 368, 484n99, 484n108, 485n113

*Nana Maru*, 95, 97, 107

*Napier*, 199

*Natori*, 340, 342–43, 365, 373

Tatsugami Maru, 95, 100, 107

Teer, Clifford, 338

Teiryu Maru, 103

Tenedos, 263, 341, 443n23

Teppes, Johan, 182

ter Poorten, Hein, 14, 207, 217

Terry, Archie, 273, 368, 384–85

Thanet, 44

Thew, Henry, 357

Thew, Norman, 323

Thorpe, Elliott R., 14, 68, 445n4

Thracian, 44

Tidore, 115

Tientsin Crisis, 438n27

Timor, seizure of, 267–68

Timor relief convoy, 151–54

Tisdale, William, 359

Tobita Kenjiro, 329

Tokitsukaze, 267, 293

Tolley, Kemp, 3, 37, 424, 438n16, 442n3

Tomioka Sadatoshi, 16

Tone, 232, 239–40

Trim, Donald "Pappy," 128

Trinity, 19–22, 32, 37, 39, 56–60, 63, 65, 86–87, 147, 444n2, 444n4, 444n6

Tripartite Pact, 15, 17

Tromp, 114, 123, 126, 143, 147, 157–59, 163–65, 175–76, 179–83, 186–87, 456n24

Truant, 160, 456n15

Tsingtao, 7–9

Tsuruga Maru, 95–97, 107

Tulagi, 152

Tulsa, 6, 424–26, 464n102

Twentieth Pursuit Squadron (Provisional), 198

Ugaki Matome, 344

Umikaze, 94

Urakaze, 250, 256

Uranami, 342

U.S. Asiatic Fleet. See Asiatic Fleet

Ushio, 267–68, 283, 429

Utsunomiya Michio, 284, 289, 320, 326–27

Van Bergen, Nick, 42

Van Cleve, Don, 210

van der Moer, Abraham, 148, 310

Van Ghent, 76, 114, 119, 147–48, 150, 310, 454n20

van Kleffens, Nicholas, 15

van Leur, Jacobus C., 290

van Mook, Hubertus, 75, 109, 111, 137, 196, 207, 447n13, 459n2

Van Stachouwer, Governor-General, 109, 111, 137, 206–7, 459n2

van Staelen, P. B. M., 330

venereal disease, 10

Verhagen, Jacobus, 240–41

Volten, H., 390–91

Wagner, Frank, 48, 271, 278, 281

Wakaba, 156, 396

Waldschmidt, Albert, 354, 379

Waller, Hector "Hec" MacDonald Laws: and Battle of Java Sea, 262, 269, 277–78, 296–97, 305–6, 309, 312, 322, 324, 329, 469n26, 472n111; and Battle of Sunda Strait, 335–36, 350–51, 355–57, 483n81; death of, 378, 483n79; and sinking of Perth and Houston, 362, 366, 369, 373, 376–78

Ward, Willard, 31

Warder, Fred, 160–62

Warnes, Bill, 214, 222–23, 227–28, 247–48, 260, 466n151

Warrego, 152

War Sirdar, 275, 341

Wassell, Corydon, 138, 453n75, 455n30, 465n121

Watanabe Daiji, 159–60, 162, 183–85

Watson, Edwin, 23

Wavell, Archibald, 70, 72, 110, 112, 196–211, 264, 445n7, 446n10, 460n7, 460n13, 461n17, 461n29

Webb, Helen, 40

Weissinger, Bill, 331–32, 473n129

Weller, Maurice "Dutch," 130

Welles, Sumner, 23

Western Striking Force, 339–42, 481n37

Whipple: and Bangka Strait sortie, 144, 454n10; and Battle of Balikpapan, 87; and Battle of Flores Sea, 137–38; and Langley episode, 214–18, 220, 224–39, 242, 245, 249, 255–59, 462n59, 464nn91–92, 464n94, 467n189; prewar locations and status of, 29; and retreat from Java, 399; at war's outbreak, 43, 63, 65

Whippoorwill, 53, 76, 424, 426, 464n102

Wiley, Herbert V., 28–30, 43, 261, 272, 441n86

Wilkes, John, 25, 49–50, 74–75, 82–83

Wilkinson, Eugene T., 119, 325

Willem van der Zaan, 215–17

William B. Preston, 7, 58, 192–93, 438n20, 442n2

Wills, Clarence R., 21–22, 440n67

Wilson, Bill, 101, 417, 419

Wilson, John V., 188

Winslow, Walter: and Battle of Flores Sea, 120–21, 131, 453n60; and Battle of Java Sea, 273–75, 291, 306, 313, 321, 324; and Battle of Sunda Strait, 339, 348; and near sinking of Houston off Timor, 459n1; and Timor relief convoy, 152, 154

Winters, Vic "Moose," 131, 134

Witte de With, 148, 157, 275, 277, 291, 310–11, 339, 400, 480n17